HF 5657.4 .W37 1988

Warren, Carl S.

W9-BKH-437

3 0147 0001 3949 6

NEW ENGLAND INSTITUTE
OF TECHNOLOGY
LEARNING RESOURCES CENTER

Managerial Accounting

Second Edition

Carl S. Warren, PhD, CPA, CMA
Professor of Accounting
University of Georgia, Athens

Philip E. Fess, PhD, CPA
Professor of Accountancy
University of Illinois, Champaign-Urbana

NEW ENGLAND INSTITUTE
OF TECHNOLOGY
LEARNING RESOURCES CENTER

A70
PUBLISHED BY
SOUTH-WESTERN PUBLISHING CO.
CINCINNATI   WEST CHICAGO, IL   CARROLLTON, TX   LIVERMORE, CA

6-96

#18171000

Copyright © 1988
by South-Western Publishing Co.
Cincinnati, Ohio

All Rights Reserved

The text of this publication, or any part thereof, may not be
reproduced or transmitted in any form or by any means,
electronic or mechanical, including photocopying, recording,
storage in an information retrieval system, or otherwise,
without the prior written permission of the publisher.

ISBN: 0-538-01730-9

Library of Congress Catalog Card Number: 87-72189

1 2 3 4 5 6 7 8 9 D 0 9 8

Printed in the United States of America

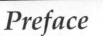

Preface

The second edition of MANAGERIAL ACCOUNTING is a student-oriented text. It presents managerial accounting concepts and principles in a logical, concise, and clear manner. MANAGERIAL ACCOUNTING provides a solid educational foundation that allows instructors to focus on clarifying issues and increasing the student's understanding of managerial accounting and its usefulness to management.

Managerial accounting concepts and principles are presented in the text in a business setting that allows students to understand managerial accounting as it is applied in serving management needs. Such an approach meets the needs of students planning careers in accounting as well as in business administration, in liberal arts areas, in law, or in other disciplines.

IMPORTANT FEATURES OF THE SECOND EDITION

The second edition of MANAGERIAL ACCOUNTING has been revised to reflect the dynamic nature of managerial accounting and current changes in the manufacturing environment in the United States. In addition, changes in coverage and new features were added, based on extensive feedback from current users and on independent reviews by scholars and educators. The most significant of these revisions and additions are described in the following paragraphs.

Nature of Managerial Accounting

Chapter 1 has been expanded to include an extended discussion of the management process, including the management functions of planning, organizing and directing, controlling, and decision making. The role of managerial accounting has been integrated into this discussion as an essential element of the management process. A discussion of the managerial accounting code of ethics has also been added.

Cost Concepts and Classifications

In Chapter 2, students are introduced to the basic cost concepts and classifications, such as product costs, period costs, differential costs, variable costs, and fixed costs.

Average Cost Method

A discussion and illustration of the average cost method has been added to the process cost chapter of the text. In this way, students will gain a better understanding of the importance of cost methods in inventory costing.

Cost Behavior and Cost Estimation

A new chapter (Chapter 5) on cost behavior and cost estimation has been added. The chapter begins with a description of the distinction between cost behavior and cost estimation, and concludes with descriptions and illustrations of the basic cost estimation methods, such as the high-low method, the scattergraph method, and the least squares method. The learning effect and current cost trends are also described. By discussing cost estimation methods early in the text, students are better able to understand subsequent topics, such as cost-volume-profit analysis.

Product Life Cycle

The use of alternative price strategies during a product's life cycle has been added to Chapter 12. In addition, a discussion of the effect of elasticity of demand and competitive market conditions on pricing strategies has also been added.

Tax Law Changes

Tax law changes have been integrated throughout the text. For example, Chapter 13 describes and illustrates the effect of the Modified Accelerated Cost Recovery Systems (MACRS) on capital investment decisions.

Statement of Cash Flows

The requirements of the Financial Accounting Standards Board pronouncement on cash flows has been incorporated into Chapter 16. The indirect method of reporting cash flows from operating activities is described and illustrated in the chapter. The direct method of reporting cash flows from operations is described and illustrated in Appendix C. Appendix D provides a work sheet approach to preparing the statement of cash flows.

Service Enterprises

A new chapter (Chapter 18) includes a description of the application of managerial accounting concepts and principles to service enterprises and activities. In addition, Appendix E contains specific applications and illustrations of managerial accounting concepts and principles for service enterprises.

Trends in Managerial Accounting

Chapter 18 also describes trends in manufacturing and in managerial accounting. Some of the trends described in this chapter include automation, controlling product quality, materials requirements planning, just-in-time inventory systems, and information technology. A selected bibliography has also been included to provide students additional readings into these current developments and trends.

Present Value and Future Value Tables

More detailed present value tables, as well as future value tables, are included in an appendix.

Chapter Objectives

The chapter objectives have been revised and expanded to enable students and instructors to integrate the chapter materials with the overall learning objectives more successfully.

Illustrations

Many additional charts, graphs, and diagrams have been added throughout the text to enable students to visualize important concepts and principles more efficiently. These charts, graphs, and diagrams are highlighted with color to enhance the learning process.

Real-World Examples

Real-world business examples have been integrated throughout the text to provide students with a flavor for the real-world impact of managerial accounting. These examples add concrete meaning to concepts and principles which might otherwise appear abstract.

Enrichment Material

Excerpts from business periodicals, such as *Management Accounting,* the *Wall Street Journal,* and *Forbes,* have been added to each chapter. Each excerpt was adapted and designed to stir the students' interest and enrich their learning experience by providing real-world information relevant to the topics that are discussed in the chapter.

Chapter Reviews

A chapter review has been added at the end of each chapter. The chapter reviews are designed to increase and enhance student retention of important chapter concepts and principles. Each chapter review includes key points, key terms, self-examination questions, and an illustrative problem and solution.

- The **key points** summarize the major concepts presented in a chapter. By studying the key points, students can quickly review the major concepts and principles of each chapter.
- Each **key term** listed in the chapter review is followed by the page number indicating where the key term was first presented in color and discussed in the chapter. Students may also refer to Appendix A, where all the key terms in the text are listed alphabetically and defined.
- Five **self-examination questions** are provided for each chapter. After studying the chapter, students can answer these questions and compare their answers with the correct ones that appear at the end of the chapter. An explanation of both the correct and incorrect answers for each question is provided in order to increase students' understanding and enhance the learning process further.
- The **illustrative problem** with suggested solution focuses on the concepts and principles discussed in the chapter. Students can use these problems as a means of building confidence in their ability to apply a chapter's concepts and principles to a problem situation.

End-of-Chapter Materials

The end-of-chapter excercises and problems have been carefully written and revised to be both practical and comprehensive. The variety and volume of the assignment materials presented at the end of each chapter provide a wide choice of subject matter and range of difficulty. In addition, selected problems may be solved using spreadsheet software that is available from South-Western Publishing Co. Each chapter contains a mini-case for stimulating student interest. Each case, which presents situations with which students can easily identify, emphasizes important chapter concepts and principles.

Real-World Focus Questions

A discussion question that requires students to interpret and respond to a real-world business situation is contained in each chapter. In some chapters, a real-world exercise is also included. These questions and exercises, which are labeled "Real World Focus," are based on actual business data.

Alternate Problems

The alternate problems appear at the end of each chapter in order to facilitate student and instructor usage.

Check Figures

As in the first edition, check figures for selected problems have been provided at the end of the text. These check figures may be used by students in checking their solutions to end-of-chapter problems. Agreement with the check figures is an indication that a significant portion of the solution is basically correct.

ORGANIZATION OF THE SECOND EDITION

MANAGERIAL ACCOUNTING has been organized to facilitate the learning of accounting and the overall educational process. Concepts and principles are introduced in a logical, step-by-step way and are reinforced by applications from the business world.

Each chapter builds on the terminology, concepts, and principles introduced in previous chapters. The chapter objectives provide students with a basis for beginning their study of each chapter. In turn, each chapter is organized around the chapter objectives in an educationally sound approach. The chapter reviews provide students with a means for review and a basis for assessing their knowledge of each chapter. The end-of-chapter discussion questions, exercises, problems, and mini-cases provide a vehicle for the instructor to assess the students' knowledge of each chapter's concepts and principles. Periodic giving of examinations provides instructors with a means for assessing students' cumulative knowledge.

The organization of the second edition of MANAGERIAL ACCOUNTING is briefly summarized in the following paragraphs.

Part 1—Fundamentals of Managerial Accounting

- Chapter 1 provides students with an overview of the nature of the management process and the essential role of managerial accounting in this process.
- Chapter 2 provides an overview of the manufacturing process and managerial accounting terminology. After completing Chapter 2, students will have been exposed to the majority of the terminology they will need in completing the first course in managerial accounting. This allows instructors flexibility in the order in which they assign subsequent chapters.

Part 2—Managerial Accounting Concepts and Systems

- Chapters 3 and 4 provide illustrations of the application of managerial accounting concepts to a manufacturing environment. Chapter 3 describes and illustrates job order cost accounting systems, and Chapter 4 describes and illustrates process cost accounting systems.

Part 3—Planning and Control

- This part emphasizes managerial accounting concepts and principles for planning and control. Chapter 5 describes and illustrates cost behavior and cost estimation.
- Chapter 6 describes and illustrates cost-volume-profit analysis.

- Chapter 7 describes and illustrates profit reporting for management analysis, including absorption costing and variable costing. The importance of the contribution margin in managerial decision making is emphasized.
- Chapter 8 describes and illustrates budgeting, including an integrated example of the preparation of the master budget.
- Chapter 9 concludes this part by describing and illustrating standard cost systems.

Part 4—Accounting for Decentralized Operations

- Chapter 10 describes responsibility accounting for decentralized operations. The chapter concludes with a description and illustration of responsibility accounting for cost and profit centers.
- Chapter 11 describes and illustrates responsibility accounting for investment centers and includes a discussion of transfer pricing.

Part 5—Analyses for Decision Making

- Chapter 12 describes and illustrates the use of differential analysis in decision making. Also included in Chapter 12 is a discussion of pricing, including short-term special pricing situations and the setting of long-term prices. Integrated into this discussion is the economic approach to pricing and the impact of a product's life cycle on setting prices.
- Chapter 13 describes and illustrates capital investment analysis, including the discounted internal rate of return method. Chapter 13 also includes a detailed illustration of the impact of MACRS depreciation on capital investment decisions.
- Chapter 14 describes and illustrates quantitative techniques for controlling inventory and making decisions under uncertainty.

Part 6—Financial Analysis for Management Use

- Chapter 15 describes and illustrates the usefulness of financial statement analysis to management. Chapter 15 also includes a description of the essential elements and content of corporate annual reports.
- Chapter 16 describes and illustrates the statement of cash flows and the use of this statement by management in planning and controlling operations.

Part 7—Modern Uses of Managerial Accounting

- Chapter 17 describes and illustrates the use of managerial accounting concepts and principles by nonprofit organizations.
- Chapter 18 describes the trends in managerial accounting, including just-in-time manufacturing systems, automation, quality control, and the use of managerial concepts and principles by service enterprises.

Appendixes

- Appendix A contains a glossary of key terms.
- Appendix B contains present value and future value tables.
- Appendix C describes and illustrates the direct method of preparing the cash flows from operating activities for the statement of cash flows.
- Appendix D describes and illustrates the work sheet approach to preparing the statement of cash flows.
- Appendix E illustrates the application of managerial accounting concepts and principles to a service enterprise.
- Appendix F contains selected financial statements for real companies.

SUPPLEMENTARY MATERIALS

MANAGERIAL ACCOUNTING is part of a well-integrated educational package that includes materials designed for the instructor's use and for the students' use. These materials are carefully prepared and reviewed to maintain consistency and high quality throughout.

Available to Instructors

Solutions Manual. This manual contains solutions to all end-of-chapter materials, including the discussion questions, exercises, problems, and mini-cases.

Spreadsheet Applications, prepared by Gaylord N. Smith of Albion College. This template diskette is used with Lotus™ 1-2-3™[1] for solving selected end-of-chapter exercises and problems that are identified with the symbol at the right. This diskette, which also provides a tutorial and "what if" analysis, may be ordered upon adoption from South-Western Publishing Co.

Instructor's Manual. This manual contains a summary of the chapter objectives, terminology, and concepts. In a section organized according to chapter objectives, a basis for developing class lectures and assigning homework is provided. In addition, exercise and problem descriptions, estimated time requirements for the problems, and suggestions for use of the appendixes and other supplementary items are included.

Transparencies. Transparencies of solutions to all exercises and problems are available.

Teaching Transparencies. The teaching transparencies are designed to aid the instructor's focus on key concepts and principles discussed in the text.

Test Bank. A collection of examination problems, multiple-choice questions, and true or false questions for each chapter, accompanied by solutions, is available in both printed and microcomputer (MicroSWAT) versions. The Test Bank is designed to save time in preparing and grading periodic and final examinations. Individual items may also be selected for use as short quizzes. The number of questions is sufficient to provide variety from year to year and from class section to class section.

Achievement Tests. Two sets of preprinted objective tests are available. Each test covers a group of chapters. A comprehensive test is also included.

The Administrator. A software management package is available to adopters. This package is specifically designed for use in maintaining a grade book, creating an interactive testing and/or study guide, and generating tests.

Available to Students

Working Papers. Appropriate printed forms on which to work end-of-chapter problems and mini-cases are available.

Study Guide, prepared by Carl S. Warren. The Study Guide is designed to assist in comprehending the concepts and principles presented in the text. This publication includes an outline and a glossary for each chapter as well as brief objective questions

---

[1]Lotus™ 1-2-3™ are trademarks of the Lotus Development Corporation. Any reference to Lotus or 1-2-3 refers to this footnote.

and problems. Solutions to these questions and problems are presented at the back of the Study Guide.

Microcomputer Study Guide. The microcomputer version of the manual Study Guide may be used with the IBM PC, the IBM PCjr,[2] and the Tandy® 1000.[3]

Practice Set, prepared by Dieter H. Weiss of Ferris State College. The short practice set is a budgeting set that emphasizes decision making rather than forms and procedures. The set is available in either a manual version or a computerized version based on Lotus 1-2-3.

ACKNOWLEDGMENTS

Throughout the textbook, relevant professional statements of the National Association of Accountants and other authoritative publications are discussed, quoted, paraphased, or footnoted. We are indebted to the American Accounting Association, the American Institute of Certified Public Accountants, the Financial Accounting Standards Board, and the National Association of Accountants for material from their publications.

We thank the following faculty who provided helpful suggestions for this revision: William K. Carter, University of Virginia; and William R. Pasewark, University of Georgia.

Carl S. Warren
Philip E. Fess

---

[2]IBM is a registered trademark of International Business Machines Corporation. Any reference to the IBM Personal Computer or the IBM PCjr refers to this footnote.

[3]Tandy® 1000 is a registered trademark of the Radio Shack Division of Tandy Corporation. Any reference to the Tandy 1000 microcomputer refers to this footnote.

About the Authors

Professor Carl S. Warren is the Arthur Andersen & Co. Alumni Professor of Accounting at the J. M. Tull School of Accounting at the University of Georgia, Athens. Professor Warren received his PhD from Michigan State University in 1973 and has taught accounting at the University of Iowa, Michigan State University, the University of Chicago, and the University of Georgia. He has received teaching awards from three different student organizations at the University of Georgia.

Professor Warren is a CMA and a CPA. He was awarded a Certificate of Distinguished Performance for his scores on the CMA examination and a Certificate of Honorable Mention for his scores on the CPA examination. He is a member of the National Association of Accountants, the American Institute of CPAs, the Georgia Society of CPAs, the American Accounting Association, the Georgia Association of Accounting Educators, and the Financial Executives Institute. Professor Warren has served on numerous professional committees and editorial boards, including a term as editor of the American Accounting Association publication *Auditing: A Journal of Practice and Theory.* He has written five textbooks and numerous articles in such journals as the *Journal of Accountancy,* the *Accounting Review,* the *Journal of Accounting Research,* the *CPA Journal, Corporate Accounting, Cost and Management,* and *Managerial Planning.* Professor Warren is also the Consulting Editor for South-Western Publishing Co.'s accounting series.

Professor Warren resides in Athens, Georgia, with his wife, Sharon, and two children, Stephanie (age 14) and Jeffrey (age 12). Professor Warren's hobbies include coaching Little League Baseball, golf, tennis, and fishing.

Professor Philip E. Fess is the Arthur Andersen & Co. Alumni Professor of Accountancy at the University of Illinois, Champaign-Urbana. Professor Fess received his PhD from the University of Illinois and has been involved in textbook writing for over twenty years. In addition to having more than 30 years of teaching experience, he has won numerous teaching awards, including the University of Illinois, College of Commerce Alumni Association Excellence in Teaching Award and the Illinois CPA Society Educator of the Year Award.

Professor Fess is a CPA and a member of the American Institute of CPAs and the Illinois Society of CPAs. He is also a member of the National Association of Accountants and the American Accounting Association. He has served many professional associations in a variety of ways, including a term as a member of the Auditing Standards Board, editorial advisor to the *Journal of Accountancy,* and chairperson of the American Accounting Association Committee on CPA Examinations. Professor Fess has written more than 100 books and articles, which have appeared in such journals as the *Journal of Accountancy,* the *Accounting Review,* the *CPA Journal,* and *Management Accounting.* He has also served as an expert witness before the U.S. Tax Court and is a member of the Cost Advisory Panel for the Secretary of the Air Force.

Professor Fess and his wife, Suzanne, have three daughters: Linda, who is completing a PhD in accounting at Arizona State University; Ginny, who is a CPA and is employed by Baxter-Travenol; and Martha, who is majoring in finance at the University of Illinois. Professor Fess' hobby is tennis, and he has represented the United States in international tennis competition.

Note to Students

This text was written with the objective of preparing you for your future professional career. Managerial accounting is a stimulating, rewarding field of study. To be effective, professionals in all areas of business, such as finance, production, marketing, personnel, and general management, must have a good understanding of managerial accounting. In addition, men and women whose careers are in nonbusiness areas can use a knowledge of managerial accounting to perform more effectively in society.

As you begin your study of managerial accounting, you may find the following suggestions helpful:

- Read each chapter objective before you begin studying a chapter.
- Take a few minutes and scan the chapter to get a flavor of the material before you begin a detailed reading of the chapter.
- As you read each chapter, you may wish to underline points that you feel are especially important. Also, you should give special attention to key terms which are identified in color when they first appear in the chapter.
- After reading the text of the chapter, carefully study the Chapter Review, giving special attention to the following items:

Key Points. You should thoroughly understand each of the key points presented in the chapter. If you have difficulty understanding any of the key points, review the section of the chapter where the key point is discussed and illustrated. The key points are organized as major chapter headings that appear sequentially throughout the chapter.

Key Terms. You should be able to define each key term. If you cannot, refer to the page of the chapter where the key term is first presented and discussed. You may also refer to Appendix A, where all of the key terms are listed in alphabetical order and defined.

Self-Examination Questions. Answer each of the self-examination questions and check your answers by referring to the answers at the end of the chapter. These answers explain the correct response.

Illustrative Problem. Study the illustrative problem and its suggested solution. Each illustrative problem applies the concepts and principles discussed in the chapter to a problem situation. If you have difficulty understanding the illustrative problem, refer to the section of the chapter where the applicable concepts and principles are discussed and illustrated.

- Work all assigned homework. In many cases, the homework is related to specific chapter illustrations, and you may find it helpful to review the relevant chapter sections before you begin a homework assignment.
- Take notes during class lectures and discussions and give attention to the topics covered by your instructor.
- In reviewing for examinations, keep in mind those topics that your instructor has emphasized, and review your class notes and the text.
- If you feel you need additional aid, you may find the Study Guide that accompanies this textbook helpful. The Study Guide can be ordered from South-Western Publishing Co. by your college or university bookstore.

Contents in Brief

Contents

TEXT OBJECTIVES

•

Describe the basic nature and structure of managerial accounting.

•

Describe and illustrate accounting systems for manufacturing operations.

•

Describe and illustrate managerial accounting concepts for planning and controlling operations and decision making.

•

Describe and illustrate financial analyses for management use.

•

Describe and illustrate managerial accounting for nonprofit organizations.

•

Part One

Fundamentals of Managerial Accounting

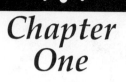

Chapter
One

CHAPTER
OBJECTIVES

•

Describe the nature of accounting as an information system.

•

Describe and illustrate four basic functions of the management process:
Planning
Organizing and directing
Controlling
Decision making

•

Describe the role of accounting in the management process.

•

Describe the basic characteristics of managerial accounting reports:
Relevance
Timeliness
Accuracy
Clarity
Conciseness

•

Describe the organization of the managerial accounting function
and its staff responsibilities.

•

Describe the similarities and differences between financial accounting
and managerial accounting.

•

Describe the profession of managerial accounting.

•

Describe the importance and future of managerial accounting.

•

Nature of Managerial Accounting

Accounting is an information system that communicates economic information for use by various groups and individuals in making informed judgments and decisions.[1] For example, investors in a business enterprise use accounting information about the firm's financial status and its future prospects to make decisions regarding their investments. Creditors seek information useful in appraising the financial soundness of a business organization and assessing the risks involved before making loans or granting credit. Government agencies require economic information for purposes of taxation and regulation. Employees and their union representatives use economic information to evaluate the stability and the profitability of the organization that employs them. The individuals most dependent upon and most involved with accounting are an organization's management, which uses accounting information in directing the operations of the enterprise.

The **management** of an organization consists of those individuals charged with the responsibility for directing the enterprise toward achieving its goals. The primary goal of most enterprises is to earn a profit by rendering services or selling products. The primary goal of nonprofit organizations, such as governmental units, churches, and the Red Cross, is the rendering of humanitarian services to the needy at the lowest possible cost. Regardless of the goals, managers of all enterprises and organizations rely heavily on accounting data in attempting to achieve their goals.

The primary focus of this text is on the accounting data needed by the management of profit-oriented entities, although many of the concepts and principles discussed are applicable to nonprofit organizations. Managerial accounting concepts and principles which have special significance to nonprofit organizations are discussed in Chapter 17.

THE MANAGEMENT PROCESS

To understand the role of accounting in providing the necessary information to management for achieving enterprise goals, it is necessary to understand the management process. The **management process** involves the four basic functions of (1) planning, (2) organizing and directing, (3) controlling, and (4) decision making. Although decision making has the central role in the management process, all four functions interact. As shown in the following

---

[1]A glossary of terms appears in Appendix A. The terms included in the glossary are printed in color the first time they appear in the text.

diagram, these functions are the driving force for an enterprise's operations. Management's actions in the management process are, to some extent, measured by the enterprise's operating results.

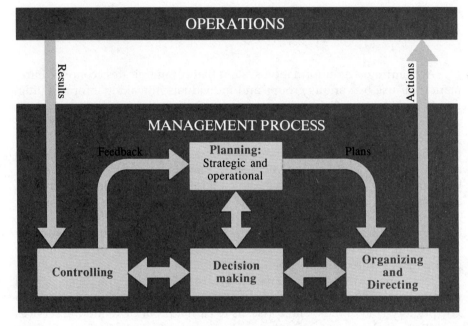

Planning
· · ·

Planning is the process by which management develops a course of action to attain enterprise goals. Planning involves such activities as setting selling prices, arranging for the financing of a plant expansion, and the development of new products. Planning can be categorized as either strategic planning or operational planning.

Strategic planning is the development of a long-range course of action to achieve goals. A strategic plan often encompasses periods ranging from five to ten years. Such a plan establishes enterprise policy and priorities for such activities as research and development, marketing, financing, and plant expansion. A strategic plan serves as the basis for the commitment of enterprise resources.

A strategic plan, which is normally approved by the highest levels of management, should integrate all aspects of the enterprise operations necessary for the achievement of long-range goals. Because the strategic plan is influenced by the changing environment within which the enterprise operates, the strategic plan should be periodically reviewed and revised. For example, rising interest rates might postpone a proposed plant expansion, or falling oil prices might postpone an enterprise's plan to expand operations into energy-saving products.

Strategic Planning

Based on a survey of 180 executives selected from manufacturing corporations listed in Standard & Poor's *Register of Corporations, Directors and Executives,* the following environmental factors were considered important to include in the development of strategic plans:

Environmental Factors
To Include In Strategic Plans

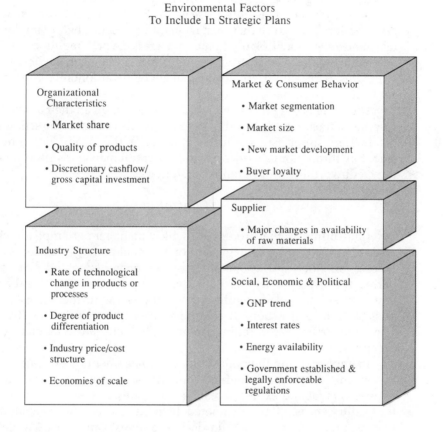

Organizational Characteristics

• Market share

• Quality of products

• Discretionary cashflow/ gross capital investment

Market & Consumer Behavior

• Market segmentation

• Market size

• New market development

• Buyer loyalty

Industry Structure

• Rate of technological change in products or processes

• Degree of product differentiation

• Industry price/cost structure

• Economies of scale

Supplier

• Major changes in availability of raw materials

Social, Economic & Political

• GNP trend

• Interest rates

• Energy availability

• Government established & legally enforceable regulations

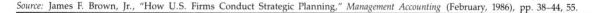

Source: James F. Brown, Jr., "How U.S. Firms Conduct Strategic Planning," *Management Accounting* (February, 1986), pp. 38–44, 55.

Operational planning, sometimes referred to as **tactical planning,** is the development of short-term plans to achieve goals identified in the strategic plan. Thus, operational plans complement the strategic plan and are typically established for time periods ranging from a week or a month to several years. Examples of operational planning are the setting of the current month's production levels by a manufacturer and determining the need for part-time employees during the holiday shopping period by a merchandising enterprise.

Effective communication between all levels of management within an enterprise is essential, so that day-to-day operations can be coordinated to meet the operational and strategic plans. An important part of this communication is the various accounting reports that management uses in planning operations.

Organizing and Directing

Organizing is the process by which management assigns responsibility to individuals for achieving enterprise goals. Each enterprise has its own unique organizational structure that management has established to implement strategic and operational plans. Some managers favor a highly centralized and autocratic organizational structure, while other managers favor decentralized structures with significant lower-management autonomy. No one organizational structure has proven best in all situations.

Directing is the process by which managers, given their assigned level of responsibilities, run day-to-day operations. Examples of directing include a production supervisor's efforts at keeping the production line moving smoothly throughout a work shift and the credit manager's efforts at assessing the creditworthiness of potential customers.

Controlling

Controlling is the process by which managers attempt to achieve the goals identified in the strategic and operational plans. This process normally involves monitoring the operating results of implemented plans and comparing the expected results with the actual results. This **feedback** allows management to isolate significant variations for further investigation and possible remedial action. It may also lead to a revision of future plans. This philosophy of controlling is sometimes referred to as **management by exception.**

In implementing the philosophy of management by exception, managers assess the estimated benefits from investigating significant differences between actual and expected results and the estimated costs of investigating these differences. If the estimated benefits exceed the estimated costs of investigating, managers should decide to investigate. For example, if actual direct materials costs exceed expected costs by $100,000, and the cost of investigation to determine the cause of the difference is estimated to be $5,000, then managers would normally investigate the materials difference and attempt to correct the problem. In this example, the cause of the difference might be the use of low-quality materials, and a change of suppliers might be warranted. On the other hand, if the difference between the actual and estimated costs is $5,000, and the cost of investigating the difference is $100,000, management would not likely decide to investigate the difference.

Decision Making

Decision making is the process by which managers determine to follow one course of action as opposed to an alternative. Decision making is inherent in each of the three management functions described in the preceding paragraphs. For example, in developing a strategic plan, managers must decide between competing courses of action to achieve long-range goals and objectives. Likewise, in organizing and directing operations, managers must decide on an organizational structure and on specific actions to take in day-to-day operations. In controlling operations, managers must decide whether variances are worth investigating.

ROLE OF MANAGERIAL ACCOUNTING

An essential ingredient for a management process to be successful is relevant information. **Managerial accounting** is the area of accounting that provides this information to management for use in planning, organizing and directing, controlling, and decision making. In this role, managerial accounting contributes to the efficient allocation of resources within a society.

Managerial accounting aids managers in planning by providing reports which estimate the effects of alternative actions on an enterprise's ability to achieve desired goals. For example, an enterprise might establish a 25% market share as a long-term strategic goal. To achieve this goal, the enterprise might consider increasing its advertising expenditures and/or decreasing its unit selling prices. Managerial accounting could report the estimated effects of the increased advertising, based on past experience, industry advertising statistics, market surveys, and other data, as well as the estimated effects of the decreased selling prices.

Managerial accounting aids managers in their organizing and directing functions by providing reports which allow them to adjust daily operations for changing conditions. For example, scrap reports could be provided to production supervisors for use in monitoring waste and efficiency of production on a daily basis. Likewise, daily or weekly sales reports could be used by a store manager in deciding which items are selling well and should be reordered and which items are not selling well and should not be reordered.

Managerial accounting aids managers in controlling operations by providing performance reports of variances between expected and actual operating results. Such reports serve as the basis for taking necessary corrective action to control operations. For example, a production supervisor might receive weekly or daily performance reports comparing actual materials costs with estimated costs. Significant variances could be isolated and corrective action could be taken. An excess of actual materials costs over estimated costs might be caused by the use of poor quality materials, in which case a change in suppliers might be warranted. Another example would be a partner in a law firm receiving weekly progress reports on the amount of staff time spent on each case. An excessive amount of staff time spent on any particular case would warrant an investigation and an explanation from the staff.

Managerial accounting aids managers in decision making by providing the basic information which the manager uses in selecting among alternative courses of action. For example, an accounting report indicating the contribution of the automotive service department to total store profits would aid the store manager in deciding whether to discontinue that department. Likewise, a similar accounting report would aid an ophthalmologist in deciding whether to sell eyeglass frames as a service to patients.

Managerial accounting thus provides information for all four basic functions of the management process. Without this information, it would be difficult for management to manage effectively and efficiently. The use of accounting information by managers is similar to the use of dashboard information by the driver of an automobile. The driver (manager) uses data on speed, oil pressure, and fuel (accounting information) to drive (manage) the automobile (enterprise) properly to an intended destination (goal).

CHARACTERISTICS OF MANAGERIAL ACCOUNTING REPORTS

As indicated, accounting reports provide much of the information useful for management in planning, organizing and directing, controlling, and decision making. The principle of "usefulness to management" is the primary criterion for the preparation of managerial accounting reports. To be useful, these reports should possess the characteristics of (1) relevance, (2) timeliness, (3) accuracy, (4) clarity, and (5) conciseness. Each of these characteristics is described in the following paragraphs.

Relevance

Relevance means that the economic information reported must be pertinent to the specific action being considered by management. In applying this concept, the accountant must be familiar with the operations of the firm and the needs of management in order to select what is important from the masses of data that are available. Especially in this modern age of the information explosion, this selection process can be difficult. To accomplish this task, the accountant must determine the needs of management for the decision at hand, examine the available data, and select only the relevant data for reporting to management. To illustrate, assume that management is considering the replacement of fully depreciated equipment, which cost $100,000, with new equipment costing $150,000. It is the $150,000 that is relevant for an analysis of financing the replacement. The original cost, $100,000, is irrelevant.

In applying the concept of relevance, it is important to recognize that some accounting information may have little or no relevance for one use but may have a high degree of relevance for another use. For example, in the previous illustration, the $100,000 was irrelevant for purposes of evaluating the financing of the replacement equipment. For tax purposes, however, the $100,000 (and its accumulated depreciation) would be relevant for determining the amount of the gain from the sale or trade-in of the old equipment and the amount of the income tax due on any gain.

Timeliness

Timeliness refers to the need for accounting reports to contain the most up-to-date information. In many cases, outdated data can lead to unwise decisions. For example, if prior years' costs are relied upon in setting the selling price of a product, the resulting selling price may not be sufficient to cover the current year's costs and to provide a satisfactory profit.

In some cases, the timeliness concept may require the accountant to prepare reports on a prearranged schedule, such as daily, weekly, or monthly. For example, daily reports of cash receipts and disbursements assist management in effectively managing the use of cash on a day-to-day basis. On the other hand, weekly reports of the cost of products manufactured may be satisfactory to assist management in the control of costs. In other cases, reports are prepared on an irregular basis or only when needed. For example, if management is evaluating a proposed advertising promotion for the month of May, a report of current costs and other current relevant data for this specific proposal would be needed in sufficient time for management to make and implement the decision.

Accuracy

Accuracy refers to the need for the report to be correct within the constraints of the use of the report and the inherent inaccuracies in the measurement process. If the report is not accurate, management's decision may not be prudent. For example, if an inaccurate report on a customer's past payment practices is presented to management, an unwise decision in granting credit may be made.

As previously indicated, the concept of accuracy must be applied within the constraint of the use to be made of the report. In other words, there are occasions when accuracy should be sacrificed for less precise data that are more useful to management. For example, in planning production, estimates (forecasts) of future sales may be more useful than more accurate data from past sales. In addition, it should be noted that there are inherent inaccuracies in accounting data that are based on estimates and approximations. For example, in determining the unit cost of a product manufactured, an estimate of depreciation expense on factory equipment used in the manufacturing process must be made. Without this estimate, the cost of the product would be of limited usefulness in establishing the product selling price.

Clarity

Clarity refers to the need for reports to be clear and understandable in both format and content. Reports that are clear and understandable will enable management to focus on significant factors in planning and controlling operations. For example, for management's use in controlling the costs of manufacturing a product, a report that compares actual costs with expected costs and clearly indicates the differences enables management to give its attention to significant differences and to take any necessary corrective action.

Conciseness
• • •

Conciseness refers to the requirement that the report should be brief and to the point. Although the report must be complete and include all relevant information, the inclusion of unnecessary information wastes management's time and makes it more difficult for management to focus on the significant factors related to a decision. For example, reports prepared for the top level of management should usually be broad in scope and present summaries of data rather than small details.

Costs vs. Benefits of Managerial Accounting Reports
• • •

The characteristics of managerial accounting reports provide general guidelines for the preparation of reports to meet the various needs of management. In applying these guidelines, consideration must be given to the specific needs of each manager, and the reports should be tailored to meet these needs. In preparing reports, costs are incurred, and a primary consideration is that the value of the management reports must at least equal the cost of producing them. The relationship between the general guidelines and the cost-benefit consideration is illustrated as follows:

• • • • • • • • •

Managerial Accounting Reports

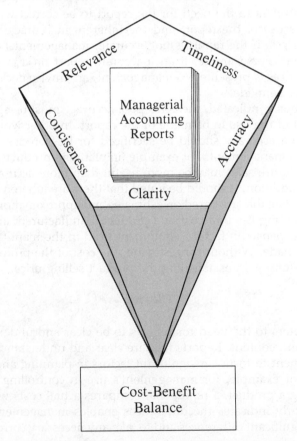

Costs and benefits must be considered, no matter how informational a report may be. A report should not be prepared if its cost exceeds the benefits derived by management.

ORGANIZATION OF THE MANAGERIAL ACCOUNTING FUNCTION

Managers organize business enterprises into departments or similar units with responsibilities for specific functions or activities. This operating structure of an enterprise can be diagrammed in an **organization chart.** An organization chart for Baker Inc., a small manufacturing enterprise, is as follows:

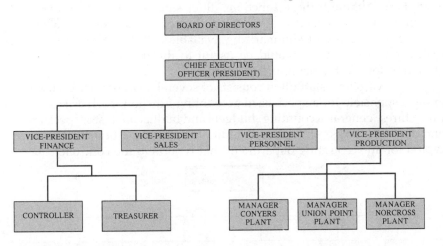

Organization Chart For Baker Inc.

The individual reporting units in an enterprise can be viewed as having either (1) line responsibilities or (2) staff responsibilities. A **line** department or unit is one directly involved in the basic objectives of the organization. For Baker Inc., the vice-president of production and the managers of the Conyers Plant, the Union Point Plant, and the Norcross Plant occupy line positions because they are responsible for an activity directly related to the generation of revenues. Likewise, the vice-president of sales occupies a line position.

A **staff** department or unit is one that provides services, assistance, and advice to the departments with line or other staff responsibilities. The organization chart for Baker Inc. indicates only two staff positions that report to the chief executive officer. In large organizations, however, staff positions may also exist for such functions as engineering, research and development, and marketing. For Baker Inc., the vice-president of personnel occupies a staff position because the personnel department assists line managers and others in staffing their departments. Likewise, the vice-president of finance occupies a staff position, to which two other staff positions—the controller and the treasurer—report.

In most business organizations, the chief accountant is called the **controller.** The controller has a staff relationship with others in the organization, providing advice and assistance to management but assuming no responsibility for the operations of the business. The controller's function might be compared to that of an airplane's navigator. The navigator, with special skills and training, assists the pilot, but the pilot is responsible for flying the airplane. Likewise, the controller, with special accounting training and skills, advises management, but management is responsible for planning and controlling operations.

The role of the treasurer is to advise management on the proper securing and handling of the enterprise's financial resources. These activities, for example, may involve the day-to-day investment of excess cash in money market securities or the long-term negotiation of a credit line from a financial institution. Although these functions differ significantly, the controller and treasurer would interact in some areas. For example, the controller's staff might prepare a report summarizing available cash balances and estimated cash needs. This report would be useful to the treasurer in planning and arranging for the financing of operations.

The controller's staff often consists of several accountants. Each accountant is responsible for a specialized accounting function, such as systems and procedures, general accounting, budgets and budget analyses, special reports and analyses, taxes, and internal audit. The following organization chart is typical for an accounting department that reports to the controller:

Organization Chart— Controller's Department

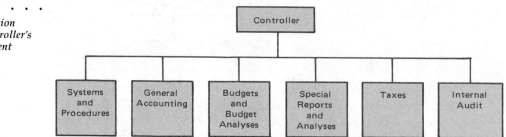

Systems and procedures is concerned with the design and implementation of procedures for the accumulation and reporting of accounting data to all interested users. In performing this function, the accountant must evaluate the usefulness of various types of data processing equipment for the firm. The systems accountant must also devise appropriate "checks and balances" to safeguard business assets and provide for an information flow that will be efficient and helpful to management. The accounting system must provide accounting data for use by various groups and individuals in making informed judgments and decisions.

General accounting is primarily concerned with the recording of transactions and periodic preparation of the basic financial statements. Of particular importance to this area is the gathering of data in conformity with the generally accepted accounting principles for preparing the basic financial statements.

Budgets and budget analyses focuses on the plan for financial operations for future periods, and through records and summaries, focuses on the comparison of actual operations with these plans. This function provides much of the information for planning and controlling operations.

Special reports and analyses is concerned with data that will be useful to management in analyzing current problems and considering alternate courses for future operations. Much of the analysis focuses on providing data related to specific problems that confront management and identifying alternative courses of action related to proposed new projects. Often the accountants who perform this function prepare special reports according to the requirements of regulatory agencies.

Taxes encompasses the preparation of tax returns and the consideration of the tax consequences of proposed business transactions or alternate courses of action. Accountants in this area must be familiar with the tax statutes affecting their business and must also keep up-to-date on administrative regulations and court decisions on tax cases.

Internal audit is a staff of company employees whose principal responsibility is to determine to what extent, if any, the various operating units are deviating from the policies and procedures prescribed by management.

The Magic of 3M

3M was listed along with 61 other corporate high achievers in the best seller, *In Search of Excellence,* by Thomas J. Peters and Robert H. Waterman, Jr. In *A Passion for Excellence,* by Peters and Nancy Austin, 3M was again listed as a model for product innovation and entrepreneurship.

Some of the reasons for 3M's success, based on interviews with 3M executives, are as follows:

"Financial expertise, long recognized as one of 3M's greatest assets, is a major contributor to the corporation's success. 3M uses its financial control system to encourage rather than curtail innovation and creativity. Numbers are used to set goals and measure performance rather than to deny expenditures or punish unmet expectations."

"... we (controllers) get intimately involved with day-to-day activities ... with forecasting and planning activities of business units. As an example, in new product development we try to lay out for the managers the cost implications of bringing on a new product and what it means in relation to their total business and whether or not they can still reach their financial targets. We work with them, developing the analysis to help them prioritize what products they want to go after. ...Our controllers view their roles as not to always challenge management, but as being a cooperative effort to develop a better business."

"3M's (division) controllers have been able to support 3M's strategic objectives while keeping management focused on operational objectives... we do a fair, if not a good, job of balancing strategic and operational considerations."

"Our organization is not a negatively focused accounting organization. We aren't always coming in and saying 'you can't do that.' We are supportive and positive in dealing with line management. We have tried to understand the business while doing our jobs."

"I (division controller) view the controller's function as the financial consultant... the person who brings to a division the financial information."

"I (vice president of finance) tell our people, 'Your job is to help the operating people achieve what they're trying to achieve. Then if you have to say no, you'll be respected for it.' The first principle is working with the operating people."

Source: Kathy Williams, "The Magic of 3M: Management Accounting Excellence," *Management Accounting* (February, 1986), pp. 20–27.

FINANCIAL ACCOUNTING AND MANAGERIAL ACCOUNTING

Although economic information can be classified in many ways, accountants often divide accounting information into two types: financial and managerial. A brief summary of the similarities and differences between these two types of accounting information may be useful in further understanding the role of managerial accounting in an organization.

Financial accounting is concerned with the recording of transactions for a business enterprise or other economic unit and with the periodic preparation of various statements from such records. In performing these functions, financial accountants use **generally accepted accounting principles (GAAP).** The financial statements, which report the results of past financial activities of the enterprise as a whole, are intended primarily for the use of persons who are "outside" or external to the enterprise, such as shareholders, creditors, governmental agencies, and the general public. However, these statements are also useful to management in directing the operations of the enterprise. For example, in planning future operations, management often begins by evaluating the results of relevant past activities as reported in the basic financial statements. For this reason, financial statements are normally prepared by the general accounting staff under the controller's direction.

Managerial accounting employs both historical and estimated data, which management uses in conducting daily operations and in planning future operations. For example, in directing day-to-day operations, management relies upon accounting to provide information concerning the amount owed to each creditor, the amount owed by each customer, and the date each amount is due. The treasurer uses these data and other data in the management of cash. Accounting data may be used by top management in determining the selling price of a new product. Production managers, by comparing past performances with planned objectives, can take steps to accelerate favorable trends and reduce those trends that are unfavorable.

Managerial accounting overlaps financial accounting to the extent that management uses the financial statements in directing current operations and planning future operations. However, managerial accounting extends beyond financial accounting by providing additional information and reports that focus on individual operating units, based on the principle of usefulness.

The distinguishing characteristics of managerial accounting in comparison to financial accounting are summarized in the following table:

· · · · · · · · ·
*Comparison of
Managerial and
Financial Accounting*

	Managerial Accounting	Financial Accounting
Primary users of reports	Management	Stockholders Creditors General public Management
Primary criteria for report preparation	Usefulness to management	Generally accepted accounting principles

	Managerial Accounting	Financial Accounting
Primary orientation	Future	Past
Frequency of report preparation	As needed by management	Monthly, quarterly, annually
Primary focus of report	Individual operating units	Enterprise as a whole

Comparison of Managerial and Financial Accounting

PROFESSION OF MANAGERIAL ACCOUNTING

As a profession, managerial accounting is gaining recognition for its importance to society and to the effective management of business enterprises. To provide some of this recognition, the **Institute of Certified Management Accounting,** which is an affiliate of the National Association of Accountants, grants the **Certificate in Management Accounting (CMA)** as evidence of professional competence in managerial accounting. The objectives of the CMA program are as follows:

1. To establish management accounting as a recognized profession by identifying the role of the management accountant and the underlying body of knowledge, and by outlining a course of study by which such knowledge can be acquired.
2. To foster higher educational standards in the field of management accounting.
3. To establish an objective measure of an individual's knowledge and competence in the field of management accounting.

The requirements for the CMA designation include the baccalaureate degree or equivalent, two years of experience in managerial accounting, and successful completion of a 2½-day examination. The examination consists of the following five parts, which reflect the interdisciplinary nature of managerial accounting:

1. Economics and business finance.
2. Organization and behavior, including ethical considerations.
3. Public reporting standards, auditing, and taxes.
4. Periodic reporting for internal and external purposes.
5. Decision analysis, including modeling and information systems.

Individual holders of the CMA certificate are also required to participate in a program of continuing education and to adhere to a professional code of ethics. The **code of ethics** requires CMAs to maintain the following attributes:[2]

---

[2]*Statement on Management Accounting No. 1C,* "Standards of Ethical Conduct for Management Accountants" (National Association of Accountants, New York, 1983).

1. Competence in the performance of their duties.
2. Confidentiality of sensitive information gathered in the performance of their duties.
3. Integrity in the performance of their duties.
4. Objectivity in communicating information.

Managerial accounting is a challenging and rewarding career path. Many Chief Executive Officers began their careers as managerial accountants. For example, former managerial accountants who later became chief executive officers include Roger B. Smith (General Motors Corp.), Charles E. Exley (NCR Corporation), Robert M. Schaeberle (Nabisco Brands, Inc.), and Ed Hennessy (Allied Corp.). The need for managerial accountants to interact with all phases of an enterprise's operations provides the managerial accountant with an excellent managerial background and understanding of enterprise operations. As society changes and businesses become more complex and more results oriented, the role of the managerial accountant will continue to be an essential element of successful business enterprises.

Chapter Review

KEY POINTS

1. The Management Process.

The management of an organization consists of those individuals charged with the responsibility of directing the enterprise toward achieving its goals. The management process involves the four basic functions of (1) planning, (2) organizing and directing, (3) controlling, and (4) decision making.

Planning is the process by which management develops a course of action to attain enterprise goals. Long-range goals involve strategic planning, while short-term goals involve operational planning. Organizing is the process by which management assigns responsibility to individuals for achieving enterprise goals, while directing is the process by which managers run day-to-day operations. Controlling is the process by which managers attempt to achieve the goals identified in the strategic and operational plans. Decision making, which involves choosing among alternative courses of action, has a central role in planning, organizing and directing, and controlling operations.

2. Role of Managerial Accounting.

Managerial accounting is the area of accounting that provides relevant information to management. Managerial accounting aids managers in planning (by providing reports which estimate the effects of alternative actions on an enterprise's ability to achieve desired goals), in organizing and directing (by providing information which is used to adjust daily operations for changing conditions), in controlling operations (by providing performance reports of variances between expected and actual operating results), and in decision making (by providing the basic information which the manager uses in selecting among alternative courses of action). Without accounting information, it would be difficult for management to manage effectively and efficiently.

3. Characteristics of Managerial Accounting Reports.

The principle of usefulness to management is the primary criterion for preparation of managerial accounting reports. In preparing useful managerial accounting reports, five characteristics should be considered. Relevance means that the economic information reported must be pertinent to the specific action being considered by management. Timeliness refers to the need for accounting reports to contain the most up-to-date information. Accuracy refers to the need for the report to be correct within the constraints of the use of the report and the inherent inaccuracies in the measurement process. Clarity refers to the need for the report to be clear and understandable in both format and content. Conciseness refers to the requirement that the report should be brief and to the point. A report should not be prepared if the cost of preparing it exceeds the benefits derived by management from its use.

4. Organization of the Managerial Accounting Function.

Managers organize business enterprises into departments or similar units with responsibilities for specific functions or activities. This operating structure of an enterprise can be diagrammed in an organization chart. Individual units in an enterprise can be viewed as having either (1) line responsibilities or (2) staff responsibilities. A line department or unit is one directly involved in the basic objectives of the organization. A staff department or unit is one that provides services, assistance, and advice to the line departments or other staff departments.

The chief accountant in a corporation is called the controller. The controller has a staff relationship with others in the organization, providing advice and assistance to management but assuming no responsibility for the operations of the business. The functions most commonly provided by the controller's staff include systems and procedures, general accounting, budgets and budget analyses, special reports and analyses, taxes, and internal audit.

5. Financial Accounting and Managerial Accounting.

Financial accounting is concerned with the recording of transactions for a business enterprise or other economic unit and with the periodic preparation of various statements from such records. In performing these functions, financial accountants use generally accepted accounting principles. Managerial accounting employs both historical and estimated data, which management uses in conducting daily operations and in planning future operations. Managerial accounting extends beyond financial accounting by providing additional information and reports for management, based on the principle of usefulness.

6. Profession of Managerial Accounting.
The Institute of Certified Management Accounting grants the Certificate in Management Accounting (CMA) as evidence of professional competence in managerial accounting. The requirements for the CMA designation include a baccalaureate degree or equivalent, two years of experience in managerial accounting, and successful completion of a $2^1/_2$-day examination. Holders of the CMA certificate are also required to participate in a program of continuing education and to adhere to a professional code of ethics.

KEY TERMS

accounting 3
management 3
management process 3
planning 4
strategic planning 4
operational planning 5
organizing 6
directing 6

controlling 6
management by exception 6
decision making 6
managerial accounting 7
controller 11
financial accounting 14
generally accepted accounting
   principles 14

SELF-EXAMINATION QUESTIONS

(Answers at End of Chapter)

1. Which of the following is *not* one of the four basic functions of the management process?
   A. Planning
   B. Controlling
   C. Decision making
   D. Operations

2. The development of a long-range course of action to achieve enterprise goals is called:
   A. operational planning
   B. controlling
   C. strategic planning
   D. organizing and directing

3. Which of the following is *not* a characteristic of managerial accounting reports?
   A. Timeliness
   B. Relevance
   C. Conciseness
   D. Cost-benefit balance

4. Which of the following departments would be considered a staff department in the organizational structure of a manufacturing enterprise?
   A. Personnel department
   B. Sales department
   C. Polishing department
   D. Assembly department

5. Which of the following designations serves as evidence of professional competence in managerial accounting?
   A. Certified Public Accountant
   B. Certified Management Accountant
   C. Certified Internal Auditor
   D. Certified Financial Planner

Discussion Questions

1–1. Identify some of the groups who use accounting information.

1–2. What are the four basic functions of the management process?

1–3. What is the term for a plan that encompasses a period ranging from five to ten years and that serves as a basis for commitment of enterprise resources?

1–4. What is the process by which management assigns responsibility to individuals for achieving enterprise goals?

1–5. What is the process by which managers determine to follow one course of action as opposed to an alternative?

1–6. Describe how managerial accounting aids managers in controlling operations.

1–7. Describe what is meant by "management by exception."

1–8. What is the dominant principle that guides the managerial accountant in preparing management reports?

1–9. Zarnoch Company is contemplating the expansion of its operations through the purchase of the assets of Keefe Lumber Company. Included among the assets of Keefe Lumber Company is lumber purchased for $150,000 and having a current replacement cost of $205,000. Which cost ($150,000 or $205,000) is relevant for the decision to be made by Zarnoch Company? Briefly explain the reason for your answer.

1–10. A bank loan officer is evaluating a request for a loan that is to be secured by a mortgage on the borrower's property. The property cost $300,000 twenty years ago and has a current market value of $450,000. Which figure, $300,000 or $450,000, is relevant for the loan officer's use in evaluating the request for the loan? Discuss.

1–11. What is meant by cost-benefit balance as it relates to the preparation of management reports?

1–12. (a) Differentiate between a department with line responsibility and a department with staff responsibility. (b) In an organization that has a sales department and a personnel department, among others, which of the two departments has (1) a line responsibility and (2) a staff responsibility?

1–13. (a) What is the role of the controller in a business organization? (b) Does the controller have a line or a staff responsibility?

1–14. What is the principal responsibility of the staff of internal auditors?

1–15. Is the information classified as financial accounting useful to management? Discuss.

1–16. In preparing the basic financial statements, must generally accepted accounting principles be used? Discuss.

1–17. In preparing reports for the use of management, must the managerial accountant use generally accepted accounting principles? Discuss.

1–18. Contrast financial accounting information with managerial accounting information in terms of those who use the information.

1–19. What do the initials CMA signify?

1–20. Briefly discuss the requirements for the CMA designation.

1–21. Real World Focus. The following paragraphs were taken from an article in *The Wall Street Journal* on April 13, 1987, describing actions taken by General Motors Corporation:

> General Motors Corp. has lowered its market-share goal in the U.S. through 1990, but "is now in a strong position to provide maximum profitability," Roger B. Smith, GM chairman, told securities analysts.
> Mr. Smith said GM's goal is to get about 40% of the U.S. car market. That is higher than the 37.9% GM got in the first quarter, but below the 42% goal that GM officials were setting a few months ago and below the 45% share that GM has averaged over the past decade. The new goal reflects GM's "changing focus towards profitability," Leon J. Krain, the company's treasurer, said in a telephone interview Friday.

Do the actions taken by General Motors Corporation impact on strategic or operational planning? Explain.

Answers to Self-Examination Questions

· · ·

1. D The four basic functions of the management process are planning (answer A), organizing and directing, controlling (answer B), and decision making (answer C). Operations (answer D) is not one of the four basic functions, but is the activity which managers attempt to manage.

2. C Strategic planning (answer C) is the development of long-range courses of action to achieve enterprise goals. Operational planning (answer A) is the development of short-term plans to achieve goals identified in the strategic plan. Controlling (answer B) is the process by which managers attempt to achieve the goals identified in the strategic and operational plans. Organizing and directing (answer D) is the process by which management assigns responsibility and runs day-to-day operations.

3. D Cost-benefit balance (answer D) is not a characteristic of managerial accounting reports, but is a general guideline for the preparation of managerial accounting reports. Timeliness (answer A), relevance (answer B), and conciseness (answer C) are all characteristics of useful managerial accounting reports.

4. A The personnel department (answer A) provides a staff function by assisting line managers and others in staffing their departments. The sales department (answer B), polishing department (answer C), and assembly department (answer D) are all line departments with a responsibility for activities directly related to the generation of enterprise revenues.

5. B The Certified Management Accountant designation (answer B) serves as evidence of professional competence in managerial accounting. A Certified Public Accountant (answer A) has professional competence in financial accounting. A Certified Internal Auditor (answer C) has professional competence in internal auditing. A Certified Financial Planner (answer D) has professional competence in financial planning.

Part Two

Managerial Accounting Concepts and Systems

Chapter
Two

Cost Concepts and Classifications

The role of managerial accounting in providing economic information to management for use in conducting daily operations and in planning future operations was discussed in general terms in Chapter 1. Although this economic information can take many forms, information related to the "costs" associated with operations is often of great significance. In this chapter, common cost terminology, classifications, and concepts used in managerial accounting are discussed.[1] Also, costs and expenses are distinguished, and financial statements for a manufacturing enterprise are illustrated.

COSTS AND EXPENSES DISTINGUISHED

The terms "cost" and "expense" are sometimes used interchangeably. However, the terms have different meanings, and the incorrect use of the terms can lead to confusion and misunderstanding.

All disbursements of cash (or the commitment to pay cash in the future) for the purpose of generating revenues are **costs**. For example, when store supplies are purchased for cash or credit (on account), the disbursement represents the cost of the supplies. In contrast, although the payment of dividends to stockholders is a disbursement, it is not a cost, since the payment of dividends does not generate revenues.

All costs initially represent assets to the enterprise. As the assets are used in generating revenues, the cost of the assets must be recognized as **expenses** in order to match revenues and expenses properly in the process of determining the net income of the period. Thus, depreciation expense is recognized as plant assets are used in generating revenues, and prepaid insurance premiums are written off as an expense over the periods benefiting from the insurance policies.

---

[1]The terminology in this chapter is consistent with the recommendations in *Statement on Management Accounting No. 2*, "Management Accounting Terminology" (Montvale, New Jersey: National Association of Accountants, 1983).

To simplify the recording process, costs that will benefit only the current period are often initially recorded as expenses rather than as assets. This procedure avoids the need to record the use of the assets as expenses, as would be the case if the costs were initially recorded as assets. For example, the payment of $1,500 for the current month's rent would be recorded by most enterprises as an expense (Rent Expense) rather than as an asset (Prepaid Rent).

The distinction between costs and expenses is summarized in the following diagram:

Costs and Expenses Distinguished

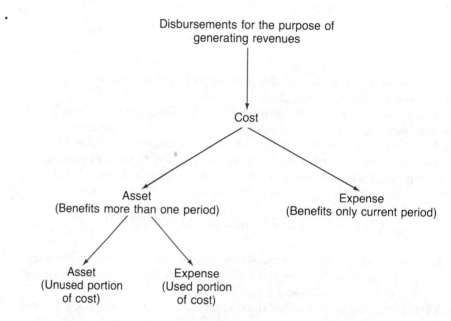

The distinction between the terms cost and expense is especially important for the preparation of financial statements for service, merchandising, and manufacturing enterprises. However, this distinction has more importance for manufacturing enterprises. Costs incurred in manufacturing products are assets, and these costs do not become expenses until the manufactured products are sold, thereby generating revenue. Likewise, products for which manufacturing has been partially or fully completed but which have not been sold should continue to be recognized as assets.

MANUFACTURING COSTS

The cost of manufacturing a product includes not only the cost of tangible materials entering into the manufacturing process, but also the costs incurred in changing the materials into a finished product ready for sale. The cost of a manufactured product generally consists of direct materials cost, direct labor cost, and factory overhead cost.

Direct Materials Cost

The cost of materials entering directly into the manufactured product is classified as **direct materials cost**, sometimes referred to as **raw materials cost.** For example, the direct materials for Seawind Company, a manufacturer of fishing boats, would include fiberglass and paint.

As a practical matter, in order for a cost to be classified as a direct materials cost, the cost must not only be an integral part of the end product, but it must be a significant dollar portion of the total cost of the product. For Seawind Company, the costs of fiberglass and paint are a significant portion of the total cost of each boat.

Other examples of direct materials costs include the cost of paper and ink for a printer, lumber for a furniture manufacturer, silicon wafers for a producer of microcomputer chips, and steel for an automobile manufacturer. The finished product of one manufacturer may become the direct materials for another manufacturer. For example, the finished products of a lumber mill become the direct materials for a construction contractor.

Direct Labor Cost

The cost of wages paid to employees directly involved in changing direct materials into finished product is classified as **direct labor cost.** For example, the direct labor cost of Seawind Company includes the wages of the employees who paint the boat hulls in the manufacturing process. Other examples of direct labor costs include the wages of carpenters for a construction contractor, mechanics' wages in an automotive repair shop, machine operators' wages in a tool manufacturing plant, and assemblers' wages in a microcomputer manufacturing plant.

As a practical matter, for the cost of employee wages to be classified as direct labor cost, the employee must not only be directly involved in the creation of the finished product, but the wages must be a significant portion of the total product cost. For Seawind Company, the painters' wages are a significant portion of the total cost of each boat.

Factory Overhead Cost

Costs other than direct materials cost and direct labor cost incurred in the manufacturing process are classified as **factory overhead cost**, sometimes referred to as **manufacturing overhead** or **factory burden.** For example, factory overhead cost includes the cost of heating and lighting the factory, repair and maintenance of factory equipment, and property taxes, insurance, and depreciation on factory plant and equipment. Factory overhead cost also includes materials and labor costs which do not enter directly into the finished product. For example, the cost of oil used to lubricate machinery is a materials cost which does not enter directly into finished products. Other examples of such costs include the wages of janitorial, supervisory, and quality control personnel.

As a practical matter, if the costs of direct materials or direct labor are not a significant portion of the total product cost, these costs are classified as factory overhead. In Seawind Company, for example, glue enters directly into the finished product (boats), but its cost is insignificant and it is therefore classified as factory overhead. For many industries, the increased use of automated machinery and robotics has decreased labor costs to a level where they are a small portion of total product costs. In this situation, direct labor costs of manufactured products are often included as part of factory overhead cost.

Prime Costs and Conversion Costs

As previously discussed, the total cost of a manufactured product consists of three elements: direct materials, direct labor, and factory overhead costs. These costs are often grouped in various classifications for analysis and reporting purposes. As will be illustrated in later chapters, two common classifications of manufacturing costs often reported to management for planning and decision making purposes are prime costs and conversion costs.

Prime costs are the combination of direct materials and direct labor costs. As the name implies, prime costs are generally the largest component of the total cost of a manufactured product. **Conversion costs** are the combination of direct labor and factory overhead costs. Conversion costs are the costs of converting the materials into a finished, manufactured product.

The diagram on page 27 summarizes the classification of manufacturing costs into prime costs and conversion costs.

NONMANUFACTURING COSTS

Nonmanufacturing costs are generally classified into two categories: selling and administrative. **Selling costs** are costs that are incurred in marketing the product and delivering the sold product to customers. Examples of selling costs include salaries of marketing personnel, advertising expenditures, sales commissions, salespersons' salaries, and depreciation on store equipment. **Administrative costs** are costs that are incurred in the administration of the business and that are not related to the manufacturing or selling functions. Examples of administrative costs include office salaries, office supplies, and depreciation on office buildings and equipment.

By classifying nonmanufacturing costs into selling and administrative, the managerial accountant enables management to establish accountability and control over the cost of two major functional activities: selling activities and administrative activities. Different levels of accountability for these activities may be shown in managerial reports. For example, selling costs may be reported by product, salespersons, departments, divisions, or geographic territories. Likewise, administrative costs may be reported by functional area, such as personnel, computer services, accounting, finance, or office support.

The accounting for nonmanufacturing costs is similar for manufacturing, merchandising, and service enterprises. Most selling and administrative costs

P R I M E   C O S T S

C O N V E R S I O N   C O S T S

Direct Materials Cost:

(1) Enters directly into the product, and

(2) Is significant amount of total product cost.

Example: Memory chips for a microcomputer manufacturer.

Direct Labor Cost:

(1) Enters directly into manufacturing the product, and

(2) Is significant amount of total product cost.

Example: Hourly wages of assemblers of microcomputers.

Factory Overhead Cost:

Is cost other than direct materials cost and direct labor cost incurred in the manufacturing of products.

Example: Depreciation on testing equipment for a microcomputer manufacturer.

are initially recognized as expenses because they benefit only the period in which they are incurred.

The concepts and principles discussed throughout this text for planning and controlling manufacturing costs are also applicable to selling and administrative costs. Where applicable, these concepts and principles will be illustrated for both manufacturing costs and selling and administrative costs.

PRODUCT COSTS AND PERIOD COSTS

In the preceding section, costs were classified as manufacturing or non-manufacturing. These costs may also be classified as either product costs or period costs.

Product costs are composed of the three elements of manufacturing cost: direct materials, direct labor, and factory overhead.[2] These costs are treated as assets until the product is sold. In other words, during the period beginning when product costs are initially incurred until the products are sold, product costs are accounted for as assets and are reported as a part of inventory on the balance sheet. In this sense, product costs are sometimes referred to as **inventoriable costs.** Thus, direct materials, direct labor, and factory overhead costs incurred in one period will not appear on the income statement as expenses until the products with which they are associated are sold.

Period costs are those costs that are used up in generating revenue during the current period and that are not involved in the manufacturing process. Selling and administrative costs are period costs. They are recognized as expenses on the current period's income statement. Many period costs are time-oriented, in the sense that the costs are incurred or used as time passes.

The diagram on page 29 relates the manufacturing and nonmanufacturing cost concepts to the product cost and period cost concepts for a furniture manufacturer.

FINANCIAL STATEMENTS FOR MANUFACTURING ENTERPRISES

The financial statements for service and merchandising enterprises are described and illustrated in textbooks on financial accounting.[3] Examples of service enterprises are law firms, medical associations, advertising firms, insurance agencies, and real estate agencies. Examples of merchandising businesses are retail stores (such as Sears, J. C. Penney, K Mart), drug stores, and hardware stores.

The financial statements for manufacturing enterprises are more complex than those for service and merchandising enterprises. Since a manufacturing enterprise manufactures the products that it sells, the manufacturing costs described in the preceding paragraphs must be properly accounted for and reported in the financial statements. These manufacturing costs primarily

---

[2]For merchandising enterprises, product costs include the costs associated with a product purchased in finished form and ready for sale.
[3]See Carl S. Warren and Philip E. Fess, *Financial Accounting* (3d ed.; Cincinnati: South-Western Publishing Co., 1988).

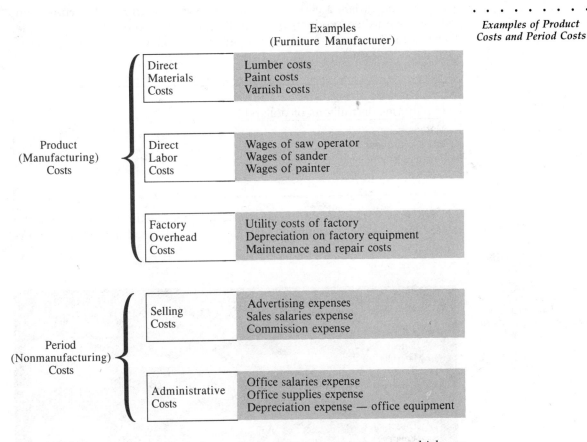

Examples
(Furniture Manufacturer)

Product
(Manufacturing)
Costs

Direct Materials Costs	Lumber costs Paint costs Varnish costs
Direct Labor Costs	Wages of saw operator Wages of sander Wages of painter
Factory Overhead Costs	Utility costs of factory Depreciation on factory equipment Maintenance and repair costs

Period
(Nonmanufacturing)
Costs

| Selling Costs | Advertising expenses
Sales salaries expense
Commission expense |
| Administrative Costs | Office salaries expense
Office supplies expense
Depreciation expense — office equipment |

affect the preparation of the balance sheet and income statement, which are described in the following paragraphs. The retained earnings and cash flow statements for merchandising and manufacturing enterprises are similar and therefore are not discussed.

Balance Sheet for a Manufacturing Enterprise

A manufacturing enterprise reports three types of inventory on its balance sheet: direct materials inventory, work in process inventory, and finished goods inventory. The **direct materials inventory** for a manufacturing enterprise consists of the cost of the direct materials which have not yet entered into the manufacturing process.[4] The **work in process inventory** for a manufacturing enterprise consists of the direct materials costs, the direct labor costs, and the factory overhead costs which have entered into the manufacturing process, but are associated with products that have not been

---

[4]Direct materials inventory, sometimes simply called materials inventory, includes only direct materials to be used in the manufacturing process. Indirect materials are classified as factory supplies.

finished. The **finished goods inventory** of a manufacturing enterprise consists of the finished products on hand that have not been sold. For example, The Proctor & Gamble Company reported the following inventories on its 1986 balance sheet:

Inventories (in millions of dollars):

Materials..	$ 782
Work in process	204
Finished products	1,053

The flow of manufacturing costs into the manufacturing process and the related inventories of a manufacturing enterprise is illustrated in the following diagram:

Flow of Manufacturing Costs to Balance Sheet

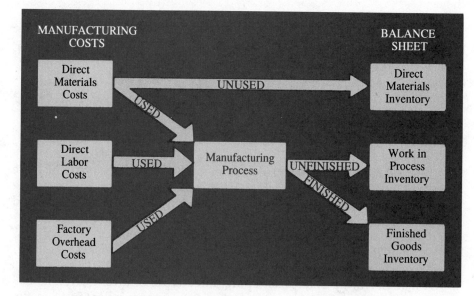

Income Statement for a Manufacturing Enterprise

The major difference in the income statements for merchandising and manufacturing enterprises is in the reporting of cost of merchandise sold for a merchandising enterprise and cost of goods sold for a manufacturing enterprise. For a merchandising enterprise, merchandise is purchased in a finished state for resale to customers. The merchandise that is sold is called the **cost of merchandise sold**.

For a manufacturing enterprise, the product to be sold is manufactured by processing direct materials, using direct labor and factory overhead. The cost of the product sold is called the **cost of goods sold.** The costs of manufacturing the product, which are comparable to the purchases reported by a merchandising enterprise, can be reported in a **statement of cost of goods manufactured.** To illustrate the difference between the income statements for a merchandising enterprise and a manufacturing enterprise, the income statements for Loose Inc., a merchandiser, and Burleson Manufacturing Company are shown below and on the following page. The Burleson Manufacturing Company income statement is supported by a statement of cost of goods manufactured.

In Burleson's statement of cost of goods manufactured, the amount listed for the work in process inventory at the beginning of the period is composed of the estimated cost of the direct materials, the direct labor, and the factory overhead applicable to the inventory of partially processed products at the end of the preceding period. The cost of the direct materials placed in production is determined by adding the beginning inventory of direct materials and the net cost of the direct materials purchased and deducting the ending inventory. The amount of direct labor is then listed. The factory overhead costs are listed individually in the statement or in a separate schedule. The sum of the costs of direct materials placed in production, the direct labor, and the factory overhead represents the total manufacturing costs incurred during the period. Addition of this amount to the beginning inventory of work in process yields the total cost of the work that has been in process during the period. The estimated cost of the ending inventory of work in process is then deducted to yield the cost of goods manufactured.

Merchandising Enterprise-Income Statement

Loose Inc.		
Income Statement		
For the Year Ended December 31, 1989		
Sales		$1,100,000
Cost of merchandise sold:		
Merchandise inventory, Jan. 1, 1989	$ 90,000	
Purchases	900,000	
Merchandise available for sale	$990,000	
Less merchandise inventory, Dec. 31, 1989	120,000	
Cost of merchandise sold		870,000
Gross profit		$ 230,000
Operating expenses:		
Selling expenses	$ 85,000	
Administrative expenses	75,000	
Total operating expenses		160,000
Net income		$ 70,000

*Manufacturing
Enterprise — Income
Statement*

Burleson Manufacturing Company
Income Statement
For Year Ended December 31, 1989

Sales		$915,800
Cost of goods sold:		
Finished goods inventory, January 1, 1989	$ 78,500	
Cost of goods manufactured	550,875	
Cost of finished goods available for sale	$629,375	
Less finished goods inventory, December 31, 1989	91,000	
Cost of goods sold		538,375
Gross profit		$377,425
Operating expenses:		
Selling expenses	$165,000	
Administrative expenses	84,425	
Total operating expenses		249,425
Net income		$128,000

*Statement of Cost of
Goods Manufactured*

Burleson Manufacturing Company
Statement of Cost of Goods Manufactured
For Year Ended December 31, 1989

Work in process inventory, January 1, 1989			$ 55,000
Direct materials:			
Inventory, January 1, 1989	$ 62,000		
Purchases	220,800		
Cost of materials available for use	$282,800		
Less inventory, December 31, 1989	58,725		
Cost of materials placed in production		$224,075	
Direct labor		218,750	
Factory overhead:			
Indirect labor	$ 49,300		
Depreciation of factory equipment	22,300		
Heat, light, and power	21,800		
Property taxes	9,750		
Depreciation of buildings	6,000		
Insurance expense	4,750		
Factory supplies expense	2,900		
Miscellaneous factory costs	2,050		
Total factory overhead		118,850	
Total manufacturing costs			561,675
Total work in process during period			$616,675
Less work in process inventory,			
December 31, 1989			65,800
Cost of goods manufactured			$550,875

ADDITIONAL COST CONCEPTS FOR MANAGERIAL PLANNING

The cost concepts and classifications described to this point are used primarily in the preparation of financial statements. For purposes of planning, organizing and directing, decision making, and controlling operations, managers require a variety of managerial reports in which cost data are classified in various ways. In the remainder of this chapter, the following cost concepts that are frequently reported to management for use in directing current operations and planning future operations are briefly described:

> Variable costs and fixed costs
> Direct costs and indirect costs
> Controllable costs and noncontrollable costs
> Differential costs
> Discretionary costs
> Opportunity costs
> Sunk costs

The use of these cost concepts by managers will be described and illustrated in more detail in later chapters.

Variable Costs and Fixed Costs

For management's use, costs are often classified by cost behavior; that is, costs are classified as to how they respond to changes in the volume of business activity. As the volume of business activity rises or falls, some costs tend to change proportionally to the rise or fall, while other costs do not change significantly as the volume of business activity changes. For directing current operations and planning future operations, a knowledge of the response pattern of costs to changing or anticipated changes in activity levels is useful.

Variable Costs. A **variable cost** varies in total dollar amount as the level of activity changes. The level of activity is normally expressed in units of production, although other activity bases may be used. Direct materials cost is a variable cost because the total direct materials cost varies directly with the number of units produced. For example, assume that Micro-Systems Inc. produces a standard microcomputer containing a 256K memory board. The cost of each memory board is a variable cost because it varies with the number of computers produced. If each memory board costs $50, the total direct materials cost of the memory boards for the production of 1,000 computers is $50,000 ($50 × 1,000); for 2,000 computers, the total cost is $100,000. Other common variable manufacturing costs include direct labor cost and factory overhead items, such as electricity, lubricants, and supplies.

The variable cost concept is also applicable to nonmanufacturing costs. For example, a 5% sales commission is a cost that varies with total sales.

Likewise, the administrative cost of billing customers is a cost that varies directly with the number of billings.

Fixed Costs. A fixed cost remains constant in total dollar amount as the level of activity changes. As with variable costs, the level of activity is normally expressed in units of production, although other activity bases may be used. Straight-line depreciation on manufacturing equipment is a fixed cost because the total annual depreciation does not vary with the number of units produced. For example, straight-line depreciation of $15,000 per year on MicroSystems Inc.'s assembly and testing equipment would not vary with the number of computers produced. The total straight-line depreciation would be $15,000, regardless of whether 1,000, 2,000, or 6,000 microcomputers are produced. Other common fixed manufacturing costs include costs of renting factory equipment or buildings, property taxes on factory plant and equipment, property insurance, and salaries of factory supervisory personnel. Although these examples are factory overhead costs, some factory overhead costs, such as electricity, are variable costs.

The fixed cost concept is also applicable to nonmanufacturing costs. For example, straight-line depreciation on store equipment and a sales manager's salary do not vary with the volume of sales. Likewise, officers' salaries is a fixed cost.

Mixed Costs. Some costs have both variable and fixed characteristics. These costs are often called **mixed costs** or **semivariable** or **semifixed** costs. These mixed costs, which are further described in Chapter 5, can be separated into their variable and fixed components. For example, the rental charge for a copier might be $100 per month plus $.01 per copy. The $100 per month portion of the rental charge is a fixed cost, and the $.01 per copy portion is a variable cost.

Direct and Indirect Costs

A **direct cost** is a cost that can be traced directly to a unit within the enterprise. Costs which are not direct are said to be **indirect costs**. Critical to separating costs into direct and indirect classifications is relating costs to some unit within the enterprise. The unit may be a product line, a department, a plant, a sales territory, or some other unit.

Direct costs for a manufactured product, such as spark plugs produced by an automobile parts manufacturer, would include direct materials and direct labor because these costs can be directly traced to the spark plugs. Indirect costs for the spark plugs product line would include factory overhead costs, such as depreciation on the factory building, because these costs cannot be directly traced to the product line. For a nonmanufacturing enterprise, such as a department store, the salaries paid to the salespersons in the shoe department would be a direct cost to that department. The store's officers' salaries would be an indirect cost to the shoe department.

Controllable Costs and Noncontrollable Costs
• • •

All costs are controllable by someone within a business enterprise, but not all costs are controllable at the same level of management. For example, plant supervisors, as members of operating management, are responsible for controlling the use of direct materials in their departments. They have no control, however, of the amount of insurance coverage or premium costs related to the buildings housing their departments. For a specific level of management, **controllable costs** are costs that it controls directly, and **noncontrollable costs** are costs that another level of management controls. This distinction, as applied to specific levels of management, is useful in fixing the responsibility for the incurrence of costs and then for reporting the cost data to those responsible for cost control.

In some cases, there is a time dimension to the classification of costs as controllable or noncontrollable. Some costs cannot be controlled in the short run but can be controlled in the long run. For example, a plant manager cannot, in the short run, control the wages of factory employees who have union contracts. In the long run, however, the wages become controllable because the contracts expire and are subject to renegotiation.

Salaries Out of Control?

From time to time in recent years, various reporting media have commented that baseball salaries were out of control. In the context of managerial accounting, however, are players' salaries a controllable cost? The answer depends upon the level of management and the time period during which the salaries are being considered for control purposes.

At top levels of baseball management, players' salaries are controllable. For example, the general manager of the Chicago Cubs has the authority to sign new players and to negotiate salaries. In contrast, the field manager of the Cubs has no authority over players' salaries and therefore no control of those salaries.

Even for the level of management that has control over salaries, that control may be available only in the long term. For example, the 1987 salary of Rick Sutcliffe, a Cubs pitcher, is noncontrollable during the 1987 season because Sutcliffe is working under a 5-year contract which he signed in 1986.

Despite the long-term controllability of players' salaries, it is obvious that these salaries have increased dramatically in recent years. Sutcliffe's 5-year salary, for example, is $9,000,000. Such salaries, which have increased the percentage of salary costs to total costs, have encouraged league owners and managers to take the following steps in an effort to achieve greater control over players' salaries:

Halted often frenzied bidding for free agents that hiked average salaries from $52,300 in 1977 to $410,732 in 1987.

Refused to sign players to contracts of longer than three years.

Insisted that many players signing two- and three-year guaranteed contracts agree to drug testing.

Decided to take more salary disputes to arbitration rather than agree to expensive contracts.

Sources: Alvin P. Sanoff, "Baseball Owners Play Tough on Salaries," *U.S. News and World Report* (February 3, 1986), p. 68; and "Baseball Owners Are Striking Back," *New York Times* (February 23, 1987).

Differential Costs

Differential cost, sometimes referred to as **incremental cost,** is the increase or decrease in cost that is expected from a particular course of action as compared with an alternative course of action. For example, the management of a microcomputer manufacturer must decide on whether to purchase carrying cases for the computers from an outside supplier or to produce the carrying cases. If the cost of purchasing the carrying cases is $20 per case and the cost of producing the carrying cases is $18 per case, the cost difference between the two alternatives ($2) is referred to as the differential cost. As another example, if an increase in advertising expenditures from $100,000 to $150,000 is being considered, the differential cost of the proposal would be $50,000.

Discretionary Costs

A **discretionary cost** is a cost that is not essential to short-term operations. For example, costs incurred in continuing education courses for management are classified as discretionary. Other examples of discretionary costs include advertising expenses, management consulting fees, sponsorship of employee social events (such as a company picnic), sponsorship of local athletic teams (such as a Little League team), charitable contributions to community activities, and a subsidized employee cafeteria.

Management reviews discretionary costs periodically, usually yearly, to determine whether the cost should continue to be incurred. Discretionary costs are usually the first to be reduced or eliminated during periods of worsening economic conditions, since their discontinuance does not affect short-term operations or profitability. Although discretionary costs do not have an immediate effect on short-term operations or profitability, their discontinuance can have a long-term impact on the enterprise. For example, research and development costs are often viewed as discretionary, but their discontinuance could be disastrous in the long run, especially in high-tech industries such as the computer industry. Likewise, the discontinuance of management continuing education could jeopardize the quality of managerial decision making in the long run.

Sunk Costs

Sunk costs are costs which have been incurred and cannot be reversed by subsequent decisions. Sunk costs are irrelevant for future decision making and are therefore excluded from managerial accounting reports prepared to assist management in making such decisions. To illustrate, assume that a major airline is currently operating a fleet of Boeing 727 passenger jets, which originally cost $300 million and on which depreciation of $250 million has been taken. In considering whether to spend $500 million to upgrade its fleet of aircraft to the newer, more fuel-efficient and technologically advanced 767 passenger jets, the original $300 million cost is irrelevant. The $300 million has been spent, and regardless of whether the original decision was wise or unwise, the $300 million expenditure cannot be reversed. For this reason, the original cost of $300 million is referred to as a sunk cost. Likewise, the $50 million book value of the 727 jets (the original cost of $300 million less accumulated depreciation of $250 million) is also irrelevant. The cost savings resulting from the use of the more fuel-efficient 767, when compared to the proposed expenditure of $500 million, are the relevant costs that would be considered by management in making the decision.

Opportunity Costs

An **opportunity cost** is the amount of income that is forgone by selecting one alternative over another. To illustrate, assume that the treasurer of Faulkner Inc. invested $100,000 in a money market account yielding 5% interest. If United States Treasury bills are currently yielding 6%, the opportunity cost of not investing in the Treasury bills is $6,000 ($100,000 × 6%). Hence, the treasurer might consider switching investments to maximize the return to Faulkner Inc. and to minimize the opportunity cost.

Opportunity cost differs fundamentally from the other classifications of costs that have been discussed previously because an opportunity cost does not represent a transaction involving a disbursement. Opportunity costs should be considered, however, in all decisions that management makes involving the commitment of resources. For example, in deciding whether to expand manufacturing capacity for the current product line, management should consider the opportunity cost of investing the resources in other product lines.

SUMMARY OF COST CONCEPTS

Many of the costs described in this chapter can be classified in more than one way, depending upon decision-making situations. For example, direct materials cost may be classified as a variable cost or a product cost. Each specific decision-making situation must be analyzed carefully by the managerial accountant in order to classify and report costs properly for managerial use. Such decision-making situations are discussed in the following chapters.

Chapter Review

KEY POINTS

1. Costs and Expenses Distinguished.
All disbursements of cash (or the commitment to pay cash in the future) for the purpose of generating revenues are costs that initially represent assets to the enterprise. As the assets are used in generating revenues, the cost of the assets must be recognized as expenses in order to match revenues and ex-

penses properly in the process of determining the net income for the period. To simplify the recording process, costs that will benefit only the current period are often initially recorded as expenses rather than as assets. This distinction between the terms cost and expense is especially important for the preparation of financial statements. This distinction has more importance for manufacturing enterprises. Costs incurred in manufacturing products are assets, and these costs do not become expenses until the manufactured products are sold.

2. Manufacturing Costs.

The cost of a manufactured product consists of direct materials cost, direct labor cost, and factory overhead cost. The cost of materials entering directly into the product is classified as direct materials cost. For a cost to be classified as a direct materials cost, the cost must not only be an integral part of the end product, but it must also be a significant dollar amount of the total cost of the product.

The cost of wages paid to employees directly involved in changing direct materials into finished products is classified as direct labor cost. For the cost of employee wages to be classified as direct labor cost, the employee must not only be directly involved in the creation of the product, but the wages must be a significant portion of the total product cost.

Costs other than direct materials cost and direct labor cost incurred in the manufacturing process are classified as factory overhead cost. If the costs of direct materials or direct labor are not a significant portion of the total product cost, these costs may be classified as factory overhead.

Two common classifications of manufacturing costs are prime costs and conversion costs. Prime costs are the combination of direct materials cost and direct labor cost. Conversion costs are the combination of direct labor cost and factory overhead cost.

3. Nonmanufacturing Costs.

Nonmanufacturing costs are generally classified into two categories: selling and administrative. These classifications enable management to establish accountability and control over the costs of each of these two major functional areas. Different levels of accountability and control may be shown in managerial reports.

4. Product Costs and Period Costs.

Product costs are composed of the three elements of manufacturing costs: direct materials, direct labor, and factory overhead. These costs are treated as assets until the product with which they are associated is sold. Product costs are sometimes referred to as inventoriable costs. Period costs are those costs that are used up in generating revenue during the current period. These costs are recognized as expenses on the current period's income statement. Many period costs are time-oriented, in the sense that the costs are incurred or used as time passes.

5. Financial Statements for Manufacturing Enterprises.

The financial statements for manufacturing enterprises are more complex than those for service and merchandising enterprises. A manufacturing enterprise reports three types of inventory on its balance sheet: direct materials, work in process, and finished goods. The direct materials inventory consists of the cost of direct materials which have not yet entered into the manufacturing process. The work in process inventory consists of direct materials costs, direct labor costs, and factory overhead costs which have entered into the manufacturing process, but are associated with products that have not been finished. The finished goods inventory consists of the finished products on hand that have not been sold.

The major difference in income statements for merchandising and manufacturing enterprises is that a merchandising enterprise reports cost of merchandise sold and a manufacturing enterprise reports cost of goods sold. For a manufacturing enterprise, the product to be sold is manufactured by processing direct materials, using direct labor and factory overhead. The cost of the product sold is called the cost of goods sold. The costs of manufacturing the product can be reported in a statement of cost of goods manufactured.

6. Additional Cost Concepts for Managerial Planning.

A variable cost varies in total dollar amount as the level of activity changes. The level of activity is normally expressed in units of production. The variable cost concept is also applicable to nonmanufacturing costs. An example of a variable cost is direct materials cost. A fixed cost remains constant in total dollar amount as the level of activity changes. The level of activity is normally expressed in units of production. The fixed cost concept is also applicable to nonmanufacturing costs. An example of a fixed cost is straight-line depreciation on factory equipment. Costs that have both variable and fixed characteristics are called mixed costs or semivariable or semifixed costs.

A direct cost is a cost that can be traced directly to a unit within the enterprise. Costs that are not direct are said to be indirect costs.

A controllable cost is one that can be controlled by a specific level of management. Over time all costs are controllable at some level of management. Therefore, when classifying a cost as controllable or noncontrollable, the time period and level of management are critical reference points.

A differential cost, sometimes referred to as an incremental cost, is the difference in cost from one course of action compared to alternative courses of action. Differential costs are an important consideration for managers in deciding among alternative courses of action.

A discretionary cost is a cost that is not essential to short-term operations. Management reviews discretionary costs periodically, usually yearly, to determine whether the costs should continue to be incurred. Although discretionary costs do not have an immediate effect on short-term operations or profitability, their discontinuance can have a long-term impact on the enterprise.

Sunk costs are costs which have been incurred and cannot be reversed by a subsequent decision. Sunk costs are irrelevant for future decision making and are therefore excluded from managerial accounting reports.

An opportunity cost is the amount of income that is forgone by selecting one alternative over another. Opportunity cost differs fundamentally from the other classifications of costs that have been discussed previously because an opportunity cost does not represent a transaction involving a disbursement. Opportunity costs should be considered in all decisions that management makes involving the commitment of resources.

Many of the costs described in this chapter can be classified in more than one way, depending upon the decision-making needs of management. Each specific decision-making situation must be analyzed carefully by the managerial accountant in order to classify and report costs properly for managerial use.

KEY TERMS

costs 23
expenses 23
direct materials cost 25
direct labor cost 25
factory overhead cost 25
prime costs 26
conversion costs 26
product costs 28
period costs 28
direct materials inventory 29
work in process inventory 29
finished goods inventory 30
cost of merchandise sold 30
cost of goods sold 31

statement of cost of goods
    manufactured 31
variable cost 33
fixed cost 34
mixed (semivariable or semifixed)
    cost 34
direct cost 34
indirect cost 34
controllable cost 35
noncontrollable cost 35
differential cost 36
discretionary cost 36
sunk cost 36
opportunity cost 37

SELF-EXAMINATION QUESTIONS

(Answers at End of Chapter)

1. Which of the following expenditures would normally be recorded initially as an expense rather than as an asset?
   A. Payment of a three-year insurance premium
   B. Payment of $3,000 for the current month's rent
   C. Purchase of office equipment
   D. Purchase of direct materials to be used in manufacturing a product

2. Which of the following is not considered a cost of manufacturing a product?
   A. Direct materials cost
   B. Factory overhead cost
   C. Sales salaries
   D. Direct labor cost

3. Which of the following costs would be included as part of the factory overhead costs of a microcomputer manufacturer?
   A. The cost of memory chips
   B. Depreciation on testing equipment
   C. Wages of computer assemblers
   D. The cost of disk drives

4. Which of the following are considered conversion costs?
   A. Direct labor cost and factory overhead cost
   B. Factory overhead cost
   C. Direct materials cost and direct labor cost
   D. Direct materials cost and factory overhead cost

5. Which of the following costs would normally be considered a variable cost?
   A. Direct materials cost
   B. Direct labor cost
   C. Electricity to operate factory equipment
   D. All of the above

ILLUSTRATIVE PROBLEM

The following pre-closing trial balance of Mahaney Inc. was prepared as of December 31, 1990, the end of the current fiscal year:

Cash	50,000	
Accounts Receivable	160,000	
Allowance for Doubtful Accounts		20,000
Finished Goods Inventory	180,000	
Work in Process Inventory	75,000	
Direct Materials Inventory	40,000	
Prepaid Insurance	12,000	
Factory Supplies	7,000	
Land	100,000	
Factory Buildings	400,000	
Accumulated Depreciation — Factory Buildings		220,000
Factory Equipment	250,000	
Accumulated Depreciation — Factory Equipment		125,000
Accounts Payable		30,000
Wages Payable		14,000
Income Tax Payable		10,000
Common Stock		100,000
Retained Earnings		711,000
Dividends	20,000	
Sales		1,500,000
Direct Materials Purchases	750,000	
Direct Labor	300,000	
Indirect Factory Labor	150,000	
Depreciation — Factory Equipment	25,000	
Factory Heat, Light, and Power	20,000	
Depreciation — Factory Building	20,000	
Factory Property Taxes	18,000	
Insurance Expense — Factory	12,000	
Factory Supplies Expense	6,000	
Miscellaneous Factory Costs	4,000	
Selling Expenses	60,000	
Administrative Expenses	50,000	
Income Tax	21,000	
	2,730,000	2,730,000

Inventories at December 31, 1990, were as follows:

Finished goods	$200,000
Work in process	70,000
Direct materials	42,000

Instructions:

1. Prepare a statement of cost of goods manufactured.
2. Prepare an income statement.
3. Prepare a retained earnings statement.
4. Prepare a balance sheet.

SOLUTION

(1)

MAHANEY INC.
Statement of Cost of Goods Manufactured
For Year Ended December 31, 1990

Work in process inventory, January 1, 1990....			$ 75,000
Direct materials:			
Inventory, January 1, 1990		$ 40,000	
Purchases		750,000	
Cost of materials available for use		$790,000	
Less inventory, December 31, 1990		42,000	
Cost of materials placed in production		$748,000	
Direct labor		300,000	
Factory overhead:			
Indirect labor	$150,000		
Depreciation—factory equipment	25,000		
Factory heat, light and power	20,000		
Depreciation—factory buildings	20,000		
Factory property taxes	18,000		
Insurance expense—factory	12,000		
Factory supplies expense	6,000		
Miscellaneous factory costs	4,000		
Total factory overhead		255,000	
Total manufacturing costs			1,303,000
Total work in process during period			$1,378,000
Less work in process inventory, December 31, 1990			70,000
Cost of goods manufactured			$1,308,000

(2)

MAHANEY INC.
Income Statement
For Year Ended December 31, 1990

Sales...		$1,500,000
Cost of goods sold:		
Finished goods inventory, January 1, 1990	$ 180,000	
Cost of goods manufactured......................	1,308,000	
Cost of finished goods available for sale	$1,488,000	
Less finished goods inventory, December 31, 1990....	200,000	
Cost of goods sold		1,288,000
Gross profit......................................		$ 212,000
Operating expenses:		
Selling expenses	$ 60,000	
Administrative expenses...........................	50,000	
Total operating expenses.......................		110,000
Income before income tax...........................		$ 102,000
Income tax..		21,000
Net income		$ 81,000

(3)

MAHANEY INC.
Retained Earnings Statement
For Year Ended December 31, 1990

Retained earnings, January 1, 1990......................		$711,000
Net income for year....................................	$81,000	
Less dividends	20,000	
Increase in retained earnings		61,000
Retained earnings, December 31, 1990		$772,000

(4)

MAHANEY INC.
Balance Sheet
December 31, 1990

Assets

Current assets:			
Cash....................................		$ 50,000	
Accounts receivable.......................	$160,000		
Less allowance for doubtful accounts	20,000	140,000	
Inventories:			
Finished goods.........................	$200,000		
Work in process	70,000		
Direct materials........................	42,000	312,000	
Prepaid insurance		12,000	
Factory supplies..........................		7,000	
Total current assets......................			$521,000
Plant assets:			
Land....................................		$100,000	
Buildings	$400,000		
Less accumulated depreciation............	220,000	180,000	
Factory equipment........................	$250,000		
Less accumulated depreciation............	125,000	125,000	
Total plant assets.......................			405,000
Total assets..................................			$926,000

Liabilities

Current liabilities:

Accounts payable..........................	$ 30,000	
Wages payable...........................	14,000	
Income tax payable.......................	10,000	
Total current liabilities.......................		$54,000

Stockholders' Equity

Common stock............................	$100,000	
Retained earnings..........................	772,000	
Total stockholders' equity....................		872,000
Total liabilities and stockholders' equity.........		$926,000

Discussion Questions

2–1. What term describes all disbursements of cash (or the commitment to pay cash in the future) for the purpose of generating revenues?

2–2. Give an example of a disbursement that is not a cost.

2–3. What are "expenses?"

2–4. What three costs make up the cost of manufacturing a product?

2–5. What manufacturing cost term is used to describe the cost of wages paid to employees directly involved in converting direct materials to a finished product?

2–6. If the cost of wages paid to employees is not a significant portion of the total product cost, the wages cost would normally be classified as what type of manufacturing cost?

2–7. Indicate whether each of the following costs of an automobile manufacturer would be classified as (a) direct materials cost, (b) direct labor cost, or (c) factory overhead cost:
(1) tires
(2) transmission
(3) factory machinery lubricants
(4) depreciation on factory machinery
(5) wages of assembly-line worker
(6) windshield
(7) engine
(8) wages of assembly-line supervisor

2–8. Distinguish between prime costs and conversion costs.

2–9. Why are nonmanufacturing costs generally classified as selling costs and administrative costs?

2–10. What is the difference between a product cost and a period cost?

2–11. Name the three inventory accounts for a manufacturing business and describe what each balance represents at the end of an accounting period.

2–12. What are the three categories of manufacturing costs included in the cost of finished goods and the cost of work in process?

2–13. What statement is used to summarize the manufacturing costs incurred during a period?

2–14. What are the terms used to describe (a) the merchandise sold by a merchandising enterprise and (b) the products sold by a manufacturing enterprise?

2–15. For a manufacturing enterprise, what is the description of the amount that is comparable to a merchandising concern's net cost of merchandise purchased?

2–16. "A variable cost remains constant in total dollar amount as the level of activity changes." Do you agree? Explain.

2–17. Classify each of the following costs as either (a) a variable cost or (b) a fixed cost:
(1) straight-line depreciation on factory equipment
(2) direct materials cost
(3) $1,000 per month rent on factory building
(4) property taxes on factory plant and equipment
(5) electricity usage
(6) direct labor cost
(7) property insurance
(8) 15% sales commission

2–18. For a company that produces microcomputers, would memory chips be considered a direct or an indirect cost of each microcomputer produced?

2–19. For a production line supervisor, would depreciation on the factory plant be considered a controllable or a noncontrollable cost?

2–20. In deciding between the purchase of truck A or truck B, what would be the differential cost?

2–21. How might the discontinuance or reduction of discretionary costs affect long-term operations? Use research and development costs as the basis for an example.

2–22. (a) What is meant by *sunk costs?* (b) A company is contemplating replacing an old piece of machinery which cost $320,000 and has $280,000 accumulated depreciation to date. A new machine costs $400,000. What is the sunk cost in this situation?

2–23. In considering the purchase of a new automobile, would the book value (the original cost less accumulated depreciation) of the automobile traded in be considered a sunk cost?

2–24. (a) What is meant by *opportunity cost?* (b) Lieu Company is currently earning 10% on $200,000 invested in marketable securities. It proposes to use the $200,000 to acquire plant facilities to manufacture a new product line that is expected to add $30,000 annually to net income. What is the opportunity cost involved in the decision to manufacture the new product?

2–25. Real World Focus. The management of Trico Products Inc., a manufacturer of windshield wipers in Buffalo, New York, was recently faced with a decision on whether to locate several new plants in New York or on the Texas-Mexico border. The management decided to locate the plants on the Texas-Mexico border. Why would the employee hourly wage rate be a major differential operating cost of the two locations for purposes of this decision?

Exercises

2-26. **Statement of cost of goods manufactured.** The following accounts were selected from the pre-closing trial balance of Jarvis Co. at July 31, 1990, the end of the current fiscal year:

Direct Labor	$192,000
Direct Materials Inventory	51,600
Direct Materials Purchases	230,100
Factory Overhead	76,800
Finished Goods Inventory	76,500
General Expense	54,750
Interest Expense	8,500
Sales	717,600
Selling Expense	76,500
Work in Process Inventory	55,500

Inventories at July 31 were as follows:

Finished Goods	$81,000
Work in Process	59,550
Direct Materials	54,000

Prepare a statement of cost of goods manufactured.

2-27. **Cost of goods sold.** On the basis of the data presented in Exercise 2-26, prepare the cost of goods sold section of the income statement.

2-28. **Terminology.** Choose the appropriate term for completing each of the following sentences.

(a) The wages of an assembly worker are considered an inventoriable or (fixed, product) cost.
(b) Direct materials costs combined with direct labor costs are called (prime, conversion) costs.
(c) Because the total wages of the assembly workers change as the level of production changes, the wages of assembly workers are considered a (fixed, variable) cost.
(d) Since the amount of overtime work by assembly workers can be determined by the production supervisor through proper scheduling, overtime pay is considered a (controllable, noncontrollable) cost for the production supervisor.
(e) Straight-line depreciation on factory equipment does not vary with changes in level of production and therefore is considered a (fixed, variable) cost.
(f) Factory overhead costs combined with direct labor costs are called (prime, conversion) costs.
(g) Sales salaries paid during the current period are shown on the income statement as an expense and are (product, period) costs.
(h) A cost that has been incurred and cannot be reversed by subsequent decisions is an example of a (fixed, sunk) cost.
(i) The (opportunity, prime) cost of not investing in U.S. Treasury securities, which are yielding 10%, is the interest forgone on the possible investment.

2-29.   Classification as product or period costs. For a manufacturing enterprise, classify each of the following costs as either a product (inventoriable) cost or period cost:

(a) Sales commissions
(b) Controller's salary
(c) Direct materials used during production
(d) Depreciation on factory equipment
(e) Depreciation on office equipment
(f) Property taxes on factory building and equipment
(g) Advertising expenses
(h) Factory supervisors' salaries
(i) Repairs and maintenance costs for factory equipment
(j) Wages of assembly workers
(k) Oil used to lubricate factory equipment
(l) Travel costs of salespersons
(m) Utility costs for office building
(n) Factory janitorial supplies
(o) Salary of production quality control supervisor

2-30.   Classification of costs. The following is a list of various costs that could be incurred in producing this textbook. With respect to the manufacture and sale of this text, classify each cost as either variable or fixed, and as either indirect or direct.

(a) paper on which the text is written
(b) wages of vice-president of marketing
(c) sales commissions paid to textbook representatives for each text sold
(d) straight-line depreciation on the printing presses used to manufacture the text
(e) electricity used to run the presses during the printing of the text
(f) hourly wages of printing press operators during production
(g) property taxes on the factory building and equipment
(h) ink used to print the text
(i) salary of staff used to develop artwork for the text
(j) royalty paid to the authors for each text sold

2-31   Analysis of differential costs. Grainger Company has been purchasing carrying cases for its portable typewriters at a price of $15 per typewriter. If Grainger Company manufactures the carrying cases, the manufacturing costs are expected to be $16. (a) What is the differential cost of manufacturing the carrying cases, compared to the alternative of purchasing the cases? (b) Should Grainger Company purchase or manufacture the cases? Explain.

Problems

2-32.   Classification as product or period costs. The following is a list of costs incurred by several business enterprises.

(a) Production supervisor's salary
(b) Steel for an automobile manufacturer
(c) Oil lubricants for factory plant and equipment
(d) Advertising costs
(e) Memory chips for a microcomputer manufacturer
(f) Wages of assembly worker on the production line
(g) Salary of the vice-president of marketing
(h) Wages of a machine operator on the production line
(i) Property taxes on factory building
(j) Factory operating supplies
(k) Salary of the president of the company
(l) Depreciation on factory equipment
(m) Wages of production quality control personnel
(n) Maintenance and repair costs for factory equipment
(o) Sales commissions
(p) Bonuses paid to president and other officers
(q) Health insurance premiums paid for factory workers
(r) Lumber used by furniture manufacturer
(s) Paper used by textbook publisher in printing texts
(t) Paper used by computer department in processing various managerial reports
(u) Insurance premiums paid on salespersons' automobiles
(v) Coffee for executive lounge
(w) Janitorial supplies used in cleaning the production line
(x) Protective glasses for factory machine operators
(y) Blank diskettes for the producer and distributor of microcomputer software
(z) Sales catalogs distributed free of charge to potential customers

Instructions:

Classify each of the preceding costs as product costs or period costs. For those costs classified as product costs, indicate whether the product cost is a direct materials cost, a direct labor cost, or a factory overhead cost. For those costs classified as period costs, indicate whether the period cost is a selling expense or an administrative expense. Use the following tabular headings for preparing your answer. Place an X in the appropriate columns.

Cost	Product Cost			Period Cost	
	Direct Materials Cost	Direct Labor Cost	Factory Overhead Cost	Selling Expense	Administrative Expense

2-33. Statement of cost of goods manufactured; cost of goods sold. The following accounts related to manufacturing operations of Henry Inc. were selected from the pre-closing trial balance at June 30, 1990, the end of the current fiscal year:

Depreciation of Factory Buildings	$ 10,000
Depreciation of Factory Equipment	14,500
Direct Labor	110,000
Direct Materials Inventory	30,000
Direct Materials Purchases	145,600
Factory Supplies Expense	3,200
Finished Goods Inventory	45,000
Heat, Light, and Power	14,300

Indirect Labor...	$ 23,500
Insurance Expense...	5,000
Miscellaneous Factory Costs	2,400
Property Taxes	6,100
Work in Process Inventory	28,400

Inventories at June 30 were as follows:

Finished Goods...	52,000
Work in Process	33,200
Direct Materials..	32,500

Instructions:

(1) Prepare a statement of cost of goods manufactured.
(2) Prepare the cost of goods sold section of the income statement.

2-34. Determination of missing income statement data. Data for Childers Inc. and Marlowe Co., manufacturing companies, are as follows:

	Childers Inc.	Marlowe Co.
Work in process inventory, Jan. 1, 1990	$ 100,000	$ 80,000
Cost of direct materials placed in production	(a)	200,000
Direct labor.....................................	300,000	105,000
Total factory overhead...........................	200,000	(f)
Total manufacturing costs........................	900,000	400,000
Work in process inventory, Dec. 31, 1990	(b)	(g)
Cost of goods manufactured	780,000	390,000
Finished goods inventory, Jan. 1, 1990	50,000	80,000
Finished goods inventory, Dec. 31, 1990............	60,000	(h)
Cost of goods sold..............................	(c)	370,000
Sales..	1,200,000	(i)
Gross profit	(d)	380,000
Total operating expenses	140,000	(j)
Net income.....................................	(e)	180,000

Instructions:

Determine the missing items, identifying each by the letters (a) through (j).

2-35. Financial statements for a manufacturing enterprise. The pre-closing trial balance of Ayers Inc. as of August 31, 1990, the end of the current fiscal year, is shown on page 50. Inventories at August 31, 1990, were as follows:

Finished Goods...	$90,000
Work in Process	60,000
Direct Materials..	55,000

Instructions:

(1) Prepare a statement of cost of goods manufactured.
(2) Prepare an income statement.
(3) Prepare a retained earnings statement.
(4) Prepare a balance sheet.

Cash	20,000	
Accounts Receivable	80,000	
Allowance for Doubtful Accounts		2,000
Finished Goods Inventory	85,000	
Work in Process Inventory	70,000	
Direct Materials Inventory	60,000	
Prepaid Insurance	9,000	
Factory Supplies	8,000	
Land	75,000	
Factory Buildings	300,000	
Accumulated Depreciation—Factory Buildings		150,000
Factory Equipment	450,000	
Accumulated Depreciation—Factory Equipment		210,000
Accounts Payable		60,000
Wages Payable		8,000
Income Tax Payable		5,000
Common Stock		100,000
Retained Earnings		578,000
Dividends	40,000	
Sales		800,000
Direct Materials Purchases	200,000	
Direct Labor	175,000	
Indirect Labor	50,000	
Depreciation—Factory Equipment	32,000	
Factory Heat, Light, and Power	22,000	
Factory Property Taxes	14,000	
Depreciation—Factory Buildings	18,000	
Insurance Expense—Factory	6,000	
Factory Supplies Expense	5,500	
Miscellaneous Factory Costs	3,500	
Selling Expenses	100,000	
Administrative Expenses	60,000	
Income Tax	30,000	
	1,913,000	1,913,000

2-36. Cost identification and classification. The management of Ferguson Inc., a boat retailer and distributor, is considering expanding operations by adding a repair and maintenance department. Originally, Ferguson Inc. built its building to accommodate future expansion. For the past several years, it has rented a 2,500-foot section of the building to Ron's Motorcycle Shop for $2,000 per month. This section of the building will be converted for use by the maintenance and repair department.

New equipment costing $10,000 will be purchased. It will be depreciated using the straight-line method. Existing equipment that has no resale value or other use and has a book value of $3,000 will be converted for use by the repair and maintenance department. A supervisory mechanic will be hired for $1,500 per month, and an assistant mechanic will be hired for $6 per hour. An inventory of $20,000 of spare parts will be ordered. Ferguson Inc.'s business insurance premiums are expected to increase by $200 per month, once the repairs and maintenance department opens for business.

To obtain as much visibility as possible, a one-time special advertising promotion is planned at a cost of $2,500.

Instructions:

(1) Classify the costs of the proposed repairs and maintenance operations into the following categories:

variable costs
fixed costs
differential costs of expansion
sunk costs of expansion

(2) What is the opportunity cost for Ferguson Inc. of expanding operations?

ALTERNATE PROBLEMS

2-32A.   Classification as product or period costs. The following is a list of costs incurred by several business enterprises.

(a) Disk drives for a microcomputer manufacturer
(b) Wages of a painter for an automotive repair shop
(c) Salary of the vice-president of finance
(d) Wages of a machine operator on the production line
(e) Life insurance premiums paid for company president
(f) Coal used to heat furnaces of steel manufacturer
(g) Ink used by textbook publisher in printing texts
(h) Pens, paper, and other supplies used by accounting department in preparing various managerial reports
(i) Employer's portion of factory workers' FICA taxes
(j) Electricity used to operate factory machinery
(k) Janitorial supplies used in cleaning the office building
(l) Fees paid lawn service for office grounds
(m) Wages of computer programmer for producer and distributor of microcomputer software
(n) Depreciation on copying machine used by the marketing department
(o) Production supervisor's salary
(p) Tires for an automobile manufacturer
(q) Oil lubricants for factory plant and equipment
(r) Cost of a 30-second television commercial
(s) Depreciation on robot used to assemble a product
(t) Wages of production quality control personnel
(u) Maintenance and repair costs for factory equipment
(v) Depreciation on tools used in production
(w) Bonuses paid to salespersons
(x) Insurance on factory building
(y) Salary of the secretary of the president of the company
(z) Cost of company picnic

Instructions:

Classify each of the preceding costs as product costs or period costs. For those costs classified as product costs, indicate whether the product cost is a direct materials cost, a direct labor cost, or a factory overhead cost. For those costs classified as period costs, indicate whether the period cost is a selling expense or an administrative expense. Use the following tabular headings for preparing your answer. Place an X in the appropriate columns.

	Product Cost			Period Cost	
Cost	Direct Materials Cost	Direct Labor Cost	Factory Overhead Cost	Selling Expense	Administrative Expense

2-33A.   Statement of cost of goods manufactured; cost of goods sold. The following accounts related to manufacturing operations of Miles Inc. were selected from the pre-closing trial balance at March 31, 1990, the end of the current fiscal year:

Depreciation of Factory Buildings	$ 56,000
Depreciation of Factory Equipment.	81,200
Direct Labor.	590,000
Direct Materials Inventory	170,000
Direct Materials Purchases.	800,000
Factory Supplies Expense	17,200
Finished Goods Inventory.	250,000
Heat, Light, and Power	80,500
Indirect Labor.	132,000
Insurance Expense.	25,400
Miscellaneous Factory Costs	13,500
Property Taxes	35,000
Work in Process Inventory	160,000

Inventories at March 31 were as follows:

Finished Goods.	$285,000
Work in Process	180,800
Direct Materials.	200,000

Instructions:

(1) Prepare a statement of cost of goods manufactured.
(2) Prepare the cost of goods sold section of the income statement.

2-34A.   Determination of missing income statement data. Data for Bormann Inc. and Fender Co., manufacturing companies, are as follows:

	Bormann Inc.	Fender Co.
Work in process inventory, Jan. 1, 1990	$ 30,000	$ 40,000
Cost of direct materials placed in production	100,000	(f)
Direct labor.	150,000	80,000
Total factory overhead.	80,000	120,000
Total manufacturing costs.	(a)	440,000
Work in process inventory, Dec. 31, 1990	20,000	(g)

	Bormann Inc.	Fender Co.
Cost of goods manufactured	(b)	390,000
Finished goods inventory, Jan. 1, 1990	(c)	100,000
Finished goods inventory, Dec. 31, 1990	70,000	80,000
Cost of goods sold	320,000	(h)
Sales	(d)	610,000
Gross profit	280,000	(i)
Total operating expenses	150,000	(j)
Net income	(e)	80,000

Instructions:

Determine the missing items, identifying each by the letters (a) through (j).

2-35A. Financial statements for a manufacturing enterprise. The following pre-closing trial balance of Whitehead Inc. was prepared as of March 31, 1990, the end of the current fiscal year:

Cash	40,000	
Accounts Receivable	120,000	
Allowance for Doubtful Accounts		10,000
Finished Goods Inventory	170,000	
Work in Process Inventory	50,000	
Direct Materials Inventory	40,000	
Prepaid Insurance	12,000	
Factory Supplies	7,000	
Land	90,000	
Factory Buildings	350,000	
Accumulated Depreciation—Factory Buildings		220,000
Factory Equipment	175,000	
Accumulated Depreciation—Factory Equipment		80,000
Accounts Payable		45,000
Wages Payable		15,000
Income Tax Payable		10,000
Common Stock		200,000
Retained Earnings		439,000
Dividends	30,000	
Sales		1,200,000
Direct Materials Purchases	500,000	
Direct Labor	250,000	
Indirect Factory Labor	110,000	
Factory Heat, Light, and Power	18,000	
Depreciation—Factory Equipment	20,000	
Factory Property Taxes	15,000	
Depreciation—Factory Buildings	14,000	
Insurance Expense—Factory	10,000	
Factory Supplies Expense	8,000	
Miscellaneous Factory Costs	5,000	
Selling Expenses	100,000	
Administrative Expenses	60,000	
Income Tax	25,000	
	2,219,000	2,219,000

Inventories at March 31, 1990, were as follows:

Finished Goods... $160,000
Work in Process   40,000
Direct Materials..   45,000

Instructions:

(1) Prepare a statement of cost of goods manufactured.
(2) Prepare an income statement.
(3) Prepare a retained earnings statement.
(4) Prepare a balance sheet.

Mini-Case 2

Rutkosky's Pizza Inc. began operations on June 20, 1986, in the garage of Helen Rutkosky. The business specializes in fast delivery of home-made pizzas on weekends. At the request of customers, Rutkosky is considering moving to a vacant office building and devoting full time to the business. Rutkosky is currently employed at Eats' Grocery as an assistant store manager, where she makes $15,000 a year.

Rutkosky has estimated the following costs of opening the new business:

Purchase of new oven $5,000
Purchase of additional delivery truck $12,000
Purchase of furnishings $8,000
Monthly rent................................. $1,000
Wages of employees .... $5.50 per hour
Insurance.................................... $500 per year
Local advertising .... $600 per month
Additional business licenses................. $300 per year

Rutkosky plans to move the existing equipment from her garage to the new business. The existing equipment has an original cost of $15,000 and accumulated depreciation of $3,000. Straight-line depreciation is used to depreciate all plant and equipment.

Instructions:

(1) Classify each of the preceding costs of opening the new business, using the following categories:
variable costs
fixed costs
differential costs
discretionary costs
opportunity costs
sunk costs
Note: Some costs may be classified into more than one category.
(2) Assuming that Rutkosky opens the new business, list (a) costs which are controllable on a day-to-day basis, and (b) costs which are noncontrollable on a day-to-day basis.
(3) List three direct costs and three indirect costs of making pizzas.

Answers to Self-Examination Questions
· · ·

1. **B** The payment of $3,000 for the current month's rent (answer B) would normally be recorded as an expense, since the disbursement benefits only the current period. Payment of a 3-year insurance premium (answer A) benefits more than one period and therefore would normally be recorded initially as an asset. The purchases of office equipment (answer C) and direct materials used in manufacturing a product (answer D) would initially be recorded as assets.

2. **C** Sales salaries (answer C) is a selling expense and is not considered a cost of manufacturing a product. Direct materials cost (answer A), factory overhead cost (answer B), and direct labor cost (answer D) are costs of manufacturing a product.

3. **B** Depreciation on testing equipment (answer B) is included as part of the factory overhead costs of the microcomputer manufacturer. The cost of memory chips (answer A) and the cost of disk drives (answer D) are both considered a part of direct materials cost. The wages of microcomputer assemblers (answer C) are part of direct labor cost.

4. **A** Conversion cost is the combination of direct labor cost and factory overhead cost (answer A). Factory overhead cost (answer B) is a separate cost of manufacturing a product. Direct materials cost and direct labor cost (answer C) are prime costs. The combination of direct materials cost and factory overhead cost (answer D) is not considered a separate cost classification.

5. **D** Direct materials cost (answer A), direct labor cost (answer B), and electricity to operate factory equipment (answer C) all vary with changes in the level of activity and are therefore variable costs.

Chapter Three

CHAPTER OBJECTIVES

•

Describe the usefulness of product costs.

•

Describe the basic types of accounting systems
used by manufacturing enterprises.

•

Describe the basic characteristics of cost accounting systems.

•

Describe and illustrate the flow of data through a cost accounting system of
a manufacturing enterprise.

•

Describe alternative cost accounting systems for manufacturing operations.

•

Describe and illustrate a job order cost accounting system.

•

Accounting Systems For Manufacturing Enterprises: Job Order Cost Systems

A variety of cost concepts and classifications were described and illustrated in Chapter 2. For manufacturing enterprises, the importance of distinguishing between product costs and period costs was emphasized. Period costs are used up in generating revenues of the current period and are shown on the current period's income statement as expenses. Product costs are composed of the three elements of manufacturing costs: direct materials, direct labor, and factory overhead. Until the units to which they relate are sold, product costs are treated as part of inventory.

To account for product costs properly, a manufacturing enterprise must use an accounting system that will accumulate and assign all product costs to the related units of production. This chapter briefly describes the basic types of accounting systems used by manufacturing enterprises. The chapter then focuses on a discussion and illustration of one of these systems, the job order cost system.

USEFULNESS OF PRODUCT COSTS

In studying product costs, it is important to keep in mind that the primary function of the managerial accountant is to provide useful information to managers for planning, organizing and directing, decision making, and controlling operations. Much of this information is developed in the process of accounting for product costs.

A primary use of product costs by managers is for preparation of the financial statements of the enterprise. To present materials, work in process, and finished goods inventories properly on the balance sheet, product costs must be accounted for and assigned to the individual units in inventory. Because the cost of materials, direct labor, and factory overhead may vary throughout the period, product costs are usually assigned to inventory on the basis of an average per unit cost for the period. For example, if 1,000,000 pounds of materials were purchased throughout the period at a total cost of $2,500,000, the materials product cost per pound would be $2.50.

The assignment of product costs to direct materials, work in process, and finished goods inventories allows for the proper determination of net income for the period. The statement of cost of goods manufactured (illustrated in Chapter 2) serves as a basis for determining the cost of goods sold. An improper assignment of product costs to inventory would lead to a misstatement of the cost of goods sold and net income.

Product costs are also needed by management for a wide variety of purposes. For example, the per unit cost of finished goods inventory is vital information for the setting of long-term product prices. Product cost information is also necessary in deciding whether to continue making a product internally for use in further processing or to purchase the product from an outside supplier. A variety of other managerial decisions which require the use of product cost information will be illustrated throughout the remainder of this text. Without accurate product cost information, managers could not effectively or efficiently manage operations.

TYPES OF ACCOUNTING SYSTEMS

Two basic accounting systems may be used by manufacturers: general accounting systems and cost accounting systems. Although accounting for manufacturing operations is usually more complex than for merchandising operations, a **general accounting system** may be used if a single product or several similar products are manufactured. A general accounting system is essentially an extension of the periodic system of inventory accounting used in merchandising enterprises to the three manufacturing inventories: direct materials, work in process, and finished goods. Because such simple manufacturing situations are rare, the basic principles of a general accounting system for manufacturing operations are not discussed further in this chapter.

Through the use of perpetual inventory systems, a **cost accounting system** achieves greater accuracy in the determination of product costs than is possible with a general accounting system that uses periodic inventory procedures. Cost accounting procedures also permit far more effective control by supplying data on the costs incurred by each manufacturing department or process and the unit cost of manufacturing each type of product. Such procedures provide not only data useful to management in minimizing costs, but also other valuable information about production methods to use and quantities to produce.

Types of Cost Accounting Systems

There are two main types of cost systems for manufacturing operations — job order cost and process cost. Each of the two systems is widely used, and a manufacturer may use a job order cost system for some of its products and a process cost system for others.

A **job order cost system** provides for a separate record of the cost of each particular quantity of product that passes through the factory. It is best suited to industries that manufacture goods to fill special orders from customers and to industries that produce different lines of products for stock. It is also appropriate when standard products are manufactured in batches rather than on a continuous basis. In a job order cost system, a summary such as the following would show the cost incurred in completing a job:

Job 565
1,000 Units of Product X200

Direct materials used	$2,380
Direct labor used	4,400
Factory overhead applied	3,080
Total cost.	$9,860
Unit cost ($9,860 ÷ 1,000)	$ 9.86

Under a **process cost system,** the costs are accumulated for each of the departments or processes within the factory. A process system is best used by manufacturers of like units of product that are not distinguishable from each other during a continuous production process.

Perpetual Inventory Procedures

In a cost accounting system, perpetual inventory controlling accounts and subsidiary ledgers are maintained for materials, work in process, and finished goods.[1] Each of these accounts is debited for all additions and is credited for all deductions. The balance of each account thus represents the inventory on hand.

All expenditures incidental to manufacturing move through the work in process account, the finished goods account, and eventually into the cost of goods sold account. The flow of costs through the perpetual inventory accounts and into the cost of goods sold account is illustrated as follows:

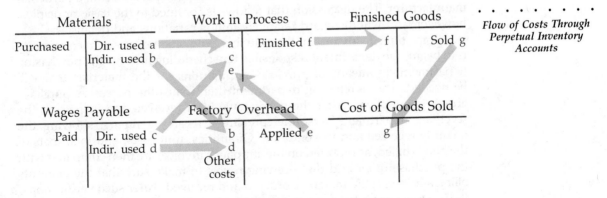

Flow of Costs Through Perpetual Inventory Accounts

Materials and labor used in production are classified as direct and indirect. The materials and the labor used directly in the process of manufacturing

---

[1] In this chapter and in subsequent chapters, the titles of the three manufacturing inventories will be shortened to "Materials," "Work in Process," and "Finished Goods."

are debited to Work in Process (a and c in the diagram). The materials and the labor used that do not enter directly into the finished product are debited to Factory Overhead (b and d in the diagram). Examples of indirect materials are oils and greases, abrasives and polishes, cleaning supplies, gloves, and brushes. Examples of indirect labor are salaries of supervisors, inspectors, material handlers, security guards, and janitors. The applied factory overhead cost is computed by using a predetermined factory overhead rate, as explained later in this chapter, and is debited to Work in Process (e in the diagram). The costs of the goods finished are transferred from Work in Process to Finished Goods (f in the diagram). When the goods are sold, their costs are transferred from Finished Goods to Cost of Goods Sold (g in the diagram).

The number of accounts presented in the flowchart was limited in order to simplify the illustration. In practice, manufacturing operations may require many processing departments, each requiring separate work in process and factory overhead accounts.

JOB ORDER COST SYSTEMS

The basic concepts of job order cost systems are illustrated in this chapter, while process cost systems are discussed in Chapter 4. In the following paragraphs, the discussion focuses attention on the source documents that serve as the basis for the entries in the job order cost system and on the managerial uses of cost accounting in planning and controlling operations.

Materials

Procedures used in the procurement and issuance of materials differ considerably among manufacturers and even among departments of a particular manufacturer. The discussion that follows is confined to the basic principles, however, and will disregard relatively minor variations and details.

Some time in advance of the date that production of a certain commodity is to begin, the department responsible for scheduling informs the purchasing department, by means of **purchase requisitions**, of the materials that will be needed. The purchasing department then issues the necessary **purchase orders** to suppliers. After the goods have been received and inspected, the receiving department personnel prepare a **receiving report**, showing the quantity received and its condition. Quantities, unit costs, and total costs of the goods billed, as reported on the supplier's invoice, are then compared with the purchase order and the receiving report to make sure that the amounts billed agree with the materials ordered and received. After such verifications, the invoice is recorded as a debit to Materials and a credit to Accounts Payable.

The account Materials in the general ledger is a controlling account. A separate account for each type of material is maintained in a subsidiary ledger called the **materials ledger**. Details as to quantity and cost of materials received are recorded in the materials ledger on the basis of the purchase invoices, or receiving reports. A typical form of materials ledger account is illustrated as follows:

MATERIAL NO. 23   ORDER POINT 1,000

RECEIVED			ISSUED			BALANCE			
REC. REPORT NO.	QUAN-TITY	AMOUNT	MAT. REQ. NO.	QUAN-TITY	AMOUNT	DATE	QUAN-TITY	AMOUNT	UNIT PRICE
						JAN. 1	1,200	600.00	.50
			672	500	250.00	4	700	350.00	.50
196	3,000	1,620.00				8	700	350.00	.50
							3,000	1,620.00	.54
			704	800	404.00	18	2,900	1,566.00	.54

The accounts in the materials ledger may also be used as an aid in maintaining proper inventory quantities of stock items. Frequent comparisons of quantity balances with predetermined order points enable management to avoid costly idle time caused by lack of materials. The subsidiary ledger form may also include columns for recording quantities ordered and dates of the purchase orders.

Materials are transferred from the storeroom to the factory in response to **materials requisitions,** which may be issued by the manufacturing department concerned or by a central scheduling department. Storeroom personnel record the issuances on the materials requisition by inserting the physical quantity data. Transfer of responsibility for the materials is evidenced by the signature or initials of the storeroom and factory personnel concerned. The requisition is then routed to the materials ledger clerk, who inserts unit prices and amounts. A typical materials requisition is illustrated as follows:

MATERIALS REQUISITION

Job No. 62   Requisition No. 704

Authorized by R. A. Sanders   Date January 18, 19--

Description	Quantity Authorized	Quantity Issued	Unit Price	Amount
Material No. 23	800	700 100	$.50 .54	$350 54
Total issued				$404

Issued by M. K.   Received by J. B.

The completed requisition serves as the basis for posting quantities and dollar data to the materials ledger accounts. In the illustration, the first-in, first-out costing method was used. A summary of the materials requisitions completed during the month serves as the basis for transferring the cost of the materials from the controlling account in the general ledger to the controlling accounts for work in process and factory overhead. The flow of materials into production is illustrated by the following entry:

Work in Process	13,000	
Factory Overhead	840	
Materials		13,840

The perpetual inventory system for materials has three important advantages: (1) it provides for prompt and accurate charging of materials to jobs and factory overhead, (2) it permits the work of inventory-taking to be spread out rather than concentrated at the end of a fiscal period, and (3) it aids in the disclosure of inventory shortages or other irregularities. As physical quantities of the various materials are determined, the actual inventories are compared with the balances of the respective subsidiary ledger accounts. The causes of significant differences between the two should be determined and the responsibility for the differences assigned to specific individuals. Remedial action can then be taken.

Factory Labor

Unlike materials, factory labor is not tangible, nor is it acquired and stored in advance of its use. Hence, there is no perpetual inventory account for labor. The two main objectives in accounting for labor are (1) determination of the correct amount to be paid each employee for each payroll period, and (2) appropriate allocation of labor costs to factory overhead and individual job orders.

The amount of time spent by an employee in the factory is usually recorded on **clock cards,** which are also called **in-and-out cards.** The amount of time spent by each employee and the labor cost incurred for each individual job, or for factory overhead, are recorded on **time tickets.** A typical time ticket form is illustrated on page 63.

The times reported on an employee's time tickets are compared with the related clock cards as an internal check on the accuracy of payroll disbursements. A summary of the time tickets at the end of each month serves as the basis for recording the direct and indirect labor costs incurred. The flow of labor costs into production is illustrated by the following entry:

Work in Process	10,000	
Factory Overhead	2,200	
Wages Payable		12,200

Time Ticket				
Employee Name Gail Berry		No. 4521		
Employee No. 240		Date January 18, 19--		
Description of work Finishing		Job No. 62		
Time Started	Time Stopped	Hours Worked	Hourly Rate	Cost
10:00 1:00	12:00 2:00	2 1	$6.50 6.50	$13.00 6.50
Total cost				$19.50
Approved by T. D.				

Factory Overhead

Factory overhead includes all manufacturing costs, except direct materials and direct labor. Examples of factory overhead costs, in addition to indirect materials and indirect labor, are depreciation, electricity, fuel, insurance, and property taxes. It is customary to have a factory overhead controlling account in the general ledger. Details of the various types of cost are accumulated in a subsidiary ledger.

Debits to Factory Overhead come from various sources. For example, the cost of indirect materials is obtained from the summary of the materials requisitions, the cost of indirect labor is obtained from the summary of the time tickets, costs of electricity and water are obtained from invoices, and the cost of depreciation and expired insurance may be recorded as adjustments at the end of the accounting period.

Although factory overhead cannot be specifically identified with particular jobs, it is as much a part of manufacturing costs as direct materials and direct labor. As the use of machines and automation has increased, factory overhead has represented an ever larger part of total costs. Many items of factory overhead cost are incurred for the entire factory and cannot be directly related to the finished product. The problem is further complicated because some items of factory overhead cost are relatively fixed in amount while others tend to vary according to changes in productivity.

To wait until the end of an accounting period to allocate factory overhead to the various jobs would be quite acceptable from the standpoint of accuracy but highly unsatisfactory in terms of timeliness. If the cost system is to be of maximum usefulness, it is imperative that cost data be available as each job is completed, even though there is a sacrifice in accuracy. It is only through timely reporting that management can make whatever adjustments seem necessary in pricing and manufacturing methods to achieve the best possible combination of revenue and cost on future jobs. Therefore, in order that job costs may be available currently, it is customary to apply factory overhead to production by using a **predetermined factory overhead rate.**

Predetermined Factory Overhead Rate. The factory overhead rate is determined by relating the estimated amount of factory overhead for the forthcoming year to some common activity base, one that will equitably apply the factory overhead costs to the goods manufactured. The common bases include direct labor costs, direct labor hours, and machine hours. For example, if it is estimated that the total factory overhead costs for the year will be $100,000 and that the total direct labor cost will be $125,000, an overhead rate of 80% ($100,000÷$125,000) will be applied to the direct labor cost incurred during the year.

As factory overhead costs are incurred, they are debited to the factory overhead account. The factory overhead costs applied to production are periodically credited to the factory overhead account and debited to the work in process account. The application of factory overhead costs to production (80% of direct labor cost of $10,000) is illustrated by the following entry:

Work in Process	8,000	
Factory Overhead		8,000

Inevitably, factory overhead costs applied and actual factory overhead costs incurred during a particular period will differ. If the amount applied exceeds the actual costs, the factory overhead account will have a credit balance and the overhead is said to be **overapplied** or **overabsorbed.** If the amount applied is less than the actual costs, the account will have a debit balance and the overhead is said to be **underapplied** or **underabsorbed.** Both cases are illustrated in the following account:

ACCOUNT FACTORY OVERHEAD   ACCOUNT NO.

Date		Item	Debit	Credit	Balance Debit	Balance Credit
May	1	Balance				200
	31	Costs incurred	8,320			
	31	Cost applied		8,000	120	

Underapplied Balance

Overapplied Balance

Disposition of Factory Overhead Balance. The balance in the factory overhead account is carried forward from month to month until the end of the year. The amount of the balance is reported on interim balance sheets as a deferred item.

The nature of the balance in the factory overhead account (underapplied or overapplied), as well as the amount, may change during the year. If there is a decided trend in either direction and the amount is substantial, the reason should be determined. If the variation is caused by alterations in manufacturing methods or by substantial changes in production goals, it may be advisable to revise the factory overhead rate. The accumulation of a large underapplied balance is more serious than a trend in the opposite direction and may indicate inefficiencies in production methods, excessive expenditures, or a combination of factors.

Despite any corrective actions that may be taken to avoid an underapplication or overapplication of factory overhead, the account will usually have a balance at the end of the fiscal year. Since the balance represents the underapplied or overapplied factory overhead applicable to the operations of the year just ended, it is not proper to report it in the year-end balance sheet as a deferred item.

There are two main alternatives for disposing of the balance of factory overhead at the end of the year: (1) by allocation of the balance among work in process, finished goods, and cost of goods sold accounts on the basis of the total amounts of applied factory overhead included in those accounts at the end of the year, or (2) by transfer of the balance to the cost of goods sold account. Theoretically, only the first alternative is sound because it represents a correction of the estimated overhead rate and brings the accounts into agreement with the costs actually incurred. On the other hand, much time and expense may be required to make the allocation and to revise the unit costs of the work in process and finished goods inventories. Furthermore, in most manufacturing enterprises, a very large part of the total manufacturing costs for the year passes through the work in process and the finished goods accounts into the cost of goods sold account before the end of the year. Therefore, unless the total amount of the underapplied or overapplied balance is great, it is satisfactory to transfer it to Cost of Goods Sold.

The Implications of Automation for Allocating Factory Overhead — A Case Study

For some departments at Amerock Corporation, the allocation of overhead on the basis of direct labor became less accurate and less useful as manufacturing processes became more automated. The solution was to change from direct labor hours to machine hours for these departments.

Amerock Corporation, a manufacturer of cabinet and decorative hardware, found that the only disadvantages to using machine hours as a basis for allocating factory overhead were the time it would take to develop the system and the need for additional reporting by the machine operators. The potential benefits clearly outweighed any disadvantages. In the accounting area, a major advantage would be the ability to allocate overhead when one worker tended several machines. Better cost estimating would also be possible because overhead allocation would be more accurate. Forecasting and the calculation of actual costs would be easier. In the manufacturing area, machine utilization information would be more useful in understanding and controlling production and reporting.

Amerock Corporation's change in its overhead allocation basis has made it possible for accounting to capture costs accurately and for manufacturing to measure performance efficiently. The results have been so successful that Amerock plans to convert most of its departments to a machine hour basis as more of its plants become automated.

Source: Gregory Hakala, "Measuring Costs with Machine Hours," *Management Accounting* (October, 1985), pp. 57–61.

Work in Process

Costs incurred for the various jobs are debited to Work in Process. The job costs described in the preceding sections may be summarized as follows:

Direct materials, $13,000 — Work in Process debited and Materials credited; data obtained from summary of materials requisitions.

Direct labor, $10,000 — Work in Process debited and Wages Payable credited; data obtained from summary of time tickets.

Factory overhead, $8,000 — Work in process debited and Factory Overhead credited; data obtained by applying overhead rate to direct labor cost (80% of $10,000).

The work in process account to which these costs were charged is illustrated as follows:

ACCOUNT WORK IN PROCESS   ACCOUNT NO.

Date		Item	Debit	Credit	Balance Debit	Balance Credit
May	1	Balance			3,000	
	31	Direct materials	13,000		16,000	
	31	Direct labor	10,000		26,000	
	31	Factory overhead	8,000		34,000	
	31	Jobs completed		31,920	2,080	

The work in process account is a controlling account that contains summary information only. The details concerning the costs incurred on each job order are accumulated in a subsidiary ledger known as the **cost ledger.** Each cost ledger account, called a **job cost sheet,** has spaces for recording all direct materials and direct labor chargeable to the job and for applying factory overhead at the predetermined rate. Postings to the job cost sheets are made from materials requisitions and time tickets or from summaries of these documents.

The four cost sheets in the subsidiary ledger for the work in process account illustrated are summarized as follows:

COST LEDGER

Job 71 (Summary)	
Balance..................	3,000
Direct materials	2,000
Direct labor...............	2,400
Factory overhead	1,920
	9,320

Job 73 (Summary)	
Direct materials	6,000
Direct labor...............	4,000
Factory overhead	3,200
	13,200

Job 72 (Summary)	
Direct materials	4,000
Direct labor...............	3,000
Factory overhead	2,400
	9,400

Job 74 (Summary)	
Direct materials	1,000
Direct labor...............	600
Factory overhead	480
	2,080

The relationship between the work in process controlling account on page 66 and the subsidiary cost ledger may be observed in the following tabulation:

Work in Process (Controlling)		Cost Ledger (Subsidiary)	
Beginning balance..........	$ 3,000 ⟷	Beginning balance Job 71	$ 3,000
Direct materials	$13,000 ⟷	Direct materials Job 71..................	$ 2,000
		Job 72.................	4,000
		Job 73.................	6,000
		Job 74.................	1,000
			$13,000
Direct labor...............	$10,000 ⟷	Direct labor Job 71..................	$ 2,400
		Job 72.................	3,000
		Job 73.................	4,000
		Job 74.................	600
			$10,000
Factory overhead..........	$ 8,000 ⟷	Factory overhead Job 71..................	$ 1,920
		Job 72.................	2,400
		Job 73.................	3,200
		Job 74.................	480
			$ 8,000

(continued)

Work in Process (Controlling)   Cost Ledger (Subsidiary)

Jobs completed

Jobs completed	$31,920 ⟷	Job 71 . . . . $ 9,320
		Job 72 9,400
		Job 73 13,200
		$31,920

Ending balance	$ 2,080 ⟷	Ending balance
		Job 74 . . . . $ 2,080

The data in the cost ledger were presented in summary form for illustrative purposes. A job cost sheet for Job 72, providing for the current accumulation of cost elements entering into the job order and for a summary when the job is completed, is as follows:

Job Cost Sheet

Job No. 72   Date _____ May 7, 19-- _____

Item 5,000 Type C Containers   Date wanted _____ May 23, 19-- _____

For Stock   Date completed _____ May 21, 19-- _____

Direct Materials		Direct Labor				Summary	
Mat. Req. No.	Amount	Time Summary No.	Amount	Time Summary No.	Amount	Item	Amount
834	800.00	2202	83.60	2248	122.50	Direct	
838	1,000.00	2204	208.40	2250	187.30	materials	4,000.00
841	1,400.00	2205	167.00	2253	155.40	Direct labor	3,000.00
864	800.00	2210	229.00		3,000.00	Factory	
	4,000.00	2211	198.30			overhead	
		2213	107.20			(80% of	
		2216	110.00			direct	
		2222	277.60			labor cost)	2,400.00
		2224	217.40			Total cost	9,400.00
		2225	106.30				
		2231	153.20			No. of units	
		2234	245.20			finished	5,000
		2237	170.00			Cost per unit	1.88
		2242	261.60				

When Job 72 was completed, the direct materials costs and the direct labor costs were totaled and entered in the Summary column. Factory overhead was added at the predetermined rate of 80% of the direct labor cost, and the total cost of the job was determined. The total cost of the job, $9,400, divided by the number of units produced, 5,000, yielded a unit cost of $1.88 for the Type C Containers produced.

Upon the completion of Job 72, the job cost sheet was removed from the cost ledger and filed for future reference. At the end of the accounting period, the sum of the total costs on all cost sheets completed during the period is determined and the following entry is made:

Finished Goods......................................	31,920	
Work in Process		31,920

The remaining balance in the work in process account represents the total cost charged to the uncompleted job cost sheets.

Finished Goods and Cost of Goods Sold

The finished goods account is a controlling account. The related subsidiary ledger, which has an account for each kind of commodity produced, is called the **finished goods ledger** or **stock ledger.** Each account in the subsidiary finished goods ledger provides columns for recording the quantity and the cost of goods manufactured, the quantity and the cost of goods shipped, and the quantity, the total cost, and the unit cost of goods on hand. An account in the finished goods ledger is illustrated as follows:

Finished Goods Ledger Account

ITEM: TYPE C CONTAINER

MANUFACTURED			SHIPPED			BALANCE			
JOB ORDER NO.	QUAN-TITY	AMOUNT	SHIP ORDER NO.	QUAN-TITY	AMOUNT	DATE	QUAN-TITY	AMOUNT	UNIT COST
						May 1	2,000	3,920.00	1.96
			643	2,000	3,920.00	8	—	—	—
72	5,000	9,400.00				21	5,000	9,400.00	1.88
			646	2,000	3,760.00	23	3,000	5,640.00	1.88

Just as there are various methods of costing materials entering into production, there are various methods of determining the cost of the finished goods sold. In the illustration, the first-in, first-out method is used. The quantities shipped are posted to the finished goods ledger from a copy of the shipping order or other memorandum. The finished goods ledger clerk then records on the copy of the shipping order the unit cost and the total amount of the commodity sold. A summary of the cost data on these shipping orders becomes the basis for the following entry:

Cost of Goods Sold	30,168	
Finished Goods		30,168

If goods are returned by a buyer and are put back in stock, it is necessary to debit Finished Goods and credit Cost of Goods Sold for the cost.

Sales

· · ·

For each sale of finished goods, it is necessary to maintain a record of both the cost price and the selling price of the goods sold. As previously stated, the cost data may be recorded on the shipping orders. As each sale occurs, the cost of the goods billed is recorded by debiting Cost of Goods Sold and crediting Finished Goods. The selling price of the goods sold is recorded by debiting Accounts Receivable (or Cash) and crediting Sales.

ILLUSTRATION OF JOB ORDER COST ACCOUNTING

·

To illustrate further a job order cost accounting system, assume that Spencer Co. has the following general ledger trial balance on January 1, the first day of the fiscal year:

Spencer Co.
Trial Balance
January 1, 19--

Cash	85,000	
Accounts Receivable	73,000	
Finished Goods	40,000	
Work in Process	20,000	
Materials	30,000	
Prepaid Expenses	2,000	
Plant Assets	850,000	
Accumulated Depreciation — Plant Assets		473,000
Accounts Payable		70,000
Wages Payable		15,000
Common Stock		500,000
Retained Earnings		42,000
	1,100,000	1,100,000

Although in practice the transactions for Spencer Co. would be recorded daily, the January transactions and adjustments are summarized as follows, along with the related journal entries:

(a) Materials purchased and prepaid expenses incurred.

Summary of invoices and receiving reports:

Material A	$29,000
Material B	17,000
Material C	16,000
Material D	4,000
Total	$66,000

Entry: Materials   66,000
Prepaid Expenses   1,000
Accounts Payable   67,000

(b) Materials requisitioned for use.

Summary of requisitions:

By Use

Job 1001	$12,000	
Job 1002	26,000	
Job 1003	22,000	$60,000
Factory Overhead		3,000
Total		$63,000

By Types

Material A	$27,000
Material B	18,000
Material C	15,000
Material D	3,000
Total	$63,000

Entry: Work in Process   60,000
Factory Overhead   3,000
Materials   63,000

(c) Factory labor used.

Summary of time tickets:

Job 1001	$60,000	
Job 1002	30,000	
Job 1003	10,000	$100,000
Factory Overhead		20,000
Total		$120,000

Entry: Work in Process   100,000
Factory Overhead   20,000
Wages Payable   120,000

(d) *Other costs incurred.*

Entry: Factory Overhead............................	56,000	
Selling Expenses	25,000	
General Expenses	10,000	
Accounts Payable..........................		91,000

(e) *Expiration of prepaid expenses.*

Entry: Factory Overhead............................	1,000	
Selling Expenses	100	
General Expenses	100	
Prepaid Expenses		1,200

(f) *Depreciation.*

Entry: Factory Overhead............................	7,000	
Selling Expenses	200	
General Expenses	100	
Accumulated Depreciation—Plant Assets ...		7,300

(g) *Application of factory overhead costs to jobs.* The predetermined rate was 90% of direct labor cost.

Summary of factory overhead applied:

Job 1001 (90% of $60,000).............	$54,000
Job 1002 (90% of $30,000).............	27,000
Job 1003 (90% of $10,000).............	9,000
Total.................................	$90,000

Entry: Work in Process	90,000	
Factory Overhead..........................		90,000

(h) *Jobs completed.*

Summary of completed job cost sheets:

Job 1001............................	$146,000
Job 1002............................	83,000
Total.................................	$229,000

Entry: Finished Goods............................	229,000	
Work in Process		229,000

(i) *Sales and cost of goods sold.*

Summary of sales invoices and shipping orders:

	Sales Price	Cost Price
Product X	$ 19,600	$ 15,000
Product Y	165,100	125,000
Product Z	105,300	80,000
Total.................	$290,000	$220,000

Entry: Accounts Receivable......................	290,000	
Sales.....................................		290,000
Entry: Cost of Goods Sold.......................	220,000	
Finished Goods...........................		220,000

(j) Cash received.

Entry: Cash.....................................	300,000	
Accounts Receivable.....................		300,000

(k) Cash disbursed.

Entry: Accounts Payable..........................	190,000	
Wages Payable............................	125,000	
Cash.....................................		315,000

The flow of costs through the manufacturing accounts, together with summary details of the subsidiary ledgers, is illustrated below. Entries in the accounts are identified by letters to facilitate comparisons with the foregoing summary journal entries.

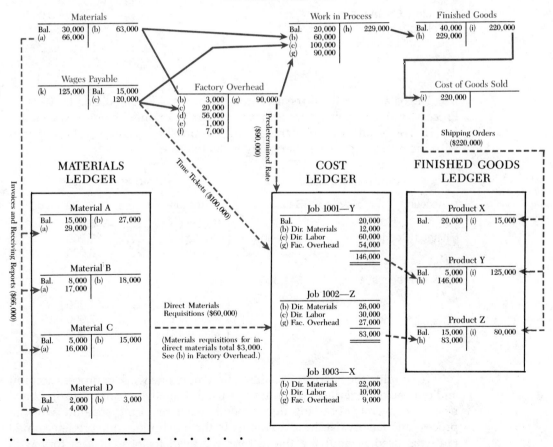

Flow of Costs Through Job Order Cost Accounts

The trial balance taken from the general ledger of Spencer Co. on January 31 is as follows:

Spencer Co.
Trial Balance
January 31, 19--

Cash	70,000	
Accounts Receivable	63,000	
Finished Goods	49,000	
Work in Process	41,000	
Materials	33,000	
Prepaid Expenses	1,800	
Plant Assets	850,000	
Accumulated Depreciation—Plant Assets		480,300
Accounts Payable		38,000
Wages Payable		10,000
Common Stock		500,000
Retained Earnings		42,000
Sales		290,000
Cost of Goods Sold	220,000	
Factory Overhead		3,000
Selling Expenses	25,300	
General Expenses	10,200	
	1,363,300	1,363,300

The balances of the three inventory accounts—Finished Goods, Work in Process, and Materials—represent the respective ending inventories on January 31. The balances of the general ledger controlling accounts are compared with their respective subsidiary ledgers as follows:

Controlling Accounts		Subsidiary Ledgers		
Account	Balance	Account	Balance	
Finished Goods	$49,000 ⟷	Product X	$ 5,000	
		Product Y	26,000	
		Product Z	18,000	$49,000
Work in Process	$41,000 ⟷	Job 1003		$41,000
Materials	$33,000 ⟷	Material A	$17,000	
		Material B	7,000	
		Material C	6,000	
		Material D	3,000	$33,000

To simplify the Spencer Co. illustration, only one work in process account and one factory overhead account were used. Usually, a manufacturing business has several processing departments, each requiring separate work in process and factory overhead accounts. In the illustration, one predetermined rate was used in applying the factory overhead to jobs. In a factory with several processing departments, a single factory overhead rate may not provide accurate product costs and effective cost control. A single rate for the entire factory cannot take into consideration such factors as differences among departments in the nature of their operations and in amounts of factory overhead incurred. In such cases, each factory department should have a separate factory overhead rate. For example, in a factory with twenty distinct operating departments, one department might have an overhead rate of 110% of direct labor cost, another a rate of $4 per direct labor hour, and another a rate of $3.50 per machine hour.

The following financial statements are based on the data for Spencer Co. It should be noted that the overapplied factory overhead on January 31 is reported on the balance sheet as a deferred item. It should also be noted that a separate statement of cost of goods manufactured, as illustrated in Chapter 2, is not shown. Under a perpetual inventory cost accounting system, the balances of the cost of goods sold, materials, work in process, and finished goods accounts are kept up to date. Hence, the finished goods ledger will indicate the costs of manufacturing the various products during the period. Likewise, the cost ledger will indicate the costs assigned to jobs still in process. The balance of the cost of goods sold account will indicate the cost of products sold during the period. The statement of cost of goods manufactured is normally prepared only for enterprises using periodic inventory procedures under a general accounting system.

Spencer Co. Income Statement For Month Ended January 31, 19--		
Sales.		$290,000
Cost of goods sold		220,000
Gross profit		$ 70,000
Operating expenses:		
Selling expenses	$25,300	
General expenses	10,200	
Total operating expenses.		35,500
Income from operations		$ 34,500

Spencer Co. Retained Earnings Statement For Month Ended January 31, 19--	
Retained earnings, January 1, 19--	$42,000
Income for the month	34,500
Retained earnings, January 31, 19--	$76,500

Spencer Co.
Balance Sheet
January 31, 19--

Assets

Current assets:

Cash..................................		$ 70,000	
Accounts receivable...................		63,000	
Inventories:			
Finished goods......................	$49,000		
Work in process....................	41,000		
Materials..........................	33,000	123,000	
Prepaid expenses.....................		1,800	
Total current assets...................			$257,800
Plant assets............................		$850,000	
Less accumulated depreciation.........		480,300	369,700
Total assets.............................			$627,500

Liabilities

Current liabilities:

Accounts payable....................	$38,000		
Wages payable.......................	10,000		
Total current liabilities.................		$ 48,000	
Deferred credits:			
Factory overhead.....................		3,000	
Total liabilities...........................			$ 51,000

Stockholders' Equity

Common stock...........................		$500,000	
Retained earnings......................		76,500	
Total stockholders' equity................			576,500
Total liabilities and stockholders' equity....			$627,500

Chapter Review

KEY POINTS

1. Usefulness of Product Costs.

Product costs are useful to managers for the preparation of financial statements. Product costs are also needed by management for a wide variety of decisions, such as setting long-term product prices. Without accurate product cost information, managers could not effectively or efficiently manage operations.

2. Types of Accounting Systems.

Two basic accounting systems may be used by manufacturers: general accounting systems and cost accounting systems. A general accounting system uses periodic inventory procedures for materials, work in process, and finished goods inventories. For more complex manufacturing operations, a cost accounting system using perpetual inventory procedures is usually employed. A cost accounting system also uses controlling accounts and subsidiary ledgers for materials, work in process, and finished goods. The two main types of cost accounting systems for manufacturing operations are the job order cost and process cost systems.

3. Job Order Cost Systems.

A job order cost system provides for a separate record of the cost of each particular quantity of product that passes through the factory. The details concerning the costs incurred on each job order are accumulated in a subsidiary ledger known as the cost ledger. Each cost ledger account, called a job cost sheet, has spaces for recording all direct materials and direct labor chargeable to the job and for applying factory overhead at the predetermined rate. Work in Process is the controlling account for the cost ledger. As a job is finished, it is transferred to the finished goods ledger, for which Finished Goods is the controlling account.

KEY TERMS

general accounting system 58
cost accounting system 58
job order cost system 58
process cost system 59
purchase requisitions 60
purchase orders 60
receiving report 60
materials ledger 60
materials requisitions 61

time tickets 62
predetermined factory
 overhead rate 64
overapplied overhead 64
underapplied overhead 64
cost ledger 66
job cost sheet 66
finished goods ledger 69

SELF-EXAMINATION QUESTIONS

(Answers at End of Chapter)

1. The account maintained by a manufacturing business for inventory of goods in the process of manufacture is:
   A. Finished Goods
   B. Materials
   C. Work in Process
   D. None of the above

2. For a manufacturing business, finished goods inventory includes:
   A. direct materials costs
   B. direct labor costs
   C. factory overhead costs
   D. all of the above

3. An example of a factory overhead cost is:
   A. wages of factory assembly-line workers
   B. salaries for factory plant supervisors
   C. bearings for electric motors being manufactured
   D. all of the above

4. For which of the following would the job order cost system be appropriate?
   A. Antique furniture repair shop   C. Coal manufacturer
   B. Rubber manufacturer   D. All of the above

5. If the factory overhead account has a credit balance, factory overhead is said to be:
   A. underapplied   C. underabsorbed
   B. overapplied   D. none of the above

ILLUSTRATIVE PROBLEM

Shelton Signs Inc. specializes in the production of neon signs and uses a job order cost system. The following data summarize the operations related to product for November, the first month of operations:

(a) Materials purchased on account, $21,750.
(b) Materials requisitioned and factory labor used:

	Materials	Factory Labor
Job No. 1	$2,750	$1,700
Job No. 2	3,800	2,000
Job No. 3	2,990	1,450
Job No. 4	5,950	3,800
Job No. 5	3,250	1,900
Job No. 6	900	600
For general factory use	595	500

(c) Factory overhead costs incurred on account, $4,300.
(d) Depreciation of machinery, $1,450.
(e) The factory overhead rate is 60% of direct labor cost.
(f) Jobs completed: Nos. 1, 2, 4, and 5.
(g) Jobs Nos. 1, 2, and 4 were shipped and customers were billed for $7,900, $10,500, and $18,100, respectively.

Instructions:

1. Prepare entries to record the foregoing summarized operations.
2. Determine the account balances for Work in Process and Finished Goods.
3. Prepare a schedule of unfinished jobs to support the balance in the work in process account.

4. Prepare a schedule of completed jobs on hand to support the balance in the finished goods account.

SOLUTION

(1)

(a)	Materials	21,750	
	Accounts Payable..........................		21,750
(b)	Work in Process	31,090	
	Factory Overhead	1,095	
	Materials		20,235
	Wages Payable		11,950
(c)	Factory Overhead	4,300	
	Accounts Payable..........................		4,300
(d)	Factory Overhead	1,450	
	Accumulated Depreciation — Machinery		1,450
(e)	Work in Process.............................	6,870	
	Factory Overhead (60% of $11,450)		6,870
(f)	Finished Goods	30,790	
	Work in Process		30,790

Computation of the cost of jobs finished:

Job	Direct Materials	Direct Labor	Overhead	Total
Job No. 1	$2,750	$1,700	$1,020	$ 5,470
Job No. 2	3,800	2,000	1,200	7,000
Job No. 4	5,950	3,800	2,280	12,030
Job No. 5	3,250	1,900	1,140	6,290
				$30,790

(g)	Accounts Receivable	36,500	
	Sales		36,500
	Cost of Goods Sold	24,500	
	Finished Goods		24,500

Computation of the cost of jobs sold:

Job No. 1...........	$ 5,470
Job No. 2...........	7,000
Job No. 4...........	12,030
	$24,500

(2) Work in Process: $7,170 ($31,090 + $6,870 − $30,790)
   Finished Goods: $6,290 ($30,790 − $24,500)

(3)   Schedule of Unfinished Jobs

	Direct Materials	Direct Labor	Factory Overhead	Total
Job No. 3	$2,990	$1,450	$870	$5,310
Job No. 6	900	600	360	1,860
Balance of Work in Process, November 30................				$7,170

(4)   Schedule of Completed Jobs

Job No. 5:	Direct materials.............................	$3,250
	Direct labor	1,900
	Factory overhead	1,140
Balance of Finished Goods, November 30		$6,290

Discussion Questions

3–1. What are two important uses of product cost information by managers?

3–2. What are the two basic accounting systems commonly used by manufacturers?

3–3. (a) Name the two principal types of cost accounting systems. (b) Which system provides for a separate record of each particular quantity of product that passes through the factory? (c) Which system accumulates the costs for each department or process within the factory?

3–4. Distinguish between the purchase requisition and the purchase order used in the procurement of materials.

3–5. Briefly discuss how the purchase order, purchase invoice, and receiving report can be used to assist in controlling cash disbursements for materials acquired.

3–6. What document is the source for (a) debiting the accounts in the materials ledger, and (b) crediting the accounts in the materials ledger?

3–7. Briefly discuss how the accounts in the materials ledger can be used as an aid in maintaining appropriate inventory quantities of stock items.

3–8. How does use of the materials requisition help control the issuance of materials from the storeroom?

3–9. Discuss the major advantages of a perpetual inventory system over a periodic system for materials.

3–10. (a) Differentiate between the clock card and the time ticket. (b) Why should the total time reported on an employee's time tickets for a payroll period be compared with the time reported on the employee's clock cards for the same period?

3-11. Which of the following items are properly classified as part of factory overhead?
    (a) factory supplies used
    (b) interest expense
    (c) amortization of factory patents
    (d) property taxes on factory buildings
    (e) sales commissions
    (f) direct materials

3-12. Discuss how the predetermined factory overhead rate can be used in job order cost accounting to assist management in pricing jobs.

3-13. (a) How is a predetermined factory overhead rate calculated? (b) Name three common bases used in calculating the rate.

3-14. (a) What is (1) overapplied factory overhead and (2) underapplied factory overhead? (b) If the factory overhead account has a debit balance, was factory overhead underapplied or overapplied? (c) If the factory overhead account has a credit balance at the end of the first month of the fiscal year, where will the amount of this balance be reported on the interim balance sheet?

3-15. At the end of a fiscal year, there was a relatively minor balance in the factory overhead account. What is the simplest satisfactory procedure for the disposition of the balance in the account?

3-16. What name is given to the individual accounts in the cost ledger?

3-17. What document serves as the basis for posting to (a) the direct materials section of the job cost sheet, and (b) the direct labor section of the job cost sheet?

3-18. Describe the source of the data for debiting Work in Process for (a) direct materials, (b) direct labor, and (c) factory overhead.

3-19. What account is the controlling account for (a) the materials ledger, (b) the cost ledger, and (c) the finished goods ledger or stock ledger?

3-20. Real World Focus. Hewlett-Packard Company manufactures printed circuit boards in which a high volume of standardized units are fabricated, machined, assembled, and tested. Is the job order cost system appropriate in this situation?

Exercises

3-21. **Cost of materials issuances by fifo and lifo methods.** The balance of Material G on April 1 and the receipts and issuances during April are as follows:

Balance: April 1 . . . . 240 units at $40.00
Received: April 6 . . . . 600 units at $42.00
              14 . . . . 480 units at $42.60
              26 . . . . 360 units at $43.20
Issued: April 7 . . . . 360 units for Job 410
              17 . . . . 300 units for Job 415
              28 . . . . 420 units for Job 430

Determine the cost of each of the three issuances under a perpetual system, using (a) the first-in, first-out method and (b) the last-in, first-out method.

3–22. Entry for issuance of materials. The issuances of materials for the current month are as follows:

Requisition No.	Material	Job No.	Amount
841	F-10	1020	$5,140
842	H-60	1060	1,690
843	W-3	1035	3,860
844	A-16	General factory use	750
845	J-48	1018	4,320

Present the journal entry to record the issuances of materials.

3–23. Entry for factory labor costs. A summary of the time tickets for the current month follows:

Job No.	Amount	Job No.	Amount
673	$1,250	677	$ 800
674	8,100	Indirect labor	1,180
675	2,670	678	6,250
676	4,500	679	5,200

Present the journal entry to record the factory labor costs.

3–24. Factory overhead rates, entries, and account balance. Logan Company, which maintains departmental accounts for work in process and factory overhead, applies factory overhead to jobs on the basis of machine hours in Department 30 and on the basis of direct labor costs in Department 40. Estimated factory overhead costs, direct labor costs, and machine hours for January are as follows:

	Department 30	Department 40
Estimated factory overhead cost for year	$65,000	$243,600
Estimated direct labor costs for year		$580,000
Estimated machine hours for year	20,000	
Actual factory overhead costs for January	$ 6,050	$ 20,100
Actual direct labor costs for January		$ 48,500
Actual machine hours for January............	1,800	

(a) Determine the factory overhead rate for Department 30. (b) Determine the factory overhead rate for Department 40. (c) Prepare the journal entries to apply factory overhead to production for January. (d) Determine the balances of the departmental factory overhead accounts as of January 31 and indicate whether the amounts represent overapplied or underapplied factory overhead.

3–25. Entry for jobs completed; cost of unfinished jobs. The following account appears in the ledger after only part of the postings have been completed for November:

Work in Process		
Balance, November 1	17,150	
Direct Materials	43,100	
Direct Labor	67,500	
Factory Overhead	37,000	

Jobs finished during November are summarized as follows:

Job 1320............	$25,400	Job 1327............	$40,800
Job 1326............	45,600	Job 1330............	26,100

(a) Prepare the journal entry to record the jobs completed and (b) determine the cost of the unfinished jobs at November 30.

3–26. Entries for factory costs and jobs completed. Hill Enterprises Inc. began manufacturing operations on February 1. Jobs 201 and 202 were completed during the month, and all costs applicable to them were recorded on the related cost sheets. Jobs 203 and 204 are still in process at the end of the month, and all applicable costs except factory overhead have been recorded on the related cost sheets. In addition to the materials and labor charged directly to the jobs, $10,500 of indirect materials and $25,200 of indirect labor were used during the month. The cost sheets for the four jobs entering production during the month are as follows, in summary form:

Job 201		Job 202	
Direct materials............	15,750	Direct materials	28,200
Direct labor	12,600	Direct labor................	20,160
Factory overhead..........	7,560	Factory overhead...........	12,096
Total	35,910	Total....................	60,456

Job 203		Job 204	
Direct materials............	21,400	Direct materials	5,500
Direct labor	17,640	Direct labor................	7,800
Factory overhead..........		Factory overhead...........	

Prepare an entry to record each of the following operations for the month (one entry for each operation):

(a) Direct and indirect materials used.
(b) Direct and indirect labor used.
(c) Factory overhead applied (a single overhead rate is used, based on direct labor cost).
(d) Completion of Jobs 201 and 202.

Problems

3–27. Entries and schedules for unfinished and completed jobs. Logan Printing Company uses a job order cost system. The following data summarize the operations related to production for June, the first month of operations:

(a) Materials purchases on account, $110,160.
(b) Materials requisitioned and factory labor used:

	Materials	Factory Labor
Job 601	$15,840	$9,500
Job 602	10,380	7,040
Job 603	13,900	5,100
Job 604	20,950	13,380
Job 605	11,440	6,680
Job 606	7,100	2,900
For general factory use...........	2,300	1,760

(c) Factory overhead costs incurred on account, $21,200.

(d) Depreciation of machinery and equipment, $7,760.

(e) The factory overhead rate is 75% of direct labor cost.

(f) Jobs completed: 601, 602, 603, and 605.

(g) Jobs 601, 602, and 605 were shipped and customers were billed for $49,250, $31,100, and $31,280 respectively.

Instructions:

(1) Prepare entries to record the foregoing summarized operations.

(2) Open T accounts for Work in Process and Finished Goods and post the appropriate entries, using the identifying letters as dates. Insert memorandum account balances as of the end of the month.

(3) Prepare a schedule of unfinished jobs to support the balance in the work in process account.

(4) Prepare a schedule of completed jobs on hand to support the balance in the finished goods account.

If the working papers correlating with the textbook are not used, omit Problem 3–28.

3–28. Job order cost sheet. Stein Furniture Company repairs, refinishes, and re-upholsters furniture. A job order cost system was installed recently to facilitate (1) the determination of price quotations to prospective customers, (2) the determination of actual costs incurred on each job, and (3) cost reductions.

In response to a prospective customer's request for a price quotation on a job, the estimated cost data are inserted on an unnumbered job cost sheet. If the offer is accepted, a number is assigned to the job and the costs incurred are recorded in the usual manner on the job cost sheet. After the job is completed, reasons for the variances between the estimated and actual costs are noted on the sheet. The data are then available to management in evaluating the efficiency of operations and in preparing quotations on future jobs.

On June 10, an estimate of $665 for reupholstering a couch was given to Nancy Westbrook. The estimate was based on the following data:

Estimated direct materials:	
10 meters at $8.50 per meter................................	$ 85
Estimated direct labor:	
20 hours at $13 per hour....................................	260
Estimated factory overhead (50% of direct labor cost)	130
Total estimated costs	$475
Markup (40% of production costs).............................	190
Total estimate...	$665

On June 14, the couch was picked up from the residence of Nancy Westbrook, 2408 Bobolink Way, Tampa, with a commitment to return it on June 28.

The job was completed on June 24. The related materials requisitions and time tickets are summarized as follows:

Materials Requisition No.	Description	Amount
3480	10 meters at $8.50	$ 85
3492	2 meters at $8.50	17

Time Ticket No.	Description	Amount
H143	15 hours at $13	$195
H151	7 hours at $13	91

Instructions:

(1) Complete that portion of the job order cost sheet that would be prepared when the estimate is given to the customer.
(2) Assign number R6-18 to the job, record the costs incurred, and complete the job order cost sheet. In commenting upon the variances between actual costs and estimated costs, assume that 2 meters of materials were spoiled, the factory overhead rate has been proved to be satisfactory, and an inexperienced employee performed the work.

3–29. **Preparation of financial statements.** The trial balance of F. R. Conrad Inc., at the beginning of the current fiscal year, is as follows:

F. R. Conrad Inc.
Trial Balance
May 1, 19--

Cash	46,300	
Accounts Receivable	70,260	
Finished Goods	66,500	
Work in Process	24,360	
Materials	32,200	
Prepaid Expenses	8,600	
Plant Assets	582,400	
Accumulated Depreciation—Plant Assets		330,500
Accounts Payable		23,700
Wages Payable		—
Common Stock		100,000
Retained Earnings		376,420
Sales		—
Cost of Goods Sold	—	
Factory Overhead	—	
Selling Expenses	—	
General Expenses	—	
	830,620	830,620

Transactions completed during May and adjustments required on May 31 are summarized as follows:

(a) Materials purchased on account................... $27,480

(b) Materials requisitioned for factory use:

Direct......................................	$25,800	
Indirect.....................................	320	26,120

(c) Factory labor costs incurred:

Direct......................................	$12,960	
Indirect.....................................	1,840	14,800

(d) Other costs and expenses incurred on account:

Factory overhead.............................	$ 6,750	
Selling expenses	6,570	
General expenses	4,800	18,120

(e) Cash disbursed:

Accounts payable.............................	$49,200	
Wages payable...............................	13,300	62,500

(f) Depreciation charged:

Factory equipment............................	$ 4,320	
Office equipment	360	4,680

(g) Prepaid expenses expired:

Chargeable to factory	$ 640	
Chargeable to selling expenses	150	
Chargeable to general expenses	140	930

(h) Applied factory overhead at a predetermined rate: 110% of direct labor cost.

(i) Total cost of jobs completed   51,600

(j) Sales, all on account:

Selling price	67,200
Cost	43,600

(k) Cash received on account   68,400

Instructions:

(1) Open T accounts and record the initial balances indicated in the May 1 trial balance, identifying each as "Bal."
(2) Record the transactions directly in the accounts, using the identifying letters in place of dates.
(3) Prepare an income statement for the month ended May 31, 19--.
(4) Prepare a retained earnings statement for the month ended May 31, 19--.
(5) Prepare a balance sheet as of May 31, 19--.

3–30. **Entries, trial balance, and financial statements.** The trial balance of the general ledger of R. Staub Co. as of March 31, the end of the first month of the current fiscal year, is as follows:

R. Staub Co.
Trial Balance
March 31, 19--

Cash....................................	92,000	
Accounts Receivable	185,300	
Finished Goods	187,600	
Work in Process...........................	62,000	
Materials.................................	72,900	
Plant Assets..............................	810,000	
Accumulated Depreciation—Plant Assets......		360,000
Accounts Payable..........................		125,000
Wages Payable		15,000
Capital Stock		100,000
Retained Earnings.........................		738,700
Sales		280,000
Cost of Goods Sold.........................	168,000	
Factory Overhead	900	
Selling and General Expenses	40,000	
	1,618,700	1,618,700

As of the same date, balances in the accounts of selected subsidiary ledgers are as follows:

Finished goods ledger:
   Commodity X, 2,000 units, $40,000; Commodity Y, 6,000 units, $90,000; Commodity Z, 3,200 units, $57,600.
Cost ledger:
   Job 700, $62,000.
Materials ledger:
   Material R15, $38,600; Material Z10, $31,600; Material W01, $2,700.

The transactions completed during April are summarized as follows:

(a) Materials were purchased on account as follows:

Material R15	$55,000
Material Z10	38,500
Material W01..	1,500

(b) Materials were requisitioned from stores as follows:

Job 700, Material R15, $21,040; Material Z10, $16,800........	$37,840
Job 701, Material R15, $27,000; Material Z10, $23,120........	50,120
Job 702, Material R15, $13,800; Material Z10, $6,130.........	19,930
For general factory use, Material W01......................	1,600

(c) Time tickets for the month were chargeable as follows:

Job 700	$19,600	Job 702	$16,400
Job 701	16,800	Indirect labor	5,000

(d) Factory payroll checks for $59,400 were issued.

(e) Various factory overhead charges of $11,200 were incurred on account.

(f) Selling and general expenses of $38,200 were incurred on account.

(g) Payments on account were $140,000.

(h) Depreciation of $10,300 on factory plant and equipment was recorded.

(i) Factory overhead was applied to jobs at 60% of direct labor cost.

(j) Jobs completed during the month were as follows: Job 700 produced 6,400 units of Commodity X; Job 701 produced 5,000 units of Commodity Y.

(k) Total sales on account were $383,200. The goods sold were as follows (use first-in, first-out method): 4,600 units of Commodity X; 7,500 units of Commodity Y; 2,000 units of Commodity Z.

(l) Cash of $250,000 was received on accounts receivable.

Instructions:

(1) Open T accounts for the general ledger, the finished goods ledger, the cost ledger, and the materials ledger. Record directly in these accounts the balances as of March 31, identifying them as "Bal." Record the quantities as well as the dollar amounts in the finished goods ledger.

(2) Prepare entries to record the April transactions. After recording each transaction, post to the T accounts, using the identifying letters as dates. When posting to the finished goods ledger, record quantities as well as dollar amounts.

(3) Prepare a trial balance.

(4) Prepare schedules of the account balances in the finished goods ledger, the cost ledger, and the materials ledger.

(5) Prepare an income statement for the two months ended April 30.

3–31. **Determination of amounts missing from selected accounts in job cost system.** Following are selected accounts for Watson Products. For the purposes of this problem, some of the debits and credits have been omitted.

Accounts Receivable

Oct. 1	Balance	47,600	Oct. 31	Collections	102,000
31	Sales	(A)			

Materials

Oct. 1	Balance	11,500	Oct. 31	Requisitions	(B)
31	Purchases	16,900			

Work in Process

Oct. 1	Balance	21,000	Oct. 31	Goods finished	(E)
31	Direct materials	(C)			
31	Direct labor	22,400			
31	Factory overhead	(D)			

Finished Goods

Oct. 1	Balance	38,900	Oct. 31	Cost of goods sold	(G)
31	Goods finished	(F)			

Factory Overhead

| Oct. | 1 | Balance | 120 | Oct. 31 | Applied (80% of | | |
| | 1–31 | Costs incurred | 17,500 | | direct labor cost) | | (H) |

Cost of Goods Sold

| Oct. 31 | | (I) | | |

Sales

| | | | Oct. 31 | | (J) |

Selected balances at October 31:

Accounts receivable......................	$52,000
Finished goods...........................	24,000
Work in process.........................	17,800
Materials	9,500

Materials requisitions for October included $500 of materials issued for general factory use. All sales are made on account, terms n/30.

Instructions:

(1) Determine the amounts represented by the letters (A) through (J), presenting your computations.

(2) Determine the amount of factory overhead overapplied or underapplied as of October 31.

ALTERNATE PROBLEMS

3–27A. Entries and schedules for unfinished and completed jobs. Owens Printing Company uses a job order cost system. The following data summarize the operations related to production for November, the first month of operations:

(a) Materials purchased on account, $57,420.

(b) Materials requisitioned and factory labor used:

	Materials	Factory Labor
Job 101	$11,600	$9,150
Job 102	3,400	1,960
Job 103	8,520	4,690
Job 104	4,280	1,900
Job 105	6,830	2,800
Job 106	6,180	4,610
For general factory use...........	1,310	3,000

(c) Factory overhead costs incurred on account, $11,300.

(d) Depreciation of machinery and equipment, $5,400.

(e) The factory overhead rate is 70% of direct labor cost.

(f) Jobs completed: 101, 102, 104, and 105.

(g) Jobs 101, 102, and 104 were shipped and customers were billed for $36,200, $8,400, and $10,350 respectively.

Instructions:

(1) Prepare entries to record the foregoing summarized operations.

(2) Open T accounts for Work in Process and Finished Goods and post the appropriate entries, using the identifying letters as dates. Insert memorandum account balances as of the end of the month.

(3) Prepare a schedule of unfinished jobs to support the balance in the work in process account.

(4) Prepare a schedule of completed jobs on hand to support the balance in the finished goods account.

If the working papers correlating with the textbook are not used, omit Problem 3–28A.

3–28A. Job order cost sheet. Katz Furniture Company repairs, refinishes, and reupholsters furniture. A job order cost system was installed recently to facilitate (1) the determination of price quotations to prospective customers, (2) the determination of actual costs incurred on each job, and (3) cost reductions.

In response to a prospective customer's request for a price quotation on a job, the estimated cost data are inserted on an unnumbered job cost sheet. If the offer is accepted, a number is assigned to the job and the costs incurred are recorded in the usual manner on the job cost sheet. After the job is completed, reasons for the variances between the estimated and actual costs are noted on the sheet. The data are then available to management in evaluating the efficiency of operations and in preparing quotations on future jobs.

On February 6, an estimate of $360 for reupholstering a chair and couch was given to John Bergman. The estimate was based on the following data:

Estimated direct materials:	
12 meters at $10 per meter..................................	$120
Estimated direct labor:	
8 hours at $15 per hour....................................	120
Estimated factory overhead (40% of direct labor cost)	48
Total estimated costs	$288
Markup (25% of production costs)............................	72
Total estimate...	$360

On February 10, the chair and couch were picked up from the residence of John Bergman, 1454 Spartan Lane, Des Moines, with a commitment to return it on February 21. The job was completed on February 19.

The related materials requisitions and time tickets are summarized as follows:

Materials Requisition No.	Description	Amount
U642	12 meters at $10	$120
U651	3 meters at $10	30

Time Ticket No.	Description	Amount
1519	6 hours at $15	$ 90
1520	3 hours at $15	45

Instructions:

(1) Complete that portion of the job order cost sheet that would be prepared when the estimate is given to the customer.

(2) Assign number 89-10-1 to the job, record the costs incurred, and complete the job order cost sheet. In commenting upon the variances between actual costs and estimated costs, assume that 3 meters of materials were spoiled, the factory overhead rate has been proved to be satisfactory, and an inexperienced employee performed the work.

3–30A. Entries, trial balance, and financial statements. The trial balance of the general ledger of Thurman Corporation as of January 31, the end of the first month of the current fiscal year, is shown as follows:

Thurman Corporation
Trial Balance
January 31, 19--

Cash.	54,840	
Accounts Receivable	111,180	
Finished Goods	106,800	
Work in Process.	36,840	
Materials	44,340	
Plant Assets	474,600	
Accumulated Depreciation—Plant Assets.		211,740
Accounts Payable		79,780
Wages Payable		9,000
Capital Stock		200,000
Retained Earnings.		311,700
Sales		160,980
Cost of Goods Sold.	120,000	
Factory Overhead	1,200	
Selling and General Expenses	23,400	
	973,200	973,200

As of the same date, balances in the accounts of selected subsidiary ledgers are as follows:

Finished goods ledger:
    Commodity E, 3,500 units, $42,000; Commodity F, 1,800 units, $27,000; Commodity G, 1,400 units, $37,800.
Cost ledger:
    Job 580, $36,840.
Materials ledger:
    Material M, $17,700; Material N, $22,140; Material O, $4,500.

The transactions completed during February are summarized as follows:

(a) Materials were purchased on account as follows:

Material M	$33,000
Material N	23,100
Material O	900

(b) Materials were requisitioned from stores as follows:

Job 580, Material M, $16,200; Material N, $14,178	$30,378
Job 581, Material M, $8,280; Material N, $3,324.	11,604
Job 582, Material M, $12,720; Material N, $10,118	22,838
For general factory use, Material O	960

(c) Time tickets for the month were chargeable as follows:

Job 580	$11,760	Job 582.	$9,840
Job 581	10,080	Indirect labor	3,600

(d) Factory payroll checks for $38,640 were issued.

(e) Various factory overhead charges of $13,425 were incurred on account.

(f) Depreciation of $5,400 on factory plant and equipment was recorded.

(g) Factory overhead was applied to jobs at 70% of direct labor cost.

(h) Jobs completed during the month were as follows: Job 580 produced 5,700 units of Commodity F; Job 582 produced 1,460 units of Commodity G.

(i) Selling and general expenses of $22,920 were incurred on account.

(j) Payments on account were $85,800.

(k) Total sales on account were $167,800. The goods sold were as follows (use first-in, first-out method): 1,500 units of Commodity E; 3,200 units of Commodity F; 1,600 units of Commodity G.

(l) Cash of $150,600 was received on accounts receivable.

Instructions:

(1) Open T accounts for the general ledger, the finished goods ledger, the cost ledger, and the materials ledger. Record directly in these accounts the balances as of January 31, identifying them as "Bal." Record the quantities as well as the dollar amounts in the finished goods ledger.

(2) Prepare entries to record the February transactions. After recording each transaction, post to the T accounts, using the identifying letters as dates. When posting to the finished goods ledger, record quantities as well as dollar amounts.

(3) Prepare a trial balance.

(4) Prepare schedules of the account balances in the finished goods ledger, the cost ledger, and the materials ledger.

(5) Prepare an income statement for the two months ended February 28.

3–31A. Determination of amounts missing from selected accounts in job cost system. Following are selected accounts for Nowell Products. For the purposes of this problem, some of the debits and credits have been omitted.

Accounts Receivable

Mar.	1	Balance	81,600	Mar. 31	Collections	120,500
	31	Sales	(A)			

Materials

Mar.	1	Balance	21,000	Mar. 31	Requisitions	(B)
	31	Purchases	41,500			

Work in Process

Mar.	1	Balance	24,000	Mar. 31	Goods finished	(E)
	31	Direct materials	(C)			
	31	Direct labor	48,200			
	31	Factory overhead	(D)			

Finished Goods

Mar.	1	Balance	12,800	Mar. 31	Cost of goods sold	(G)
	31	Goods finished	(F)			

Factory Overhead

Mar.	1	Balance	300	Mar. 31	Applied (60% of direct labor cost)	(H)
	1–31	Costs incurred	28,800			

Cost of Goods Sold

Mar. 31		(I)	

Sales

	Mar. 31	(J)

Selected balances at March 31:
Accounts receivable $78,750
Finished goods.   22,000
Work in process.   27,300
Materials   15,000

Materials requisitions for March included $1,300 of materials issued for general factory use. All sales are made on account, terms n/30.

Instructions:

(1) Determine the amounts represented by the letters (A) through (J), presenting your computations.
(2) Determine the amount of factory overhead overapplied or underapplied as of March 31.

Mini-Case 3

As an assistant cost accountant for Atkinson Industries, you have been assigned to review the activity base for the predetermined factory overhead rate. The president, J. C. Atkinson, has expressed concern that the over- or underapplied overhead has fluctuated excessively over the years.

An analysis of the company's operations and use of the current overhead base (direct materials usage) have narrowed the possible alternative overhead bases to direct labor cost and machine hours. For the past five years, the following data have been gathered:

	1990	1989	1988	1987	1986
Actual overhead...	$ 840,000	$ 820,000	$ 900,000	$ 735,000	$ 705,000
Applied overhead...	812,000	847,500	921,000	750,000	656,000
(Over) under-applied over-head	$ 28,000	$ (27,500)	$ (21,000)	$ (15,000)	$ 49,000
Direct labor cost	$3,350,000	$3,300,000	$3,625,000	$2,925,000	$2,800,000
Machine hours......	663,000	645,000	726,000	597,000	569,000

Instructions:

(1) Calculate a predetermined factory overhead rate for each alternative base, assuming that the rates would have been determined by relating the amount of factory overhead for the past five years to the base.
(2) For each of the past five years, determine the over- or underapplied overhead, based on the two predetermined overhead rates developed in (1).
(3) Which predetermined overhead rate would you recommend? Discuss the basis for your recommendation.

Answers to Self-Examination Questions

· · ·

1. **C** Three inventory accounts are maintained by manufacturing businesses for (1) goods in the process of manufacture (Work in Process—answer C), (2) goods in the state in which they are to be sold (Finished Goods—answer A), and (3) goods in the state in which they were acquired (Materials—answer B).

2. **D** The finished goods inventory is composed of three categories of manufacturing costs: direct materials (answer A), direct labor (answer B), and factory overhead (answer C).

3. **B** Factory overhead includes all manufacturing costs, except direct materials and direct labor. Salaries of plant supervisors (answer B) is an example of a factory overhead item. Wages of factory assembly-line workers (answer A) is a direct labor item, and bearings for electric motors (answer C) are direct materials.

4. **A** Job order cost systems are best suited to businesses manufacturing for special orders from customers, such as would be the case for a repair shop for antique furniture (answer A). A process cost system is best suited for manufacturers of homogeneous units of product, such as rubber (answer B) and coal (answer C).

5. **B** If the amount of factory overhead applied during a particular period exceeds the actual overhead costs, the factory overhead account will have a credit balance and is said to be overapplied (answer B) or overabsorbed. If the amount applied is less than the actual costs, the account will have a debit balance and is said to be underapplied (answer A) or underabsorbed (answer C).

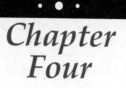

Chapter Four

CHAPTER OBJECTIVES

•

Distinguish process cost accounting systems from
job order cost accounting systems.

•

Describe and illustrate the basic concepts for
a process cost accounting system.

•

Describe and illustrate the preparation and the
use of a cost of production report.

•

Describe and illustrate the accounting for joint products.

•

Describe and illustrate the accounting for by-products.

•

Describe and illustrate the use of the average cost method of inventory
costing for process cost accounting systems.

•

Process Cost Systems

In many industries, job orders as described in Chapter 3 are not suitable for scheduling production and accumulating the manufacturing costs. Companies manufacturing cement, flour, or paint, for example, do so on a continuous basis. The principal product is a homogeneous mass rather than a collection of distinct units. No useful purpose would be served by maintaining job orders for particular amounts of a product as the material passes through the several stages of production.

PROCESS COST AND JOB ORDER COST SYSTEMS DISTINGUISHED

Many of the methods, procedures, and managerial applications presented in the preceding chapter in the discussion of job order cost systems apply equally to process cost systems. For example, perpetual inventory accounts with subsidiary ledgers for materials, work in process, and finished goods are requisites of both systems. In job order cost accounting, however, the costs of direct materials, direct labor, and factory overhead are charged directly to job orders. In process cost accounting, the costs are charged to processing departments, and the cost of a finished unit is determined by dividing the total cost incurred in each process among the number of units produced. Since all goods produced in a department are identical units, it is not necessary to classify production into job orders.

In factories with departmentalized operations, costs are accumulated in factory overhead and work in process accounts maintained for each department. If there is only one processing department in a factory, the cost accounting procedures are simple. The manufacturing cost elements are charged to the single work in process account, and the unit cost of the finished product is determined by dividing the total cost by the number of units produced.

When the manufacturing procedure requires a sequence of different processes, the output of Process 1 becomes the direct materials of Process 2, the output of Process 2 becomes the direct materials of Process 3, and so on until the finished product emerges. Additional direct materials requisitioned from stores may also be introduced during subsequent processes.

A work in process account for Haworth Manufacturing Company, which is departmentalized, is illustrated as follows. In this illustration, the total cost of $96,000 is divided by the output, 10,000 units, to obtain a unit cost of $9.60.

Work in Process — Assembly Department		
Direct materials	32,000	To Sanding Dept., 10,000 units 96,000
Direct labor	40,000	Cost per unit:
Factory overhead	24,000	$96,000 ÷ 10,000 = $9.60
	96,000	
		96,000

A New Way To Build Cars

One of the major industries that uses process cost accounting is the automobile manufacturing industry. Typically, cars are built as they move along an assembly line that provides little flexibility for the installation of the many options common to today's vehicles. Therefore, automakers are turning to modern technology in modifying the traditional assembly line. For example, in two new assembly plants in Kansas City, Kansas, and Doraville, Georgia, General Motors Corporation is using hundreds of motorized, unmanned carriers to move cars through the assembly process. The effect of using these carriers, called automated guided vehicles, in the production of cars is described in the following excerpts from an article in the *New York Times*:

When Henry Ford perfected the assembly line, he was making only one type of car, the Model T, which came in just one color, black. Since then, options have proliferated and today there can be as much as a 30 percent difference in the content of a stripped-down model and one fully loaded.

Because current lines move at a constant speed, regardless of the model mix, plant managers have had to hire enough workers to build the most complex car in the assigned amount of time. This means that some people are idle when base models come down the line. And because stopping the line to fix some-

thing would idle thousands, most workers only tag an incorrectly fitting part and hope it will be repaired at the end of the line.

With the carriers, the notion of a "line" begins to fade, although the vehicles generally follow a prescribed path, receiving their instructions from wires buried in the plant floor. If a particular car has a heavy load of options, though, the vehicle may be directed to move out of the main [path] to have those parts installed, while less heavily equipped models continue along the route. G.M. engineers call this "decoupling the line." With this flexibility, plant managers will be able to balance the work force more closely with the workload....

The carriers also fit into the modular assembly concept that G.M. officials have called one of the keys to cutting manufacturing costs in its Saturn program. Instead of installing thousands of parts, one by one, on a car, a whole module, such as an instrument panel, will be built off the line, tested and only installed if it passes the tests. Since a carrier can be programmed to stop and go as needed, it could roll to the completed instrument panels and then stop to ease the installation....

"We couldn't have done this a few years ago," said David D. Campbell, the director of operations for G.M.'s Chevrolet-Pontiac-Canada group. "We need computers that can keep track of hundreds of carriers and decide on a minute-by-minute basis what station to assign them to, based on variations in the model mix."

Source: John Holusha, "A New Way to Build Cars," *The New York Times*, March 13, 1986.

SERVICE DEPARTMENTS AND PROCESS COSTS

In a factory with several processes, there may be one or more **service departments** that do not process the materials directly. Examples of service departments are the factory office, the power plant, and the maintenance and repair shop. These departments perform services for the benefit of other production departments. The costs that they incur, therefore, are part of the total manufacturing costs and must be charged to the processing departments.

The services performed by a service department give rise to internal transactions with the processing departments benefited. These internal transactions are recorded periodically in order to charge the factory overhead accounts of the processing departments with their share of the costs incurred by the service departments. The period usually chosen is a month, although a different period of time may be used. To illustrate, assume that the Power Department of Haworth Manufacturing Company produced 600 000 kilowatt-hours (kwh) during the month at a total cost of $30,000, or 5¢ per kilowatt-hour ($30,000 ÷ 600 000). The factory overhead accounts for the departments that used the power are accordingly charged for power at the 5¢ rate. Assuming that during the month the Assembly Department used 100 000 kwh, the Sanding Department used 300 000 kwh, and the Polishing Department used 200 000 kwh, the accounts affected by the interdepartmental transfer of cost would appear as follows:

Power Department

Fuel	12,000	To Factory Overhead —	
Wages	8,500	Assembly Dept.	5,000
Depreciation	3,000	To Factory Overhead —	
Maintenance	2,500	Sanding Dept.	15,000
Insurance	2,000	To Factory Overhead —	
Taxes	1,500	Polishing Dept.	10,000
Miscellaneous	500		
	30,000		30,000

Service Department Costs Charged to Processing Departments

Factory Overhead — Assembly Dept.

Power	5,000

Factory Overhead — Sanding Dept.

Power	15,000

Factory Overhead — Polishing Dept.

Power	10,000

Some service departments render services to other service departments. For example, the power department may supply electric current to light the factory office and to operate data processing equipment. At the same time, the factory office provides general supervision for the power department, maintains its payroll records, buys its fuel, and so on. In such cases, the costs of the department rendering the greatest service to other service departments may be distributed first, despite the fact that it receives benefits from other service departments.

PROCESSING COSTS

The accumulated costs transferred from preceding departments and the costs of direct materials and direct labor incurred in each processing department are debited to the related work in process account. Each work in process account is also debited for the factory overhead applied. The costs incurred are summarized periodically, usually at the end of the month. The costs related to the output of each department during the month are then transferred to the next processing department or to Finished Goods, as the case may be. This flow of costs through a work in process account is illustrated as follows:

Work in Process — Sanding Department

10,000 units at $9.60 from Assembly Dept.		96,000	To Polishing Dept., 10,000 units 160,000
Direct labor	36,800		Cost per unit:
Factory overhead	27,200	64,000	$160,000 ÷ 10,000 = $16
		160,000	160,000

The three debits in the preceding account may be grouped into two separate categories: (1) direct materials or partially processed materials received from another department, which in this case is composed of 10,000 units received from the Assembly Department, with a total cost of $96,000, and (2) direct labor and factory overhead applied in the Sanding Department, which in this case totaled $64,000. This second group of costs, as described in Chapter 2, is called the **conversion cost.**

Again referring to the illustration, all of the 10,000 units were completely processed in the Sanding Department and were passed on to the Polishing Department. The $16 unit cost of the product transferred to the Polishing Department is made up of Assembly Department cost of $9.60 ($96,000 ÷ 10,000 units) and conversion cost of $6.40 ($64,000 ÷ 10,000 units) incurred in the Sanding Department.

INVENTORIES OF PARTIALLY PROCESSED MATERIALS

In the preceding illustration, all materials entering a process were completely processed at the end of the accounting period. In such a case, the determination of unit costs is quite simple. The total of the costs transferred from other departments, the direct materials, the direct labor, and the factory overhead charged to a department is divided by the number of units completed and passed on to the next department or to finished goods. Often, however, some partially processed materials remain in various stages of production in a department at the end of a period. In this case, the costs in work in process must be allocated between the units that have been completed and transferred to the next process or to finished goods and those that are only partially completed and remain within the department.

Flow of Manufacturing Costs

To allocate direct materials and transferred costs between the output completed and transferred to the next process and inventory of goods within the department, it is necessary to determine the manner in which materials are placed in production and flow through the production processes. For some products, materials may be added to production in about the same proportion as conversion costs are incurred. In still other situations, materials may enter the process at relatively few points, which may or may not be evenly spaced throughout the process. For most manufacturing processes, however, the materials are on hand when production begins, and they move through the production processes in a first-in, first-out flow; that is, the first units entering the production process are the first to be completed. Therefore, the following discussion and illustrations will assume a normal production process, whereby all materials are placed into the process in a fifo (first-in, first-out) order. The manufacturing costs associated with such a process will also be allocated by the fifo cost method. Later in the chapter, an alternate method — the average cost method — will be discussed.

Equivalent Units of Production

To allocate processing costs between the output completed and transferred to the next process and the inventory of goods within the process, it is necessary to determine the number of *equivalent units* of production during the period. The **equivalent units of production** are the number of units that could have been manufactured from start to finish during the period. To illustrate, assume that there is no inventory of goods in process in a certain processing department at the beginning of the period, that 1,000 units of materials enter the process during the period, and that at the end of the period all of the units are 75% completed. The equivalent production in the processing department for the period would be 750 units (75% of 1,000).

Usually there is an inventory of partially processed units in the department at the beginning of a period. These units are normally completed during the period and transferred to the next department along with units started and completed in the current period. Other units started in the period are only partially processed and thus make up the ending inventory. To illustrate the computation of equivalent units under such circumstances, the following data are assumed for the Polishing Department of Haworth Manufacturing Company:

Inventory within Polishing Department on March 1 . . . .   600 units, 1/3 completed
Completed in Polishing Department and transferred to
   finished goods during March . . . .   9,800 units, completed
Inventory within Polishing Department on March 31 . . . . . .   800 units, 2/5 completed

The equivalent units of production are determined as follows:

Determination of Equivalent Units of Production

To process units in inventory on March 1 . . . . 600 units × 2/3   400
To process units started and completed in March . . . . .9,800 units − 600 units   9,200
To process units in inventory on March 31 . . . . 800 units × 2/5   320

Equivalent units of production in March.   9,920

The 9,920 equivalent units of production represent the number of units that would have been produced if there had been no inventories within the process either at the beginning or at the end of the period.

Continuing with the illustration, the next step is to allocate the costs incurred in the Polishing Department between the units completed during March and those remaining in process at the end of the month. If all materials were introduced at the beginning of the process, the full materials cost per unit must be assigned to the uncompleted units. The conversion costs would then be allocated to the finished and the uncompleted units on the basis of equivalent units of production, as shown in the following account:

ACCOUNT WORK IN PROCESS — POLISHING DEPARTMENT   ACCOUNT NO.

Date		Item	Debit	Credit	Balance Debit	Balance Credit
Mar.	1	Bal., 600 units, 1/3 completed			10,200	
	31	Sanding Dept., 10,000 units				
		at $16	160,000		170,200	
	31	Direct labor	26,640		196,840	
	31	Factory overhead	18,000		214,840	
	31	Goods finished, 9,800 units		200,600		
	31	Bal., 800 units, 2/5 completed			14,240	

The conversion costs incurred in the Polishing Department during March total $44,640 ($26,640 + $18,000). The equivalent units of production for March, determined above, is 9,920. The conversion cost per equivalent unit is therefore $4.50 ($44,640 ÷ 9,920). Of the $214,840 debited to the Polishing

Department, $200,600 was transferred to Finished Goods and $14,240 remained in the account as work in process inventory. The computation of the allocations to finished goods and to inventory is as follows:

Goods Finished During March

600 units:	Inventory on March 1, 1/3 completed	$ 10,200	
	Conversion cost in March:		
	600 × 2/3, or 400 units at $4.50	1,800	
	Total.		$ 12,000
	(Unit cost: $12,000 ÷ 600 = $20)		
9,200 units:	Materials cost in March, at $16 per unit	$147,200	
	Conversion cost in March:		
	9,200 at $4.50 per unit	41,400	
	Total.		188,600
	(Unit cost: $188,600 ÷ 9,200 = $20.50)		
9,800 units:	Goods finished during March.		$200,600

Polishing Department Inventory on March 31

800 units:	Materials cost in March, at $16 per unit	$ 12,800	
	Conversion cost in March:		
	800 × 2/5, or 320 at $4.50	1,440	
800 units:	Polishing Department inventory on March 31. . .		$ 14,240

Allocation of Departmental Charges to Finished Goods and Inventory

COST OF PRODUCTION REPORT

A report prepared periodically for each processing department summarizes (1) the units for which the department is accountable and the disposition of these units, and (2) the costs charged to the department and the allocation of these costs. This report, termed the **cost of production report,** may be used as the source of the computation of unit production costs and the allocation of the processing costs in the general ledger to the finished and the uncompleted units. More importantly, the report is used to control costs. Each department head is held responsible for the units entering production and the costs incurred in the department. Any differences in unit product costs from one month to another are studied carefully and the causes of significant differences are determined.

The cost of production report based on the data presented in the preceding section for the Polishing Department of Haworth Manufacturing Company is shown on page 104.

Haworth Manufacturing Company
Cost of Production Report — Polishing Department
For the Month Ended March 31, 19--

Quantities:
Charged to production:
In process, March 1.................................... 600
Received from Sanding Department 10,000
Total units to be accounted for 10,600

Units accounted for:
Transferred to finished goods 9,800
In process, March 31.............................. 800
Total units accounted for.......................... 10,600

Costs:
Charged to production:
In process, March 1............................... $ 10,200
March costs:
Direct materials from Sanding Department
($16 per unit)................................ 160,000
Conversion costs:
Direct labor .... $ 26,640
Factory overhead 18,000
Total conversion costs ($4.50 per unit) 44,640
Total costs to be accounted for.................... $214,840

Costs allocated as follows:
Transferred to finished goods:
600 units at $20 .... $ 12,000
9,200 units at $20.50 188,600
Total cost of finished goods...................... $200,600
In process, March 31:
Direct materials (800 units at $16) .... $ 12,800
Conversion costs (800 units × 2/5 × $4.50)...... 1,440
Total cost of inventory in process, March 31 14,240
Total costs accounted for $214,840

Computations:
Equivalent units of production:
To process units in inventory on March 1:
600 units × 2/3 400
To process units started and completed in March:
9,800 units − 600 units......................... 9,200
To process units in inventory on March 31:
800 units × 2/5 320
Equivalent units of production................. 9,920

Unit conversion cost:
$44,640 ÷ 9,920............................... $ 4.50

JOINT PRODUCTS AND BY-PRODUCTS

In some manufacturing processes, more than one product is produced. In processing cattle, for example, the meat packer produces dressed beef, hides, and other products. In processing logs, the lumber mill produces several grades of lumber in addition to scraps and sawdust. When the output of a manufacturing process consists of two or more different products, the products may be joint products, or one or more of the products may be a by-product.

When two or more goods of significant value are produced from a single principal direct material, the products are termed **joint products.** Similarly, the costs incurred in the manufacture of joint products are called **joint costs.** Common examples of joint products are gasoline, naphtha, kerosene, paraffin, benzine, and other related goods, all of which come from the processing of crude oil.

If one of the products resulting from a process has little value in relation to the main product or joint products, it is known as a **by-product.** The emergence of a by-product is only incidental to the manufacture of the main product or joint products. By-products may be leftover materials, such as sawdust and scraps of wood in a lumber mill, or they may be separated from the material at the beginning of production, as in the case of cottonseed from raw cotton.

Accounting for Joint Products

In management decisions concerning the production and sale of joint products, only the relationship of the total revenue to be derived from the entire group to their total production cost is relevant. Nothing is to be gained from an allocation of joint costs to each product because one product cannot be produced without the others. A decision to produce a single joint product is in effect a decision to produce all of the joint products.

Since joint products come from the processing of a common parent material, the assignment of cost to each separate product cannot be based on actual expenditures. It is impossible to determine the amount of cost incurred in the manufacture of each separate product. However, for purposes of inventory valuation, it is necessary to allocate joint costs among the joint products.

One method of allocation commonly used is the **market (sales) value method.** Its main feature is the assignment of costs to the different products according to their relative sales values. To illustrate, assume that 10,000 units of Product X and 50,000 units of Product Y were produced at a total cost of $63,000. The sales values of the two products and the allocation of the joint costs are as follows:

Allocation of Joint Costs

Joint Costs	Joint Product	Units Produced	Sales Value per Unit	Total Sales Value
$63,000	X	10,000	$3.00	$30,000
	Y	50,000	1.20	60,000
Total sales value				$90,000

Allocation of joint costs:

X: $\dfrac{\$30,000}{\$90,000} \times \$63,000$ $21,000

Y: $\dfrac{\$60,000}{\$90,000} \times \$63,000$ 42,000

Unit cost:

X: $21,000 ÷ 10,000 units $2.10

Y: $42,000 ÷ 50,000 units 84

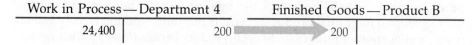

Accounting for By-Products

The amount of manufacturing cost usually assigned to a by-product is the sales value of the by-product reduced by any additional costs necessary to complete and sell it. The amount of cost thus determined is removed from the proper work in process account and transferred to a finished goods inventory account. To illustrate, assume that for a certain period the costs accumulated in Department 4 total $24,400, and during the same period of time, 1,000 units of by-product B emerge from the processing in Department 4. If the estimated value of the by-product is $200, after estimated completion and selling costs have been deducted, Finished Goods—Product B would be debited for $200 and Work in Process—Department 4 would be credited for the same amount, as illustrated in the following accounts:

Work in Process—Department 4		Finished Goods—Product B	
24,400	200	200	

ILLUSTRATION OF PROCESS COST ACCOUNTING

To illustrate further the basic procedures of the process costing system, assume that Conway Company manufactures Product A. The manufacturing activity begins in Department 1, where all materials enter production. The materials remain in Department 1 for a relatively short time, and there is usually no inventory of work in process in that department at the end of the accounting period. From Department 1, the materials are transferred to Department 2. In Department 2, there are usually inventories at the end of the accounting period. Separate factory overhead accounts are maintained for Departments 1 and 2. Factory overhead is applied at 80% and 50% of direct labor cost for Departments 1 and 2 respectively. There are two service departments, Maintenance and Power. All inventories are costed by the first-in, first-out method.

The trial balance of the general ledger on January 1, the first day of the fiscal year, is as follows:

Conway Company
Trial Balance
January 1, 19--

Cash	39,400	
Accounts Receivable.	45,000	
Finished Goods — Product A (1,000 units at $36.50)	36,500	
Work in Process — Department 2		
(800 units, 1/2 completed).	24,600	
Materials.	32,000	
Prepaid Expenses	6,150	
Plant Assets.	510,000	
Accumulated Depreciation — Plant Assets		295,000
Accounts Payable.		51,180
Wages Payable.		3,400
Common Stock		250,000
Retained Earnings		94,070
	693,650	693,650

To reduce the illustrative entries to a manageable number and to avoid repetition, the transactions and the adjustments for January are stated as summaries. In practice, the transactions would be recorded from day to day in various journals. The descriptions of the transactions, followed in each case by the entry, are as follows:

(a) Materials purchased and prepaid expenses incurred.

Entry: Materials.	80,500	
Prepaid Expenses.	3,300	
Accounts Payable.		83,800

(b) Materials requisitioned for use.

Entry: Maintenance Department	1,200	
Power Department	6,000	
Factory Overhead — Department 1	3,720	
Factory Overhead — Department 2	2,700	
Work in Process — Department 1	58,500	
Materials.		72,120

(c) Factory labor used.

Entry: Maintenance Department 3,600
Power Department 4,500
Factory Overhead—Department 1 2,850
Factory Overhead—Department 2 2,100
Work in Process—Department 1 24,900
Work in Process—Department 2 37,800
Wages Payable............................ 75,750

(d) Other costs incurred.

Entry: Maintenance Department 600
Power Department 900
Factory Overhead—Department 1 1,800
Factory Overhead—Department 2 1,200
Selling Expenses............................ 15,000
General Expenses 13,500
Accounts Payable......................... 33,000

(e) Expiration of prepaid expenses.

Entry: Maintenance Department 300
Power Department 750
Factory Overhead—Department 1 1,350
Factory Overhead—Department 2 1,050
Selling Expenses............................ 900
General Expenses 600
Prepaid Expenses.......................... 4,950

(f) Depreciation.

Entry: Maintenance Department 300
Power Department 1,050
Factory Overhead—Department 1 1,800
Factory Overhead—Department 2 2,700
Selling Expenses............................ 600
General Expenses 300
Accumulated Depreciation—Plant Assets...... 6,750

(g) Distribution of Maintenance Department costs.
The portion of services rendered was 5%, 45%, and 50% for the Power Department, Department 1, and Department 2, respectively.

Entry: Power Department 300
Factory Overhead—Department 1 2,700
Factory Overhead—Department 2 3,000
Maintenance Department 6,000

(h) Distribution of Power Department costs.
Power was provided at 5¢ per kwh for 108 000 and 162 000 kwh for Departments 1 and 2, respectively.

Entry: Factory Overhead—Department 1 5,400
       Factory Overhead—Department 2 8,100
           Power Department 13,500

(i) *Application of factory overhead costs to work in process.*
The predetermined rates were 80% and 50% of direct labor cost for Departments 1 and 2 respectively. See transaction (c) for the monthly direct labor costs.

Entry: Work in Process—Department 1 19,920
       Work in Process—Department 2 18,900
           Factory Overhead—Department 1 19,920
           Factory Overhead—Department 2 18,900

(j) *Transfer of production costs from Department 1 to Department 2.*
4,100 units were fully processed, and there is no work in process in Department 1 at the beginning or at the end of the month.

Total costs charged to Department 1:
  Direct materials .... $ 58,500
  Direct labor.................................... 24,900
  Factory overhead 19,920
      Total costs $103,320

Unit cost of product transferred to Department 2:
  $103,320 ÷ 4,100........................... $ 25.20

Entry: Work in Process—Department 2 103,320
           Work in Process—Department 1 103,320

(k) *Transfer of production costs from Department 2 to Finished Goods.*
4,000 units were completed, and the remaining 900 units were 2/3 completed at the end of the month.

Equivalent units of production:
  To process units in inventory on January 1:
    800 × 1/2................................... 400
  To process units started and completed in January:
    4,000 − 800................................ 3,200
  To process units in inventory on January 31:
    900 × 2/3.................................. 600
  Equivalent units of production in January........... 4,200

Conversion costs:
  Direct labor [transaction (c)] .... $ 37,800
  Factory overhead [transaction (i)] 18,900
      Total conversion costs .... $ 56,700

Unit conversion cost:
$56,700 ÷ 4,200 .... $ 13.50

Allocation of costs of Department 2:
  Units started in December, completed in January:
    Inventory on January 1, 800 units 1/2 completed .... $ 24,600
    Conversion costs in January, 400 at $13.50........... 5,400
      Total ($30,000 ÷ 800 = $37.50 unit cost) .... $ 30,000

  Units started and completed in January:
    From Department 1, 3,200 units at $25.20............ $ 80,640
    Conversion costs, 3,200 at $13.50................... 43,200
      Total ($123,840 ÷ 3,200 = $38.70 unit cost)......... 123,840
      Total transferred to Product A.................... $153,840

  Units started in January, 2/3 completed:
    From Department 1, 900 units at $25.20.............. $ 22,680
    Conversion costs, 600 at $13.50.................... 8,100
      Total work in process — Department 2............. 30,780
  Total costs charged to Department 2................... $184,620

Entry: Finished Goods — Product A 153,840
         Work in Process — Department 2................ 153,840

(l) Cost of goods sold.

  Product A, 3,800 units:
    1,000 units at $36.50 .... $ 36,500
      800 units at $37.50 30,000
    2,000 units at $38.70 77,400
      Total cost of goods sold..................... $143,900

  Entry: Cost of Goods Sold 143,900
           Finished Goods — Product A 143,900

(m) Sales.

  Entry: Accounts Receivable 210,500
           Sales................................... 210,500

(n) Cash received.

  Entry: Cash 200,000
           Accounts Receivable 200,000

(o) Cash disbursed.

  Entry: Accounts Payable......................... 120,000
           Wages Payable.......................... 72,500
           Cash 192,500

A chart of the flow of costs from the service and processing department accounts into the finished goods account and then to the cost of goods sold account is as follows. Entries in the accounts are identified by letters to aid the comparison with the summary journal entries.

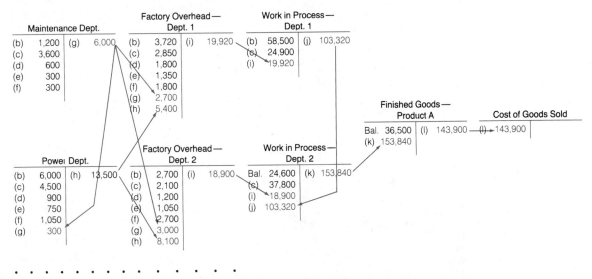

Flow of Costs Through Process Cost Accounts

Cost of Production Reports

The cost of production reports for Departments 1 and 2 are as follows:

Conway Company
Cost of Production Report—Department 1
For Month Ended January 31, 19--

Quantities:	
Units charged to production and to be accounted for............	4,100
Units accounted for and transferred to Department 2	4,100
Costs:	
Costs charged to production in January:	
Direct materials..	$ 58,500
Direct labor	24,900
Factory overhead	19,920
Total costs to be accounted for......................	$103,320
Total costs accounted for and transferred to Department 2	
(4,100 units × $25.20)................................	$103,320

Conway Company
Cost of Production Report — Department 2
For Month Ended January 31, 19--

Quantities:
Charged to production:

In process, January 1	800
Received from Department 1	4,100
Total units to be accounted for	4,900

Units accounted for:

Transferred to finished goods	4,000
In process, January 31	900
Total units accounted for............................	4,900

Costs:
Charged to production:

In process, January 1		$ 24,600
January costs:		
Direct materials from Department 1		
($25.20 per unit)................................		103,320
Conversion costs:		
Direct labor	$ 37,800	
Factory overhead	18,900	
Total conversion costs ($13.50 per unit)		56,700
Total costs to be accounted for.....................		$184,620

Costs allocated as follows:
Transferred to finished goods:

800 units at $37.50.............................	$ 30,000	
3,200 units at $38.70...........................	123,840	
Total cost of finished goods......................		$153,840
In process, January 31:		
Direct materials (900 units at $25.20)	$ 22,680	
Conversion costs (900 units × 2/3 × $13.50).....	8,100	
Total cost of inventory in process, January 31.....		30,780
Total costs accounted for		$184,620

Computations:
Equivalent units of production:

To process units in inventory on January 1:	
800 units × 1/2	400
To process units started and completed in January:	
4,000 units − 800 units...........................	3,200
To process units in inventory on January 31:	
900 units × 2/3	600
Equivalent units of production	4,200
Unit conversion cost:	
$56,700 ÷ 4,200.................................	$13.50

Financial Statements
· · ·

The financial statements for process cost systems are similar to those for job order cost systems. To illustrate, the trial balance and the condensed financial statements for Conway Company are presented as follows. Note that the net underapplied factory overhead of $1,650 ($1,950 − $300) on January 31 is reported on the balance sheet as a deferred item.

Conway Company
Trial Balance
January 31, 19--

Cash	46,900	
Accounts Receivable.	55,500	
Finished Goods — Product A (1,200 units at $38.70)	46,440	
Work in Process — Department 2 (900 units, 2/3 completed). . . .	30,780	
Materials.	40,380	
Prepaid Expenses	4,500	
Plant Assets.	510,000	
Accumulated Depreciation — Plant Assets		301,750
Accounts Payable.		47,980
Wages Payable.		6,650
Common Stock		250,000
Retained Earnings		94,070
Sales.		210,500
Cost of Goods Sold	143,900	
Factory Overhead — Department 1.		300
Factory Overhead — Department 2.	1,950	
Selling Expenses	16,500	
General Expenses	14,400	
	911,250	911,250

Conway Company
Income Statement
For Month Ended January 31, 19--

Sales.		$210,500
Cost of goods sold.		143,900
Gross profit		$ 66,600
Operating expenses:		
Selling expenses.	$16,500	
General expenses	14,400	
Total operating expenses		30,900
Income from operations		$ 35,700

Conway Company
Retained Earnings Statement
For Month Ended January 31, 19--

Retained earnings, January 1, 19--..........................	$ 94,070
Income for the month...........................	35,700
Retained earnings, January 31, 19--............................	$129,770

Conway Company
Balance Sheet
January 31, 19--

Assets

Current assets:

Cash		$ 46,900	
Accounts receivable		55,500	
Inventories:			
Finished goods.........................	$46,440		
Work in process	30,780		
Materials.............................	40,380	117,600	
Prepaid expenses........................		4,500	
Total current assets			$224,500
Plant assets		$510,000	
Less accumulated depreciation		301,750	208,250
Deferred debits:			
Factory overhead underapplied			1,650
Total assets			$434,400

Liabilities

Current liabilities:

Accounts payable........................		$ 47,980	
Wages payable...........................		6,650	
Total liabilities			$ 54,630

Stockholders' Equity

Common stock		$250,000	
Retained earnings		129,770	
Total stockholders' equity...................			379,770
Total liabilities and stockholders' equity.......			$434,400

INVENTORY COSTING METHODS

In the preceding discussion and illustrations, the **first-in, first-out (fifo) cost method** was used to determine unit product costs. Another method, known as the average cost method, is sometimes used in practice. Under the **average cost method**, all costs incurred in manufacturing the goods completed during a period are averaged, and this average is used in determining the unit product cost of the goods completed during the period and the work in process at the end of the period. Although the average cost method is not as accurate and not as useful to management in controlling costs as the fifo method, it is simpler to use and is therefore encountered in practice.

First-In, First-Out (Fifo) Cost Method

In most manufacturing processes, the products flow through the processes in a first-in, first-out manner; that is, the first units entering the process are the first completed. In such processes, the work in process at the beginning of the period is completed before work is completed on additional materials entered into the process. The fifo cost method is consistent with the flow of products in such manufacturing processes and is widely used.

When the fifo cost method is used, the beginning work in process inventory costs are kept separate from the costs incurred during the current period. As a result, the fifo cost method generally provides two unit cost figures for products completed during a period: (1) units completed from the beginning work in process, and (2) units started and completed during the current period. These two unit cost figures are useful to management in controlling manufacturing costs because current costs are used to determine the cost of products started and completed during the current period. Management can therefore focus on these current costs in evaluating and controlling current operations.

Using two separate costs adds some complexity to the calculation of unit costs. It also complicates the determination of product costs when the products completed by one process are used in subsequent processes. Primarily for these reasons, some enterprises prefer to use the average cost method.

Average Cost Method

The average cost method is *based on the assumption that the work in process at the beginning of the current period was started and completed during the current period.* Using this method, one unit cost figure for all products completed during the current period is determined. Although not as accurate as the fifo cost method, the average cost method avoids the problem of having two unit cost figures for products completed during a period. When the average cost method is used, it is more difficult for management to evaluate and control current operations, since past costs and current costs are averaged.

To illustrate the use of the average cost method, assume the following data for the Cutting Department of Perrin Company for July of the current year. In addition, assume that all materials used in the Cutting Department are added at the beginning of the process.

Inventory in process, July 1, 500 units:	
Materials cost, 500 units	$24,550
Conversion costs, 500 units, 60% completed	3,600
Materials cost for July, 1,000 units	50,000
Conversion costs for July, 1,000 units	9,660
Goods finished in July (includes units in process on July 1), 1,100 units	—
Inventory in process, July 31, 400 units, 50% completed	—

To apply the average cost method in the determination of the unit cost for the 1,100 units finished in July and the 400 units that are 50% completed on July 31, the average materials cost and the average conversion cost are determined as follows:

Materials cost for 500 units in process at July 1	$24,550
Materials cost for 1,000 units for July.	50,000
Total materials cost (1,500 units).	$74,550
Average materials cost per unit ($74,550 ÷ 1,500).	$ 49.70
Conversion costs for units in process at July 1	$ 3,600
Conversion costs for July	9,660
Total conversion costs	$13,260
Equivalent units of production:	
To process units in inventory on July 1	500
To process units started and completed in July (1,100 units − 500 units)	600
To process units in inventory on July 31 (400 units × 50%)	200
Equivalent units of production in July	1,300
Average conversion cost per unit ($13,260 ÷ 1,300)	$ 10.20

It should be noted that in determining the average unit materials cost, the cost of materials in work in process on July 1 (the beginning inventory) is added to the materials cost for July before dividing by the total units of materials in the cutting process during July. A similar procedure is followed for computing the average unit conversion cost. The conversion costs in work in process on July 1 (the beginning inventory) are added to the conversion costs for July before dividing by the equivalent units of production for July. As mentioned earlier, in computing these equivalent units, the units in the beginning inventory are treated as if they were all started and completed during the current period. In other words, the beginning inventory of

500 units is treated as 500 units fully completed during the current period, not 500 units 40% completed (200 units) during the current period.

The average unit costs for Perrin Company are used to determine the cost of goods finished during July and the cost of the work in process on July 31 (the ending inventory), as follows:

Goods finished during July:
```
1,100 units:  1,100 units at $49.70 for materials costs ............   $54,670
              1,100 units at $10.20 for conversion costs...........     11,220
                Total (1,100 units at $59.90) .....................    $65,890
```

Work in process, July 31:
```
400 units:  400 units at $49.70 for materials costs...............   $19,880
            400 units × 50% × $10.20 for conversion costs .......     2,040
                Total.............................................    $21,920
```

In many manufacturing processes, there is no significant difference between the unit cost figures determined under the average cost and the fifo cost methods. This similarity in unit costs is especially true where the beginning and ending work in process inventories are uniform and materials costs do not fluctuate widely from period to period. Therefore, the simplification of the calculations by using the average cost method and the lack of significant variation in unit costs under the two methods have been the principal reasons for the use of the average cost method. Computers, however, have removed the complexity from the calculations of unit product costs.

Chapter Review

KEY POINTS

1. Process Cost and Job Order Cost Systems Distinguished.

No useful purpose would be served for companies manufacturing a homogeneous product, such as cement, flour, or paint, to maintain job orders for each particular amount of product. In these cases, a process cost system is normally utilized. In process cost accounting, costs are charged to processing departments, and the cost of the finished unit is determined by dividing the total cost incurred in each process among the number of units produced.

2. Service Departments and Process Costs.

In a factory with several processes, there may be one or more service departments that do not process the materials directly. Examples include the factory office, the power plant, and the maintenance and repair shop. Periodically, the costs incurred by service departments are allocated to the factory overhead accounts of the processing departments.

3. Processing Costs.

The accumulated costs transferred from preceding departments and the costs of direct materials and direct labor incurred in each processing department are debited to the related work in process account. Each work in process account is also debited for the factory overhead applied. The direct labor and the factory overhead applied are referred to as the conversion costs.

4. Inventories of Partially Processed Materials.

Frequently, partially processed materials remain in various stages of production in a department at the end of a period. In this case, the manufacturing costs must be allocated between the units that have been completed and those that are only partially completed and remain within the department. In allocating costs between completed products and work remaining in process, either the first-in, first-out method or the average cost method may be used. To allocate processing costs between the output completed and the inventory of goods within the department, it is necessary to determine the number of equivalent units of production during the period. The equivalent units of production are the number of units that could have been manufactured from start to finish during the period.

5. Cost of Production Report.

A report prepared periodically for each processing department summarizes (1) the units for which the department is accountable and the disposition of these units and (2) the costs charged to the department and the allocation of these costs. This report, termed the cost of production report, may be used as the source of the computation of unit production costs and the allocation of the processing costs to the finished and the uncompleted units. More importantly, the report is used to control costs.

6. Joint Products and By-Products.

In some manufacturing processes, more than one product is produced. When the output of a manufacturing process consists of two or more different products, the products are either joint products or by-products. When two or more goods of significant value are produced from a single principal direct material, the products are termed joint products. Similarly, the costs incurred in the manufacture of joint products are called joint costs. If one of the products resulting from a process has little value in relation to the main product or joint products, it is known as a by-product.

Since joint products come from the processing of a common parent material, the assignment of cost to each separate product cannot be based on actual expenditures. The allocation of joint costs among the joint products is usually

performed using the market (sales) value method. The amount of manufacturing cost usually assigned to a by-product is the sales value of the by-
product reduced by any additional costs necessary to complete and sell it.

7. Inventory Costing Methods.

The first-in, first-out (fifo) cost method of accounting for manufacturing costs
is consistent with the flow of product costs through most manufacturing
processes. The average cost method, although not as useful for cost control as
the fifo method, is also used in practice. The simplification of the computations of unit product costs under the average cost method is the major
reason for use of the method. Under the average cost method, one unit cost
figure (rather than two, as under the fifo method) for all products completed
during a period is computed.

KEY TERMS

service departments 99
conversion cost 100
equivalent units of production 101
cost of production report 103
joint products 105

joint costs 105
by-product 105
market (sales) value method 105
first-in, first-out method 115
average cost method, 115

SELF-EXAMINATION QUESTIONS

(Answers at End of Chapter)

1. For which of the following businesses would the process cost system be
   most appropriate?
   A. Custom furniture manufacturer C. Crude oil refinery
   B. Commercial building contractor D. None of the above

2. The group of manufacturing costs referred to as *conversion costs* includes:
   A. direct materials and direct labor
   B. direct materials and factory overhead
   C. direct labor and factory overhead
   D. none of the above

3. Information relating to production in Department A for May is as follows:

May 1	Balance, 1,000 units, 3/4 completed	$22,150
31	Direct materials, 5,000 units	75,000
31	Direct labor	32,500
31	Factory overhead	16,250

   If 500 units were 1/4 completed at May 31, 5,500 units were completed
   during May, and inventories are costed by the first-in, first-out method,
   what was the number of equivalent units of production for May?
   A. 4,500   C. 5,500
   B. 4,875   D. None of the above

4. Based on the data presented in Question 3, what is the unit conversion cost?
   A. $10   C. $25
   B. $15   D. None of the above

5. If one of the products resulting from a process has little value in relation to the principal products, it is known as a:
   A. joint product   C. direct material
   B. by-product   D. none of the above

ILLUSTRATIVE PROBLEM

Tate Company manufactures Product A by a series of four processes, all materials being introduced in Department 1. From Department 1 the materials pass through Departments 2, 3, and 4, emerging as finished Product A. All inventories are costed by the first-in, first-out method.

The balances in the accounts Work in Process—Department 4 and Finished Goods were as follows on May 1:

Work in Process—Department 4 (1,000 units, 1/4 completed) $17,800
Finished Goods (1,800 units at $23.50 a unit)   42,300

The following costs were charged to Work in Process—Department 4 during May:

Direct materials transferred from Department 3: 4,700 units at
  $16 a unit. $75,200
Direct labor.   25,500
Factory overhead   15,300

During May, 5,000 units of A were completed and 4,800 units were sold. Inventories on May 31 were as follows:

Work in Process—Department 4: 700 units, 1/2 completed
Finished Goods: 2,000 units

Instructions:

Determine the following, presenting the computations in good order:
   (a) Equivalent units of production for Department 4 during May.
   (b) Unit conversion cost for Department 4 for May.
   (c) Total and unit cost of Product A started in a prior period and finished in May.
   (d) Total and unit cost of Product A started and finished in May.
   (e) Total cost of goods transferred to finished goods.
   (f) Work in process inventory for Department 4, May 31.
   (g) Cost of goods sold (indicate number of units and unit costs.)
   (h) Finished goods inventory, May 31.

SOLUTION

(a) Equivalent units of production:
To process units in inventory on May 1:
1,000 units × 3/4   750
To process units started and completed
in May: 5,000 units − 1,000 units   4,000
To process units in inventory on May 31:
700 units × 1/2   350
Equivalent units of production in May   5,100

(b) Unit conversion cost: $\dfrac{\$25,500 + \$15,300}{5,100} = \$8$

(c) Cost of Product A started in a prior period and
finished in May:
1,000 units: Inventory on May 1, 1/4 completed . . . . . $ 17,800
Conversion cost in May, 750 × $8   6,000
Total . . . . $ 23,800

Unit cost: $23,800 ÷ 1,000 = $23.80

(d) Cost of Product A started and finished in May:
4,000 units: Materials from Department 3,
4,000 × $16 . . . . $ 64,000
Conversion cost in May, 4,000 × $8   32,000
Total . . . . $ 96,000

Unit cost: $96,000 ÷ 4,000 = $24

(e) Total cost of goods transferred to finished goods:
Cost of Product A started in a prior period
and finished in May (1,000 units at $23.80) . . . . $ 23,800
Cost of Product A started and finished in May
(4,000 units at $24)   96,000
Total $119,800

(f) Work in process inventory, May 31:
700 units: Materials cost, 700 × $16 . . . . $ 11,200
Conversion costs in May, 350 × $8   2,800
Work in process inventory, May 31 . . . . . $ 14,000

(g) Cost of goods sold:

1,800 units at $23.50	$ 42,300
1,000 units at $23.80	23,800
2,000 units at $24.00	48,000
4,800 units	$114,100

(h) Finished goods inventory, May 31:

2,000 units at $24	$ 48,000

Discussion Questions

4–1. Which type of cost system, process or job order, would be best suited for each of the following: (a) paint manufacturer, (b) oil refinery, (c) furniture upholsterer, (d) building contractor, (e) refrigerator manufacturer? Give reasons for your answers.

4–2. Are perpetual inventory accounts for materials, work in process, and finished goods generally used for (a) job order cost systems and (b) process cost systems?

4–3. In job order cost accounting, the three elements of manufacturing cost are charged directly to job orders. Why is it not necessary to charge manufacturing costs in process cost accounting to job orders?

4–4. (a) How does a service department differ from a processing department? (b) Give two examples of a service department.

4–5. Cowen Company maintains a cafeteria for its employees at a cost of $2,250 per month. On what basis would the company most likely allocate the cost of the cafeteria among the production departments?

4–6. What two groups of manufacturing costs are referred to as conversion costs?

4–7. In the manufacture of 1,000 units of a product, direct materials cost incurred was $20,000, direct labor cost incurred was $8,000, and factory overhead applied was $4,000. (a) What is the total conversion cost? (b) What is the conversion cost per unit? (c) What is the total manufacturing cost? (d) What is the manufacturing cost per unit?

4–8. What is meant by the term "equivalent units"?

4–9. If Department A had no work in process at the beginning of the period, 5,000 units were completed during the period, and 1,000 units were 25% completed at the end of the period, what was the number of equivalent units of production for the period?

4–10. The following information concerns production in the Mixing Department for January. All direct materials are placed in process at the beginning of production. Determine the number of units in work in process inventory at the end of the month.

WORK IN PROCESS—MIXING DEPARTMENT

Date		Item	Debit	Credit	Balance Debit	Balance Credit
Jan.	1	Bal., 6,000 units, ¾ completed			9,500	
	31	Direct materials, 15,000 units	7,500			
	31	Direct labor	14,450			
	31	Factory overhead	7,225			
	31	Goods finished, 13,500 units		28,550		
	31	Bal., _____ units, ½ completed			10,125	

4–11. For Question No. 4–10, determine the equivalent units of production for January, assuming that the first-in, first-out method is used to cost inventories.

4–12. What data are summarized in the two principal sections of the cost of production report?

4–13. What is the most important purpose of the cost of production report?

4–14. Distinguish between a joint product and a by-product.

4–15. The Refining Department produces two products. How should the costs be allocated (a) if the products are joint products and (b) if one of the products is a by-product?

4–16. Factory employees in the Assembly Department of Farr Co. are paid widely varying wage rates. In such circumstances, would direct labor hours or direct labor cost be the more equitable base for applying factory overhead to the production of the department? Explain.

4–17. In a factory with several processing departments, a separate factory overhead rate may be determined for each department. Why is a single factory overhead rate often inadequate in such circumstances?

4–18. What are the two common inventory costing methods used in process cost accounting?

4–19. What are the principal advantages of the use of the first-in, first-out method for costing inventories for process cost systems?

4–20. What are the principal advantages of the use of the average method for costing inventories for process cost systems?

4–21. Real World Focus. As production processes become more and more automated in what many see as the "age of robotics," materials may enter into and leave a production process without human intervention. For example, in the manufacture of automobiles, General Motors uses state-of-the-art paint systems, which are operated from an automated video control room. The control room supervisor monitors the preparation of the bare metal body of the automobile as it is submerged in a primer. Next, the body passes through nine pairs of robot painters teamed with other robot devices that open and close doors and paint inside surfaces. (a) In this type of production environment, would direct labor hours be an appropriate base for allocation of predetermined factory overhead? (b) Can you suggest other possible factory overhead bases?

Exercises

·

4–22. Flowchart of accounts related to service and processing departments. Yates Co. manufactures two products. The entire output of Department 1 is transferred to Department 2. Part of the fully processed goods from Department 2 are sold as Product P and the remainder of the goods are transferred to Department 3 for further processing into Product Q. The service department, Factory Office, provides services for each of the processing departments.

Prepare a chart of the flow of costs from the service and processing department accounts into the finished goods accounts and then into the cost of goods sold account. The relevant accounts are as follows:

Cost of Goods Sold	Finished Goods — Product P
Factory Office	Finished Goods — Product Q
Factory Overhead — Department 1	Work in Process — Department 1
Factory Overhead — Department 2	Work in Process — Department 2
Factory Overhead — Department 3	Work in Process — Department 3

4–23. Entry for allocation of service department costs. The Maintenance and Repair Department provides services to processing departments C, D, and E. During July of the current year, the total cost incurred by the Maintenance and Repair Department was $80,000. During July, it was estimated that 60% of the services were provided to Department C, 25% to Department D, and 15% to Department E.

Prepare an entry to record the allocation of the Maintenance and Repair Department cost for July to the processing departments.

4–24. Entries for flow of factory costs for process cost system. Lunn Company manufactures a single product by a continuous process, involving four production departments. The records indicate that $65,000 of direct materials were issued to and $90,000 of direct labor was incurred by Department 1 in the manufacture of the product; the factory overhead rate is 60% of direct labor cost; work in process in the department at the beginning of the period totaled $37,500; and work in process at the end of the period totaled $35,000.

Prepare entries to record (a) the flow of costs into Department 1 during the period for (1) direct materials, (2) direct labor, and (3) factory overhead; (b) the transfer of production costs to Department 2.

4–25. Factory overhead rate, entry for application of factory overhead, and factory overhead account balance. The chief cost accountant for R. D. Evans Co. estimates total factory overhead cost for the Blending Department for the year at $72,000 and total direct labor costs at $96,000. During March, the actual direct labor cost totaled $8,100, and factory overhead cost incurred totaled $6,250. (a) What is the predetermined factory overhead rate based on direct labor cost? (b) Prepare the entry to apply factory overhead to production for March. (c) What is the March 31 balance of the account Factory Overhead — Blending Department? (d) Does the balance in (c) represent overapplied or underapplied factory overhead?

4-26. Equivalent units of production and related costs. The charges to Work in Process—Finishing Department for a period, together with information concerning production, are as follows. All direct materials are placed in process at the beginning of production, and the first-in, first-out method is used to cost inventories.

Work in Process—Finishing Department

2,000 units, 80% completed	49,100	To Dept. 2, 6,200 units	169,600
Direct materials, 4,200 at $15	63,000		
Direct labor	46,000		
Factory overhead	11,500		

Determine the following, presenting your computations: (a) equivalent units of production, (b) conversion cost per equivalent unit of production, (c) total and unit cost of product started in prior period and completed in the current period, and (d) total and unit cost of product started and completed in the current period.

4-27. Cost of production report. Prepare a cost of production report for the Assembly Department of Cohen Company for May of the current fiscal year, using the following data and assuming that the first-in, first-out method is used to cost inventories:

Inventory, May 1, 5,000 units, 40% completed....................	$120,000
Materials from the Sanding Department, 15,000 units	337,500
Direct labor for May	51,875
Factory overhead for May......................................	31,125
Goods finished during May (includes units in process, May 1)	
16,500 units......................................	—
Inventory, May 31, 3,500 units, 60% completed..................	—

4-28. Allocation of costs for by-product and joint products. The charges to Work in Process—Department 4, together with units of product completed during the period, are indicated in the following account:

Work in Process—Department 4

From Department 3	125,600	By-product A, 1,000 units
Direct labor	30,300	Joint product P, 4,000 units
Factory overhead	10,100	Joint product Q, 10,000 units

There is no inventory of goods in process at either the beginning or the end of the period. The value of A is $1 a unit; P sells at $25 a unit, and Q sells at $15 a unit.

Allocate the costs to the three products and determine the unit cost of each, presenting your computations.

4–29. Unit cost of product by average cost method. The debits to Work in Process — Melting Department for a period, together with information concerning production, are as follows:

Work in process, beginning of period:	
Materials costs, 2,000 units	$28,760
Conversion costs, 2,000 units, 80% completed	15,000
Materials added during period, 4,200 units	63,000
Conversion costs during period	46,000
Work in process, end of period, 200 units, 50% completed..........	—
Goods finished during period, 6,000 units.......................	—

All direct materials are placed in process at the beginning of the process, and the average cost method is used to cost inventories. Determine the following, presenting your computations: (a) average materials cost per unit for period, (b) equivalent units of production for period, (c) average conversion cost per unit for period, (d) cost of goods finished during the period, and (e) cost of work in process at end of period.

Problems

·

4–30. Entries for process cost system. Sellers Company manufactures Product Z. Material A is placed in process in Department 1, where it is ground and partially refined. The output of Department 1 is transferred to Department 2, where Material B is added at the beginning of the process and the refining is completed. On June 1, Sellers Company had the following inventories:

Finished goods (6,150 units)	$107,625
Work in process — Department 1	—
Work in process — Department 2 (3,150 units, 2/3 completed)	51,345
Materials...	61,470

Departmental accounts are maintained for factory overhead, and there is one service department, Factory Office. The first-in, first-out method is used to cost inventories. Manufacturing operations for June are summarized as follows:

(a) Materials purchased on account...........................	$32,700
(b) Materials requisitioned for use:	
Material A..	$51,705
Material B..	9,840
Indirect materials — Department 1	2,160
Indirect materials — Department 2	540

(c) Labor used:

Direct labor—Department 1	$73,050
Direct labor—Department 2	29,175
Indirect labor—Department 1	4,200
Indirect labor—Department 2	1,920
Factory Office	3,450

(d) Depreciation charged on plant assets:

Department 1	$29,850
Department 2	14,400
Factory Office	1,650

(e) Miscellaneous costs incurred on account:

Department 1	$ 5,535
Department 2	3,465
Factory Office	1,800

(f) Expiration of prepaid expenses:

Department 1	$ 3,420
Department 2	735
Factory Office	1,125

(g) Distribution of Factory Office costs:

Department 1	60% of total Factory Office costs
Department 2	40% of total Factory Office costs

(h) Application of factory overhead costs:

Department 1	70% of direct labor cost
Department 2	80% of direct labor cost

(i) Production costs transferred from Department 1 to Department 2:
12,300 units were fully processed, and there was no inventory of work in process in Department 1 at June 30.

(j) Production costs transferred from Department 2 to finished goods:
11,250 units, including the inventory at June 1, were fully processed. There were 4,200 units 3/5 completed at June 30.

(k) Cost of goods sold during June:
12,000 units (Use the first-in, first-out method in crediting the finished goods account.)

Instructions:

(1) Prepare entries to record the foregoing operations. Identify each entry by letter.
(2) Compute the June 30 work in process inventory for Department 2.

4–31. Cost of production report. The data related to production during June of the current year for Department 2 of Sellers Company are presented in Problem 4–30.

Instructions:

Prepare a cost of production report for Department 2 for June.

4–32. Financial statements for process cost system. The trial balance of Sarnoff Inc. at January 31, the end of the first month of the current fiscal year, is as follows:

READSHEET
PROBLEM

Sarnoff Inc.
Trial Balance
January 31, 19--

Cash	80,600	
Marketable Securities	60,000	
Accounts Receivable	245,000	
Allowance for Doubtful Accounts		9,900
Finished Goods—Product A1	91,600	
Finished Goods—Product A2	155,000	
Work in Process—Department 1	17,750	
Work in Process—Department 2	33,150	
Work in Process—Department 3	29,400	
Materials	60,500	
Prepaid Insurance	14,750	
Office Supplies	5,250	
Land	105,000	
Buildings	660,000	
Accumulated Depreciation—Buildings		319,200
Machinery and Equipment	342,000	
Accumulated Depreciation—Machinery and Equipment		216,600
Office Equipment	59,400	
Accumulated Depreciation—Office Equipment		25,560
Patents	66,000	
Accounts Payable		122,150
Wages Payable		19,750
Income Tax Payable		6,500
Mortgage Note Payable (due 1995)		120,000
Common Stock ($15 par)		600,000
Retained Earnings		518,220
Sales		755,500
Cost of Goods Sold	502,300	
Factory Overhead—Department 1	400	
Factory Overhead—Department 2	370	
Factory Overhead—Department 3		290
Selling Expenses	99,750	
General Expenses	68,800	
Interest Expense	1,000	
Interest Income		350
Income Tax	16,000	
	2,714,020	2,714,020

Instructions:

(1) Prepare an income statement.
(2) Prepare a retained earnings statement.
(3) Prepare a balance sheet.

4-33. Equivalent units and related costs; cost of production report. Drysdale Company manufactures Product C by a series of four processes, all materials being introduced in Department 1. From Department 1, the materials pass through Departments 2, 3, and 4, emerging as finished Product C. All inventories are costed by the first-in, first-out method.

The balances in the accounts Work in Process—Department 4 and Finished Goods were as follows on July 1:

Work in Process—Department 4 (6,000 units, 3/4 completed) .	$ 66,300
Finished Goods (8,000 units at $13 a unit)	104,000

The following costs were charged to Work in Process—Department 4 during July:

Direct materials transferred from Department 3: 26,000 units at $5.20 a unit	$135,200
Direct labor.	144,000
Factory overhead.	72,000

During July, 25,000 units of C were completed and 26,800 units were sold. Inventories on July 31 were as follows:

Work in Process—Department 4: 7,000 units, 1/2 completed
Finished Goods: 6,200 units

Instructions:

(1) Determine the following, presenting computations in good order:
   (a) Equivalent units of production for Department 4 during July.
   (b) Unit conversion cost for Department 4 for July.
   (c) Total and unit cost of Product C started in a prior period and finished in July.
   (d) Total and unit cost of Product C started and finished in July.
   (e) Total cost of goods transferred to finished goods.
   (f) Work in process inventory for Department 4, July 31.
   (g) Cost of goods sold (indicate number of units and unit costs).
   (h) Finished goods inventory, July 31.
(2) Prepare a cost of production report for Department 4 for July.

4-34. Entries for process cost system, including joint products. I. C. Han Products manufactures joint products A and B. Materials are placed in production in Department 1, and after processing, are transferred to Department 2, where more materials are added. The finished products emerge from Department 2. There are two service departments: Factory Office, and Maintenance and Repair.

There were no inventories of work in process at the beginning or at the end of January. Finished goods inventories at January 1 were as follows:

Product A, 2,500 units..................... $75,000
Product B, 900 units 45,000

Transactions related to manufacturing operations for January are summarized as follows:

(a) Materials purchased on account, $91,750.
(b) Materials requisitioned for use: Department 1, $47,000 ($42,540 entered directly into the products); Department 2, $31,385 ($27,320 entered directly into the products); Maintenance and Repair, $1,990.
(c) Labor costs incurred: Department 1, $36,100 ($31,500 entered directly into the products); Department 2, $38,800 ($33,600 entered directly into the products); Factory Office, $5,850; Maintenance and Repair, $13,650.
(d) Miscellaneous costs and expenses incurred on account: Department 1, $5,570; Department 2, $4,150; Factory Office, $1,400; and Maintenance and Repair, $2,170.
(e) Depreciation charged on plant assets: Department 1, $6,900; Department 2, $5,360; Factory Office, $900; and Maintenance and Repair, $980.
(f) Expiration of various prepaid expenses: Department 1, $450; Department 2, $330; Factory Office, $350; and Maintenance and Repair, $490.
(g) Factory office costs allocated on the basis of hours worked: Department 1, 2,200 hours; Department 2, 1,760 hours; Maintenance and Repair, 440 hours.
(h) Maintenance and repair costs allocated on the basis of services rendered: Department 1, 60%; Department 2, 40%.
(i) Factory overhead applied to production at the predetermined rates: 120% and 90% of direct labor cost for Departments 1 and 2 respectively.
(j) Output of Department 1: 8,100 units.
(k) Output of Department 2: 4,000 units of Product A and 1,600 units of Product B. Unit selling price is $45 for Product A and $75 for Product B.
(l) Sales on account: 4,500 units of Product A at $45 and 1,700 units of Product B at $75. Credits to the finished goods accounts are to be made according to the first-in, first-out method.

Instructions:

Present entries to record the transactions, identifying each by letter. Include as an explanation for entry (k) the computations for the allocation of the production costs for Department 2 to the joint products, and as an explanation for entry (l) the number of units and the unit costs for each product sold.

4–35. **Work in process account data for two months and determination of difference in unit product cost between months.** A process cost system is used to record the costs of manufacturing Product C, which requires a series of three processes. The inventory of Work in Process—Department 3 on July 1 and debits to the account during July were as follows:

Balance, 1,200 units, 2/3 completed..........................	$11,640
From Department 2, 5,250 units............................	9,450
Direct labor...	50,676
Factory overhead..	12,669

During July, the 1,200 units in process on July 1 were completed, and of the 5,250 units entering the department, all were completed except 2,000 units, which were 3/4 completed.

Charges to Work in Process—Department 3 for August were as follows:

From Department 2, 6,100 units............................	$10,675
Direct labor...	63,500
Factory overhead..	15,875

During August, the units in process at the beginning of the month were completed, and of the 6,100 units entering the department, all were completed except 500 units, which were 1/2 completed. All inventories are costed by the first-in, first-out method.

Instructions:

(1) Set up an account for Work in Process—Department 3. Enter the balance as of July 1 and record the debits and credits in the account for July. Present computations for the determination of (a) equivalent units of production, (b) unit conversion cost, (c) cost of goods finished, differentiating between units started in the prior period and units started and finished in July, and (d) work in process inventory.

(2) Record the transactions for August in the account. Present the computations listed in (1).

(3) Determine the difference in unit cost between the product started and completed in July and the product started and completed in August. Determine also the amount of the difference attributable collectively to operations in Departments 1 and 2 and the amount attributable to operations in Department 3.

4–36. Unit cost of finished product by average cost method; cost of production report. Tupper Company manufactures Product F by a series of four processes, all materials being introduced in Department 1. From Department 1, the materials pass through Departments 2, 3, and 4, emerging as finished Product F. All inventories are costed by the average method.

The balance in the account Work in Process—Department 4 was as follows on March 1:

Materials cost (4,000 units).....................................	$ 18,640
Conversion costs (4,000 units, 3/4 completed)....................	14,000

The following costs were charged to Work in Process—Department 4 during March:

Direct materials transferred from Department 3: 24,000 units	
at $4.80 per unit	$115,200
Direct labor...	138,460
Factory overhead	42,420

During March, 21,600 units of Product F were completed and the work in process inventory on March 31 was 6,400 units, 1/4 completed.

Instructions:

(1) Determine the following for Department 4, presenting computations in good order:
    (a) Average materials cost per unit.
    (b) Equivalent units of production in March.
    (c) Average conversion cost per unit for March.
    (d) Cost of goods finished during March.
    (e) Cost of work in process at March 31.
(2) Prepare a cost of production report for Department 4 for March.

ALTERNATE PROBLEMS

4–30A. Entries for process cost system. Ryan Company manufacturers Product W. Material E is placed in process in Department 1, where it is ground and partially refined. The output of Department 1 is transferred to Department 2, where Material F is added at the beginning of the process and the refining is completed. On April 1, Ryan Company had the following inventories:

Finished goods (7,000 units)	$169,400
Work in process—Department 1	—
Work in process—Department 2 (1,400 units, 3/4 completed)	28,140
Materials	37,650

Departmental accounts are maintained for factory overhead, and there is one service department, Factory Office. All inventories are costed by the first-in, first-out method. Manufacturing operations for April are summarized as follows:

(a) Materials purchased on account		$68,500
(b) Materials requisitioned for use:		
	Material E	$37,114
	Material F	30,800
	Indirect materials—Department 1	2,460
	Indirect materials—Department 2	1,770
(c) Labor used:		
	Direct labor—Department 1	$77,000
	Direct labor—Department 2	54,950
	Indirect labor—Department 1	2,900
	Indirect labor—Department 2	2,750
	Factory Office	2,618
(d) Miscellaneous costs incurred on account:		
	Department 1	$ 9,950
	Department 2	7,250
	Factory Office	2,996
(e) Expiration of prepaid expenses:		
	Department 1	$ 1,490
	Department 2	975
	Factory Office	420

(f) Depreciation charged on plant assets:

Department 1 .... $20,500

Department 2 17,500

Factory Office 1,330

(g) Distribution of Factory Office costs:

Department 1 .... 75% of total Factory Office costs

Department 2 .... 25% of total Factory Office costs

(h) Application of factory overhead costs:

Department 1 .... 55% of direct labor cost

Department 2 .... 60% of direct labor cost

(i) Production costs transferred from Department 1 to Department 2:

12,320 units were fully processed, and there was no inventory of work in process in Department 1 at April 30.

(j) Production costs transferred from Department 2 to finished goods:

11,200 units, including the inventory at April 1, were fully processed. 2,520 units were 1/3 completed at April 30.

(k) Cost of goods sold during April:

13,300 units (Use the first-in, first-out method in crediting the finished goods account.)

Instructions:

(1) Prepare entries to record the foregoing operations. Identify each entry by letter.

(2) Compute the April 30 work in process inventory for Department 2.

4–33A. Equivalent units and related costs; cost of production report.
Bowers Company manufactures Product Z by a series of three processes, all materials being introduced in Department 1. From Department 1, the materials pass through Departments 2 and 3, emerging as finished Product Z. All inventories are costed by the first-in, first-out method.

The balances in the accounts Work in Process—Department 3 and Finished Goods were as follows on March 1:

Work in Process—Department 3 (7,000 units, 1/2 completed) . $212,100

Finished Goods (12,000 units at $36.20 a unit) 434,400

The following costs were charged to Work in Process—Department 3 during March:

Direct materials transferred from Department 2: 37,000 units

at $24 a unit.. $888,000

Direct labor... 232,600

Factory overhead....................................... 140,000

During March, 35,000 units of Z were completed and 37,200 units were sold. Inventories on March 31 were as follows:

Work in Process—Department 3: 9,000 units, 1/3 completed

Finished Goods: 9,800 units

Instructions:

(1) Determine the following, presenting computations in good order:
    (a) Equivalent units of production for Department 3 during March.
    (b) Unit conversion cost for Department 3 for March.
    (c) Total and unit cost of Product Z started in a prior period and finished in March.
    (d) Total and unit cost of Product Z started and finished in March.
    (e) Total cost of goods transferred to finished goods.
    (f) Work in process inventory for Department 3, March 31.
    (g) Cost of goods sold (indicate number of units and unit costs).
    (h) Finished goods inventory, March 31.
(2) Prepare a cost of production report for Department 3 for March.

4–35A. Work in process account data for two months and determination of difference in unit product cost between months. A process cost system is used to record the costs of manufacturing Product F10, which requires a series of four processes. The inventory of Work in Process—Department 4 on June 1 and debits to the account during June were as follows:

Balance, 800 units, 1/4 completed $13,040
From Department 3, 4,600 units........................... 51,520
Direct labor... 77,000
Factory overhead.. 19,250

During June, the 800 units in process on June 1 were completed, and of the 4,600 units entering the department, all were completed except 1,100 units, which were 1/4 completed.

Charges to Work in Process—Department 4 for July were as follows:

From Department 3, 4,125 units........................... $47,850
Direct labor... 83,448
Factory overhead.. 20,862

During July, the units in process at the beginning of the month were completed, and of the 4,125 units entering the department, all were completed except 750 units, which were 1/2 completed. All inventories are costed by the first-in, first-out method.

Instructions:

(1) Set up an account for Work in Process—Department 4. Enter the balance as of June 1 and record the debits and the credits in the account for June. Present computations for the determination of (a) equivalent units of production, (b) unit conversion cost, (c) cost of goods finished, differentiating between units started in the prior period and units started and finished in June, and (d) work in process inventory.
(2) Record the transactions for July in the account. Present the computations listed in (1).
(3) Determine the difference in unit cost between the product started and completed in June and the product started and completed in July. Determine also the amount of the difference attributable collectively to operations in Departments 1 through 3 and the amount attributable to operations in Department 4.

Mini-Case 4

H and S Inc. manufactures product 3D by a series of four processes. All materials are placed in production in the Die Casting Department and, after processing, are transferred to the Tooling, Assembly, and Polishing Departments, emerging as a finished product 3D.

On June 1, the balance in the account Work in Process—Polishing was $201,960, determined as follows:

Direct materials: 12,000 units	$122,040
Direct labor: 12,000 units, 3/4 completed	64,530
Factory overhead: 12,000 units, 3/4 completed	15,390
Total	$201,960

The following costs were charged to Work in Process—Polishing during June:

Direct materials transferred from Assembly Dept., 136,000 units	$1,428,000
Direct labor	988,920
Factory overhead	217,080

During June, 138,000 units of 3D were completed and transferred to Finished Goods. On June 30, the inventory in the Polishing Department consisted of 10,000 units, one-half completed. All inventories are costed by the first-in, first-out method.

As a new cost accountant for H and S Inc., you have just received a phone call from Ann Pearlstein, the superintendent of the Polishing Department. She was extremely upset with the cost of production report, which she says does not balance. In addition, she commented:

"I give up! These reports are a waste of time. My department has always been the best department in the plant, so why should I bother with these reports? Just what purpose do they serve?"

The report to which Pearlstein referred is as follows:

H and S Inc.
Cost of Production Report—Polishing Department
For Month Ended June 30, 19--

Quantities:		
Charged to production:		
In process, June 1......................		9,000
Received from Assembly Department.....		136,000
Total units to be accounted for...........		145,000
Units accounted for:		
Transferred to finished goods............		138,000
In process, June 30		5,000
Total units accounted for		143,000

Costs:		
Charged to production:		
In process, June 1......................		$ 201,960
June costs:		
Direct materials from Assembly Department		
($9.42 per unit)		1,428,000
Conversion costs:		
Direct labor.........................	$988,920	
Factory overhead....................	217,080	
Total conversion costs ($8.04 per unit)..		1,206,000
Total costs to be accounted for		$2,835,960

Costs allocated as follows:		
Transferred to finished goods:		
138,000 units at $17.46 ($9.42+$8.04) .		$2,409,480
In process, June 30:		
Materials (5,000 units×$9.42)..........	$ 47,100	
Conversion costs (5,000 units×$8.04) ..	40,200	
Total cost of inventory in process.......		87,300
Total costs accounted for.................		$2,496,780

Computations:		
Equivalent units of production:		
To process units in inventory on June 1:		
12,000 units×3/4		9,000
To process units started and completed		
in June.............................		136,000
To process units in inventory on June 30:		
10,000 units×1/2		5,000
Equivalent units of production..........		150,000
Unit conversion cost:		
$1,206,000÷150,000		$8.04

Instructions:

(1) Based upon the data for June, prepare a revised cost of production report for the Polishing Department.
(2) Assume that for May, the unit direct materials cost was $10.17 and the unit conversion cost was $8.88. Determine the change in the direct materials unit cost and unit conversion cost for June.
(3) Based on (2), what are some possible explanations for the changing unit costs?
(4) Describe how you would explain to Pearlstein that cost of production reports are useful.

Answers to Self-Examination Questions

· · ·

1. C The process cost system is most appropriate for a business where manufacturing is conducted by continuous operations and involves a series of uniform production processes, such as the processing of crude oil (answer C). The job order cost system is most appropriate for a business where the product is made to customers' specifications, such as custom furniture manufacturing (answer A) and commercial building construction (answer B).

2. C The manufacturing costs that are necessary to convert direct materials into finished products are referred to as conversion costs. The conversion costs include direct labor and factory overhead (answer C).

3. B The number of units that could have been produced from start to finish during a period is termed equivalent units. The 4,875 equivalent units (answer B) is determined as follows:

To process units in inventory on May 1:	
1,000 units × 1/4	250
To process units started and completed	
in May: 5,500 units − 1,000 units	4,500
To process units in inventory on May 31:	
500 units × 1/4	125
Equivalent units of production in May	4,875

4. A The conversion costs (direct labor and factory overhead) totaling $48,750 are divided by the number of equivalent units (4,875) to determine the unit conversion cost of $10 (answer A).

5. B The product resulting from a process that has little value in relation to the principal product or joint products is known as a by-product (answer B). When two or more commodities of significant value are produced from a single direct material, the products are termed joint products (answer A). The raw material that enters directly into the finished product is termed direct material (answer C).

Part Three

Planning and Control

Chapter
Five

•

Distinguish between cost behavior and cost estimation.

•

Describe and illustrate variable costs.

•

Describe the behavior of total and unit variable costs.

•

Describe and illustrate fixed costs.

•

Describe the behavior of total and unit fixed costs.

•

Describe and illustrate mixed costs.

•

Describe and illustrate the use of the high-low method
to estimate total costs.

•

Describe and illustrate the use of the scattergraph method
to estimate total costs.

•

Describe and illustrate the use of the least squares method
to estimate total costs.

•

Describe the judgmental and engineering methods of estimating total costs.

•

Explain how the learning effect may influence cost estimation.

•

Describe cost trends in the United States.

•

Cost Behavior and Cost Estimation

A variety of managerial cost and expense terms, classifications, and concepts were introduced in Chapter 2. This chapter continues the discussion of cost concepts by focusing on cost behavior and cost estimation.

Cost behavior refers to the manner in which a cost changes in relation to its activity base. For example, direct materials costs vary proportionately with changes in the number of units produced. If the total units produced doubles, direct materials costs will also double. **Cost estimation** refers to the methods used to estimate costs for use in managerial decision making. For example, the managerial accountant must develop reliable product cost estimates for use by managers in setting selling prices.

A thorough understanding of cost behavior and cost estimation methods is essential for planning and controlling operations. For example, classifying costs by their behavior as production varies allows management to establish standards for evaluating (controlling) the efficiency of current operations and for predicting (planning) the costs of future levels of operations. Cost estimation methods may be used to analyze past cost behavior so that future production costs can be estimated.

COST BEHAVIOR

The behavior of costs can be classified in a variety of ways. The three most common cost classifications are variable costs, fixed costs, and mixed costs. Each of these classifications was briefly described in Chapter 2. This chapter expands upon this discussion to include additional issues which must be considered if the managerial accountant is to classify cost behavior properly into these three types.

Variable Costs

Variable costs are costs that vary in total in direct proportion to changes in an activity base. As mentioned in Chapter 2, direct materials and direct labor costs are generally treated as variable costs because, as production volume changes, the totals of these costs change proportionately. To illustrate, assume that Wilson Inc. produces stereophonic sound systems under the brand name of JimBo. The parts for the stereo systems are purchased from outside suppliers for $10 per unit and are assembled in Wilson's Augusta plant. The direct materials costs for Model JW-12 for differing levels of production are summarized in the following table:

Number of Units of Model JW-12 Produced	Direct Materials Cost per Unit	Total Direct Materials Cost
5,000 units	$10	$ 50,000
10,000 units	10	100,000
15,000 units	10	150,000
20,000 units	10	200,000
25,000 units	10	250,000
30,000 units	10	300,000

As the table illustrates, the total direct materials cost varies in direct proportion to the number of units of Model JW-12 produced. The direct materials cost for 25,000 units ($250,000) is 5 times the direct materials cost for 5,000 units ($50,000). However, the unit direct materials cost of $10 remains constant over all levels of production. A constant per unit cost is a characteristic of variable costs.

The following graphs illustrate how the variable costs for direct materials for Model JW-12 behave in total and on a per unit basis as production changes:

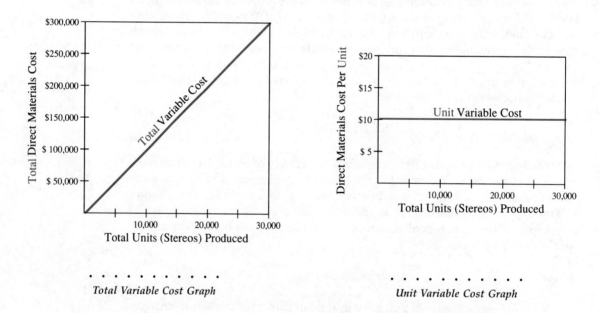

Total Variable Cost Graph   *Unit Variable Cost Graph*

Activity Base for Variable Costs. The preceding illustration of a variable cost used units produced as the activity base. The relevant activity base for a cost depends upon which base is most closely associated with the cost and the decision-making needs of management in using the cost in planning and controlling operations. To illustrate, food costs for a hospital are closely associated with the number of patients in the hospital. Thus, the number of patients would be the most appropriate activity base for making decisions related to food costs. On the other hand, because patients' diagnoses differ, the number of x-rays taken rather than the number of patients is a better activity base for decisions related to the cost of x-ray film.

To provide relevant information to management for decision making, managerial accountants must be thoroughly familiar with the operations of the entity, so that the most appropriate activity bases for various cost classifications are selected. Units sold and units produced are commonly used activity bases, but they may not always be the most appropriate. For example, miles driven rather than the number of orders delivered would be the most appropriate activity base for gasoline costs of a moving company.

Step-Wise Variable Costs. True variable costs remain constant on a per unit basis and change in total on a proportionate basis with changes in an activity base. For example, in the previous illustration of Wilson Inc., each additional Model JW-12 unit produced required $10 of direct materials. The materials cost per unit remained constant at $10, and the total materials cost increased by $10 with each additional unit produced. Hence, as the number of units of Model JW-12 produced doubled from 5,000 units to 10,000 units, the total direct materials cost doubled from $50,000 to $100,000. Likewise, as the number of units of Model JW-12 tripled, the total direct materials cost tripled.

In practice, some costs may be classified as variable costs, even though they may not change in exact proportion to changes in the activity base. For example, direct labor costs are generally treated as a variable cost. However, direct labor may be acquired in units that increase or decrease with a batch of products produced. In such cases, the direct labor cost is a step-wise variable cost. To illustrate, assume that Horn Inc. manufactures machine tools using semi-automated lathes. During an 8-hour work shift, a machine operator normally produces 50 tools. Thus, for each increase in production of 50 tools, an additional machine operator is required. If scheduled production for a machine operator is less than 50 tools, the operator is still paid for an 8-hour shift. Assuming that machine operators earn $12.50 per hour, the direct labor costs for increasing levels of production are summarized in the following table and graph:

Number of Units Produced	Total Direct Labor Cost
0– 50	$100
51–100	200
101–150	300
151–200	400
201–250	500
251–300	600

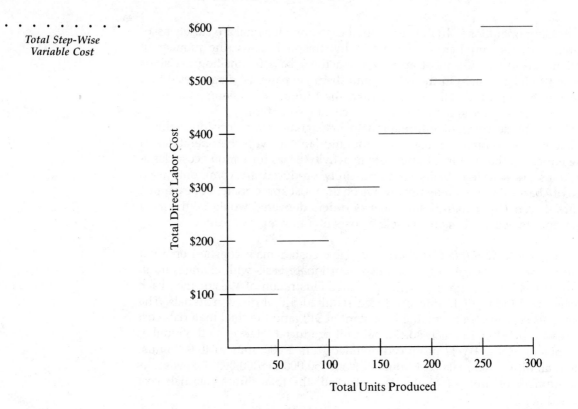

Step-wise variable costs derive their name from their step-wise nature, as indicated in the preceding graph. In practice, when the length of the steps is relatively small, step-wise variable costs are often treated as simple variable costs. For example, in the preceding illustration, the direct labor cost could be treated as a variable cost with a constant per unit cost of $2, as illustrated in the following table:

Number of Units Produced	Total Direct Labor Cost	Direct Labor Cost per Unit
50	$100	$2
100	200	2
150	300	2
200	400	2
250	500	2
300	600	2

These direct labor costs are shown in the following graph, where the step-wise variable cost data are indicated by dotted lines and the estimated variable cost data are indicated by a solid line.

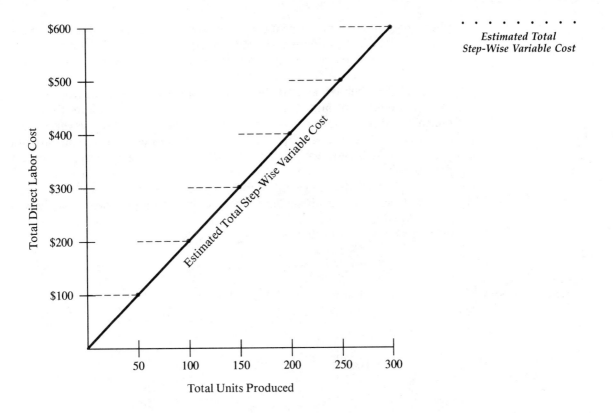

When dealing with step-wise variable costs, management must exercise extra care in planning and scheduling production in order to maximize the efficiency of production. At production levels between steps, production efficiency is not maximized. For example, in the preceding illustration, the production of 40 tools is inefficient in the sense that, for the same direct labor cost, 50 tools could have been produced. In addition, step-wise variable costs may be difficult to reduce when production decreases, thus creating further inefficiencies. For example, if workers are laid off every time a significant decrease in production occurs, employee morale may suffer, additional training costs may be necessary in hiring replacement workers when production resumes, and the company may have difficulty hiring workers who view the likelihood of layoffs as high.

Relevant Range for Variable Costs. Because variable costs are assumed to change in a constant proportion with changes in the activity base, the graph of a variable cost when plotted against the activity base appears as a straight line, as illustrated on page 142. In this sense, variable costs are said to be **linear** in nature.

Over a wide range of production, some costs vary in differing proportions to changes in an activity base, rather than vary in a constant proportion. This phenomenon of changing proportions of costs to changes in an activity base is referred to by economists as the principle of **economies of scale.** This principle recognizes that, when production facilities are limited, some variable costs increase but at a decreasing rate as production increases from a relatively low level. This behavior occurs because, as operations expand, workers learn to be more efficient and division of labor is possible. Therefore, the rate of increase in direct labor costs is not constant. At some point, however, variable costs may begin to increase at an increasing rate, rather than at a constant rate, because of inefficiencies created by such factors as employee fatigue and poor morale.

Graphically, the effect of differing proportions of costs to changes in an activity base is a curvilinear line rather than a straight line. The following graph illustrates the principle of economies of scale for the direct labor costs of John Manufacturing Inc.:

Economies of Scale

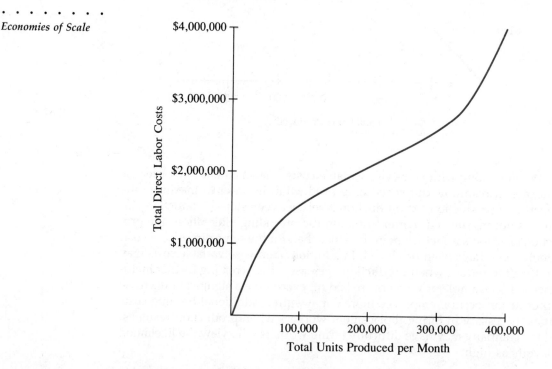

Managerial accountants recognize the curvilinear nature of total costs for wide ranges of production. However, most operating decisions by management focus on a narrow range of relevant activity within which the enterprise is planning to operate. This range of activity is referred to as the **relevant range.** Generally, within the relevant range, variable costs vary so closely to a constant rate that they may be represented by a straight line without a significant loss of accuracy. For example, the direct labor costs of John Manufacturing Inc. are considered to be linear in nature for the relevant range of production, 100,000 units to 300,000 units, as shown in the following graph:

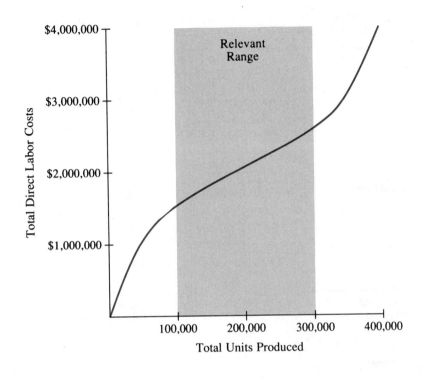

Relevant Range for Variable Costs

Fixed Costs

Fixed costs are costs that remain constant in total dollar amount as the level of activity changes. Examples of fixed manufacturing costs include straight-line depreciation on factory equipment and buildings, rent on factory plant and equipment, property insurance on factory plant and equipment, and salaries of factory supervisory personnel.

To illustrate, assume that Gossage Inc. manufactures, bottles, and distributes La Fleur Perfume at its Los Angeles plant. The production supervisor at the Los Angeles plant is Jane Sovissi, who is paid a salary of $75,000 per year. Sovissi's salary is a fixed cost that does not vary with production. Regardless of whether 50,000, 100,000, or 300,000 bottles are produced, Sovissi will still receive a salary of $75,000.

Although fixed costs remain constant in total dollar amount as the level of production changes, the fixed cost per unit of production changes. As additional units are produced, the total fixed costs are spread over a larger number of units, and hence the fixed cost per unit decreases.

The relationship of total fixed cost and fixed cost per unit is illustrated in the following table and graphs for the $75,000 salary of Jane Sovissi:

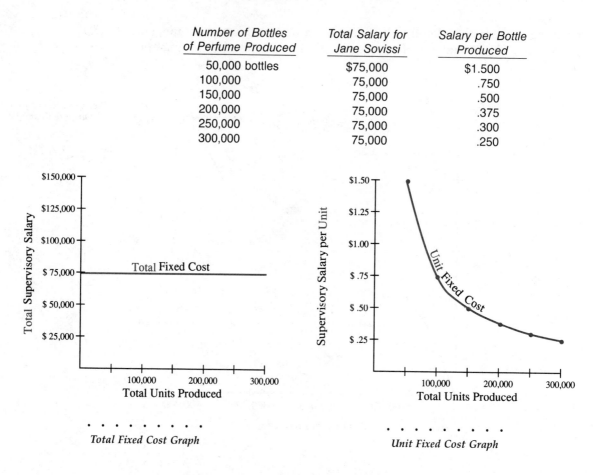

Number of Bottles of Perfume Produced	Total Salary for Jane Sovissi	Salary per Bottle Produced
50,000 bottles	$75,000	$1.500
100,000	75,000	.750
150,000	75,000	.500
200,000	75,000	.375
250,000	75,000	.300
300,000	75,000	.250

Total Fixed Cost Graph

Unit Fixed Cost Graph

Activity Base for Fixed Costs. Like variable costs, fixed costs are defined relative to an activity base. In most situations, the activity base for fixed costs will be expressed as either units produced, units sold, or sales dollars. In the preceding illustration, the activity base was expressed in terms of units of production—bottles of perfume produced.

Step-Wise Fixed Costs. As discussed earlier, many costs behave in a step-wise fashion over a wide range of production. **Step-wise fixed costs** differ from step-wise variable costs in the width of the range of production over which total costs change: the steps are longer for step-wise fixed costs than for step-wise variable costs. For example, a step-wise variable cost might vary with every 50 units produced, while a step-wise fixed cost might vary with every 300,000 units produced.

To illustrate, assume that Gossage Inc. can only produce 300,000 bottles of La Fleur Perfume during an 8-hour shift. To produce between 300,000 to 600,000 bottles of perfume, an additional shift has to be added and another production supervisor hired at a salary of $75,000. Likewise, to produce between 600,000 to 900,000 bottles of perfume, yet another production supervisor must be hired. Graphically, the step-wise nature of the production supervisory salary costs is illustrated as follows:

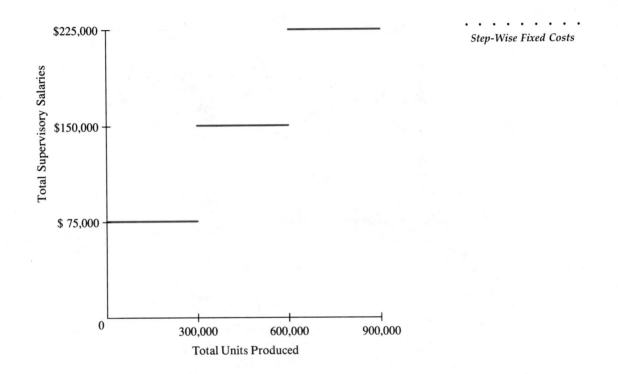

Step-Wise Fixed Costs

Another example of step-wise fixed costs is straight-line depreciation on machinery. As demand for a product increases and new machines are purchased to produce additional units, total straight-line depreciation costs will vary in a step-wise fashion.

Step-wise fixed costs tend to be long-term in nature and therefore are not easily changed. For this reason, managers should be careful in incurring step-wise fixed costs. Since fixed costs cannot be easily changed, managers often focus on maximizing the usage of existing resources. Later chapters will discuss commonly used methods by which managers evaluate decisions that involve the incurrence of fixed costs.

Relevant Range for Fixed Costs. As discussed in the preceding paragraphs, there exists a relevant range of activity for which management normally focuses its attention for operating purposes. The usefulness of this relevant range for classifying step-wise variable costs was discussed previously. The relevant range is also useful in classifying step-wise fixed costs for management decision-making purposes. To illustrate, if the relevant range of production for Gossage Inc. is between 300,000 and 600,000 bottles of perfume, the salary cost of production supervisors is a fixed cost of $150,000, as shown in the following graph:

Relevant Range for
Fixed Costs

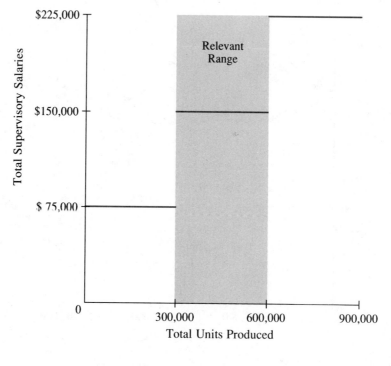

Mixed Costs

A **mixed cost** has characteristics of both a variable and a fixed cost. For example, over one range of the activity base, the mixed cost may remain constant in total amount, and it will therefore be a fixed cost. Over another range of activity, the mixed cost may change in proportion to changes in the activity base, and it will therefore be a variable cost. Mixed costs are sometimes referred to as **semivariable** or **semifixed** costs.

To illustrate, assume that Simpson Inc. manufactures sails, using rented machinery. The rental charges are $20,000 per year plus $1 for each machine hour used. If the machinery is used 20,000 hours, the total rental charge is $40,000 [$20,000 + (20,000 × $1)]. If the machinery is used 30,000 hours, the total rental charge is $50,000 [$20,000 + (30,000 × $1)], and so on. This mixed cost behavior is illustrated graphically at the top of page 151.

In this illustration, which is the most common type of mixed cost behavior, a rental cost of $20,000 will be incurred, even if the machinery is not used at all. The $20,000 is constant over all levels of production and represents the fixed cost component of the mixed cost. The rental charge of $1 per hour, which represents the variable cost component of the mixed cost, causes the total mixed cost to increase as machine hours are used.

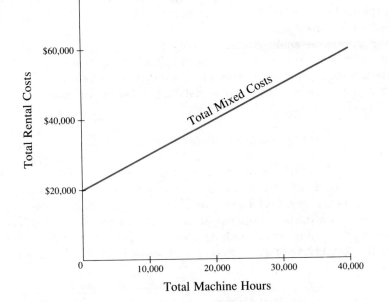

Mixed Costs –
$20,000 + $1 per Hour

The behavior of mixed costs can vary widely. For example, if the rental charges in the preceding illustration had been $15,000 per year plus $1 for each machine hour used over 10,000 hours, the mixed cost graph would appear as follows:

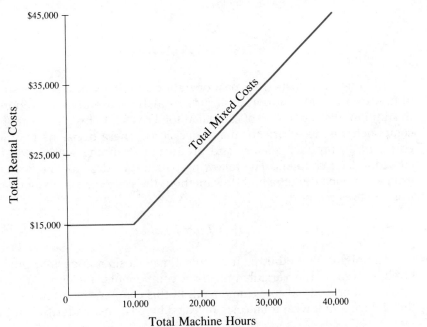

Mixed Costs –
$15,000 + $1 per Hour
Over 10,000 Hours

In this graph, the fixed cost component is $15,000 and the rental charge of $1 per hour is the variable cost component of the mixed cost. The variable cost component causes the total mixed cost to increase after 10,000 machine hours have been used.

For purposes of analysis, mixed costs can generally be separated into their variable and fixed cost components. The remainder of this chapter describes techniques for such separation, as well as for estimating costs, so that the variable, fixed, and mixed costs can be used by management in decision making.

Summary of Cost Behavior Concepts

As indicated in the preceding paragraphs, costs can be classified as variable costs, fixed costs, or mixed costs. Step-wise variable costs and step-wise fixed costs are normally treated as either simple variable costs or fixed costs. Likewise, for purposes of analysis, mixed costs are generally separated into their variable and fixed cost components. The following table summarizes the cost behavior characteristics of variable costs and fixed costs:

| | Effect of Changing Activity Level | |
Cost	Total Amount	Per Unit Amount
Variable	Increases and decreases proportionately with activity level.	Remains constant regardless of activity level.
Fixed	Remains constant regardless of activity level.	Increases and decreases proportionately with activity level.

COST ESTIMATION

Although the costs from past operations are known, it is the estimation of future costs that is important for many analyses useful in decison making. In addition, the separation of estimated total costs into fixed and variable cost components is necessary for many decisions. These decisions may involve cost control, product pricing, and production planning, which will be discussed in later chapters. The following paragraphs describe methods of cost estimation, including the high-low method, the scattergraph method, and the least squares method.

High-Low Method

The **high-low method** is used to estimate costs at a desired production level, as well as the variable and fixed components, for either a particular mixed cost or for total costs in general. In this chapter, the examples will use the highest and lowest total costs revealed by past cost patterns. The activity base associated with past cost patterns is usually units of production, although other activity bases, such as machine hours, direct labor hours, or direct labor cost, could be used.

To estimate the variable cost per unit and the fixed cost, the following steps are used:

1. a. The difference between the *total costs* at the highest and lowest levels of production is determined.
   b. The difference between the *total units* produced at the highest and lowest levels of production is determined.
2. Since only the total variable cost will change as the number of units of production changes, the difference in total costs as determined in (1a) is divided by the diference in units produced as determined in (1b) to determine the variable cost per unit.
3. The total variable cost (variable cost per unit × total units produced) at either the highest or the lowest level of production is determined, and the amount is subtracted from the total cost at that level to determine the fixed cost per period.

To illustrate, assume that Sutton Company, which produces sports jerseys, has incurred total costs for the following levels of production during the past 5 months:

	Units Produced	Total Costs
June....................................	175,000 units	$185,000
July.....................................	75,000	80,000
August..................................	200,000	210,000
September	325,000	320,000
October	300,000	270,000

The units produced and the total costs at the highest and lowest levels of production and the differences are as follows:

	Units Produced	Total Costs
Highest level............................	325,000 units	$320,000
Lowest level	75,000	80,000
Differences	250,000 units	$240,000

Since the total fixed cost does not change with changes in volume of production, the $240,000 difference in the total cost represents the change in the total variable cost. Hence, dividing the difference in total costs by the change in production provides an estimate of the variable cost per unit. In this illustration, the variable cost per unit is $.96, as shown in the following computation:

$$\text{Variable Cost per Unit} = \frac{\text{Difference in Total Costs}}{\text{Difference in Production}}$$

$$\text{Variable Cost per Unit} = \frac{\$240{,}000}{250{,}000 \text{ units}} = \$.96 \text{ per unit}$$

The fixed costs will be the same at both the highest and the lowest levels of production. Thus, the fixed cost of $8,000 per month can be estimated by subtracting the estimated total variable cost from the total cost at either the highest or the lowest levels of production, using the total cost equation as follows:

$$\text{Total Cost} = (\text{Variable Cost per Unit} \times \text{Units of Production}) + \text{Fixed Cost}$$

Highest level:

$$\$320{,}000 = (\$.96 \times 325{,}000) \mid \text{Fixed Cost}$$
$$\$320{,}000 = \$312{,}000 + \text{Fixed Cost}$$
$$\$\ \ \ 8{,}000 = \text{Fixed Cost}$$

Lowest level:

$$\$\ 80{,}000 = (\$.96 \times 75{,}000) + \text{Fixed Cost}$$
$$\$\ 80{,}000 = \$72{,}000 + \text{Fixed Cost}$$
$$\$\ \ \ 8{,}000 = \text{Fixed Cost}$$

The variable and fixed cost components of the total cost have now been identified and can be incorporated into the total cost equation:

$$\text{Total Cost} = (\text{Variable Cost per Unit} \times \text{Units of Production}) + \text{Fixed Cost}$$
$$\text{Total Cost} = (\$.96 \times \text{Units of Production}) + \$8{,}000$$

The cost data and the related total cost for Sutton Company are plotted on the graph illustrated on page 155. The graph is constructed in the following manner:

1. Levels of units of production are spread along the horizontal axis. For Sutton Company, it is assumed that a maximum of 400,000 units could be produced per month.
2. The total costs are spread along the vertical axis. For Sutton Company, it is assumed that the total costs could not exceed $400,000 per month.
3. The total cost at the highest and lowest levels of production is then plotted on the graph. For example, the total cost of September's 325,000 units of production would be indicated on the graph by a point representing $320,000. The total cost of July's 75,000 units would be indicated by a point representing $80,000.

4. After the total costs for the highest and lowest levels of production have been plotted on the graph, a straight line (the total cost line) is drawn through the highest and lowest total cost points. The point at which the total cost line intersects the vertical axis represents the estimated fixed cost per month, approximately $8,000. The variable cost per unit, $.96, is represented by the slope of the total cost line. The relevant range on the graph represents the range from which the cost data were gathered.

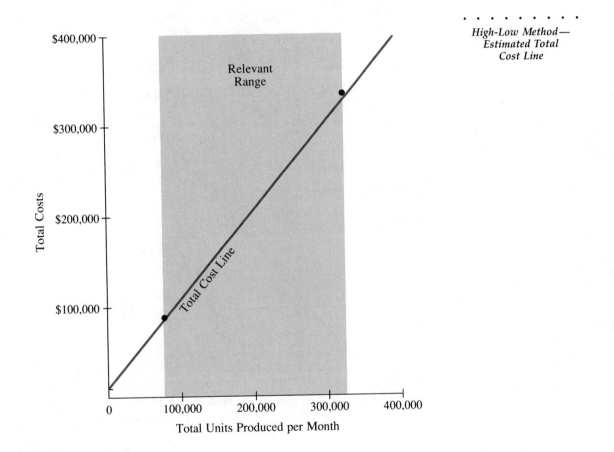

High-Low Method— Estimated Total Cost Line

For any level of production within the relevant range, total costs can be estimated using either the graph or the total cost equation. For example, for 200,000 units of production in one month, the estimated total cost would be determined as follows, using the total cost equation:

Total Cost = ($.96 × 200,000 units) + $8,000
Total Cost = $200,000

Alternatively, the total cost can be estimated directly from the graph by locating the total units of production on the horizontal axis, proceeding vertically upward until the total cost line is intersected, and then proceeding horizontally to the left until the vertical axis is intersected. In this way, the estimated total cost of producing 200,000 units is determined to be $200,000, as shown in the following graph:

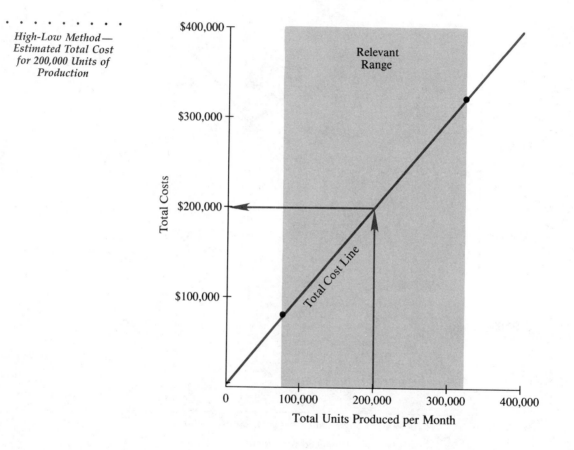

High-Low Method—Estimated Total Cost for 200,000 Units of Production

Scattergraph Method

The **scattergraph method** of estimating costs uses a graph format similar to that used for the high-low method. A distinguishing characteristic of the scattergraph method relative to the high-low method is that the scattergraph method uses total costs at all the levels of past production, rather than just the highest and lowest levels. Because the scattergraph method uses all the data available, it tends to be more accurate than the high-low method.

The following cost and production data for Sutton Company, which were used in illustrating the high-low method, are used to illustrate the scattergraph method:

	Units Produced	Total Costs
June......................................	170,000	$185,000
July......................................	75,000	80,000
August..................................	200,000	210,000
September	325,000	320,000
October	300,000	270,000

The following scattergraph was constructed with these data:

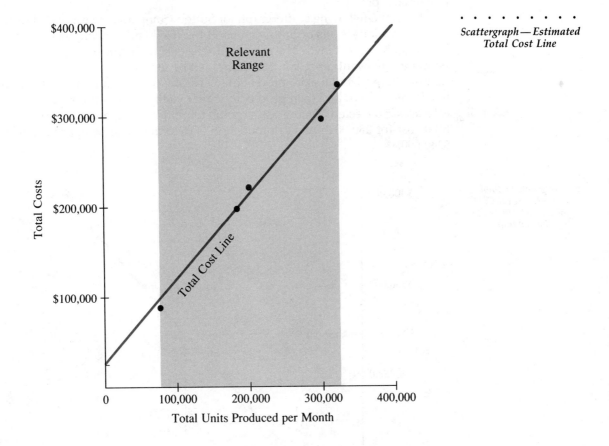

Scattergraph — Estimated Total Cost Line

The scattergraph is constructed in the following manner:

1. Levels of units of production are spread along the horizontal axis. For Sutton Company, it is assumed that a maximum of 400,000 units could be produced per month.
2. The total costs are spread along the vertical axis. For Sutton Company, it is assumed that the total costs could not exceed $400,000 per month.
3. The total cost at each past level of production is then plotted on the graph. For example, the total cost of June's 175,000 units of production would be

indicated on the graph by a point representing $185,000. The total cost of July's 75,000 units would be indicated by a point representing $80,000.

4. After the total costs for the past levels of production have been plotted on the graph, a straight line representing the total costs is drawn on the graph. *This line is drawn so that the differences between each point and the line are at a minimum in the judgment of the preparer of the graph.*

The scattergraph is similar to the high-low graph, except for the total cost line. In the high-low method, the total cost line connects the highest and lowest cost points.

From the following scattergraph for Sutton Company, the estimated total costs for various levels of production and the fixed and variable cost components can be determined. The estimated total cost for any level of production within the relevant range can be determined by locating the units of production on the horizontal axis, proceeding vertically upward until the total cost line is intersected, and then proceeding horizontally to the left until the vertical axis is intersected. On the scattergraph for Sutton Company, the estimated total cost for 250,000 units of production is determined to be approximately $240,000.

Scattergraph Method— Estimated Total Cost for 250,000 Units of Production

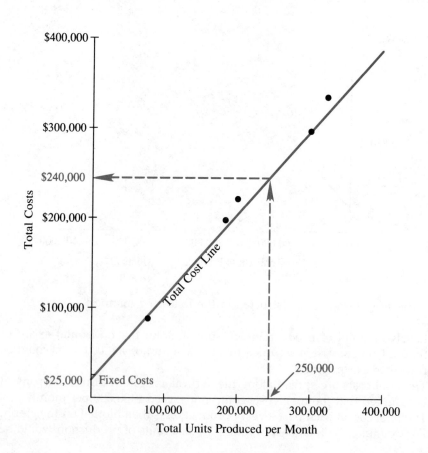

The point at which the total cost line intersects the vertical axis of the scattergraph indicates the estimated fixed cost of production. For Sutton Company, the fixed cost component is approximately $25,000 per month.

The total variable cost for any level of production within the relevant range is the difference between the estimated total cost and the estimated fixed cost. For Sutton Company, the estimated total variable cost for 250,000 units of production is $215,000 ($240,000 − $25,000). The estimated variable cost per unit is $.86 ($215,000 ÷ 250,000 units).

For 200,000 units of production, the estimated total cost would be determined as follows, using the total cost equation:

Total Cost = (Variable Cost per Unit × Units of Production) + Fixed Cost
Total Cost = ($.86 × Units of Production) + $25,000
Total Cost = ($.86 × 200,000 units) + $25,000
Total Cost = $197,000

Least Squares Method

While the scattergraph method requires the judgmental drawing of a total cost line through the plotted total cost points, the **least squares method** uses statistics to determine the total cost line. Thus, the resulting estimated total cost line is based on more objective statistical criteria.

The least squares method fits a straight line through the plotted total cost points according to the following total cost equation:

Total Cost = (Variable Cost per Unit × Units of Production) + Fixed Cost

The variable cost per unit component of this equation is estimated statistically, using the following computational formula:

$$\text{Variable Cost per Unit} = \frac{n(\Sigma P_i C_i) - (\Sigma P_i)(\Sigma C_i)}{n(\Sigma P_i^2) - (\Sigma P_i)^2}$$

The symbols in the preceding formula are explained as follows:

n is the number of total cost observations
Σ is the sum of the numbers
P_i is an observed level of production, in units, at period i
C_i is an observation of total cost, in dollars, at period i
P_i^2 is the square of the value P_i; likewise, $(\Sigma P_i)^2$ is the square of the value (ΣP_i)

The formula can be easily solved through the use of a computational table with columns for P_i, C_i, P_i^2, and $P_i C_i$. To illustrate, the following computational table for the estimation of the variable cost per unit for Sutton Company is prepared, based on the cost and production data that were used in the preceding illustrations. To simplify the computations, the thousands have been deleted from both the cost and production data.

Units Produced (P_i)	Total Costs (C_i)	P_i^2	P_iC_i
175	$ 185	30,625	$ 32,375
75	80	5,625	6,000
200	210	40,000	42,000
325	320	105,625	104,000
300	270	90,000	81,000
1,075	$1,065	271,875	$265,375
$\uparrow$	$\uparrow$	$\uparrow$	$\uparrow$
ΣP_i	ΣC_i	ΣP_i^2	ΣP_iC_i

Using the values from the table, the computational formula yields the following results:

$$\text{Variable Cost per Unit} = \frac{n(\Sigma P_iC_i) - (\Sigma P_i)(\Sigma C_i)}{n(\Sigma P_i^2) - (\Sigma P_i)^2}$$

$$\text{Variable Cost per Unit} = \frac{5(\$265,375) - (1,075)(\$1,065)}{5(271,875) - (1,075)^2}$$

$$\text{Variable Cost per Unit} = \frac{\$1,326,875 - \$1,144,875}{1,359,375 - 1,155,625}$$

$$\text{Variable Cost per Unit} = \frac{\$182,000}{203,750} = \$.89 \text{ per unit}$$

The fixed cost component of total cost is estimated statistically, using the following computational formula:

$$\text{Fixed Cost} = \overline{C} - (\text{Variable Cost per Unit} \times \overline{P})$$

The symbols are explained as follows:

$\overline{C}$ is the average of the monthly total costs
$\overline{P}$ is the average of the monthly units of production

For Sutton Company, the average total cost is $213,000 ($1,065,000 ÷ 5), and the average units of production is 215,000 units (1,075,000 units ÷ 5). When these values are substituted into the formula, the fixed cost per month is computed as follows:

Fixed Cost = $213,000 − ($.89 × 215,000 units)
Fixed Cost = $213,000 − $191,350
Fixed Cost = $21,650

The estimated fixed cost of $21,650 per month and the variable cost of $.89 per unit are represented in the total cost equation as follows:

Total Cost = Variable Cost + Fixed Cost
Total Cost = ($.89 × Total Units of Production) + $21,650

The estimated total cost can be shown graphically by fitting the estimated total cost line to the plotted data, as illustrated in the following graph of the Sutton Company data. This line, which is sometimes referred to as a **regression line,** is fitted so that the sum of the squares of deviations from each plotted point to the line is smaller (hence, the name *least squares*) than it would be for any other line. Regression lines are discussed in detail in more advanced texts.

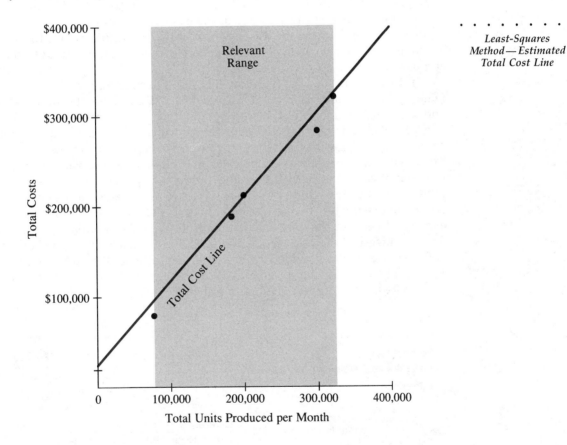

Least-Squares Method—Estimated Total Cost Line

For 200,000 units of production in one month, the estimated total cost could be determined by using the preceding graph or the total cost equation, as follows:

Total Cost = ($.89 × 200,000 units) + $21,650
Total Cost = $199,650

Comparison of Cost Estimation Methods
. . .

Each of the three methods described provided different estimates of fixed and variable costs, summarized as follows:

	Variable Cost per Unit	Fixed Cost per Month
High-low method	$.96	$ 8,000
Scattergraph method	.86	25,000
Least squares method	.89	21,650

The cost estimation method that should be used in any given situation depends on such considerations as the cost of gathering data for the estimates and the importance of the accuracy of the estimates. Although the high-low method is the easiest and the least costly to apply, it is also normally the least accurate. The least squares method is generally more accurate, but it is more complex and more costly to use.

In this illustration, the high-low method differs significantly in its estimates of variable and fixed costs, $.96 and $8,000, compared to the variable and fixed cost estimates of the scattergraph and least squares method, $.86 and $25,000, and $.89 and $21,650, respectively. These differences result because the high-low method uses only two cost and production observations to estimate costs for all levels of production. If these two observations are not representative of the normal cost and production patterns for all levels of production, then inaccurate variable and fixed cost estimates may be obtained. To illustrate, if the July production and total cost data for Sutton Company are eliminated because they are seasonal and not typical of normal operations, then the high-low method yields representative estimates which are comparable to the estimates provided by the scattergraph and least squares methods, as shown in the following computations. In these computations, the fixed cost is estimated at the highest level of production.

	Total Units Produced	Total Costs
Highest level	325,000 units	$320,000
Lowest level (excluding July data)...............	175,000	185,000
Differences......................................	150,000 units	$135,000

$$\text{Variable Cost per Unit} = \frac{\text{Difference in Total Cost}}{\text{Difference in Production}}$$

$$\text{Variable Cost per Unit} = \frac{\$135,000}{150,000 \text{ units}} = \$.90 \text{ per unit}$$

Total Cost = (Variable Cost per Unit × Units of Production) + Fixed Cost
$320,000 = ($.90 × 325,000 units) + Fixed Cost
$320,000 = $292,500 + Fixed Cost
 $27,500 = Fixed Cost

Care should also be exercised in using the scattergraph and least squares methods. The scattergraph method depends on the judgment of the individual who draws the total cost line through the points on the graph. Different individuals could fit different lines and thereby arrive at different estimates of the total cost. The least squares method is more objective, but it is difficult to use without a computer. Additional complications of the least squares method are described in more advanced texts.

Regardless of which cost estimation method is used, the estimated total costs should be compared periodically with actual costs. Large differences between estimated total costs and actual costs might indicate that the way in which total costs are estimated should be revised. For example, a change in the manufacturing process will likely require the gathering of total cost and production data related to the new process and the estimation of a new total cost equation, using one of the three methods discussed in this section.

Other Methods of Cost Estimation

The preceding paragraphs have described three common methods of cost estimation. Two other methods used in practice include the judgmental method and the engineering method. Each of these methods is briefly discussed in the following paragraphs.

Judgmental Method. The use of the **judgmental method** is viewed by some accountants as an alternative method of cost estimation. Under this method, managers use their experience and past observations of cost-volume relationships to estimate fixed and variable costs. The advantage of this method is its simplicity and its reliance on the seasoned experience of the manager. In some cases, managers use either the high-low, scattergraph, or least-squares method as an initial starting point and then refine the estimates, using experienced judgment. The use of the judgmental method has the further advantage of allowing the manager to incorporate anticipated cost trends into the estimates, rather than relying solely on past cost data. The disadvantage of the judgmental method is its heavy reliance on the judgment of the manager or the accountant who is estimating the costs. If this individual does not exercise good judgment, a significant potential for errors exists. Such errors could have a major effect on related managerial decisions.[1]

Engineering Method. In situations where little or no past cost data are available for use in estimating costs, the **engineering method** may be used to estimate costs. Under this method, industrial engineers provide estimates based on studies of such factors as production methods, materials and labor requirements, equipment needs, and utility demands. The following excerpt taken from a National Association of Accountants Research Report summarizes the use of the engineering method:

---

[1] A recent study sponsored by the National Association of Accountants concluded that managerial judgment is a widely used method of estimating costs. Maryanne M. Mowen, *Accounting for Costs as Fixed and Variable* (National Association of Accountants: Montvale, New Jersey, 1986), p. 19.

> *The industrial engineering approach to determination of how costs should vary with volume proceeds by systematic study of materials, labor, services, and facilities needed at varying volumes.... These studies generally make use of...results obtained by direct study of the production methods and facilities. Where no past experience is available, as with a new product, plant, or method, this approach can be applied to estimate the changes in cost that will accompany changes in volume.* [2]

THE LEARNING EFFECT IN ESTIMATING COSTS

Total costs are affected by how efficiently and effectively employees perform their tasks. In a manufacturing environment, costs will be affected by how rapidly new employees learn their jobs and by how rapidly experienced employees learn new job assignments. For example, after production for a new product begins or as a new manufacturing process is implemented, workers usually increase their efficiency as more units are produced and they become more experienced. This **learning effect** is known as the **learning curve phenomenon.** When learning occurs, it can have a significant impact on costs and should be considered in estimating costs.

To illustrate, assume that Barker Company manufactures yachts and has added a new yacht to its product line. Past experience indicates that every time a new line of yachts is added, the total time to manufacture each yacht declines by 10% as each of the next 5 yachts is produced. Thus, the second yacht requires 90% of the total time to manufacture the first yacht, the third yacht requires 90% of the time of the second yacht, and so on. However, past experience also indicates that after the sixth yacht is produced, further reductions in time are insignificant.

For Barker Company, it is estimated that the first yacht will require 500 direct labor hours at $20 per hour, and that 10 yachts are scheduled for initial production. The following table illustrates the learning effect on the total direct labor cost per yacht:

Yacht	Total Direct Labor Hours per Yacht	Direct Labor Cost per Hour	Total Direct Labor Cost per Yacht
1	500	$20	$10,000
2	450	20	9,000
3	405	20	8,100
4	365	20	7,300
5	329	20	6,580
6	296	20	5,920
7	296	20	5,920
8	296	20	5,920
9	296	20	5,920
10	296	20	5,920

[2]National Association of Accountants, *The Analysis of Cost-Volume-Profit Relationships: Research Report No. 16* (New York, 1960).

In this table, the total direct labor hours per yacht declined by 10% each time an additional yacht was produced, from a high of 500 hours to a low of 296 hours. The total direct labor cost per yacht declined from a high of $10,000 to a low of $5,920. After the sixth yacht was produced, the employees had learned enough from their experience in building the first 6 yachts that no additional reductions in time could be achieved.

The learning effect for Barker Company in terms of total direct labor hours per yacht is shown in the following graph:

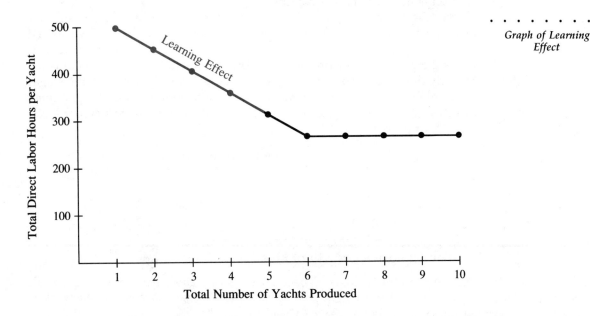

Graph of Learning Effect

The learning effect does not occur for all production processes, nor does it affect all production processes in the same way. In the preceding illustration of Barker Company, for example, instead of a 10% learning effect each time an additional yacht was produced, the learning effect could have been 10% for the first 3 yachts and 5% for the following 3 yachts. Generally, the more labor that is used in the production process, the greater the opportunity for the learning effect to occur. As production processes become more automated, less opportunity for learning exists.

The learning effect is important to managers, since it directly affects cost estimation. Estimated costs affect the development of reports and analyses used by management in decision making.

COST TRENDS

There are several important cost trends in the United States which may be relevant in the preparation of reports for use by managers in decision making. One such trend is the increased automation of manufacturing processes through the use of robotics and advanced technology. As a result of this automation, the percentage of product cost that is attributable to direct labor cost has steadily declined over the years. In contrast, an increasing percentage of the product cost is fixed cost and factory overhead cost. The increasing fixed cost is due in large measure to increased depreciation charges, rental charges, property taxes, and insurance costs. Since fixed costs are often more difficult to reduce than variable costs, incurring an increasing percentage of fixed costs may limit the ability of an enterprise's managers to react quickly to changing environmental and market conditions.

As the percentage of direct labor costs has decreased significantly for many businesses in recent years, some managerial accountants have started to classify direct labor cost for such businesses as part of factory overhead cost, rather than as a separate product cost. This treatment is especially valid when the only direct labor cost entering into a manufacturing process is the wages of machine operators who operate or monitor several machines at one time. In this situation, it is difficult to trace the direct labor cost to any particular product or process.

The Explosive Growth of Overhead Costs

In order for American industry to remain competitive in world markets, it is critical for managers to control overhead costs and the forces behind them. Yet control of overhead costs is more difficult to achieve as overhead costs become a more significant part of product cost. This growth in overhead costs is described in the following excerpts from an article in the *Harvard Business Review*:

While the world's attention is focused on the fight to increase productivity and develop new technologies, manufacturing managers—especially those in the electronics and mechanical equipment (machinery) industries—are quietly waging a different battle: the battle to conquer [increasing] overhead costs. Indeed, our research shows that overhead costs rank *behind only quality and getting new products out on schedule as a primary concern of manufacturing executives.*

...Overhead costs as a percentage of value added in American industry and as a percentage of overall manufacturing costs have been rising steadily for more than 100 years as the ratio of direct labor costs to value added has declined [as indicated in the graph on page 167]. Moreover, in today's environment, production managers have more direct leverage on improving productivity through cutting overhead than they do through pruning direct labor.

As America's factories step up the pace of automation, they find that they are being hit twice: first, overhead costs grow in percentage terms as direct labor costs fall (everything has to add up to 100%); and second, overhead costs grow in real terms because of the increased support costs associated with maintaining and running automated equipment....

Components of value added

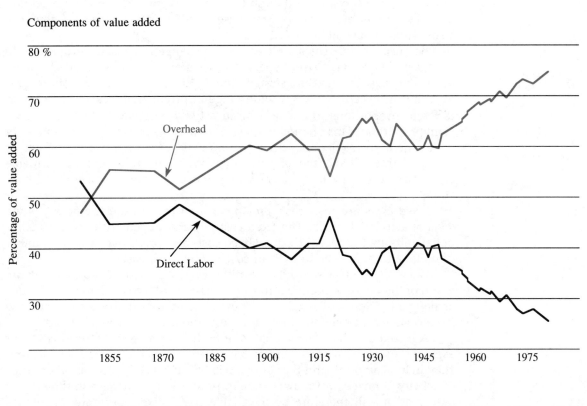

Source: Jeffrey G. Miller and Thomas E. Vollmann, "The Hidden Factory," *Harvard Business Review* (September–October, 1985),pp. 142–150.

Chapter Review

KEY POINTS

1. Cost Behavior.

Cost behavior refers to the manner in which a cost changes as its activity base changes. The three most common cost classifications are variable costs, fixed costs, and mixed costs.

Variable costs are costs that vary in total in direct proportion to changes in an activity base. Variable costs remain constant on a per unit basis with changes in the activity base. The relevant activity base for a variable cost depends upon which base is most closely associated with the cost and the decision-making needs of management. In practice, some costs may be classified as variable costs, even though they may not change in exact proportion to changes in the activity base. Step-wise variable costs change on a step-wise basis with changes in an activity base.

Because variable costs are assumed to change in constant proportion to changes in the activity base, the graph of a variable cost when plotted against the activity base appears as a straight line. In this sense, variable costs are said to be linear in nature. Over a wide range of production, costs often vary in different proportions to changes in an activity base, rather than in a constant proportion. This phenomenon is known as the principle of economies of scale. The narrow range of activity within which an enterprise is planning to operate is referred to as the relevant range. Within the relevant range, variable costs vary so closely to a constant rate that they may be represented by a straight line.

Fixed costs are costs that remain constant in total dollar amount as the level of activity changes. The fixed cost per unit of activity varies. As additional units are produced, the total fixed costs are spread over a larger number of units, and hence the total fixed cost per unit decreases.

Generally, step-wise fixed costs differ from step-wise variable costs in the width of the range of production over which the total costs change. The steps are longer for step-wise fixed costs than for step-wise variable costs. Step-wise fixed costs tend to be long-term in nature and are not easily changed.

A mixed cost has characteristics of both a variable and a fixed cost. For example, over one range of the activity base, a mixed cost may remain constant in total amount, and therefore it will be a fixed cost. Over another range of activity, a mixed cost may change in proportion to changes in the activity base, and it will therefore be a variable cost. Mixed costs are sometimes referred to as semivariable or semifixed costs. For purposes of analysis, mixed costs can generally be separated into their variable or fixed cost components.

2. Cost Estimation.

Cost estimation refers to the methods used to estimate costs for use in managerial decision making. For either a particular mixed cost or for total costs in general, the high-low method is used to estimate costs at a desired production level, as well as the variable and fixed cost components, by using the highest and the lowest total costs revealed by past cost patterns. To estimate the variable costs per unit and the fixed cost per period, the following steps are used:

1. a. The difference between the total costs at the highest and lowest levels of production is determined.
   b. The difference between the total units produced at the highest and lowest levels of production is determined.
2. The difference in total costs as determined in (1a) is divided by the difference in units produced as determined in (1b) to determine the variable cost per unit.
3. The total variable cost (variable cost per unit × total units produced) at either the highest or the lowest level of production is determined, and the

amount is subtracted from the total cost at that level to determine the fixed cost per period.

The estimated total cost line for the high-low method can be plotted on a graph by connecting the highest and the lowest total cost points by a straight line. The point at which the total cost line intersects the vertical axis represents the estimated fixed cost per period. The variable cost per unit is represented by the slope of the total cost line.

The scattergraph method of estimating costs uses a graph format similar to that used for the high-low method. A distinguishing characteristic of the scattergraph method relative to the high-low method is that the scattergraph method uses total costs at all the levels of past production, rather than just the highest and lowest levels.

The scattergraph is constructed using similar procedures as for the high-low graph, except that the total cost line is drawn so that the differences between each plotted point and the line are at a minimum in the judgment of the preparer of the graph.

The least squares method of estimating costs uses statistics to determine the total cost line. The least squares method fits a straight line through the plotted total cost points according to the following total cost equation:

$$\text{Total Cost} = (\text{Variable Cost per Unit} \times \text{Units of Production}) + \text{Fixed Cost}$$

The variable cost per unit component of the equation is estimated statistically, using the following computational formula:

$$\text{Variable Cost per Unit} = \frac{n(\Sigma P_i C_i) - (\Sigma P_i)(\Sigma C_i)}{n(\Sigma P_i^2) - (\Sigma P_i)^2}$$

The fixed cost component of total cost is estimated statistically, using the following computational formula:

$$\text{Fixed Cost} = \overline{C} - (\text{Variable Cost per Unit} \times \overline{P})$$

The high-low method, scattergraph method, and least squares method provide different estimates of fixed and variable costs. The cost estimation method that should be used in any given situation depends upon such considerations as the cost of gathering data for the estimates and the importance of the accuracy of the estimates. Although the high-low method is the easiest and the least costly to apply, it is also normally the least accurate. The least squares method is generally more accurate, but it is more complex and more costly to use.

Two other methods of cost estimation used in practice include the judgmental method and the engineering method. Under the judgmental method, managers use their experience and past observations to estimate fixed and variable costs. Under the engineering method, industrial engineers estimate fixed and variable costs by studying such factors as production methods, materials and labor requirements, equipment needs, and utility demands.

3. The Learning Effect in Estimating Costs.

Total costs are affected by how efficiently and effectively employees perform their tasks. After production for a new product begins or as a manufacturing process is implemented, workers usually increase their efficiency as more units are produced and they become more experienced. This learning effect is known as the learning curve phenomenon.

4. Cost Trends.

There are several important cost trends in the United States which may be relevant to managers for decision making. One such trend is the increased automation of manufacturing processes through the use of robotics and advanced technology. As a result of this automation, the percentage of product cost that is attributable to direct labor cost has declined. In contrast, an increasing percentage of product cost is fixed cost and factory overhead cost. Since fixed costs are often more difficult to reduce, an increasing percentage of fixed costs may limit the ability of an enterprise's managers to react quickly to changing environmental and market conditions.

KEY TERMS
·

cost behavior 141	semivariable costs 150
cost estimation 141	high-low method 152
variable costs 141	scattergraph method 156
step-wise variable costs 144	least squares method 159
economies of scale 146	judgmental method 163
relevant range 146	engineering method 163
fixed costs 147	learning effect 164
step-wise fixed costs 148	learning curve 164
mixed costs 150	

SELF-EXAMINATION QUESTIONS
·
(Answers at End of Chapter)

1. Which of the following statements describes variable costs?
   A. Costs that vary on a per unit basis as the activity base changes
   B. Costs that vary in total in direct proportion to changes in the activity base
   C. Costs that remain constant in total dollar amount as the level of activity changes
   D. Costs that vary on a per unit basis, but remain constant in total as the level of activity changes

2. Which of the following is an example of a mixed cost?
   A. Straight-line depreciation on factory equipment
   B. Direct materials cost
   C. Utility costs of $5,000 per month plus $.50 per kilowatt-hour
   D. Supervisory salaries of $10,000 per month

3. The point at which the total cost line intersects the vertical axis of the scattergraph indicates:
   A. total variable cost
   B. total fixed cost
   C. variable cost per unit
   D. none of the above

4. Which of the following methods of cost estimation always uses statistical formulas to determine the total cost and the variable and fixed cost components?
   A. High-low method
   B. Judgmental method
   C. Least squares method
   D. Scattergraph method

5. Which of the following methods is normally considered the least accurate method of estimating total costs and fixed and variable cost components?
   A. High-low method
   B. Scattergraph method
   C. Least squares method
   D. Engineering method

ILLUSTRATIVE PROBLEM

Hinderman Manufacturing Inc., which began operations in January, 1990, is in the process of estimating variable costs per unit and fixed costs based upon the past year's results. The following production and cost data have been gathered from the accounting and production records for the past 10 months:

	Units Produced	Total Costs
March.	80,000	$170,000
April	90,000	190,000
May	100,000	200,000
June.	110,000	220,000
July.	120,000	224,000
August	115,000	218,000
September	110,000	210,000
October	100,000	205,000
November.	110,000	215,000
December.	120,000	220,000

January and February cost and production data have been excluded, since operations during these months were in a start-up stage and were not typical.

Instructions:
1. Estimate (a) the variable cost per unit and (b) the fixed cost per month, using the high-low method of cost estimation. Use the cost data for De-

cember's production of 120,000 units, rather than the July cost data, since the December costs are more recent.

2. Prepare a least squares computational table for the estimation of variable cost per unit, using the following form. Do not include thousands in the table.

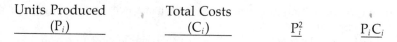

Units Produced (P_i)	Total Costs (C_i)	P_i^2	P_i C_i

3. Determine the estimated variable cost per unit, using the table in (2) and the appropriate least squares formula. Round to the nearest cent.
4. Determine the estimated fixed cost per month, using (2) and (3) and the appropriate least squares formula.
5. Estimate the total cost of 100,000 units of production per month, using (a) the high-low method and (b) the least squares method.

SOLUTION

(1) (a)

	Units Produced	Total Costs
Highest level.....................	120,000	$220,000
Lowest level	80,000	170,000
Difference.....................	40,000	$ 50,000

$$\text{Variable Cost per Unit} = \frac{\text{Difference in Total Costs}}{\text{Difference in Production}}$$

$$\text{Variable Cost per Unit} = \frac{\$220,000 - \$170,000}{120,000 \text{ units} - 80,000 \text{ units}}$$

$$\text{Variable Cost per Unit} = \frac{\$50,000}{40,000} = \$1.25 \text{ per unit}$$

(b) The fixed cost per month can be determined by subtracting the estimated total variable cost from the total cost at either the highest or lowest level of production, as follows:

$$\text{Total Cost} = (\text{Variable Cost per Unit} \times \text{Units of Production}) + \text{Fixed Cost}$$

Highest Level:

$220,000 = (\$1.25 \times 120,000 \text{ units}) + \text{Fixed Cost}$
$220,000 = \$150,000 + \text{Fixed Cost}$
$ 70,000 = \text{Fixed Cost}$

Lowest Level:

$170,000 = (\$1.25 \times 80,000 \text{ units}) + \text{Fixed Cost}$
$170,000 = \$100,000 + \text{Fixed Cost}$
$ 70,000 = \text{Fixed Cost}$

(2)

Units Produced (P_i)	Total Costs (C_i)	P_i^2	$P_i C_i$
80	$ 170	6,400	$ 13,600
90	190	8,100	17,100
100	200	10,000	20,000
110	220	12,100	24,200
120	224	14,400	26,880
115	218	13,225	25,070
110	210	12,100	23,100
100	205	10,000	20,500
110	215	12,100	23,650
120	220	14,400	26,400
1,055	$2,072	112,825	$220,500

(3) Variable Cost per Unit $= \dfrac{n(\Sigma P_i C_i) - (\Sigma P_i)(\Sigma C_i)}{n(\Sigma P_i^2) - (\Sigma P_i)^2}$

Variable Cost per Unit $= \dfrac{10(\$220,500) - (1,055)(\$2,072)}{10(112,825) - (1,055)^2}$

Variable Cost per Unit $= \dfrac{\$2,205,000 - \$2,185,960}{1,128,250 - 1,113,025}$

Variable Cost per Unit $= \dfrac{\$19,040}{15,225} = \$1.25$ per unit

(4) Fixed Cost $= \overline{C} - ($Variable Cost per Unit $\times \overline{P})$

$\overline{C} = (\$2,072,000 \div 10) = \$207,200$

$\overline{P} = (1,055,000$ units $\div 10) = 105,500$ units

Fixed Cost $= \$207,200 - (\$1.25 \times 105,500$ units$)$

Fixed Cost $= \$207,200 - \$131,875$

Fixed Cost $= \$75,325$

(5) (a) Total Cost $= ($Variable Cost per Unit $\times$ Units of Production$)$ + Fixed Cost

Total Cost $= (\$1.25 \times 100,000$ units$) + \$70,000$

Total Cost $= \$125,000 + \$70,000$

Total Cost $= \$195,000$

(b) Total Cost $= ($Variable Cost per Unit $\times$ Units of Production$)$ + Fixed Cost

Total Cost $= (\$1.25 \times 100,000$ units$) + \$75,325$

Total Cost $= \$125,000 + \$75,325$

Total Cost $= \$200,325$

Discussion Questions

5–1. Distinguish between cost behavior and cost estimation.

5–2. What are the three most common classifications used for classifying cost behavior?

5–3. Describe how total variable costs and unit variable costs behave with changes in the activity base.

5–4. Which of the following costs would be classified as variable costs for units produced?
   (a) Direct materials cost
   (b) Straight-line depreciation
   (c) Factory supervisor's salary
   (d) Electricity costs of $.25 per kilowatt-hour
   (e) Insurance premiums on factory plant and equipment of $3,000 per month
   (f) Direct labor costs
   (g) Oil used in operating factory machinery
   (h) Janitorial supplies of $750 per month

5–5. Which of the following graphs illustrates how total variable costs behave with changes in total units produced?

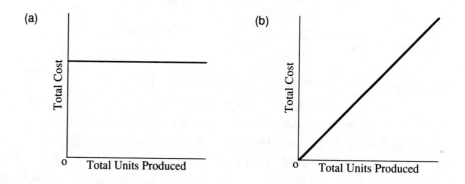

5–6. Which of the following graphs illustrates how unit variable costs behave with changes in total units produced?

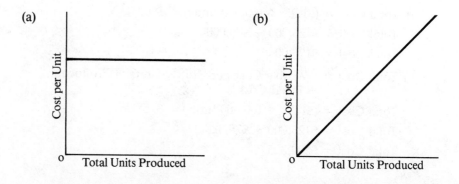

5–7. For Weber Tree Farm Inc., match each cost in the following table with the activity base most appropriate to it. An activity base may be used more than once.

<table>
<tr><td align="center">Cost</td><td align="center">Activity Base</td></tr>
<tr><td>(1) Fertilizer</td><td>(a) Number of trees planted in the fields</td></tr>
<tr><td>(2) Dirt and packaging materials for shipping mature trees</td><td>(b) Number of trees shipped</td></tr>
<tr><td>(3) The cost of water used to water the trees</td><td>(c) Number of fields
(d) Dollar amount of trees sold</td></tr>
<tr><td>(4) Sales commissions</td><td>(e) Dollar amount of trees planted in the fields</td></tr>
<tr><td>(5) Field managers' salaries</td><td></td></tr>
</table>

5–8. Which of the following graphs best illustrates the nature of a step-wise cost?

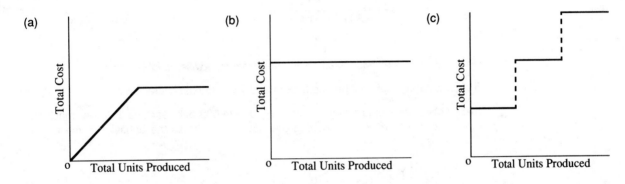

5–9. Why must management exercise added care in planning and scheduling production in order to maximize the efficiency of operations for step-wise costs?

5–10. Does the total cost graph of a variable cost appear as a straight line or as a curvilinear line when plotted against its activity base?

5–11. What term refers to the economic phenomenon of changing proportions of costs to changes in an activity base?

5–12. What term refers to the narrow range of activity within which the enterprise is planning to operate?

5–13. Describe the behavior of (a) total fixed costs and (b) unit fixed costs as the activity base increases.

5–14. Which of the following costs are fixed costs of production?
  (a) Property insurance premiums of $4,000 per month on plant and equipment
  (b) Straight-line depreciation on plant and equipment
  (c) Direct labor costs
  (d) Salary of factory supervisor, $40,000 per year
  (e) Rent of $25,000 per month on factory building
  (f) Electricity used in running machinery, $.02 per kilowatt-hour
  (g) Direct materials
  (h) Oil and other lubricants used on factory machinery

5–15. Which of the following graphs best illustrates fixed costs per unit as the activity base changes?

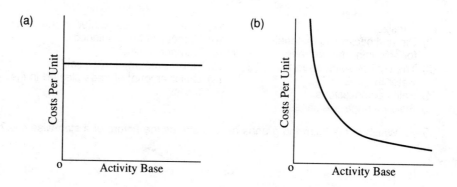

5–16. How do step-wise fixed costs differ from step-wise variable costs?

5–17. What type of cost has both fixed and variable cost characteristics?

5–18. Miller Inc. rents factory machinery for $14,000 per year and $.25 per machine hour. Which of the following graphs best illustrates the behavior of the rental costs?

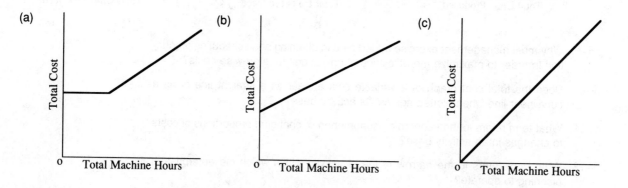

5–19. Name five methods of cost estimation that may be useful to the managerial accountant.

5–20. In applying the high-low method of cost estimation, how is the total fixed cost estimated?

5–21. If the variable cost per unit is $2.50 and the total fixed cost is $300,000, what is the estimated total cost for the production of 50,000 units?

5–22. Describe how the total cost line is drawn on a scattergraph.

5–23. How is the scattergraph method used to determine the estimated total cost for any level of production?

5–24. Assuming that the least squares method of cost estimation is used to estimate a variable cost per unit of $1.30, the average of the observed total costs is $82,000, and the average of the observed levels of production is 40,000 units, what is the least squares estimate of the total fixed cost?

5–25. What might be indicated by large differences between estimated total costs and actual costs?

5–26. As production for a new product begins or as a new manufacturing process is implemented, workers usually increase their efficiency as they produce more units and acquire more experience. What is this phenomenon called?

5–27. Why is the learning effect important to managers?

5–28. What is an implication of the increasing percentage of fixed costs to total product costs?

5–29. How have some managerial accountants classified direct labor costs as the percentage of direct labor costs to total product costs has declined significantly?

5–30. Real World Focus. From the following list of activity bases for an automobile dealership, select the base that would be most appropriate for each of these costs: (1) preparation costs (cleaning, oil, and gasoline costs) for each car received, (2) salespersons' commission of 5% for each car sold, and (3) property taxes at the end of the year.

Activity Base

(a) Number of cars sold
(b) Number of cars received
(c) Number of cars ordered
(d) Number of cars on hand
(e) Dollar amount of cars sold
(f) Dollar amount of cars received
(g) Dollar amount of cars ordered
(h) Dollar amount of cars on hand

Exercises

5–31. Classification of costs. Following is a list of various costs incurred in producing pencils. With respect to the manufacture and sale of pencils, classify each cost as either variable, fixed, or mixed.

1. Erasers for the end of each pencil.
2. Salary of the plant superintendent.
3. Straight-line depreciation on the factory equipment.
4. Gold paint for each pencil.
5. Number 2 lead.
6. Property taxes on factory building and equipment.
7. Hourly wages of machine operators.
8. Pension cost of $.20 per employee hour on the job.

(continued)

9. Lubricants used to oil machinery.
10. Rent on warehouse of $3,000 per month plus $2 per square foot of storage used.
11. Metal to hold the eraser on the end of the pencil.
12. Electricity costs of $.025 per kilowatt-hour.
13. Janitorial costs of $2,000 per month.
14. Wood costs per pencil.
15. Property insurance premiums of $1,500 per month plus $.003 for each dollar of insurance over $2,000,000.

5–32. Identification of cost graphs. The following cost graphs illustrate various types of cost behavior:

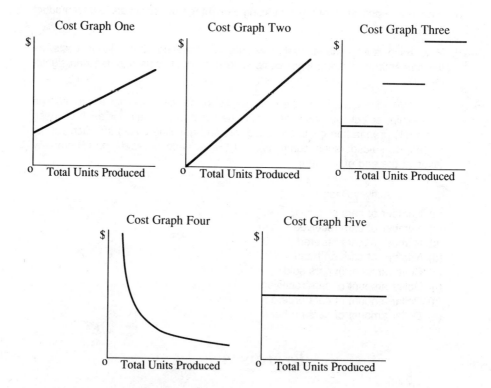

For each of the following costs, identify the cost graph that best illustrates its cost behavior as the number of units produced increases.
(a) Total direct materials cost.
(b) Per unit cost of straight-line depreciation on factory equipment.
(c) Utility costs of $2,000 per month plus $.0002 per kilowatt-hour.
(d) Salary of quality control supervisor, $2,500 per month. One quality control supervisor is needed for each 10,000 units produced.
(e) Per unit cost of direct labor.

5–33. Relevant range and computation of fixed and variable costs.
Reynolds Inc. manufactures tool sets within a relevant range of 100,000 to 300,000 sets a year. Within this range, the following partially completed manufacturing cost schedule has been prepared:

	Tool Sets Produced		
	100,000	200,000	300,000
Total costs:			
Total variable costs	$ 700,000	(d)	(j)
Total fixed costs	450,000	(e)	(k)
Total costs	$1,150,000	(f)	(l)
Cost per unit:			
Variable cost per unit.................	(a)	(g)	(m)
Fixed cost per unit	(b)	(h)	(n)
Total cost per unit...................	(c)	(i)	(o)

Complete the cost schedule, identifying each cost by the appropriate letter (a) through (o).

5–34. Terminology. Choose the appropriate term for completing each of the following sentences.

(a) The term (cost behavior, cost estimation) refers to the manner in which a cost changes as the activity base of the cost changes.

(b) (Variable, Fixed) costs vary in total in direct proportion to changes in an activity base.

(c) A cost which increases by $50,000 for every additional 100,000 units produced is called a (mixed, step-wise) cost.

(d) The phenomenon of changing proportions of costs to changes in an activity base is known as the economic principle of (economies of scale, marginal productivity of inputs).

(e) The range of activity within which the enterprise is planning to operate is the (relevant, tactical) range.

(f) A (mixed, sunk) cost has characteristics of both a variable and a fixed cost.

(g) The (high-low, scattergraph) method uses total costs at all levels of past production in estimating costs.

(h) The (least squares, scattergraph) method uses statistics to determine the total cost line.

(i) The (engineering, judgmental) method uses such inputs as studies of production processes, material and labor requirements, and utility demands in estimating costs.

(j) When new equipment or a new process is implemented, the increase in efficiency as more units are produced is known as the (economies of scale, learning effect.)

5–35. Cost estimation, using the high-low method. McKean Company has decided to use the high-low method to estimate the total cost and the fixed and variable cost components of the total cost. The data for the highest and lowest levels of production are as follows:

EADSHEET
ROBLEM

	Units Produced	Total Costs
Highest level...................	80,000	$370,000
Lowest level	40,000	220,000

(a) Determine the variable cost per unit and the fixed cost for McKean Company.

(b) Based on (a), estimate the total cost for 60,000 units of production.

5–36. Cost estimation, using the scattergraph method. Using data for an 8-month period, a cost accountant for Kadrmas Company has prepared the following scattergraph as a basis for cost estimation:

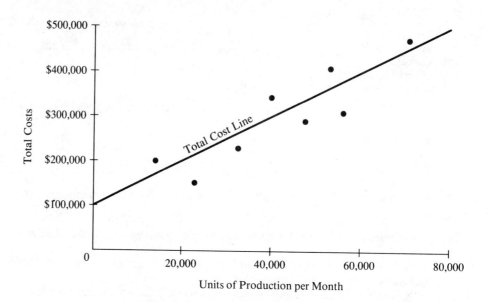

(a) Determine the estimated fixed cost per month for Kadrmas Company.
(b) Determine the estimated total cost for 40,000 units of production.
(c) Compute the estimated variable cost per unit, based on the total cost of producing 40,000 units.

5–37. Cost estimation, using the least squares method. Using data for the first six months of the year, the assistant controller for Zavor Company prepared the following table for use in estimating costs:

Units Produced (P_i)	Total Costs (C_i)	P_i^2	P_iC_i
50	$ 200	2,500	$ 10,000
100	302	10,000	30,200
80	258	6,400	20,640
60	220	3,600	13,200
90	280	8,100	25,200
70	240	4,900	16,800
450	$1,500	35,500	$116,040

The thousands have been deleted from the table. Thus, 50 units in the table represents 50,000 units of production, and $100 represents $100,000.
(a) Determine the estimated variable cost per unit, using the table and the appropriate least squares formula. Round to the nearest cent.
(b) Determine the estimated fixed cost per month, using the preceding data and the appropriate least squares formula.
(c) Based on (a) and (b), estimate the total cost for 65,000 units of production.

5–38. Learning effect. Miles Sails Inc. manufactures sailboats and has added a new model of sailboat to its product line. Past experience indicates that every time a new model of sailboat is added, the total time to manufacture each sailboat declines by 8% as each of the next six sailboats is produced. After the seventh sailboat, no further reduction in time is possible. It is estimated that the first sailboat will require 500 direct labor hours at a cost of $12 per hour.

(a) Complete the following table for the manufacture of the first ten sailboats. Round to the nearest direct labor hour.

Sailboat	Total Direct Labor Hours per Sailboat	Direct Labor Cost per Hour	Total Direct Labor Cost per Sailboat
1	500	$12	$6,000

(b) Graph the learning effect for Miles Sails Inc. in terms of total direct labor hours per sailboat.

Problems

5–39. Classification of costs. Wiley Inc. manufactures sofas for distribution to several major retail chains. The following costs are incurred in the production and sale of sofas:

(a) Fabric for sofa coverings.
(b) Springs.
(c) Hourly wages of sewing machine operators.
(d) Foam rubber for cushion fillings.
(e) Insurance premiums on property plant and equipment, $5,000 per year plus $.002 per insured value over $8,000,000.
(f) Straight-line depreciation on factory equipment.
(g) Wood for framing the sofas.
(h) Salary of designers.
(i) Salary of production vice-president.
(j) Rent on experimental equipment, $50 for every sofa produced.
(k) Consulting fee of $15,000 paid to efficiency specialists.
(l) Janitorial supplies, $40 for each sofa produced.
(m) Salesperson's salary, $12,000 plus 5% of the selling price of each sofa sold.
(n) Employer's FICA taxes on controller's salary of $65,000.
(o) Sewing supplies.
(p) Cartons used to ship sofas.
(q) Rental costs of warehouse, $14,000 per month.
(r) Legal fees paid to attorneys in defense of the company in a patent infringement suit, $10,000 plus $30 per hour.
(s) Property taxes on property, plant, and equipment.
(t) Electricity costs of $.00035 per kilowatt-hour.

Instructions:

Classify the preceding costs as either variable, fixed, or mixed. Use the following tabular headings and place an X in the appropriate column:

Cost	Variable Cost	Fixed Cost	Mixed Cost

5–40. Identification of cost graphs. The following costs were incurred by Johnson Manufacturing Co. in the production of utility trailers:

(a) Aluminum for sides of trailers.

(b) Hourly wages of assemblers, $15 per hour plus time and one half for all hours in excess of 40 per week.

(c) Property taxes paid to city, $1,000, unless 200 trailers are produced, in which case no tax is paid.

(d) Per unit cost of straight-line depreciation.

(e) Electricity costs of $1,000 per month plus $.0004 per kilowatt-hour.

(f) Safety chain, where the cost per foot of chain is $.06 per foot for the first 1,000 feet purchased, and $.05 per foot after the purchase of 1,000 feet.

(g) Rental of welding equipment, $500 for the first 100 trailers produced plus $3 for each trailer after 100.

(h) Water costs according to the following schedule:

First 1,000 gallons	$.20 per gallon
1,001–3,000 gallons..................	$.18 per gallon
3,001–8,000 gallons.................	$.15 per gallon
over 8,000 gallons	$.12 per gallon

(i) Salary of superintendent of production, $60,000.

(j) Rental costs for metal stamping equipment, per machine:

1–100 trailers	$600 per month
101–200 trailers	$500 per month
201–300 trailers	$400 per month

(k) Health insurance costs, $200 per employee plus $.003 per hour worked for first 2,000 hours and $.005 per hour worked for all hours over 2,000.

(l) Maintenance contract for factory overhead: $1,000 for first 100 trailers produced, $1,200 for second 100 trailers produced, and $1,400 for third 100 trailers produced.

Instructions:

For each of the costs, identify the cost graph, from the following group of various graphs, that best describes the cost behavior as the number of units produced increases. For each graph, the vertical axis represents dollars of cost and the horizontal axis represents units of production.

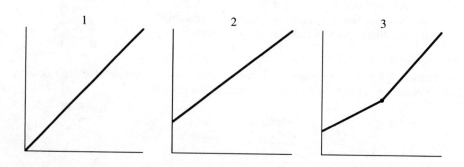

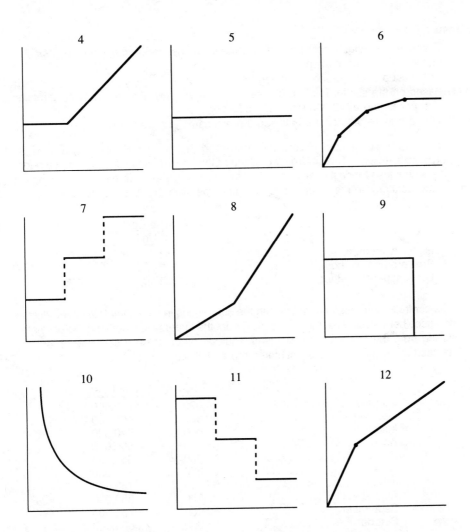

5–41. Cost estimation, using high-low and scattergraph methods. The controller for Shaut Company is preparing some preliminary cost projections for the 1990 budget and has accumulated the following cost and production data for 1989:

	Units Produced	Total Costs
January	20,000	$250,000
February...............	50,000	500,000
March	40,000	400,000
April..................	30,000	300,000
May...................	60,000	550,000
June	65,000	600,000
July	70,000	620,000
August	85,000	750,000
September.............	80,000	700,000
October	45,000	410,000
November	25,000	280,000
December	10,000	150,000

Instructions:

(1) Estimate the variable cost per unit and the fixed cost per month, using the high-low method of cost estimation.
(2) Construct a scattergraph, including the total cost line.
(3) Based on the scattergraph in (2), estimate the variable cost per unit and the fixed cost per month at 40,000 units of production.
(4) Why are there differences between the estimates in (1) and (3)?

5–42. Analysis of cost estimates, using high-low, scattergraph, and least squares methods. The controller of Sauter Company recently decided to use quantitative techniques for cost estimation purposes. Cost estimates were prepared using the high-low, scattergraph, and least squares methods, with the following results:

	Variable Cost per Unit	Fixed Costs per Month
High-low method	$8.25	$35,000
Scattergraph method	8.02	60,000
Least squares method	8.00	57,300

The controller expressed concern with the differences in the estimates, especially the differences between the estimates resulting from the high-low method and the estimates resulting from the scattergraph and least squares methods. The cost and production data used in developing these estimates are as follows:

	Units Produced	Total Costs
January	20,000	$200,000
February................	50,000	460,000
March	60,000	540,000
April.	65,000	600,000
May.....................	40,000	380,000
June	65,000	580,000
July.....................	94,000	780,000
August	100,000	860,000
September.............	80,000	700,000
October	75,000	665,000

Instructions:

(1) Based on each of the preceding cost estimates for the high-low, scattergraph, and least squares methods, (a) compute the estimated total cost for 75,000 units of production, and (b) compute the differences between each of the total cost estimates in (a) and the actual cost of $665,000.
(2) Assuming that the January production and cost data are not typical of normal operations, recompute the variable cost per unit and the fixed cost per month, using the high-low method.
(3) Based on (2), recompute the estimated total cost for 75,000 units of production, using the high-low method.
(4) Based on the total cost estimate computed in (3), what is the difference between this estimate and the actual cost of $665,000?
(5) Regardless of which cost estimation method is used, why should the estimated total cost be compared periodically with the actual cost?

5-43. Cost estimation, using least squares method. Mitchell Company began operations in January, 1989, and has decided to use the least squares method for estimating variable costs per unit and fixed costs. The following production and cost data have been gathered from the accounting and production records for the past 10 months:

	Units Produced	Total Costs
March	300,000	$ 665,000
April.	400,000	810,000
May.	650,000	1,170,000
June	690,000	1,250,000
July	720,000	1,270,000
August	780,000	1,400,000
September.	510,000	980,000
October	320,000	700,000
November	270,000	600,000
December	90,000	350,000

January and February cost and production data have been excluded, since operations during these months were in a start-up stage and were not typical.

Instructions:

(1) Prepare a computational table for the estimation of the variable cost per unit, using the following form. Do not include thousands in the table.

Units Produced (P_i)	Total Costs (C_i)	P_i^2	P_iC_i

(2) Determine the estimated variable cost per unit, using the table in (1) and the appropriate least squares formula. Round to the nearest cent.
(3) Determine the estimated fixed cost per month, using (1) and (2) and the appropriate least squares formula.
(4) Estimate the total cost of 600,000 units of production, using the results of (2) and (3).

ALTERNATE PROBLEMS

5-39A. Classification of costs. Gardner Inc. manufactures blue jeans for distribution to several major retail chains. The following costs are incurred in the production and sale of blue jeans:
- (a) Blue denim fabric.
- (b) Insurance premiums on property, plant, and equipment, $10,000 per year plus $.003 per insured value over $5,000,000.
- (c) Hourly wages of sewing machine operators.
- (d) Property taxes on property, plant, and equipment.
- (e) Thread.
- (f) Brass buttons.
- (g) Legal fees paid to attorneys in defense of the company in a patent infringement suit, $20,000 plus $50 per hour.
- (h) Salary of designers.
- (i) Salary of production vice-president.
- (j) Rent on experimental equipment, $15,000 per year.

(k) Consulting fee of $80,000 paid to industry specialist for marketing advice.
(l) Janitorial supplies, $1,000 per month.
(m) Salesperson's salary, $12,000 plus 5% of the total sales.
(n) Electricity costs of $.00040 per kilowatt-hour.
(o) Sewing supplies.
(p) Shipping boxes used to ship orders.
(q) Rental costs of warehouse, $2,000 per month plus $.50 per square foot of storage used.
(r) Leather for patches identifying each jean style.
(s) Blue dye.
(t) Straight-line depreciation on sewing machines.

Instructions:

Classify the preceding costs as either variable, fixed, or mixed. Use the following tabular headings and place an X in the appropriate column:

Cost	Variable Cost	Fixed Cost	Mixed Cost

5–40A. Identification of cost graphs. The following costs were incurred by Brown Manufacturing Co. in the production of ironing boards:

(a) Wood for top of board.
(b) Hourly wages of assemblers, $15 per hour plus time and one half for all hours in excess of 40 per week.
(c) Property taxes paid to city, $5,000, unless 10,000 ironing boards are produced, in which case no tax is paid.
(d) Per unit cost of straight-line depreciation.
(e) Electricity costs of $500 per month plus $.0006 per kilowatt-hour.
(f) Rental of experimental shipping equipment, $1,000 for first 5,000 shipments and $.04 for each shipment after 5,000.
(g) Special heat-resistant cloth for covering top of board, where the cost per yard is $1.50 per yard for the first 5,000 yards, and $1 per yard thereafter.
(h) Water costs according to the following schedule:

First 5,000 gallons	$.30 per gallon
5,001–10,000 gallons...................	$.25 per gallon
10,001–15,000 gallons	$.20 per gallon
over 15,000 gallons	$.15 per gallon

(i) Maintenance contract for factory equipment; $600 for first 2,000 hours of use, $900 for next 500 hours of use, and $1,200 for remaining hours of use.
(j) Rental of cutting machine according to the following schedule:

1–500 hours of use	$700
501–1,000 hours of use	$500
1,001–2,000 hours of use.....................	$300

(k) Health insurance costs, $300 per employee plus $.002 per hour worked for first 2,000 hours and $.004 per hour worked for all hours over 2,000.
(l) Salary of superintendent of production, $80,000.

Instructions:

For each of the costs, identify the cost graph, from the following group of various graphs, that best describes the cost behavior as the number of units produced increases. For each graph, the vertical axis represents dollars of cost, and the horizontal axis represents units of production.

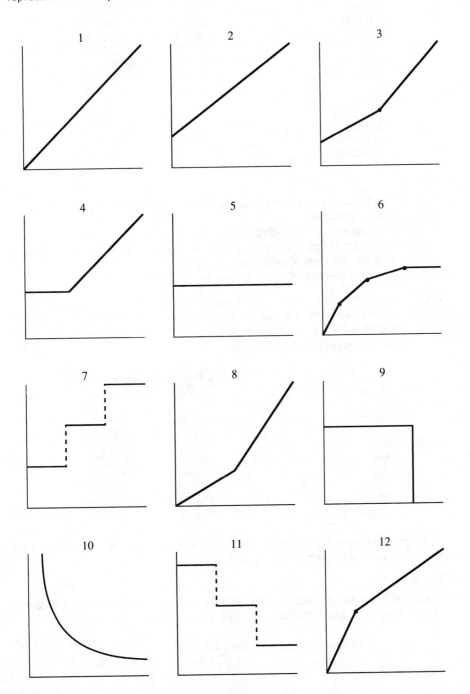

5–41A. Cost estimation, using high-low and scattergraph methods. The controller for Valdes Company is preparing some preliminary cost projections for the 1990 budget and has accumulated the following cost and production data for 1989:

	Units Produced	Total Costs
January	30,000	$380,000
February..............	20,000	330,000
March	10,000	210,000
April.................	35,000	360,000
May..................	42,000	450,000
June	60,000	490,000
July.................	70,000	595,000
August	80,000	695,000
September............	90,000	650,000
October	75,000	570,000
November	65,000	550,000
December	50,000	450,000

Instructions:

(1) Estimate the variable cost per unit and the fixed cost per month, using the high-low method of cost estimation.
(2) Construct a scattergraph, including the total cost line.
(3) Based on the scattergraph in (2), estimate the variable cost per unit and the fixed cost per month at 40,000 units of production.
(4) Why are there differences between the estimates in (1) and (3)?

5–43A. Cost estimation, using least squares method. The management of Lindgren Company has decided to use the least squares method for estimating variable costs per unit and fixed costs. The following production and cost data have been gathered from the accounting and production records:

	Units Produced	Total Costs
January	20,000	$125,000
February..............	40,000	180,000
March	50,000	205,000
April.................	55,000	222,000
May..................	60,000	240,000
June	70,000	270,000
July.................	75,000	282,000
August	80,000	291,000
September............	65,000	258,000
October	45,000	200,000

Cost and production data for November and December have been excluded, since operations during these months were not typical.

Instructions:

(1) Prepare a computational table for the estimation of the variable cost per unit, using the following form. Do not include thousands in the table.

Units Produced (P_i)	Total Costs (C_i)	P_i^2	$P_i C_i$

(2) Determine the estimated variable cost per unit, using the table in (1) and the appropriate least squares formula. Round to the nearest cent.

(3) Determine the estimated fixed cost per month, using (1) and (2) and the appropriate least squares formula.

(4) Estimate the total cost of 35,000 units of production, using the results of (2) and (3).

Mini-Case 5

Beckel Company has recently become concerned with the accuracy of its cost estimates because of large monthly differences between actual and estimated total costs. In the past, the senior managerial accountant has used the high-low method to develop estimates of variable costs per unit and fixed costs. These cost estimates are as follows:

Variable cost per unit......................	$1.50
Fixed cost	$52,500

As a new junior accountant, the controller has asked you to determine whether the least squares method of cost estimation would provide more accurate estimates. The following twelve-month cost and production data have been gathered as a basis for developing the least squares cost estimates:

	Units Produced	Total Costs
January	40,000	$127,000
February................	45,000	131,000
March..................	50,000	136,000
April...................	55,000	143,000
May....................	60,000	150,000
June	70,000	155,000
July....................	80,000	170,000
August	85,000	180,000
September..............	75,000	157,000
October	65,000	144,000
November	46,000	133,000
December	25,000	90,000

Instructions:

(1) Prepare a least squares computational table for the estimation of variable cost per unit, using the following form. Do not include thousands in the table.

Units Produced (P_i)	Total Costs (C_i)	P_i^2	$P_i C_i$

(2) Determine the estimated variable cost per unit, using the table in (1) and the appropriate least squares formula. Round to the nearest cent.

(3) Determine the estimated fixed cost per month, using (1) and (2) and the appropriate least squares formula.

(4) Prepare a table comparing the monthly differences between actual and estimated total costs for the high-low and least squares methods. Use the following headings:

Month	Units Produced	Total Actual Costs	Total Estimated Costs High-Low Method	Total Estimated Costs Least Squares Method	Monthly Differences High-Low Method	Monthly Differences Least Squares Method

(5) Which method is more accurate in estimating total costs? Explain.

(6) Which cost estimation method would you recommend to the controller?

Answers to Self-Examination Questions

· · ·

1. **B** Variable costs vary in total in direct proportion to changes in the activity base (answer B). Costs that vary on a per unit basis as the activity base changes (answer A) or remain constant in total dollar amount as the level of activity changes (answer C), or both (answer D), are fixed costs.

2. **C** Mixed costs have characteristics of both variable and fixed costs. Utility costs of $5,000 per month (the fixed component) plus $.50 per kilowatt-hour (the variable component) (answer C) are a mixed cost. Straight-line depreciation on factory equipment (answer A) and supervisory salaries of $10,000 per month (answer D) are fixed costs. Direct materials cost (answer B) is a variable cost.

3. B The point at which the total cost line intersects the vertical axis of the scattergraph indicates the estimated total fixed cost of production (answer B). The total variable cost (answer A) for any level of production is the difference between the estimated total cost indicated on the scattergraph and the estimated total fixed cost. The estimated variable cost per unit (answer C) can be computed by dividing the total variable cost by the total units of production for a given level of production.

4. C The least squares method (answer C) uses statistical formulas to estimate the total cost and the variable and fixed cost components. The high-low method (answer A) uses only data for the highest and lowest levels of production in estimating costs. The scattergraph method (answer D) uses a graph to estimate costs. The judgmental method (answer B) uses experience and past observations of cost-volume relationships to estimate costs. It may also use the high-low, scattergraph, or least squares method as a starting point.

5. A The high-low method (answer A) is normally considered the least accurate method of estimating costs because it uses data for only the highest and lowest levels of production. On the other hand, the scattergraph method (answer B) and the least squares method (answer C) both utilize data for all the observed levels of production. The engineering method (answer D) will provide estimates that are as accurate as the engineering studies upon which the estimates are based.

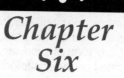

Chapter Six

CHAPTER OBJECTIVES

•

Describe the use of analyses of cost-volume-profit relationships
in planning operations.

•

Describe and illustrate the mathematical approach to
cost-volume-profit analysis.

•

Describe and illustrate the graphic approach to cost-volume-profit analysis.

•

Describe the use of computers in cost-volume-profit analysis.

•

Describe and illustrate the impact of sales mix considerations in
cost-volume-profit analysis.

•

Describe and illustrate special cost-volume-profit relationships.

•

Describe the limitations of cost-volume-profit analysis.

•

Cost-Volume-Profit Analysis

Cost-volume-profit analysis is a commonly used tool that provides management with useful information for decision making. For example, cost-volume-profit analysis may be used in setting selling prices, selecting the mix of products to sell, choosing among alternative marketing strategies, and analyzing the effects of cost increases or decreases on the profitability of the business enterprise. In this chapter, the study of the relationship of costs to volume and profit is based on the cost behavior and cost estimation discussion of Chapter 5. Cost-volume-profit analysis is then applied in the calculation of the break-even point, desired profit, sales mix, margin of safety, and contribution margin ratio.

COST-VOLUME-PROFIT RELATIONSHIPS

Cost-volume-profit analysis is the systematic examination of the interrelationships between selling prices, volume of sales and production, costs, expenses, and profits. This analysis is a complex matter, since these relationships are often affected by forces entirely or partially beyond management's control. For example, the determination of the selling price of a product is often affected by not only the costs of production, but also by uncontrollable factors in the marketplace. On the other hand, the cost of producing the product is affected by such controllable factors as the efficiency of operations and the volume of production.

Accountants can play an important role in cost-volume-profit analysis by providing management with information on the relative profitability of its various products, the probable effects of changes in selling price, and other variables. Such information can help management improve the relationship between these variables. For example, an analysis of sales and cost data can be helpful in determining the level of sales volume necessary for the business to earn a satisfactory profit.

In cost-volume-profit analysis, all costs[1] must be classified into two categories: (1) variable and (2) fixed. As described in Chapter 5, variable costs are costs that change, in total, as the volume of activity changes. Fixed costs remain constant, in total, as the volume of activity changes. Mixed costs, sometimes referred to as **semivariable** or **semifixed costs,** are costs that have

---

[1]In this chapter, the term "costs" is often used as a convenience to represent both "costs" and "expenses."

both variable and fixed characteristics. Using the cost estimation methods described in Chapter 5, a mixed cost can generally be separated into its variable and fixed components.

MATHEMATICAL APPROACH TO COST-VOLUME-PROFIT ANALYSIS

After the costs and expenses have been classified into fixed and variable components, the effect on profit of these costs and expenses, along with revenues and volume, can be expressed in the form of cost-volume-profit analysis. Although accountants have proposed various approaches for cost-volume-profit analysis, the mathematical approach is one of two common approaches described and illustrated in this chapter.

The mathematical approach to cost-volume-profit analysis generally uses equations (1) to indicate the revenues necessary to achieve the break-even point in operations or (2) to indicate the revenues necessary to achieve a desired or target profit. These two equations and their use by management in profit planning are described and illustrated in the paragraphs that follow.

Break-Even Point

The level of operations of an enterprise at which revenues and expired costs are exactly equal is called the **break-even point.** At this level of operations, an enterprise will neither realize an operating income nor incur an operating loss. Break-even analysis can be applied to past periods, but it is most useful when applied to future periods as a guide to business planning, particularly if either an expansion or a curtailment of operations is expected. In such cases, it is concerned with future prospects and future operations and hence relies upon estimates. The reliability of the analysis is greatly influenced by the accuracy of the estimates.

The break-even point can be computed by means of a mathematical formula which indicates the relationship between revenue, costs, and capacity. The data required are (1) total estimated fixed costs for a future period, such as a year, and (2) the total estimated variable costs for the same period, stated as a percent of net sales. To illustrate, assume that fixed costs are estimated at $90,000 and that variable costs are expected to be 60% of sales. The break-even point is $225,000 of sales, computed as follows:

Break-Even Sales (in $) = Fixed Costs (in $) + Variable Costs (as % of Break-Even Sales)

$$S = \$90,000 + 60\%S$$
$$40\%S = \$90,000$$
$$S = \$225,000$$

The validity of the preceding computation is shown in the following income statement:

Sales		$225,000
Expenses:		
Variable costs ($225,000 × 60%)	$135,000	
Fixed costs	90,000	225,000
Operating profit		-0-

The break-even point can be expressed either in terms of total sales dollars, as in the preceding illustration, or in terms of units of sales. For example, in the preceding illustration, if the unit selling price is $25, the break-even point can be expressed as either $225,000 of sales or 9,000 units ($225,000 ÷ $25).

The break-even point can be affected by changes in the fixed costs, unit variable costs, and unit selling price. The effect of each of these factors on the break-even point is briefly described in the following paragraphs.

Effect of Changes in Fixed Costs. Although fixed costs do not change in total with changes in volume of activity, they may change because of other factors, such as changes in property tax rates and salary increases given to factory supervisors. Increases in fixed costs will raise the break-even point. Similarly, decreases in fixed costs will lower the break-even point.

To illustrate, assume that Bishop Co. is evaluating a proposal to budget an additional $100,000 for advertising. Fixed costs (before the additional expenditure of $100,000 is considered) are estimated at $600,000, and variable costs are estimated at 75% of sales. The break-even point (before the additional expenditure is considered) is $2,400,000, computed as follows:

Break-Even Sales (in $) = Fixed Costs (in $) + Variable Costs (as % of Break-Even Sales)
$$S = \$600,000 + 75\%S$$
$$25\%S = \$600,000$$
$$S = \$2,400,000$$

If advertising expense is increased by $100,000, the break-even point is raised to $2,800,000, computed as follows:

Break-Even Sales (in $) = Fixed Costs (in $) + Variable Costs (as % of Break-Even Sales)
$$S = \$700,000 + 75\%S$$
$$25\%S = \$700,000$$
$$S = \$2,800,000$$

The increased fixed cost of $100,000 increases the break-even point by $400,000 of sales, since 75 cents of each sales dollar must cover variable costs. Hence, $4 of additional sales are needed for each $1 increase in fixed costs if the operating profit for Bishop Co. is to remain unchanged.

Effect of Changes in Variable Costs. Although unit variable costs do not change with changes in volume of activity, they may change because of other factors, such as changes in the price of direct materials and salary increases given to factory workers providing direct labor. Increases in unit variable costs will raise the break-even point. Similarly, decreases in unit variable costs will lower the break-even point.

To illustrate, assume that Park Co. is evaluating a proposal to pay an additional 2% sales commission to its sales representatives as an incentive to increase sales. Fixed costs are estimated at $84,000, and variable costs are estimated at 58% of sales (before the additional 2% commission is considered). The break-even point (before the additional commission is considered) is $200,000, computed as follows:

Break-Even Sales (in $) = Fixed Costs (in $) + Variable Costs (as % of Break-Even Sales)
$$S = \$84,000 + 58\%S$$
$$42\%S = \$84,000$$
$$S = \$200,000$$

If the sales commission proposal is adopted, the break-even point is raised to $210,000, computed as follows:

Break-Even Sales (in $) = Fixed Costs (in $) + Variable Costs (as % of Break-Even Sales)
$$S = \$84,000 + 60\%S$$
$$40\%S = \$84,000$$
$$S = \$210,000$$

The additional 2% sales commission (a variable cost) increases the break-even point by $10,000 of sales. If the proposal is adopted, 2% less of each sales dollar is available to cover the fixed costs of $84,000.

Effect of Changing Unit Selling Price. Increases in the unit selling price will lower the break-even point, while decreases in the unit selling price will raise the break-even point. To illustrate the effect of changing the unit selling price, assume that Graham Co. is evaluating a proposal to increase the unit selling price of its product from its current price of $50 to $60 and has accumulated the following relevant data:

	Current	Proposed
Unit selling price................................	$50	$60
Unit variable cost	$30	$30
Variable costs (as % of break-even sales):		
$30 unit variable cost ÷ $50 unit selling price.....	60%	
$30 unit variable cost ÷ $60 unit selling price.....		50%
Total fixed costs	$600,000	$600,000

The break-even point based on the current selling price is $1,500,000, computed as follows:

Break-Even Sales (in $) = Fixed Costs (in $) + Variable Costs (as % of Break-Even Sales)
$$S = \$600,000 + 60\%S$$
$$40\%S = \$600,000$$
$$S = \$1,500,000$$

If the selling price is increased by $10 per unit, the break-even point is decreased to $1,200,000, computed as follows:

Break-Even Sales (in $) = Fixed Costs (in $) + Variable Costs (as % of Break-Even Sales)
$$S = \$600,000 + \$50\%S$$
$$50\%S = \$600,000$$
$$S = \$1,200,000$$

The increase in selling price of $10 per unit decreases the break-even point by $300,000 (from $1,500,000 to $1,200,000). In terms of units of sales, the decrease is from 30,000 units ($1,500,000 ÷ $50) to 20,000 units ($1,200,000 ÷ $60).

Desired Profit

At the break-even point, sales and costs are exactly equal. However, business enterprises do not use the break-even point as their goal for future operations. Rather, they seek to achieve the largest possible volume of sales above the break-even point. By modifying the break-even equation, the sales volume required to earn a desired amount of profit may be estimated. For this purpose, a factor for desired profit is added to the standard break-even formula. To illustrate, assume that fixed costs are estimated at $200,000, variable costs are estimated at 60% of sales, and the desired profit is $100,000. The sales volume is $750,000, computed as follows:

Sales (in $) = Fixed Costs (in $) + Variable Costs (as % of Sales) + Desired Profit
$$S = \$200,000 + 60\%S + \$100,000$$
$$40\%S = \$300,000$$
$$S = \$750,000$$

The validity of the preceding computation is shown in the following income statement:

Sales		$750,000
Expenses:		
Variable costs ($750,000 × 60%)	$450,000	
Fixed costs...............................	200,000	650,000
Operating profit		$100,000

GRAPHIC APPROACH TO COST-VOLUME-PROFIT ANALYSIS

Cost-volume-profit analysis can be presented graphically as well as in equation form. Many managers prefer the graphic format because the operating profit or loss for any given level of capacity can be readily determined, without the necessity of solving an equation. The following paragraphs describe two graphic approaches which managers find useful.

Cost-Volume-Profit (Break-Even) Chart

A **cost-volume-profit chart,** sometimes called a **break-even chart,** is used to assist management in understanding the relationships between costs, sales, and operating profit or loss. To illustrate the cost-volume-profit chart, assume that fixed costs are estimated at $90,000, and variable costs are estimated as 60% of sales. The maximum sales at 100% of capacity is $400,000. The following cost-volume-profit chart is based on the foregoing data:

Cost-Volume-Profit Chart

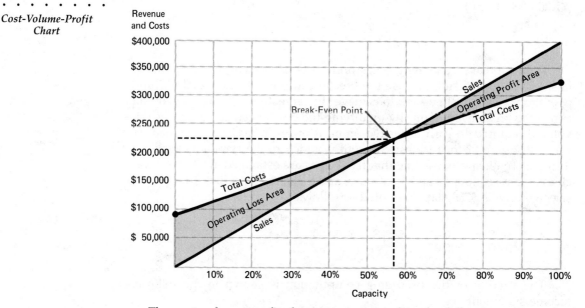

The cost-volume-profit chart is constructed in the following manner:

1. Percentages of capacity of the enterprise are spread along the horizontal axis, and dollar amounts representing operating data are spread along the vertical axis. The outside limits of the chart represent 100% of capacity and the maximum sales potential at that level of capacity.
2. A diagonal line representing sales is drawn from the lower left corner to the upper right corner.
3. A point representing fixed costs is plotted on the vertical axis at the left, and a point representing total costs at maximum capacity is plotted at the right edge of the chart. A diagonal line representing total costs at various percentages of capacity is then drawn connecting these two points.
4. Horizontal and vertical lines are drawn at the point of intersection of the sales and cost lines, which is the break-even point, and the areas representing operating profit and operating loss are identified.

In the illustration, the total costs at maximum capacity are $330,000 (fixed costs of $90,000 plus variable costs of $240,000, which is 60% of $400,000). The dotted line drawn from the point of intersection to the vertical axis identifies the break-even sales amount of $225,000. The dotted line drawn from the point of intersection to the horizontal axis identifies the break-even point in terms of capacity of approximately 56%. Operating profits will be earned when sales levels are to the right of the break-even point (operating profit area), and operating losses will be incurred when sales levels are to the left of the break-even point (operating loss area).

Changes in the unit selling price, total fixed costs, and unit variable costs can also be analyzed using a cost-volume-profit chart. To illustrate, using the preceding example, assume that a proposal to reduce fixed costs by $42,000 is to be evaluated. In this situation, the total fixed costs would be $48,000 ($90,000 − $42,000), and the total costs at maximum capacity would amount to $288,000 ($48,000 of fixed costs plus variable costs of $240,000). The preceding cost-volume-profit chart is revised by plotting the points representing the total fixed cost and the total cost and drawing a line between the two points, indicating the proposed total cost line. The following revised chart indicates that the break-even point would decrease to $120,000 of sales (30% of capacity).

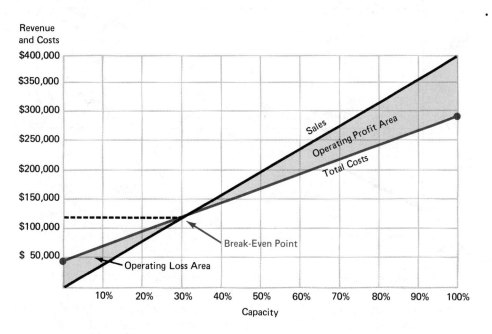

Revised Cost-Volume-Profit Chart

Profit-Volume Chart

Rather than focusing on sales revenues and costs, as was the case for the cost-volume-profit chart, another graphic approach to cost-volume-profit analysis, called the **profit-volume chart**, focuses on profitability. On the profit-volume chart, only the difference between total sales revenues and total costs is plotted, which enables management to determine the operating profit (or loss) for various levels of operations.

To illustrate the profit-volume chart, assume that fixed costs are estimated at $50,000, variable costs are estimated at 75% of sales, and the maximum capacity is $500,000 of sales. The maximum operating loss is equal to the fixed costs of $50,000, and the maximum operating profit at 100% of capacity is $75,000, computed as follows:

Sales		$500,000
Expenses:		
Variable costs ($500,000 × 75%)	$375,000	
Fixed costs................................	50,000	425,000
Operating profit		$ 75,000

The following profit-volume chart is based on the foregoing data:

Profit-Volume Chart

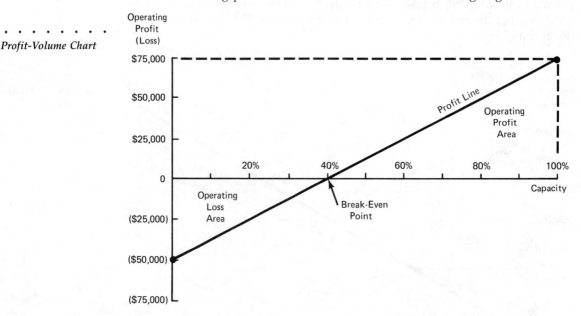

The profit-volume chart is constructed in the following manner:

1. Percentages of capacity of the enterprise are spread along the horizontal axis, and dollar amounts representing operating profits and losses are spread along the vertical axis.
2. A point representing the maximum operating loss is plotted on the vertical axis at the left. This loss is equal to the total fixed costs at 0% of capacity.
3. A point representing the maximum operating profit at 100% of capacity is plotted on the right.
4. A diagonal profit line is drawn connecting the maximum operating loss point with the maximum operating profit point.

5. The profit line intersects the horizontal axis at the break-even point expressed as a percentage of capacity, and the areas representing operating profit and operating loss are identified.

In the illustration, the break-even point is 40% of productive capacity, which can be converted to $200,000 of total sales (maximum capacity of $500,000 × 40%). Operating profit will be earned when sales levels are to the right of the break-even point (operating profit area), and operating losses will be incurred when sales levels are to the left of the break-even point (operating loss area). For example, at 60% of productive capacity, an operating profit of $25,000 will be earned, as indicated in the following profit-volume chart:

Profit-Volume Chart

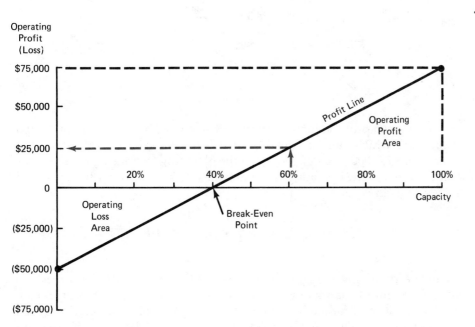

The effect of changes in the unit selling price, total fixed costs, and unit variable costs on profit can be analyzed using a profit-volume chart. To illustrate, using the preceding example, assume that the effect on profit of an increase of $25,000 in fixed costs is to be evaluated. In this case, the total fixed costs would be $75,000 ($50,000 + $25,000), and the maximum operating loss at 0% of capacity would be $75,000. The maximum operating profit at 100% of capacity would be $50,000, computed as follows:

Sales		$500,000
Expenses:		
Variable costs ($500,000 × 75%)	$375,000	
Fixed costs	75,000	450,000
Operating profit		$ 50,000

A revised profit-volume chart is constructed by plotting the maximum operating loss and maximum operating profit points and drawing a line between the two points, indicating the revised profit line. The original and the revised profit-volume charts are as follows:

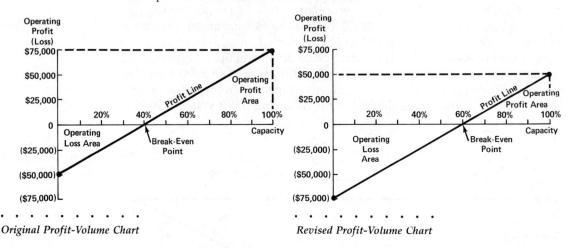

Original Profit-Volume Chart   *Revised Profit-Volume Chart*

The revised profit-volume chart indicates that the break-even point is 60% of capacity, which can be converted to total sales of $300,000 (maximum capacity of $500,000 × 60%). Note that the operating loss area of the chart has increased, while the operating profit area has decreased under the proposed change in fixed costs.

USE OF COMPUTERS IN COST-VOLUME-PROFIT ANALYSIS

In the preceding paragraphs, the use of the mathematical approach to cost-volume-profit analysis and the use of the cost-volume-profit chart and the profit-volume chart for analyzing the effect of changes in selling price, costs, and volume on profits have been demonstrated. Both the mathematical and graphic approaches are becoming increasingly popular and easy to use when managers have access to a computer terminal or a microcomputer. With the wide variety of computer software that is available, managers can vary assumptions regarding selling prices, costs, and volume and can instantaneously analyze the effects of each assumption on the break-even point and profit.

Break-Even Analysis — A Case Study

A break-even analysis based on a multidimensional approach, rather than the traditional two-dimensional approach, was described in an article in *The Journal of Accountancy*. Such an approach is used by The Motor Convoy Inc.'s Chief Financial Officer, who prepared the following break-even chart. The Motor Convoy Inc. is a Georgia-based common carrier operating primarily in the southeastern United States.

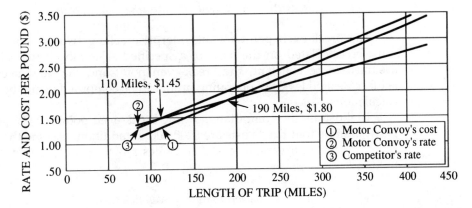

The chart illustrates a typical break-even analysis at The Motor Convoy for a normal load of 2,000 pounds over a relevant range of trips — from about 100 miles to 450 miles. The rate and cost per pound are plotted along the vertical axis, while the length of the trip (in miles) is plotted along the horizontal axis. The rate charged by The Motor Convoy's primary competitor is also graphed, so that the company can assess the effect of competition on developing its operating strategy.

In the above chart, the rate and cost curves are drawn only in the relevant range. The competitor's rate curve is parallel to The Motor Convoy's cost curve, and both rate curves cross at 110 miles. At this volume, The Motor Convoy's business should be concentrated on trips between 110 miles and 190 miles. On shorter trips, the competition is cheaper than The Motor Convoy, while on longer trips, The Motor Convoy is losing money.

Source: "Multidimensional Break-Even Analysis," *The Journal of Accountancy* (January, 1987), pp. 132–133.

SALES MIX CONSIDERATIONS

In many businesses, more than one product is sold at varying selling prices. In addition, the products often have different unit variable costs, and each product makes a different contribution to profits. Thus, the total business profit, as well as the break-even point, depends upon the proportions in which the products are sold.

Sales mix is the relative distribution of sales among the various products sold by an enterprise. For example, assume that the sales for Cascade Company during the past year, a typical year for the company, are as follows:

Product	Units Sold	Sales Mix
A	8,000	80%
B	2,000	20
	10,000	100%

The sales mix for products A and B can be expressed as a relative percentage, as shown above, or as the ratio of 80:20.

Sales Mix and the Break-Even Point

The break-even point for an enterprise selling two or more products must be calculated on the basis of a specified sales mix. If the sales mix is assumed to be constant, the break-even point and the sales necessary to achieve desired levels of operating profit can be computed using the standard calculations.

To illustrate the computation of the break-even point for Cascade Company, assume that fixed costs are $200,000. In addition, assume that the unit selling prices, unit variable costs, and sales mix for products A and B are as follows:

Product	Selling Price per Unit	Variable Cost per Unit	Sales Mix
A	$ 90	$70	80%
B	140	95	20

To compute the break-even point when several products are sold, it is useful to think of the individual products as components of one overall enterprise product. For Cascade Company, assume that this overall enterprise product is arbitrarily labeled E. The unit selling price of E can be thought of as equal to the total of the unit selling prices of the individual products A and B, multiplied by their respective sales mix percentages. Likewise, the unit variable cost of E can be thought of as equal to the total of the unit variable costs of products A and B, multiplied by the sales mix percentages. These computations are as follows:

Unit selling price of E: ($90 × .8) + ($140 × .2) = $100
Unit variable cost of E: ($70 × .8) + ($95 × .2) = $75

The variable costs for enterprise product E are therefore expected to be 75% of sales ($75 ÷ 100). The break-even point can be determined in the normal manner, using the equation, as follows:

Break-Even Sales (in $) = Fixed Costs (in $) + Variable Costs (as % of Break-Even Sales)
S = $200,000 + 75%S
25%S = $200,000
S = $800,000

The break-even point of $800,000 of sales of enterprise product E is equivalent to 8,000 total sales units ($800,000 ÷ $100). Since the sales mix for products A and B is 80% and 20% respectively, the break-even quantity of A is 6,400 (8,000 × 80%) and B is 1,600 (8,000 × 20%) units.

The validity of the preceding analysis can be verified by preparing the following income statement:

Cascade Company
Income Statement
For Year Ended December 31, 19--

	Product A	Product B	Total
Sales:			
6,400 units × $90	$576,000		$576,000
1,600 units × $140		$224,000	224,000
Total sales	$576,000	$224,000	$800,000
Variable costs:			
6,400 units × $70	$448,000		$448,000
1,600 units × $95		$152,000	152,000
Total variable costs	$448,000	$152,000	$600,000
Fixed costs			200,000
Total costs			$800,000
Operating profit			-0-

The effects of changes in the sales mix on the break-even point can be determined by repeating the preceding analysis, assuming a different sales mix.

Sales Mix and Desired Profit

The sales volume needed to earn an amount of profit when an enterprise sells two or more products can be computed using an approach similar to that described in the previous section. For example, the total sales necessary for Cascade Company to earn an operating profit of $40,000, with the original sales mix of 80% and 20% (where fixed costs were $200,000 and variable costs were 75% of sales), can be computed by use of the concept of an overall enterprise product E and solving the following equation:

Sales (in $) = Fixed Costs (in $) + Variable Costs (as a % of Sales) + Desired Profit
$$S = \$200,000 + 75\%S + \$40,000$$
$$25\%S = \$240,000$$
$$S = \$960,000$$

Sales of $960,000 of enterprise product E is equivalent to 9,600 total sales units ($960,000 ÷ $100). Since the sales mix for products A and B is 80% and 20% respectively, the quantity of A to be sold is 7,680 (9,600 × 80%) and B is

1,920 (9,600 × 20%) units. The validity of this approach can be verified by preparing the following income statement:

Cascade Company
Income Statement
For Year Ended December 31, 19--

	Product A	Product B	Total
Sales:			
7,680 units × $90	$691,200		$691,200
1,920 units × $140		$268,800	268,800
Total sales.........................	$691,200	$268,800	$960,000
Variable costs:			
7,680 units × $70	$537,600		$537,600
1,920 units × $95		$182,400	182,400
Total variable costs	$537,600	$182,400	$720,000
Fixed costs			200,000
Total costs.........................			$920,000
Operating profit.....................			$ 40,000

SPECIAL COST-VOLUME-PROFIT RELATIONSHIPS

Additional relationships can be developed from the information presented in both the mathematical and graphic approaches to cost-volume-profit analysis. Two of these relationships that are especially useful to management in decision making are discussed in the following paragraphs.

Margin of Safety

The difference between the current sales revenue and the sales at the break-even point is called the **margin of safety**. It represents the possible decrease in sales revenue that may occur before an operating loss results, and it may be stated either in terms of dollars or as a percentage of sales. For example, if the volume of sales is $250,000 and sales at the break-even point amount to $200,000, the margin of safety is $50,000 or 20%, as shown by the following computation:

$$\text{Margin of Safety} = \frac{\text{Sales} - \text{Sales at Break-Even Point}}{\text{Sales}}$$

$$\text{Margin of Safety} = \frac{\$250,000 - \$200,000}{\$250,000} = 20\%$$

The margin of safety is useful in evaluating past operations and as a guide to business planning. For example, if the margin of safety is low, management should carefully study forecasts of future sales because even a small decline in sales revenue will result in an operating loss.

Contribution Margin Ratio

Another relationship between cost, volume, and profits that is especially useful in business planning because it gives an insight into the profit potential of a firm is the **contribution margin ratio,** sometimes called the **profit-volume ratio.** This ratio indicates the percentage of each sales dollar available to cover the fixed expenses and to provide operating income. For example, if the volume of sales is $250,000 and variable expenses amount to $175,000, the contribution margin ratio is 30%, as shown by the following computation:

$$\text{Contribution Margin Ratio} = \frac{\text{Sales} - \text{Variable Expenses}}{\text{Sales}}$$

$$\text{Contribution Margin Ratio} = \frac{\$250,000 - \$175,000}{\$250,000} = 30\%$$

The contribution margin ratio permits the quick determination of the effect on operating income of an increase or a decrease in sales volume. To illustrate, assume that the management of a firm with a contribution margin ratio of 30% is studying the effect on operating income of adding $25,000 in sales orders. Multiplying the ratio (30%) by the change in sales volume ($25,000) indicates an increase in operating income of $7,500 if the additional orders are obtained. In using the analysis in such a case, factors other than sales volume, such as the amount of fixed expenses, the percentage of variable expenses to sales, and the unit sales price, are assumed to remain constant. If these factors are not constant, the effect of any change must be considered in applying the analysis.

The contribution margin ratio is also useful in setting business policy. For example, if the contribution margin ratio of a firm is large and production is at a level below 100% capacity, a comparatively large increase in operating income can be expected from an increase in sales volume. On the other hand, a comparatively large decrease in operating income can be expected from a decline in sales volume. A firm in such a position might decide to devote more effort to additional sales promotion because of the large change in operating income that will result from changes in sales volume. On the other hand, a firm with a small contribution margin ratio will probably want to give more attention to reducing costs and expenses before concentrating large efforts on additional sales promotion.

LIMITATIONS OF COST-VOLUME-PROFIT ANALYSIS

The reliability of cost-volume-profit analysis depends upon the validity of several assumptions. One major assumption is that there is no change in inventory quantities during the year; that is, the quantity of units in the beginning inventory equals the quantity of units in the ending inventory. When changes in inventory quantities occur, the computations for cost-volume-profit analysis become more complex.

For cost-volume-profit analysis, a relevant range of activity is assumed, within which all costs can be classified as either fixed or variable. Within the relevant range, which is usually a range of activity within which the company is likely to operate, the unit variable costs and the total fixed costs will not change. For example, within the relevant range of activity, factory supervisory salaries are fixed. For cost-volume-profit analysis, it is assumed that a significant change in activity that would cause these salaries to change, such as adding a night shift that would double production, will not occur.

These assumptions simplify cost-volume-profit relationships, and since substantial variations in the assumptions are often uncommon in practice, cost-volume-profit analysis can be used quite effectively in decision making. Under conditions of substantial variations from the assumptions, the analysis of the cost-volume-profit relationships must be used cautiously.

Chapter Review

KEY POINTS

1. Cost-Volume-Profit Relationships.

Cost-volume-profit analysis is the systematic examination of the interrelationships between selling prices, volume of sales and production, costs, expenses, and profits. Accountants can play an important role in cost-volume-profit analysis by providing management with information on the relative profitability of its various products, the probable effects of changes in selling price, and other variables.

In cost-volume-profit analysis, costs are subdivided into two categories: (1) variable and (2) fixed. Variable costs are costs that change, in total, as the volume of activity changes. Fixed costs remain constant, in total, as the volume of activity changes. Mixed costs are costs that have both variable and fixed characteristics. For purposes of analysis, mixed costs can generally be separated into variable and fixed components.

2. Mathematical Approach to Cost-Volume-Profit Analysis.

The mathematical approach to cost-volume-profit analysis uses equations (1) to indicate the revenues necessary to achieve the break-even point in operations or (2) to indicate the revenues necessary to achieve a desired or target profit. The level of operations of an enterprise at which revenues and expired costs are exactly equal is called the break-even point. The break-even point can be determined using the following equation:

Break-Even Sales (in $) = Fixed Costs (in $) + Variable Costs (as % of Break-Even Sales)

The break-even point is raised by increases in fixed costs, increases in variable costs, or decreases in the unit selling price. The break-even point is lowered by decreases in fixed costs, decreases in variable costs, or increases in the unit selling price. By modifying the break-even equation and adding a factor for desired profit, the sales volume required to earn a desired amount of profit may be estimated.

3. Graphic Approach to Cost-Volume-Profit Analysis.

Many managers prefer to use a graphic format for cost-volume-profit analysis because the operating profit or loss for any given level of capacity can be readily determined, without the necessity of solving an equation. A cost-volume-profit chart is used to assist management in understanding the relationships between costs, sales, and operating profit or loss. Changes in the unit selling price, total fixed costs, and unit variable costs can also be analyzed using a cost-volume-profit chart. Another graphic approach to cost-volume-profit analysis, called the profit-volume chart, focuses on profitability rather than on sales revenues and costs. The effect of changes in unit selling price, total fixed costs, and unit variable costs on profit can also be analyzed using a profit-volume chart.

4. Use of Computers in Cost-Volume-Profit Analysis.

Both the mathematical and graphic approaches to cost-volume-profit analysis are becoming increasing popular and easy to use when managers have access to a computer terminal or a microcomputer. With the wide variety of computer software that is available, managers can vary assumptions regarding selling prices, costs, and volume and can instantaneously analyze the effects of each assumption on the break-even point and profit.

5. Sales Mix Considerations.

The break-even point for an enterprise selling two or more products must be calculated on the basis of a specified sales mix. If the sales mix is assumed to be constant, the break-even point can be computed using the standard approaches.

6. Special Cost-Volume-Profit Relationships.

The difference between the current sales revenue and the sales at the break-even point is called the margin of safety. The margin of safety is useful in evaluating past operations and as a guide to business planning. Another relationship between costs, volume, and profits that is especially useful in business planning because it gives an insight into the profit potential of a firm is the contribution margin ratio. This ratio indicates the percentage of each sales dollar available to cover the fixed costs and expenses and to provide operating income. The contribution margin ratio permits the quick determination of the effect on operating income of an increase or a decrease in sales volume.

7. Limitations of Cost-Volume-Profit Analysis.

The reliability of cost-volume-profit analysis depends upon the validity of several assumptions. One major assumption is that there is no change in inventory quantities during the year. Another assumption is that the analysis is conducted within a relevant range of activity within which all costs can be classified as fixed or variable. These assumptions simplify cost-volume-profit relationships, and since substantial variations in the assumptions are often uncommon in practice, cost-volume-profit analysis can be used quite effectively in decision making.

KEY TERMS
·

cost-volume-profit analysis 193
variable costs 193
fixed costs 193
mixed costs 193
break-even point 194

cost-volume-profit chart 198
profit-volume chart 199
sales mix 203
margin of safety 206
contribution margin ratio 207

SELF-EXAMINATION QUESTIONS
·
(Answers at End of Chapter)

1. For cost-volume-profit analysis, costs must be classified as either fixed or variable. Variable costs:
   A. change in total as the volume of activity changes
   B. do not change in total as the volume of activity changes
   C. change on a per unit basis as the volume of activity changes
   D. none of the above

2. If variable costs are 40% of sales and fixed costs are $240,000, what is the break-even point?
   A. $200,000 C. $400,000
   B. $240,000 D. None of the above

3. Based on the data presented in Question 2, how much sales would be required to realize operating profit of $30,000?
   A. $400,000 C. $600,000
   B. $450,000 D. None of the above

4. If sales were $500,000, variable costs are $200,000, and fixed costs are $240,000, what is the margin of safety?
   A. 20%   C. 60%
   B. 40%   D. None of the above

5. Based on the data presented in Question 4, what is the contribution margin ratio?
   A. 40%   C. 88%
   B. 48%   D. None of the above.

ILLUSTRATIVE PROBLEM

Nissat Company expects to maintain the same inventories at the end of the year as at the beginning of the year. The estimated fixed costs and expenses for the year are $360,000 and the estimated variable costs and expenses per unit are $9. It is expected that 75,000 units will be sold at a selling price of $15 per unit. Capacity output is 80,000 units.

Instructions:

1. Determine the break-even point (a) in dollars of sales, (b) in units, and (c) in terms of capacity.
2. Construct a cost-volume-profit chart, indicating the break-even point in dollars of sales.
3. Construct a profit-volume chart, indicating the break-even point as a percentage of capacity.
4. What is the expected margin of safety?
5. What is the contribution margin ratio?

SOLUTION

(1) (a) Break-even point in dollars of sales:
$$S = \$360,000 + 60\%S$$
$$S - 60\%S = \$360,000$$
$$S = \$900,000$$

(b) Break-even point in units:
$$\$900,000 \div \$15 = 60,000 \text{ units}$$

(c) Break-even point in terms of capacity:
$$60,000 \div 80,000 = 75\%$$

(2)

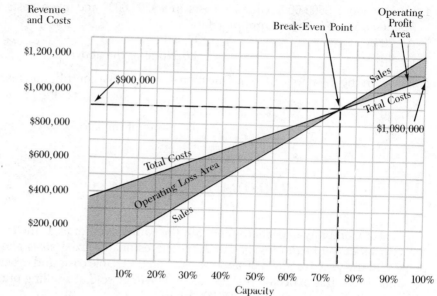

(3)

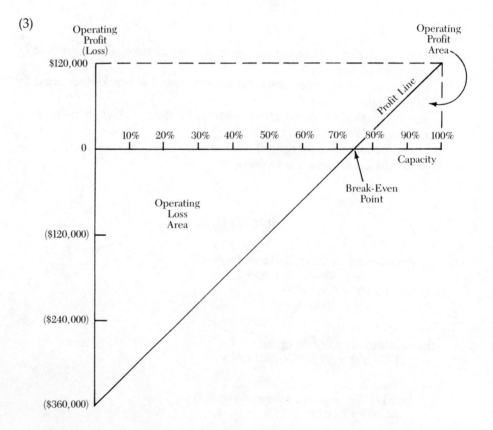

(4) Margin of safety:

Expected sales (75,000 units @ $15)............. $1,125,000
Break-even point............................... 900,000
Margin of safety .... $ 225,000 or 20%

(5) Contribution margin ratio $= \dfrac{\text{Sales} - \text{Variable Expenses}}{\text{Sales}}$

$$= \dfrac{\$1,125,000 - (75,000 \times \$9)}{\$1,125,000}$$

$$= \dfrac{\$450,000}{\$1,125,000}$$

$$= 40\%$$

Discussion Questions

6–1. How do changes in volume of activity affect (a) total variable costs and (b) total fixed costs?

6–2. If total fixed costs are $84,000, what is the unit fixed cost if production is (a) 20,000 units and (b) 35,000 units?

6–3. (a) What is the break-even point? (b) What equation can be used to determine the break-even point?

6–4. If sales are $800,000, variable costs are $520,000, and fixed costs are $175,000, what is the break-even point?

6–5. If fixed costs are $320,000 and variable costs are 60% of sales, what is the break-even point?

6–6. If the unit cost of direct materials is decreased, what effect will this change have on the break-even point?

6–7. If the property tax rates are increased, what effect will this change in fixed costs have on the break-even point?

6–8. If fixed costs are $250,000 and variable costs are 65% of sales, what sales are required to realize an operating profit of $100,000?

6–9. What is the advantage of presenting cost-volume-profit analysis in the chart form over the equation form?

6–10. Name the following chart and identify the items represented by the letters *a* through *f*.

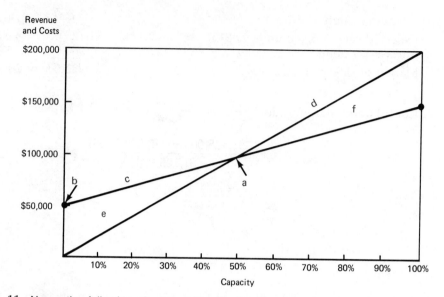

6–11. Name the following chart and identify the items represented by the letters *a* through *f*.

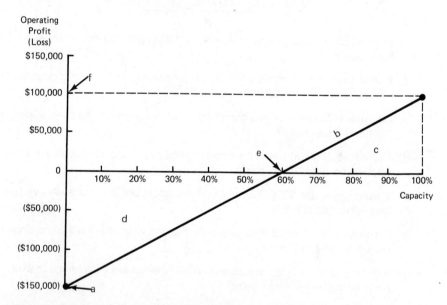

6–12. Both Harris Company and Lammers Company had the same sales, total costs, and operating profit for the current fiscal year, yet Harris Company had a lower break-even point than Lammers Company. Explain the reason for this difference in break-even points.

6–13. (a) What is meant by *sales mix*? (b) For conventional break-even analysis, is the sales mix assumed to be constant?

6–14. (a) What is meant by the term *margin of safety?* (b) If sales are $600,000, net income is $50,400, and sales at the break-even point are $480,000, what is the margin of safety?

6–15. What ratio indicates the percentage of each sales dollar that is available to cover fixed costs and to provide a profit?

6–16. (a) If sales are $180,000 and variable costs are $126,000, what is the contribution margin ratio? (b) What is the contribution margin ratio if variable costs are 65% of sales?

6–17. An examination of the accounting records of Cardel Company disclosed a high contribution margin ratio and production at a level below maximum capacity. Based on this information, suggest a likely means of improving operating profit. Explain.

6–18. Real World Focus. The 1986 annual report of William Wrigley Jr. Company indicates that, compared to the previous year, net sales were approximately $80,000,000 higher, and income from operations was approximately $10,000,000 higher. The William Wrigley Jr. Company has operated above the break-even point throughout the 1980s. Assuming that fixed costs and expenses did not change significantly from the prior year, what is the estimated contribution margin for William Wrigley Jr. Company?

Exercises

6–19. **Break-even point and sales to realize operating profit.** For the current year ending October 31, Duval Company expects fixed costs and expenses of $72,000 and variable costs and expenses equal to 64% of sales.

(a) Compute the anticipated break-even point.
(b) Compute the sales required to realize operating profit of $43,200.

6–20. **Break-even point.** For the past year, DeLong Company had fixed costs of $342,000 and variable costs equal to 55% of sales. All revenues and costs are expected to remain constant for the coming year, except that property taxes are expected to increase by $27,000 during the year.

EADSHEET
ROBLEM

(a) Compute the break-even point for the past year.
(b) Compute the anticipated break-even point for the coming year.

6–21. **Break-even point.** For the current year ending May 31, Lynch Company expects fixed costs of $420,000 and variable costs equal to 65% of sales. For the coming year, a new wage contract will increase variable costs to 70% of sales.

(a) Compute the break-even point for the current year.
(b) Compute the anticipated break-even point for the coming year, assuming that all revenues and costs are to remain constant, with the exception of the costs represented by the new wage contract.

6–22. Break-even point. Currently the unit selling price of a product is $40, the unit variable cost is $27, and the total fixed costs are $52,000. A proposal is being evaluated to increase the unit selling price to $45.

(a) Compute the current break-even point.
(b) Compute the anticipated break-even point, assuming that the unit selling price is increased and all costs remain constant.

6–23. Profit-volume chart. For the coming year, Inwood Inc. anticipates fixed costs of $200,000, variable costs equal to 60% of sales, and maximum capacity of $1,000,000 of sales.

(a) What is the maximum possible operating loss?
(b) Compute the maximum possible operating profit.
(c) Construct a profit-volume chart.
(d) Determine the break-even point as a percentage of capacity by using the profit-volume chart constructed in (c).

6–24. Margin of safety. (a) If Tucker Company, with a break-even point at $420,000 of sales, has actual sales of $700,000, what is the margin of safety expressed (1) in dollars and (2) as a percentage of sales? (b) If the margin of safety for Faust Company was 25%, fixed costs were $240,000, and variable costs were 60% of sales, what was the amount of actual sales?

6–25. Contribution margin ratio. (a) If Woodall Company budgets sales of $750,000, fixed costs and expenses of $120,000, and variable costs and expenses of $480,000, what is the anticipated contribution margin ratio? (b) If the contribution margin ratio for Austin Company is 28%, sales were $850,000, and fixed costs and expenses were $88,000, what was the operating profit?

6–26. Computation of break-even point, variable and fixed costs, and operating profit. For the past year, Gonzales Company had sales of $1,200,000, a margin of safety of 15%, and a contribution margin ratio of 40%. Compute:

(a) The break-even point.
(b) The variable costs and expenses.
(c) The fixed costs and expenses.
(d) The operating profit.

6–27. Computation of break-even point, sales, and operating profit. For 1989, a company had sales of $1,800,000, fixed costs of $300,000, and a contribution margin ratio of 25%. During 1990, the variable costs were 75% of sales, the fixed costs did not change from the previous year, and the margin of safety was 20%.

(a) What was the operating profit for 1989?
(b) What was the break-even point for 1990?
(c) What was the amount of sales for 1990?
(d) What was the operating profit for 1990?

6–28. Real World Focus. The following income statement data were taken from the 1986 financial statements of Pillsbury Company:

	(In millions)
Net sales.....................................	$5,847.9
Costs and expenses:	
Cost of sales	$4,102.6
Selling, general, and administrative expenses	1,270.9
Interest expense	97.3
	$5,470.8
Income before income tax............................	$ 377.1

Assume that the costs and expenses have been classified into the following fixed and variable components:

	Fixed	Variable
Cost of sales	20%	80%
Selling, general, and administrative expenses	40%	60%
Interest expense	100%	0%

Based on the above data, determine (a) the break-even point for Pillsbury Company and (b) the margin of safety expressed in sales dollars and as a percentage of 1986 sales. Round computations to one decimal place.

Problems

.

6–29. Break-even point and cost-volume-profit chart. For the coming year, Peak Company anticipates fixed costs of $300,000 and variable costs equal to 70% of sales.

Instructions:

(1) Compute the anticipated break-even point.
(2) Compute the sales required to realize an operating profit of $90,000.
(3) Construct a cost-volume-profit chart, assuming sales of $2,000,000 at full capacity.
(4) Determine the probable operating profit if sales total $1,600,000.

6–30. Break-even point and cost-volume-profit chart. Hooper Company operated at 80% of capacity last year, when sales were $800,000. Fixed costs were $240,000, and variable costs were 60% of sales. Hooper Company is considering a proposal to spend an additional $40,000 on billboard advertising during the current year in an attempt to increase sales and utilize additional capacity.

Instructions:

(1) Construct a cost-volume-profit chart indicating the break-even point for last year.
(2) Using the cost-volume-profit chart prepared in (1), determine (a) the operating profit for last year and (b) the maximum operating profit that could have been realized during the year.

(continued)

(3) Construct a cost-volume-profit chart indicating the break-even point for the current year, assuming that a noncancelable contract is signed for the additional billboard advertising. No changes are expected in unit selling price or other costs.

(4) Using the cost-volume-profit chart prepared in (3), determine (a) the operating profit if sales total $800,000 and (b) the maximum operating profit that could be realized during the year.

6–31. Break-even point and profit-volume chart. Last year, Randall Company had sales of $300,000, fixed costs of $50,000, and variable costs of $225,000. Randall Company is considering a proposal to spend $12,500 to hire a public relations firm, hoping that the company's image can be improved and sales increased. Maximum operating capacity is $500,000 of sales.

Instructions:

(1) Construct a profit-volume chart for last year.
(2) Using the profit-volume chart prepared in (1), determine for last year (a) the break-even point, (b) the operating profit, and (c) the maximum operating profit that could have been realized.
(3) Construct a profit-volume chart for the current year, assuming that the additional $12,500 expenditure is made and there is no change in unit selling price or other costs.
(4) Using the profit-volume chart prepared in (3), determine (a) the break-even point, (b) the operating profit if sales total $300,000, and (c) the maximum operating profit that could be realized.

6–32. Sales mix and break-even point. Data related to the expected sales of products A and B for Gowdy Company for the current year, which is typical of recent years, are as follows:

Product	Selling Price per Unit	Variable Cost per Unit	Sales Mix
A	$160	$ 88	75%
B	200	144	25

The estimated fixed costs for the current year are $544,000.

Instructions:

(1) Determine the estimated sales revenues necessary to reach the break-even point for the current year.
(2) Based on the break-even point in (1), determine the unit sales of both A and B for the current year.
(3) Determine the estimated sales revenues necessary for Gowdy Company to realize an operating profit of $136,000 for the current year.
(4) Based on the sales revenues determined in (3), determine the unit sales of both A and B for the current year.

6–33. Break-even point and cost-volume-profit chart, margin of safety, and contribution margin ratio. Joyce Company expects to maintain the same inventories at the end of 1990 as at the beginning of the year. The total of all production costs for the year is therefore assumed to be equal to the cost of goods sold. With this in mind, the various department heads were asked to submit estimates of the expenses for their departments during 1990. A summary report of these estimates is as follows:

	Estimated Fixed Expense	Estimated Variable Expense (per unit sold)
Production costs:		
Direct materials	—	$ 5.40
Direct labor........................	—	12.60
Factory overhead	$150,000	2.00
Selling expenses:		
Sales salaries and commissions	50,000	.60
Advertising	25,400	—
Travel...........................	5,600	—
Miscellaneous selling expense	1,200	.15
General expenses:		
Office and officers' salaries..........	30,000	—
Supplies..........................	5,100	.20
Miscellaneous general expense	2,700	.05
	$270,000	$21.00

It is expected that 40,000 units will be sold at a selling price of $30 a unit. Capacity output is 50,000 units.

Instructions:

(1) Determine the break-even point (a) in dollars of sales, (b) in units, and (c) in terms of capacity.
(2) Prepare an estimated income statement for 1990.
(3) Construct a cost-volume-profit chart, indicating the break-even point in dollars of sales.
(4) What is the expected margin of safety?
(5) What is the expected contribution margin ratio?

6–34. Break-even point under present and proposed conditions. Fain Company operated at full capacity during 1990. Its income statement for 1990 is as follows:

Sales		$4,000,000
Cost of goods sold		2,400,000
Gross profit..............................		$1,600,000
Operating expenses:		
Selling expenses.......................	$850,000	
General expenses.......................	250,000	
Total operating expenses...............		1,100,000
Operating profit		$ 500,000

The division of costs and expenses between fixed and variable is as follows:

	Fixed	Variable
Cost of goods sold	15%	85%
Selling expenses.	10%	90%
General expenses	22%	78%

Management is considering a plant expansion program that will permit an increase of $800,000 in yearly sales. The expansion will increase fixed costs and expenses by $150,000, but will not affect the relationship between sales and variable costs and expenses.

Instructions:

(1) Determine for present capacity (a) the total fixed costs and expenses and (b) the total variable costs and expenses.
(2) Determine the percentage of total variable costs and expenses to sales.
(3) Compute the break-even point under present conditions.
(4) Compute the break-even point under the proposed program.
(5) Determine the amount of sales that would be necessary under the proposed program to realize the $500,000 of operating profit that was earned in 1990.
(6) Determine the maximum operating profit possible with the expanded plant.
(7) If the proposal is accepted and sales remain at the 1990 level, what will the operating profit or loss be for 1991?
(8) Based on the data given, would you recommend accepting the proposal? Explain.

ALTERNATE PROBLEMS

6–29A.   **Break-even point and cost-volume-profit chart.**   For the coming year, Reece Company anticipates fixed costs of $140,000 and variable costs equal to 60% of sales.

Instructions:

(1) Compute the anticipated break-even point.
(2) Compute the sales required to realize an operating profit of $40,000.
(3) Construct a cost-volume-profit chart, assuming sales of $500,000 at full capacity.
(4) Determine the probable operating profit if sales total $400,000.

6–30A.   **Break-even point and cost-volume-profit chart.**   Chadwick Company operated at 70% of capacity last year, when sales totaled $700,000. Fixed costs were $125,000, and variable costs were 75% of sales. Chadwick Company is considering a proposal to spend an additional $25,000 on billboard advertising during the current year in an attempt to increase sales and utilize additional capacity.

Instructions:

(1) Construct a cost-volume-profit chart indicating the break-even point for last year.
(2) Using the cost-volume-profit chart prepared in (1), determine (a) the operating profit for last year and (b) the maximum operating profit that could have been realized during the year.

(3) Construct a cost-volume-profit chart indicating the break-even point for the current year, assuming that a noncancelable contract is signed for the additional billboard advertising. No changes are expected in unit selling price or other costs.

(4) Using the cost-volume-profit chart prepared in (3), determine (a) the operating profit if sales total $700,000 and (b) the maximum operating profit that could be realized during the year.

6–31A. Break-even point and profit-volume chart. Last year, Coggins Company had sales of $400,000, fixed costs of $50,000, and variable costs of $320,000. Coggins Company is considering a proposal to spend $10,000 to hire a public relations firm, hoping that the company's image can be improved and sales increased. Maximum operating capacity is $500,000 of sales.

Instructions:

(1) Construct a profit-volume chart for last year.

(2) Using the profit-volume chart prepared in (1), determine for last year (a) the break-even point, (b) the operating profit, and (c) the maximum operating profit that could have been realized.

(3) Construct a profit-volume chart for the current year, assuming that the additional $10,000 expenditure is made and there is no change in unit selling price or other costs.

(4) Using the profit-volume chart prepared in (3), determine (a) the break-even point, (b) the operating profit if sales total $400,000, and (c) the maximum operating profit that could be realized.

6–33A. Break-even point and cost-volume-profit chart, margin of safety, and contribution margin ratio. Spencer Company expects to maintain the same inventories at the end of 1990 as at the beginning of the year. The total of all production costs for the year is therefore assumed to be equal to the cost of goods sold. With this in mind, the various department heads were asked to submit estimates of the expenses for their departments during 1990. A summary report of these estimates is as follows:

SPREADSHEET PROBLEM

	Estimated Fixed Expense	Estimated Variable Expense (per unit sold)
Production costs:		
Direct materials	—	$ 3.25
Direct labor	—	8.70
Factory overhead	$120,000	1.80
Selling expenses:		
Sales salaries and commissions	60,000	.80
Advertising	35,200	—
Travel	21,800	—
Miscellaneous selling expense	7,000	.20
General expenses:		
Office and officers' salaries	40,000	—
Supplies	11,600	.15
Miscellaneous general expense	4,400	.10
	$300,000	$15.00

It is expected that 50,000 units will be sold at a selling price of $25 a unit. Capacity output is 60,000 units.

Instructions:

(1) Determine the break-even point (a) in dollars of sales, (b) in units, and (c) in terms of capacity.
(2) Prepare an estimated income statement for 1990.
(3) Construct a cost-volume-profit chart, indicating the break-even point in dollars of sales.
(4) What is the expected margin of safety?
(5) What is the expected contribution margin ratio?

Mini-Case 6

Owens Company manufactures product M, which sold for $45 per unit in 1989. For the past several years, sales and operating profit have been declining. On sales of $495,000 in 1989, the company operated near the break-even point and used only 55% of its productive capacity. Bill Owens, your father-in-law, is considering several proposals to reverse the trend of declining sales and operating profit, and to more fully use production facilities. One proposal under consideration is to reduce the unit selling price to $40.

Your father-in-law has asked you to aid him in assessing the proposal to reduce the sales price by $5. For this purpose, he provided the following summary of the estimated fixed and variable costs and expenses for 1990, which are unchanged from 1989:

Variable costs and expenses:
Production costs	$18.60 per unit
Selling expenses	6.20 per unit
General expenses	4.00 per unit

Fixed costs and expenses:
Production costs	$120,000
Selling expenses	30,000
General expenses	26,400

Instructions:

(1) Determine the break-even point for 1990 in dollars, assuming (a) no change in sales price and (b) the proposed sales price.
(2) How much additional sales are necessary for Owens Company to break even in 1990 under the proposal?
(3) Determine the operating profit for 1990, assuming (a) no change in sales price and volume from 1989 and (b) the new sales price and no change in volume from 1989.
(4) Determine the maximum operating profit for 1990, assuming the proposed sales price.
(5) Briefly list factors that you would discuss with your father-in-law in evaluating the proposal.

Answers to Self-Examination Questions

· · ·

1. **A** Variable costs change in total as the volume of activity changes (answer A) or, expressed in another way, the unit variable cost remains constant with changes in volume.

2. **C** The break-even point of $400,000 (answer C) is that level of operations at which revenue and expired costs are exactly equal and is determined as follows:

$$\text{Break-Even Sales (in \$)} = \text{Fixed Costs (in \$)} + \text{Variable Costs (as \% of Sales)}$$
$$S = \$240,000 + 40\%S$$
$$60\%S = \$240,000$$
$$S = \$400,000$$

3. **B** $450,000 of sales (answer B) would be required to realize operating profit of $30,000, computed as follows:

$$\text{Sales (in \$)} = \text{Fixed Costs (in \$)} + \text{Variable Costs (as \% of Sales)} + \text{Desired Profit}$$
$$S = \$240,000 + 40\%S + \$30,000$$
$$60\%S = \$270,000$$
$$S = \$450,000$$

4. A The margin of safety of 20% (answer A) represents the possible decrease in sales revenue that may occur before an operating loss results and is determined as follows:

$$\text{Margin of Safety} = \frac{\text{Sales} - \text{Sales at Break-Even Point}}{\text{Sales}}$$

$$= \frac{\$500,000 - \$400,000}{\$500,000}$$

$$= 20\%$$

The margin of safety can also be expressed in terms of dollars and would amount to $100,000, determined as follows:

Sales...	$500,000
Less sales at break-even point..............................	400,000
Margin of safety...	$100,000

5. D The contribution margin ratio indicates the percentage of each sales dollar available to cover the fixed expenses and provide operating income and is determined as follows:

$$\frac{\text{Contribution Margin}}{\text{Ratio}} = \frac{\text{Sales} - \text{Variable Expenses}}{\text{Sales}}$$

$$\frac{\text{Contribution Margin}}{\text{Ratio}} = \frac{\$500,000 - \$200,000}{\$500,000}$$

$$= 60\%$$

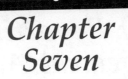

Chapter Seven

Profit Reporting for Management Analysis
7

The basic accounting systems used by manufacturers to provide accounting information useful to management in planning, organizing and directing, controlling, and decision making were described and illustrated in preceding chapters. In planning operations, the use of cost-volume-profit analysis, which was based on the discussion of cost behavior and cost estimation, was also discussed. In this chapter, two additional concepts useful to management in planning and controlling operations—gross profit analysis and variable costing—are described and illustrated.

GROSS PROFIT ANALYSIS

Gross profit is often considered the most significant intermediate figure in the income statement. It is common to determine its percentage relationship to sales and to make comparisons with prior periods. However, the mere knowledge of the percentages and the degree and direction of change from prior periods is insufficient. Management needs information about the causes. The procedure used in developing such information is termed **gross profit analysis**.

Since gross profit is the excess of sales over the cost of goods sold, a change in the amount of gross profit can be caused by (1) an increase or decrease in the amount of sales and (2) an increase or decrease in the amount of the cost of goods sold. An increase or decrease in either element may in turn be due to (1) a change in the number of units sold and (2) a change in the unit price. The effect of these two factors on either sales or cost of goods sold may be stated as follows:

1. **Quantity factor.** The effect of a change in the number of units sold, assuming no change in unit price.
2. **Price factor.** The effect of a change in unit price on the number of units sold.

The following data are to be used as the basis for illustrating gross profit analysis. For the sake of simplicity, a single commodity is assumed. The amount of detail entering into the analysis would be greater if a number of different commodities were sold, but the basic principles would not be affected.

	1990	1989	*Increase Decrease**
Sales	$900,000	$800,000	$100,000
Cost of goods sold	650,000	570,000	80,000
Gross profit.....................	$250,000	$230,000	$ 20,000
Number of units sold	125,000	100,000	25,000
Unit sales price	$7.20	$8.00	$.80*
Unit cost price	$5.20	$5.70	$.50*

The following analysis of these data shows that the favorable increase in the number of units sold was partially offset by a decrease in unit selling price. Also, the increase in the cost of goods sold due to increased quantity was partially offset by a decrease in unit cost.

Analysis of Increase in Gross Profit
For Year Ended December 31, 1990

*Gross Profit
Analysis Report*

Increase in amount of sales attributed to:
Quantity factor:
Increase in number of units sold
in 1990 25,000
Unit sales price in 1989............. × $8 $200,000

Price factor:
Decrease in unit sales price in 1990.. $.80
Number of units sold in 1990........ ×125,000 100,000

Net increase in amount of sales $100,000
Increase in amount of cost of goods sold attributed to:
Quantity factor:
Increase in number of units sold
in 1990 25,000
Unit cost price in 1989 .... × $5.70 $142,500

Price factor:
Decrease in unit cost price in 1990 .. $.50
Number of units sold in 1990........ ×125,000 62,500

Net increase in amount of cost of
goods sold........................ 80,000
Increase in gross profit................ $ 20,000

The data presented in the report may be useful both in evaluating past performance and in planning for the future. The importance of the cost reduction of $.50 a unit is quite clear. If the unit cost had not changed from the preceding year, the net increase in the amount of sales ($100,000) would have been more than offset by the increase in the cost of goods sold ($142,500), causing a decrease of $42,500 in gross profit. The $20,000 increase in gross profit actually attained was made possible, therefore, by the ability of management to reduce the unit cost of the commodity.

The means by which the $.50 reduction in the unit cost of the commodity was accomplished is also significant. If it was due to the spreading of fixed factory overhead costs over the larger number of units produced, the decision to reduce the sales price in order to achieve a larger volume was probably wise. On the other hand, if the $.50 reduction in unit cost was due to operating efficiencies entirely unrelated to the increased production, the $.80 reduction in the unit sales price was unwise. The accuracy of the conclusion can be demonstrated by comparing actual results with hypothetical results. The hypothetical results are based on (1) a sales volume that did not change from the 1989 level and (2) a unit cost reduction to $5.20 due to operating efficiencies. The following analysis shows the possible loss of an opportunity to have realized an additional gross profit of $30,000 ($280,000 − $250,000).

	Actual		Hypothetical	
Number of units sold......	125,000		100,000	
Unit sales price	$7.20		$8.00	
Sales		$900,000		$800,000
Unit cost price	$5.20		$5.20	
Cost of goods sold		650,000		520,000
Gross profit.............		$250,000		$280,000

If the reduction in unit cost had been achieved by a combination of spreading the fixed factory overhead over more production units and achieving operating efficiencies related to the increased production, the approximate effects of each could be determined by additional analyses. The methods used in gross profit analysis may also be extended, with some changes, to the analysis of changes in selling and general expenses.

ABSORPTION COSTING AND VARIABLE COSTING

In the preceding illustration of gross profit analysis, the importance of the cost of goods sold in determining income was emphasized. In determining the cost of goods sold, two alternate costing concepts can be used. These two costing concepts are absorption costing and variable costing.

The cost of manufactured products consists of direct materials, direct labor, and factory overhead. All such costs become a part of the finished goods inventory and remain there as an asset until the goods are sold. This conventional treatment of manufacturing costs is sometimes called **absorption costing** because all costs are "absorbed" into finished goods. Although the concept is necessary in determining historical costs and taxable income, another costing concept may be more useful to management in making decisions.

In **variable costing**, which is also termed **direct costing**, the cost of goods manufactured is composed only of variable costs—those manufacturing costs that increase or decrease as the volume of production rises or falls. These costs are the direct materials, direct labor, and only those factory overhead costs which vary with the rate of production. The remaining factory overhead costs, which are the fixed or nonvariable items, are related to the productive capacity of the manufacturing plant and are not affected by changes in the quantity of product manufactured. Accordingly, the fixed factory overhead does not become a part of the cost of goods manufactured, but is considered an expense of the period.

The distinction between absorption costing and variable costing is illustrated in the following diagram. Note that the difference between the two costing concepts is in the treatment of the fixed manufacturing costs, which consist of the fixed factory overhead costs.

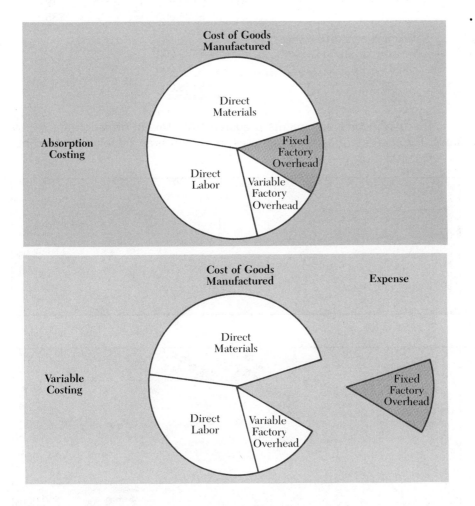

Absorption Costing Compared with Variable Costing

Variable Costing and the Income Statement

The arrangement of data in the variable costing income statement differs considerably from the format of the conventional income statement. Variable costs and expenses are presented separately from fixed costs and expenses, with significant summarizing amounts inserted at intermediate points. As a basis for illustrating the differences between the two forms, assume that 15,000 units were manufactured and sold at a unit price of $50 and the costs and expenses were as follows:

	Total Cost or Expense	Number of Units	Unit Cost
Manufacturing costs:			
Variable........................	$375,000	15,000	$25
Fixed	150,000	15,000	10
Total........................	$525,000		$35
Selling and general expenses:			
Variable ($5 per unit sold).........	$ 75,000		
Fixed	50,000		
Total........................	$125,000		

The two income statements prepared from this information are as follows. The computations in parentheses are shown as an aid to understanding.

Absorption Costing Income Statement

Absorption Costing Income Statement	
Sales (15,000 × $50)...	$750,000
Cost of goods sold (15,000 × $35)............................	525,000
Gross profit...	$225,000
Selling and general expenses ($75,000 + $50,000)...............	125,000
Income from operations......................................	$100,000

Variable Costing Income Statement

Variable Costing Income Statement		
Sales (15,000 × $50).....................................		$750,000
Variable cost of goods sold (15,000 × $25)..............		375,000
Manufacturing margin		$375,000
Variable selling and general expenses..................		75,000
Contribution margin		$300,000
Fixed costs and expenses:		
Fixed manufacturing costs	$150,000	
Fixed selling and general expenses	50,000	200,000
Income from operations.................................		$100,000

The absorption costing income statement does not distinguish between variable and fixed costs and expenses. All manufacturing costs are included in the cost of goods sold. The deduction of the cost of goods sold from sales yields the intermediate amount, gross profit. Deduction of selling and general expenses then yields income from operations.

In contrast, the variable costing income statement includes only the variable manufacturing costs in the cost of goods sold. Deduction of the cost of goods sold from sales yields an intermediate amount, termed **manufacturing margin.** Deduction of the variable selling and general expenses yields the **contribution margin,** or **marginal income.** The fixed costs and expenses are then deducted from the contribution margin to yield income from operations.

Units Manufactured Equal Units Sold. In the preceding illustration, 15,000 units were manufactured and sold. Both the absorption and the variable costing income statements reported the same income from operations of $100,000. Assuming no other changes, this equality of income will always be the case when the number of units manufactured and the number of units sold are equal. Only when the number of units manufactured and the number of units sold are not equal, which creates a change in the quantity of finished goods in inventory, will the income from operations differ under the two concepts.

Units Manufactured Exceed Units Sold. For any period in which the number of units manufactured exceeds the number of units sold, the operating income reported under the absorption costing concept will be larger than the operating income reported under the variable costing concept. To illustrate, assume that in the preceding example only 12,000 units of the 15,000 units manufactured were sold. The two income statements that result are as follows. Computations are inserted parenthetically as an aid to understanding.

Absorption Costing Income Statement		
Sales (12,000 × $50)		$600,000
Cost of goods sold:		
Cost of goods manufactured (15,000 × $35)	$525,000	
Less ending inventory (3,000 × $35)	105,000	
Cost of goods sold		420,000
Gross profit		$180,000
Selling and general expenses ($60,000 + $50,000)		110,000
Income from operations		$ 70,000

Variable Costing Income Statement		
Sales (12,000 × $50)................................		$600,000
Variable cost of goods sold:		
Variable cost of goods manufactured		
(15,000 × $25)...........................	$375,000	
Less ending inventory (3,000 × $25)................	75,000	
Variable cost of goods sold		300,000
Manufacturing margin		$300,000
Variable selling and general expenses...................		60,000
Contribution margin		$240,000
Fixed costs and expenses:		
Fixed manufacturing costs	$150,000	
Fixed selling and general expenses................	50,000	200,000
Income from operations..............................		$ 40,000

The $30,000 difference in the amount of income from operations ($70,000 − $40,000) is due to the different treatment of the fixed manufacturing costs. The entire amount of the $150,000 of fixed manufacturing costs is included as an expense of the period in the variable costing statement. The ending inventory in the absorption costing statement includes $30,000 (3,000 × $10) of fixed manufacturing costs. This $30,000, by being included in inventory on hand, is thus excluded from the current cost of goods sold and instead is deferred to another period.

Units Manufactured Less Than Units Sold. For any period in which the number of units manufactured is less than the number of units sold, the operating income reported under the absorption costing concept will be less than the operating income reported under the variable costing concept. To illustrate, assume that 5,000 units of inventory were on hand at the beginning of a period, 10,000 units were manufactured during the period, and 15,000 units were sold (10,000 units manufactured during the period plus the 5,000 units on hand at the beginning of the period) at $50 per unit. The manufacturing costs and selling and general expenses are as follows:

	Total Cost or Expense	Number of Units	Unit Cost
Beginning inventory:			
Manufacturing costs:			
Variable	$125,000	5,000	$25
Fixed....................	50,000	5,000	10
Total	$175,000		$35

	Total Cost or Expense	Number of Units	Unit Cost
Current period:			
Manufacturing costs:			
Variable	$250,000	10,000	$25
Fixed.	150,000	10,000	15
Total	$400,000		$40
Selling and general expenses:			
Variable ($5 per unit sold) .	$ 75,000		
Fixed.	50,000		
Total	$125,000		

The two income statements prepared from this information are as follows. Computations are inserted parenthetically as an aid to understanding.

. . . .

Absorption Costing Income Statement

Absorption Costing Income Statement		
Sales (15,000 × $50).		$750,000
Cost of goods sold:		
Beginning inventory (5,000 × $35).	$175,000	
Cost of goods manufactured (10,000 × $40)	400,000	
Cost of goods sold.		575,000
Gross profit.		$175,000
Selling and general expenses ($75,000 + $50,000).		125,000
Income from operations.		$ 50,000

. . . .

Variable Costing Income Statement

Variable Costing Income Statement		
Sales (15,000 × $50).		$750,000
Variable cost of goods sold:		
Beginning inventory (5,000 × $25).	$125,000	
Variable cost of goods manufactured		
(10,000 × $25).	250,000	
Variable cost of goods sold		375,000
Manufacturing margin		$375,000
Variable selling and general expenses.		75,000
Contribution margin		$300,000
Fixed costs and expenses:		
Fixed manufacturing costs	$150,000	
Fixed selling and general expenses.	50,000	200,000
Income from operations.		$100,000

The $50,000 difference ($100,000 − $50,000) in the amount of income from operations is attributable to the different treatment of the fixed manufacturing costs. The beginning inventory in the absorption costing income statement includes $50,000 (5,000 units × $10) of fixed manufacturing costs incurred in the preceding period. By being included in the beginning inventory, this $50,000 is included in the cost of goods sold for the current period. Under variable costing, however, this $50,000 was included as an expense in an income statement of a prior period. Therefore, none of it is included as an expense in the current period variable costing income statement.

Comparison of Income Reported Under the Two Concepts

The examples presented in the preceding sections illustrated the effects of the absorption costing and variable costing concepts on income from operations when the level of inventory changes during a period. These effects may be summarized as follows:

Units manufactured:

Equal units sold...............	Absorption costing income equals variable costing income.
Exceed units sold.............	Absorption costing income is greater than variable costing income.
Less than units sold...........	Absorption costing income is less than variable costing income

Income Analysis Under Absorption Costing

As was illustrated in the preceding examples, changes in the quantity of the finished goods inventory, caused by differences in the levels of sales and production, directly affect the amount of income from operations reported under absorption costing. Management should therefore be aware of the possible effects of changing inventory levels on operating income reported under absorption costing in analyzing and evaluating operations. To illustrate, assume that the following two proposed production levels are being evaluated by the management of Brownstein Manufacturing Company:

Proposal 1: 20,000 Units To Be Manufactured

	Total Cost or Expense	Number of Units	Unit Cost
Manufacturing costs:			
Variable	$ 700,000	20,000	$35
Fixed......................	400,000	20,000	20
Total	$1,100,000		$55
Selling and general expenses:			
Variable ($5 per unit sold) ...	$ 100,000		
Fixed......................	100,000		
Total	$ 200,000		

Proposal 2: 25,000 Units To Be Manufactured

	Total Cost or Expense	Number of Units	Unit Cost
Manufacturing costs:			
Variable	$ 875,000	25,000	$35
Fixed.....................	400,000	25,000	16
Total	$1,275,000		$51
Selling and general expenses:			
Variable ($5 per unit sold) ...	$ 100,000		
Fixed.....................	100,000		
Total	$ 200,000		

Brownstein Manufacturing Company has no beginning inventory, and sales are estimated to be 20,000 units at $75 per unit, regardless of production levels. If the company manufactures 20,000 units, which is an amount equal to the estimated sales, income from operations under absorption costing would be $200,000. However, the reported income from operations could be increased by $80,000 by manufacturing 25,000 units and adding 5,000 units to the finished goods inventory. The absorption costing income statements illustrating this effect are as follows:

Absorption Costing Income Statements		
	20,000 Units Manufactured	25,000 Units Manufactured
Sales (20,000 units × $75)...................	$1,500,000	$1,500,000
Cost of goods sold:		
Cost of goods manufactured:		
(20,000 units × $55)...................	$1,100,000	
(25,000 units × $51)...................		$1,275,000
Less ending inventory:		
(5,000 units × $51)...................		255,000
Cost of goods sold....................	$1,100,000	$1,020,000
Gross profit.........................	$ 400,000	$ 480,000
Selling and general expenses ($100,000 + $100,000)...................	200,000	200,000
Income from operations....................	$ 200,000	$ 280,000

· · · · · · · · · ·

Absorption Costing Income Statements

The $80,000 increase in operating income would be caused by the allocation of the fixed manufacturing costs of $400,000 over a greater number of units of production. Specifically, an increase in production from 20,000 units to 25,000 units meant that the fixed manufacturing costs per unit decreased from $20 ($400,000 ÷ 20,000 units) to $16 ($400,000 ÷ 25,000 units). Thus, the cost of goods sold when 25,000 units are manufactured would be $4 per unit less, or $80,000 less in total (20,000 units sold times $4). Since the cost of goods sold is less, operating income is $80,000 more when 25,000 units are manufactured rather than 20,000 units.

Under the variable costing concept, income from operations would have been $200,000, regardless of the amount by which units manufactured exceeded sales, because no fixed manufacturing costs are allocated to the units manufactured. To illustrate, the following variable costing income statements are presented for Brownstein for the production of 20,000 units, 25,000 units, and 30,000 units. In each case, the income from operations is $200,000.

Variable Costing Income Statements

Variable Costing Income Statements			
	20,000 Units Manufactured	25,000 Units Manufactured	30,000 Units Manufactured
Sales (20,000 units × $75).....	$1,500,000	$1,500,000	$1,500,000
Variable cost of goods sold:			
Variable cost of goods manufactured:			
(20,000 units × $35)........	$ 700,000		
(25,000 units × $35)........		$ 875,000	
(30,000 units × $35)........			$1,050,000
Less ending inventory:			
(0 units × $35)............	0		
(5,000 units × $35)........		175,000	
(10,000 units × $35)........			350,000
Variable cost of goods sold	$ 700,000	$ 700,000	$ 700,000
Manufacturing margin	$ 800,000	$ 800,000	$ 800,000
Variable selling and general expenses..................	100,000	100,000	100,000
Contribution margin	$ 700,000	$ 700,000	$ 700,000
Fixed costs and expenses:			
Fixed manufacturing costs	$ 400,000	$ 400,000	$ 400,000
Fixed selling and general expenses.................	100,000	100,000	100,000
Total fixed costs and expenses.................	$ 500,000	$ 500,000	$ 500,000
Income from operations........	$ 200,000	$ 200,000	$ 200,000

As illustrated, if absorption costing is used, management should be careful in analyzing income from operations when large changes in inventory levels occur. Otherwise, increases or decreases in income from operations due to changes in inventory levels could be misinterpreted to be the result of operating efficiencies or inefficiencies.

MANAGEMENT'S USE OF VARIABLE COSTING AND ABSORPTION COSTING

Both variable costing and absorption costing serve useful purposes for management. However, there are limitations to the use of both concepts in certain circumstances. Therefore, managerial accountants must carefully analyze each situation in evaluating whether variable costing reports or absorption costing reports would be more useful. In many situations, the preparation of reports under both concepts will provide useful insights. Such reports and their advantages and disadvantages are discussed in the following paragraphs.

Cost Control

As discussed in Chapter 2, all costs are controllable by someone within a business enterprise, but they are not all controllable at the same level of management. For example, plant supervisors, as members of operating management, are responsible for controlling the use of direct materials in their departments. They have no control, however, of the amount of insurance coverage or premium costs related to the buildings housing their departments. For a specific level of management, **controllable costs** are costs that it controls directly, and **noncontrollable costs** are costs that another level of management controls. This distinction, as applied to specific levels of management, is useful in fixing the responsibility for incurrence of costs and then for reporting the cost data to those responsible for cost control.

Variable manufacturing costs are controlled at the operating level because the amount of such costs varies with changes in the volume of production. By including only variable manufacturing costs in the cost of the product, variable costing provides a product cost figure that can be controlled by operating management. The fixed factory overhead costs are ordinarily the responsibility of a higher level of management. When the fixed factory overhead costs are reported as a separate item in the variable costing income statement, they are easier to identify and control than when they are spread among units of product as they are under absorption costing.

As is the case with the fixed and variable manufacturing costs, the control of the variable and fixed operating expenses is usually the responsibility of different levels of management. Under variable costing, the variable selling and general expenses are reported in a separate category from the fixed selling and general expenses. Because they are reported in this manner, both types of operating expenses are easier to identify and control than is the case under absorption costing, where they are not reported separately.

Product Pricing
· · ·

Many factors enter into the determination of the selling price of a product. The cost of making the product is clearly significant. Microeconomic theory deduces, from a set of restrictive assumptions, that income is maximized by expanding output to the volume where the revenue realized by the sale of the final unit (marginal revenue) equals the cost of that unit (marginal cost). Although the degree of exactness assumed in economic theory is rarely attainable, the concepts of marginal revenue and marginal cost are useful in setting selling prices.

In the short run, an enterprise is committed to the existing capacity of its manufacturing facilities. The pricing decision should be based upon making the best use of such capacity. The fixed costs and expenses cannot be avoided, but the variable costs and expenses can be eliminated if the company does not manufacture the product. The selling price of a product, therefore, should at least be equal to the variable costs and expenses of making and selling it. Any price above this minimum selling price contributes an amount toward covering fixed costs and expenses and providing operating income. Variable costing procedures yield data that emphasize these relationships.

In the long run, plant capacity can be increased or decreased. If an enterprise is to continue in business, the selling prices of its products must cover all costs and expenses and provide a reasonable operating income. Hence, in establishing pricing policies for the long run, information provided by absorption costing procedures is needed.

The results of a recent research study sponsored by the National Association of Accountants indicated that the companies studied used absorption costing in making routine pricing decisions. However, these companies regularly used variable costing as a basis for setting prices in many short-run situations.[1]

There are no simple solutions to most pricing problems. Consideration must be given to many factors of varying importance. Accounting can contribute by preparing analyses of various pricing plans for both the short run and the long run.

Variable Costing in Pricing Decisions — Two Case Studies

A firm may find it profitable to sell its existing products in new markets. For example, consumer products may be targeted for industrial usage, or the firm may decide to expand into national or international markets. Variable costing can aid management in pricing decisions related to such products, as the following case studies illustrate.

---

[1]Thomas M. Bruegelmann, Gaile A. Haessly, Michael Schiff, and Claire P. Wolfangel, *The Use of Variable Costing in Pricing Decisions*, National Association of Accountants (Montvale, New Jersey, 1986), p. vii.

Case One

This company is a division of a Fortune 500 firm. The division identified good opportunities in Third World countries for selling its products through distributors. Since there is usually an independent agent acting as an intermediary in arranging sales between the company and the distributors in the United States, dealing with distributors eliminates the commission paid to these agents. In addition, freight costs are lower, since the distributors provide the transportation. The company passes on these cost savings and quotes prices based on variable costs rather than full costs. In this way, the company is able to meet stiff foreign competition.

Case Two

This company is engaged primarily in the manufacture and sale of wire and cable made from nonferrous metals. The company has 25 major product lines. In the initial stages of introducing a product to a new market, price is not a major factor—quality, reliability, and timeliness of delivery are far more important. Hence, in this initial introductory stage, a full cost approach is used to establish the product price. However, once a product has passed the introductory stage and has achieved a good market share, it normally runs into stiff price competition from within the market. It is at this point that variable costing enters into the pricing decision to determine the price floor. If management decides to remain in the market, a price will be set, based upon variable cost, to fight off short-run price wars from competitors.

Source: Thomas M. Bruegelmann, Gaile A. Haessly, Michael Schiff, and Claire P. Wolfangel, *The Use of Variable Costing in Pricing Decisions,* National Association of Accountants (Montvale, New Jersey, 1986), pp. 45–46.

Production Planning
· · ·

Production planning also has both short-run and long-run implications. In the short run, production is limited to existing capacity, and operating decisions must be made quickly before opportunities are lost. For example, a company manufacturing products with a seasonal demand may have an opportunity to obtain an off-season order that will not interfere with its production schedule nor reduce the sales of its other products. The relevant factors for such a short-run decision are the revenues and the variable costs and expenses. If the revenues from the special order will provide a contribution margin, the order should be accepted because it will increase the company's operating income. For long-run planning, management must also consider the fixed costs and expenses.

Sales Analysis
· · ·

The primary objective of the marketing and sales functions is to offer the company's products for sale at prices that will result in an adequate amount of income relative to the total assets employed. To evaluate these functions properly, management needs information concerning the profitability of various types of products and sales mixes, sales territories, and salespersons. Variable costing can make a significant contribution to management decision making in such areas.

Sales Mix Analysis. **Sales mix,** sometimes referred to as product mix, is generally defined as the relative distribution of sales among the various products sold. Some products are more profitable than others, and management should concentrate its sales efforts on those that will provide the maximum total operating income.

Sales mix studies are based on assumptions, such as the ability to sell one product in place of another and the ability to convert production facilities to accommodate the manufacture of one product instead of another. Proposed changes in the sales mix often affect only small segments of a company's total operations. In such cases, changes in sales mix may be possible within the limits of existing capacity, and the presentation of cost and revenue data in the variable costing form is useful in achieving the most profitable sales mix.

Two very important factors that should be determined for each product are (1) the production facilities needed for its manufacture and (2) the amount of contribution margin to be gained from its manufacture. If two or more products require equal use of limited production facilities, then management should concentrate its sales and production efforts on the product or products with the highest contribution margin per unit. The following report, which focuses on product contribution margins, is an example of the type of data needed for an evaluation of sales mix. The enterprise, which manufactures two products and is operating at full capacity, is considering whether to change the emphasis of its advertising and other promotional efforts.

Contribution Margin Statement — Unit of Product

Contribution Margin by Unit of Product
April 15, 19--

	Product A	Product B
Sales price....................................	$6.00	$8.50
Variable cost of goods sold	3.50	5.50
Manufacturing margin	$2.50	$3.00
Variable selling and general expenses..............	1.00	1.00
Contribution margin	$1.50	$2.00

The statement indicates that Product B yields a greater amount of contribution margin per unit than Product A. Therefore, Product B provides the larger contribution to the recovery of fixed costs and expenses and realization of operating income. If the amount of production facilities used for each product is assumed to be equal, it would be desirable to increase the sales of Product B.

If two or more products require unequal use of production resources, management should concentrate its sales and production efforts on that product or products with the highest contribution margin per unit of resource. For example, assume that in the above illustration, to manufacture Product B requires twice the machine hours required for Product A. Specifically, Product B requires 2 machine hours per unit, while Product A requires only 1 machine hour per unit. Under this assumption, the contribution margin per unit of resource (machine hours) is $1.50 ($1.50 contribution margin ÷ 1 machine hour) for Product A and $1 ($2 contribution margin ÷ 2 machine hours) for Product B. Under such circumstances, a change in sales mix designed to increase sales of Product A would be desirable.

To illustrate, if 2,000 additional units of Product A (requiring 2,000 machine hours) could be sold in place of 1,000 units of Product B (also requiring 2,000 machine hours), the total company contribution margin would increase by $1,000, as follows:

Additional contribution margin from sale of additional 2,000 units of Product A ($1.50 × 2,000 units)	$3,000
Less contribution margin from forgoing production and sale of 1,000 units of Product B ($2 × 1,000 units)	2,000
Increase in total contribution margin	$1,000

Sales Territory Analysis. An income statement presenting the contribution margin by sales territories is often useful to management in appraising past performance and in directing future sales efforts. The following income statement is prepared in such a format, in abbreviated form:

Contribution Margin Statement by Sales Territory
For Month Ended July 31, 19--

	Territory A	Territory B	Total
Sales	$315,000	$502,500	$817,500
Less variable costs and expenses	189,000	251,250	440,250
Contribution margin	$126,000	$251,250	$377,250
Less fixed costs and expenses			242,750
Income from operations.			$134,500

Contribution Margin Statement — Sales Territories

In addition to the contribution margin, the **contribution margin ratio** (contribution margin divided by sales) for each territory is useful in evaluating sales territories and directing operations toward more profitable activities. For Territory A, the contribution margin ratio is 40% ($126,000 ÷ $315,000), and for Territory B the ratio is 50% ($251,250 ÷ $502,500). Consequently, more profitability could be achieved by efforts to increase the sales of Territory B relative to Territory A.

Salespersons' Analysis. A report to management for use in evaluating the sales performance of each salesperson could include total sales, gross profit, gross profit percentage, total selling expenses, and contribution to company profit. Such a report is illustrated as follows:

Salespersons' Analysis
For Six Months Ended June 30, 19--

Sales-person	Total Sales	Gross Profit	Gross Profit Percentage	Total Selling Expenses	Contribution to Company Profit
A	$300,000	$120,000	40%	$24,000	$ 96,000
B	250,000	75,000	30	22,500	52,500
C	500,000	125,000	25	35,000	90,000
D	180,000	72,000	40	18,000	54,000
E	460,000	197,800	43	27,600	170,200
F	320,000	112,000	35	22,400	89,600

The preceding report illustrates that the total sales figure is not the only consideration in evaluating a salesperson. For example, although salesperson C has the highest total sales, C's sales are not contributing as much to overall company profits as are the sales of A and E, primarily because C's sales have the lowest gross profit percentage. Of the six salespersons, E is generating the highest dollar contribution to company profit and is selling the most profitable mix of products, as measured by a gross profit percentage of 43%.

Other factors should also be considered in evaluating the performance of salespersons. For example, sales growth rates, years of experience, and actual performance compared to budgeted performance may be more important than total sales.

Chapter Review

KEY POINTS

1. Gross Profit Analysis.
A change in the amount of gross profit can be caused by (1) an increase or decrease in the amount of sales and (2) an increase or decrease in the amount of the cost of goods sold. An increase or decrease in either element may in turn be due to (1) a change in the number of units sold and (2) a change in the unit price. These two factors are known as the quantity factor and the price factor respectively.

2. Absorption Costing and Variable Costing.
The costs of manufacturing are direct materials, direct labor, and factory overhead. Under absorption costing, all such costs become part of the cost of

goods manufactured. Under variable costing, the cost of goods manufactured is composed of only variable costs—those manufacturing costs that increase or decrease as the volume of production rises or falls. These costs are the direct materials, direct labor, and only those factory overhead costs which vary with the rate of production. The fixed factory overhead costs do not become a part of the cost of goods manufactured, but are considered an expense of the period. In the variable costing income statement, the deduction of the cost of goods sold from sales yields an intermediate amount, termed manufacturing margin. Deduction of the variable selling and general expenses yields the contribution margin. Fixed costs and expenses are then deducted from the contribution margin to yield income from operations.

A comparison of income reported under the absorption costing and variable costing concepts when the level of inventory changes during the period is summarized in the following table:

Units manufactured:

Equal units sold. . . . . Absorption costing income equals variable costing income.

Exceed units sold . . . . Absorption costing income is greater than variable costing income.

Less than units sold . . . . Absorption costing income is less than variable costing income.

The possible effects of any changes in inventory levels on operating income should be considered when management analyzes and evaluates operations.

3. Management's Use of Variable Costing and Absorption Costing.

Variable costing is especially useful at the operating level of management because the amount of variable manufacturing costs varies with changes in the volume of production and thus is controllable at this level. The fixed factory overhead costs are ordinarily controllable by a higher level of management.

In the short run, variable costing may be useful in establishing the selling price of a product. This price should be at least equal to the variable costs and expenses of making and selling the product. In the long run, however, absorption costing procedures are useful in establishing selling prices, in that all costs and expenses and a reasonable amount of operating income must be earned.

Variable costing can make a significant contribution to management decision making in analyzing and evaluating sales. Management should concentrate its sales efforts on those products that will provide the maximum total operating income. Sales mix studies emphasize the contribution margin of each product in evaluating sales territories and directing operations towards more profitable activities. In addition, a salespersons' analysis report may be useful to management in evaluating the sales performance of each salesperson. Such a report emphasizes the contribution of each salesperson to the overall company profit.

KEY TERMS

.

gross profit analysis 226
absorption costing 228
variable costing 228
manufacturing margin 231
contribution margin 231

controllable costs 237
noncontrollable costs 237
sales mix 240
contribution margin ratio 241

SELF-EXAMINATION QUESTIONS

.

(Answers at End of Chapter)

1. If sales totaled $800,000 for the current year (80,000 units at $10 each) and $765,000 for the preceding year (85,000 units at $9 each), the effect of the quantity factor on the change in sales is:
   A. a $50,000 increase
   B. a $35,000 decrease
   C. a $45,000 decrease
   D. none of the above

2. The concept that considers the cost of products manufactured to be composed only of those manufacturing costs that vary with the rate of production is known as:
   A. absorption costing
   B. variable costing
   C. replacement cost
   D. none of the above

3. In an income statement prepared under the variable costing concept, the deduction of the variable cost of goods sold from sales yields an intermediate amount referred to as:
   A. gross profit
   B. contribution margin
   C. manufacturing margin
   D. none of the above

4. Sales were $750,000, variable cost of goods sold was $400,000, variable selling and general expenses were $90,000, and fixed costs and expenses were $200,000. The contribution margin was:
   A. $60,000
   B. $260,000
   C. $350,000
   D. none of the above

5. During a year in which the number of units manufactured exceeded the number of units sold, the operating income reported under the absorption costing concept would be:
   A. larger than the operating income reported under the variable costing concept
   B. smaller than the operating income reported under the variable costing concept
   C. the same as the operating income reported under the variable costing concept
   D. none of the above

ILLUSTRATIVE PROBLEM

During the current period, McLaughlin Company sold 60,000 units of product at a selling price of $30 per unit. At the beginning of the period, there were 10,000 units in inventory and McLaughlin Company manufactured 50,000 units during the period. The manufacturing costs and selling and general expenses were as follows:

	Total Cost or Expense	Number of Units	Unit Cost
Beginning inventory:			
Direct materials.........................	$ 67,000	10,000	$ 6.70
Direct labor............................	155,000	10,000	15.50
Variable factory overhead...............	18,000	10,000	1.80
Fixed factory overhead	20,000	10,000	2.00
Total.....................................	$ 260,000		$26.00
Current period costs:			
Direct materials.........................	$ 350,000	50,000	$ 7.00
Direct labor............................	810,000	50,000	16.20
Variable factory overhead...............	90,000	50,000	1.80
Fixed factory overhead	100,000	50,000	2.00
Total.....................................	$1,350,000		$27.00
Selling and general expenses:			
Variable..............................	$ 65,000		
Fixed	45,000		
Total.................................	$ 110,000		

Instructions:

1. Prepare an income statement based on the absorption costing concept.
2. Prepare an income statement based on the variable costing concept.
3. Explain the reason for the difference in the amount of operating income reported in 1 and 2.

SOLUTION

(1)   Absorption Costing Income Statement

Sales (60,000 × $30)......................		$1,800,000
Cost of goods sold:		
Beginning inventory (10,000 × $26).......	$ 260,000	
Cost of goods manufactured (50,000 × $27).	1,350,000	
Cost of goods sold....................		1,610,000
Gross profit		$ 190,000
Selling and general expenses ($65,000 + $45,000)		110,000
Income from operations		$ 80,000

(2) Variable Costing Income Statement

Sales (60,000 × $30)......................		$1,800,000
Variable cost of goods sold:		
Beginning inventory (10,000 × $24).......	$ 240,000	
Variable cost of goods manufactured		
(50,000 × $25)	1,250,000	
Variable cost of goods sold............		1,490,000
Manufacturing margin.....................		$ 310,000
Variable selling and general expenses.......		65,000
Contribution margin		$ 245,000
Fixed costs and expenses:		
Fixed manufacturing costs	$ 100,000	
Fixed selling and general expenses	45,000	145,000
Income from operations		$ 100,000

(3) The difference of $20,000 ($100,000 − $80,000) in the amount of income from operations is attributable to the different treatment of the fixed manufacturing costs. The beginning inventory in the absorption costing income statement includes $20,000 (10,000 units × $2) of fixed manufacturing costs incurred in the preceding period. This $20,000 was included as an expense in a variable costing income statement of a prior period, however. Therefore, none of it is included as an expense in the current period variable costing income statement.

Discussion Questions
·

7–1. Discuss the two factors affecting both sales and cost of goods sold to which a change in gross profit can be attributed.

7–2. The analysis of increase in gross profit for a company includes the effect that an increase in the quantity of goods sold has had on the cost of goods sold. How is this figure determined?

7–3. What types of costs are customarily included in the cost of manufactured products under (a) the *absorption costing* concept and (b) the *variable costing* concept?

7–4. Which type of manufacturing cost (direct materials, direct labor, variable factory overhead, fixed factory overhead) is included in the cost of goods manufactured under the absorption costing concept but is excluded from the cost of goods manufactured under the variable costing concept?

7–5. At the end of the first year of operations, 500 units remained in the finished goods inventory. The unit manufacturing costs during the year were as follows:

Direct materials..........................	$ 3.00
Direct labor..............................	24.00
Fixed factory overhead	1.50
Variable factory overhead	.50

What would be the cost of the finished goods inventory reported on the balance sheet under (a) the absorption costing concept and (b) the variable costing concept?

7–6. Which of the following costs would be included in the cost of a manufactured product according to the variable costing concept: (a) electricity purchased to operate factory equipment, (b) property taxes on factory building, (c) direct labor, (d) salary of factory supervisor, (e) direct materials, (f) depreciation on factory building, and (g) rent on factory building?

7–7. In the following equations, based on the variable costing income statement, identify the items designated by **X**:
(a) Net sales − **X** = manufacturing margin
(b) Manufacturing margin − **X** = contribution margin
(c) Contribution margin − **X** = income from operations

7–8. In the variable costing income statement, how are the fixed manufacturing costs reported and how are the fixed selling and general expenses reported?

7–9. If the quantity of the ending inventory is larger than that of the beginning inventory, will the amount of income from operations determined by absorption costing be more than or less than the amount determined by variable costing? Explain.

7–10. Since all costs of operating a business are controllable, what is the significance of the term *noncontrollable cost?*

7–11. Discuss how financial data prepared on the basis of variable costing can assist management in the development of short-run pricing policies.

7–12. What term is used to refer to the relative distribution of sales among the various products manufactured?

7–13. A company, operating at full capacity, manufactures two products, with Product E requiring three times the production facilities as Product F. The contribution margin is $50 per unit for Product E and $15 per unit for Product F. How much would the total contribution margin be increased or decreased for the coming year if the sales of Product E could be increased by 1,000 units by changing the emphasis of promotional efforts?

7–14. Explain why rewarding sales personnel on the basis of total sales might not be in the best interests of an enterprise whose goal is to maximize profits.

7–15. Real World Focus. Dutch Pantry Inc. operates 53 full-service family restaurants in 12 eastern states. To assure consistent quality, many of the items served in the restaurants are prepared in a central food processing plant. Classify each of the following costs and expenses of the food processing plant as either variable or fixed.

(a) Cooking oil
(b) Office salaries
(c) Electricity
(d) Experimental costs and expenses
(e) Depreciation on equipment (straight-line method)
(f) Garbage collection expense
(g) Water
(h) Cleaning supplies
(i) Property taxes
(j) Salad dressing
(k) Spices

Exercises

7–16. Gross profit analysis report. The following data for Driscoll Company are available:

	For Year Ended March 31			
	1990		1989	
Sales.........	60,000 units at $20	$1,200,000	40,000 units at $25.00	$1,000,000
Cost of goods sold........	60,000 units at $14	840,000	40,000 units at $13.50	540,000
Gross profit ...		$ 360,000		$ 460,000

Prepare an analysis of the decrease in gross profit for the year ended March 31, 1990.

7–17. Income statements under absorption costing and variable costing. Casey Company began operations on July 1 and operated at 100% of capacity during the first month. The following data summarize the results for July:

Sales (12,000 units)		$600,000
Production costs (15,000 units):		
Direct materials	$150,000	
Direct labor..............................	180,000	
Variable factory overhead	45,000	
Fixed factory overhead....................	30,000	405,000
Selling and general expenses:		
Variable selling and general expenses	$ 60,000	
Fixed selling and general expenses	18,000	78,000

(a) Prepare an income statement in accordance with the absorption costing concept. (b) Prepare an income statement in accordance with the variable costing concept. (c) What is the reason for the difference in the amount of operating income reported in (a) and (b)?

7–18. Cost of goods manufactured, using variable costing and absorption costing. On October 31, the end of the first year of operations, Kanter Company manufactured 40,000 units and sold 35,000 units. The following income statement was prepared, based on the variable costing concept:

Kanter Company
Income Statement
For Year Ended October 31, 19--

Sales....................................		$700,000
Variable cost of goods sold:		
Variable cost of goods manufactured...............	$480,000	
Less ending inventory	60,000	
Variable cost of goods sold......................		420,000
Manufacturing margin		$280,000
Variable selling and general expenses................		70,000
Contribution margin		$210,000
Fixed costs and expenses:		
Fixed manufacturing costs	$ 60,000	
Fixed selling and general expenses................	50,000	110,000
Income from operations............................		$100,000

Determine the unit cost of goods manufactured, based on (a) the variable costing concept and (b) the absorption costing concept.

7–19. Variable costing income statement. On June 30, the end of the first month of operations, Lloyd Company prepared the following income statement, based on the absorption costing concept:

Lloyd Company
Income Statement
For Month Ended June 30, 19--

Sales (4,400 units)................................		$66,000
Cost of goods sold:		
Cost of goods manufactured	$45,000	
Less ending inventory (600 units).................	5,400	
Cost of goods sold.............................		39,600
Gross profit		$26,400
Selling and general expenses		15,800
Income from operations...........................		$10,600

If the fixed manufacturing costs were $15,000 and the variable selling and general expenses were $7,700, prepare an income statement in accordance with the variable costing concept.

7–20. Absorption costing income statement. On April 30, the end of the first month of operations, Moyer Company prepared the following income statement, based on the variable costing concept:

Moyer Company
Income Statement
For Month Ended April 30, 19--

Sales (18,000 units)		$360,000
Variable cost of goods sold:		
Variable cost of goods manufactured	$200,000	
Less ending inventory (2,000 units)	20,000	
Variable cost of goods sold.		180,000
Manufacturing margin		$180,000
Variable selling and general expenses..............		36,000
Contribution margin		$144,000
Fixed costs and expenses:		
Fixed manufacturing costs	$ 50,000	
Fixed selling and general expenses	29,000	79,000
Income from operations.		$ 65,000

Prepare an income statement in accordance with the absorption costing concept.

7–21. Estimated income statements, using absorption and variable costing. Prior to the first month of operations ending January 31, Lester Company estimated the following operating results:

Sales (1,000 × $50)	$50,000
Manufacturing costs (1,000 units):	
Direct materials	15,000
Direct labor.	10,000
Variable factory overhead	7,000
Fixed factory overhead.	4,800
Fixed selling and general expenses	6,500
Variable selling and general expenses	2,000

The company is evaluating a proposal to manufacture 1,200 units instead of 1,000 units.

(a) Assuming no change in sales, unit variable manufacturing costs, and fixed factory overhead and total selling and general expenses, prepare an estimated income statement, comparing operating results if 1,000 and 1,200 units are manufactured, in the (1) absorption costing format and (2) variable costing format. (b) What is the reason for the difference in income from operations reported for the two levels of production by the absorption costing income statement?

7–22. Change in sales mix and contribution margin. Van Cleave Company manufactures Products A and B and is operating at full capacity. To manufacture Product A requires four times the number of machine hours as required for Product B. Market research indicates that 2,000 additional units of Product B could be sold. The contribution margin by unit of product is as follows:

	Product A	Product B
Sales price	$120	$50
Variable cost of goods sold.	70	36
Manufacturing margin.........................	$ 50	$14
Variable selling and general expenses	32	9
Contribution margin.	$ 18	$ 5

Prepare a tabulation indicating the increase or decrease in total contribution margin if 2,000 additional units of Product B are produced and sold.

7-23. Real World Focus. The following data were adapted from the income statement of General Electric Company for the year ended December 31, 1986:

	In Millions
Sales of products and services to customers	$35,211
Operating costs:	
Cost of goods sold	26,187
Selling, general, and administrative expense.	5,963
Operating costs	$32,150
Income from operations	$ 3,061

Assume that the variable amount of each category of operating costs is as follows:

Cost of goods sold	$19,500
Selling, general, and administrative expense.	3,600

Based on the above data, prepare a variable costing income statement for General Electric Company for the year ended December 31, 1986.

Problems
·

7-24. Gross profit analysis report. Towns Company manufactures only one product. In 1989, the plant operated at full capacity. At a meeting of the board of directors on November 17, 1989, it was decided to raise the price of this product from $60, which had prevailed last year, to $65, effective January 1, 1990. Although the cost price was expected to rise about $2.40 per unit in 1990 because of increases in the cost of direct materials and direct labor, the increase in selling price was expected to cover these increases and also add to operating income. The comparative income statement for 1989 and 1990 is as follows:

SPREADSHEET PROBLEM

	1990		1989	
Sales.		$227,500		$240,000
Cost of goods sold: variable	$120,400		$128,000	
fixed	14,000	134,400	14,000	142,000
Gross profit		$ 93,100		$ 98,000
Operating expenses: variable	$ 16,800		$ 19,200	
fixed	40,000	56,800	40,000	59,200
Operating income.		$ 36,300		$ 38,800

Instructions:

(1) Prepare a gross profit analysis report for the year 1990.

(2) At a meeting of the board of directors on April 3, 1991, the president, after reading the gross profit analysis report, made the following comment:

It looks as if the increase in unit cost price was $2.90 and not the anticipated $2.40. The failure of operating management to keep these costs within the bounds of those in 1989, except for the anticipated $2.40 increase in direct materials and direct labor cost, was a major factor in the decrease in gross profit.

Do you agree with this analysis of the increase in unit cost price? Explain.

7–25. Absorption and variable costing income statements. During the first month of operations ended October 31, Woodruff Company manufactured 150,000 units, of which 120,000 were sold. Operating data for the month are summarized as follows:

Sales		$840,000
Manufacturing costs:		
Direct materials	$150,000	
Direct labor...............................	330,000	
Variable factory overhead	120,000	
Fixed factory overhead......................	60,000	660,000
Selling and general expenses:		
Variable	$ 72,000	
Fixed	48,000	120,000

Instructions:

(1) Prepare an income statement based on the absorption costing concept.
(2) Prepare an income statement based on the variable costing concept.
(3) Explain the reason for the difference in the amount of operating income reported in (1) and (2).

7–26. Income statements under absorption costing and variable costing. The demand for Product H, one of numerous products manufactured by Sommer Inc., has dropped sharply because of recent competition from a similar product. The company's chemists are currently completing tests of various new formulas, and it is anticipated that the manufacture of a superior product can be started on June 1, one month hence. No changes will be needed in the present production facilities to manufacture the new product because only the mixture of the various materials will be changed.

The controller has been asked by the president of the company for advice on whether to continue production during May or to suspend the manufacture of Product H until June 1. The controller has assembled the following pertinent data:

Sommer Inc.
Estimated Income Statement—Product H
For Month Ending April 30, 19--

Sales (20,000 units).......................	$800,000
Cost of goods sold........................	760,500
Gross profit	$ 39,500
Selling and general expenses...............	84,000
Loss from operations......................	$ 44,500

The estimated production costs and selling and general expenses, based on a production of 20,000 units, are as follows:

Direct materials	$14.50 per unit
Direct labor.....................................	18.00 per unit
Variable factory overhead	2.50 per unit
Variable selling and general expenses	3.00 per unit
Fixed factory overhead...........................	$60,500 for April
Fixed selling and general expenses	24,000 for April

Sales for May are expected to drop about 30% below those of the preceding month. No significant changes are anticipated in the production costs or operating expenses. No extra costs will be incurred in discontinuing operations in the portion of the plant associated with Product H. The inventory of Product H at the beginning and end of May is expected to be inconsequential.

Instructions:

(1) Prepare an estimated income statement in absorption costing form for May for Product H, assuming that production continues during the month.
(2) Prepare an estimated income statement in variable costing form for May for Product H, assuming that production continues during the month.
(3) State the estimated operating loss arising from the activities associated with Product H for May if production is temporarily suspended.
(4) Prepare a brief statement of the advice the controller should give.

7–27. Salespersons' report and analysis. Lin Company employs seven salespersons to sell and distribute its product throughout the state. Data extracted from reports received from the salespersons during the current year ended December 31 are as follows:

Salesperson	Total Sales	Cost of Goods Sold	Total Selling Expenses
Barr	$900,000	$585,000	$217,500
Farmer	675,000	418,500	175,500
Griffith	560,000	341,600	118,400
Murray	600,000	372,000	141,000
Owens	375,000	225,000	78,000
Thom	480,000	278,400	112,500
York	525,000	315,000	114,000

Instructions:

(1) Prepare a report for the year, indicating total sales, gross profit, gross profit percentage, total selling expenses, and contribution to company profit by salesperson.
(2) Which salesperson contributed the highest dollar amount to company profit during the year?
(3) Briefly list factors other than contribution to company profit that should be considered in evaluating the performance of salespersons.

7–28. Variable costing income statement and effect on income of change in operations. T. E. Collins Company manufactures three styles of folding chairs, A, B, and C. The income statement has consistently indicated a net loss for Style B, and management is considering three proposals: (1) continue Style B, (2) discontinue Style

B and reduce total output accordingly, or (3) discontinue Style B and conduct an advertising campaign to expand the sales of Style A so that the entire plant capacity can continue to be used.

If Proposal 2 is selected and Style B is discontinued and production curtailed, the annual fixed production costs and fixed operating expenses could be reduced by $22,500 and $12,000 respectively. If Proposal 3 is selected, it is anticipated that an additional annual expenditure of $40,000 for advertising Style A would yield an increase of 40% in its sales volume, and that the increased production of Style A would utilize the plant facilities released by the discontinuance of Style B.

The sales, costs, and expenses have been relatively stable over the past few years, and they are expected to remain so for the foreseeable future. The income statement for the past year ended August 31 is:

| | Style | | | |
	A	B	C	Total
Sales........................	$650,000	$190,000	$600,000	$1,440,000
Cost of goods sold:				
Variable costs................	$370,000	$132,300	$330,000	$ 832,300
Fixed costs	125,000	40,700	120,000	285,700
Total cost of goods sold	$495,000	$173,000	$450,000	$1,118,000
Gross profit	$155,000	$ 17,000	$150,000	$ 322,000
Less operating expenses:				
Variable expenses	$ 64,800	$ 18,900	$ 60,000	$ 143,700
Fixed expenses	36,000	16,000	35,000	87,000
Total operating expenses	$100,800	$ 34,900	$ 95,000	$ 230,700
Income from operations	$ 54,200	$(17,900)	$ 55,000	$ 91,300

Instructions:

(1) Prepare an income statement for the past year in the variable costing format. Use the following headings:

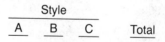

Data for each style should be reported through contribution margin. The fixed costs and expenses should be deducted from the total contribution margin, as reported in the "Total" column, to determine income from operations.

(2) Based on the income statement prepared in (1) and the other data presented above, determine the amount by which total annual operating income would be reduced below its present level if Proposal 2 is accepted.

(3) Prepare an income statement in the variable costing format, indicating the projected annual operating income if Proposal 3 is accepted. Use the following headings:

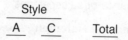

Data for each style should be reported through contribution margin. The fixed costs and expenses should be deducted from the total contribution margin as reported in the "Total" column. For purposes of this problem, the additional expenditure of $40,000 for advertising can be added to the fixed operating expenses.

(4) By how much would total annual income increase above its present level if Proposal 3 is accepted? Explain.

ALTERNATE PROBLEMS

7–24A. Gross profit analysis report. Ayers Company manufactures only one product. In 1989, the plant operated at full capacity. At a meeting of the board of directors on December 1, 1989, it was decided to raise the price of this product from $36, which had prevailed for the past few years, to $40, effective January 1, 1990. Although the cost price was expected to rise about $2 per unit in 1990 because of a direct materials and direct labor wage increase, the increase in selling price was expected to cover this increase and also add to operating income. The comparative income statement for 1989 and 1990 is as follows:

	1990		1989	
Sales........................		$640,000		$720,000
Cost of goods sold: variable	$377,600		$432,000	
fixed	48,000	425,600	48,000	480,000
Gross profit		$214,400		$240,000
Operating expenses: variable	$ 96,000		$120,000	
fixed	50,000	146,000	50,000	170,000
Operating income................		$ 68,400		$ 70,000

Instructions:

(1) Prepare a gross profit analysis report for the year 1990.

(2) At a meeting of the board of directors on March 10, 1991, the president, after reading the gross profit analysis report, made the following comment:

It looks as if the increase in unit cost price was $2.60 and not the anticipated $2. The failure of operating management to keep these costs within the bounds of those in 1989, except for the anticipated $2 increase in direct materials and direct labor cost, was a major factor in the decrease in gross profit.

Do you agree with this analysis of the increase in unit cost price? Explain.

7–25A. Absorption and variable costing income statements. During the first month of operations ended April 30, Hyatt Company manufactured 80,000 units, of which 60,000 were sold. Operating data for the month are summarized as follows:

Sales		$480,000
Manufacturing costs:		
Direct materials	$ 96,000	
Direct labor..............................	192,000	
Variable factory overhead	60,000	
Fixed factory overhead.....................	120,000	468,000
Selling and general expenses:		
Variable	$ 66,000	
Fixed	35,000	101,000

Instructions:

(1) Prepare an income statement based on the absorption costing concept.
(2) Prepare an income statement based on the variable costing concept.
(3) Explain the reason for the difference in the amount of operating income reported in (1) and (2).

7–26A. Income statements under absorption costing and variable costing.
The demand for Product X, one of numerous products manufactured by Engel Inc., has dropped sharply because of recent competition from a similar product. The company's chemists are currently completing tests of various new formulas, and it is anticipated that the manufacture of a superior product can be started on August 1, one month hence. No changes will be needed in the present production facilities to manufacture the new product because only the mixture of the various materials will be changed.

The controller has been asked by the president of the company for advice on whether to continue production during July or to suspend the manufacture of Product X until August 1. The controller has assembled the following pertinent data:

Engel Inc.
Estimated Income Statement — Product X
For Month Ending June 30, 19--

Sales (10,000 units)........................	$200,000
Cost of goods sold.........................	157,000
Gross profit	$ 43,000
Selling and general expenses...............	50,000
Loss from operations......................	$ 7,000

The estimated production costs and selling and general expenses, based on a production of 10,000 units, are as follows:

Direct materials	$4.50 per unit
Direct labor..	6.00 per unit
Variable factory overhead	1.20 per unit
Variable selling and general expenses	2.00 per unit
Fixed factory overhead............................	$40,000 for June
Fixed selling and general expenses	30,000 for June

Sales for July are expected to drop about 50% below those of the preceding month. No significant changes are anticipated in the production costs or operating expenses. No extra costs will be incurred in discontinuing operations in the portion of the plant associated with Product X. The inventory of Product X at the beginning and end of July is expected to be inconsequential.

Instructions:

(1) Prepare an estimated income statement in absorption costing form for July for Product X, assuming that production continues during the month.
(2) Prepare an estimated income statement in variable costing form for July for Product X, assuming that production continues during the month.

(3) State the estimated operating loss arising from the activities associated with Product X for July if production is temporarily suspended.
(4) Prepare a brief statement of the advice the controller should give.

Mini-Case 7

REYNOLDS
COMPANY

Reynolds Company is a family-owned business in which you own 15% of the common stock and your brothers and sisters own the remaining shares. The employment contract of Reynolds' new president, Grace McKean, stipulates a base salary of $60,000 per year plus 8% of income from operations in excess of $2,000,000. Reynolds uses the absorption costing method of reporting income from operations, which has averaged approximately $2,000,000 for the past several years.

Sales for 1990, McKean's first year as president of Reynolds Company, are estimated at 50,000 units at a selling price of $180 per unit. To maximize the use of Reynolds' productive capacity, McKean has decided to manufacture 60,000 units, rather than the 50,000 units of estimated sales. The beginning inventory at January 1, 1990, is insignificant in amount, and the manufacturing costs and selling and general expenses for the production of 50,000 and 60,000 units are as follows:

50,000 Units To Be Manufactured

	Total Cost or Expense	Number of Units	Unit Cost
Manufacturing costs:			
Variable.....................................	$4,000,000	50,000	$ 80
Fixed.......................................	1,500,000	50,000	30
Total.....................................	$5,500,000		$110
Selling and general expenses:			
Variable.....................................	$1,000,000		
Fixed.......................................	500,000		
Total.....................................	$1,500,000		

60,000 Units To Be Manufactured

	Total Cost or Expense	Number of Units	Unit Cost
Manufacturing costs:			
Variable..................................	$4,800,000	60,000	$ 80
Fixed.....................................	1,500,000	60,000	25
Total.......................................	$6,300,000		$105
Selling and general expenses:			
Variable..................................	$1,000,000		
Fixed.....................................	500,000		
Total.......................................	$1,500,000		

Instructions:

(1) Prepare absorption costing income statements for the year ending December 31, 1990, based upon sales of 50,000 units and the manufacture of (a) 50,000 units and (b) 60,000 units.
(2) Explain the difference in the income from operations reported in (1).
(3) Compute McKean's total salary for 1990, based on sales of 50,000 units and the manufacture of (a) 50,000 units and (b) 60,000 units.
(4) In addition to maximizing the use of Reynolds Company's productive capacity, why might McKean wish to manufacture 60,000 units rather than 50,000 units?
(5) Can you suggest an alternative way in which McKean's salary could be determined, using a base salary of $60,000 and 8% of income from operations in excess of $2,000,000, so that the salary could not be increased by simply manufacturing more units?

Answers to Self-Examination Questions

· · ·

1. **C** A change in sales revenue from one period to another can be attributed to (1) a change in the number of units sold—quantity factor and (2) a change in the unit price—price factor. The $45,000 decrease (answer C) attributed to the quantity factor is determined as follows:

Decrease in number of units sold in current year....................................	5,000
Unit sales price in preceding year................	× $9
Quantity factor—decrease	$45,000

The price factor can be determined as follows:

Increase in unit sales price in current
year. $1
Number of units sold in current year . . . . ×80,000
Price factor — increase. $80,000

The increase of $80,000 attributed to the price factor less the decrease of $45,000 attributed to the quantity factor accounts for the $35,000 increase in total sales for the current year.

2. B Under the variable costing concept (answer B), the cost of products manufactured is composed of only those manufacturing costs that increase or decrease as the volume of production rises or falls. These costs include direct materials, direct labor, and variable factory overhead. Under the absorption costing concept (answer A), all manufacturing costs become a part of the cost of the products manufactured. The absorption costing concept is required in the determination of historical cost and taxable income. The variable costing concept is often useful to management in making decisions.

3. C In the variable costing income statement, the deduction of the variable cost of goods sold from sales yields the manufacturing margin (answer C). Deduction of the variable selling and general expenses from manufacturing margin yields the contribution margin (answer B).

4. B The contribution margin of $260,000 (answer B) is determined by deducting all of the variable costs and expenses ($400,000 + $90,000) from sales ($750,000).

5. A In a period in which the number of units manufactured exceeds the number of units sold, the operating income reported under the absorption costing concept is larger than the operating income reported under the variable costing concept (answer A) because a portion of the fixed manufacturing costs are deferred when the absorption costing concept is used. This deferment has the effect of excluding a portion of the fixed manufacturing costs from the current cost of goods sold.

Chapter Eight

CHAPTER OBJECTIVES

·

Describe the nature and objectives of budgeting and the budget process.

·

Describe and illustrate the master budget and the preparation
of the following components of a master budget
for a small manufacturing enterprise:
Sales budget
Production budget
Direct materials purchases budget
Direct labor cost budget
Factory overhead cost budget
Cost of goods sold budget
Operating expenses budget
Budgeted income statement
Capital expenditures budget
Cash budget
Budgeted balance sheet

·

Describe and illustrate budget performance reports.

·

Describe and illustrate flexible budgets.

·

Describe automated budgeting systems.

·

Describe the impact of budgeting on human behavior.

·

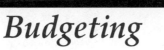

Budgeting

Effective planning and control are requisites of successful operations. Various uses of accounting data by management in performing these functions have been described and illustrated in earlier chapters. For example, the role of accounting in planning production and controlling costs has been discussed and illustrated. This chapter and Chapter 9 are devoted to budgeting and standard costs, two additional accounting devices that aid management in planning and controlling the operations of the business.

NATURE AND OBJECTIVES OF BUDGETING

A **budget** is a formal written statement of management's plans for the future, expressed in financial terms. A budget charts the course of future action. Thus, it serves management's primary functions in the same manner that the architect's blueprints aid the builder and the navigator's flight plan aids the pilot.

A budget, like a blueprint and flight plan, should contain sound, attainable objectives. If the budget is to contain such objectives, planning must be based on careful study, investigation, and research. Management's reliance on data thus obtained lessens the role of guesswork and intuition in managing a business enterprise.

In a recent survey, the corporate boards of directors of 600 of the 1,000 largest U.S. corporations emphasized the importance of planning to the success of a business. The results of this survey, which asked the boards to identify the most important issues facing them now, and five years from now, are shown in the following bar graph:[1]

---

[1]Deloitte Haskins & Sells, "Major Issues Facing Boards of Directors," *DH+S Review,* October 25, 1987, p. 3.

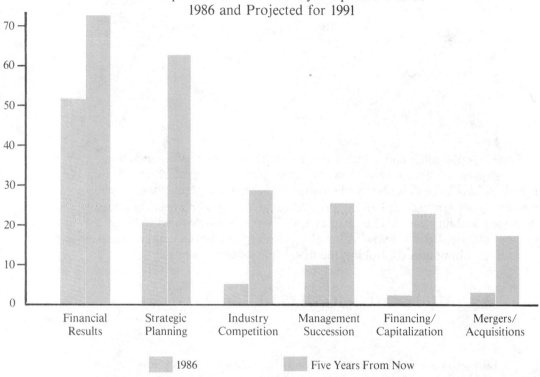

Most Important Issues Faced by Corporate Boards
1986 and Projected for 1991

The essentials of budgeting are (1) the establishment of specific goals for future operations and (2) the periodic comparison of actual results with these goals. The establishment of specific goals for future operations encompasses the planning function of management. The periodic comparison of actual results with these goals encompasses the control function of management.

Although budgets are commonly associated with profit-making enterprises, they play an important role in operating most instrumentalities of government, ranging from rural school districts and small villages to gigantic agencies of the federal government. They are also an important part of the operations of churches, hospitals, and other nonprofit institutions. Individuals and family units often use budgeting techniques as an aid to careful management of resources. In this chapter, the principles of budgeting are discussed in the context of profit-making enterprises.[2]

---

[2]The application of the basic budgeting principles to nonprofit organizations is presented in Chapter 17.

BUDGET PERIOD

Budgets of operating activities usually include the fiscal year of an enterprise. A year is short enough to make possible fairly dependable estimates of future operations, and yet long enough to make it possible to view the future in a reasonably broad context. However, to achieve effective control, the annual budgets must be subdivided into shorter time periods, such as quarters of the year, months, or weeks. It is also necessary to review the budgets from time to time and make any changes that become necessary as a result of unforeseen changes in general business conditions, in the particular industry, or in the individual enterprise.

A frequent variant of fiscal-year budgeting, sometimes called **continuous budgeting,** provides for maintenance of a twelve-month projection into the future. At the end of each time interval used, the twelve-month budget is revised by removing the data for the period just ended and adding the newly estimated budget data for the same period next year.

BUDGETING PROCEDURES

The details of budgeting systems are affected by the type and degree of complexity of a particular company, the amount of its revenues, the relative importance of its various divisions, and many other factors. Budget procedures used by a large manufacturer of automobiles would obviously differ in many ways from a system designed for a small manufacturer of paper products. The differences between a system designed for factory operations of any type and a financial enterprise such as a bank would be even more marked.

The development of budgets for a following fiscal year usually begins several months prior to the end of the current year. The responsibility for their development is ordinarily assigned to a committee made up of the budget director and such high-level executives as the controller, treasurer, production manager, and sales manager. The process is started by requesting estimates of sales, production, and other operating data from the various administrative units concerned. It is important that all levels of management and all departments participate in the preparation and submission of budget estimates. The involvement of all supervisory personnel fosters cooperation both within and among departments and also heightens awareness of each department's importance in the overall processes of the company. All levels of management are thus encouraged to set goals and to control operations in a manner that strengthens the possibilities of achieving the goals.

The process of developing budget estimates differs among enterprises. One method is to require all levels of management to start from zero and estimate sales, production, and other operating data as though operations were being started for the first time. Although this concept, called **zero-base budgeting,** has received wide attention in regard to budgeting for governmental units, it is equally useful to commercial enterprises. Another method of developing estimates is for each level of management to modify last year's budgeted amounts in light of last year's operating results and expected changes for the coming year.

The various estimates received by the budget committee are revised, reviewed, coordinated, cross-referenced, and finally put together to form the **master budget.** The estimates submitted should not be substantially revised by the committee without first giving the originators an opportunity to defend their proposals. After agreement has been reached and the master budget has been adopted by the budget committee, copies of the pertinent sections are distributed to the proper personnel in the chain of accountability. Periodic reports comparing actual results with the budget should likewise be distributed to all supervisory personnel.

As a framework for describing and illustrating budgeting, a small manufacturing enterprise will be assumed. The major parts of its master budget are as follows:

Components of Master Budget

Budgeted income statement
  Sales budget
  Cost of goods sold budget
    Production budget
    Direct materials purchases budget
    Direct labor cost budget
    Factory overhead cost budget
  Operating expenses budget

Budgeted balance sheet
  Capital expenditures budget
  Cash budget

Sales Budget

The first budget to be prepared is usually the sales budget. An estimate of the dollar volume of sales revenue serves as the foundation upon which the other budgets are based. Sales volume will have a significant effect on all of the factors entering into the determination of operating income.

The sales budget ordinarily indicates (1) the quantity of forecasted sales for each product and (2) the expected unit selling price of each product. These data are often classified by areas and/or sales representatives.

In forecasting the quantity of each product expected to be sold, the starting point is generally past sales volumes. These amounts are revised for various factors expected to affect future sales, such as a backlog of unfilled sales orders, planned advertising and promotion, expected industry and general economic conditions, productive capacity, projected pricing policy, and market research study findings. Statistical analysis can be used in this process to evaluate the effect of these factors on past sales volume. Such analysis can provide a mathematical association between past sales and the several variables expected to affect future sales.

Once the forecast of sales volume is completed, the anticipated sales revenue is then determined by multiplying the volume of forecasted sales by the expected unit sales price, as shown in the following sales budget:

Sales Budget

Bowers Company
Sales Budget
For Year Ending December 31, 19--

Product and Area	Unit Sales Volume	Unit Selling Price	Total Sales
Product X:			
Area A....................	208,000	$ 9.90	$2,059,200
Area B....................	162,000	9.90	1,603,800
Area C	158,000	9.90	1,564,200
Total.....................	528,000		$5,227,200
Product Y:			
Area A....................	111,600	$16.50	$1,841,400
Area B....................	78,800	16.50	1,300,200
Area C	89,600	16.50	1,478,400
Total.....................	280,000		$4,620,000
Total revenue from sales........			$9,847,200

Frequent comparisons of actual sales with the budgeted volume, by product, area, and/or sales representative, will show differences between the two. Management is then able to investigate the probable cause of the significant differences and attempt corrective action.

Production Budget

The number of units of each commodity expected to be manufactured to meet budgeted sales and inventory requirements is set forth in the production budget. The budgeted volume of production is based on the sum of (1) the expected sales volume and (2) the desired year-end inventory, less (3) the inventory expected to be available at the beginning of the year. A production budget is illustrated as follows:

Production Budget

Bowers Company
Production Budget
For Year Ending December 31, 19--

	Units	
	Product X	Product Y
Sales.......................................	528,000	280,000
Plus desired ending inventory, December 31, 19--....	80,000	60,000
Total..	608,000	340,000
Less estimated beginning inventory, January 1, 19--..	88,000	48,000
Total production	520,000	292,000

The production needs must be carefully coordinated with the sales budget to assure that production and sales are kept in balance during the period.

Ideally, manufacturing operations should be maintained at capacity, and inventories should be neither excessive nor insufficient to fill sales orders.

Direct Materials Purchases Budget

The production needs shown by the production budget, combined with data on direct materials needed, provide the data for the direct materials purchases budget. The quantities of direct materials purchases necessary to meet production needs is based on the sum of (1) the materials expected to be needed to meet production requirements and (2) the desired year-end inventory, less (3) the inventory expected to be available at the beginning of the year. The quantities of direct materials required are then multiplied by the expected unit purchase price to determine the total cost of direct materials purchases.

In the following direct materials purchases budget, materials A and C are required for Product X, and materials A, B, and C are required for Product Y.

· · · · · · · · · ·

Direct Materials Purchases Budget

Bowers Company
Direct Materials Purchases Budget
For Year Ending December 31, 19--

	Direct Materials		
	A	B	C
Units required for production:			
Product X....................................	390,000	—	520,000
Product Y....................................	146,000	292,000	294,200
Plus desired ending inventory, Dec. 31, 19--....	80,000	40,000	120,000
Total	616,000	332,000	934,200
Less estimated beginning inventory, Jan. 1, 19-- .	103,000	44,000	114,200
Total units to be purchased.................	513,000	288,000	820,000
Unit price....................................	$ .60	$ 1.70	$ 1.00
Total direct materials purchases...............	$307,800	$489,600	$820,000

The timing of the direct materials purchases requires close coordination between the purchasing and production departments so that inventory levels can be maintained within reasonable limits.

Direct Labor Cost Budget

The needs indicated by the production budget provide the starting point for the preparation of the direct labor cost budget. The direct labor hours necessary to meet production needs are multiplied by the estimated hourly rate to yield the total direct labor cost. The manufacturing operations for both

Products X and Y are performed in Departments 1 and 2. A direct labor cost budget is illustrated as follows:

Direct Labor Cost Budget

Bowers Company
Direct Labor Cost Budget
For Year Ending December 31, 19--

	Department 1	Department 2
Hours required for production:		
Product X....	75,000	104,000
Product Y....	46,800	116,800
Total	121,800	220,800
Hourly rate....	$10	$8
Total direct labor cost....	$1,218,000	$1,766,400

The direct labor requirements must be carefully coordinated with available labor time to assure that sufficient labor will be available to meet production needs. Efficient manufacturing operations minimize idle time and labor shortages.

Factory Overhead Cost Budget

The factory overhead costs estimated to be necessary to meet production needs are presented in the factory overhead cost budget. For use as part of the master budget, the factory overhead cost budget usually presents the total estimated cost for each item of factory overhead. A factory overhead cost budget is illustrated as follows:

Factory Overhead Cost Budget

Bowers Company
Factory Overhead Cost Budget
For Year Ending December 31, 19--

Indirect factory wages	$ 732,800
Supervisory salaries	360,000
Power and light	306,000
Depreciation of plant and equipment	288,000
Indirect materials....	182,800
Maintenance....	140,280
Insurance and property taxes....	79,200
Total factory overhead cost....	$2,089,080

Supplemental schedules are often prepared to present the factory overhead cost for each individual department. Such schedules enable department supervisors to direct attention to those costs for which each is solely responsible. They also aid the production manager in evaluating performance in each department.

Cost of Goods Sold Budget

The budget for the cost of goods sold is prepared by combining data on estimated inventories with the relevant estimates of quantities and costs in the budgets for (1) direct materials purchases, (2) direct labor costs, and (3) factory overhead costs. A cost of goods sold budget is illustrated as follows:

Cost of Goods Sold Budget

Bowers Company
Cost of Goods Sold Budget
For Year Ending December 31, 19--

Finished goods inventory, January 1, 19--..			$1,095,600
Work in process inventory, January 1, 19--..		$ 214,400	
Direct materials:			
Direct materials inventory, January 1, 19--.....................	$ 250,800		
Direct materials purchases	1,617,400		
Cost of direct materials available for use .	$1,868,200		
Less direct materials inventory, December 31, 19--.................	236,000		
Cost of direct materials placed in production......................	$1,632,200		
Direct labor..........................	2,984,400		
Factory overhead......................	2,089,080		
Total manufacturing costs		6,705,680	
Total work in process during period		$6,920,080	
Less work in process inventory, December 31, 19--....................		220,000	
Cost of goods manufactured.............			6,700,080
Cost of finished goods available for sale ..			$7,795,680
Less finished goods inventory, December 31, 19--...................			1,195,000
Cost of goods sold			$6,600,680

Operating Expenses Budget

Based on past experiences, which are adjusted for future expectations, the estimated selling and general expenses are set forth in the operating expenses budget. For use as part of the master budget, the operating expenses budget ordinarily presents the expenses by nature or type of expenditure, such as sales salaries, rent, insurance, and advertising. An operating expenses budget is illustrated as follows:

Bowers Company
Operating Expenses Budget
For Year Ending December 31, 19--

Selling expenses:		
Sales salaries expense	$595,000	
Advertising expense	360,000	
Travel expense	115,000	
Telephone expense — selling	95,000	
Miscellaneous selling expense	25,000	
Total selling expenses		$1,190,000
General expenses:		
Officers salaries expense	$360,000	
Office salaries expense	105,000	
Heating and lighting expense	75,000	
Taxes expense	60,000	
Depreciation expense — office equipment	27,000	
Telephone expense — general	18,000	
Insurance expense	17,500	
Office supplies expense	7,500	
Miscellaneous general expense	25,000	
Total general expenses		695,000
Total operating expenses		$1,885,000

Detailed supplemental schedules based on departmental responsibility are often prepared for major items in the operating expenses budget. The advertising expense schedule, for example, should include such details as the advertising media to be used (newspaper, direct mail, television), quantities (column inches, number of pieces, minutes), cost per unit, frequency of use, and sectional totals. A realistic budget is prepared through careful attention to details, and effective control is achieved through assignment of responsibility to departmental supervisors.

Budgeted Income Statement

A budgeted income statement can usually be prepared from the estimated data presented in the budgets for sales, cost of goods sold, and operating expenses, with the addition of data on other income, other expense, and income tax. A budgeted income statement is illustrated as follows:

Bowers Company
Budgeted Income Statement
For Year Ending December 31, 19--

Revenue from sales.		$9,847,200
Cost of goods sold		6,600,680
Gross profit		$3,246,520
Operating expenses:		
Selling expenses	$1,190,000	
General expenses	695,000	
Total operating expenses.		1,885,000
Income from operations		$1,361,520
Other income:		
Interest income.	$ 98,000	
Other expense:		
Interest expense.	90,000	8,000
Income before income tax.		$1,369,520
Income tax.		610,000
Net income		$ 759,520

The budgeted income statement brings together in condensed form the projection of all profit-making phases of operations and enables management to weigh the effects of the individual budgets on the profit plan for the year. If the budgeted net income in relationship to sales or to stockholders' equity is disappointingly low, additional review of all factors involved should be undertaken in an attempt to improve the plans.

Capital Expenditures Budget

The capital expenditures budget summarizes future plans for acquisition of plant facilities and equipment.[3] Substantial expenditures may be needed to replace machinery and other plant assets as they wear out, become obsolete, or for other reasons fall below minimum standards of efficiency. In addition, an expansion of plant facilities may be planned to keep pace with increasing demand for a company's product or to provide for additions to the product line.

The useful life of many plant assets extends over relatively long periods of time, and the amount of the expenditures for such assets usually changes a great deal from year to year. The customary practice, therefore, is to project

---

[3]The methods of evaluating alternate capital expenditure proposals are discussed in Chapter 13.

the plans for a number of years into the future in preparing the capital expenditures budget. A five-year capital expenditures budget is illustrated as follows:

Capital Expenditures Budget

Bowers Company
Capital Expenditures Budget
For Five Years Ending December 31, 1992

Item	1988	1989	1990	1991	1992
Machinery— Department 1	$400,000			$280,000	$360,000
Machinery— Department 2	180,000	$260,000	$560,000	200,000	
Office equipment		90,000			60,000
Total	$580,000	$350,000	$560,000	$480,000	$420,000

The various proposals recognized in the capital expenditures budget must be considered in preparing certain operating budgets. For example, the expected amount of depreciation on new equipment to be acquired in the current year must be taken into consideration when the budgets for factory overhead and operating expenses are prepared. The manner in which the proposed expenditures are to be financed will also affect the cash budget.

Cash Budget

The cash budget presents the expected inflow and outflow of cash for a day, week, month, or longer period. Receipts are classified by source and disbursements by purpose. The expected cash balance at the end of the period is then compared with the amount established as the minimum balance and the difference is the anticipated excess or deficiency for the period.

The minimum cash balance represents a safety buffer for mistakes in cash planning and for emergencies. However, the amount stated as the minimum balance need not remain fixed. It should perhaps be larger during periods of "peak" business activity than during the "slow" season. In addition, for effective cash management, much of the minimum cash balance can often be deposited in interest-bearing accounts.

The interrelationship of the cash budget with other budgets may be seen from the following illustration. Data from the sales budget, the various budgets for manufacturing costs and operating expenses, and the capital expenditures budget affect the cash budget. Consideration must also be given to dividend policies, plans for equity or long-term debt financing, and other projected plans that will affect cash.

Bowers Company
Cash Budget
For Three Months Ending March 31, 19--

	January	February	March
Estimated cash receipts from:			
Cash sales..............................	$168,000	$185,000	$115,000
Collections of accounts receivable	699,000	712,800	572,000
Other sources (issuance of securities, interest, etc.)..........................	—	—	27,000
Total cash receipts	$867,000	$897,800	$714,000
Estimated cash disbursements for:			
Manufacturing costs	$541,200	$557,000	$536,000
Operating expenses	150,200	151,200	140,800
Capital expenditures.....................	—	144,000	80,000
Other purposes (notes, income tax, etc.)....	47,000	20,000	160,000
Total cash disbursements	$738,400	$872,200	$916,800
Cash increase (decrease)	$128,600	$ 25,600	$(202,800)
Cash balance at beginning of month	280,000	408,600	434,200
Cash balance at end of month..............	$408,600	$434,200	$231,400
Minimum cash balance.....................	300,000	300,000	300,000
Excess (deficiency)........................	$108,600	$134,200	$ (68,600)

In some cases, it is useful to present supplemental schedules to indicate the details of some of the amounts in the cash budget. For example, the following schedule illustrates the determination of the estimated cash receipts arising from collections of accounts receivable. For the illustration, it is assumed that the accounts receivable balance was $295,800 on January 1, and sales for each of the three months ending March 31 are $840,000, $925,000, and $575,000, respectively. Bowers Company expects to sell 20% of its merchandise for cash. Of the sales on account, 60% are expected to be collected in the month of the sale and the remainder in the following month.

Bowers Company
Schedule of Collections of Accounts Receivable
For Three Months Ending March 31, 19--

	January	February	March
January 1 balance..........................	$295,800		
January sales on account (80% × $840,000):			
Collected in January (60% × $672,000)......	403,200		
Collected in February (40% × $672,000).....		$268,800	
February sales on account (80% × $925,000):			
Collected in February (60% × $740,000).....		444,000	
Collected in March (40% × $740,000).......			$296,000
March sales on account (80% × $575,000):			
Collected in March (60% × $460,000).......			276,000
Totals	$699,000	$712,800	$572,000

The importance of accurate cash budgeting can scarcely be over-emphasized. An unanticipated lack of cash can result in loss of discounts, unfavorable borrowing terms on loans, and damage to the credit rating. On the other hand, an excess amount of idle cash also shows poor management. When the budget shows periods of excess cash, such funds can be used to reduce loans or purchase investments in readily marketable income-producing securities. Reference to the Bowers Company cash budget shows excess cash during January and February and a deficiency during March.

Getting the Most Out of Your Cash

Most businesses could reduce their interest expenses if they would improve their management of cash. The goal of cash management is to use the company's money to maximize earnings while paying all liabilities and maintaining adequate liquidity. Accelerating collections, delaying disbursements, and getting the needed information about the cash status are the foundation of effective cash management.

One of the most efficient cash management tools is the wire transfer, which is the safest and fastest way to move a large sum of money quickly. It is used by having your customers who monthly pay you large amounts wire the money directly to your bank.

Another efficient cash management tool is the lockbox, which is a system that has your customers mail their remittance checks directly to a post office box in the name of your company. You authorize your bank to collect the customers' payments, and each item is deposited directly to the bank, according to your instructions. A lockbox greatly accelerates the transformation of your receivables into cash, and it eliminates delays from mail and processing.

If your company is borrowing from a bank and not using its cash as effectively as it can, your company is losing interest every day. If the money is not needed on a day-by-day basis, you should invest the excess money in overnight, one- or two-week or 30-day instruments. If you are required to keep a compensating balance, monitor the account so that you do not keep more than the required amount.

Every morning, through phone calls or through a third party, you can receive information on your previous night's bank balances, credits, and disbursements in order to determine what you have available for investments that day. You can arrange for your bank to transfer the money out of your account and into investments every day.

Source: Allen E. Fishman, "Getting the Most Out of Your Cash," *St. Louis Post-Dispatch* (May 5, 1986), p. 14A.

Budgeted Balance Sheet

The budgeted balance sheet may reveal weaknesses in financial position, such as an abnormally large amount of current liabilities in relation to current assets, or excessive long-term debt in relation to stockholders' equity. If such conditions are indicated, the relevant factors should be given further study, so that the proper corrective action may be taken.

The budgeted balance sheet presents estimated details of financial condition at the end of a budget period, assuming that all budgeted operating and financing plans are fulfilled. A budgeted balance sheet is illustrated as follows:

Budgeted Balance Sheet

Bowers Company
Budgeted Balance Sheet
December 31, 19--

Assets

Current assets:

Cash		$ 360,000
Accounts receivable		214,000
Marketable securities		650,000

Inventories:

Finished goods	$1,195,000		
Work in process	220,000		
Materials	236,000	1,651,000	
Prepaid expenses		37,500	
Total current assets			$2,912,500

Plant assets:	Cost	Accumulated Depreciation	Book Value
Land	$ 275,000	——	$ 275,000
Buildings	3,100,000	$1,950,000	1,150,000
Machinery	950,000	380,000	570,000
Office equipment	180,000	75,000	105,000
Total plant assets	$4,505,000	$2,405,000	2,100,000
Total assets			$5,012,500

Liabilities

Current liabilities:

Accounts payable	$ 580,000	
Accrued liabilities	175,000	
Total current liabilities		$ 755,000

Long-term liabilities:

Mortgage note payable		900,000
Total liabilities		$1,655,000

Stockholders' Equity

Common stock	$2,000,000	
Retained earnings	1,357,500	
Total stockholders' equity		3,357,500
Total liabilities and stockholders' equity		$5,012,500

BUDGET PERFORMANCE REPORTS

A **budget performance report** comparing actual results with the budgeted figures should be prepared periodically for each budget. This "feedback" enables management to investigate significant differences to determine their cause and to seek means of preventing their recurrence. If corrective action cannot be taken because of changed conditions that have occurred since the budget was prepared, future budget figures should be revised accordingly. A budget performance report is illustrated as follows:

Bowers Company
Budget Performance Report—Factory Overhead Cost, Department 1
For Month Ended June 30, 19--

	Budget	Actual	Over	Under
Indirect factory wages....................	$30,200	$30,400	$200	
Supervisory salaries......................	15,000	15,000		
Power and light..........................	12,800	12,750		$ 50
Depreciation of plant and equipment.......	12,000	12,000		
Indirect materials	7,600	8,250	650	
Maintenance	5,800	5,700		100
Insurance and property taxes	3,300	3,300		
	$86,700	$87,400	$850	$150

Budget Performance Report

The amounts reported in the "Budget" column were obtained from supplemental schedules accompanying the master budget. The amounts in the "Actual" column are the costs actually incurred. The last two columns show the amounts by which actual costs exceeded or were below budgeted figures. As shown in the illustration, there were differences between the actual and budgeted amounts for some of the items of overhead cost. The cause of the significant difference in indirect materials cost should be investigated, and an attempt to find means of corrective action should be made. For example, if the difference in indirect materials cost were found to be caused by a marketwide increase in the price of materials used, a corrective action may not be possible. On the other hand, if the difference resulted from the inefficient use of materials in the production process, it may be possible to eliminate the inefficiency and effect a savings in future indirect materials costs.

FLEXIBLE BUDGETS

In the discussion of budget systems, it has been assumed that the amount of sales and the level of manufacturing activity achieved during a period approximated the goals established in the budgets. When substantial changes in expectations occur during a budget period, the budgets should be revised to give effect to such changes. Otherwise, they will be of questionable value as incentives and instruments for controlling costs and expenses.

The effect of changes in volume of activity can be "built in" to the system by what are termed **flexible budgets**. Particularly useful in estimating and controlling factory overhead costs and operating expenses, a flexible budget is in reality a series of budgets for varying rates of activity. To illustrate, assume that because of extreme variations in demand and other uncontrollable factors, the output of a particular manufacturing enterprise fluctuates widely from month to month. In such circumstances, the total factory overhead costs incurred during periods of high activity are certain to be greater than during periods of low activity. It is equally certain, however, that fluctuations in total factory overhead costs will not be exactly proportionate to the volume of production. For example, if $100,000 of factory overhead costs are usually incurred during a month in which production totals 10,000 units, the factory overhead for a month in which only 5,000 units are produced would unquestionably be more than $50,000.

As discussed in previous chapters, items of factory cost and operating expense that tend to remain constant in amount regardless of changes in volume of activity may be said to be **fixed.** Real estate taxes, property insurance, and depreciation expense on buildings are examples of fixed costs. The amounts incurred are substantially independent of the level of operations. Costs and expenses which tend to fluctuate in amount according to changes in volume of activity are called **variable.** Supplies and indirect materials used and sales commissions are examples of variable costs and expenses. The degree of variability is not the same for all variable items; few, if any, vary in exact proportion to sales or production. The terms **mixed cost, semivariable cost,** or **semifixed cost** are sometimes applied to items that have both fixed and variable characteristics to a significant degree. An example is electric power, for which there is often an initial flat fee and a rate for additional usage. For example, the charge for electricity used might be $700 for the first 10 000 kwh consumed during a month and $.05 per kwh used above 10 000.

Although there are many approaches to the preparation of a flexible budget, the first step is to identify the fixed and variable components of the various factory overhead and operating expenses being budgeted. The costs and expenses can then be presented in variable and fixed categories. For example, in the following flexible budget for factory overhead cost for one department and one product, "electric power" is broken down into its fixed and variable cost components for three different levels of production.

Flexible Budget for
Factory Overhead Cost

Collins Manufacturing Company
Monthly Factory Overhead Cost Budget

	8,000	9,000	10,000
Units of product			
Variable cost:			
Indirect factory wages	$ 32,000	$ 36,000	$ 40,000
Electric power	24,000	27,000	30,000
Indirect materials	12,000	13,500	15,000
Total variable cost	$ 68,000	$ 76,500	$ 85,000
Fixed cost:			
Supervisory salaries	$ 40,000	$ 40,000	$ 40,000
Depreciation of plant and equipment	25,000	25,000	25,000
Property taxes	15,000	15,000	15,000
Insurance	12,000	12,000	12,000
Electric power	10,000	10,000	10,000
Total fixed cost	$102,000	$102,000	$102,000
Total factory overhead cost	$170,000	$178,500	$187,000

The fixed portion of electric power is $10,000 for all levels of production. The variable portion is $30,000 for 10,000 units of product, $27,000 ($30,000 × 9,000/10,000) for 9,000 units of product, and $24,000 ($30,000 × 8,000/10,000) for 8,000 units of product.

In practice, the number of production levels and the interval between levels in a flexible budget will vary with the range of production volume. For example, instead of budgeting for 8,000, 9,000, and 10,000 units of product, it might be necessary to provide for levels, at intervals of 500, from 6,000 to 12,000 units. Alternative bases, such as hours of departmental operation or direct labor hours, may also be used in measuring the volume of activity.

In preparing budget performance reports, the actual results would be compared with the flexible budget figures for the level of operations achieved. For example, if Collins Manufacturing Company manufactured 10,000 units during a month, the budget figures reported in the budget performance report would be those appearing in the "10,000 units" column of Collins' flexible budget.

AUTOMATED BUDGETING SYSTEMS

Many firms use computers in the budgeting process. Computers can not only speed up the budgeting process, but they can also reduce the cost of budget preparation when large quantities of data need to be processed. Computers are especially useful in preparing flexible budgets and in continuous budgeting. Budget performance reports can also be prepared on a timely basis by the use of the computer.

By using computerized simulation models, which are mathematical statements of the relationships among various operating activities, management can determine the impact of various operating alternatives on the master budget. For example, if management wishes to evaluate the impact of a proposed change in direct labor wage rates, the computer can quickly provide a revised master budget that reflects the new rates. If management wishes to evaluate a proposal to add a new product line, the computer can quickly update current budgeted data and indicate the effect of the proposal on the master budget.

BUDGETING AND HUMAN BEHAVIOR

The budgeting process sets the overall goals of the business as well as the specific goals for individual units. Significant human behavior problems can develop if these goals are viewed as unrealistic or unachievable by management personnel. In such a case, management may become discouraged as well as uncommitted to the achievement of the goals. As a result, the budget becomes worthless as a tool for planning and controlling operations. On the other hand, goals set within a range that management considers attainable are likely to inspire management's efforts to achieve the goals. Therefore, it is important that all levels of management be involved in establishing the goals which they will be expected to achieve. In such an environment, the budget is a planning tool that will favorably affect human behavior and increase the possibility of achieving the goals.

Human behavior problems can also arise when the budgeted and actual results are compared and reported. These problems can be minimized if budget performance reports are used exclusively to evaluate operating performance and to initiate corrective action when performance can be improved. However, if budget performance reports are also used to evaluate management performance, management may concentrate more on defending its performance than on using the budgeting system to plan and control operations.

There is little doubt that budgets and budget performance reports can have a significant influence on management behavior. Behavioral factors have received increased attention by management accountants and behavioral scientists in recent years, and many behavioral issues are the subject of ongoing research.

Chapter Review

KEY POINTS

1. Nature and Objectives of Budgeting.
The essentials of budgeting are (1) the establishment of specific goals for future operations and (2) the periodic comparison of actual results with these goals. The establishment of specific goals for future operations encompasses the planning function of management. The periodic comparison of actual results with these goals encompasses the control function of management.

2. Budget Period.
Although budgets may be prepared for quarters of the year, months, or weeks, budgets of operating activities usually include the fiscal year of an enterprise. A variant of fiscal-year budgeting, continuous budgeting, provides for maintenance of a twelve-month projection into the future.

3. Budgeting Procedures.
All levels of management should be encouraged to participate in the budgeting process. Usually a budget committee has final responsibility for preparation of the master budget.

The sales budget is usually the first component of the master budget that is prepared. The production budget sets forth the number of units of each commodity expected to be manufactured to meet budgeted sales and inventory requirements. The direct materials budget is based on the needs shown by the production budget. The production budget also serves as a starting point for the preparation of the direct labor cost budget and factory overhead cost budget. The cost of goods sold budget is prepared by combining data on estimated inventories with the relevant estimates of quantities and costs in the budgets for (1) direct materials purchases, (2) direct labor costs, and (3) factory overhead costs. After the operating expenses budget is prepared, the budgeted income statement can be prepared.

The capital expenditures budget summarizes future plans for the acquisition of plant facilities and equipment, while the cash budget represents the expected inflow and outflow of cash for a day, week, month, or a longer period. The budgeted balance sheet presents estimated details of financial condition at the end of a budget period, assuming that all the budgeted operating and financing plans are fulfilled.

4. Budget Performance Reports.
A budget performance report provides feedback to management by reporting actual results compared with budgeted figures. Significant differences can then be investigated and corrective action taken.

5. Flexible Budgets.
Through the use of flexible budgets, the effect of changes in volume of activity can be built into the budgetary system. The preparation of flexible budgets requires the separation of costs and expenses into fixed and variable components. The use of flexible budgets facilitates the preparation of budget performance reports based on the actual level of operations achieved.

6. Automated Budgeting Systems.
Computers can be useful in speeding up the budgetary process and in preparing timely budget performance reports. In addition, through the use of simulation models, management can determine the impact of operating alternatives on the various budgets.

7. Budgeting and Human Behavior.
Significant human behavior problems can develop if managers view a budget as unrealistic or unachievable. Human behavior problems can also arise when budgeted and actual results are compared. These problems can be minimized if managers are involved in establishing budgets initially and budgets are revised for changes and expectations that occur during a budget period.

KEY TERMS

budget 261
continuous budgeting 263
zero-base budgeting 263
master budget 264
budget performance report 274

flexible budgets 275
fixed costs and expenses 276
variable cost and expenses 276
mixed costs 276

SELF-EXAMINATION QUESTIONS

(Answers at End of Chapter)

1. Budgeting of operating activities to provide at all times for maintenance of a twelve-month projection into the future is called:
   A. fixed budgeting
   B. variable budgeting
   C. continuous budgeting
   D. none of the above

2. The budget that summarizes future plans for acquisition of plant facilities and equipment is the:
   A. cash budget
   B. sales budget
   C. capital expenditures budget
   D. none of the above

3. A report comparing actual results with the budget figures is called a:
   A. budget report
   B. budget performance report
   C. flexible budget report
   D. none of the above

4. Costs that tend to remain constant in amount, regardless of variations in volume of activity, are called:
   A. fixed costs
   B. variable costs
   C. semifixed costs
   D. semivariable costs

5. The system that "builds in" the effect of fluctuations in volume of activity into the various budgets is termed:
   A. budget performance reporting
   B. continuous budgeting
   C. flexible budgeting
   D. none of the above

ILLUSTRATIVE PROBLEM

Hamilton Company prepared the following factory overhead cost budget for the Finishing Department for June of the current year:

Hamilton Company
Factory Overhead Cost Budget — Finishing Department
For Month Ending June 30, 19--

Direct labor hours budgeted		9,000
Variable cost:		
Indirect factory wages.........................	$9,450	
Indirect materials.............................	6,750	
Power and light	5,400	
Total variable cost.........................		$21,600
Fixed cost:		
Supervisory salaries	$8,000	
Indirect factory wages.........................	3,300	
Depreciation of plant and equipment............	3,100	
Insurance	1,500	
Power and light	1,200	
Property taxes	900	
Total fixed cost..........................		18,000
Total factory overhead cost......................		$39,600

Instructions:

1. Prepare a flexible budget for the month of July, indicating capacities of 8,000, 9,000, 10,000, and 11,000 direct labor hours.
2. Prepare a budget performance report for July. The Finishing Department was operated for 8,000 direct labor hours and the following factory overhead costs were incurred:

Indirect factory wages.....................................	$11,500
Supervisory salaries	8,000
Power and light	6,350
Indirect materials..	6,050
Depreciation of plant and equipment.........................	3,100
Insurance..	1,500
Property taxes	900
Total factory overhead costs incurred	$37,400

SOLUTION

(1)

Hamilton Company
Factory Overhead Cost Budget—Finishing Department
For Month Ending July 31, 19--

	8,000	9,000	10,000	11,000
Direct labor hours.................	8,000	9,000	10,000	11,000
Budgeted factory overhead:				
Variable cost:				
Indirect factory wages	$ 8,400	$ 9,450	$10,500	$11,550
Indirect materials.............	6,000	6,750	7,500	8,250
Power and light..............	4,800	5,400	6,000	6,600
Total variable cost	$19,200	$21,600	$24,000	$26,400
Fixed cost:				
Supervisory salaries	$ 8,000	$ 8,000	$ 8,000	$ 8,000
Indirect factory wages	3,300	3,300	3,300	3,300
Depreciation of plant and equipment.................	3,100	3,100	3,100	3,100
Insurance....................	1,500	1,500	1,500	1,500
Power and light..............	1,200	1,200	1,200	1,200
Property taxes	900	900	900	900
Total fixed cost.............	$18,000	$18,000	$18,000	$18,000
Total factory overhead cost........	$37,200	$39,600	$42,000	$44,400

(2)

Hamilton Company
Budget Performance Report—Finishing Department
For Month Ended July 31, 19--

	Budget	Actual	Over	Under
Variable cost:				
Indirect factory wages	$ 8,400	$ 8,200		$ 200
Indirect materials.........	6,000	6,050	$ 50	
Power and light..........	4,800	5,150	350	
Total variable cost	$19,200	$19,400		
Fixed cost:				
Supervisory salaries	$ 8,000	$ 8,000		
Indirect factory wages	3,300	3,300		
Depreciation of plant and equipment.............	3,100	3,100		
Insurance...............	1,500	1,500		
Power and light..........	1,200	1,200		
Property taxes	900	900		
Total fixed cost.........	$18,000	$18,000		
Total factory overhead cost..	$37,200	$37,400	$400	$ 200

Discussion Questions

8–1. What is a budget?

8–2. (a) Name the two basic functions of management in which accounting is involved. (b) How does a budget aid management in the discharge of these basic functions?

8–3. What is meant by *continuous budgeting?*

8–4. Why should all levels of management and all departments participate in the preparation and submission of budget estimates?

8–5. Which budgetary concept requires all levels of management to start from zero and estimate sales, production, and other operating data as though the operations were being initiated for the first time?

8–6. Why should the production requirements as set forth in the production budget be carefully coordinated with the sales budget?

8–7. Why should the timing of direct materials purchases be closely coordinated with the production budget?

8–8. What is a capital expenditures budget?

8–9. (a) Discuss the purpose of the cash budget. (b) If the cash budget for the first quarter of the fiscal year indicates excess cash at the end of each of the first two months, how might the excess cash be used?

8–10. What is a budget performance report?

8–11. What is a flexible budget?

8–12. Distinguish between (a) fixed costs and (b) variable costs.

8–13. Which of the following costs incurred by a manufacturing enterprise tend to be fixed and which tend to be variable: (a) cost of direct materials entering into finished product, (b) salary of factory superintendent, (c) indirect materials, (d) rent on factory building, (e) depreciation on factory building, (f) property taxes on factory building, (g) direct labor entering into finished product?

8–14. What is a mixed cost?

8–15. Drake Corporation uses flexible budgets. For each of the following variable operating expenses, indicate whether there has been a saving or an excess of expenses, assuming that actual sales were $500,000.

Expense Item	Actual Amount	Budget Allowance Based on Sales
Factory supplies expense.......	$15,800	3%
Uncollectible accounts expense .	9,500	2%

8–16. Briefly discuss the type of human behavior problem that might arise if goals used in developing budgets are unrealistic or unachievable.

8–17. Real World Focus. During a ten-year period from 1977 to 1986, the ratio of cost of sales to net sales for PepsiCo Inc. declined from 48.2% to 40.2%. During this same period, the net sales of PepsiCo increased by approximately 400%. As the sales increase, why would management normally expect the ratio of cost of sales to net sales to decline?

Exercises

·

SPREADSHEET
PROBLEM

8–18. Sales and production budgets. Husley Company manufactures two models of humidifiers, M3 and P4. Based on the following production and sales data for June of the current year, prepare (a) a sales budget and (b) a production budget.

	M3	P4
Estimated inventory (units), June 1..................	45,000	27,600
Desired inventory (units), June 30..................	54,000	24,000
Expected sales volume (units):		
Region A......................................	81,500	40,800
Region B......................................	66,200	24,800
Unit sales price	$14.50	$20

SPREADSHEET PROBLEM

8–19. Schedule of cash collections of accounts receivable. Mattox Company was organized on August 1 of the current year. Projected sales for each of the first three months of operations are as follows:

August	$160,000
September	200,000
October	280,000

The company expects to sell 25% of its merchandise for cash. Of sales on account, 60% are expected to be collected in the month of the sale, 30% in the month following the sale, and the remainder in the following month. Prepare a schedule indicating cash collections of accounts receivable for August, September, and October.

8–20. Schedule of cash disbursements. Sirmons Company was organized on February 28 of the current year. Projected operating expenses for each of the first three months of operations are as follows:

March	$ 98,000
April	122,000
May	136,000

Depreciation, insurance, and property taxes represent $18,000 of the estimated monthly operating expenses. Insurance was paid on February 28, and property taxes will be paid in December. Three fourths of the remainder of the operating expenses are expected to be paid in the month in which they are incurred, with the balance to be paid in the following month. Prepare a schedule indicating cash disbursements for operating expenses for March, April, and May.

8–21. Flexible budget for operating expenses. Daniel Company uses flexible budgets that are based on the following data:

Sales commissions	6% of sales
Advertising expense	$10,000 for $200,000 of sales
	$15,000 for $300,000 of sales
	$20,000 for $400,000 of sales
Miscellaneous selling expense	$1,000 plus 1/2% of sales
Office salaries expense	$15,000
Office supplies expense	2% of sales
Miscellaneous general expense	$500 plus 1/4% of sales

Prepare a flexible operating expenses budget for November of the current year for sales volumes of $200,000, $300,000, and $400,000.

8–22. Budget performance report. The operating expenses incurred during November of the current year by Daniel Company were as follows:

Sales commissions	$23,800
Advertising expense	22,600
Miscellaneous selling expense	3,050
Office salaries expense	15,000
Office supplies expense	7,810
Miscellaneous general expense	1,620

Assuming that the total sales for November were $400,000, prepare a budget performance report for operating expenses on the basis of the data presented above and in Exercise 8–21.

8–23.   Flexible factory overhead cost budget.   Spang Company prepared the following factory overhead cost budget for Department L for March of the current year, during which it expected to manufacture 20,000 units:

Variable cost:		
Indirect factory..............................	$16,000	
Power and light	12,500	
Indirect materials............................	4,000	
Total variable cost.........................		$32,500
Fixed cost:		
Supervisory salaries	$15,000	
Depreciation of plant and equipment............	4,000	
Insurance and property taxes..................	2,000	
Total fixed cost............................		21,000
Total factory overhead cost......................		$53,500

Assuming that the estimated costs in March are applicable to April operations, prepare a flexible factory overhead cost budget for Department L for April for 18,000, 20,000, and 22,000 units of product.

8–24.   Budget performance report.   During April, Spang Company manufactured 22,000 units, and the factory overhead costs incurred in Department L were: indirect factory wages, $17,300; power and light, $14,000; indirect materials, $4,500; supervisory salaries, $15,000; depreciation of plant and equipment, $4,000; and insurance and property taxes, $2,000.

Prepare a budget performance report for Department L for April. To be useful for cost control, the budgeted amounts should be based on the data for 22,000 units, as revealed in Exercise 8–23.

Problems
·

8–25.   Sales, production, direct materials, and direct labor budgets.   The budget director of Greaves Company requests estimates of sales, production, and other operating data from the various administrative units every month. Selected information concerning sales and production for August of the current year are summarized as follows:

(a) Estimated sales for August by sales territory:
   Northeast:
      Product A: 24,000 units at $45 per unit
      Product B: 20,000 units at $60 per unit
   Southeast:
      Product A: 15,000 units at $45 per unit
      Product B: 27,000 units at $60 per unit
   Southwest:
      Product A: 32,000 units at $45 per unit
      Product B: 43,000 units at $60 per unit

(b) Estimated inventories at August 1:
   Direct materials:
      Material W: 21,000 lbs.   Material Y: 21,500 lbs.
      Material X: 15,600 lbs.   Material Z: 27,600 lbs.
   Finished products:
      Product A: 10,000 units   Product B: 15,000 units

(c) Desired inventories at August 31:
   Direct materials:
      Material W: 18,000 lbs.   Material Y: 28,000 lbs.
      Material X: 22,000 lbs.   Material Z: 20,000 lbs.
   Finished products:
      Product A: 12,000 units   Product B: 25,000 units

(d) Direct materials used in production:
   In manufacture of Product A:
      Material X: 1.2 lbs. per unit of product
      Material Y: .8 lbs. per unit of product
      Material Z: 1.0 lb. per unit of product
   In manufacture of Product B:
      Material W: 1.5 lbs. per unit of product
      Material Y: .9 lbs. per unit of product
      Material Z: 1.4 lbs. per unit of product

(e) Anticipated purchase price for direct materials:
      Material W: $1.40 per lb.   Material Y: $2.00 per lb.
      Material X: $ .50 per lb.   Material Z: $1.75 per lb.

(f) Direct labor requirements:
      Product A:
         Department 20: 1.0 hour at $14 per hour
         Department 30: .6 hours at $20 per hour
      Product B:
         Department 10: 1.4 hours at $15 per hour
         Department 20: .5 hours at $14 per hour

Instructions:

(1) Prepare a sales budget for August.
(2) Prepare a production budget for August.
(3) Prepare a direct materials purchases budget for August.
(4) Prepare a direct labor cost budget for August.

8–26. Budgeted income statement and supporting budgets. The budget director of Martin Inc., with the assistance of the controller, treasurer, production manager, and sales manager, has gathered the following data for use in developing the budgeted income statement for July:

(a) Estimated sales for July:
   Product J: 50,000 units at $120 per unit
   Product K: 30,000 units at $90 per unit

(b) Estimated inventories at July 1:
   Direct materials: Finished products:
      Material A: 5,000 lbs.   Product J: 10,000 units at $92 per unit
      Material B: 40,000 lbs.   Product K: 7,000 units at $75 per unit
      Material C: 8,000 lbs.

(c) Desired inventories at July 31:
   Direct materials: Finished products:
      Material A: 8,000 lbs.   Product J: 15,000 units at $92 per unit
      Material B: 35,000 lbs.   Product K: 9,000 units at $75 per unit
      Material C: 10,000 lbs.

(d) Direct materials used in production:
   In manufacture of Product J:
      Material A: .75 lbs. per unit of product
      Material B: 1.5 lbs. per unit of product
   In manufacture of Product K:
      Material B: 1.0 lb. per unit of product
      Material C: 1.2 lbs. per unit of product

(e) Anticipated cost of purchases and beginning and ending inventory of direct materials:
      Material A: $14.00 per lb.
      Material B: $ .80 per lb.
      Material C: $20.00 per lb.

(f) Direct labor requirements:
   Product J:
      Department 100: 3.0 hours at $15 per hour
      Department 200: 1.0 hour at $20 per hour
   Product K:
      Department 200: .5 hours at $20 per hour
      Department 300: 2.0 hours at $18 per hour

(g) Estimated factory overhead costs for July:

Indirect factory wages	$250,000
Depreciation of plant and equipment	220,000
Supervisory salaries	125,000
Power and light	115,700
Indirect materials	81,000
Maintenance	33,400
Insurance and property taxes	25,900

(h) Estimated operating expenses for July:

Sales salaries expense...............................	$462,000
Officers salaries expense............................	300,000
Advertising expense	286,000
Office salaries expense..............................	125,000
Depreciation expense — office equipment...............	84,500
Telephone expense — selling..........................	47,900
Telephone expense — general.........................	22,000
Travel expense — selling.............................	14,500
Travel expense — general............................	8,300
Office supplies expense	4,000
Miscellaneous selling expense	11,200
Miscellaneous general expense	7,500

(i) Estimated other income and expense for July:

Interest income.....................................	$180,000
Interest expense....................................	145,000

(j) Estimated tax rate: 30%.

Instructions:

(1) Prepare a sales budget for July.

(2) Prepare a production budget for July.

(3) Prepare a direct materials purchases budget for July.

(4) Prepare a direct labor cost budget for July.

(5) Prepare a factory overhead cost budget for July.

(6) Prepare a cost of goods sold budget for July. Work in process at the beginning of July is estimated to be $140,000, and work in process at the end of July is estimated to be $150,000.

(7) Prepare an operating expenses budget for July. Classify the expenses as either selling or general expenses.

(8) Prepare a budgeted income statement for July.

8–27. Cash budget. The treasurer of Flores Company instructs you to prepare a monthly cash budget for the next three months. You are presented with the following budget information:

	April	May	June
Sales	$600,000	$550,000	$700,000
Manufacturing costs	390,000	360,000	450,000
Operating expenses	125,000	115,000	145,000
Capital expenditures..............	—	160,000	—

The company expects to sell about 25% of its merchandise for cash. Of sales on account, 60% are expected to be collected in full in the month following the sale and the remainder the following month. Depreciation, insurance, and property taxes represent $30,000 of the estimated monthly manufacturing costs and $5,000 of the probable monthly operating expenses. Insurance and property taxes are paid in December. Of the remainder of the manufacturing costs and operating expenses, 70% are expected to be paid in the month in which they are incurred and the balance in the following month.

Current assets as of April 1 are composed of cash of $70,200, marketable securities of $60,000, and accounts receivable of $570,000 ($442,000 from March sales and $128,000 from February sales). Current liabilities as of April 1 are composed of a $100,000, 12%, 120-day note payable due June 20, $105,000 of accounts payable incurred in March for manufacturing costs, and accrued liabilities of $30,200 incurred in March for operating expenses.

It is expected that $4,000 in dividends will be received in May. An estimated income tax payment of $31,200 will be made in June. Flores Company's regular semiannual dividend of $20,000 is expected to be declared in May and paid in June. Management desires to maintain a minimum cash balance of $60,000.

Instructions:

(1) Prepare a monthly cash budget for April, May, and June.
(2) On the basis of the cash budget prepared in (1), what recommendation should be made to the treasurer?

8–28. Forecast sales volume and sales budget. Ingram Company prepared the following sales budget for the current year:

Ingram Company
Sales Budget
For Year Ending December 31, 1989

Product and Area	Unit Sales Volume	Unit Selling Price	Total Sales
Product R:			
East.	20,000	$15.00	$ 300,000
Central	30,000	15.00	450,000
West	50,000	15.00	750,000
Total	100,000		$1,500,000
Product S:			
East.	15,000	$10.00	$ 150,000
Central	12,000	10.00	120,000
West	8,000	10.00	80,000
Total	35,000		$ 350,000
Total revenue from sales			$1,850,000

At the end of September, 1989, the following unit sales data were reported for the first nine months of the year:

	Unit Sales	
	Product R	Product S
East.	14,100	11,475
Central	23,400	9,270
West	36,000	5,700

For the year ending December 31, 1990, unit sales are expected to follow the patterns established during the first nine months of the year ending December 31, 1989. The unit selling price for Product R is not expected to change, and the unit selling price for Product S is expected to be increased to $10.50, effective January 1, 1990.

Instructions:

(1) Compute the increase or decrease of actual *unit* sales for the nine months ended September 30, 1989, over expectations for this nine-month period. Since sales have historically occurred evenly throughout the year, budgeted sales for the first nine months of a year would be 75% of the year's budgeted sales. Comparison of this amount with actual sales will indicate the percentage increase or decrease of actual sales for the nine months over budgeted sales for the nine months. (Round percent changes to the nearest whole percent.) Place your answers in a columnar table with the following format:

	Unit Budgeted Sales		Actual Sales	Increase (Decrease)	
	Year	Nine Months	for Nine Months	Amount	Percent
Product R					
East					
Central					
West					
Product S					
East					
Central					
West					

(2) Assuming that the trend of sales indicated in (1) is to continue in 1990, compute the unit sales volume to be used for preparing the sales budget for the year ending December 31, 1990. Place your answers in a columnar table with the following format:

	1989 Budgeted Units	Percentage Increase (Decrease)	1990 Budgeted Units
Product R			
East			
Central			
West			
Product S			
East			
Central			
West			

(3) Prepare a sales budget for the year ending December 31, 1990.

8–29. Flexible factory overhead cost budget and budget performance report. Sims Inc. prepared the following factory overhead cost budget for July of the current year for 12,000 units of product:

Sims Inc.
Factory Overhead Cost Budget
For Month Ending July 31, 19--

Variable cost:		
Indirect factory wages	$36,000	
Indirect materials......................................	21,000	
Power and light..	13,200	
Total variable cost.............................		$ 70,200
Fixed cost:		
Supervisory salaries...............................	$16,200	
Indirect factory wages	13,800	
Depreciation of plant and equipment	10,000	
Insurance..	7,100	
Power and light.......................................	6,300	
Property taxes......................................	2,000	
Total fixed cost		55,400
Total factory overhead cost...........................		$125,600

The following factory overhead costs were incurred in producing 11,000 units in July:

Indirect factory wages	$ 47,500
Supervisory salaries...	16,200
Power and light..	18,000
Indirect materials...	19,100
Depreciation of plant and equipment	10,000
Insurance...	7,100
Property taxes...	2,000
Total factory overhead cost incurred..........................	$119,900

Instructions:

(1) Prepare a flexible factory overhead cost budget for July, indicating capacities of 9,000, 10,000, 11,000, and 12,000 units of product.
(2) Prepare a budget performance report for July.

8–30. Budgeted income statement and balance sheet. As a preliminary to requesting budget estimates of sales, costs, and expenses for the fiscal year beginning January 1, 1990, the following tentative trial balance as of December 31 of the preceding year is prepared by the accounting department of Calmer Company:

Cash	85,000	
Accounts Receivable	90,000	
Finished Goods....................................	150,000	
Work in Process	78,800	
Materials.......................................	52,200	
Prepaid Expenses..................................	10,200	
Plant and Equipment	800,000	
Accumulated Depreciation—Plant and Equipment		320,000
Accounts Payable....................................		100,000
Notes Payable......................................		60,000
Common Stock, $20 par		150,000
Retained Earnings		636,200
	1,266,200	1,266,200

Factory output and sales for 1990 are expected to total 60,000 units of product, which are to be sold at $20 per unit. The quantities and costs of the inventories (lifo method) at December 31, 1990, are expected to remain unchanged from the balances at the beginning of the year.

Budget estimates of manufacturing costs and operating expenses for the year are summarized as follows:

	Estimated Costs and Expenses	
	Fixed (Total for Year)	Variable (Per Unit Sold)
Cost of goods manufactured and sold:		
Direct materials......................	—	$2.50
Direct labor	—	6.00
Factory overhead:		
Depreciation of plant and equipment ...	$25,000	—
Other factory overhead	18,000	1.95
Selling expenses:		
Sales salaries and commissions	30,000	.60
Advertising..........................	15,000	—
Miscellaneous selling expense..........	1,000	.05
General expenses:		
Office and officers salaries.............	40,000	.30
Supplies	2,000	.10
Miscellaneous general expense.........	1,000	.04

Balances of accounts receivable, prepaid expenses, and accounts payable at the end of the year are expected to differ from the beginning balances by only inconsequential amounts.

For purposes of this problem, assume that federal income tax of $160,500 on 1990 taxable income will be paid during 1990. Regular quarterly cash dividends of $.30 a share are expected to be declared and paid in March, June, September, and December. It is anticipated that plant and equipment will be purchased for $200,000 cash in November.

Instructions:

(1) Prepare a budgeted income statement for 1990.
(2) Prepare a budgeted balance sheet as of December 31, 1990.

ALTERNATE PROBLEMS

8–27A. Cash budget. The treasurer of Inman Company instructs you to prepare a monthly cash budget for the next three months. You are presented with the following budget information:

	October	November	December
Sales...........................	$240,000	$360,000	$410,000
Manufacturing costs..............	140,000	220,000	250,000
Operating expenses..............	38,000	54,000	62,000
Capital expenditures..............	—	90,000	—

The company expects to sell about 30% of its merchandise for cash. Of sales on account, 80% are expected to be collected in full in the month following the sale and the remainder the following month. Depreciation, insurance, and property taxes represent $20,000 of the estimated monthly manufacturing costs and $8,000 of the probable monthly operating expenses. Insurance and property taxes are paid in March and August respectively. Of the remainder of the manufacturing costs and operating expenses, 65% are expected to be paid in the month in which they are incurred and the balance in the following month.

Current assets as of October 1 are composed of cash of $28,500, marketable securities of $40,000, and accounts receivable of $176,400 ($140,000 from September sales and $36,400 from August sales). Current liabilities as of October 1 are composed of a $50,000, 10%, 90-day note payable due November 5, $42,500 of accounts payable incurred in September for manufacturing costs, and accrued liabilities of $10,200 incurred in September for operating expenses.

It is expected that $2,000 in dividends will be received in October. An estimated income tax payment of $15,000 will be made in November. Inman Company's regular quarterly dividend of $10,000 is expected to be declared in November and paid in December. Management desires to maintain a minimum cash balance of $25,000.

Instructions:

(1) Prepare a monthly cash budget for October, November, and December.
(2) On the basis of the cash budget prepared in (1), what recommendation should be made to the treasurer?

8–28A. Forecast sales volume and sales budget. Johnson Company prepared the following sales budget for the current year:

Johnson Company
Sales Budget
For Year Ending December 31, 1989

Product and Area	Unit Sales Volume	Unit Selling Price	Total Sales
Product R:			
East.	20,000	$18.00	$ 360,000
Central	30,000	18.00	540,000
West	40,000	18.00	720,000
Total	90,000		$1,620,000
Product S:			
East.	50,000	$20.00	$1,000,000
Central	60,000	20.00	1,200,000
West	75,000	20.00	1,500,000
Total	185,000		$3,700,000
Total revenue from sales			$5,320,000

At the end of September, 1989, the following unit sales data were reported for the first nine months of the year:

	Unit Sales	
	Product R	Product S
East..................................	14,400	39,750
Central	22,950	44,100
West	28,500	60,750

For the year ending December 31, 1990, unit sales are expected to follow the patterns established during the first nine months of the year ending December 31, 1989. The unit selling price for Product R is expected to be increased to $19, effective January 1, 1990, and the unit selling price for Product S is not expected to change.

Instructions:

(1) Compute the increase or decrease of actual *unit* sales for the nine months ended September 30, 1989, over expectations for this nine-month period. Since sales have historically occurred evenly throughout the year, budgeted sales for the first nine months of a year would be 75% of the year's budgeted sales. Comparison of this amount with actual sales will indicate the percentage increase or decrease of actual sales for the nine months over budgeted sales for the nine months. Place your answers in a columnar table with the following format:

	Unit Budgeted Sales		Actual Sales	Increase (Decrease)	
	Year	Nine Months	for Nine Months	Amount	Percent
Product R					
East					
Central					
West					
Product S					
East					
Central					
West					

(2) Assuming that the trend of sales indicated in (1) is to continue in 1990, compute the unit sales volume to be used for preparing the sales budget for the year ending December 31, 1990. Place your answers in a columnar table with the following format:

	1989 Budgeted Units	Percentage Increase (Decrease)	1990 Budgeted Units
Product R			
East			
Central			
West			
Product S			
East			
Central			
West			

(3) Prepare a sales budget for the year ending December 31, 1990.

8–29A. Flexible factory overhead cost budget and budget performance report. Southern Company prepared the following factory overhead cost budget for June of the current year for 20,000 units of product:

Southern Company
Factory Overhead Cost Budget
For Month Ending June 30, 19--

Variable cost:		
Indirect factory wages	$30,000	
Indirect materials.................................	18,500	
Power and light....................................	9,500	
Total variable cost..............................		$ 58,000
Fixed cost:		
Supervisory salaries..............................	$25,000	
Indirect factory wages	7,500	
Depreciation of plant and equipment	6,000	
Insurance..	4,500	
Power and light...................................	4,000	
Property taxes....................................	3,000	
Total fixed cost		50,000
Total factory overhead cost.........................		$108,000

The following factory overhead costs were incurred in producing 19,000 units in June:

Indirect factory wages	$ 36,800
Supervisory salaries...	25,000
Indirect materials...	17,100
Power and light...	12,600
Depreciation of plant and equipment	6,000
Insurance...	4,500
Property taxes..	3,000
Total factory overhead cost incurred.........................	$105,000

Instructions:

(1) Prepare a flexible factory overhead cost budget for June, indicating capacities of 18,000, 19,000, 20,000, and 21,000 units of product.
(2) Prepare a budget performance report for June.

Mini-Case 8

Your father is president and chief operating officer of Barnes Manufacturing Company and has hired you as a summer intern to assist the controller. The controller has asked you to visit with the production supervisor of the Polishing Department and evaluate the supervisor's concern with the budgeting process. After this evaluation, you are to meet with the controller to discuss suggestions for improving the budgeting process.

This morning, you met with the supervisor, who expressed dissatisfaction with the budgets and budget performance reports prepared for the factory overhead costs for the Polishing Department. Specifically, July's budget performance report was mentioned as an example. The supervisor indicated that this report is not useful in evaluating the efficiency of the department, because most of the overages for the individual factory overhead items are not caused by inefficiencies, but by variations in the volume of activity between actual and budget. Although you were not provided with a copy of the budget for July, the supervisor indicated that it is standard practice for the plant manager to prepare a budget based on the production of 20,000 units. Actual production varies widely, however, with approximately 22,000 to 24,000 units being produced each month for the past several months. You are provided with the following budget performance report for July of the current year, when actual production was 24,000 units. All of the overages relate to variable costs, and the other costs are fixed.

Barnes Manufacturing Company
Budget Performance Report — Factory Overhead Cost, Polishing Department
For Month Ended July 31, 19--

	Budget	Actual	Over	Under
Indirect factory wages	$18,000	$21,800	$3,800	
Electric power	15,000	17,500	2,500	
Supervisory salaries.................	12,000	12,000		
Depreciation of plant assets..........	8,100	8,100		
Indirect materials....................	7,500	9,100	1,600	
Insurance and property taxes.........	5,000	5,000		
	$65,600	$73,500	$7,900	$0

In your discussion, you learned that the department supervisor has little faith in the budgeting process. The supervisor views the budgets as worthless and the budget performance reports as a waste of time, because they require an explanation of the budget overages, which, for the most part, are not departmentally controlled.

Instructions:

Prepare a list of suggestions for improving the budgeting process. Include any reports that you might find useful when you meet with the controller to discuss your suggestions.

Answers to Self-Examination Questions

1. C Continuous budgeting (answer C) is a type of budgeting that continually provides for maintenance of a twelve-month projection into the future.

2. C The capital expenditures budget (answer C) summarizes the plans for the acquisition of plant facilities and equipment for a number of years into the future. The cash budget (answer A) presents the expected inflow and outflow of cash for a budget period, and the sales budget (answer B) presents the expected sales for the budget period.

3. B A budget performance report (answer B) compares actual results with budgeted figures.

4. A Costs that tend to remain constant in amount, regardless of variations in volume of activity, are called fixed costs (answer A). Costs that tend to fluctuate in amount in accordance with variations in volume are called variable costs (answer B). Costs that have both fixed and variable characteristics are called semifixed costs (answer C) or semivariable costs (answer D).

5. C Flexible budgeting (answer C) provides a series of budgets for varying rates of activity and thereby builds into the budgeting system the effect of fluctuations in volume of activity. Budget performance reporting (answer A) is a system of reports that compares actual results with budgeted figures. Continuous budgeting (answer B) is a variant of fiscal-year budgeting that provides for continuous twelve-month projections into the future. This is achieved by periodically deleting from the current budget the data for the elapsed period and adding newly estimated budget data for the same period next year.

Chapter Nine

CHAPTER OBJECTIVES

•

Describe the nature and objectives of standards.

•

Describe the use of standard cost systems in planning
and controlling operations.

•

Describe the use of variance analysis in controlling operations.

•

Compute and illustrate the use of the following variances
in controlling costs:
Direct materials quantity variance
Direct materials price variance
Direct labor time variance
Direct labor rate variance
Factory overhead volume variance
Factory overhead controllable variance

•

Describe and illustrate the use of standards in the accounts.

•

Describe and illustrate the reporting of variances on the income statement.

•

Describe the conditions requiring the revision of standards.

•

Describe the use of standards for nonmanufacturing expenses.

•

Standard Cost Systems

The preceding chapter focused on the use of budgets as an aid to management in planning and controlling the operations of a business. This chapter will focus on standard cost systems and variance analysis, which can also be used by management in planning and controlling operations.

THE NATURE AND OBJECTIVES OF STANDARDS

Standards are used to measure and evaluate performance in many areas of life. For example, colleges and universities set standards for graduation, such as a C average. They may establish a B+ average for graduation with honors. Golfers use par as a standard in evaluating their play on the golf course. In each of these cases, the predetermined standard is used to measure and evaluate an individual's performance. In a like manner, business enterprises may use carefully predetermined standards to evaluate and control operations.

Service, merchandising, and manufacturing enterprises can all use standards. For example, an automobile repair garage may use a *standard* amount of time, as expressed in service manuals, as the basis for computing the labor charges for automobile repairs and measuring the performance of the mechanic. The driver of a truck delivering merchandise may be expected to make a *standard* number of deliveries each day. The widest use of standards is by manufacturing enterprises, which establish standard costs for the three categories of manufacturing costs: direct materials, direct labor, and factory overhead.

Accounting systems that use standards for each element of manufacturing cost entering into the finished product are sometimes called standard cost systems. Such systems enable management to determine how much a product should cost (standard), how much it does cost (actual), and the causes of any difference (variance) between the two. Standard costs thus serve as a device for measuring efficiency. If the actual costs are compared with the standard costs, unfavorable conditions can be determined and corrective actions taken. Thus, management has a device for controlling costs and motivating employees to become more cost conscious.

Setting Standards

The starting point in setting standards is often a review of past operations. In this review, management and the management accountant rely on their knowledge and judgment of past processes and costs to estimate the costs to produce a unit of product. However, standards should not be merely an extension of past costs. Inefficiencies may be reflected in past costs, and these inefficiencies should be considered in determining what the costs should be (standards). In addition, changes in technology, machinery, production methods, and economic conditions must be considered.

The setting of standards is both an art and a science. Although the standard-setting process varies among enterprises, it often requires the joint efforts of accountants, engineers, personnel administrators, and other management personnel. The management accountant plays an important role by expressing the results of judgments and studies in terms of dollars and subsequently reporting how actual results compare with these standards. Engineers contribute to the standard-setting process by studying the requirements of the product and the production process. For example, direct materials requirements can be determined by studying such factors as the materials specifications for the product and the normal spoilage in production. Time and motion studies may be used to determine the length of time required for each of the various manufacturing operations. Engineering studies may also be used to determine standards for some of the elements of factory overhead, such as the amount of power needed to operate machinery.

The Development of Standard Costs

An example of a company that uses standard costs is Dutch Pantry Inc., which operates 53 family restaurants in 12 eastern states. To assure consistent quality in the items served in these restaurants, much of the food preparation is done in a central commissary. Because the commissary produces more than 150 different items, it uses a standard cost system based on the production of a batch of product. This system allows the costs for the many products to flow through the various operations involved in food preparation.

The food processing activity of the central commissary consists of the following operations:

Spice room	Trim
Butcher shop	Weigh
Pan/stuffing	Pop-out
Bake/roast	Sure flow
Meat/broth	Bulk pack
Cooking kettles	Salad dressing
Frying	Case packing
Slicing	Warehouse

As production passes through each of these operations, the various elements of cost are incurred. How standard costs are developed for Dutch Pantry's raw materials, ingredients, packaging, and direct labor is described in the following excerpts from an article in *Management Accounting:*

... The standard costs of raw materials, ingredients and packaging are calculated by the use of a Recipe Sheet..., which is actually a bill of materials for a batch of the product. For costing purposes, the recipes are input to a computer program called the Recipe Master List. All costs are calculated on a hundred weight (CWT) basis....

The standard costs of the component items are updated monthly on the Inventory Master Listing. At the same time, the updated costs are input to the Recipe Master List. This permits a timely revision of the costs of the finished products for changes in the standards of any components.

Direct labor dollars are [incurred in] production [as] the product passes through [the various operations.] A labor grid is prepared for each product. This grid lists the various [operations] for the product and the number of workers required to staff each [operation]. The various worker classifications and hourly rates are used to calculate a weighted-average cost per hour for direct labor.

Next, a standard poundage of product processed per hour is developed for each [operation]. A weighted average of the actual production runs from the prior year is used for this calculation. The direct labor cost per CWT is recorded on the product rate master (report) by [operation]....

[Finally, the] budgeted direct labor dollars for the warehouse are divided by the forecasted quantity of production (cases). The result is the warehousing cost per case....

Source: Dennis M. Boll, "How Dutch Pantry Accounts for Standard Costs," *Management Accounting* (December, 1982), pp. 32–35.

Types of Standards

Implicit in the use of standards is the concept of an acceptable level of production efficiency. One of the major objectives in selecting this performance level is to motivate workers to expend the efforts necessary to achieve the most efficient operations.

Standards that are too high, that is, standards that are unrealistic, may have a negative impact on performance because workers may become frustrated with their inability to meet the standards and, therefore, may not be motivated to do their best. Such standards represent levels of performance that can be achieved only under perfect operating conditions, such as no idle time, no machine breakdown, and no materials spoilage. Such standards, often called theoretical standards or **ideal standards,** are not widely used.

Standards that are too low might not motivate employees to perform at their best because the standard level of performance can be reached too easily. As a result, productivity may be lower than that which could be achieved.

Most companies use currently attainable standards (sometimes called **normal standards**), which represent levels of operation that can be attained with reasonable effort. Such currently attainable standards allow for reasonable production problems and errors, such as normal materials spoilage and machinery downtime for maintenance. When reasonable standards are used, employees often become cost conscious and expend their best efforts to achieve the best possible results at the lowest possible cost. Also, if employees are given bonuses for exceeding normal standards, the standards may be even more effective in motivating employees to perform at their best.

VARIANCES FROM STANDARDS

One of the primary purposes of a standard cost system is to facilitate control over costs by comparing actual costs with standard costs. Control is achieved by the action of management in investigating significant deviations of performance from standards and taking corrective action. Differences between the standard costs of a department or product and the actual costs incurred are termed **variances.** If the actual cost incurred is less than the standard cost, the variance is favorable. If the actual cost exceeds the standard cost, the variance is unfavorable. When actual costs are compared with standard costs, only the "exceptions" or variances are reported to the person responsible for cost control. This reporting by the "principle of exceptions" enables the one responsible for cost control to concentrate on the cause and correction of the variances.

When manufacturing operations are automated, standard cost data can be integrated with the computer that directs operations. Variances can then be detected and reported automatically by the computer system, and adjustments can be made to operations in progress.

The total variance for a certain period is usually made up of several variances, some of which may be favorable and some unfavorable. There may be variances from standards in direct materials costs, in direct labor costs, and in factory overhead costs. Illustrations and analyses of these variances for Ballard Company, a manufacturing enterprise, are presented in the following paragraphs. For illustrative purposes, it is assumed that only one type of direct material is used, that there is a single processing department, and that Product X is the only commodity manufactured by the enterprise. The standard costs for direct materials, direct labor, and factory overhead for a unit of Product X are as follows:

Direct materials:	
2 pounds at $1 per pound	$ 2.00
Direct labor:	
.4 hour at $16 per hour.	6.40
Factory overhead:	
.4 hour at $8.40 per hour	3.36
Total per unit.	$11.76

Direct Materials Cost Variance

Two major factors enter into the determination of standards for direct materials cost: (1) the quantity (usage) standard and (2) the price standard. If the actual quantity of direct materials used in producing a commodity differs from the standard quantity, there is a **quantity variance.** If the actual unit price of the materials differs from the standard price, there is a **price variance.** To illustrate, assume that the standard direct materials cost of producing

10,000 units of Product X and the direct materials cost actually incurred during June were as follows:

Actual: 20,600 pounds at $1.04............ $21,424
Standard: 20,000 pounds at $1.00............ 20,000

The unfavorable variance of $1,424 resulted in part from an excess usage of 600 pounds of direct materials and in part from an excess cost of $.04 per pound. The analysis of the direct materials cost variance is as follows:

Quantity variance:
  Actual quantity .... 20,600 pounds
  Standard quantity......... 20,000 pounds
    Variance—unfavorable. . 600 pounds × standard price, $1 ...... $ 600

Price variance:
  Actual price .... $1.04 per pound
  Standard price .... 1.00 per pound
    Variance—unfavorable. . $ .04 per pound × actual quantity, 20,600 . 824
Total direct materials cost variance—unfavorable $1,424

Direct Materials Cost Variance

Direct Materials Quantity Variance. The direct materials quantity variance is the difference between the actual quantity used and the standard quantity, multiplied by the standard price per unit. If the standard quantity exceeds the actual quantity used, the variance is favorable. If the actual quantity of materials used exceeds the standard quantity, the variance is unfavorable, as shown for Ballard Company in the following illustration:

$$\text{Direct Materials Quantity Variance} = \text{Actual Quantity Used} - \text{Standard Quantity} \times \text{Standard Price per Unit}$$

Quantity variance = (20,600 pounds − 20,000 pounds) × $1.00 per pound
Quantity variance = 600 pounds   × $1.00 per pound
Quantity variance = $600 unfavorable

Direct Materials Quantity Variance

Direct Materials Price Variance. The direct materials price variance is the difference between the actual price per unit and the standard price per unit, multiplied by the actual quantity used. If the standard price per unit exceeds the actual price per unit, the variance is favorable. If the actual price per unit exceeds the standard price per unit, the variance is unfavorable, as shown for Ballard Company in the following illustration:

$$\text{Direct Materials Price Variance} = \text{Actual Price per Unit} - \text{Standard Price} \times \text{Actual Quantity Used}$$

Price variance = ($1.04 per pound − $1.00 per pound) × 20,600 pounds
Price variance = $.04 per pound   × 20,600 pounds
Price variance = $824 unfavorable

Direct Materials Price Variance

Reporting Direct Materials Cost Variance. The physical quantity and the dollar amount of the quantity variance should be reported to the factory superintendent and other personnel responsible for production. If excessive amounts of direct materials were used because of the malfunction of equipment or some other failure within the production department, those responsible should correct the situation. However, an unfavorable direct materials quantity variance is not necessarily the result of inefficiency within the production department. If the excess usage of 600 pounds of materials in the example above had been caused by inferior materials, the purchasing department should be held responsible.

The unit price and the total amount of the materials price variance should be reported to the purchasing department, which may or may not be able to control this variance. If materials of the same quality could have been purchased from another supplier at the standard price, the variance was controllable. On the other hand, if the variance resulted from a marketwide price increase, the variance was not subject to control.

Direct Labor Cost Variance

As in the case of direct materials, two major factors enter into the determination of standards for direct labor cost: (1) the time (usage or efficiency) standard, and (2) the rate (price or wage) standard. If the actual direct labor hours spent producing a product differ from the standard hours, there is a time variance. If the wage rate paid differs from the standard rate, there is a rate variance. The standard cost and the actual cost of direct labor in the production of 10,000 units of Product X during June are assumed to be as follows:

> Actual: 3,950 hours at $16.40 . . . . $64,780
> Standard: 4,000 hours at 16.00   64,000

The unfavorable direct labor variance of $780 is made up of a favorable time variance and an unfavorable rate variance, determined as follows:

Direct Labor Cost Variance

Time variance:
Actual time.	3,950 hours	
Standard time	4,000 hours	
Variance — favorable. . . .	−50 hours × standard rate, $16.	$ 800

Rate variance:
Actual rate	$16.40 per hour	
Standard rate	16.00 per hour	
Variance — unfavorable. .	$ .40 per hour × actual time, 3,950 hours .	1,580
Total direct labor cost variance — unfavorable.		$ 780

Direct Labor Time Variance. The direct labor time variance is the difference between the actual hours worked and the standard hours, multiplied by the standard rate per hour. If the actual hours worked exceed the standard hours, the variance is unfavorable. If the actual hours worked are less than the standard hours, the variance is favorable, as shown for Ballard Company in the following illustration:

$$\frac{\text{Direct Labor}}{\text{Time Variance}} = \frac{\text{Actual Hours Worked} -}{\text{Standard Hours}} \times \frac{\text{Standard Rate}}{\text{per Hour}}$$

Time variance = (3,950 hours − 4,000 hours) × $16 per hour
Time variance = −50 hours   × $16 per hour
Time variance = $800 favorable

Direct Labor Time Variance

In the illustration, when the standard hours (4,000) are subtracted from the actual hours worked (3,950), the difference is "−50 hours." The minus sign indicates that the variance of 50 hours, or $800 (50 hours × $16), is favorable.

Direct Labor Rate Variance. The direct labor rate variance is the difference between the actual rate per hour and the standard rate per hour, multiplied by the actual hours worked. If the standard rate per hour exceeds the actual rate per hour, the variance is favorable. If the actual rate per hour exceeds the standard rate per hour, the variance is unfavorable, as shown for Ballard Company in the following illustration:

$$\frac{\text{Direct Labor}}{\text{Rate Variance}} = \frac{\text{Actual Rate per Hour} -}{\text{Standard Rate}} \times \frac{\text{Actual Hours}}{\text{Worked}}$$

Rate variance = ($16.40 per hour − $16.00 per hour) × 3,950 hours
Rate variance = $.40 per hour   × 3,950 hours
Rate variance = $1,580 unfavorable

Direct Labor Rate Variance

Reporting Direct Labor Cost Variance. The control of direct labor cost is often in the hands of production supervisors. To aid them, periodic reports analyzing the cause of any direct labor variance may be prepared. A comparison of standard direct labor hours and actual direct labor hours will provide the basis for an investigation into the efficiency of direct labor (time variance). A comparison of the rates paid for direct labor with the standard rates highlights the efficiency of the supervisors or the personnel department in selecting the proper grade of direct labor for production (rate variance).

Factory Overhead Cost Variance

Some of the difficulties encountered in allocating factory overhead costs among products manufactured have been considered in Chapter 3. These difficulties stem from the great variety of costs that are included in factory overhead and their nature as indirect costs. For the same reasons, the procedures used in determining standards and variances for factory overhead cost are more complex than those used for direct materials cost and direct labor cost.

A flexible budget, described in Chapter 8, is used to establish the standard factory overhead rate and to aid in determining subsequent variations from standard. The standard rate is determined by dividing the standard factory overhead costs by the standard amount of productive activity, generally expressed in direct labor hours, direct labor cost, or machine hours. A flexible budget showing the standard factory overhead rate for a month is as follows:

. . . .
Factory Overhead Cost
Budget Indicating
Standard Factory
Overhead Rate

Ballard Company
Factory Overhead Cost Budget
For Month Ending June 30, 19--

	80%	90%	100%	110%
Percent of productive capacity..........	80%	90%	100%	110%
Direct labor hours	4,000	4,500	5,000	5,500
Budgeted factory overhead:				
Variable cost:				
Indirect factory wages	$12,800	$14,400	$16,000	$17,600
Power and light	5,600	6,300	7,000	7,700
Indirect materials.................	3,200	3,600	4,000	4,400
Maintenance.....................	2,400	2,700	3,000	3,300
Total variable cost	$24,000	$27,000	$30,000	$33,000
Fixed cost:				
Supervisory salaries	$ 5,500	$ 5,500	$ 5,500	$ 5,500
Depreciation of plant and equipment	4,500	4,500	4,500	4,500
Insurance and property taxes.......	2,000	2,000	2,000	2,000
Total fixed cost.................	$12,000	$12,000	$12,000	$12,000
Total factory overhead cost...........	$36,000	$39,000	$42,000	$45,000

Factory overhead rate per direct labor hour ($42,000 ÷ 5,000) ... $8.40

The standard factory overhead cost rate is determined on the basis of the projected factory overhead costs at 100% of productive capacity, where this level of capacity represents the general expectation of business activity under normal operating conditions. In the illustration, the standard factory overhead rate is $8.40 per direct labor hour. This rate can be subdivided into $6 per hour for variable factory overhead ($30,000 ÷ 5,000 hours) and $2.40 per hour for fixed factory overhead ($12,000 ÷ 5,000 hours).

Variances from standard for factory overhead cost result (1) from operating at a level above or below 100% of capacity and (2) from incurring a total amount of factory overhead cost greater or less than the amount budgeted for the level of operations achieved. The first factor results in the **volume variance**, which is a measure of the penalty of operating at less than 100% of productive capacity or the benefit from operating at a level above 100% of productive capacity. The second factor results in the **controllable variance**, which is the difference between the actual amount of factory overhead incurred and the amount of factory overhead budgeted for the level of production achieved during the period. To illustrate, assume that the actual cost and standard cost of factory overhead for Ballard Company's production of 10,000 units of Product X during June were as follows:

Actual: Variable factory overhead............ $24,600
          Fixed factory overhead...............   12,000 $36,600
Standard: 4,000 hours at $8.40.................   33,600

The unfavorable factory overhead cost variance of $3,000 is made up of a volume variance and a controllable variance, determined as follows:

Volume variance:
  Productive capacity of 100%.......................   5,000 hours
  Standard for amount produced......................   4,000 hours

  Productive capacity not used......................   1,000 hours
  Standard fixed factory overhead cost rate .... ×$2.40

      Variance—unfavorable..................................... $2,400
Controllable variance:
  Actual factory overhead cost incurred................ $36,600
  Budgeted factory overhead for standard product produced.   36,000

      Variance—unfavorable.....................................   600
Total factory overhead cost variance—unfavorable..................... $3,000

· · · · · · · ·
Factory Overhead Cost Variance

Factory Overhead Volume Variance. The factory overhead volume variance is the difference between the productive capacity at 100% and the standard productive capacity, multiplied by the standard fixed factory overhead rate. If the standard capacity for the amount produced exceeds the productive capacity at 100%, the variance is favorable. If the productive capacity at 100% exceeds the standard capacity for the amount produced, the variance is unfavorable, as shown for Ballard Company in the following illustration:

$$\text{Factory Overhead Volume Variance} = \frac{\text{Productive Capacity at 100\%} -}{\text{Standard Capacity for Amount Produced}} \times \frac{\text{Standard Fixed Factory}}{\text{Overhead Rate}}$$

Volume variance = (5,000 hours − 4,000 hours)   × $2.40 per hour
Volume variance = 1,000 hours   × $2.40 per hour
Volume variance = $2,400 unfavorable

· · · · · · · ·
Factory Overhead Volume Variance

In the illustration, the unfavorable volume variance of $2,400 can be viewed as the cost of the available but unused productive capacity (1,000 hours). It should also be noted that the variable portion of the factory overhead cost rate was ignored in determining the volume variance. Variable factory overhead costs vary with the level of production. Thus, a curtailment of production should be accompanied by a comparable reduction of such costs. On the other hand, fixed factory overhead costs are not affected by changes in the volume of production. The fixed factory overhead costs represent the costs of providing the capacity for production, and the volume variance measures the amount of the fixed factory overhead cost due to the variance between capacity used and 100% of capacity.

The idle time that resulted in a volume variance may be due to such factors as failure to maintain an even flow of work, machine breakdowns or repairs causing work stoppages, and failure to obtain enough sales orders to keep the factory operating at full capacity. Management should determine the causes of the idle time and should take corrective action. A volume variance caused by failure of supervisors to maintain an even flow of work, for example, can be remedied. Volume variances caused by lack of sales orders may be corrected through increased advertising or other sales effort, or it may be advisable to develop other means of using the excess plant capacity.

Factory Overhead Controllable Variance. The factory overhead controllable variance is the difference between the actual factory overhead and the budgeted factory overhead for the standard amount produced. If the budgeted factory overhead for the standard amount produced exceeds the actual factory overhead, the variance is favorable. If the actual factory overhead exceeds the budgeted factory overhead for the standard amount produced, the variance is unfavorable. For Ballard Company, the standard direct labor hours for the amount produced during June was 4,000 (80% of productive capacity). Therefore, the factory overhead budgeted at this level of production, according to the budget on page 306, was $36,000. When this budgeted factory overhead is compared with the actual factory overhead, as shown in the following illustration for Ballard Company, an unfavorable variance results.

. . . .
*Factory Overhead
Controllable Variance*

Factory Overhead Controllable Variance	=	Actual Factory Overhead	−	Budgeted Factory Overhead for Standard Amount Produced

Controllable variance = $36,600 − $36,000

Controllable variance = $600 unfavorable

The amount and the direction of the controllable variance show the degree of efficiency in keeping the factory overhead costs within the limits established by the budget. Most of the controllable variance is related to the cost of the variable factory overhead items because generally there is little or no variation in the costs incurred for the fixed factory overhead items. Therefore, responsibility for the control of this variance generally rests with department supervisors.

Reporting Factory Overhead Cost Variance. The best means of presenting standard factory overhead cost variance data is through a factory overhead cost variance report. Such a report, illustrated as follows, can present both the controllable variance and the volume variance in a format that pinpoints the causes of the variances and aids in placing the responsibility for control.

Ballard Company
Factory Overhead Cost Variance Report
For Month Ended June 30, 19--

	Budget	Actual	Variances Favorable	Variances Unfavorable
Productive capacity for the month				5,000 hours
Actual production for the month				4,000 hours
Variable cost:				
Indirect factory wages	$12,800	$13,020		$ 220
Power and light	5,600	5,550	$50	
Indirect materials	3,200	3,630		430
Maintenance	2,400	2,400		
Total variable cost	$24,000	$24,600		
Fixed cost:				
Supervisory salaries	$ 5,500	$ 5,500		
Depreciation of plant and equipment	4,500	4,500		
Insurance and property taxes	2,000	2,000		
Total fixed cost	$12,000	$12,000		
Total factory overhead cost	$36,000	$36,600		
Total controllable variances			$50	$ 650
Net controllable variance—unfavorable				$ 600
Volume variance—unfavorable:				
Idle hours at the standard rate for fixed factory overhead—				
1,000 × $2.40				2,400
Total factory overhead cost variance—unfavorable				$3,000

The variance in many of the individual cost items in factory overhead can be subdivided into quantity and price variances, as were the variances in direct materials and direct labor. For example, the indirect factory wages variance may include both time and rate variances, and the indirect materials variance may be made up of both a quantity variance and a price variance.

The foregoing brief introduction to analysis of factory overhead cost variance suggests the many difficulties that may be encountered in actual practice. The rapid increase of automation in factory operations has been accompanied by increased attention to factory overhead costs. The use of predetermined standards and the analysis of variances from such standards provides management with the best possible means of establishing responsibility and controlling factory overhead costs.

STANDARDS IN THE ACCOUNTS

Although standard costs can be used solely as a statistical device apart from the ledger, it is generally considered preferable to incorporate them in the accounts. One approach, when this plan is used, is to identify the variances in the accounts at the time the manufacturing costs are recorded in the accounts. To illustrate, assume that Marin Corporation purchased, on account, 10,000 pounds of direct materials at $1 per pound, when the standard price was $.95 per pound. The entry to record the purchase and the unfavorable direct materials price variance is as follows:

Materials..	9,500	
Direct Materials Price Variance	500	
Accounts Payable......................................		10,000

The materials account is debited for the 10,000 pounds at the standard price of $.95 per pound. The unfavorable direct materials price variance is $500 [($1.00 actual price per pound − $.95 standard price per pound) × 10,000 pounds purchased] and is recorded by a debit to Direct Materials Price Variance. Accounts Payable is credited for the actual amount owed, $10,000 (10,000 pounds at $1 per pound). If the variance had been favorable, Direct Materials Price Variance would have been credited for the amount of the variance.

The accounts affected by the purchase of direct materials would appear as follows:

ACCOUNT MATERIALS   ACCOUNT NO.

Date	Item	Debit	Credit	Balance Debit	Balance Credit
	Purchased	9,500		9,500	

ACCOUNT DIRECT MATERIALS PRICE VARIANCE   ACCOUNT NO.

Date	Item	Debit	Credit	Balance Debit	Balance Credit
	Purchased	500		500	

ACCOUNT ACCOUNTS PAYABLE   ACCOUNT NO.

Date	Item	Debit	Credit	Balance Debit	Balance Credit
	Actual cost		10,000		10,000

Variances in other manufacturing costs are recorded in a manner similar to the direct materials price variance. For example, if Marin Corporation used 4,900 pounds of direct materials to produce a product with a standard of 5,000 pounds, the entry to record the variance and the materials used would be as follows:

Work in Process	4,750	
Materials.		4,655
Direct Materials Quantity Variance		95

The work in process account is debited for the standard price of the standard amount of direct materials required, $4,750 (5,000 pounds × $.95). Materials is credited for the actual amount of materials used at the standard price, $4,655 (4,900 pounds × $.95). The favorable direct materials quantity variance of $95 [(5,000 standard pounds − 4,900 actual pounds) × $.95 standard price per pound] is credited to Direct Materials Quantity Variance. If the variance had been unfavorable, Direct Materials Quantity Variance would have been debited for the amount of the variance.

The accounts affected by the use of direct materials would appear as follows:

ACCOUNT MATERIALS   ACCOUNT NO.

				Balance	
Date	Item	Debit	Credit	Debit	Credit
	Purchased	9,500		9,500	
	Used		4,655	4,845	

ACCOUNT DIRECT MATERIALS QUANTITY VARIANCE   ACCOUNT NO.

				Balance	
Date	Item	Debit	Credit	Debit	Credit
	Used		95		95

ACCOUNT WORK IN PROCESS   ACCOUNT NO.

				Balance	
Date	Item	Debit	Credit	Debit	Credit
	Direct materials (actual)	4,750		4,750	

For Marin Corporation, the entries for direct labor, factory overhead, and other variances are recorded in a manner similar to the entries for direct materials. The work in process account is debited for the standard costs of direct labor and factory overhead as well as direct materials. Likewise, the work in process account is credited for the standard cost of the product completed and transferred to the finished goods account.

In a given period, it is possible to have both favorable and unfavorable variances. For example, if a favorable variance has been recorded, such as the direct materials quantity variance for Marin Corporation, and unfavorable direct materials quantity variances occur later in the period, the unfavorable variances would be recorded as debits in the direct materials quantity variance account. Analyses of this account may provide management with insights for controlling direct materials usage.

Another means of incorporating standards in the accounts is to debit the work in process account for the actual cost of direct materials, direct labor, and factory overhead entering into production. The same account is credited for the standard cost of the product completed and transferred to the finished goods account. The balance remaining in the work in process account is then made up of the ending inventory of work in process and the variances of actual cost from standard cost. In the following illustrative accounts for Ballard Company, there is assumed to be no ending inventory of work in process:

Standard Costs in Accounts

ACCOUNT WORK IN PROCESS   ACCOUNT NO.

Date		Item	Debit	Credit	Balance Debit	Balance Credit
June	30	Direct materials (actual)	21,424		21,424	
	30	Direct labor (actual)	64,780		86,204	
	30	Factory overhead (actual)	36,600		122,804	
	30	Units finished (standard)		117,600		
	30	Balance (variances)			5,204	

ACCOUNT FINISHED GOODS   ACCOUNT NO.

Date		Item	Debit	Credit	Balance Debit	Balance Credit
June	1	Inventory (standard)			88,800	
	30	Units finished (standard)	117,600		206,400	
	30	Units sold (standard)		113,500	92,900	

The balance in the work in process account is the sum of the variances between the standard and actual costs. In the illustration, the debit balance of $5,204 indicates a net unfavorable variance. If the balance had been a credit, it would have indicated a net favorable variance.

REPORTING VARIANCES ON THE INCOME STATEMENT

Variances from standard costs are usually not reported to stockholders and others outside of management. If standards are recorded in the accounts, however, it is customary to disclose the variances on income statements prepared for management. An interim monthly income statement prepared for Ballard Company's internal use is illustrated as follows:

Ballard Company Income Statement For Month Ended June 30, 19--				
Sales				$185,400
Cost of goods sold — at standard				113,500
Gross profit — at standard				$ 71,900
		Favorable	Unfavorable	
Less variances from standard cost:				
Direct materials quantity			$ 600	
Direct materials price			824	
Direct labor time		$800		
Direct labor rate			1,580	
Factory overhead volume			2,400	
Factory overhead controllable		___	600	5,204
Gross profit				$ 66,696
Operating expenses:				
Selling expenses			$22,500	
General expenses			19,225	41,725
Income before income tax				$ 24,971

At the end of the fiscal year, the variances from standard are usually transferred to the cost of goods sold account. However, if the variances are significant or if many of the products manufactured are still on hand, the variances should be allocated to the work in process, finished goods, and cost of goods sold accounts. The result of such an allocation is to convert these account balances from standard cost to actual cost.

REVISION OF STANDARDS

Standard costs should be continuously reviewed, and when they no longer represent the conditions that were present when the standards were set, they should be changed. Standards should not be revised merely because they differ from actual costs, but because they no longer reflect the conditions that they were intended to measure. For example, the direct labor cost standard would not be revised simply because workers were unable to meet properly determined standards. On the other hand, standards should be revised when prices, product designs, labor rates, manufacturing methods, or other circumstances change to such an extent that the current standards no longer represent a useful measure of performance.

STANDARDS FOR NONMANUFACTURING EXPENSES

The use of standards for nonmanufacturing expenses is not as common as the use of standards for manufacturing costs. This difference in the use of

314 · Part 3 · Planning and Control

standards is due in part to the fact that nonmanufacturing expenses are, in many cases, not nearly as large as the manufacturing costs. Another major reason is that while many manufacturing operations are repetitive and thus subject to the determination of a per unit cost of output, many non-manufacturing expenses do not lend themselves to such measurement. In many cases, for example, the costs associated with an assembly line can be measured and related to a uniform product unit. On the other hand, the expenses associated with the work of the office manager are not easily related to any unit of output.

When nonmanufacturing activities are repetitive and generate a somewhat homogeneous product, the concept of standards can be applied. In these cases, the process of estimating and using standards can be similar to that described for a manufactured product. For example, standards can be applied to the work of office personnel who process sales orders, and a standard unit expense for processing a sales order could be determined. The variance between the actual cost of processing a sales order with the standard expense can then be evaluated by management and corrective action taken.

In practice, standards are not widely used for nonmanufacturing expenses. Instead, these expenses are generally controlled by the use of budgets and budget performance reports, as discussed in Chapter 8. However, the use of standards appears to be gaining in acceptance as more attention is being given to the nonmanufacturing expenses by the managerial accountant.

Chapter Review

KEY POINTS

1. The Nature and Objectives of Standards.

Accounting systems that use standards for each element of manufacturing cost entering into the finished product are called standard cost systems. Such systems enable management to determine how much a product should cost (standard), how much it does cost (actual), and the causes of any difference (variance) between the two. Standard costs thus serve as a device for measuring efficiency.

The setting of standards is both an art and a science. Although the standard-setting process varies among enterprises, it often requires the joint efforts of accountants, engineers, personnel administrators, and other management personnel. Standards that represent levels of performance that can be achieved only under perfect operating conditions, such as no idle time, no machine breakdowns, and no materials spoilage, are called theoretical standards or ideal standards. Standards that represent levels of operation that can be attained with reasonable effort are called currently attainable standards or normal standards.

2. Variances from Standards.

One of the primary purposes of a standard cost system is to facilitate control over costs by comparing actual costs with standard costs and thus determining variances. The two major variances for direct materials cost are the (1) direct materials quantity variance and (2) direct materials price variance. The two major variances for direct labor costs are the (1) direct labor time variance and (2) direct labor rate variance. The two major variances for factory overhead costs are the (1) factory overhead volume variance and (2) factory overhead controllable variance.

3. Standards in the Accounts.

It is generally preferable to incorporate standards in the accounts. One approach is to identify the variances in the accounts at the time the manufacturing costs are recorded in the accounts. Under this approach, the work in process account is debited for the standard costs of direct materials, direct labor, and factory overhead. Likewise, the work in process account is credited for the standard cost of the product completed and transferred to the finished goods account.

Another approach to incorporating standards in the accounts is to debit the work in process account for the actual costs of direct materials, direct labor, and factory overhead entering into production. The same account is then credited for the standard costs of the product completed and transferred to the finished goods account. Thus, the variances of actual costs from standard costs are isolated along with the ending inventory in the work in process account. At the end of the fiscal year, the variances are usually transferred to the cost of goods sold account.

4. Reporting Variances on the Income Statement.

Variances from standard costs are usually not reported to stockholders and others outside management. If standards are recorded in the accounts, however, it is customary to disclose the variances on interim income statements prepared for management. At the end of the year, the variances from standard are usually transferred to the cost of goods sold account. However, if the variances are significant or if many of the products manufactured are still on hand, the variances should be allocated to the work in process, finished goods, and cost of goods sold accounts.

5. Revision of Standards.

Established standards should be continually reviewed. If the standards no longer represent present conditions, they should be revised.

6. Standards for Nonmanufacturing Expenses.

The use of standards for nonmanufacturing expenses is not as common as the use of standards for manufacturing costs. When nonmanufacturing activities are repetitive and generate a somewhat homogeneous product, the concept of standards can be applied. In these cases, the process of estimating and using standards is similar to that described for a manufactured product.

KEY TERMS
·

standard cost systems 299
standard costs 299
variances 299
theoretical standards 301
currently attainable standards 301
direct materials quantity
  variance 302

direct materials price variance 302
direct labor time variance 304
direct labor rate variance 304
factory overhead volume
  variance 306
factory overhead controllable
  variance 306

SELF-EXAMINATION QUESTIONS
·
(Answers at End of Chapter)

1. The actual and standard direct materials costs for producing a specified quantity of product are as follows:

    Actual: 51,000 pounds at $5.05 . . . . $257,550
    Standard: 50,000 pounds at $5.00 250,000

The direct materials price variance is:
A. $2,500 unfavorable   C. $7,550 unfavorable
B. $2,550 unfavorable   D. none of the above

2. The actual and standard direct labor costs for producing a specified quantity of product are as follows:

    Actual: 990 hours at $10.90 . . . . $10,791
    Standard: 1,000 hours at $11.00 11,000

The direct labor cost time variance is:
A. $99 favorable   C. $110 favorable
B. $99 unfavorable   D. $110 unfavorable

3. The actual and standard factory overhead costs for producing a specified quantity of product are as follows:

Actual: Variable factory overhead $72,500
           Fixed factory overhead 40,000 $112,500
Standard: 19,000 hours at $6
           ($4 variable and $2 fixed)......   114,000

If 1,000 hours of productive capacity were unused, the factory overhead volume variance would be:
A. $1,500 favorable
B. $2,000 unfavorable
C. $4,000 unfavorable
D. none of the above

4. Based on the data in Question 3, the factory overhead controllable variance would be:
A. $3,500 favorable
B. $3,500 unfavorable
C. $1,500 favorable
D. none of the above

5. Variances from standard costs are reported on interim income statements as:
A. selling expenses
B. general expenses
C. other expenses
D. none of the above

ILLUSTRATIVE PROBLEM

Wolfram Inc. manufactures Product S for distribution nationally. The standard costs and actual costs for direct materials, direct labor, and factory overhead incurred for the manufacture of 1,000 units of Product S were as follows:

	Standard Costs	Actual Costs
Direct materials.............	1,000 pounds at $75	980 pounds at $75.50
Direct labor.................	12,500 hours at $9	12,600 hours at $8.95
Factory overhead	Rates per direct labor hour, based on 100% of capacity of 15,000 labor hours:	
	Variable cost, $3.50	$44,150 variable cost
	Fixed cost, $1.00	$15,000 fixed cost

Instructions:

1. Determine the quantity variance, price variance, and total direct materials cost variance for Product S.
2. Determine the time variance, rate variance, and total direct labor cost variance for Product S.
3. Determine the volume variance, controllable variance, and total factory overhead cost variance for Product S.

SOLUTION

(1)   Direct Materials Cost Variance

Quantity Variance:

Actual quantity	980 pounds	
Standard quantity	1,000 pounds	
Variance — favorable . . .	20 pounds × standard price, $75 .	$1,500

Price Variance:

Actual price	$75.50 per pound	
Standard price	75.00 per pound	
Variance — unfavorable	$ .50 per pound × actual quantity, 980	490

Total Direct Materials Cost Variance — favorable $1,010

(2)   Direct Labor Cost Variance

Time Variance:

Actual time	12,600 hours	
Standard time	12,500 hours	
Variance — unfavorable	100 hours × standard rate, $9 . .	$ 900

Rate Variance:

Actual rate	$8.95	
Standard rate	9.00	
Variance — favorable . .	$ .05 per hour × actual time, 12,600	630

Total Direct Labor Cost Variance — unfavorable . . . . $ 270

(3)   Factory Overhead Cost Variance

Volume Variance:

Productive capacity of 100%	15,000 hours	
Standard for amount produced	12,500 hours	
Productive capacity not used	2,500 hours	
Standard fixed factory overhead cost rate	× $1	
Variance — unfavorable		$2,500

Controllable Variance:

Actual factory overhead cost incurred	$59,150	
Budgeted factory overhead for 12,500 hrs.	58,750	
Variance — unfavorable		400

Total Factory Overhead Cost Variance — unfavorable $2,900

Discussion Questions

9–1. What are the basic objectives in the use of standard costs?

9–2. (a) Describe theoretical (ideal) standards and discuss the possible impact of theoretical standards on worker performance. (b) Describe currently attainable (normal) standards and discuss the possible impact of currently attainable standards on worker performance.

9–3. How can standards be used by management to achieve control over costs?

9–4. As the term is used in reference to standard costs, what is a *variance*?

9–5. What is meant by reporting by the "principle of exceptions" as the term is used in reference to cost control?

9–6. (a) What are the two variances between actual cost and standard cost for direct materials? (b) Discuss some possible causes of these variances.

9–7. The materials cost variance report for Jachino Inc. indicates a large favorable materials price variance and a significant unfavorable materials quantity variance. What might have caused these offsetting variances?

9–8. (a) What are the two variances between actual cost and standard cost for direct labor? (b) Who generally has control over the direct labor cost?

9–9. A new assistant controller recently was heard to remark: "All the assembly workers in this plant are covered by union contracts, so there should be no labor variances." Was the controller's remark correct? Discuss.

9–10. (a) Describe the two variances between actual costs and standard costs for factory overhead. (b) What is a factory overhead cost variance report?

9–11. If variances are recorded in the accounts at the time the manufacturing costs are incurred, what does a credit balance in Direct Materials Price Variance represent?

9–12. If variances are recorded in the accounts at the time the manufacturing costs are incurred, what does a debit balance in Direct Materials Quantity Variance represent?

9–13. If standards are recorded in the accounts and Work in Process is debited for the actual manufacturing costs and credited for the standard cost of products produced, what does the balance in Work in Process represent?

9–14. Are variances from standard costs usually reported in financial statements issued to stockholders and others outside the firm?

9–15. Assuming that the variances from standards are not significant at the end of the period, to what account are they transferred?

9–16. How often should standards be revised?

9–17. Are standards for nonmanufacturing expenses as widely used as standards for manufacturing costs?

9–18. Real World Focus.   Concrete Pipe & Products Co. Inc. manufactures concrete pipe in its operations in Richmond, Virginia. The primary materials used in producing concrete are cement, sand, and gravel. The costs for a batch of concrete weighing 13,250 pounds are as follows:

	Pounds per batch	Price per pound
Cement	2,350	$.03000
Sand	6,700	.00205
Gravel	4,200	.00270
	13,250	

Assuming 5% waste, compute the standard cost per pound for concrete. Use the following tabular headings for organizing the computations:

	Pounds per batch	Price per pound	Batch cost	5% waste	Total batch cost	Cost per pound
Cement...	2,350	$.03000				
Sand	6,700	.00205				
Gravel	4,200	.00270				
	13,250					

Exercises

·

9–19. Direct materials variances. The following data relate to the direct materials cost for the production of 30,000 units of product:

Actual: 78,000 pounds at $1.82 .... $141,960
Standard: 75,000 pounds at 1.80   135,000

Determine the quantity variance, price variance, and total direct materials cost variance.

9–20. Standard direct materials cost per unit from variance data. The following data relating to direct materials cost for July of the current year are taken from the records of J. Ledbetter Company:

Quantity of direct materials used .... 16,000 pounds
Unit cost of direct materials .... $2.50 per pound
Units of finished product manufactured .... 20,625 units
Standard direct materials per unit of finished product....... .8 pounds
Direct materials quantity variance—favorable $1,200
Direct materials price variance—unfavorable............. $1,600

Determine the standard direct materials cost per unit of finished product, assuming that there was no inventory of work in process at either the beginning or the end of the month. Present your computations.

9-21. Direct labor variances. The following data relate to direct labor cost for the production of 15,000 units of product:

Actual: 42,500 hours at $15.80...................... $671,500
Standard: 42,000 hours at $16.00...................... 672,000

Determine the time variance, rate variance, and total direct labor cost variance.

9-22. Factory overhead cost variances. The following data relate to factory overhead cost for the production of 40,000 units of product:

Actual: Variable factory overhead.................... $152,000
           Fixed factory overhead...................... 120,000
Standard: 60,000 hours at $4.......................... 240,000

If productive capacity of 100% was 80,000 hours and the factory overhead costs budgeted at the level of 60,000 standard hours was $270,000, determine the volume variance, controllable variance, and total factory overhead cost variance. The fixed factory overhead rate was $1.50 per hour.

9-23. Flexible budget. Blackmon Company prepared the following factory overhead cost budget for Department M for November of the current year, when the company expected to operate at 9,900 direct labor hours:

Variable cost:		
Indirect factory wages	$21,600	
Power and light....................................	12,600	
Indirect materials..................................	7,380	
Total variable cost..............................		$41,580
Fixed cost:		
Supervisory salaries................................	$15,000	
Depreciation of plant and equipment	10,700	
Insurance and property taxes.......................	4,000	
Total fixed cost		29,700
Total factory overhead cost..........................		$71,280

Blackmon Company has decided to install a standard cost system and has determined that productive capacity is 11,000 direct labor hours. Prepare a flexible budget indicating production levels of 8,800, 9,900, and 11,000 direct labor hours and showing the standard factory overhead rate.

9-24. Entries for recording standards in accounts. Smith Manufacturing Company incorporates standards in the accounts and identifies variances at the time the manufacturing costs are incurred. Prepare entries to record the following transactions:

(a) Purchased 1,000 units of direct material W at $15.50 per unit. The standard price is $15 per unit.
(b) Used 400 units of direct material W in the process of manufacturing 140 units of finished product. Three units of material W are required, at standard, to produce a finished unit.

Problems

SPREADSHEET
PROBLEM

9–25. Direct materials, direct labor, and factory overhead cost variance analysis. Standard costs and actual costs for direct materials, direct labor, and factory overhead incurred for the manufacture of 5,000 units of product were as follows:

	Standard Costs	Actual Costs
Direct materials.........	7,000 pounds at $12	7,200 pounds at $11.50
Direct labor	2,000 hours at $15	1,850 hours at $15.50
Factory overhead.......	Rates per direct labor, based on 100% of capacity of 2,500 labor hours:	
	Variable cost, $13.20	$28,000 variable cost
	Fixed cost, $8.00	$20,000 fixed cost

Instructions:

Determine (a) the quantity variance, price variance, and total direct materials cost variance; (b) the time variance, rate variance, and total direct labor cost variance; and (c) the volume variance, controllable variance, and total factory overhead cost variance.

9–26. Standard factory overhead variance report. Hiram Company prepared the following factory overhead cost budget for Department F for April of the current year. The company expected to operate the department at 100% of capacity of 15,000 direct labor hours.

Variable cost:		
Indirect factory wages	$25,000	
Power and light....................................	14,600	
Indirect materials..................................	6,400	
Total variable cost................................		$46,000
Fixed cost:		
Supervisory salaries...............................	$18,000	
Depreciation of plant and equipment	10,000	
Insurance and property taxes......................	3,500	
Total fixed cost		31,500
Total factory overhead cost..........................		$77,500

During April, the department operated at 12,750 direct labor hours, and the factory overhead costs incurred were: indirect factory wages, $22,100; power and light, $12,000; indirect materials, $6,000; supervisory salaries, $18,000; depreciation of plant and equipment, $10,000; and insurance and property taxes, $3,500.

Instructions:

Prepare a standard factory overhead variance report for April. To be useful for cost control, the budgeted amounts should be based on 12,750 direct labor hours.

SPREADSHEET
PROBLEM

9–27. Flexible factory overhead cost budget and variance report. Yates Company prepared the following factory overhead cost budget for the Painting Department for October of the current year:

Yates Company
Factory Overhead Cost Budget—Painting Department
For Month Ending October 31, 19--

Direct labor hours:		
Productive capacity of 100%		20,000
Hours budgeted.....................................		16,000
Variable cost:		
Indirect factory wages	$24,000	
Indirect materials.................................	9,600	
Power and light....................................	4,800	
Total variable cost................................		$38,400
Fixed cost:		
Supervisory salaries...............................	$18,000	
Indirect factory wages	12,400	
Depreciation of plant and equipment	7,500	
Insurance	6,200	
Power and light....................................	4,100	
Property taxes.....................................	3,800	
Total fixed cost		52,000
Total factory overhead cost........................		$90,400

During October, the Painting Department was operated for 16,000 direct labor hours, and the following factory overhead costs were incurred:

Indirect factory wages.....................................	$38,000
Supervisory salaries	18,000
Indirect materials...	9,400
Power and light	9,100
Depreciation of plant and equipment........................	7,500
Insurance	6,200
Property taxes	3,800
Total factory overhead cost incurred......................	$92,000

Instructions:

(1) Prepare a flexible budget for October, indicating capacities of 14,000, 16,000, 18,000, and 20,000 direct labor hours and the determination of a standard factory overhead rate per direct labor hour.

(2) Prepare a standard factory overhead cost variance report for October.

9–28.   **Entries and standard cost variance analysis.** Walters Inc. maintains perpetual inventory accounts for materials, work in process, and finished goods and uses a standard cost system based on the following data:

	Standard Cost per Unit
Direct materials: 4 kilograms at $1.25 per kg	$ 5
Direct labor: 3 hours at $15 per hour	45
Factory overhead: $1.00 per direct labor hour	3
Total..	$53

There was no inventory of work in process at the beginning or end of January, the first month of the current fiscal year. The transactions relating to production completed during January are summarized as follows:

(a) Materials purchased on account, $75,600.
(b) Direct materials used, $36,400. The amount represented 28 000 kilograms at $1.30 per kilogram.
(c) Direct labor paid, $315,700. This amount represented 20,500 hours at $15.40 per hour. There were no accruals at either the beginning or the end of the period.
(d) Factory overhead incurred during the month was composed of depreciation on plant and equipment, $8,500; indirect labor, $7,400; insurance, $4,750; and miscellaneous factory costs, $4,150. The indirect labor and miscellaneous factory costs were paid during the period, and the insurance represents an expiration of prepaid insurance. Of the total factory overhead of $24,800, fixed costs amounted to $12,000 and variable costs were $12,800.
(e) Goods finished during the period, 6,900 units.

Instructions:

(1) Prepare entries to record the transactions, assuming that the work in process account is debited for actual production costs and credited with standard costs for goods finished.
(2) Prepare a T account for Work in Process and post to the account, using the identifying letters as dates.
(3) Prepare schedules of variances for direct materials cost, direct labor cost, and factory overhead cost. Productive capacity for the plant is 30,000 direct labor hours.
(4) Total the amount of the standard cost variances and compare this total with the balance of the work in process account.

9–29. Income statement indicating standard cost variances. The following data were taken from the records of Watkins Company for May of the current year:

Cost of goods sold (at standard)	$390,000
Direct materials quantity variance—unfavorable	2,560
Direct materials price variance—favorable	1,320
Direct labor time variance—unfavorable	3,270
Direct labor rate variance—favorable	900
Factory overhead volume variance—unfavorable	10,000
Factory overhead controllable variance—favorable	1,600
General expenses	25,000
Sales	500,000
Selling expenses	42,000

Instructions:

Prepare an income statement for presentation to management.

ALTERNATE PROBLEMS

SPREADSHEET
PROBLEM

9–25A. Direct materials, direct labor, and factory overhead cost variance analysis. Standard costs and actual costs for direct materials, direct labor, and factory overhead incurred for the manufacture of 2,000 units of product were as follows:

	Standard Costs	Actual Costs
Direct materials..........	3,000 pounds at $8	3,100 pounds at $8.20
Direct labor	6,200 hours at $12	6,000 hours at $13.25
Factory overhead........	Rates per direct labor hour, based on 100% of capacity of 8,000 labor hours:	
	Variable cost, $1.20	$8,200 variable cost
	Fixed cost, $3.50	$28,000 fixed cost

Instructions:

Determine (a) the quantity variance, price variance, and total direct materials cost variance; (b) the time variance, rate variance, and total direct labor cost variance; and (c) the volume variance, controllable variance, and total factory overhead cost variance.

9–27A. Flexible factory overhead cost budget and variance report. Wooten Inc. prepared the following factory overhead cost budget for the Polishing Department for March of the current year:

Wooten Inc.
Factory Overhead Cost Budget—Polishing Department
For Month Ending March 31, 19--

Direct labor hours:		
Productive capacity of 100%		25,000
Hours budgeted.....................................		28,750
Variable cost:		
Indirect factory wages	$16,100	
Indirect materials.................................	9,430	
Power and light....................................	7,360	
Total variable cost................................		$32,890
Fixed cost:		
Supervisory salaries..............................	$13,500	
Indirect factory wages	7,780	
Depreciation of plant and equipment	5,220	
Insurance	3,160	
Power and light....................................	2,800	
Property taxes.....................................	1,940	
Total fixed cost		34,400
Total factory overhead cost...........................		$67,290

During March, the Polishing Department was operated for 28,750 direct labor hours, and the following factory overhead costs were incurred:

Indirect factory wages......................................	$25,780
Supervisory salaries	13,500
Power and light	10,000
Indirect materials...	9,700
Depreciation of plant and equipment.......................	5,220
Insurance	3,160
Property taxes	1,940
Total factory overhead cost incurred.....................	$69,300

Instructions:

(1) Prepare a flexible budget for March, indicating capacities of 17,500, 21,250, 25,000, and 28,750 direct labor hours and the determination of a standard factory overhead rate per direct labor hour.
(2) Prepare a standard factory overhead cost variance report for March.

9–28A.   Entries and standard cost variance analysis.   Duckworth Inc. maintains perpetual inventory accounts for materials, work in process, and finished goods and uses a standard cost system based on the following data:

	Standard Cost per Unit
Direct materials: 4 kilograms at $2.50 per kg	$10
Direct labor: 2 hours at $16.50 per hour.	33
Factory overhead: $2.50 per direct labor hour	5
Total.	$48

There was no inventory of work in process at the beginning or end of August, the first month of the current fiscal year. The transactions relating to production completed during August are summarized as follows:

(a) Materials purchased on account, $120,600.
(b) Direct materials used, $49,920. This represented 20 800 kilograms at $2.40 per kilogram.
(c) Direct labor paid, $169,320. This represented 10,200 hours at $16.60 per hour. There were no accruals at either the beginning or the end of the period.
(d) Factory overhead incurred during the month was composed of depreciation on plant and equipment, $13,700; indirect labor, $9,480; insurance, $2,400; and miscellaneous factory costs, $5,320. The indirect labor and miscellaneous factory costs were paid during the period, and the insurance represents an expiration of prepaid insurance. Of the total factory overhead of $30,900, fixed costs amounted to $18,000, and variable costs were $12,900.
(e) Goods finished during the period, 5,000 units.

Instructions:

(1) Prepare entries to record the transactions, assuming that the work in process account is debited for actual production costs and credited with standard costs for goods finished.
(2) Prepare a T account for Work in Process and post to the account, using the identifying letters as dates.
(3) Prepare schedules of variances for direct materials cost, direct labor cost, and factory overhead cost. Productive capacity for the plant is 15,000 direct labor hours.
(4) Total the amount of the standard cost variances and compare this total with the balance of the work in process account.

Mini-Case 9

PC Pany Company

Pany Company operates a plant in Columbus, Iowa, where you have been assigned as the new cost analyst. To familiarize yourself with your new responsibilities, you have gathered the following cost variance data for May. During May, 34,000 units of product were manufactured.

Factory Overhead Cost Variance Report

Productive capacity for the month (100%) ....20,000 hours
Standard for amount produced during month........................17,000 hours

	Budget	Actual	Variances Favorable	Variances Unfavorable
Variable cost:				
Indirect factory wages...........	$27,200	$28,000		$ 800
Power and light	17,850	18,000		150
Indirect materials	10,200	10,000	$200	
Maintenance	4,250	4,000	250	
Total variable cost	$59,500	$60,000		
Fixed cost:				
Supervisory salaries	$20,000	$20,000		
Depreciation of plant and				
equipment	15,000	15,000		
Insurance and property taxes	3,000	3,000		
Total fixed cost..............	$38,000	$38,000		
Total factory overhead cost	$97,500	$98,000		
Total controllable variances			$450	$ 950

Net controllable variance—unfavorable .... $ 500
Volume variance—unfavorable:
  Idle hours at the standard rate for
    fixed factory overhead − 3,000 × $1.90....................... 5,700
Total factory overhead cost variance—unfavorable................. $6,200

Direct Materials Cost Variance

Quantity variance:
Actual quantity . . . .   41,000 pounds
Standard quantity . . . .   40,800 pounds

   Variance — unfavorable.   200 pounds × standard price, $2.25 . . . . $ 450

Price variance:
Actual price . . . . $2.40 per pound
Standard price . . . .   2.25 per pound

   Variance — unfavorable. $ .15 per pound × actual quantity, 41,000   6,150

Total direct materials cost variance — unfavorable $6,600

Direct Labor Cost Variance

Time variance:
Actual time . . . .   17,500 hours
Standard time . . . .   17,000 hours

   Variance — unfavorable.   500 hours × standard rate, $12 . . . . $6,000

Rate variance:
Actual rate . . . . $11.50 per hour
Standard rate . . . .   12.00 per hour

   Variance — favorable . . . $ .50 per hour × actual hours, 17,500   8,750

Total direct labor cost — favorable $2,750

After your review of the May cost variance data, you arranged a meeting with the factory superintendent to discuss manufacturing operations. During this meeting, the factory superintendent made the following comment:

"Why do you have to compute a factory overhead volume variance? I don't have any control over the level of operations. I can only control costs for the level of production at which I am told to operate. Why not just eliminate the volume variance from the factory overhead cost variance report?"

You next discussed the direct materials variance analyses with the purchasing department manager, who made the following comment:

"The materials price variance is computed incorrectly. The computations should be actual price minus standard price times the standard quantity of materials for the amount produced. By multiplying the difference in the actual and standard price by the actual quantity of materials used, my department is being penalized for the inefficiencies of the production department."

During June, the standard costs were not changed, productive capacity was 20,000 hours, and the following data were taken from the records for the production of 36,000 units of product:

Quantity of direct materials used........................	43,500 pounds
Cost of direct materials	$2.42 per pound
Quantity of direct labor used	18,600 hours
Cost of direct labor.................................	$11.60 per hour
Factory overhead costs:	
Indirect factory wages	$29,800
Supervisory salaries................................	20,000
Power and light....................................	19,400
Depreciation of plant and equipment	15,000
Indirect materials.................................	10,700
Maintenance	4,450
Insurance and property taxes.......................	3,000

Instructions:

(1) Prepare a factory overhead cost variance report for June.
(2) Determine (a) the quantity variance, price variance, and total direct materials cost variance, and (b) the time variance, rate variance, and total direct labor cost variance for June.
(3) Based upon the cost variances for May and June, what areas of operations would you investigate and why?
(4) How would you respond to the comments of the factory superintendent?
(5) How would you respond to the comments of the manager of the purchasing department?

Answers to Self-Examination Questions

1. B The unfavorable direct materials price variance of $2,550 (answer B) is determined as follows:

Actual price...	$5.05 per pound
Standard price	5.00 per pound
Price variance—unfavorable.........................	$ .05 per pound

    $.05 × 51,000 actual quantity = $2,550

2. C The favorable direct labor cost time variance of $110 (answer C) is determined as follows:

Actual time.	990 hours
Standard time	1,000 hours
Time variance — favorable	10 hours
10 hours × $11 standard	$110

3. B The unfavorable factory overhead volume variance of $2,000 (answer B) is determined as follows:

Productive capacity not used	1,000 hours
Standard fixed factory overhead cost rate	× $2
Factory overhead volume variance — unfavorable	$2,000

4. A The favorable factory overhead controllable variance of $3,500 (answer A) is determined as follows:

Actual factory overhead cost incurred.	$112,500
Budgeted factory overhead for standard product produced [(19,000 hours at $4 variable) + (20,000 hours at $2 fixed)]	116,000
Factory overhead controllable variance — favorable.	$ 3,500

5. D Since variances from standard costs represent the differences between the standard cost of manufacturing a product and the actual costs incurred, the variances relate to the product. Therefore, they should be reported on interim income statements as an adjustment to gross profit — at standard.

Part
Four

Accounting for
Decentralized
Operations

Chapter Ten

Responsibility Accounting for Cost and Profit Centers

In a small business, virtually all plans and decisions can be made by one individual. As a business grows or its operations become more diverse, it becomes difficult, if not impossible, for one individual to perform these functions. For example, the responsibility for planning and controlling operations is clear in a one-person real estate agency. If the agency expands by opening an office in a distant city, some of the authority and responsibility for planning and decision making in a given area of operations might be delegated to others. In other words, if centralized operations become unwieldy as a business grows, the need to delegate responsibility for portions of operations arises. This separation of a business into more manageable units is termed **decentralization.** In a decentralized business, an important function of the managerial accountant is to assist individual managers in evaluating and controlling their areas of responsibility.

A term frequently applied to the process of measuring and reporting operating data by areas of responsibility is **responsibility accounting.** Some of the concepts useful in responsibility accounting were presented in preceding chapters. For example, in discussing budgetary control of operations, the use of the master budget, budgets for various departments, and budget performance reports in controlling operations by areas of responsibility were discussed. In this chapter, the concept of responsibility accounting as it relates to two types of decentralized operations is described and illustrated. A third type of decentralization is discussed in Chapter 11.

CENTRALIZED AND DECENTRALIZED OPERATIONS

A completely centralized business organization is one in which all major planning and operating decisions are made by the top echelon of management. For example, a one-person, owner-manager-operated business is centralized because all plans and decisions are made by one person. In a small owner-manager-operated business, centralization may be desirable, since the owner-manager's close supervision ensures that the business will be operated in conformity with the manager's wishes and desires.

In a decentralized business organization, responsibility for planning and controlling operations is delegated among managers. These managers have the authority to make decisions without first seeking the approval of higher management. The level of decentralization varies significantly, and there is no one best level of decentralization for all businesses. In some companies, for example, plant managers have authority over all plant operations, including plant asset acquisitions and retirements. In other companies, a plant manager may only have authority for scheduling production and for controlling the costs of direct materials, direct labor, and factory overhead. The proper level of decentralization for a company depends on the advantages and disadvantages of decentralization as they apply to a company's specific, unique circumstances.

Advantages of Decentralization

As a business grows, it becomes more difficult for top management to maintain close daily contact with all operations. Hence, a top management that delegates authority in such circumstances has a better chance of sound decisions being made, and the managers closest to the operations may anticipate and react to operating information more quickly. In addition, as a company diversifies into a wide range of products and services, it becomes more difficult for top management to maintain operating expertise in all product lines and services. In such cases, decentralization allows managers to concentrate on acquiring expertise in their areas of responsibility. For example, in a company that maintains diversified operations in oil refining, banking, and the manufacture of office equipment, individual managers could become "expert" in the area of their responsibility.

The delegation of responsibility for day-to-day operations from top management to middle management frees top management to concentrate more on strategic planning. **Strategic planning** is the process of establishing long-term goals for an enterprise and developing plans to achieve these goals. For example, a goal to expand an enterprise's product line into new markets and a plan to finance this expansion through the issuance of long-term debt rather than additional common stock are examples of strategic planning decisions. As the business environment becomes more complex and as companies grow, strategic planning assumes an increasingly important role in the long-run success of a company.

Decentralized decision making provides excellent training for managers, which may be a factor in enabling a company to retain quality managers. Since the art of management can best be acquired through experience, the delegation of responsibility enables managers to acquire and develop managerial expertise early in their careers. Also, the operating personnel may be more creative in suggesting operating improvements, since personnel in a decentralized company tend to identify closely with the operations for which they are responsible.

The delegation of responsibility also serves as a positive reinforcement for managers, in that they may view such delegation as an indication of top management's confidence in their abilities. Thus, manager morale tends to increase because managers feel that they have more control over factors affecting their careers and their performance evaluation.

Disadvantages of Decentralization

The primary disadvantage of decentralized operations is that decisions made by one manager may affect other managers in such a way that the profitability of the entire company may suffer. For example, two managers competing in a common product market may engage in price cutting to win customers. However, the overall company profits are less than the profits that could have been if the price cutting had not occurred.

Other potential disadvantages of decentralized operations may be the duplication of various assets and costs in the operating divisions. For example, each manager of a product line might have a separate sales force and administrative office staff, but centralization of these personnel could save money. Likewise, the costs of gathering and processing operating information in a decentralized operation might be greater than if such information were gathered and processed centrally.

Thinking Small

One company that experienced positive results from decentralizing was NCR (formerly National Cash Register Co.), a Dayton-based multi-national electronics and computer manufacturing corporation. In 1979, NCR was a troubled company. Management began to examine NCR's problems and to reevaluate the company's structure, which appeared to be inhibiting NCR'S ability to innovate and adapt. Additional background and the results of NCR's changes were reported in *Inc.*, as follows:

As part of this reevaluation process, NCR commissioned the McKinsey & Co. consulting group to study the attributes of a number of highly successful companies. The researchers looked at such corporations as Sperry, IBM, and Hewlett-Packard, to determine what they had done that might be applied to NCR.

Using this study as background, NCR developed a plan for restructuring itself. Analyzing the path of a product from idea to implementation, it discovered

some obvious impediments. The development, production, and marketing of a new product involved three separate divisions. This cumbersome system created opportunities for false starts and misinterpreting. . . the market. . . . It took a long time to get a product through this entire process, and sometimes products got lost in translation. . . .

So NCR proceeded to break up its product-management organization and move the parts to units that would develop, manufacture, and market products. In consulting jargon, this is called shifting from a "functional" to a "divisional" organization, and it has been done many times before in other industries. . . .

These changes transformed NCR Corp. from a highly centralized operation into a series of stand-alone [or decentralized] units. Today there is no requirement that one unit buy components from another NCR unit if it can find better or cheaper products outside the company. Moreover, based upon the nature of their products, the different divisions make their own decisions about how they want to structure themselves with regard to such activities as marketing.

Source: Eugene Linden, "Let a Thousand Flowers Bloom," *Inc.*, April, 1984, pp. 64–76.

TYPES OF DECENTRALIZED OPERATIONS

Decentralized operations can be classified by the scope of responsibility assigned and the decision making authority given to individual managers. The three common types of decentralized operations are referred to as cost centers, profit centers, and investment centers. Each of these types of decentralized operations is briefly described in the following paragraphs. Responsibility accounting for cost centers and profit centers is then discussed and illustrated in the remainder of this chapter, while responsibility accounting for investment centers is discussed in Chapter 11.

Cost Centers

In a **cost center,** the department or division manager has responsibility for the control of costs incurred and the authority to make decisions that affect these costs. For example, the marketing manager has responsibility for the costs of the Marketing Department, and the supervisor of the Power Department has responsibility for the costs incurred in providing power. The department manager does not make decisions concerning sales of the cost center's output, nor does the department manager have control over the plant assets available to the cost center.

Cost centers are the most widely used type of decentralization, because the organization and operation of most businesses allow for an easy identification of areas where managers can be assigned responsibility for and authority over costs. Cost centers may vary in size from a small department with a few employees to an entire manufacturing plant. In addition, cost centers may exist within other cost centers. For example, a manager of a manufacturing plant organized as a cost center may treat individual departments within the plant as separate cost centers, with the department managers reporting directly to the plant manager.

Profit Centers

In a **profit center**, the manager has the responsibility and the authority to make decisions that affect both costs and revenues (and thus profits) for the department or division. For example, a retail department store might decentralize its operations by product line. The manager of each product line would have responsibility for the cost of merchandise and decisions regarding revenues, such as the determination of sales prices. The manager of a profit center does not make decisions concerning the plant assets available to the center. For example, the manager of the Sporting Goods Department does not make the decision to expand the available floor space for that department.

Profit centers are widely used in businesses in which individual departments or divisions sell products or services to those outside the company.

A partial organization chart for a department store decentralized by retail departments as profit centers is as follows:

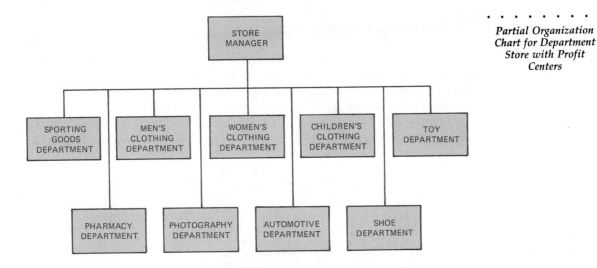

Partial Organization Chart for Department Store with Profit Centers

Occasionally, profit centers are established when the center's product or service is consumed entirely within the company. For example, a Repairs and Maintenance Department of a manufacturing plant could be treated as a profit center if its manager were allowed to bill other departments, such as the various production departments, for services rendered. Likewise, the Data Processing Department of a company might bill each of the company's administrative and operating units for computing services.

In a sense, a profit center may be viewed as a business within a business. While the primary concern of a cost center manager is the control of costs, the profit center is concerned with both revenues and costs.

Profit centers are often viewed as an excellent training assignment for new managers. For example, Lester B. Korn, Chairman and Chief Executive Officer of Korn/Ferry International, recently offered the following strategy for young executives enroute to top management positions:

Get Profit-Center Responsibility—Obtain a position where you can prove yourself as both a specialist with particular expertise and a generalist who can exercise leadership, authority, and inspire enthusiasm among colleagues and subordinates.

Investment Centers

In an **investment center**, the manager has the responsibility and the authority to make decisions that affect not only costs and revenues, but also the plant assets available to the center. For example, a plant manager sets selling prices of products and establishes controls over costs. In addition, the plant manager could, within general constraints established by top management, expand production facilities through equipment acquisitions and retirements.

The manager of an investment center has more authority and responsibility than the manager of either a cost center or a profit center. The manager of an investment center occupies a position similar to that of a chief operating officer or president of a separate company. As such, an investment center manager is evaluated in much the same way as a manager of a separate company is evaluated.

Investment centers are widely used in highly diversified companies. A partial organizational chart for a diversified company with divisions organized as investment centers is as follows:

Partial Organization Chart for Diversified Company with Investment Centers

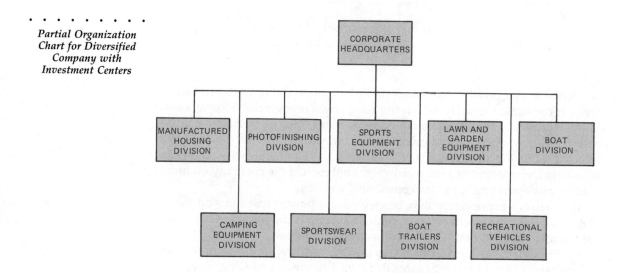

RESPONSIBILITY ACCOUNTING FOR COST CENTERS

Since managers of cost centers have responsibility for and authority to make decisions regarding costs, responsibility accounting for cost centers focuses on costs. The primary accounting tools appropriate for controlling and reporting costs are budgets and standard costs. Since budgets and standard costs were described and illustrated in Chapters 8 and 9, they will not be discussed in detail in this chapter. Instead, responsibility accounting for a cost center which uses budgeting to assist in the control of costs will be illustrated.

The basic concepts of responsibility accounting, as illustrated, are equally applicable to cost centers that use standard cost systems to aid in cost control.

For purposes of illustration, assume that the responsibility for the manufacturing operations of an enterprise is as represented in the following organization chart:

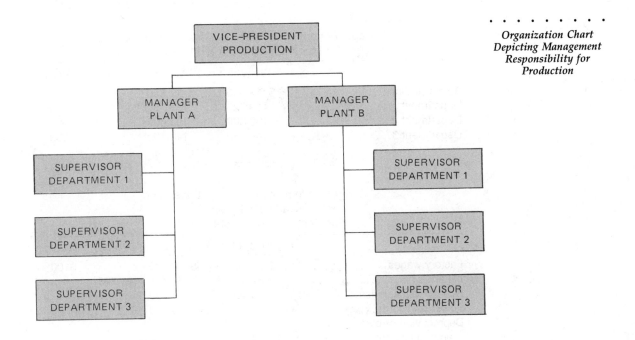

Organization Chart Depicting Management Responsibility for Production

Within the organizational structure illustrated, there are three levels of cost centers. At the operating level, each department is a cost center, with the department supervisors responsible for controlling costs within their departments. At the next level of the organization, each plant is a cost center, with each plant manager responsible for controlling plant administrative costs as well as supervising the control of costs in the plant departments. Finally, at the top level, the office of the vice-president of production is a cost center with responsibility for controlling the administrative costs of the office as well as supervising the control of costs in each plant.

Managerial accounting reports aid each level of management in carrying out its assigned responsibilities for the control of costs. To illustrate, the following budget performance reports are part of a responsibility accounting system for the enterprise:

Budget Performance Report—
Vice-President, Operations
For Month Ended October 31, 19--

	Budget	Actual	Over	Under
Administration	$ 19,500	$ 19,700	$ 200	
Plant A	467,475	470,330	2,855	
Plant B	395,225	394,300		$925
	$882,200	$884,330	$3,055	$925

Budget Performance Report—Manager, Plant A
For Month Ended October 31, 19--

	Budget	Actual	Over	Under
Administration	$ 17,500	$ 17,350		$150
Department 1	109,725	111,280	$1,555	
Department 2	190,500	192,600	2,100	
Department 3	149,750	149,100		650
	$467,475	$470,330	$3,655	$800

Budget Performance Report—Supervisor,
Department 1-Plant A
For Month Ended October 31, 19--

	Budget	Actual	Over	Under
Factory wages	$ 58,100	$ 58,000		$100
Materials	32,500	34,225	$1,725	
Supervisory salaries	6,400	6,400		
Power and light	5,750	5,690		60
Depreciation of plant and equipment	4,000	4,000		
Maintenance	2,000	1,990		10
Insurance and property taxes	975	975		
	$109,725	$111,280	$1,725	$170

The amount of detail presented in the budget performance report depends upon the level of management to which the report is directed. The reports prepared for the department supervisors present details of the budgeted and actual manufacturing costs for their departments. Each supervisor can then concentrate on the individual items that resulted in significant variations. In the illustration, the budget performance report for Department 1-Plant A indicates a significant variation between the budget and actual amounts for materials. It is clear that supplemental reports providing detailed data on the causes of the variation would aid the supervisor in taking corrective action. One such report, a scrap report, is illustrated as follows. This report indicates the cause of a significant part of the variation.

Materials Scrap Report—Department 1-Plant A
For Month Ended October 31, 19--

Material No.	Units Spoiled	Unit Cost	Dollar Loss	Remarks
A392	50	$3.10	$ 155.00	Machine malfunction
C417	76	.80	60.80	Inexperienced employee
G118	5	1.10	5.50	
J510	120	8.25	990.00	Substandard materials
K277	2	1.50	3.00	
P719	7	2.10	14.70	
V112	22	4.25	93.50	Machine malfunction
			$1,322.50	

The scrap report is one example of the type of supplemental report that can be provided to department supervisors. Other examples would include reports on factory wages and the cost of idle time.

The budget performance reports for the plant managers contain summarized data on the budgeted and actual costs for the departments under their jurisdiction. These reports enable them to identify the department supervisors responsible for significant variances. The report for the vice-president in charge of operations summarizes the data by plant. The persons responsible for plant operations can thus be held accountable for significant variations from predetermined objectives.

RESPONSIBILITY ACCOUNTING FOR PROFIT CENTERS

Since managers of profit centers have responsibility for and authority to make decisions regarding expenses and revenues, responsibility accounting reports for profit centers are normally in the form of income statements. These income statements for individual profit centers report expenses and revenues by departments through either gross profit or operating income. Alternatively, profit center income statements may include a breakdown of revenues and expenses by responsibility for their incurrence, and may identify contributions made by each department to overall company profit.

Since profit centers are widely used by merchandising enterprises, such as department stores, a merchandising enterprise is used as the basis for the following discussion and illustration of responsibility accounting for profit centers. Although the degree to which profit centers are used by a merchandising enterprise varies, profit centers are typically established for each major retail department. The enterprise in the illustrations, Garrison Company, has established Departments A and B as profit centers.

Gross Profit by Departments

To compute gross profit by departments, it is necessary to determine by departments each element entering into gross profit. An income statement showing gross profit by departments for Garrison Company appears below. For illustrative purposes, the operating expenses are shown in condensed form. Usually they would be listed in detail.

For a merchandising enterprise, the gross profit is one of the most significant figures in the income statement. Since the sales and the cost of goods sold are both controlled by departmental management, the reporting of gross profit by departments is useful in cost analysis and control. In addition, such reports aid management in directing its efforts toward obtaining a mix of sales that will maximize profits. For example, after studying the reports, management may decide to change sales or purchases policies to achieve a higher gross profit for each department. Caution must be exercised in the use of such

Income Statement Departmentalized Through Gross Profit

		Garrison Income For Year Ended
		Department A	
Revenue from sales:			
Sales		$630,000	
Less sales returns and allowances		15,300	
Net sales			$614,700
Cost of goods sold:			
Inventories, January 1, 19--		$ 80,150	
Purchases	$334,550		
Less purchases discounts	6,200	328,350	
Goods available for sale		$408,500	
Less inventories, December 31, 19--		85,150	
Cost of goods sold			323,350
Gross profit			$291,350
Operating expenses:			
Selling expenses			
General expenses			
Total operating expenses			
Income from operations			
Other expense:			
Interest expense			
Income before income tax			
Income tax			
Net income			

reports to insure that proposed changes affecting gross profit do not have an adverse effect on net income. A change that increases gross profit could result in an even greater increase in operating expenses and thereby decrease net income.

Operating Income by Departments

Departmental reporting may be extended to operating income. In such cases, each department must be assigned not only the related revenues and the cost of goods sold (as in the preceding illustration), but also that part of operating expenses incurred for its benefit. Some of these expenses may be easily identified with the department benefited. For example, if each sales-person is restricted to a certain sales department, the sales salaries may be assigned to the proper departmental salary accounts each time the payroll is prepared. On the other hand, the salaries of company officers, executives, and

Company Statement December 31, 19--						
	Department B			Total		
....	$270,000	....	....	$900,000	....
....	7,100	....	....	22,400	....
....	....	$262,900	....	....	$877,600
....	$ 61,750	....	....	$141,900	....
$200,350	....	....	$534,900	....	....
2,400	197,950	....	8,600	526,300	....
....	$259,700	....	....	$668,200	....
....	78,950	....	....	164,100	....
....	....	180,750	....	....	504,100
....	....	$ 82,150	....	....	$373,500
....	....	....	....	$113,000	....
....	....	....	....	110,200	....
....	....	....	....	....	223,200
....	....	....	....	....	$150,300
....	....	....	....	....	2,500
....	....	....	....	....	$147,800
....	....	....	....	....	37,800
....	....	....	....	....	$110,000

office personnel are not identifiable with specific sales departments and must therefore be allocated if an equitable and reasonable basis for allocation exists.

When operating expenses are allocated, they should be apportioned to the respective departments as nearly as possible in accordance with the cost of services rendered to them. Determining the amount of an expense chargeable to each department is not always a simple matter. In the first place, it requires the exercise of judgment; and accountants of equal ability may well differ in their opinions as to the proper basis for the apportionment of operating expenses. Second, the cost of collecting data for use in making an apportionment must be kept within reasonable bounds. Consequently, information that is readily available and is substantially reliable may be used instead of more accurate information that would be more costly to collect.

To illustrate the apportionment of operating expenses, assume that Garrison Company extends its departmental reporting through income from operations. The company's operating expenses for the year and the methods used in apportioning them are presented in the paragraphs that follow.

Sales Salaries Expense is apportioned to the two departments according to the distributions shown in the payroll records. Of the $84,900 total in the account, $54,000 is chargeable to Department A and $30,900 is chargeable to Department B.

Advertising Expense, covering billboard advertising and newspaper advertising, is apportioned according to the amount of advertising incurred for each department. The billboard advertising totaling $5,000 emphasizes the name and the location of the company. This expense is allocated on the basis of sales, the assumption being that this basis represents a fair allocation of billboard advertising to each department. Analysis of the newspaper space costing $14,000 indicates that 65% of the space was devoted to Department A and 35% to Department B. The computations of the apportionment of the total advertising expense are as follows:

	Total	Department A	Department B
Sales—dollars	$900,000	$630,000	$270,000
Sales—percent	100%	70%	30%
Billboard advertising .	$ 5,000	$ 3,500	$1,500
Newspaper space— percent	100%	65%	35%
Newspaper advertising	14,000	9,100	4,900
Advertising expense . .	$19,000	$12,600	$6,400

Depreciation Expense—Store Equipment is apportioned according to the average cost of the equipment in each of the two departments. The computations for the apportionment of the depreciation expense are as follows:

	Total	Department A	Department B
Cost of store equipment:			
January 1	$28,300	$16,400	$11,900
December 31	31,700	19,600	12,100
Total	$60,000	$36,000	$24,000
Average	$30,000	$18,000	$12,000
Percent	100%	60%	40%
Depreciation expense	$ 4,400	$ 2,640	$ 1,760

Officers' Salaries Expense and **Office Salaries Expense** are apportioned on the basis of the relative amount of time devoted to each department by the officers and by the office personnel. Obviously, this can be only an approximation. The number of sales transactions may have some bearing on the matter, as may billing and collection procedures and other factors such as promotional campaigns that might vary from period to period. Of the total officers' salaries of $52,000 and office salaries of $17,600, it is estimated that 60%, or $31,200 and $10,560 respectively, is chargeable to Department A and that 40%, or $20,800 and $7,040 respectively, is chargeable to Department B.

Rent Expense and **Heating and Lighting Expense** are usually apportioned on the basis of floor space devoted to each department. In apportioning rent expense for a multistory building, differences in the value of the various floors and locations may be taken into account. For example, the space near the main entrance of a department store is more valuable than the same amount of floor space located far from the elevator on the sixth floor. For Garrison Company, rent expense is apportioned on the basis of floor space used because there is no significant difference in the value of the floor areas used by each department. In allocating heating and lighting expense, it is assumed that the number of lights, their wattage, and the extent of use are uniform throughout the sales departments. If there are major variations and the total lighting expense is material, further analysis and separate apportionment may be advisable. The rent expense and the heating and lighting expense are apportioned as follows:

	Total	Department A	Department B
Floor space, square feet	160,000	104,000	56,000
Percent	100%	65%	35%
Rent expense	$15,400	$10,010	$ 5,390
Heating and lighting expense.	$ 5,100	$ 3,315	$ 1,785

Property Tax Expense and **Insurance Expense** are related primarily to the cost of the inventories and the store equipment. Although the cost of these assets may differ from their assessed value for tax purposes and their value for insurance purposes, the cost is most readily available and is considered to be satisfactory as a basis for apportioning these expenses. The computations of the apportionment of the personal property tax expense and the insurance expense are as follows:

	Total	Department A	Department B
Inventories:			
January 1	$141,900	$ 80,150	$ 61,750
December 31	164,100	85,150	78,950
Total.	$306,000	$165,300	$140,700
Average	$153,000	$ 82,650	$ 70,350
Average cost of store equipment (computed previously)	30,000	18,000	12,000
Total.	$183,000	$100,650	$ 82,350
Percent	100%	55%	45%
Property tax expense	$ 6,800	$ 3,740	$ 3,060
Insurance expense	$ 3,900	$ 2,145	$ 1,755

Uncollectible Accounts Expense, Miscellaneous Selling Expense, and **Miscellaneous General Expense** are apportioned on the basis of sales. Although the uncollectible accounts expense may be apportioned on the basis of an analysis of accounts receivable written off, it is assumed that the expense is closely related to sales. The miscellaneous selling and general expenses are apportioned on the basis of sales, which are assumed to be a reasonable measure of the benefit to each department. The computation of the apportionment is as follows:

	Total	Department A	Department B
Sales	$900,000	$630,000	$270,000
Percent	100%	70%	30%
Uncollectible accounts expense	$ 4,600	$ 3,220	$ 1,380
Miscellaneous selling expense	$ 4,700	$ 3,290	$ 1,410
Miscellaneous general expense	$ 4,800	$ 3,360	$ 1,440

An income statement presenting income from operations by departments for Garrison Company appears on pages 348 and 349. The amounts for sales and the cost of goods sold are presented in condensed form. Details could be reported if desired, in the manner illustrated on pages 342 and 343.

Departmental Margin

In a recent research study, 85% of the companies surveyed indicated that they allocate some operating expenses to profit centers (departments), as discussed in the preceding section.[1] Caution should be used, however, in relying on income statements departmentalized through income from operations, since the use of arbitrary bases in allocating operating expenses is likely to yield incorrect amounts of departmental operating income. In addition, the reporting of operating income by departments may be misleading, since the departments are not independent operating units. The departments are segments of a business enterprise, and no single department of a business can earn an income independently. For these reasons, income statements of segmented businesses may follow a somewhat different format than the one illustrated on pages 348 and 349. The alternative format emphasizes the contribution of each department to overall company net income and to covering the overall operating expenses incurred on behalf of the business. Income statements prepared in this alternative format are said to follow the **departmental margin** or **contribution margin** approach to responsibility accounting.

Prior to the preparation of an income statement in the departmental margin format, it is necessary to differentiate between operating expenses that are direct and those that are indirect. The two categories may be described in general terms as follows:

1. **Direct expense** — Operating expenses directly traceable to or incurred for the sole benefit of a specific department and usually subject to the control of the department manager.
2. **Indirect expense** — Operating expenses incurred for the entire enterprise as a unit and hence not subject to the control of individual department managers.

The details of departmental sales and the cost of goods sold are presented on the income statement in the usual manner. The direct expenses of each department are then deducted from the related departmental gross profit, yielding balances which are identified as the departmental margin. The remaining expenses, including the indirect operating expenses, are not departmentalized. They are reported separately below the total departmental margin.

---

[1]James M. Fremgen and Shu S. Liao, *The Allocation of Corporate Indirect Costs* (New York: National Association of Accountants, 1981), pp. 33–34.

Garrison
Income
For Year Ended

	Department A		
Net sales			$614,700
Cost of goods sold			323,350
Gross profit			$291,350
Operating expenses:			
Selling expenses:			
Sales salaries expense	$ 54,000		
Advertising expense	12,600		
Depreciation expense—store			
equipment	2,640		
Miscellaneous selling expense	3,290		
Total selling expenses		$ 72,530	
General expenses:			
Officers' salaries expense	$ 31,200		
Office salaries expense	10,560		
Rent expense	10,010		
Property tax expense	3,740		
Heating and lighting expense	3,315		
Uncollectible accounts expense	3,220		
Insurance expense	2,145		
Miscellaneous general expense	3,360		
Total general expenses		67,550	
Total operating expenses			140,080
Income (loss) from operations			$151,270
Other expense:			
Interest expense			
Income before income tax			
Income tax			
Net income			

Company
Statement
December 31, 19--

	Department B			Total	
....	....	$262,900	....	....	$877,600
....	....	180,750	....	....	504,100
....	....	$ 82,150	....	....	$373,500
$ 30,900	....	....	$ 84,900	....	....
6,400	....	....	19,000	....	....
1,760	....	....	4,400	....	....
1,410	....	....	4,700	....	....
....	$ 40,470	....	....	$113,000	....
$ 20,800	....	....	$ 52,000	....	....
7,040	....	....	17,600	....	....
5,390	....	....	15,400	....	....
3,060	....	....	6,800	....	....
1,785	....	....	5,100	....	....
1,380	....	....	4,600	....	....
1,755	....	....	3,900	....	....
1,440	....	....	4,800	....	....
....	42,650	....	....	110,200	....
....	....	83,120	....	....	223,200
....	....	$ (970)	....	....	$150,300
....	....	....	....	....	2,500
....	....	....	....	....	$147,800
....	....	....	....	....	37,800
....	....	....	....	....	$110,000

An income statement in the departmental margin format for Garrison Company is presented on the following page. The basic revenue, cost, and expense data for the period are identical with those reported in the earlier illustration. The expenses identified as "direct" are sales salaries, property tax, uncollectible accounts, insurance, depreciation, and the newspaper advertising portion of advertising. The billboard portion of advertising, which is for the benefit of the business as a whole, as well as officers' and office salaries, and the remaining operating expenses, are identified as "indirect." Although a $970 net loss from operations is reported for Department B on page 349, a departmental margin of $38,395 is reported for the same department on the statement on page 351.

With departmental margin income statements, the manager of each department can be held responsible for operating expenses traceable to the department. A reduction in the direct expenses of a department will have a favorable effect on that department's contribution to the net income of the enterprise.

The departmental margin income statement may also be useful to management in making plans for future operations. For example, this type of analysis can be used when the discontinuance of a certain operation or department is being considered. If a specific department yields a departmental margin, it generally should be retained, even though the allocation of the indirect operating expenses would result in a net loss for that department. This observation is based upon the assumption that the department in question represents a relatively small segment of the enterprise. Its termination, therefore, would not cause any significant reduction in the amount of indirect expenses.

To illustrate the application of the departmental margin approach to long-range planning, assume that a business occupies a rented three-story building. If the enterprise is divided into twenty departments, each occupying about the same amount of space, termination of the least profitable department would probably not cause any reduction in rent or other occupancy expenses. The space vacated would probably be absorbed by the remaining nineteen departments. On the other hand, if the enterprise were divided into three departments, each occupying approximately equal areas, the discontinuance of one could result in vacating an entire floor and significantly reducing occupancy expenses. When the departmental margin analysis is applied to problems of this type, consideration should be given to proposals for the use of the vacated space.

To further illustrate the departmental margin approach, assume that an enterprise with six departments has earned $70,000 before income tax during the past year, which is fairly typical of recent operations. Assume also that recent income statements, in which all operating expenses are allocated, indicate that Department F has been incurring losses, the net loss having amounted to $5,000 for the past year. Departmental margin analysis shows that, in spite of the losses, Department F should not be discontinued unless there is enough assurance that a proportionate increase in the gross profit of other departments or a decrease in indirect expenses can be effected. The

Garrison Company
Income Statement
For Year Ended December 31, 19--

	Department A		Department B		Total	
Net sales		$614,700		$262,900		$877,600
Cost of goods sold		323,350		180,750		504,100
Gross profit		$291,350		$ 82,150		$373,500
Direct departmental expenses:						
Sales salaries expense	$54,000		$30,900		$84,900	
Advertising expense	9,100		4,900		14,000	
Property tax expense	3,740		3,060		6,800	
Uncollectible accounts expense	3,220		1,380		4,600	
Depreciation expense—store equipment	2,640		1,760		4,400	
Insurance expense	2,145		1,755		3,900	
Total direct departmental expenses		74,845		43,755		118,600
Departmental margin		$216,505		$ 38,395		$254,900
Indirect expenses:						
Officers' salaries expense					$52,000	
Office salaries expense					17,600	
Rent expense					15,400	
Heating and lighting expense					5,100	
Advertising expense					5,000	
Miscellaneous selling expense					4,700	
Miscellaneous general expense					4,800	
Total indirect expenses						104,600
Income from operations						$150,300
Other expense:						
Interest expense						2,500
Income before income tax						$147,800
Income tax						37,800
Net income						$110,000

· ·

Income Statement Departmentalized Through Departmental Margin following analysis, which is considerably condensed, shows a possible reduction of $10,000 in net income (the amount of the departmental margin for Department F) if Department F is discontinued.

Proposal to Discontinue Department F
January 25, 19--

	Current Operations			Discontinuance of Department F
	Department F	Departments A–E	Total	
Sales........................	$100,000	$900,000	$1,000,000	$900,000
Cost of goods sold	70,000	540,000	610,000	540,000
Gross profit..................	$ 30,000	$360,000	$ 390,000	$360,000
Direct departmental expenses ...	20,000	210,000	230,000	210,000
Departmental margin	$ 10,000	$150,000	$ 160,000	$150,000
Indirect expenses			90,000	90,000
Income before income tax......			$ 70,000	$ 60,000

In addition to departmental margin analysis, there are other factors that may need to be considered. For example, there may be problems regarding the displacement of sales personnel. Or customers attracted by the least profitable department may make large purchases in other departments, so that discontinuance of that department may adversely affect the sales of other departments.

The foregoing discussion of departmental income statements has suggested various ways in which income data may be made useful to management in making important policy decisions. Note that the format selected for the presentation of income data to management must be that which will be most useful for evaluating, controlling, and planning departmental operations.

Chapter Review

KEY POINTS

1. Centralized and Decentralized Operations.

Responsibility accounting is the process of measuring and reporting operating data to management by areas of responsibility. In a centralized business organization, all major planning and operating decisions are made by the top echelon of management. In a decentralized business organization, the responsibility for planning and controlling operations is delegated among managers who have authority to make decisions without first seeking the approval of higher management. In a decentralized organization, an important function of the managerial accountant is to assist managers in the process of measuring and reporting data by their areas of responsibility.

2. Types of Decentralized Operations.

Decentralized operations can be classified by the scope of the responsibility assigned and the decision-making authority given to individual managers. In a cost center, the manager has the responsibility for the control of costs incurred and the authority to make decisions that affect those costs. In a profit center, the manager has the responsibility and the authority to make decisions that affect both costs and revenue (and thus profits) for the department or division. In an investment center, the manager has the responsibility and the authority to make decisions that affect not only costs and revenues, but also the plant assets available to the center.

3. Responsibility Accounting for Cost Centers.

Since managers of cost centers have responsibility for and authority to make decisions regarding costs, responsibility accounting for cost centers focuses on costs. The primary accounting tools for planning and controlling costs for a cost center are budgets and standard costs.

4. Responsibility Accounting for Profit Centers.

Since managers of profit centers have responsibility for and authority to make decisions regarding expenses and revenues, responsibility accounting reports for profit centers are normally in the form of income statements. One such statement determines gross profit by departments. Departmental reporting may be extended to operating income, in which case the operating expenses incurred by the company must be allocated to the departments. These expenses are usually allocated on the basis of the departmental benefit received from the expenditure. Some accountants, who consider the allocation of operating expenses to be arbitrary, advocate the preparation of departmental income statements based upon departmental margin or contribution margin. Departmental margin is determined by deducting the direct expenses of each department from departmental gross profit. The remaining expenses are not allocated to a department, but are reported in the income statement separately below the total departmental margin.

KEY TERMS

decentralization 333
responsibility accounting 333
strategic planning 334
cost center 336
profit center 336

investment center 337
departmental margin 347
contribution margin 347
direct expense 347
indirect expense 347

SELF-EXAMINATION QUESTIONS

(Answers at End of Chapter)

1. When the manager has the responsibility and authority to make decisions that affect costs and revenues, but no responsibility for or authority over assets invested in the department, the department is referred to as:

    A. a cost center
    B. a profit center
    C. an investment center
    D. none of the above

2. Which of the following would be the most appropriate basis for allocating rent expense for use in arriving at operating income by departments?

    A. Departmental sales
    B. Physical space occupied
    C. Cost of inventory
    D. Time devoted to departments

3. The term used to describe the excess of departmental gross profit over direct departmental expenses is:

    A. income from operations
    B. net income
    C. departmental margin
    D. none of the above

4. On an income statement departmentalized through departmental margin, sales commissions expense would be reported as:

    A. a direct expense
    B. an indirect expense
    C. an other expense
    D. none of the above

5. On an income statement departmentalized through departmental margin, office salaries would be reported as:

    A. a direct expense
    B. an indirect expense
    C. an other expense
    D. none of the above

ILLUSTRATIVE PROBLEM

Perry Home Appliances operates two sales departments—Department F for freezers, and Department R for ranges and ovens. The following data were obtained from the ledger on April 30, the end of the current fiscal year:

Sales—Department F..	350,000
Sales—Department R..	650,000
Sales Returns and Allowances—Department F	6,400

Sales Returns and Allowances — Department R	10,200
Cost of Goods Sold — Department F	280,200
Cost of Goods Sold — Department R	526,800
Sales Salaries	43,400
Advertising Expense	10,800
Depreciation Expense — Store Equipment	8,800
Store Supplies Expense	1,250
Miscellaneous Selling Expense	800
Office Salaries	10,000
Rent Expense	9,800
Heating and Lighting Expense	4,000
Property Tax Expense	3,000
Insurance Expense	1,800
Uncollectible Accounts Expense	1,100
Miscellaneous General Expense	900
Interest Income	1,000
Income Tax	15,700

The bases to be used in apportioning expenses, together with other essential information, are as follows:

Sales salaries — payroll records: Department F, $17,300; Department R, $26,100

Advertising expense — usage: Department F, $4,000; Department R, $6,800.

Depreciation expense — average cost of equipment. Equipment balances at beginning of year: Department F, $17,000; Department R, $26,000. Equipment balances at end of year: Department F, $18,200; Department R, $26,800.

Store supplies expense — requisitions: Department F, $550; Department R, $700.

Office salaries — Department F, 30%; Department R, 70%.

Rent expense and heating and lighting expense — floor space: Department F, 1,200 sq. ft.; Department R, 2,800 sq. ft.

Property tax expense and insurance expense — average cost of equipment plus average cost of inventories. Inventory balances at the beginning of the year: Department F, $17,200; Department R, $36,000. Inventory balances at the end of the year: Department F, $17,600; Department R, $41,200.

Uncollectible accounts expense, miscellaneous selling expense, and miscellaneous general expense — volume of gross sales.

Instructions:

Prepare an income statement departmentalized through income from operations.

SOLUTION

PERRY HOME
Income
For Year Ended

		Department F	
Revenue from sales:			
Sales.........................	....	$350,000	....
Less sales returns and allowances	....	6,400	....
Net sales........................	....	......	$343,600
Cost of goods sold	....	......	280,200
Gross profit	....	......	$ 63,400
Operating expenses:			
Selling expenses:			
Sales salaries	$17,300	......	....
Advertising expense	4,000	......	....
Depreciation expense—			
store equipment	3,520	......	....
Store supplies expense	550	......	....
Miscellaneous selling expense..	280	......	....
Total selling expenses	....	$ 25,650	....
General expenses:			
Office salaries	$ 3,000	......	....
Rent expense.................	2,940	......	....
Heating and lighting expense ..	1,200	......	....
Property tax expense..........	1,050	......	....
Insurance expense	630	......	....
Uncollectible accounts expense .	385	......	....
Miscellaneous general expense .	315	......	....
Total general expenses	....	9,520	....
Total operating expenses	....	......	35,170
Income from operations	....	......	$ 28,230
Other income:			
Interest income	....	......	....
Income before income tax..........	....	......	....
Income tax	....	......	....
Net income.......................	....	......	....

APPLIANCES
Statement
April 30, 19--

Department R			Total		
. . . .	$650,000	. . . .	. . . . . .	$1,000,000	. . . . . .
. . . .	10,200	. . . .	. . . . . .	16,600	. . . . . .
. . . .	. . . . . .	$639,800	. . . . . .	. . . .	$983,400
. . . .	. . . . . .	526,800	. . . . . .	. . . .	807,000
. . . .	. . . . . .	$113,000	. . . . . .	. . . .	$176,400
$26,100	. . . . . .	. . . .	$43,400	. . . .	. . . . . .
6,800	. . . . . .	. . . .	10,800	. . . .	. . . . . .
5,280	. . . . . .	. . . .	8,800	. . . .	. . . . . .
700	. . . . . .	. . . .	1,250	. . . .	. . . . . .
520	. . . . . .	. . . .	800	. . . .	. . . . . .
. . . .	$ 39,400	. . . .	. . . . . .	$ 65,050	. . . . . .
$ 7,000	. . . . . .	. . . .	$10,000	. . . .	. . . . . .
6,860	. . . . . .	. . . .	9,800	. . . .	. . . . . .
2,800	. . . . . .	. . . .	4,000	. . . .	. . . . . .
1,950	. . . . . .	. . . .	3,000	. . . .	. . . . . .
1,170	. . . . . .	. . . .	1,800	. . . .	. . . . . .
715	. . . . . .	. . . .	1,100	. . . .	. . . . . .
585	. . . . . .	. . . .	900	. . . .	. . . . . .
. . . .	21,080	. . . .	. . . . . .	30,600	. . . . . .
. . . .	. . . . . .	60,480	. . . . . .	. . . .	95,650
. . . .	. . . . . .	$ 52,520	. . . . . .	. . . .	$ 80,750
. . . .	. . . . . .	. . . .	. . . . . .	. . . .	1,000
. . . .	. . . . . .	. . . .	. . . . . .	. . . .	$ 81,750
. . . .	. . . . . .	. . . .	. . . . . .	. . . .	15,700
. . . .	. . . . . .	. . . .	. . . . . .	. . . .	$ 66,050

Discussion Questions

10–1. What is responsibility accounting?

10–2. What is a decentralized business organization?

10–3. Name three common types of responsibility centers for decentralized operations.

10–4. Differentiate between a cost center and a profit center.

10–5. Differentiate between a profit center and an investment center.

10–6. In what major respect would budget performance reports prepared for the use of plant managers of a manufacturing enterprise with cost centers differ from those prepared for the use of the various department supervisors who report to the plant managers?

10–7. The newly appointed manager of the Appliance Department in a department store is studying the income statements presenting gross profit by departments in an attempt to adjust operations to achieve the highest possible gross profit for the department. (a) Suggest ways in which an income statement departmentalized through gross profit can be used in achieving this goal. (b) Suggest reasons why caution must be exercised in using such statements.

10–8. Describe the underlying principle of apportionment of operating expenses to departments for income statements departmentalized through income from operations.

10–9. For each of the following types of expenses, select the allocation basis listed that is most appropriate for use in arriving at operating income by departments.

Expense:
(a) Property tax expense
(b) Sales salaries
(c) Rent expense
(d) Advertising expense

Basis of allocation:
(1) Cost of inventory and equipment
(2) Departmental sales
(3) Time devoted to departments
(4) Physical space occupied

10–10. Describe an appropriate basis for apportioning Officers' Salaries Expense among departments for purposes of the income statement departmentalized through income from operations.

10–11. Differentiate between a direct and an indirect operating expense.

10–12. Indicate whether each of the following operating expenses incurred by a department store is a direct or an indirect expense:
(a) Uncollectible accounts expense   (d) Insurance expense on building
(b) General manager's salary   (e) Sales commissions
(c) Depreciation of store equipment   (f) Heating and lighting expense

10–13. What term is applied to the dollar amount representing the excess of departmental gross profit over direct departmental expenses?

10–14. Recent income statements departmentalized through income from operations report operating losses for Department J, a relatively minor segment of the business. Management studies indicate that discontinuance of Department J would not affect sales of other departments or the volume of indirect expenses. Under what circumstances would the discontinuance of Department J result in a decrease of net income of the enterprise?

10–15. A portion of an income statement in condensed form, departmentalized through departmental margin for the year just ended, is as follows:

	Department 9
Net sales.	$135,750
Cost of goods sold	109,500
Gross profit.	$ 26,250
Direct expenses.	30,000
Departmental margin	$ (3,750)

    It is believed that the discontinuance of Department 9 would not affect the sales of the other departments nor reduce the indirect expenses of the enterprise. Based on this information, what would have been the effect on the income from operations of the enterprise if Department 9 had been discontinued prior to the year just ended?

10–16. Real World Focus. Many business enterprises maintain a computer information system. In such systems, there are three types of costs: systems development costs, operating costs, and software maintenance costs. Systems development costs include feasibility analysis, design, testing, and training costs. Operating costs are the expenses incurred in the day-to-day operation of the data processing facility. They include the use of hardware, software, and telecommunications resources. Software maintenance costs include the costs of assuring that all valid transactions are processed properly, and that new procedures are designed, tested, and used.
    For purposes of allocating information system costs to user departments, which allocation base — labor time or machine processing time — would be most appropriate for each type of information system cost?

Exercises

10–17. Budget performance report. The budget for Department P of Plant 11 for the current month ended April 30 is as follows:

Direct materials	$140,000
Direct labor	157,500
Power and light	51,000
Supervisory salaries	36,000
Indirect materials	7,000
Indirect factory wages	10,500
Depreciation of plant and equipment	21,300
Maintenance	19,300
Insurance and property taxes	12,000

During April, the costs incurred in Department P of Plant 11 were: direct materials, $145,130; direct labor, $158,200; power and light, $50,400; supervisiory salaries, $36,000; indirect materials, $7,020; indirect factory wages, $10,550; depreciation of plant and equipment, $21,300; maintenance, $19,180; insurance and property taxes, $12,000. (a) Prepare a budget performance report for the supervisor of Department P, Plant 11, for the month of April. (b) For what significant variations might the supervisor be expected to request supplemental reports?

10–18. Idle time report. The chief accountant of Allen Company prepares weekly reports of idleness of direct labor employees. These reports for the plant manager classify the idle time by departments. Idle time data for the week ended June 11 of the current year are as follows:

Department	Standard Hours	Actual Hours
A	5,200	4,940
B	3,700	3,700
C	4,100	4,018
D	2,000	1,880

The hourly direct labor rates are $22, $19, $24, and $16 respectively for Departments A through D. The idleness was caused by a machine breakdown in Department A, a materials shortage in Department C, and a lack of sales orders in Department D. Prepare an idle time report, classified by departments, for the week ended June 11. Use the following columnar headings for the report:

	Production			Idle Time		
Dept.	Standard Hours	Actual Hours	Percentage of Standard	Hours	Cost of Idle Time	Remarks

10–19. Apportionment of rent expense to departments. Hobbs Company occupies a two-story building. The departments and the floor space occupied by each department are as follows:

Receiving and Storage	basement	1,800 sq. ft.
Department 1	basement	4,200
Department 2	first floor	3,500
Department 3	first floor	6,500
Department 4	second floor	1,000
Department 5	second floor	1,600
Department 6	second floor	1,400

The building is leased at an annual rental of $100,000, allocated to the floors as follows: basement, 30%; first floor, 50%; second floor, 20%. Determine the amount of rent to be apportioned to each department.

10–20. Apportionment of depreciation and property tax expense to departments. In income statements prepared for Beeman Company, depreciation expense on equipment is apportioned on the basis of the average cost of the equipment, and property tax expense is apportioned on the basis of the combined total of the average cost of the equipment and the average cost of the inventories. Depreciation expense on equipment amounted to $150,000, and property tax expense amounted to $30,000 for the year. Determine the apportionment of the depreciation expense and the property tax expense, based on the following data:

	Average Cost	
Departments	Equipment	Inventories
Service:		
A	$ 360,000	
B	240,000	
Sales:		
X	720,000	$360,000
Y	480,000	120,000
Z	600,000	120,000
Total	$2,400,000	$600,000

ADSHEET
BLEM

10–21. Departmental income statement. The following data were summarized from the accounting records for Crow Company for the current year ended October 31:

Cost of goods sold:	
Department E	$166,800
Department F	237,000
Direct expenses:	
Department E	88,000
Department F	119,200
Income tax	38,400
Indirect expenses	76,400
Interest Income	16,000
Net sales:	
Department E	328,400
Department F	466,200

Prepare an income statement departmentalized through departmental margin.

10–22. Decision on discontinuance of department. A portion of an income statement in condensed form, departmentalized through loss from operations for the year just ended, is as follows:

	Department C
Net sales	$271,200
Cost of goods sold	218,700
Gross profit	$ 52,500
Operating expenses.................	64,000
Loss from operations	$(11,500)

The operating expenses of Dept. C include $20,000 for indirect expenses. It is believed that the discontinuance of Department C would not affect the sales of the other departments nor reduce the indirect expenses of the enterprise. Based on this information, determine the increase or decrease in income from operations of the enterprise if Department C had been discontinued prior to the year just ended.

Problems

·

If the working papers correlating with the textbook are not used, omit Problem 10–23.

10–23. Budget performance reports. The organization chart for the manufacturing operations of Hubble Inc. is presented in the working papers, along with the completed budget performance reports for the Machine Shop and Assembly Departments of Plant 2. Partially completed budget performance reports for the Painting Department of Plant 2 and the vice-president in charge of operations are also presented.

Instructions:

(1) Complete the budget performance report for the supervisor of the Painting Department of Plant 2.
(2) Prepare a budget performance report for the use of the manager of Plant 2, detailing the relevant data from the three departments in the plant. Assume that the budgeted and actual administration expenses for the plant were $22,600 and $23,850, respectively.
(3) Complete the budget performance report for the vice-president in charge of operations.

10–24. Departmental income statement through income from operations. Waller Appliances operates two sales departments—Department S for small appliances, such as radios and televisions, and Department L for large appliances, such as refrigerators and washing machines. The following data were obtained from the ledger on October 31, the end of the current fiscal year:

SPREADSHEET PROBLEM

Sales—Department S	280,000
Sales—Department L	520,000
Sales Returns and Allowances—Department S	2,800
Sales Returns and Allowances—Department L	4,200
Cost of Goods Sold—Department S	171,360
Cost of Goods Sold—Department L	344,640
Sales Salaries Expense	33,900
Advertising Expense	12,090
Depreciation Expense—Store Equipment	6,200
Store Supplies Expense	1,620
Miscellaneous Selling Expense	2,600
Office Salaries Expense	30,000
Rent Expense	12,000
Heating and Lighting Expense	10,200
Property Tax Expense	3,800
Insurance Expense	1,800
Uncollectible Accounts Expense	1,500
Miscellaneous General Expense	1,700
Interest Expense	1,800
Income Tax	46,500

Inventories at the beginning of the year: Department S, $15,600; Department L, $49,400. Inventories at the end of the year: Department S, $12,240; Department L, $42,760.

The bases to be used in apportioning expenses, together with other essential information, are as follows:

Sales salaries expense—payroll records: Department S, $11,800; Department L, $22,100.

Advertising expense—usage: Department S, $4,250; Department L, $7,840.

Depreciation expense—average cost of equipment. Equipment balances at beginning of year: Department S, $19,360; Department L, $29,320. Equipment balances at end of year: Department S, $22,240; Department L, $33,080.

Store supplies expense—requisitions: Department S, $580; Department L, $1,040.

Office salaries expense—Department S, 32%; Department L, 68%.

Rent expense and heating and lighting expense—floor space: Department S, 4,200 sq. ft.; Department L, 10,800 sq. ft.

Property tax expense and insurance expense—average cost of equipment plus average cost of inventories.

Uncollectible accounts expense, miscellaneous selling expense, and miscellaneous general expense—volume of gross sales.

Instructions:

Prepare an income statement departmentalized through income from operations.

10–25. Decision on discontinuance of department. Wood-Cutler Company is considering discontinuance of one of its ten departments. If operations in Department 4 are discontinued, it is estimated that the indirect operating expenses and the level of operations in the other departments will not be affected.

Data from the income statement for the past year ended December 31, which is considered to be a typical year, are as follows:

	Department 4		Other Departments	
Sales........................		$61,500		$995,500
Cost of goods sold.............		40,000		603,100
Gross profit		$21,500		$392,400
Operating expenses:				
Direct expenses	$18,400		$208,000	
Indirect expenses	9,500	27,900	114,000	322,000
Income (loss) before income tax .		$(6,400)		$ 70,400

Instructions:

(1) Prepare an estimated income statement for the current year ending December 31, assuming the discontinuance of Department 4.
(2) On the basis of the data presented, would it be advisable to retain Department 4?

10–26. Departmental income statement through departmental margin.
Coastland Fashions has 16 departments. Those with the least sales volume are Department G and Department K, which were established about eighteen months ago on a trial basis. The board of directors believes that it is now time to consider the retention or the termination of these two departments. The following adjusted trial balance as of August 31, the end of the first month of the current fiscal year, is severely condensed. August is considered to be a typical month. The income tax accrual has no bearing on the decision and is excluded from consideration.

Coastland Fashions
Trial Balance
August 31, 19--

Current Assets..................................	228,700	
Plant Assets....................................	792,900	
Accumulated Depreciation—Plant Assets...........		218,600
Current Liabilities		150,100
Common Stock..................................		250,000
Retained Earnings		403,505
Cash Dividends.................................	50,000	
Sales—Department G............................		37,500
Sales—Department K............................		26,900
Sales—Other Departments		998,900
Cost of Goods Sold—Department G...............	26,125	
Cost of Goods Sold—Department K...............	20,480	
Cost of Goods Sold—Other Departments	619,160	
Direct Expenses—Department G..................	8,125	
Direct Expenses—Department K..................	7,490	
Direct Expenses—Other Departments	227,665	
Indirect Expenses...............................	94,860	
Interest Expense................................	10,000	
	2,085,505	2,085,505

Instructions:

(1) Prepare an income statement for August, departmentalized through departmental margin.
(2) State your recommendations concerning the retention of Departments G and K, giving reasons.

10–27. Departmental income statement through departmental margin.

Wilson Corporation consists of two departments, J and M. The bases to be used in apportioning expenses between the two departments, together with other essential data, are as follows:

> Sales salaries and commissions expense—basic salary plus 5% of sales. Basic salaries for Department J, $40,800; Department M, $18,200.
>
> Advertising expense for brochures—usage within each department advertising specific products: Department J, $9,400; Department M, $4,350.
>
> Depreciation expense—average cost of store equipment: Department J, $63,800, Department M, $46,200.
>
> Insurance expense—average cost of store equipment plus average cost of inventories. Average cost of inventories was $49,950 for Department J and $15,050 for Department M.
>
> Uncollectible accounts expense—.4% of sales. Departmental managers are responsible for the granting of credit on the sales made by their respective departments.

The following data are obtained from the ledger on May 31, the end of the current fiscal year:

Sales—Department J		550,000
Sales—Department M		220,000
Cost of Goods Sold—Department J	357,500	
Cost of Goods Sold—Department M	145,200	
Sales Salaries and Commissions Expense	97,500	
Advertising Expense	13,750	
Depreciation Expense—Store Equipment	9,500	
Miscellaneous Selling Expense	1,520	
Administrative Salaries Expense	32,800	
Rent Expense	18,000	
Utilities Expense	11,200	
Insurance Expense	4,800	
Uncollectible Accounts Expense	3,080	
Miscellaneous General Expense	720	
Interest Income		5,000
Income Tax	24,200	

Instructions:

(1) Prepare an income statement departmentalized through departmental margin.
(2) Determine the rate of gross profit for each department.
(3) Determine the rate of departmental margin to sales for each department.

ALTERNATE PROBLEMS

If the working papers correlating with the textbook are not used, omit Problem 10–23A.

10–23A. Budget performance reports.
The organization chart for the manufacturing operations of Hubble Inc. is presented in the working papers, along with the completed budget performance reports for the Machine Shop and Assembly Departments of Plant 2. Partially completed budget performance reports for the Painting Department of Plant 2 and the vice-president in charge of operations are also presented.

Instructions:

(1) Complete the budget performance report for the supervisor of the Painting Department of Plant 2.

(2) Prepare a budget performance report for the use of the manager of Plant 2, detailing the relevant data from the three departments in the plant. Assume that the budgeted and actual administration expenses for the plant were $15,800 and $14,300, respectively.

(3) Complete the budget performance report for the vice-president in charge of operations.

10–24A.   Departmental income statement through income from operations.
Sparkman Co. operates two sales departments — Department S for sporting goods and Department T for camping equipment. The following data were obtained from the ledger on June 30, the end of the current fiscal year.

Sales — Department S	280,000
Sales — Department T	120,000
Sales Returns and Allowances — Department S	2,500
Sales Returns and Allowances — Department T	1,700
Cost of Goods Sold — Department S	134,030
Cost of Goods Sold — Department T	68,770
Sales Salaries Expense	70,000
Advertising Expense	11,000
Depreciation Expense — Store Equipment	5,500
Store Supplies Expense	3,600
Miscellaneous Selling Expense	3,000
Office Salaries Expense	30,000
Rent Expense	10,000
Heating and Lighting Expense	6,000
Property Tax Expense	3,200
Insurance Expense	2,800
Uncollectible Accounts Expense	2,200
Miscellaneous General Expense	1,050
Interest Expense	1,100
Income Tax	6,500

Inventories at the beginning of the year: Department S, $26,730; Department T, $14,770. Inventories at the end of the year: Department S, $24,300; Department T, $16,400.

The bases to be used in apportioning expenses, together with other essential information, are as follows:

Sales salaries expense — payroll records: Department S, $45,000; Department T, $25,000.

Advertising expense — usage: Department S, $7,200; Department T, $3,800.

Depreciation expense — average cost of equipment. Balances of equipment at beginning of year: Department S, $48,490; Department T, $26,110. Balances at end of year: Department S, $54,080; Department T, $29,120.

Store supplies expense—requisitions: Department S, $2,420; Department T, $1,180.

Office salaries expense—Department S, 80%; Department T, 20%.

Rent expense and heating and lighting expense—floor space: Department S, 14,400 sq. ft.; Department T, 5,600 sq. ft.

Property tax expense and insurance expense—average cost of equipment plus average cost of inventories.

Uncollectible accounts expense, miscellaneous selling expense, and miscellaneous general expense—volume of gross sales.

Instructions:

Prepare an income statement departmentalized through income from operations.

10–25A.   Decision on discontinuance of department.   R. E. Ziegler Company is considering discontinuance of one of its twelve departments. If operations in Department L are discontinued, it is estimated that the indirect operating expenses and the level of operations in the other departments will not be affected.

Data from the income statement for the past year ended December 31, which is considered to be a typical year, are as follows:

	Department L		Other Departments	
Sales........................		$66,000		$855,000
Cost of goods sold............		35,250		510,750
Gross profit		$30,750		$344,250
Operating expenses:				
Direct expenses	$24,750		$192,500	
Indirect expenses	13,500	38,250	99,000	291,500
Income (loss) before income tax .		$ (7,500)		$ 52,750

Instructions:

(1) Prepare an estimated income statement for the current year ending December 31, assuming the discontinuance of Department L.

(2) On the basis of the data presented, would it be advisable to retain Department L?

10–26A.   Departmental income statement through departmental margin. Weaver's Department Store has 18 departments. Those with the least sales volume are Department 16 and Department 17, which were established about a year ago on a trial basis. The board of directors feels that it is now time to consider the retention or the termination of these two departments. The following adjusted trial balance as of May 31, the end of the first month of the current fiscal year, is severely condensed. May is considered to be a typical month. The income tax accrual has no bearing on the decision and is excluded from consideration.

Weaver's Department Store
Trial Balance
May 31, 19--

Current Assets.	383,200	
Plant Assets.	692,700	
Accumulated Depreciation—Plant Assets.		282,370
Current Liabilities		190,920
Common Stock		200,000
Retained Earnings		291,860
Cash Dividends.	20,000	
Sales—Department 16		40,000
Sales—Department 17		25,000
Sales—Other Departments		881,750
Cost of Goods Sold—Department 16	31,500	
Cost of Goods Sold—Department 17	15,200	
Cost of Goods Sold—Other Departments	531,750	
Direct Expenses—Department 16	12,750	
Direct Expenses—Department 17	5,800	
Direct Expenses—Other Departments	125,000	
Indirect Expenses.	85,000	
Interest Expense.	9,000	
	1,911,900	1,911,900

Instructions:

(1) Prepare an income statement for May, departmentalized through departmental margin.

(2) State your recommendations concerning the retention of Departments 16 and 17, giving reasons.

Mini-Case 10

◆ HARDWARE

Assume that you recently started to work in your family-owned hardware store as an assistant store manager. Your father, the store manager and major stockholder, is considering the elimination of the Garden Supply Department, which has been incurring net losses for several years. Condensed revenue and expense data for the most recent year ended December 31, are presented on the following page. These data are typical of recent years. Bases

Petry Hardware
Income Statement
For Year Ended December 31, 19--

	Garden Supply Department	Other Departments	Total
Net sales	$68,000	$796,800	$864,800
Cost of goods sold	49,600	500,000	549,600
Gross profit	$18,400	$296,800	$315,200
Operating expenses:			
Selling expenses:			
Sales commissions expense	$5,440	$63,744	$69,184
Advertising expense	2,040	24,000	26,040
Depreciation expense—store equipment	1,600	18,800	20,400
Miscellaneous selling expense	1,020	11,952	12,972
Total selling expenses	$10,100	$118,496	$128,596
General expenses:			
Administrative salaries expense	$6,920	$62,280	$69,200
Rent expense	2,272	18,176	20,448
Utilities expense	2,044	16,360	18,404
Insurance and property tax expense	1,400	13,360	14,760
Miscellaneous general expense	612	7,172	7,784
Total general expenses	13,248	117,348	130,596
Total operating expenses	23,348	235,844	259,192
Income (loss) from operations	$ (4,948)	$ 60,956	$ 56,008
Other expense:			
Interest expense			1,700
Income before income tax			$ 54,308
Income tax			8,500
Net income			$ 45,808

used in allocating operating expenses among departments are as follows:

Expense	Basis
Sales commissions expense	Actual: 8% of net sales
Advertising expense	Actual: all advertising consists of brochures distributed by the various departments advertising specific products
Depreciation expense	Average cost of store equipment used
Miscellaneous selling expense	Amount of net sales
Administrative salaries expense	Each of the 10 departments apportioned an equal share
Rent expense	Floor space occupied
Utilities expense	Floor space occupied
Insurance and property tax expense	Average cost of equipment used plus average cost of inventory
Miscellaneous general expense	Amount of net sales

Since the Garden Supply Department is under your supervision, your father has asked your opinion as to whether the Garden Supply Department should be eliminated.

Instructions:

Prepare a brief statement of your recommendation to your father, supported by such schedule(s) as you think will be helpful to him in reaching a decision.

Answers to Self-Examination Questions

1. B The manager of a profit center (answer B) has responsibility for and authority over costs and revenues. If the manager has responsibility and authority for only costs, the department is referred to as a cost center (answer A). If the responsibility and authority extend to the investment in assets as well as costs and revenues, it is referred to as an investment center (answer C).

2. B Operating expenses should be apportioned to the various departments as nearly as possible in accordance with the cost of services rendered to them. For rent expense, generally the most appropriate basis is the floor space devoted to each department (answer B).

3. C When the departmental margin approach to income reporting is employed, the direct departmental expenses for each department are deducted from the gross profit for each department to yield departmental margin for each department (answer C). The indirect expenses are deducted from the total departmental margin to yield income from operations (answer A). The final total income is identified as net income (answer B).

4. A Operating expenses traceable to or incurred for the sole benefit of a specific department, such as sales commissions expense, are termed direct expenses (answer A) and should be so reported on the income statement departmentalized through departmental margin.

5. B Operating expenses incurred for the entire enterprise as a unit and hence not subject to the control of individual department managers, such as office salaries, are termed indirect expenses (answer B) and should be so reported on the income statement departmentalized through departmental margin.

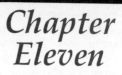

Chapter Eleven

•

Describe and illustrate responsibility accounting for investment centers, including three common measures of management performance:
Operating income
Rate of return on investment
Residual income

•

Describe the nature of transfer pricing for decentralized operations.

•

Describe and illustrate three common approaches to establishing transfer prices:
Market price approach
Negotiated price approach
Cost price approach

•

Describe and illustrate the effect of transfer prices on the evaluation of decentralized performance.

•

Describe and illustrate the potential impact of transfer prices on overall enterprise income.

•

Responsibility Accounting for Investment Centers; Transfer Pricing

Businesses that are separated into two or more manageable units in which divisional managers have authority and responsibility for operations are said to be decentralized. Three types of decentralized operations—cost centers, profit centers, and investment centers—were described in Chapter 10. The role of the managerial accountant in providing useful reports to assist individual managers in evaluating and controlling cost centers and profit centers was also described.

This chapter completes the discussion of decentralized business operations by focusing on responsibility accounting and reporting for investment centers. In addition, the pricing of products or services that are transferred between decentralized segments of a company is discussed.

RESPONSIBILITY ACCOUNTING FOR INVESTMENT CENTERS

Since investment center managers have responsibility for revenues and expenses, operating income is an essential part of investment center reporting. In addition, because the investment center manager also has responsibility for the assets invested in the center, two additional measures of performance are often used. These additional measures are the rate of return on investment and residual income. Each of these measures of investment center performance will be described and illustrated for Marsh Company, a diversified company with three operating divisions, as shown in the following organization chart:

MARSH COMPANY

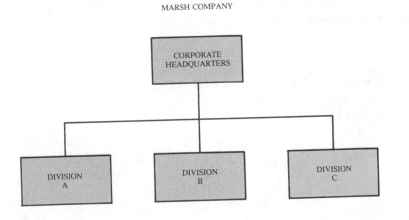

Partial Organization Chart for a Decentralized Company with Investment Centers

373

Operating Income

Because investment centers are evaluated as if they were separate companies, traditional financial statements are normally prepared for each center. For purposes of assessing profitability, operating income is the focal point of analysis. Since the determination of operating income for decentralized operations was described and illustrated in Chapter 10, only condensed divisional income statements will be used for illustrative purposes. The condensed divisional income statements for Marsh Company are as follows:

Marsh Company
Divisional Income Statements
For Year Ended December 31, 19--

	Division A	Division B	Division C
Sales	$560,000	$672,000	$750,000
Cost of goods sold	336,000	470,400	562,500
Gross profit	$224,000	$201,600	$187,500
Operating expenses	154,000	117,600	112,500
Operating income	$ 70,000	$ 84,000	$ 75,000

Based on the amount of divisional operating income, Division B is the most profitable of Marsh Company's divisions, with income from operations of $84,000. Divisions A and C are less profitable, with Division C reporting $5,000 more operating income than Division A.

Although operating income is a useful measure of investment center profitability, it does not reflect the amount of investment in assets committed to each center. For example, if the amount of assets invested in Division B is twice that of the other divisions, then Division B is the least profitable of the divisions in terms of the rate of return on investment. Since investment center managers also control the amount of assets invested in their centers, they should be held accountable for the use of invested assets.

Rate of Return on Investment

One of the most widely used measures of divisional performance for investment centers is the **rate of return on investment (ROI)**, or **rate of return on assets**. This rate is computed as follows:

$$\text{Rate of Return on Investment (ROI)} = \frac{\text{Operating Income}}{\text{Invested Assets}}$$

The rate of return on investment is useful because the three factors subject to control by divisional managers (revenues, expenses, and invested assets) are considered in its computation. By measuring profitability relative to the amount of assets invested in each division, the rate of return on investment can be used to compare divisions. The higher the rate of return on investment, the more effectively the division is utilizing its assets in generating income. To illustrate, the rate of return on investment for each division of Marsh Company, based on the book value of invested assets, is as follows:

	Operating Income	Invested Assets	Rate of Return on Investment
Division A	$70,000	$350,000	20%
Division B	84,000	700,000	12
Division C	75,000	500,000	15

Although Division B generated the largest operating income, its rate of return on investment (12%) is the lowest. Hence, relative to the assets invested, Division B is the least profitable division. In comparison, the rates of return on investment of Divisions A and C are 20% and 15% respectively. These differences in the rates of return on investment may be analyzed by restating the expression for the rate of return on investment in expanded form, as follows:

$$\text{Rate of Return on Investment (ROI)} = \frac{\text{Operating Income}}{\text{Sales}} \times \frac{\text{Sales}}{\text{Invested Assets}}$$

In the expanded form, the rate of return on investment is the product of two factors: (1) the ratio of operating income to sales, often termed the **profit margin**, and (2) the ratio of sales to invested assets, often termed the **investment turnover**. As shown in the following computation, the use of this expanded expression yields the same rate of return for Division A, 20%, as the previous expression for the rate of return on investment:

$$\text{Rate of Return on Investment (ROI)} = \frac{\text{Operating Income}}{\text{Sales}} \times \frac{\text{Sales}}{\text{Invested Assets}}$$

$$\text{ROI} = \frac{\$70,000}{\$560,000} \times \frac{\$560,000}{\$350,000}$$

$$\text{ROI} = 12.5\% \times 1.6$$

$$\text{ROI} = 20\%$$

The expanded expression for the rate of return on investment is useful in management's evaluation and control of decentralized operations because the profit margin and the investment turnover focus on the underlying operating relationships of each division. The profit margin component focuses on profitability by indicating the rate of profit earned on each sales dollar. When efforts are aimed at increasing a division's profit margin by changing the division's sales mix, for example, the division's rate of return on investment may increase.

The investment turnover component focuses on efficiency in the use of assets and indicates the rate at which sales are being generated for each dollar of invested assets. The more sales per dollar invested, the greater the efficiency in the use of the assets. When efforts are aimed at increasing a division's investment turnover through special sales promotions, for example, the division's rate of return on investment may increase.

The rate of return on investment, using the expanded expression for each division of Marsh Company, is summarized as follows:

$$\text{Rate of Return on Investment (ROI)} = \text{Profit Margin} \times \text{Investment Turnover}$$

$$\text{ROI} = \frac{\text{Operating Income}}{\text{Sales}} \times \frac{\text{Sales}}{\text{Invested Assets}}$$

Division A:
$$\text{ROI} = \frac{\$70,000}{\$560,000} \times \frac{\$560,000}{\$350,000}$$
$$\text{ROI} = 12.5\% \times 1.6$$
$$\text{ROI} = 20\%$$

Division B:
$$\text{ROI} = \frac{\$84,000}{\$672,000} \times \frac{\$672,000}{\$700,000}$$
$$\text{ROI} = 12.5\% \times .96$$
$$\text{ROI} = 12\%$$

Division C:
$$\text{ROI} = \frac{\$75,000}{\$750,000} \times \frac{\$750,000}{\$500,000}$$
$$\text{ROI} = 10\% \times 1.5$$
$$\text{ROI} = 15\%$$

Although Divisions A and B have the same profit margins, Division A's investment turnover is larger than that of Division B (1.6 to .96). Thus, by more efficiently utilizing its invested assets, Division A's rate of return on investment is higher than Division B's. Division C's profit margin of 10% and investment turnover of 1.5 are lower than the corresponding factors for Division A. The product of these factors results in a return on investment of 15% for Division C, as compared to 20% for Division A.

To determine possible ways of increasing the rate of return on investment, the profit margin and investment turnover for a division should be analyzed. For example, if Division A is in a highly competitive industry where the profit margin cannot be easily increased, the division manager should concentrate on increasing the investment turnover. To illustrate, assume that sales of Division A could be increased by $56,000 through changes in advertising expenditures. The cost of goods sold is expected to be 60% of sales, and operating expenses will increase to $169,400. If the advertising changes are undertaken, Division A's operating income would increase from $70,000 to $77,000, as shown in the following condensed income statement:

Sales ($560,000 + $56,000)	$616,000
Cost of goods sold ($616,000 × 60%)	369,600
Gross profit	$246,400
Operating expenses	169,400
Operating income	$ 77,000

The rate of return on investment for Division A, using the expanded expression, is recomputed as follows:

$$\text{Rate of Return on Investment (ROI)} = \frac{\text{Operating Income}}{\text{Sales}} \times \frac{\text{Sales}}{\text{Invested Assets}}$$

$$\text{ROI} = \frac{\$77,000}{\$616,000} \times \frac{\$616,000}{\$350,000}$$

$$\text{ROI} = 12.5\% \times 1.76$$

$$\text{ROI} = 22\%$$

Although Division A's profit margin remains the same (12.5%), the division's investment turnover has increased from 1.6 to 1.76, an increase of 10% (.16 ÷ 1.6). The 10% increase in investment turnover has the effect of also increasing the rate of return on investment by 10% (from 20% to 22%).

The major advantage of the use of the rate of return on investment instead of operating income as a divisional performance measure is that the amount of divisional investment is directly considered. Thus, divisional performances can be compared, even though the sizes of the divisions may vary significantly.

In addition to its use as a performance measure, the rate of return on investment can assist management in other ways. For example, in considering a decision to expand the operations of Marsh Company, management should consider giving priority to Division A because it earns the highest rate of return on investment. If the current rates of return on investment can be maintained in the future, an investment in Division A will return 20 cents (20%) on each dollar invested, while investments in Divisions B and C will return only 12 cents and 15 cents respectively.

A major disadvantage of the rate of return on investment as a performance measure is that it may lead divisional managers to reject new investment proposals, even though the rate of return on these investments exceeds the minimum considered acceptable by the company. For example, a division might have an overall rate of return on investment of 25%, and the company might have an overall rate of return on investment of 15%. If the division accepts a new investment that would earn a 20% rate of return on investment, the overall rate of return for the division would decrease, but the overall rate of return for the company as a whole would increase. Thus, the division manager might reject the proposal, even though its acceptance would be in the best interests of the company.

Measuring a Foreign Subsidiary's Performance

Managers of foreign subsidiaries face a major problem: achieving accurately measured levels of performance. Because a foreign subsidiary is not isolated from its environment, it is influenced significantly by local sociological, economic, political-legal, and educational factors. Between countries, these factors are likely to be quite different, which destroys the comparability of subsidiary operating results. For example, there may be differences in social structures and religious customs that interact with inflation, foreign exchange rates, and taxes. A country's attitudes toward foreigners may cause the country's government to issue laws and regulations that affect a foreign subsidiary's operations in that country. Special

training programs may be required for a foreign subsidiary operating in an educationally underdeveloped country.

The following table illustrates the variability of traditional measures between the foreign subsidiaries of four U.S.-based corporations. Because of the factors mentioned above, the managers of multinational corporations must be especially careful in using such measures to evaluate their foreign subsidiary operations. For example, the relatively high 100% profit margin and the relatively low 4% rate of return on investment for Company Four's Venezuelan subsidiary would be totally misleading if the local environmental factors were not considered.

The name of the company (assumed)	Industry	Foreign Countries
Company One	Measuring, Analyzing, and Control Instruments	Canada, the U.K., Belgium, Australia, and South Africa
Company Two	Oil and Gas	Canada, Mexico, Brazil, the Philippines, and Thailand
Company Three	Electric and Electronic	Germany, Canada, South Africa, Brazil, and Australia
Company Four	Fabricated Metal	Italy, Spain, France, Mexico, and Venezuela

Actual Financial Information (in millions of dollars)

Foreign Country	(1) Total Assets	(2) Gross Revenues	(3) Income After Taxes	(4) Profit Margin (3) ÷ (2)	(5) Investment Turnover (2) ÷ (1)	(6) Actual ROI (3) ÷ (1)
			Company One			
Canada	9	6.50	1.60	24.6%	0.72	17.8%
The U.K.	6	4.20	1.20	28.6%	0.70	20 %
Belgium	15	13.60	.40	2.9%	0.90	2.7%
Australia	12	11.80	2.00	22.0%	0.98	21.7%
South Africa	9	7.60	1.40	18.4%	0.84	15.6%
			Company Two			
Canada	60	110	10	9.1%	1.83	16.7%
Mexico	80	130	16	12.3%	1.63	20 %
Brazil	30	30	6	20 %	1.00	20 %
Phillippines	20	50	8	16 %	2.50	40 %
Thailand	15	30	12	40 %	2.00	80 %
			Company Three			
Germany	5.4	1.96	1.22	62.2%	0.36	22.6%
Canada	6.0	1.80	.94	52.2%	0.30	15.7%
South Africa	2.4	1.44	.80	55.6%	0.60	33.3%
Brazil	1.0	.52	.30	57.7%	0.52	30 %
Australia	6.0	2.52	1.32	52.4%	0.42	22 %
			Company Four			
Italy	29.6	29.8	14.4	48.3%	1.01	48.6%
Spain	18.6	13.4	10.2	76.1%	0.72	54.8%
France	5.2	4.8	1.60	33.3%	0.92	30.8%
Mexico	7	4.4	2.0	45.5%	0.63	28.6%
Venezuela	15	0.60	.60	100 %	.04	4 %

Source: Wagdy M. Abdallah, "Change the Environment or Change the System," *Management Accounting* (October, 1986), pp. 33–36.

Residual Income

· · ·

In the previous illustration for Marsh Company, two measures of evaluating divisional performance were discussed and illustrated. The advantages and disadvantages of both measures were also discussed. An additional measure, residual income, is useful in overcoming some of the disadvantages associated with the operating income and rate of return on investment measures.

Residual income is the excess of divisional operating income over a minimum amount of desired operating income. The minimum amount of desired divisional operating income is set by top management by establishing a minimum rate of return for the invested assets and then multiplying this rate by the amount of divisional assets. To illustrate, assume that the top management of Marsh Company has established 10% as the minimum rate of return on divisional assets. The residual incomes for Divisions A, B, and C are computed as follows:

	Division A	Division B	Division C
Divisional operating income............	$70,000	$84,000	$75,000
Minimum amount of divisional operating income:			
$350,000 × 10%	35,000		
$700,000 × 10%		70,000	
$500,000 × 10%			50,000
Residual income.....................	$35,000	$14,000	$25,000

The major advantage of residual income as a performance measure is that it gives consideration not only to a minimum rate of return on investment, but also to the total magnitude of the operating income earned by each division. For example, Division A has more residual income than the other divisions of Marsh Company, even though it has the least operating income. Also, Division C earns $11,000 more residual income than Division B, even though Division B generates more operating income than Division C. The reason for this difference is that Division B has $200,000 more assets than Division C. Hence, Division B's operating income is reduced by $20,000 ($200,000 × 10%) more than Division C's operating income in determining residual income.

The preceding paragraphs have described and illustrated three measures—operating income, rate of return on investment, and residual income—which management can use in evaluating and controlling investment center performance. In practice, most companies use some combination of all these measures.

TRANSFER PRICING

The use of responsibility accounting and reporting in measuring performance in decentralized companies can be important in motivating managers to achieve common profit goals. However, when decentralized units transfer products or render services to each other, the **transfer price**—the price to charge for the products or services—becomes an issue. Since transfer prices affect the revenues and expenses of both the receiving unit and the unit providing the product or service, transfer prices affect the performance measures used for evaluating divisional performance.

The objective of transfer pricing is to encourage each divisional manager to transfer goods and services between divisions if overall company income can be increased by doing so. As will be illustrated, however, transfer prices may be misused to the detriment of overall company income.

The following paragraphs describe and illustrate various approaches to establishing transfer prices, the effect of transfer prices on the evaluation of decentralized performance, and their potential impact on overall company income. Three commonly used approaches are (1) the market price approach, (2) the negotiated price approach, and (3) the cost price approach.

Although transfer prices may apply when decentralized units are organized as cost or profit centers, a diversified company (Wilson Company) with two operating divisions (M and N) organized as investment centers will be used for the illustrations in the remainder of this chapter. Condensed income statements for Wilson Company's divisions, with no intracompany transfers and a breakdown of expenses into variable and fixed components, are as follows:

	Division M	Division N	Total
Wilson Company **Divisional Income Statements** **For Year Ended December 31, 19--**			
Sales:			
50,000 units × $20 per unit..........	$1,000,000		$1,000,000
20,000 units × $40 per unit..........		$800,000	800,000
			$1,800,000
Expenses:			
Variable:			
50,000 units × $10 per unit.........	$ 500,000		$ 500,000
20,000 units × $30* per unit........		$600,000	600,000
Fixed.....................	300,000	100,000	400,000
Total expenses	$ 800,000	$700,000	$1,500,000
Operating income	**$ 200,000**	**$100,000**	**$ 300,000**

*$20 of the $30 per unit represents materials costs, and the remaining $10 per unit represents other expenses incurred within Division N.

Market Price Approach

Under the **market price approach,** the transfer price is the price at which the product or service transferred could be sold to outside buyers. If an outside market exists for the product or service transferred, then the current market price at which the purchasing division could buy the product or service outside the company would seem to be a reasonable transfer price for intracompany transfers. However, the appropriateness of the market price approach depends on whether the division supplying the product or service is operating at full capacity and can sell all it produces.

To illustrate, assume that materials used by Wilson Company in producing Division N's product are currently purchased from an outside supplier at $20 per unit. The same materials are produced by Division M. If Division M is operating at full capacity of 50,000 units and can sell all it produces to either Division N or to outside buyers, then the use of a transfer price of $20 per unit (the market price) has no effect on the income of Division M or total company income. Division M will earn revenues of $20 per unit on all its production and sales, regardless of who buys its product, and Division N will pay $20 per unit for materials, regardless of whether it purchases the materials from Division M or from an outside supplier. In this situation, the use of the market price as the transfer price is appropriate. The condensed divisional income statements for Wilson Company under such circumstances would be as shown on the previous page.

If unused capacity exists in the supplying division, the use of the market price approach may not lead to the maximization of total company income. To illustrate, assume that Division M has unused capacity of 20,000 units and it can continue to sell only 50,000 units to outside buyers. In this situation, the transfer price should be set to motivate the manager of Division N to purchase from Division M if the variable cost per unit of product of Division M is less than the market price. If the variable costs are less than $20 per unit but the transfer price is set equal to the market price of $20, then the manager of Division N is indifferent as to whether materials are purchased from Division M or from outside suppliers, since the cost per unit to Division N would be the same, $20. However, Division N's purchase of 20,000 units of materials from outside suppliers at a cost of $20 per unit would not maximize overall company income, since this market price per unit is greater than the unit variable expenses of Division M, $10. Hence, the intracompany transfer could save the company the difference between the market price per unit and Division M's unit variable expenses. This savings of $10 per unit would add $200,000 (20,000 units × $10) to overall company income.

Negotiated Price Approach

In the previous illustration, the manager of Division N should be encouraged to purchase from Division M by establishing a transfer price at an amount less than the market price of $20 per unit. Division N's materials cost per unit would thus decrease, and its operating income would increase. In such situations, the negotiated price approach can be used to establish an appropriate transfer price.

The **negotiated price approach** allows the managers of decentralized units to agree (negotiate) among themselves as to the proper transfer price. If agreement cannot be reached among the division managers, the company's top management may have to intervene to set the transfer price. To illustrate, assume that Wilson Company's division managers agree to a transfer price of $15 for Division M's product. By purchasing from Division M, Division N would then report $5 per unit less materials cost. At the same time, Division M would increase its sales to a total of 70,000 units (50,000 units to outside buyers and 20,000 units to Division N). The effect of increasing Division M's sales by $300,000 (20,000 units × $15 per unit) is to increase its income by $100,000 ($300,000 sales − $200,000 variable expenses). The effect of reducing Division N's materials cost by $100,000 (20,000 units × $5 per unit) is to increase its income by $100,000. Therefore, Wilson Company's income is increased by $200,000 ($100,000 reported by Division M and $100,000 reported by Division N), as shown in the following condensed income statements:

Wilson Company
Divisional Income Statements
For Year Ended December 31, 19--

	Division M	Division N	Total
Sales:			
50,000 units × $20 per unit	$1,000,000		$1,000,000
20,000 units × $15 per unit	300,000		300,000
20,000 units × $40 per unit		$800,000	800,000
	$1,300,000	$800,000	$2,100,000
Expenses:			
Variable:			
70,000 units × $10 per unit	$ 700,000		$ 700,000
20,000 units × $25* per unit		$500,000	500,000
Fixed	300,000	100,000	400,000
Total expenses	$1,000,000	$600,000	$1,600,000
Operating income	$ 300,000	$200,000	$ 500,000

*$10 per unit of the $25 is incurred solely within Division N, and $15 per unit represents the transfer price per unit from Division M.

In the Wilson Company illustration, any transfer price less than the market price of $20 but greater than Division M's unit variable expenses of $10 would increase each division's income and would increase overall company income by $200,000. By establishing a range of $20 to $10 for the negotiated transfer price, each division manager will have an incentive to negotiate the intracompany transfer of the materials. For example, a transfer price of $18 would increase Division M's income by $160,000 (from $200,000 to $360,000) and Division N's income by $40,000 (from $100,000 to $140,000). Overall company income would still be increased by $200,000 (from $300,000 to $500,000), as shown in the following condensed income statements:

Wilson Company
Divisional Income Statements
For Year Ended December 31, 19--

	Division M	Division N	Total
Sales:			
50,000 units × $20 per unit	$1,000,000		$1,000,000
20,000 units × $18 per unit	360,000		360,000
20,000 units × $40 per unit		$800,000	800,000
	$1,360,000	$800,000	$2,160,000
Expenses:			
Variable:			
70,000 units × $10 per unit	$ 700,000		$ 700,000
20,000 units × $28* per unit		$560,000	560,000
Fixed	300,000	100,000	400,000
Total expenses	$1,000,000	$660,000	$1,660,000
Operating income	$ 360,000	$140,000	$ 500,000

*$10 per unit of the $28 is incurred solely within Division N, and $18 per unit represents the transfer price per unit from Division M.

Cost Price Approach

Under the **cost price approach,** cost is used as the basis for setting transfer prices. With this approach, a variety of cost concepts may be used. For example, cost may refer to either total product cost per unit or variable product cost per unit. If total product cost per unit is used, direct materials, direct labor, and factory overhead are included in the transfer price. If variable product cost per unit is used, the fixed factory overhead component of total product cost is excluded from the transfer price.

Either actual costs or standard (budgeted) costs may be used in applying the cost price approach. If actual costs are used, inefficiencies of the producing division are transferred to the purchasing division, and thus there is little incentive for the producing division to control costs carefully. For this reason, most companies use standard costs in the cost price approach, so that differences between actual and standard costs are isolated in the producing divisions for cost control purposes.

When division managers have responsibility for only costs incurred in their divisions, the cost price approach to transfer pricing is frequently used. However, many accountants argue that the cost price approach is inappropriate for decentralized operations organized as profit or investment centers. In profit and investment centers, division managers have responsibility for both revenues and expenses. The use of cost as a transfer price, however, ignores the supplying division manager's responsibility over revenues. When a supplying division's sales are all intracompany transfers, for example, the use of the cost price approach would prevent the supplying division from reporting any operating income. A cost-based transfer price would therefore not motivate the division manager to make intracompany transfers, even though they are in the best interests of the company.

Transfer Pricing for an Automobile Dealership — A Case Analysis

The importance of developing appropriate transfer prices can be demonstrated by the following case, which was reported in *Management Accounting*. The case is based on an actual company, an automobile dealership that is one of the largest volume import dealers in the state of Pennsylvania.

... With sales expected to exceed 1,000 new units in [the] calendar year, ... the dealership serves as a leader in the field. Dollar sales of new units will top $9 million by calendar year-end. In addition to the sales department, the dealership also has separate parts and service departments. [The sales department] is a major customer of both [the] service and parts [departments]....

[The transfer prices for floormats, rustproofing, paint protection, AM-FM stereo cassettes, and air conditioning transferred from the parts and service departments to the sales department were determined as follows:]

Item	Cost*	Markup	Transfer Price
Deluxe floormats ..	$ 27.49	27%	$ 35.00
Rustproofing	25.54	135	60.00
Paint protection....	25.54	135	60.00
AM-FM stereo cassette	225.60	13	255.00
A/C	484.70	34	650.00

*Includes installation costs.

All of the above prices were set by the dealer-owner in conjunction with his service manager and parts manager with the implied intention of giving

these departments a share of the sales department's profit. These prices are not retail prices, nor are they legitimate wholesale prices; they are simply arbitrary transfer prices.

[The above transfer prices illustrate] the haphazard method by which [the sales department] is charged for goods from the two supporting departments. Notice that floormats are charged to sales at approximately a 27% mark-up on cost, rustproofing and paint protection at 135% mark-up, and air conditioning at 34% mark-up. The lowest mark-up occurs on radios, a mere 13% increase....

Because of perceived excess charges, the frustrated sales manager looked outside the company for the products and services he needed. After minimal investigation he found a subcontractor willing to supply comparable performance radios and air conditioners at considerable savings. He was able to and did buy radios for $227.00 installed and air conditioners for $525.00 installed. This practice continued for approximately two years. During this period the sales manager was noticeably ecstatic over his increased bonuses, while the parts and service managers were long-faced and moody due to declining profits. In this period 618 air conditioners and 267 AM-FM stereo cassettes were sold by the sales department. Of these, 112 air conditioners and three stereo cassettes were purchased internally. Although the sales department saved $63,250.00 (506 units @ $125.00 savings) on air conditioners, and [$7,392.00 (264 units @ $28.00 savings)] on cassette radios, the company as a whole lost money. By buying 506 air conditioners from a third party the company lost $20,391.80 [506 units × ($525.00 price paid − $484.70 cost to internally install.)]. By purchasing 264 AM-FM stereo cassettes from an outsider the company gave up $369.60 [264 units × ($227.00 price paid − $225.60 cost to internally install)]. Total company losses totalled $20,761.40.

After two years the dealer-owner realized the extent of his lost profits and immediately called all three managers together in conference to discuss the problem.... After several days of negotiation,... the parties settled on what they believed were fair and reasonable transfer prices for the products involved as well as all other products sold internally to the sales department....

Source: Joseph A. Scarpo, Jr., "Auto Dealers Lag in Transfer Pricing," *Management Accounting* (July, 1984), pp. 54–56.

Chapter Review

KEY POINTS

1. Responsibility Accounting for Investment Centers.

Since investment center managers have responsibility for expenses and revenues of the center and plant assets assigned to the center, they are evaluated as if they were managers of separate companies. Three common measures of performance for investment centers are (1) operating income, (2) rate of return on investment, and (3) residual income.

Because investment centers are evaluated as if they were separate companies, traditional financial statements are normally prepared for each center. For purposes of assessing profitability, operating income is the focal point of the analysis.

The rate of return on investment is one of the most widely used measures of divisional performance for investment centers and is computed as follows:

$$\text{Rate of Return on Investment (ROI)} = \frac{\text{Operating Income}}{\text{Invested Assets}}$$

The rate of return on investment may be expressed in expanded form as follows:

$$\text{Rate of Return on Investment (ROI)} = \frac{\text{Operating Income}}{\text{Sales}} \times \frac{\text{Sales}}{\text{Invested Assets}}$$

In the expanded form, the rate of return on investment is the product of two factors: (1) the ratio of operating income to sales, often termed the profit margin, and (2) the ratio of sales to invested assets, often termed the investment turnover.

Residual income is the excess of divisional operating income over a minimum amount of desired operating income. The minimum amount of desired divisional operating income is set by top management by establishing a minimum rate of return for the invested assets and then multiplying this rate by the amount of divisional assets.

2. Transfer Pricing.

The transfer price is the price charged by a unit for products or services provided to another unit in a decentralized company. The objective of transfer pricing is to encourage each divisional manager to transfer goods and services between divisions if overall company income can be increased by doing so. Three commonly used approaches to establishing transfer prices are (1) the market price approach, (2) the negotiated price approach, and (3) the cost price approach.

Under the market price approach to transfer pricing, the transfer price is set at the price at which the product or services transferred between units could be sold to outsider buyers.

Under the negotiated price approach to transfer pricing, the transfer price is the price agreed to (negotiated) among the managers of the decentralized units.

Under the cost price approach, cost is used as the basis for setting transfer prices. The cost may be either total product cost per unit or variable product cost per unit, and most companies use the standard cost rather than the actual cost.

KEY TERMS
·

rate of return on investment
   (ROI) 374
profit margin 375
investment turnover 375
residual income 379

transfer price 380
market price approach 381
negotiated price approach 382
cost price approach 384

Self-Examination Questions
·
(Answers at End of Chapter)

1. Managers of what type of decentralized units have authority and responsibility over revenues, expenses, and invested assets?
   A. Profit center
   B. Cost center
   C. Investment center
   D. None of the above

2. Division A of Kern Co. has sales of $350,000, cost of goods sold of $200,000, operating expenses of $30,000, and invested assets of $600,000. What is the rate of return on investment for Division A?

A. 20%   C. 40%
B. 25%   D. None of the above

3. Which of the following expressions is frequently referred to as the turnover factor in determining the rate of return on investment?

A. Operating Income ÷ Sales
B. Operating Income ÷ Invested Assets
C. Sales ÷ Invested Assets
D. None of the above

4. Division L of Liddy Co. has a rate of return on investment of 24% and an investment turnover of 1.6. What is the profit margin?

A. 6%   C. 24%
B. 15%   D. None of the above

5. Which approach to transfer pricing uses the price at which the product or service transferred could be sold to outside buyers as the transfer price?

A. Cost price approach   C. Market price approach
B. Negotiated price approach D. None of the above

ILLUSTRATIVE PROBLEM

Reese Company has two divisions, A and B. Invested assets and condensed income statement data for each division for the past year ended December 31 are as follows:

	Division A	Division B
Sales	$3,125,000	$5,100,000
Cost of goods sold	2,500,000	4,000,000
Operating expenses......	150,000	590,000
Invested assets..........	2,500,000	3,000,000

Instructions:

1. Prepare condensed income statements for the past year for each division.
2. Using the expanded expression, determine the profit margin, investment turnover, and rate of return on investment for each division.
3. If management desires a minimum rate of return of 12%, determine the residual income for each division.

SOLUTION

(1)

Reese Company
Divisional Income Statements
For Year Ended December 31, 19--

	Division A	Division B
Sales	$3,125,000	$5,100,000
Cost of goods sold	2,500,000	4,000,000
Gross profit...................................	$ 625,000	$1,100,000
Operating expenses	150,000	590,000
Operating income	$ 475,000	$ 510,000

(2)

Rate of Return on Investment (ROI) = Profit Margin × Investment Turnover

$$ROI = \frac{Operating\ Income}{Sales} \times \frac{Sales}{Invested\ Assets}$$

$$Division\ A:\ ROI = \frac{\$475,000}{\$3,125,000} \times \frac{\$3,125,000}{\$2,500,000}$$

$$ROI = 15.2\% \times 1.25$$

$$ROI = 19\%$$

$$Division\ B:\ ROI = \frac{\$510,000}{\$5,100,000} \times \frac{\$5,100,000}{\$3,000,000}$$

$$ROI = 10\% \times 1.7$$

$$ROI = 17\%$$

(3) Division A: $175,000 ($475,000 − $300,000)
    Division B: $150,000 ($510,000 − $360,000)

Discussion Questions

11–1. What are three ways in which decentralized operations may be organized?

11–2. Name three performance measures useful in evaluating investment centers.

11–3. What is the major shortcoming of using operating income as a performance measure for investment centers?

11–4. Why should the factors under the control of the investment center manager (revenues, expenses, and invested assets) be considered in the computation of the rate of return on investment?

11–5. Halbert Co. has $300,000 invested in Division R, which earned $81,000 of operating income. What is the rate of return on investment for Division R?

11–6. If Halbert Co. in Question 11–5 had sales of $540,000, what is (a) the profit margin and (b) the investment turnover for Division R?

11–7. What are two ways of expressing the rate of return on investment?

11–8. In evaluating investment centers, what does multiplying the profit margin by the investment turnover equal?

11–9. In a decentralized company in which the divisions are organized as investment centers, how could a division be considered the least profitable, even though it earned the largest amount of operating income?

11–10. Which component of the rate of return on investment (profit margin factor or investment turnover factor) focuses on efficiency in the use of assets and indicates the rate at which sales are generated for each dollar of invested assets?

11–11. Division C of Austin Co. has a rate of return on investment of 20%. (a) If Division C increases its investment turnover by 15%, what would be the new rate of return on investment? (b) If Division C also increases its profit margin from 10% to 12%, what would be the new rate of return on investment?

11–12. How does the use of the rate of return on investment facilitate comparability of divisions of decentralized companies?

11–13. The rates of return on investment for Horn Co.'s three divisions, X, Y, and Z, are 22%, 18%, and 12%, respectively. In expanding operations, which of Horn Co.'s divisions should be given priority? Explain.

11–14. What term is used to describe the excess of divisional operating income over a minimum amount of desired operating income?

11–15. Division M of Jones Co. reported operating income of $260,000, based on invested assets of $800,000. If the minimum rate of return on divisional investments is 15%, what is the residual income for Division M?

11–16. What term is used to describe the amount charged for products transferred or services rendered to other decentralized units in a company?

11–17. What is the objective of transfer pricing?

11–18. Name three commonly used approaches to establishing transfer prices.

11–19. What transfer price approach uses the price at which the product or service transferred could be sold to outside buyers as the transfer price?

11–20. When is the negotiated price approach preferred over the market price approach in setting transfer prices?

11–21. If division managers cannot agree among themselves on a transfer price when using the negotiated price approach, how is the transfer price established?

11–22. When using the negotiated price approach to transfer pricing, within what range should the transfer price be established?

11–23. **Real World Focus.** Tandy Corporation's annual report for the year ended June 30, 1987 reports a profit margin of 7.0% and an investment turnover rate of 1.76. (a) What was the rate of return on investment for the year ended June 30, 1987? (b) If the investment turnover rate does not change for the year ended June 30, 1988, what must the profit margin be to earn a rate of return on investment of 15%? (Round to the nearest tenth of one percent.)

Exercises
.

11–24. **Determination of missing items on income statements.** One item is omitted from each of the following condensed divisional income statements of Bormann Company:

	Division G	Division H	Division I
Sales	$450,000	$640,000	(e)
Cost of goods sold	270,000	(c)	320,000
Gross profit....................	(a)	$330,000	$260,000
Operating expenses	30,000	(d)	100,000
Operating income	(b)	$130,000	(f)

(a) Determine the amount of the missing items, identifying them by letter. (b) Based on operating income, which division is the most profitable?

11–25. **Rate of return on investment.** The operating income and the amount of invested assets in each division of Enders Company are as follows:

	Operating Income	Invested Assets
Division A	$221,000	$850,000
Division B	158,400	480,000
Division C	136,800	720,000

(a) Compute the rate of return on investment for each division. (b) Which division is the most profitable per dollar invested?

11–26. **Residual income.** Based on the data in Exercise 11–25, assume that management has established a minimum rate of return for invested assets of 15%. (a) Determine the residual income for each division. (b) Based on residual income, which of the divisions is the most profitable?

11–27. **Determination of missing items for computations of rate of return on investment.** One item is omitted from each of the following computations of the rate of return on investment:

Rate of Return on Investment	=	Profit Margin	×	Investment Turnover
26%		20%		(a)
(b)		12%		1.5
36%		(c)		2.4
24%		15%		(d)
(e)		15%		.8

Determine the missing items, identifying each by the appropriate letter.

11–28. Profit margin, investment turnover, and rate of return on investment. The condensed income statement for Division E of Farmer Company is as follows:

Sales......................................	$600,000
Cost of goods sold........................	360,000
Gross profit	$240,000
Operating expenses........................	144,000
Operating income.........................	$ 96,000

The manager of Division E is considering ways to increase the rate of return on investment. (a) Using the expanded expression, determine the profit margin, investment turnover, and rate of return on investment of Division E, assuming that $400,000 of assets have been invested in Division E. (b) If expenses could be reduced by $12,000 without decreasing sales, what would be the impact on the profit margin, investment turnover, and rate of return on investment for Division E?

11–29. Determination of missing items for computations of rate of return on investment and residual income. One or more items is missing from the following tabulation of rate of return on investment and residual income:

Invested Assets	Operating Income	Rate of Return on Investment	Minimum Rate of Return	Minimum Amount of Operating Income	Residual Income
$750,000	$150,000	(a)	16%	(b)	(c)
$420,000	(d)	15%	(e)	$42,000	$21,000
$600,000	(f)	(g)	(h)	$72,000	$36,000
$900,000	$216,000	(i)	20%	(j)	(k)

Determine the missing items, identifying each item by the appropriate letter.

11–30. Decision on transfer pricing. Materials used by Burr Company in producing Division C's product are currently purchased from outside suppliers at a cost of $40 per unit. However, the same materials are available from Division W. Division W has unused capacity and can produce the materials needed by Division C at a variable cost of $30 per unit. (a) If a transfer price of $35 per unit is established and 50,000 units of material are transferred, with no reduction in Division W's current sales, how much would Burr Company's total operating income increase? (b) How much would operating income of Division C increase? (c) How much would the operating income of Division W increase?

11–31. Decision on transfer pricing. Based on the Burr Company data in Exercise 11–30, assume that a transfer price of $32 has been established and 50,000 units of materials are transferred, with no reduction in Division W's current sales. (a) How much would Burr Company's total operating income increase? (b) How much would Division C's operating income increase? (c) How much would Division W's operating income increase? (d) If the negotiated price approach is used, what would be the range of acceptable transfer prices?

Problems

·

ADSHEET
BLEM

11–32. Divisional income statements and rate of return on investment analysis. Mitchell Company is a diversified company with three operating divisions organized as investment centers. Condensed data taken from the records of the three divisions for the year ended August 31 are as follows:

	Division A	Division B	Division C
Sales	$1,000,000	$1,500,000	$1,800,000
Cost of goods sold	600,000	975,000	1,350,000
Operating expenses	280,000	345,000	252,000
Invested assets	800,000	1,000,000	1,200,000

The management of Mitchell Company is evaluating each division as a basis for planning a future expansion of operations.

Instructions:

(1) Prepare condensed divisional income statements for Divisions A, B, and C.
(2) Using the expanded expression, compute the profit margin, investment turnover, and rate of return on investment for each division.
(3) If available funds permit the expansion of operations of only one division, which of the divisions would you recommend for expansion, based on (1) and (2)?

11–33. Effect of proposals on divisional performance. A condensed income statement for Division H of Searcy Company for the year ended October 31 is as follows:

Sales.	$2,400,000
Cost of goods sold.	1,440,000
Gross profit	$ 960,000
Operating expenses.	660,000
Operating income.	$ 300,000

The president of Searcy Company is concerned with Division H's rate of return on invested assets of $2,000,000, and has indicated that the division's rate of return on investment must be increased to at least 18% by the end of the next year if operations are to continue. The division manager is considering the following three proposals:

Proposal 1: Transfer equipment with a book value of $400,000 to other divisions at no gain or loss and lease similar equipment. The annual lease payments would exceed the amount of depreciation expense on the old equipment by $16,800. This increase in expense would be included as part of the cost of goods sold. Sales would remain unchanged.

Proposal 2: Reduce invested assets by discontinuing a product line. This action would eliminate sales of $150,000, cost of goods sold of $120,000, and operating expenses of $45,000. Assets of $200,000 would be transferred to other divisions at no gain or loss.

Proposal 3: Purchase new and more efficient machinery and thereby reduce the cost of goods sold by $134,400. Sales would remain unchanged, and the old machinery, which has no remaining book value, would be scrapped at no gain or loss. The new machinery would increase invested assets by $400,000 for the year.

Instructions:

(1) Using the expanded expression, determine the profit margin, investment turnover, and rate of return on investment for Division H for the past year.
(2) Prepare condensed estimated income statements for Division H for each proposal.
(3) Using the expanded expression, determine the profit margin, investment turnover, and rate of return on investment for Division H under each proposal.
(4) Which of the three proposals would meet the required 18% rate of return on investment?
(5) If Division H were in an industry where the investment turnover could not be increased, how much would the profit margin have to increase to meet the president's required 18% rate of return on investment?

11–34. Determination of missing items from computations. Data for Divisions A, B, C, D, and E of Young Company are as follows:

	Sales	Operating Income	Invested Assets	Rate of Return on Investment	Profit Margin	Investment Turnover
Division A....	$750,000	$120,000	$500,000	(a)	(b)	(c)
Division B....	(d)	(e)	$600,000	12%	(f)	1.25
Division C....	$420,000	(g)	(h)	(i)	15%	1.2
Division D....	$375,000	(j)	(k)	(l)	16%	1.25
Division E....	(m)	$ 88,000	(n)	22%	11%	(o)

Instructions:

(1) Determine the missing items, identifying each by letters (a) through (o).
(2) Determine the residual income for each division, assuming that the minimum rate of return established by management is 10%.
(3) Which division is the most profitable?

11–35. Divisional performance analysis and evaluation. The vice-president of operations of Carney Company is evaluating the performance of two divisions organized as investment centers. Division F generates the largest amount of operating income but has the lowest rate of return on investment. Division E has the highest rate of return on investment but generates the smallest operating income. Invested assets and condensed income statement data for the past year for each division are as follows:

	Division E	Division F
Sales.	$5,000,000	$6,750,000
Cost of goods sold.	3,000,000	4,320,000
Operating expenses.	1,200,000	1,620,000
Invested assets.	4,000,000	4,500,000

Instructions:

(1) Prepare condensed divisional income statements for each division for the year ended October 31.
(2) Using the expanded expression, determine the profit margin, investment turnover, and rate of return on investment for each division.
(3) If management desires a minimum rate of return of 12%, determine the residual income for each division.
(4) Discuss the evaluation of Divisions E and F, using the performance measures determined in (1), (2), and (3).

11–36. Divisional performance analysis and evaluation. The vice-president of operations of Swann Inc. recently resigned, and the president is considering which one of two division managers to promote to the vacated position. Both division managers have been with the company approximately ten years. Operating data for each division for the past three years are as follows:

	1990	1989	1988
Division M:			
Sales.	$ 1,520,000	$ 1,360,000	$ 1,200,000
Cost of goods sold	900,000	800,000	720,000
Gross profit	$ 620,000	$ 560,000	$ 480,000
Operating expenses.	460,400	410,400	345,600
Operating income.	$ 159,600	$ 149,600	$ 134,400
Invested assets.	$ 950,000	$ 800,000	$ 600,000
Total industry sales.	$15,200,000	$10,880,000	$ 8,000,000
Division N:			
Sales.	$ 900,000	$ 770,000	$ 500,000
Cost of goods sold	540,000	460,000	300,000
Gross profit	$ 360,000	$ 310,000	$ 200,000
Operating expenses.	216,000	194,500	128,000
Operating income.	$ 144,000	$ 115,500	$ 72,000
Invested assets.	$ 600,000	$ 550,000	$ 400,000
Total industry sales.	$11,250,000	$11,000,000	$10,000,000

Instructions:

(1) For each division for each of the three years, use the expanded expression to determine the profit margin, investment turnover, and rate of return on investment.

(2) Assuming that 15% has been established as a minimum rate of return, determine the residual income for each division for each of the three years.

(3) Determine each division's market share (division sales divided by total industry sales) for each of the three years.

(4) Based on (1), (2), and (3), which division manager would you recommend for promotion to vice-president of operations?

(5) What other factors should be considered in the promotion decision?

11–37. Real World Focus. The following data (in millions) for the four primary business segments of Rockwell International Corporation were taken from Rockwell International's 1986 financial statements:

	Sales	Operating Income	Assets
Aerospace......................	$5,545	$571.1	$1,431
Electronics.....................	4,221	400.5	3,549
Automotive.....................	1,588	153.6	995
General Industries	942	87.9	567

Instructions:

(1) For each of the four segments, use the expanded expression to determine the profit margin, investment turnover, and rate of return on investment. Round the profit margin to one decimal place, round the investment turnover to two decimal places, and determine the rate of return on investment by multiplying the profit margin by the investment turnover.

(2) Rank the segments from the highest to the lowest in terms of rate of return on investment.

11–38. Transfer pricing. Pane Company is diversified, with two operating divisions, X and Y. Condensed divisional income statements, which involve no intracompany transfers and which include a breakdown of expenses into variable and fixed components, are as follows:

Pane Company
Divisional Income Statements
For Year Ended December 31, 19--

	Division X	Division Y	Total
Sales:			
75,000 units × $120 per unit.....	$9,000,000		$ 9,000,000
25,000 units × $160 per unit.....		$4,000,000	4,000,000
			$13,000,000
Expenses:			
Variable:			
75,000 units × $60 per unit....	$4,500,000		$ 4,500,000
25,000 units × $100* per unit..		$2,500,000	2,500,000
Fixed........................	3,000,000	1,000,000	4,000,000
Total expenses	$7,500,000	$3,500,000	$11,000,000
Operating income................	$1,500,000	$ 500,000	$ 2,000,000

*$80 of the $100 per unit represents materials costs, and the remaining $20 per unit represents other expenses incurred within Division Y.

Division X is operating at three fourths of capacity of 100,000 units. Materials used in producing Division Y's product are currently purchased from outside suppliers at a price of $80 per unit. The materials used by Division Y are produced by Division X. Except for the possible transfer of materials between divisions, no changes are expected in sales and expenses.

Instructions:

(1) Would the market price of $80 per unit be an appropriate transfer price for Pane Company? Explain.

(2) If Division Y purchases 25,000 units from Division X and a transfer price of $70 per unit is negotiated between the managers of Divisions X and Y, how much would the operating income of each division and total company operating income increase?

(3) Prepare condensed divisional income statements for Pane Company, based on the data in (2).

(4) If a transfer price of $65 per unit is negotiated, how much would the operating income of each division and total company income increase?

(5) (a) What is the range of possible negotiated transfer prices that would be acceptable for Pane Company?

  (b) Assuming that the division managers of X and Y cannot agree on a transfer price, what price would you suggest as the transfer price?

ALTERNATE PROBLEMS

11–32A. Divisional income statements and rate of return on investment analysis. Zavor Company is a diversified company with three operating divisions organized as investment centers. Condensed data taken from the records of the three divisions for the year ended August 31 are as follows:

	Division X	Division Y	Division Z
Sales	$960,000	$1,875,000	$1,350,000
Cost of goods sold	624,000	1,200,000	810,000
Operating expenses	192,000	525,000	324,000
Invested assets	800,000	750,000	900,000

The management of Zavor Company is evaluating each division as a basis for planning a future expansion of operations.

Instructions:

(1) Prepare condensed divisional income statements for Divisions X, Y, and Z.

(2) Using the expanded expression, compute the profit margin, investment turnover, and rate of return on investment for each division.

(3) If available funds permit the expansion of operations of only one division, which of the divisions would you recommend for expansion, based on (1) and (2)?

11–34A. Determination of missing items from computations. Data for Divisions M, N, O, P, and Q of Reid Company are as follows:

	Sales	Operating Income	Invested Assets	Rate of Return on Investment	Profit Margin	Investment Turnover
Division M...	$ 500,000	$ 60,000	$400,000	(a)	(b)	(c)
Division N...	$1,080,000	(d)	$600,000	18%	(e)	(f)
Division O...	(g)	$174,000	(h)	(i)	24%	1.25
Division P...	$ 840,000	(j)	(k)	24%	20%	(l)
Division Q...	(m)	$ 75,600	$360,000	(n)	(o)	1.5

Instructions:

(1) Determine the missing items, identifying each by letters (a) through (o).
(2) Determine the residual income for each division, assuming that the minimum rate of return established by management is 12%.
(3) Which division is the most profitable?

11–35A. Divisional performance analysis and evaluation. The vice-president of operations of Eaton Company is evaluating the performance of two divisions organized as investment centers. Division Y has the highest rate of return on investment, but generates the smallest amount of operating income. Division X generates the largest operating income, but has the lowest rate of return on investment. Invested assets and condensed income statement data for the past year for each division are as follows:

	Division X	Division Y
Sales......................	$3,375,000	$3,840,000
Cost of goods sold...........	2,025,000	2,496,000
Operating expenses..........	756,000	768,000
Invested assets.............	2,700,000	2,400,000

Instructions:

(1) Prepare condensed divisional income statements for each division for the year ended October 31.
(2) Using the expanded expression, determine the profit margin, investment turnover, and rate of return on investment for each division.
(3) If management desires a minimum rate of return of 16%, determine the residual income for each division.
(4) Discuss the evaluation of Divisions X and Y, using the performance measures determined in (1), (2), and (3).

11–38A. Transfer pricing. Cowen Company is diversified, with two operating divisions, F and G. Condensed divisional income statements, which involve no intracompany transfers and which include a breakdown of expenses into variable and fixed components, are as follows:

Cowen Company
Divisional Income Statements
For Year Ended December 31, 19--

	Division F	Division G	Total
Sales:			
240,000 units × $20 per unit ..	$4,800,000		$4,800,000
80,000 units × $25 per unit ...		$2,000,000	2,000,000
			$6,800,000
Expenses:			
Variable:			
240,000 units × $12 per unit	$2,880,000		$2,880,000
80,000 units × $16* per unit		$1,280,000	1,280,000
Fixed........................	920,000	520,000	1,440,000
Total expenses	$3,800,000	$1,800,000	$5,600,000
Operating income.............	$1,000,000	$ 200,000	$1,200,000

*$14 of the $16 per unit represents materials costs, and the remaining $2 per unit represents other expenses incurred within Division G.

Division F is operating at two thirds of its capacity of 360,000 units. Materials used in producing Division G's product are currently purchased from outside suppliers at a price of $14 per unit. The materials used by Division G are produced by Division F. Except for the possible transfer of materials between divisions, no changes are expected in sales and expenses.

Instructions:

(1) Would the market price of $14 per unit be an appropriate transfer price for Cowen Company? Explain.
(2) If Division G purchases 80,000 units from Division F and a transfer price of $13 per unit is negotiated between the managers of Divisions F and G, how much would the operating income of each division and total company operating income increase?
(3) Prepare condensed divisional income statements for Cowen Company, based on the data in (2).
(4) If a transfer price of $13.50 per unit had been negotiated, how much would the operating income of each division and total company income have increased?
(5) (a) What is the range of possible negotiated transfer prices that would be acceptable for Cowen Company?
    (b) If the division managers of F and G cannot agree on a transfer price, what price would you suggest as the transfer price?

Mini-Case 11

NEWMAN
COMPANY■ ■ ■ ■ ■ ■ ■ ■

Your father is the president of Newman Company, a privately held, diversified company with five separate divisions organized as investment centers. A condensed income statement for the Sporting Goods Division for the past year is as follows:

Newman Company—Sporting Goods Division
Income Statement
For Year Ended December 31, 19--

Sales	$22,500,000
Cost of goods sold	13,500,000
Gross profit	$ 9,000,000
Operating expenses	5,400,000
Operating income	$ 3,600,000

The manager of the Sporting Goods Division was recently presented with the opportunity to add an additional product line, which would require invested assets of $5,000,000. A projected income statement for the new product line is as follows:

New Product Line
Projected Income Statement
For Year Ended December 31, 19--

Sales	$ 6,000,000
Cost of goods sold	3,600,000
Gross profit	$ 2,400,000
Operating expenses	1,500,000
Operating income	$ 900,000

The Sporting Goods Division currently has $15,000,000 in invested assets, and Newman Company's overall rate of return on investment, including all divisions, is 15%. Each division manager is evaluated on the basis of divisional rate of return on investment, and a bonus equal to $4,000 for each percentage point by which the division's rate of return on investment exceeds the company average is awarded each year.

Your father is concerned that the manager of the Sporting Goods Division rejected the addition of the new product line, when all estimates indicated that the product line would be profitable and would increase overall company income. You have been asked to analyze the possible reasons why the Sporting Goods Division manager rejected the new product line.

Instructions:

(1) Determine the rate of return on investment for the Sporting Goods Division for the past year.
(2) Determine the Sporting Goods Division manager's bonus for the past year.
(3) Determine the estimated rate of return on investment for the new product line.
(4) Why might the manager of the Sporting Goods Division decide to reject the new product line?
(5) Can you suggest an alternative performance measure for motivating division managers to accept new investment opportunities that would increase the overall company income and rate of return on investment?

Answers to Self-Examination Questions

$\cdot$ $\cdot$ $\cdot$

1. **C** Managers of investment centers (answer C) have authority and responsibility for revenues, expenses, and assets. Managers of profit centers (answer A) have authority and responsibility for revenues and expenses. Managers of cost centers (answer B) have authority and responsibility for costs.

2. **A** The rate of return on investment for Division A is 20% (answer A), computed as follows:

$$\frac{\text{Rate of Return on}}{\text{Investment (ROI)}} = \frac{\text{Operating Income}}{\text{Invested Assets}}$$

$$\text{ROI} = \frac{\$350,000 - \$200,000 - \$30,000}{\$600,000}$$

$$\text{ROI} = \frac{\$120,000}{\$600,000}$$

$$\text{ROI} = 20\%$$

3. **C** Investment turnover is the ratio of sales to invested assets (answer C). The ratio of operating income to sales is the profit margin (answer A). The ratio of operating income to invested assets is the rate of return on investment (answer B).

4. **B** The profit margin for Division L of Liddy Co. is 15% (answer B), computed as follows:

$$\text{Rate of Return on Investment (ROI)} = \text{Profit Margin} \times \text{Investment Turnover}$$
$$24\% = \text{Profit Margin} \times 1.6$$
$$15\% = \text{Profit Margin}$$

5. **C** The market price approach (answer C) to transfer pricing uses the price at which the product or service transferred could be sold to outside buyers as the transfer price. The cost price approach (answer A) uses cost as the basis for setting transfer prices. The negotiated price approach (answer B) allows managers of decentralized units to agree (negotiate) among themselves as to the proper transfer price.

Part Five

Analyses For Decision Making

Chapter Twelve

CHAPTER OBJECTIVES

•

Describe the nature of differential analysis.

•

Illustrate the use of differential analysis in decisions involving:
Leasing or selling
Discontinuing an unprofitable segment
Making or buying
Replacing equipment
Processing or selling
Accepting business at a special price

•

Describe and illustrate the setting of normal product prices, using the:
Total cost concept
Product cost concept
Variable cost concept

•

Describe and illustrate the economic theory of product pricing.

•

Describe the use of alternative price strategies
during a product's life cycle.

•

Differential Analysis and Product Pricing

A primary objective of accounting is to provide management with analyses and reports that will be useful in resolving current problems and planning for the future. The types of analyses and reports depend on the nature of the decisions to be made. However, all decisions require careful consideration of the consequences of alternative courses of action. This chapter discusses differential analysis, which provides management with data on the differences in total revenues and costs associated with alternative actions.

This chapter also describes and illustrates practical approaches frequently used by managers in setting normal product prices. The relationship of economic theory to the more practical approaches to product pricing is briefly discussed. Finally, the alternative price strategies used by management during a product's life cycle are discussed.

DIFFERENTIAL ANALYSIS

Planning for future operations is chiefly decision making. For some decisions, revenue and cost information drawn from the general ledger and other basic accounting records is very useful. For example, historical cost data in the absorption costing format are helpful in planning production for the long run. Historical cost data in the variable costing format are useful in planning production for the short run. However, the revenue and cost data needed to evaluate courses of future operations or to choose among competing alternatives are often not available in the basic accounting records.

The relevant revenue and cost data in the analysis of future possibilities are the differences between the alternatives under consideration. The amounts of such differences are called **differentials** and the area of accounting concerned with the effect of alternative courses of action on revenues and costs is called **differential analysis**.

Differential revenue is the amount of increase or decrease in revenue expected from a particular course of action as compared with an alternative. To illustrate, assume that certain equipment is being used to manufacture a product that provides revenue of $150,000. If the equipment could be used to make another product that would provide revenue of $175,000, the differential revenue from the alternative would be $25,000.

Differential cost is the amount of increase or decrease in cost that is expected from a particular course of action as compared with an alternative. For example, if an increase in advertising expenditures from $100,000 to $150,000 is being considered, the differential cost of the action would be $50,000.

The main advantage of differential analysis is its selection of relevant revenues and costs related to alternative courses of action. Differential analysis reports emphasize the significant factors bearing on the decision, help to clarify the issues, and save the time of the reader.

Differential analysis can aid management in making decisions on a variety of alternatives, including (1) whether equipment should be leased or sold, (2) whether to discontinue an unprofitable segment, (3) whether to manufacture or purchase a needed part, (4) whether to replace usable plant assets, (5) whether to process further or sell an intermediate product, and (6) whether to accept additional business at a special price. The following discussion relates to the use of differential analysis in analyzing these alternatives.

Lease or Sell

Management often has a choice between leasing or selling a piece of equipment that is no longer needed in the business. In deciding which option is best, management can use differential analysis. To illustrate, assume that Company A is considering the disposal of equipment that originally cost $200,000 and has been depreciated a total of $120,000 to date. Company A can sell the equipment through a broker for $100,000 less a 6% commission. Alternatively, Company B has tentatively offered to lease the equipment for a number of years for a total of $160,000, after which Company A would sell it for a small amount as scrap. During the period of the lease, Company A would incur repair, insurance, and property tax expenses estimated at $35,000. Company A's analysis of whether to lease or sell the equipment is as follows:

Differential Analysis Report — Lease or Sell

Proposal To Lease or Sell Equipment
June 22, 19--

Differential revenue from alternatives:		
Revenue from lease	$160,000	
Revenue from sale	100,000	
Differential revenue from lease		$60,000
Differential cost of alternatives:		
Repair, insurance, and property tax expenses	$ 35,000	
Commission expense on sale	6,000	
Differential cost of lease		29,000
Net advantage of lease alternative		$31,000

It should be noted that it was not necessary to consider the $80,000 book value ($200,000 − $120,000) of the equipment. The $80,000 is a **sunk cost**; that is, it is a cost that will not be affected by later decisions. In the illustration, the expenditure to acquire the equipment had already been made, and the choice is now between leasing or selling the equipment. The relevant factors to be considered are the differential revenues and differential costs associated with the lease or sell decision. The undepreciated cost of the equipment is irrelevant. The validity of the foregoing report can be shown by the following conventional analysis:

Lease alternative:

Revenue from lease		$160,000	
Depreciation expense	$80,000		
Repair, insurance, and property tax expenses..	35,000	115,000	
Net gain			$45,000

Sell alternative:

Sale price		$100,000	
Book value of equipment	$80,000		
Commission expense	6,000	86,000	
Net gain			14,000
Net advantage of lease alternative			$31,000

The alternatives presented in the illustration were relatively uncomplicated. Regardless of the number and complexity of the additional factors that may be involved, the approach to differential analysis remains basically the same. Two factors that often need to be considered are (1) the differential revenue from investing the funds generated by the alternatives and (2) the income tax differential. In the example, there would undoubtedly be a differential advantage to the immediate investment of the $94,000 net proceeds ($100,000 − $6,000) from the sale over the investment of the net proceeds from the lease arrangement, which would become available over a period of years. The income tax differential would be that related to the differences in timing of the income from the alternatives and the differences in the amount of investment income.

Discontinuance of an Unprofitable Segment

When a department, branch, territory, or other segment of an enterprise has been operating at a loss, management should consider eliminating the unprofitable segment. It might be natural to assume (sometimes mistakenly) that the total operating income of the enterprise would be increased if the operating loss could be eliminated. Discontinuance of the unprofitable segment will usually eliminate all of the related variable costs and expenses. However, if the segment represents a relatively small part of the enterprise, the fixed costs and expenses (depreciation, insurance, property taxes, etc.)

will not be reduced by its discontinuance. It is entirely possible in this situation for the total operating income of a company to be reduced rather than increased by eliminating an unprofitable segment. As a basis for illustrating this type of situation, the following income statement is presented for the year just ended, which was a normal year. For purposes of the illustration, it is assumed that discontinuance of Product A, on which losses are incurred annually, will have no effect on total fixed costs and expenses.

Condensed Income Statement
For Year Ended August 31, 19--

	Product			
	A	B	C	Total
Sales....................	$100,000	$400,000	$500,000	$1,000,000
Cost of goods sold:				
Variable costs...............	$ 60,000	$200,000	$220,000	$ 480,000
Fixed costs	20,000	80,000	120,000	220,000
Total cost of goods sold	$ 80,000	$280,000	$340,000	$ 700,000
Gross profit...................	$ 20,000	$120,000	$160,000	$ 300,000
Operating expenses:				
Variable expenses	$ 25,000	$ 60,000	$ 95,000	$ 180,000
Fixed expenses	6,000	20,000	25,000	51,000
Total operating expenses	$ 31,000	$ 80,000	$120,000	$ 231,000
Income (loss) from operations....	$ (11,000)	$ 40,000	$ 40,000	$ 69,000

Data on the estimated differential revenue and differential cost related to discontinuing Product A, on which an operating loss of $11,000 was incurred during the past year, may be assembled in a report such as the following. This report emphasizes the significant factors bearing on the decision.

· · · · · · · · ·
Differential Analysis Report—Discontinuance of Unprofitable Segment

Proposal To Discontinue Product A
September 29, 19--

Differential revenue from annual sales of product:		
Revenue from sales		$100,000
Differential cost of annual sales of product:		
Variable cost of goods sold	$60,000	
Variable operating expenses	25,000	85,000
Annual differential income from sales of Product A......		$ 15,000

Instead of an increase in annual operating income to $80,000 (Product B, $40,000; Product C, $40,000) that might seem to be indicated by the income statement, the discontinuance of Product A would reduce operating income to an estimated $54,000 ($69,000 − $15,000). The validity of this conclusion can be shown by the following conventional analysis:

Proposal To Discontinue Product A
September 29, 19--

	Current Operations			Discontinuance of Product A
	Product A	Products B and C	Total	
Sales.	$100,000	$900,000	$1,000,000	$900,000
Cost of goods sold:				
Variable costs	$ 60,000	$420,000	$ 480,000	$420,000
Fixed costs	20,000	200,000	220,000	220,000
Total cost of goods sold .	$ 80,000	$620,000	$ 700,000	$640,000
Gross profit	$ 20,000	$280,000	$ 300,000	$260,000
Operating expenses:				
Variable expenses	$ 25,000	$155,000	$ 180,000	$155,000
Fixed expenses	6,000	45,000	51,000	51,000
Total operating expenses	$ 31,000	$200,000	$ 231,000	$206,000
Income (loss) from operations	$ (11,000)	$ 80,000	$ 69,000	$ 54,000

For purposes of the illustration, it was assumed that the discontinuance of Product A would not cause any significant reduction in the volume of fixed costs and expenses. If plant capacity made available by discontinuance of a losing operation can be used in some other manner or if plant capacity can be reduced, with a resulting reduction in fixed costs and expenses, additional analysis would be needed.

In decisions involving the elimination of an unprofitable segment, management must also consider such other factors as its effect on employees and customers. If a segment of the business is discontinued, some employees may have to be laid off and others may have to be relocated and retrained. Also important is the possible decline in sales of the more profitable products to customers who were attracted to the firm by the discontinued product.

Make or Buy

The assembly of many parts is often a substantial element in manufacturing operations. Many of the large factory complexes of automobile manufacturers are specifically called assembly plants. Some of the parts of the finished automobile, such as the motor, are produced by the automobile manufacturer, while other parts, such as tires, are often purchased from other manufacturers. Even in manufacturing the motors, such items as spark plugs and nuts and bolts may be acquired from suppliers in their finished state. When parts or components are purchased, management has usually evaluated the question of "make or buy" and has concluded that a savings in cost results from buying the part rather than manufacturing it. However, "make or buy" options are likely to arise anew when a manufacturer has excess productive capacity in the form of unused equipment, space, and labor.

As a basis for illustrating such alternatives, assume that a manufacturer has been purchasing a component, Part X, for $5 a unit. The factory is currently operating at 80% of capacity, and no significant increase in production is anticipated in the near future. The cost of manufacturing Part X, determined by absorption costing methods, is estimated at $1 for direct materials, $2 for direct labor, and $3 for factory overhead (at the predetermined rate of 150% of direct labor cost), or a total of $6. The decision based on a simple comparison of a "make" price of $6 with a "buy" price of $5 is obvious. However, to the extent that unused capacity could be used in manufacturing the part, there would be no increase in the total amount of fixed factory overhead costs. Hence, only the variable factory overhead costs need to be considered. Variable factory overhead costs such as power and maintenance are determined to amount to approximately 65% of the direct labor cost of $2, or $1.30. The cost factors to be considered are summarized in the following report:

Differential Analysis Report — Make or Buy

Proposal To Manufacture Part X
February 15, 19--

Purchase price of part..................................		$5.00
Differential cost to manufacture part:		
Direct materials.....................................	$1.00	
Direct labor	2.00	
Variable factory overhead............................	1.30	4.30
Cost reduction from manufacturing Part X.................		$ .70

Other possible effects of a change in policy should also be considered, such as the possibility that a future increase in volume of production would require the use of the currently idle capacity of 20%. The possible effect of the alternatives on employees and on future business relations with the supplier of the part, who may be providing other essential components, are additional factors that might need study.

Equipment Replacement

The usefulness of plant assets may be impaired long before they are considered to be "worn out." Equipment may no longer be ideally adequate for the purpose for which it is used, but on the other hand it may not have reached the point of complete inadequacy. Similarly, the point in time when equipment becomes obsolete may be difficult to determine. Decisions to replace usable plant assets should be based on studies of relevant costs rather than on whims or subjective opinions. The costs to be considered are the alternative future costs of retention as opposed to replacement. The book values of the plant assets being replaced are sunk costs and are irrevelant.

To illustrate some of the factors involved in replacement decisions, assume that an enterprise is considering the disposal of several identical machines having a total book value of $100,000 and an estimated remaining life of five years. The old machines can be sold for $25,000. They can be replaced by a single high-speed machine at a cost of $250,000, with an estimated useful life of five years and no residual value. Analysis of the specifications of the new machine and of accompanying changes in manufacturing methods indicate an estimated annual reduction in variable manufacturing costs from $225,000 to $150,000. No other changes in the manufacturing costs or the operating expenses are expected. The basic data to be considered are summarized in the following report:

Proposal To Replace Equipment
November 28, 19--

Differential Analysis Report — Equipment Replacement

Annual variable costs — present equipment..............	$225,000	
Annual variable costs — new equipment.................	150,000	
Annual differential decrease in cost.....................	$ 75,000	
Number of years applicable...........................	× 5	
Total differential decrease in cost......................	$375,000	
Proceeds from sale of present equipment	25,000	$400,000
Cost of new equipment................................		250,000
Net differential decrease in cost, 5-year total............		$150,000
Annual differential decrease in cost — new equipment		$ 30,000

Complicating features could be added to the foregoing illustration, such as a disparity between the remaining useful life of the old equipment and the estimated life of the new equipment, or possible improvement in the product due to the new machine, with a resulting increase in selling price or volume of sales. Another factor that should be considered is the importance of alternative uses for the cash outlay needed to obtain the new equipment. The amount of income that would result from the best available alternative to the proposed use of cash or its equivalent is sometimes called **opportunity cost**. If, for example, it is assumed that the cash outlay of $250,000 for the new equipment, less the $25,000 proceeds from the sale of the present equipment, could be used to yield a 10% return, the opportunity cost of the proposal would amount to 10% of $225,000, or $22,500.

The term "opportunity cost" introduces a new concept of "cost." In reality, it is not a cost in any usual sense of the word. Instead, it represents the forgoing of possible income associated with a lost opportunity. Although opportunity cost computations do not appear as a part of historical accounting data, they are unquestionably useful in analyses involving choices between alternative courses of action.

Process or Sell

When a product is manufactured, it progresses through various stages of production. Often, a product can be sold at an intermediate stage of production, or it can be processed further and then sold. In deciding whether to sell a product at an intermediate stage or to process it further, the differential revenues that would be provided and the differential costs that would be incurred from further processing must be considered. Since the costs of producing the intermediate product do not change, regardless of whether the intermediate product is sold or processed further, these costs are not differential costs and are not considered.

To illustrate, assume that an enterprise produces Product Y in batches of 4,000 gallons by processing standard quantities of 4,000 gallons of direct materials, which cost $1.20 per gallon. Product Y can be sold without further processing for $2 per gallon. It is possible for the enterprise to process Product Y further to yield Product Z, which can be sold for $5 per gallon. Product Z will require additional processing costs of $5,760 per batch, and 20% of the gallons of Product Y will evaporate during production. The differential revenues and costs to be considered in deciding whether to process Product Y to produce Product Z are summarized in the following report:

· · · · · · · ·
Differential Analysis
Report—Process or Sell

Proposal To Process Product Y Further
October 1, 19--

Differential revenue from further processing per batch:		
Revenue from sale of Product Z [(4,000 gallons − 800		
gallons evaporation) × $5]........................	$16,000	
Revenue from sale of Product Y (4,000 gallons × $2) ...	8,000	
Differential revenue		$8,000
Differential cost per batch:		
Additional cost of producing Product Z...............		5,760
Net advantage of further processing Product Y per batch..		$2,240

The net advantage of further processing Product Y into Product Z is $2,240 per batch. Note that the initial cost of producing the intermediate Product Y, $4,800 (4,000 gallons × $1.20), is not considered in deciding whether to process Product Y further. This initial cost will be incurred regardless of whether Product Z is produced.

Acceptance of Business at a Special Price

· · ·

In determining whether to accept additional business at a special price, management must consider the differential revenue that would be provided and the differential cost that would be incurred. If the company is operating at full capacity, the additional production will increase both fixed and variable production costs. But if the normal production of the company is below full capacity, additional business may be undertaken without increasing fixed production costs. In the latter case, the variable costs will be the differential cost of the additional production. Variable costs are the only costs to be considered in making a decision to accept or reject the order. If the operating expenses are likely to increase, these differentials must also be considered.

To illustrate, assume that the usual monthly production of an enterprise is 10,000 units of a certain commodity. At this level of operation, which is well below capacity, the manufacturing cost is $20 per unit, composed of variable costs of $12.50 and fixed costs of $7.50. The normal selling price of the product in the domestic market is $30. The manufacturer receives an offer from an exporter for 5,000 units of the product at $18 each. Production costs can be spread over a three-month period without interfering with normal production or incurring overtime costs. Pricing policies in the domestic market will not be affected. Comparison of a sales price of $18 with the present unit cost of $20 would indicate that this offer should be rejected. However, if attention is limited to the differential cost, which in this case is composed of the variable costs and expenses, the conclusion is quite different. The essentials of the analysis are presented in the following brief report:

Proposal To Sell to Exporter
March 10, 19--

Differential revenue from acceptance of offer:	
Revenue from sale of 5,000 additional units at $18....................	$90,000
Differential cost of acceptance of offer:	
Variable costs and expenses of 5,000 additional units at $12.50........	62,500
Gain from acceptance of offer.......................................	$27,500

Differential Analysis Report — Sale at Special Price

Proposals to sell an increased output in the domestic market at a reduction from the normal price may require additional considerations of a difficult nature. It would clearly be unwise to increase sales volume in one territory by means of a price reduction if sales volume would thereby be jeopardized in other areas. Manufacturers must also exercise care to avoid violations of the Robinson-Patman Act, which prohibits price discrimination within the United States unless the difference in price can be justified by a difference in the cost of serving different customers.

SETTING NORMAL PRODUCT PRICES

Differential analysis, as illustrated, is useful to management in setting product selling prices for special short-run decisions, such as whether to accept business at a price lower than the normal price. In such situations, the short-run price is set high enough to cover all variable costs and expenses plus provide an excess to cover some of the fixed costs and perhaps provide for profit. Such a pricing plan will improve profits in the short run. In the long run, however, the normal selling price must be set high enough to cover all costs and expenses (both fixed and variable) and provide a reasonable amount for profit. Otherwise, the long-run survival of the firm may be jeopardized.

The normal selling price can be viewed as the target selling price which must be achieved in the long run, but which may be deviated from in the short run because of such factors as competition and general market conditions. A practical approach to setting the normal price is the cost-plus approach. Using this approach, managers determine product prices by adding to a "cost" amount a plus, called a **markup,** so that all costs plus a profit are covered in the price.

Three cost concepts commonly used in applying the cost-plus approach are (1) total cost, (2) product cost, and (3) variable cost. Each of these cost concepts is described and illustrated in the following paragraphs.

Total Cost Concept

Using the **total cost concept** of determining the product price, all costs of manufacturing a product plus the selling and general expenses are included in the cost amount to which the markup is added. Since all costs and expenses are included in the cost amount, the dollar amount of the markup equals the desired profit.

The first step in applying the total cost concept is to determine the total cost of manufacturing the product. Under the absorption costing system of accounting for manufacturing operations, the costs of direct materials, direct labor, and factory overhead should be available from the accounting records. The next step is to add the estimated selling and general expenses to the total cost of manufacturing the product. The cost amount per unit is then computed by dividing the total costs and expenses by the total units expected to be produced and sold.

After the cost amount per unit has been determined, the dollar amount of the markup is determined. For this purpose, the markup is expressed as a percentage of cost. This percentage is then multiplied by the cost amount per unit. The dollar amount of the markup is then added to the cost amount per unit to arrive at the selling price.

The markup percentage for the total cost concept is determined by applying the following formula:

$$\text{Markup Percentage} = \frac{\text{Desired Profit}}{\text{Total Costs and Expenses}}$$

The numerator of the markup percentage formula includes only the desired profit, since all costs and expenses will be covered by the cost amount to which the markup will be added. The denominator of the formula includes the total costs and expenses, which are covered by the cost amount.

To illustrate the use of the total cost concept, assume that the costs and expenses for Product N of Moyer Co. are as follows:

Variable costs and expenses:	
Direct materials	$ 3.00 per unit
Direct labor	10.00
Factory overhead	1.50
Selling and general expenses . .	1.50
Total	$16.00 per unit

Fixed costs and expenses:
Factory overhead $50,000
Selling and general expenses . . 20,000

Moyer Co. desires a profit equal to a 20% rate of return on assets, $800,000 of assets are devoted to producing Product N, and 100,000 units are expected to be produced and sold. The cost amount for Product N is $1,670,000, or $16.70 per unit, computed as follows:

Variable costs and expenses ($16.00 × 100,000 units)		$1,600,000
Fixed costs and expenses:		
Factory overhead.	$50,000	
Selling and general expenses.	20,000	70,000
Total costs and expenses		$1,670,000
Cost amount per unit ($1,670,000 ÷ 100,000 units)		$16.70

The desired profit is $160,000 (20% × $800,000), and the markup percentage for Product N is 9.6%, computed as follows:

$$\text{Markup Percentage} = \frac{\text{Desired Profit}}{\text{Total Costs and Expenses}}$$

$$\text{Markup Percentage} = \frac{\$160,000}{\$1,670,000}$$

$$\text{Markup Percentage} = 9.6\%$$

Based on the cost amount per unit and the markup percentage for Product N, Moyer Co. would price Product N at $18.30 per unit, as shown in the following computation:

Cost amount per unit.	$16.70
Markup ($16.70 × 9.6%)	1.60
Selling price	$18.30

The ability of the selling price of $18.30 to generate the desired profit of $160,000 is shown in the following condensed income statement for Moyer Co.:

Moyer Co. Income Statement For Year Ended December 31, 19--		
Sales (100,000 units × $18.30).		$1,830,000
Expenses:		
Variable (100,000 units × $16.00)	$1,600,000	
Fixed ($50,000 + $20,000).	70,000	1,670,000
Income from operations.		$ 160,000

The total cost concept of applying the cost-plus approach to product pricing is frequently used by contractors who sell products to government agencies. In many cases, government contractors are required by law to be reimbursed for their products on a total-cost-plus-profit basis.

Product Cost Concept

Using the **product cost concept** of determining the product price, only the costs of manufacturing the product, termed the product cost, are included in the cost amount to which the markup is added. Selling expenses, general expenses, and profit are covered in the markup. The markup percentage is determined by applying the following formula:

$$\text{Markup Percentage} = \frac{\text{Desired Profit} + \text{Total Selling and General Expenses}}{\text{Total Manufacturing Costs}}$$

The numerator of the markup percentage formula includes the desired profit plus the total selling and general expenses. Selling and general expenses must be covered by the markup, since they are not covered by the cost amount to which the markup will be added. The denominator of the formula includes the costs of direct materials, direct labor, and factory overhead, which are covered by the cost amount.

To illustrate the use of the product cost concept, assume the same data that were used in the preceding illustration. The cost amount for Moyer Co.'s Product N is $1,500,000, or $15 per unit, computed as follows:

Direct materials ($3 × 100,000 units)		$ 300,000
Direct labor ($10 × 100,000 units)		1,000,000
Factory overhead:		
Variable ($1.50 × 100,000 units)	$150,000	
Fixed	50,000	200,000
Total manufacturing costs		$1,500,000
Cost amount per unit ($1,500,000 ÷ 100,000 units)		$15

The desired profit is $160,000 (20% × $800,000), and the total selling and general expenses are $170,000 [(100,000 units × $1.50 per unit) + $20,000]. The markup percentage for Product N is 22%, computed as follows:

$$\text{Markup Percentage} = \frac{\text{Desired Profit} + \text{Total Selling and General Expenses}}{\text{Total Manufacturing Costs}}$$

$$\text{Markup Percentage} = \frac{\$160,000 + \$170,000}{\$1,500,000}$$

$$\text{Markup Percentage} = \frac{\$330,000}{\$1,500,000}$$

$$\text{Markup Percentage} = 22\%$$

Based on the cost amount per unit and the markup percentage for Product N, Moyer Co. would price Product N at $18.30 per unit, as shown in the following computation:

Cost amount per unit	$15.00
Markup ($15 × 22%)	3.30
Selling price	$18.30

Variable Cost Concept

Using the **variable cost concept** of determining the product price, only variable costs and expenses are included in the cost amount to which the markup is added. All variable manufacturing costs, as well as variable selling and general expenses, are included in the cost amount. Fixed manufacturing costs, fixed selling and general expenses, and profit are covered in the markup.

The markup percentage for the variable cost concept is determined by applying the following formula:

$$\text{Markup Percentage} = \frac{\text{Desired Profit + Total Fixed Manufacturing Costs +}}{\text{Total Variable Costs and Expenses}}$$
$$\frac{\text{Total Fixed Selling and General Expenses}}{}$$

The numerator of the markup percentage formula includes the desired profit plus the total fixed manufacturing costs and the total fixed selling and general expenses. Fixed manufacturing costs and fixed selling and general expenses must be covered by the markup, since they are not covered by the cost amount to which the markup will be added. The denominator of the formula includes the total variable costs and expenses, which are covered by the cost amount.

To illustrate the use of the variable cost concept, assume the same data that were used in the two preceding illustrations. The cost amount for Product N is $1,600,000, or $16.00 per unit, computed as follows:

Variable costs and expenses:	
Direct materials ($3 × 100,000 units)	$ 300,000
Direct labor ($10 × 100,000 units)	1,000,000
Factory overhead ($1.50 × 100,000 units)	150,000
Selling and general expenses ($1.50 × 100,000 units) . .	150,000
Total variable costs and expenses	$1,600,000
Cost amount per unit ($1,600,000 ÷ 100,000 units)	$16.00

The desired profit is $160,000 (20% × $800,000), the total fixed manufacturing costs are $50,000, and the total fixed selling and general expenses are $20,000. The markup percentage for Product N is 14.4%, computed as follows:

$$\text{Markup Percentage} = \frac{\text{Desired Profit} + \text{Total Fixed Manufacturing Costs} + \text{Total Fixed Selling and General Expenses}}{\text{Total Variable Costs and Expenses}}$$

$$\text{Markup Percentage} = \frac{\$160,000 + \$50,000 + \$20,000}{\$1,600,000}$$

$$\text{Markup Percentage} = \frac{\$230,000}{\$1,600,000}$$

Markup Percentage = 14.4%

Based on the cost amount per unit and the markup percentage for Product N, Moyer Co. would price Product N at $18.30 per unit, as shown in the following computation:

Cost amount per unit.............................	$16.00
Markup ($16.00 × 14.4%)	2.30
Selling price....................................	$18.30

The variable cost concept emphasizes the distinction between variable and fixed costs and expenses in product pricing. This distinction is similar to the distinction between absorption and variable costing described in Chapter 7.

Choosing a Cost-Plus Approach Cost Concept

The three cost concepts commonly used in applying the cost-plus approach to product pricing are summarized as follows:

Cost Concept	Covered in Cost Amount	Covered in Markup
Total cost	Total costs and expenses	Desired profit
Product cost	Total manufacturing costs	Desired profit + Total selling and general expenses
Variable cost	Total variable costs and expenses	Desired profit + Total fixed manufacturing costs + Total fixed selling and general expenses

As demonstrated in the Moyer Co. illustration, all three cost concepts will yield the same selling price ($18.30) when the concepts are properly applied. Which of the three cost concepts should be used by management depends on such factors as the cost of gathering the data and the decision needs of management. For example, the data for the product cost concept can be easily gathered by a company using an absorption cost accounting system.

To reduce the costs of gathering data, standard costs rather than actual costs may be used with any of the three cost concepts. However, caution should be exercised by management when using standard costs in applying the cost-plus approach. As discussed in Chapter 9, the standards should be based on normal (attainable) operating levels and not theoretical (ideal) levels of performance. In product pricing, the use of standards based on ideal or maximum capacity operating levels might lead to the establishment of product prices which are too low, since the costs of such factors as normal spoilage or normal periods of idle time would not be covered in the price. As a result, the desired profit would be reduced by these costs and expenses.

ECONOMIC THEORY OF PRODUCT PRICING

In addition to costs, as discussed in the preceding paragraphs, other factors may influence the pricing decision. In considering these factors, which include the general economic conditions of the marketplace, a knowledge of the economic theory underlying product pricing is useful to the managerial accountant. Although the study of **price theory** is generally considered a separate discipline in the area of microeconomics, the following paragraphs present an overview of the economic models for explaining pricing behavior.

Maximization of Profits

In microeconomic theory, management's primary objective is assumed to be the maximization of profits. Profits will be maximized at the point at which the difference between total revenues and total costs and expenses is the greatest amount. Consequently, microeconomic theory focuses on the behavior of total revenues as price and sales volume vary and the behavior of total costs and expenses as production varies.

Revenues

Generally, it is not possible to sell an unlimited number of units of product at the same price. At some point, price reductions will be necessary in order to sell more units. Total revenue may increase as the price is reduced, but there comes a point when further price decreases will reduce total revenue. To illustrate, the following revenue schedule shows the effect on revenue when each $1 reduction in the unit selling price increases by 1 unit the number of units sold:

REVENUE SCHEDULE

Price	Units Sold	Total Revenue	Marginal Revenue
$11	1	$11	$11
10	2	20	9
9	3	27	7
8	4	32	5
7	5	35	3
6	6	36	1
5	7	35	−1

In the revenue schedule illustrated, a price reduction from $11 to $10 increases total revenue by $9 (from $11 to $20). This increase (or decrease) in total revenue realized from the sale of an additional unit of product is called the **marginal revenue**. With each successive price reduction from $11 to $6, the total revenue increase is less. Finally, a price reduction from $6 to $5 decreases total revenue by $1.

Costs

As production and sales increase, the total cost increases. The amount by which total cost increases, however, varies as more and more production and sales are squeezed from limited facilities. Economists assume that as the total number of units produced and sold increases from a relatively low level, the total cost increases but in decreasing amounts. This assumption is based on efficiencies created by **economies of scale**. Economies of scale generally imply that, for a given amount of facilities, it is more efficient to produce and sell large quantities than small quantities. At some point, however, the total cost will begin to increase by increasing amounts because of inefficiencies created by such factors as employees getting in each other's way and machine break-downs caused by heavy use. The increase in total cost from producing and selling an additional unit of product is known as **marginal cost**. To illustrate, the following cost schedule shows the effect on cost when one additional unit is produced and sold:

COST SCHEDULE

Units Produced and Sold	Total Cost	Marginal Cost
1	$ 9	$9
2	17	8
3	24	7
4	30	6
5	37	7
6	45	8
7	54	9

In the cost schedule, the cost of producing 1 unit is $9, and for each additional unit the total cost per unit increases by $8, $7, $6, $7, $8, and $9 respectively. The marginal cost of producing and selling the second unit is $8, which is the difference between the total cost of producing and selling 2 units ($17) and the total cost of producing and selling 1 unit ($9). As production and sales increase from 1 unit to 4 units, the marginal cost decreases from $9 to $6. After the production and sale of 4 units, however, the marginal cost increases from $6 for the fourth unit to $7 for producing and selling the fifth unit.

Product Price Determination

A price-cost combination that maximizes the total profit of an enterprise can be determined by plotting the marginal revenues and marginal costs on a **price graph.** To illustrate, the marginal revenues and marginal costs for the preceding illustration are plotted on the following graph:

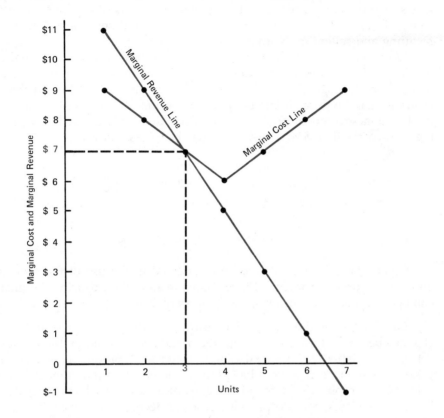

Price Graph

A price graph is constructed in the following manner:

1. The horizontal axis is drawn to represent units of production and sales.
2. The vertical axis is drawn to represent dollars for marginal revenues and marginal costs.
3. The marginal revenue for each unit of sales is plotted on the graph by first locating the number of units of sales along the horizontal axis and then proceeding upward until the proper amount of marginal revenue is indicated on the vertical axis.
4. The marginal revenue line is drawn on the price graph by connecting the marginal revenue points.
5. The marginal cost for each unit of production is plotted on the graph by first locating the number of units of production along the horizontal axis and then proceeding upward until the proper amount of marginal cost is indicated on the vertical axis.
6. The marginal cost line is drawn on the price graph by connecting the marginal cost points.

The point at which the marginal revenue line intersects the marginal cost line on the price graph indicates a level of sales and production at which profits are maximized. In other words, there is no other level of production and sales that will provide a larger amount of profit. For example, at higher levels of production and sales, the change in total cost is greater than the change in total revenue. Therefore, less profit would be achieved by manufacturing and selling more units.

In the illustration, the marginal revenue line intersects the marginal cost line at 3 units of sales and production. At this point, marginal revenue and marginal cost equal $7. To sell 3 units, the revenue schedule on page 419 indicates that the price should be set at $9 per unit. A price of $9 per unit will provide total revenue of $27, and the cost schedule on page 420 indicates that the total cost will be $24. Thus, profit will be $3, as follows:

Total revenue (3 units × $9)	$27
Total cost (from cost schedule).	24
Profit	$ 3

Other Considerations and Limitations
• • •

Several other factors should be considered in the use of the economic approach to product pricing. These factors include the elasticity of demand, competitive market conditions, and data availability.

Elasticity of demand. The degree by which the number of units sold changes because of a change in product price is measured by the economic concept of **elasticity of demand.** The demand for a product is **inelastic** if a price increase or decrease will have little or no effect on the number of units sold. For example, the demand for a medical drug, such as penicillin or insulin, is inelastic because price increases or decreases will have little or no effect on the quantity of the drug sold to consumers (patients).

The demand for a product is **elastic** if a price increase or decrease will have a significant effect on the number of units sold. For example, the demand for most automobiles is elastic. As a consequence, automobile manufacturers will periodically offer special rebates or other price reductions to consumers in order to stimulate sales.[1]

Economists employ various techniques to estimate the elasticity of demand. A description of these techniques is normally covered in economic texts and is not described in this chapter.

Competitive market conditions. One limitation of the economic concepts described in the preceding paragraphs is that the concepts directly apply only to conditions of monopoly and monopolistic competition. In a **monopoly market,** no competing products exist. For example, many cable television companies offer their services in a monopoly market. In a **monopolistic com-**

---

[1]Managers must be careful in classifying the demand for products as either elastic or inelastic. For example, although the demand for most automobiles is elastic, the demand for specialty automoblies, such as Porsches and Ferraris, is inelastic.

petitive market, there exist many sellers of similar products, with no one seller having a large enough share of the market to influence the total sales of the other products. For example, many retail businesses operate within monopolistic competitive markets.

The concepts described in the preceding paragraphs are not directly applicable to purely competitive and oligopoly markets. In a **purely competitive market,** the price for the product is established solely by the market conditions, and the quantity that a firm sells has no impact on the total market for the product. Thus, a firm can sell all it produces at the market price. Agriculture is an example of a purely competitive market.

In an **oligopoly market,** there exist a few large sellers competing against each other with similar products. Hence, the amount sold by each seller has a direct effect on the sales of the other companies. An example is the auto industry. In this market, price increases by a company will bring no response by competitors and will result in a decrease in total units sold because competitors will not change their prices. In contrast, a price decrease will bring retaliatory price decreases by competitors.

Data availability. The economic approach to product pricing is not often used because the data required to estimate demand elasticity and marginal revenue are often unavailable. For example, it is difficult to estimate the amount that consumers will purchase over a range of prices without actually offering the product for sale at those prices. Since total cost data can be estimated reliably from accounting records, the cost-plus approach to product pricing is frequently used.

The Art of Pricing Air Fares

One industry in which pricing plays a very significant role is the airline industry, which operates in an oligopoly market. Fare wars and constantly changing fares are commonplace among the major airlines. The fine tuning involved in pricing fares is described in the following excerpt from an article in *The Wall Street Journal.*

The latest round of fare wars... has put a spotlight on how carriers use state-of-the-art computer software, complex forecasting techniques and a little intuition to divine how many seats at what prices they will offer on any given flight....

Too many wrong projections can lead to huge losses of revenue, or even worse. The inability of People Express to manage its inventory of seats properly, for example, was one of the major causes of its demise.

"It's a sophisticated guessing game," said [the] vice president of pricing and product planning at American Airlines.... "You don't want to sell a seat to a guy for $69 when he's willing to pay $400."

With the industry now adopting very low discount but nonrefundable fares, the complex task of managing seat inventory may become easier because airlines will be better able to predict how many people will show up for a flight.

Some airlines have already seen a drop in their no-shows, which means they can overbook less and spare more customers from being bumped. The nonrefundable fares could also enable carriers to sell more discount seats weeks before a flight, rather than putting them on sale at the last minute in an effort to fill up the plane.

American's inventory operation illustrates just how complicated the process can be. At the airline's corporate headquarters [in Dallas], 90 yield managers are linked by terminals to five International Business Machines mainframe computers in Tulsa, Okla. The managers monitor and adjust the fare mixes on 1,600 daily flights as well as 528,000 future flights involving nearly 50 million passengers. Their work is hectic: A fare's average life span is two weeks, and industrywide about 200,000 fares change daily.

American and the other airlines base their forecasts largely on historical profiles of each flight. Business travelers, for example, book heavily on many Friday afternoon flights, but often not until the day of departure. The airlines reserve blocks of seats for those frequent fliers. Few, if any, discounts are made available....

For the bargain hunter, finding a discount will increasingly depend on the season, day and time of travel, destination and length of stay....

The following table indicates the difference between the number of seats sold at each fare for a Wednesday and Friday flight of American Airlines:

How Two Flights Compare on Type of Seats Sold

Both examples are based on one-way fares for actual American Airlines flights from LaGuardia to Dallas/Fort Worth on a DC-10, which has coach capacity of 258 passengers.

PEAK FLIGHT — **Friday, Feb. 13, 5 P.M.**

Full coach ($230 or more)	89 seats
Intermediate discount ($80–$229)	146 seats
Deepest discount ($79 or less)	0 seats*
Empty	23 seats

OFF-PEAK FLIGHT — **Wednesday, Feb. 11, 1 P.M.**

Full coach ($230 or more)	6 seats
Intermediate discount ($80–$229)	138 seats
Deepest discount ($79 or less)	40 seats
Empty	74 seats

*Such seats may have been available, with certain restrictions on sales, but none were sold.

Source: American Airlines

Source: Eric Schmitt, "The Art of Pricing Air Fares," The Wall Street Journal, March 4, 1987.

PRICING STRATEGIES

Within the constraints of market conditions, managers must decide upon a pricing strategy for a company's various products. The pricing strategy chosen for a product depends upon the factors previously discussed. In addition, the stage in the product's life cycle at which the product is offered for sale has an important effect. The **product life cycle** concept is based on the idea that a product normally passes through various stages from the time that it is introduced until the time that it disappears from the market.

The normal life cycle for a product is divided into five stages: the introductory stage, the rapid growth stage, the turbulent stage, the maturity stage, and the terminating stage. Graphically, the relationship of these stages to total dollar sales during a product's life cycle can be illustrated as follows:

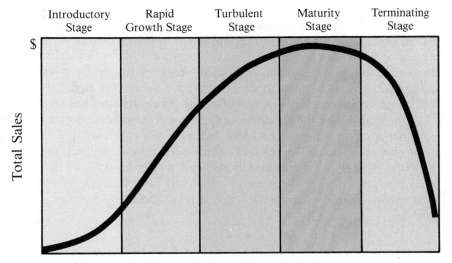

| Introductory Stage | Rapid Growth Stage | Turbulent Stage | Maturity Stage | Terminating Stage |

Product Life Cycle

In the introductory stage, the product is new to the market and no direct competition exists. During this stage, management normally spends large amounts on promotional activities in order to develop a market for the product. Since no competition exists, prices are normally set to provide coverage of all costs and to provide high profit margins. Total sales begin low and expand rapidly as more consumers discover the product.

In the rapid growth stage, the product has caught on with consumers and competitors begin to enter the market. Total sales expand rapidly, since the industry cannot meet consumer demand for the product. Prices normally remain high during this stage, but begin to decrease as competition increases. Management normally continues to set prices high enough to cover all costs and provide for a reasonable profit.

In the turbulent stage, competition increases dramatically as more and more competitors enter the market. Although sales continue to be strong, increasing price competition causes total sales to increase at a decreasing rate.

Management normally continues to set prices high enough to cover all costs, but profit margins are reduced to meet competition. For short periods of time, management may offer the product for sale at special prices that cover only variable costs. During this stage, one or two companies may achieve dominant positions in the market as less efficient competitors are driven out of the market.

In the maturity stage, competition stabilizes and few, if any, new competitors enter the market. Management normally sets prices at a relatively low level to cover all costs and to allow for a low profit margin. The consumer demand for the product levels off and may decline. Total sales reach a maximum and begin to decline.

In the terminating stage, the strategy of management is to reduce the chance of any losses and to get as much profit out of the remaining product demand as possible. Near the end of this stage, prices are often set to cover only product variable costs in order to reduce the chance that the company will be left with excess inventories after consumer demand has disappeared.

One example of the product life cycle concept is the market for the IBM personal computer during the early and mid-1980's. During this period, the price of a standard IBM personal computer decreased from approximately $3,500 in 1980, when it was first introduced, to less than $1,000 in 1987. IBM attempted to prolong the computer's relatively brief life cycle by introducing new enhancements, such as hard disk drives, additional memory, and color monitors.

Chapter Review

KEY POINTS

1. Differential Analysis.

The area of accounting concerned with the effect of alternative courses of action on revenues and costs is called differential analysis. Differential revenue is the amount of increase or decrease in revenue expected from a particular course of action as compared with an alternative. Differential cost is the amount of increase or decrease in cost that is expected from a particular course of action as compared with an alternative.

Different analysis can aid management in making decisions on a variety of alternatives, including (1) whether equipment should be leased or sold, (2) whether to discontinue an unprofitable segment, (3) whether to manufacture or purchase a needed part, (4) whether to replace plant assets, (5) whether to process further or sell an intermediate product, and (6) whether to accept additional business at a special price.

2. Setting Normal Product Prices.

The normal selling price can be viewed as the target selling price, which must be achieved in the long run but may be deviated from in the short run because of such factors as competition and general market conditions. A practical approach to setting the normal price is the cost-plus approach. Using this approach, managers determine product prices by adding to a "cost" amount a markup, so that all costs plus a profit are covered in the price.

The three cost concepts commonly used in applying the cost-plus approach to product pricing are summarized as follows:

Cost Concept	Covered in Cost Amount	Covered in Markup
Total cost	Total costs and expenses	Desired profit
Product cost	Total manufacturing costs	Desired profit + Total selling and general expenses
Variable cost	Total variable costs and expenses	Desired profit + Total fixed manufacturing costs + Total fixed selling and general expenses

The markup percentage for each cost concept is determined by dividing the amount covered in the markup by the amount covered in the cost.

3. Economic Theory of Product Pricing.

The theory underlying product pricing is a separate economic discipline known as price theory. In this theory, management's primary objective is assumed to be the maximization of profits. The increase (decrease) in total revenue realized from the sale of an additional unit of product is called marginal revenue. The increase in total cost from producing and selling an additional unit of product is called marginal cost. A cost schedule prepared under the assumption of economies of scale is used for determining marginal costs. The point on the price graph where the marginal revenue line and the marginal cost line intersect indicates the level of sales and production at which profits are maximized.

In using the economic approach to product pricing, elasticity of demand, competitive market conditions, and data availability should be considered.

4. Pricing Strategies.

The stage in its life cycle at which a product is offered for sale has an important effect on management's choice of a pricing strategy. During the introductory stage, product prices are set to cover all costs and to provide for high profit margins. During the rapid growth stage, product prices remain high, but begin to decrease as new competitors enter the market. During the turbulent stage, profit margins are reduced as prices fall and special prices covering only variable costs may be established for short periods. During the maturity stage, prices remain at low levels as total sales reach a maximum and begin to fall. During the terminating stage, prices may be lowered to cover only variable costs in order to reduce losses and excess inventories.

KEY TERMS

differential analysis 405
differential revenue 405
differential cost 406
sunk cost 407
opportunity cost 411
markup 414
total cost concept 414
product cost concept 416
variable cost concept 417
price theory 419
marginal revenue 420
economies of scale 420

marginal cost 420
price graph 421
elasticity of demand 422
inelastic demand 422
elastic demand 422
monopoly market 422
monopolistic competitive
   market 422
purely competitive market 423
oligopoly market 423
product life cycle 425

SELF-EXAMINATION QUESTIONS

(Answers at End of Chapter)

1. The amount of increase or decrease in cost that is expected from a particular course of action as compared with an alternative is referred to as:
   A. differential cost
   B. replacement cost
   C. sunk cost
   D. none of the above

2. Victor Company is considering the disposal of equipment that was originally purchased for $200,000 and has accumulated depreciation to date of $150,000. The same equipment would cost $310,000 to replace. What is the sunk cost?
   A. $50,000
   B. $150,000
   C. $200,000
   D. None of the above

3. The amount of income that would result from the best available alternative to a proposed use of cash or its equivalent is referred to as:
   A. actual cost
   B. historical cost
   C. opportunity cost
   D. none of the above

4. For which cost concept used in applying the cost-plus approach to product pricing are fixed manufacturing costs, fixed selling and general expenses, and desired profit allowed for in the determination of markup?
   A. Total cost
   B. Product cost
   C. Variable cost
   D. None of the above

5. According to microeconomic theory, profits of a business enterprise will be maximized at the point where:
   A. marginal revenue equals marginal cost
   B. the change in total revenue is greater than the change in total cost
   C. the change in total cost is greater than the change in total revenue
   D. none of the above

ILLUSTRATIVE PROBLEM
·

Berry Company recently began production of a new product, M, which required the investment of $2,000,000 in assets. The costs and expenses of producing and selling 100,000 units of Product M are estimated as follows:

Variable costs and expenses:
Direct materials............................	$ 2.40 per unit
Direct labor..............................	6.50
Factory overhead	.90
Selling and general expenses	.20
Total.....................................	$10.00 per unit

Fixed costs and expenses:
Factory overhead	$ 60,000
Selling and general expenses	140,000

Berry Company is currently considering the establishment of a selling price for Product M. The president of Berry Company has decided to use the cost-plus approach to product pricing and has indicated that Product M must earn an 18% rate of return on invested assets.

Instructions:
1. Determine the amount of desired profit from the production and sale of Product M.
2. Assuming that the total cost concept is used, determine (a) the cost amount per unit, (b) the markup percentage, and (c) the selling price of Product M.
3. Assuming that the product cost concept is used, determine (a) the cost amount per unit, (b) the markup percentage, and (c) the selling price of Product M.
4. Assuming thet the variable cost concept is used, determine (a) the cost amount per unit, (b) the markup percentage, and (c) the selling price of Product M.

SOLUTION
·

(1) $360,000 ($2,000,000 × 18%)

(2) (a) Total costs and expenses:
Variable ($10 × 100,000 units).....................	$1,000,000
Fixed ($60,000 + $140,000)........................	200,000
Total	$1,200,000

Cost amount per unit: $1,200,000 ÷ 100,000 units = $12

(b) $\text{Markup Percentage} = \dfrac{\text{Desired Profit}}{\text{Total Costs and Expenses}}$

$\text{Markup Percentage} = \dfrac{\$360,000}{\$1,200,000}$

Markup Percentage = 30%

(c)
Cost amount per unit	$12.00
Markup ($12 × 30%)	3.60
Selling price...	$15.60

(3) (a) Total manufacturing costs:

Variable ($9.80 × 100,000 units)	$ 980,000
Fixed factory overhead	60,000
Total	$1,040,000

Cost amount per unit: $1,040,000 ÷ 100,000 units = $10.40

(b) $\text{Markup Percentage} = \dfrac{\text{Desired Profit} + \substack{\text{Total Selling and} \\ \text{General Expenses}}}{\text{Total Manufacturing Costs}}$

$\text{Markup Percentage} = \dfrac{\$360,000 + \$140,000 + (\$.20 \times 100,000 \text{ units})}{\$1,040,000}$

$\text{Markup Percentage} = \dfrac{\$360,000 + \$140,000 + \$20,000}{\$1,040,000}$

$\text{Markup Percentage} = \dfrac{\$520,000}{\$1,040,000}$

Markup Percentage = 50%

(c)
Cost amount per unit	$10.40
Markup ($10.40 × 50%)	5.20
Selling price...	$15.60

(4) (a) Total variable costs and expenses: $10 × 100,000 units = $1,000,000
Cost amount per unit: $1,000,000 ÷ 100,000 units = $10

(b) $\text{Markup Percentage} = \dfrac{\substack{\text{Desired Profit} + \\ \text{Total Fixed Manufacturing Costs} \\ + \text{ Total Fixed Selling and General Expenses}}}{\text{Total Variable Costs and Expenses}}$

$\text{Markup Percentage} = \dfrac{\$360,000 + \$60,000 + \$140,000}{\$1,000,000}$

$\text{Markup Percentage} = \dfrac{\$560,000}{\$1,000,000}$

Markup Percentage = 56%

(c) Cost amount per unit $10.00
 Markup ($10 × 56%) 5.60
 Selling price.. $15.60

Discussion Questions

12–1. What term is applied to the type of analysis that emphasizes the difference between the revenues and costs for proposed alternative courses of action?

12–2. Explain the meaning of (a) *differential revenue* and (b) *differential cost.*

12–3. Phillips Lumber Company incurs a cost of $80 per thousand board feet in processing a certain "rough-cut" lumber which it sells for $120 per thousand board feet. An alternative is to produce a "finished-cut" at a total processing cost of $96 per thousand board feet, which can be sold for $160 per thousand board feet. What is the amount of (a) the differential revenue and (b) the differential cost associated with the alternative?

12–4. (a) What is meant by *sunk costs?* (b) A company is contemplating replacing an old piece of machinery which cost $320,000 and has $280,000 accumulated depreciation to date. A new machine costs $400,000. What is the sunk cost in this situation?

12–5. The condensed income statement for Irving Company for the current year is as follows:

| | Product | | | |
	A	B	C	Total
Sales...........................	$200,000	$170,000	$ 80,000	$450,000
Less variable costs and expenses ..	120,000	100,000	60,000	280,000
Contribution margin	$ 80,000	$ 70,000	$ 20,000	$170,000
Less fixed costs and expenses.....	40,000	31,000	30,000	101,000
Income (loss) from operations......	$ 40,000	$ 39,000	$(10,000)	$ 69,000

Management decided to discontinue the manufacture and sale of Product C. Assuming that the discontinuance will have no effect on the total fixed costs and expenses or on the sales of Products A and B, has management made the correct decision? Explain.

12–6. (a) What is meant by *opportunity cost?* (b) Lieu Company is currently earning 10% on $200,000 invested in marketable securities. It proposes to use the $200,000 to acquire plant facilities to manufacture a new product that is expected to add $30,000 annually to net income. What is the opportunity cost involved in the decision to manufacture the new product?

12–7. In the long run, the normal selling price must be set high enough to cover what factors?

12–8. What are three cost concepts commonly used in applying the cost-plus approach to product pricing?

12–9. In using the product cost concept of applying the cost-plus approach to product pricing, what factors are included in the markup?

12–10. The variable cost concept used in applying the cost-plus approach to product pricing includes what costs in the cost amount to which the markup is added?

12–11. In determining the markup percentage for the variable cost concept of applying the cost-plus approach, what is included in the denominator?

12–12. Why might the use of ideal standards in applying the cost-plus approach to product pricing lead to setting product prices which are too low?

12–13. Although the cost-plus approach to product pricing may be used by management as a general guideline, what are some examples of other factors that managers should also consider in setting product prices?

12–14. In microeconomic theory, what is assumed to be management's primary objective for a business enterprise?

12–15. Why is it generally not possible to sell an unlimited number of units of product at the same price?

12–16. As the terms are used in microeconomic theory, what is meant by (a) marginal revenue and (b) marginal cost?

12–17. If the total revenue for selling 4 units of Product F is $40 and the total revenue for selling 5 units is $45, what is the marginal revenue associated with selling the fourth unit?

12–18. What does the concept of economies of scale generally imply?

12–19. For a given amount of facilities, why will the total costs and expenses begin to increase by increasing amounts at some point?

12–20. What point on the price graph indicates a maximum level of profit?

12–21. (a) If an increase in a price of a product has little or no effect on the number of units sold, is the demand for the product said to be elastic or inelastic? (b) Is the demand for bath soap by college students elastic or inelastic?

12–22. What is the economic term used to describe the market for a product in which there are many sellers of similar products, with no one seller having a large enough share of the market to influence the total sales of the other products?

12–23. Why is the more theoretical economic approach to product pricing not used as often as the cost-plus approach?

12–24. For the following graph of total sales for a product, identify each stage of the product's life cycle.

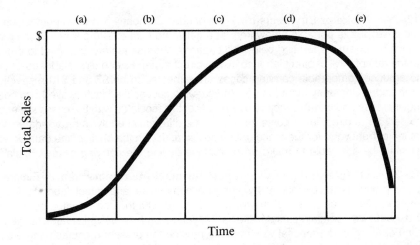

12–25. Real World Focus. In the personal computer hardware market, at what stage in the product life cycle is the 5 1/4-inch disk drive and the 3 1/2-inch drive?

12–26. Real World Focus. In July, 1986, *The Wall Street Journal* reported that the brakes that General Motors produces at its Delco Moraine division for its auto-mobile assembly plants cost up to 15% more to make than they would cost to buy from an outside supplier. The same article reported that Ford Motor Co. and Chrysler Corp. buy almost all their brakes from outside suppliers as far away as Brazil, and these companies save money in the process. The decision of General Motors to produce its brakes internally is an example of what type of decision illustrated in this chapter?

Exercises

12–27. Differential analysis report for discontinuance of product. A condensed income statement by product line for Chow Co. indicated the following for Product H for the past year:

Sales.	$120,000
Cost of goods sold.	70,000
Gross profit	$ 50,000
Operating expenses.	60,000
Loss from operations.	$ (10,000)

It is estimated that 20% of the cost of goods sold represents fixed factory overhead costs and that 40% of operating expenses is fixed. Since Product H is only one of many products, the fixed costs and expenses will not be materially affected if the product is discontinued. (a) Prepare a differential analysis report, dated January 3 of the current year, for the proposed discontinuance of Product H. (b) Should Product H be retained? Explain.

12–28.   Make or buy decision.   Hernandez Company has been purchasing carrying cases for its portable typewriters at a delivered cost of $20 per unit. The company, which is currently operating below full capacity, charges factory overhead to production at the rate of 40% of direct labor cost. The direct materials and direct labor costs per unit to produce comparable carrying cases are expected to be $7 and $10 respectively. If Hernandez Company manufactures the carrying cases, fixed factory overhead costs will not increase and variable factory overhead costs associated with the cases are expected to be 15% of direct labor costs. (a) Prepare a differential analysis report, dated May 10 of the current year, for the make or buy decision. (b) On the basis of the data presented, would it be advisable to make or to continue buying the carrying cases? Explain.

SPREADSHEET
PROBLEM

12–29.   Differential analysis report for machine replacement.   Elmore Company produces a commodity by applying a machine and direct labor to the direct material. The original cost of the machine is $270,000, the accumulated depreciation is $160,000, its remaining useful life is 10 years, and its salvage value is negligible. On February 10, a proposal was made to replace the present manufacturing procedure with a fully automatic machine that will cost $500,000. The automatic machine has an estimated useful life of 10 years and no significant salvage value. For use in evaluating the proposal, the accountant accumulated the following annual data on present and proposed operations:

	Present Operations	Proposed Operations
Sales	$650,000	$650,000
Direct materials	277,200	277,200
Direct labor	118,800	—
Power and maintenance	20,400	47,200
Taxes, insurance, etc.	13,200	19,200
Selling and general expenses	52,800	52,800

(a) Prepare a differential analysis report for the proposal to replace the machine. Include in the analysis both the net differential decrease in costs and expenses anticipated over the 10 years and the annual differential decrease in costs and expenses anticipated. (b) Based only on the data presented, should the proposal be accepted? (c) What are some of the other factors that should be considered before a final decision is made?

12–30.   Decision on acceptance of additional business.   Bailey Company has a plant capacity of 60,000 units, and current production is 40,000 units. Monthly fixed costs and expenses are $130,000, and variable costs and expenses are $14.20 per unit. The present selling price is $25 per unit. On November 23, the company received an offer from EMI Company for 10,000 units of the product at $16 each. The EMI Company will market the units in a foreign country under its own brand name. The additional business is not expected to affect the regular selling price or quantity of sales of Bailey Company. (a) Prepare a differential analysis report for the proposed sale to EMI Company. (b) Briefly explain the reason why the acceptance of this additional business will increase operating income. (c) What is the minimum price per unit that would produce a contribution margin?

12–31.   Use of absorption costing or variable costing in bidding on contract.   Adams Company expects to operate at 90% of productive capacity during

November. The total manufacturing costs for November for the production of 18,000 grinders are budgeted as follows:

Direct materials..	$ 23,400
Direct labor..	45,000
Variable factory overhead.................................	10,800
Fixed factory overhead	27,000
Total manufacturing costs................................	$106,200

The company has an opportunity to submit a bid for 2,000 grinders to be delivered by November 30 to a government agency. If the contract is obtained, it is anticipated that the additional activity will not interfere with normal production during November or increase the selling or general expenses. (a) What is the unit cost below which Adams Company should not go in bidding on the government contract? (b) Is a unit cost figure based on absorption costing or one based on variable costing more useful in arriving at a bid on this contract? Explain.

12–32. Total cost concept of product pricing. Hargrave Company uses the total cost concept of applying the cost-plus approach to product pricing. The costs and expenses of producing and selling 10,000 units of Product M are as follows:

Variable costs and expenses:	
Direct materials.....................................	$ 5.60 per unit
Direct labor...	2.80
Factory overhead	.60
Selling and general expenses	1.50
Total...	$10.50 per unit
Fixed costs and expenses:	
Factory overhead	$30,000
Selling and general expenses	15,000

Hargrave Company desires a profit equal to an 18% rate of return on invested assets of $100,000. (a) Determine the amount of desired profit from the production and sale of Product M. (b) Determine the total costs and expenses and the cost amount per unit for the production and sale of 10,000 units of Product M. (c) Determine the markup percentage for Product M. (d) Determine the selling price of Product M.

12–33. Product cost concept of product pricing. Based on the data presented in Exercise 12–32, assume that Hargrave Company uses the product cost concept of applying the cost-plus approach to product pricing. (a) Determine the total manufacturing costs and the cost amount per unit for the production and sale of 10,000 units of Product M. (b) Determine the markup percentage for Product M. (c) Determine the selling price of Product M.

12–34. Variable cost concept of product pricing. Based on the data presented in Exercise 12–32, assume that Hargrave Company uses the variable cost concept of applying the cost-plus approach to product pricing. (a) Determine the cost amount per unit for the production and sale of 10,000 units of Product M. (b) Determine the markup percentage for Product M. (c) Determine the selling price of Product M.

12–35. Price graph and analysis. For the following revenue schedule and cost schedule for Product E, (a) construct a price graph, (b) determine the level of sales and production at which the marginal cost and marginal revenue lines intersect, (c) determine the unit sales price at the level of sales determined in (b), and (d) determine the maximum profit for Product E at the level of sales determined in (b).

Revenue Schedule

Price	Units Sold	Total Revenue	Marginal Revenue
$10	1	$10	$10
9	2	18	8
8	3	24	6
7	4	28	4
6	5	30	2
5	6	30	0
4	7	28	−2

Cost Schedule

Units Produced and Sold	Total Cost	Marginal Cost
1	$ 7	$ 7
2	13	6
3	18	5
4	22	4
5	25	3
6	29	4
7	34	5

Problems

·

12–36. Differential analysis report involving opportunity costs. On August 1, Waters Company is considering leasing a building and purchasing the necessary equipment to operate a public warehouse. The project would be financed by selling $800,000 of 9% U.S. Treasury bonds that mature in 20 years. The bonds were purchased at face value and are currently selling at face value. The following data have been assembled:

Cost of equipment...	$800,000
Life of equipment..	20 years
Estimated residual value of equipment	$200,000
Yearly costs to operate the warehouse, in addition to depreciation of equipment	$ 50,000
Yearly expected revenues—first 8 years	$180,000
Yearly expected revenues—next 12 years..........................	$150,000

Instructions:

(1) Prepare a differential analysis report presenting the differential revenue and the differential cost associated with the proposed operation of the warehouse for the 20 years as compared with present conditions.

(2) Based on the results disclosed by the differential analysis, should the proposal be accepted?

(3) If the proposal is accepted, what is the total estimated income from operation of the warehouse for the 20 years?

12-37. Differential analysis report for machine replacement proposal. Lee Company is considering the replacement of a machine that has been used in its factory for three years. Relevant data associated with the operations of the old machine and the new machine, neither of which has any residual value, are as follows:

Old Machine

Cost of machine, 9-year life	$300,000
Annual depreciation	33,333
Annual manufacturing costs, exclusive of depreciation	510,000
Related annual operating expenses	320,000
Associated annual revenue	1,120,000
Current estimated selling price	180,000

New Machine

Cost of machine, 6-year life	$630,000
Annual depreciation	105,000
Estimated annual manufacturing costs, exclusive of depreciation	380,000

Annual operating expenses and revenue are not expected to be affected by purchase of the new machine.

Instructions:

(1) Prepare a differential analysis report as of October 4 of the current year, comparing operations utilizing the new machine with operations using the present equipment. The analysis should indicate the total differential decrease or increase in costs that would result over the 6-year period if the new machine is acquired.

(2) List other factors that should be considered before a final decision is reached.

12-38. Differential analysis report for sales promotion proposal. Gorksi Company is planning a one-month campaign for June to promote sales of one of its two products. A total of $35,000 has been budgeted for advertising, contests, redeemable coupons, and other promotional activities. The following data have been assembled for their possible usefulness in deciding which of the products to select for the campaign:

	Product D	Product E
Unit selling price	$50	$60
Unit production costs:		
Direct materials	$14	$18
Direct labor	10	14
Variable factory overhead	8	8
Fixed factory overhead	6	6
Total unit production costs	$38	$46
Unit variable operating expenses	5	5
Unit fixed operating expenses	3	3
Total unit costs and expenses	$46	$54
Operating income per unit	$ 4	$ 6

No increase in facilities would be necessary to produce and sell the increased output. It is anticipated that 10,000 additional units of Product D or 8,000 additional units of Product E could be sold without changing the unit selling price of either product.

Instructions:

(1) Prepare a differential analysis report as of May 5 of the current year, presenting the additional revenue and additional costs and expenses anticipated from the promotion of Product D and Product E.
(2) The sales manager had tentatively decided to promote Product E, estimating that operating income would be increased by $13,000 ($6 operating income per unit for 8,000 units, less promotion expenses of $35,000). It was also believed that the selection of Product D would increase operating income by only $5,000 ($4 operating income per unit for 10,000 units, less promotion expenses of $35,000). State briefly your reasons for supporting or opposing the tentative decision.

12–39. Differential analysis report for further processing. The management of Beeman Company is considering whether to process further Product X into Product Y. Product Y can be sold for $50 per pound, and Product X can be sold without further processing for $10 per pound. Product X is produced in batches of 300 pounds by processing 400 pounds of raw material, which costs $7 per pound. Product Y will require additional processing costs of $2.50 per pound of Product X, and 3 pounds of Product X will produce 1 pound of Product Y.

Instructions:

(1) Prepare a differential analysis report as of April 10, presenting the differential revenue and differential cost per batch associated with the further processing of Product X to produce Product Y.
(2) Briefly report your recommendations.

12–40. Differential analysis report for further processing. Childers Refining Inc. refines Product V in batches of 100,000 gallons, which it sells for $4.80 per gallon. The associated unit costs and expenses are currently as follows:

Direct materials..............................	$2.70
Direct labor	.72
Variable factory overhead......................	.28
Fixed factory overhead........................	.18
Sales commissions	.48
Fixed selling and general expenses..............	.12

The company is presently considering a proposal to put Product V through several additional processes to yield Products V and W. Although the company had determined such further processing to be unwise, new processing methods have now been developed. Existing facilities can be used for the additional processing, but since the factory is operating at full 8-hour-day capacity, the processing would have to be performed at night. Additional costs of processing would be $6,500 per batch, and there would be an evaporation loss of 10%, with 65% of the processed material evolving as Product V and 25% as Product W. The selling price of Product W is $7.20 per gallon. Sales commissions are a uniform percentage based on the sales price.

Instructions:

(1) Prepare a differential analysis report as of January 20, presenting the differential revenue and the differential cost per batch associated with the processing to produce Products V and W, compared with processing to produce Product V only.

(2) Briefly report your recommendations.

12–41. Product pricing using the cost-plus approach concepts. Wilson Company recently began production of a new product, J, which required the investment of $500,000 in assets. The costs and expenses of producing and selling 50,000 units of Product J are estimated as follows:

Variable costs and expenses:	
Direct materials.....................................	$ 6.20
Direct labor...	7.40
Factory overhead	1.40
Selling and general expenses	1.00
Total...	$16.00
Fixed costs and expenses:	
Factory overhead	$150,000
Selling and general expenses	50,000

Wilson Company is currently considering the establishment of a selling price for Product J. The president of Wilson Company has decided to use the cost-plus approach to product pricing and has indicated that Product J must earn a 16% rate of return on invested assets.

Instructions:

(1) Determine the amount of desired profit from the production and sale of Product J.

(2) Assuming that the total cost concept is used, determine (a) the cost amount per unit, (b) the markup percentage, and (c) the selling price of Product J.

(3) Assuming that the product cost concept is used, determine (a) the cost amount per unit, (b) the markup percentage, and (c) the selling price of Product J.

(4) Assuming that the variable cost concept is used, determine (a) the cost amount per unit, (b) the markup percentage, and (c) the selling price of Product J.

(5) Comment on any additional considerations that could influence the establishment of the selling price for Product J.

ALTERNATE PROBLEMS

SPREADSHEET
PROBLEM

12–36A. Differential analysis report involving opportunity costs. On July 1, Stuart Company is considering leasing a building and purchasing the necessary equipment to operate a public warehouse. The project would be financed by selling $750,000 of 8% U.S. Treasury bonds that mature in 10 years. The bonds were purchased at face value and are currently selling at face value. The following data have been assembled:

Cost of equipment	$750,000
Life of equipment	10 years
Estimated residual value of equipment	$ 50,000
Yearly costs to operate the warehouse, in addition to depreciation of equipment	$ 74,000
Yearly expected revenues—first 6 years	$220,000
Yearly expected revenues—next 4 years.	$200,000

Instructions:

(1) Prepare a differential analysis report presenting the differential revenue and the differential cost associated with the proposed operation of the warehouse for the 10 years as compared with present conditions.

(2) Based on the results disclosed by the differential analysis, should the proposal be accepted?

(3) If the proposal is accepted, what is the total estimated income from operation of the warehouse for the 10 years?

12–37A. Differential analysis report for machine replacement proposal.

Greeley Company is considering the replacement of a machine that has been used in its factory for four years. Relevant data associated with the operations of the old machine and the new machine, neither of which has any residual value, are as follows:

Old Machine

Cost of machine, 9-year life.	$585,000
Annual depreciation.	65,000
Annual manufacturing costs, exclusive of depreciation	375,000
Related annual operating expenses.	138,500
Associated annual revenue	920,000
Current estimated selling price	210,000

New Machine

Cost of machine, 5-year life.	$750,000
Annual depreciation.	150,000
Estimated annual manufacturing costs, exclusive of depreciation	220,000

Annual operating expenses and revenue are not expected to be affected by purchase of the new machine.

Instructions:

(1) Prepare a differential analysis report as of April 2 of the current year, comparing operations utilizing the new machine with operations using the present equipment. The analysis should indicate the total differential decrease or increase in costs that would result over the 5-year period if the new machine is acquired.

(2) List other factors that should be considered before a final decision is reached.

12–41A. Product pricing using the cost-plus approach concepts.

Alman Company recently began production of a new product, W, which required the investment of $800,000 in assets. The costs and expenses of producing and selling 25,000 units of Product W are as follows:

Variable costs and expenses:

Direct materials.....................................	$ 6.00
Direct labor...	2.75
Factory overhead	1.25
Selling and general expenses	2.00
Total...	$12.00

Fixed costs and expenses:

Factory overhead	$70,000
Selling and general expenses	30,000

Alman Company is currently considering the establishment of a selling price for Product W. The president of Alman Company has decided to use the cost-plus approach to product pricing and has indicated that Product W must earn a 10% rate of return on invested assets.

Instructions:

(1) Determine the amount of desired profit from the production and sale of Product W.

(2) Assuming that the total cost concept is used, determine (a) the cost amount per unit, (b) the markup percentage, and (c) the selling price of Product W.

(3) Assuming that the product cost concept is used, determine (a) the cost amount per unit, (b) the markup percentage, and (c) the selling price of Product W. Round to the nearest cent.

(4) Assuming that the variable cost concept is used, determine (a) the cost amount per unit, (b) the markup percentage, and (c) the selling price of Product W.

(5) Comment on any additional considerations that could influence the establishment of the selling price for Product W.

Mini-Case 12

Your father operates a family-owned automotive dealership. Recently, the city government has requested bids on the purchase of 10 sedans for use by the city police department. Although the city prefers to purchase from local dealerships, state law requires the acceptance of the lowest bid. The past several contracts for automotive purchases have been granted to dealerships from surrounding communities.

The following data were taken from the dealership records for the normal sale of the automobile for which current bids have been requested:

Retail list price of sedan.	$13,600
Cost allocated to normal sale:	
Dealer cost from manufacturer.	10,800
Fixed overhead	500
Shipping charges from manufacturer.	420
Preparation charges	100
Sales commission based on selling price.	6%

Your father has asked you to help him in arriving at a "winning" bid price for this contract. In the past, your father has always bid $300 above the total cost (including fixed overhead). No sales commissions will be paid if the bid is accepted, and your father has indicated that the bid price must contribute at least $300 per car to the profits of the dealership.

Instructions:

(1) Do you think that your father has used good bidding procedures for prior contracts? Explain.
(2) What should be the bid price, based upon your father's profit objectives?
(3) Explain why the bid price determined in (2) would not be an acceptable price for normal customers.

Answers to Self-Examination Questions
· · ·

1. **A** Differential cost (answer A) is the amount of increase or decrease in cost that is expected from a particular course of action compared with an alternative. Replacement cost (answer B) is the cost of replacing an asset at current market prices, and sunk cost (answer C) is a past cost that will not be affected by subsequent decisions.

2. **A** A sunk cost is not affected by later decisions. For Victor Company, the sunk cost is the $50,000 (answer A) book value of the equipment, which is equal to the original cost of $200,000 (answer C) less the accumulated depreciation of $150,000 (answer B).

3. **C** The amount of income that could have been earned from the best available alternative to a proposed use of cash is called opportunity cost (answer C). Actual cost (answer A) or historical cost (answer B) is the cash or equivalent outlay for goods or services actually acquired.

4. C Under the variable cost concept of product pricing (answer C), fixed manufacturing costs, fixed general and selling expenses, and desired profit are allowed for in the determination of the markup. Only desired profit is allowed for in the markup under the total cost concept (answer A). Under the product cost concept (answer B), total selling and general expenses, and desired profit are allowed for in the determination of markup.

5. A Microeconomic theory indicates that profits of a business enterprise will be maximized at the point where marginal revenue equals marginal cost (answer A). At lower levels of production and sales, the change in total revenue is greater than the change in total cost (answer B); hence, more profit can be achieved by manufacturing and selling more units. At higher levels of production and sales, the change in total cost is greater than the change in total revenue (answer C); hence, less profit will be achieved by manufacturing and selling more units.

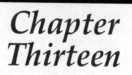

Chapter Thirteen

CHAPTER
OBJECTIVES

•

Describe the nature and importance of long-term investment decisions involving property, plant, and equipment.

•

Describe and illustrate the use of the present value concept in capital investment decisions.

•

Describe the nature of capital investment analysis and illustrate the evaluation of capital investment proposals by the following methods:
Average rate of return
Cash payback
Discounted cash flow
Discounted internal rate of return

•

Describe and illustrate factors that complicate capital investment analysis, including:
Income tax
Unequal proposal lives
Lease versus capital investment
Uncertainty
Changes in price levels

•

Describe and illustrate the capital rationing process.

•

Describe the basic concepts for planning and controlling capital investment expenditures.

•

Capital Investment Analysis

With the accelerated growth of American industry, increasing attention has been given to long-term investment decisions involving property, plant, and equipment. The process by which management plans, evaluates, and controls such investments is called **capital investment analysis**, or **capital budgeting.** This chapter describes analyses useful for making capital investment decisions, which may involve thousands, millions, or even billions of dollars. The similarities and differences between the most commonly used methods of evaluating capital investment proposals, as well as the uses of each method, are emphasized. Finally, considerations complicating capital investment analyses, the process of allocating available investment funds among competing proposals (capital rationing), and planning and controlling capital expenditures are briefly discussed.

NATURE OF CAPITAL INVESTMENT ANALYSIS

Capital investment expenditures normally involve a long-term commitment of funds and thus affect operations for many years. These expenditures must earn a reasonable rate of return, so that the enterprise can meet its obligations to creditors and provide dividends to stockholders. Because capital investment decisions are some of the most important decisions that management makes, the systems and procedures for evaluating, planning, and controlling capital investments must be carefully developed and implemented.

A capital investment program should include a plan for encouraging employees at all levels of an enterprise to submit proposals for capital investments. The plan should provide for communicating to the employees the long-range goals of the enterprise, so that useful proposals are submitted. In addition, the plan may provide for rewarding employees whose proposals are implemented. All reasonable proposals should be given serious consideration, and the effects of the economic implications expected from these proposals should be identified.

METHODS OF EVALUATING CAPITAL INVESTMENT PROPOSALS

The methods of evaluating capital investment proposals can be grouped into two general categories that can be referred to as (1) methods that ignore present value and (2) present value methods. The characteristic that distinguishes one category from the other is the way in which the concept of the time value of money is treated. Both the time value of money and the concept of present value are discussed in more detail later in this chapter. Because cash on hand can be invested to earn more cash, while cash to be received in the future cannot, money has a time value. However, the methods that ignore present value do not give consideration to the fact that cash on hand is more valuable than cash to be received in the future. The two methods in this category are (1) the average rate of return method and (2) the cash payback method.

By converting dollars to be received in the future into current dollars, using the concept of present value, the present value methods take into consideration the fact that money has a time value. The two common present value methods used in evaluating capital investment proposals are (1) the discounted cash flow method and (2) the discounted internal rate of return method.

Each of the four methods of analyzing capital investment proposals has both advantages and limitations. Often management will use some combination of the four methods in evaluating the various economic aspects of capital investment proposals.

Methods That Ignore Present Value

The average rate of return and the cash payback methods of evaluating capital investment proposals are simple to use and are especially useful in screening proposals. Management often establishes a minimum standard, and proposals not meeting this minimum standard are dropped from further consideration. When several alternative proposals meet the minimum standard, management will often rank the proposals from the most desirable to the least desirable.

The methods that ignore present value are also useful in evaluating capital investment proposals that have relatively short useful lives. In such situations, the timing of the cash flows is less important, and management generally focuses its attention on the amount of income to be earned from the investment and the total net cash flows to be received from the investment.

Average Rate of Return Method. The expected **average rate of return,** sometimes referred to as the **accounting rate of return,** is a measure of the expected profitability of an investment in plant assets. The amount of income expected to be earned from the investment is stated as an annual average over the number of years the asset is to be used. The amount of the investment may be considered to be the original cost of the plant asset, or recognition may be given to the effect of depreciation on the amount of the investment. According to the latter view, the investment gradually declines from the original cost to the estimated residual value at the end of its useful life. If straight-line depreciation and no residual value are assumed, the average investment would be equal to one half of the original expenditure.

To illustrate, assume that management is considering the purchase of a certain machine at a cost of $500,000. The machine is expected to have a useful life of 4 years, with no residual value, and its use during the 4 years is expected to yield total income of $200,000. The estimated average annual income is therefore $50,000 ($200,000 ÷ 4), and the average investment is $250,000 [($500,000 + $0 residual value) ÷ 2]. Accordingly, the expected average rate of return on the average investment is 20%, computed as follows:

$$\text{Average Rate of Return} = \frac{\text{Estimated Average Annual Income}}{\text{Average Investment}}$$

$$\text{Average Rate of Return} = \frac{\$200,000 \div 4}{(\$500,000 + \$0) \div 2}$$

$$\text{Average Rate of Return} = 20\%$$

The expected average rate of return of 20% should be compared with the rate established by management as the minimum reward for the risks involved in the investment. The attractiveness of the proposed purchase of additional equipment is indicated by the difference between the expected rate and the minimum desired rate.

When several alternative capital investment proposals are being considered, the proposals can be ranked by their average rates of return. The higher the average rate of return, the more desirable the proposal. For example, assume that management is considering the following alternative capital investment proposals and has computed the indicated average rates of return:

	Proposal A	Proposal B
Estimated average annual income.........	$ 30,000	$ 36,000
Average investment	$120,000	$180,000
Average rate of return:		
$30,000 ÷ $120,000...................	25%	
$36,000 ÷ $180,000...................		20%

If only the average rate of return is considered, Proposal A, based on its average rate of return of 25%, would be preferred over Proposal B.

The primary advantages of the average rate of return method are its ease of computation and the fact that it emphasizes the amount of income earned over the entire life of the proposal. Its main disadvantages are its lack of consideration of the expected cash flows from the proposal and the timing of these cash flows. These cash flows are important because cash coming from an investment can be reinvested in other income-producing activities. Therefore, the more funds and the sooner the funds become available, the more income that can be generated from their reinvestment.

Cash Payback Method. The expected period of time that will pass between the date of a capital investment and the complete recovery in cash (or equivalent) of the amount invested is called the **cash payback period.** To simplify the analysis, the revenues and the out-of-pocket operating expenses expected to be associated with the operation of the plant assets are assumed to be entirely in the form of cash. The excess of the cash flowing in from revenue over the cash flowing out for expenses is termed **net cash flow.** The time required for the net cash flow to equal the initial outlay for the plant asset is the payback period.

For purposes of illustration, assume that the proposed investment in a plant asset with an 8-year life is $200,000 and that the annual net cash flow is expected to be $40,000. The estimated cash payback period for the investment is 5 years, computed as follows:

$$\frac{\$200,000}{\$40,000} = \text{5-year cash payback period}$$

In the preceding illustration, the annual net cash flows were equal ($40,000 per year). If these annual net cash flows are not equal, the cash payback period is determined by summing the annual net cash flows until the cumulative sum equals the amount of the proposed investment. To illustrate, assume that for a proposed investment of $400,000, the annual net cash flows and cumulative net cash flows over the proposal's 6-year life are as follows:

Year	Net Cash Flow	Cumulative Net Cash Flow
1	$ 60,000	$ 60,000
2	80,000	140,000
3	105,000	245,000
4	155,000	400,000
5	140,000	540,000
6	90,000	630,000

The cumulative net cash flow at the end of the fourth year equals the amount of the investment, $400,000. Therefore, the payback period is 4 years.

The cash payback method is widely used in evaluating proposals for expansion and for investment in new projects. A relatively short payback period is desirable, because the sooner the cash is recovered the sooner it becomes available for reinvestment in other projects. In addition, there is likely to be less possibility of loss from changes in economic conditions, obsolescence, and other unavoidable risks when the commitment is short-term. The cash payback concept is also of interest to bankers and other creditors who may be dependent upon net cash flow for the repayment of claims associated with the initial capital investment. The sooner the cash is recovered, the sooner the debt or other liabilities can be paid. Thus, the cash payback method would be especially useful to managers whose primary concern is liquidity.

One of the primary disadvantages of the cash payback method as a basis for decisions is its failure to take into consideration the expected profitability of a proposal. A project with a very short payback period, coupled with relatively poor profitability, would be less desirable than one with a longer payback period but with satisfactory profitability. Another disadvantage of the cash payback method is that the cash flows occurring after the payback period are ignored. A 5-year project with a 3-year payback period and two additional years of substantial cash flows is more desirable than a 5-year project with a 3-year payback period that has lower cash flows in the last two years.

Present Value Methods

An investment in plant and equipment may be viewed as the acquisition of a series of future net cash flows composed of two elements: (1) recovery of the initial investment and (2) income. The period of time over which these net cash flows will be received may be an important factor in determining the value of an investment.

The concept of the time value of money is that any specified amount of cash to be received at some date in the future is not the equivalent of the same amount of cash held at an earlier date. A sum of cash to be received in the future is not as valuable as the same sum on hand today, because cash on hand today can be invested to earn income. For example, $10,000 on hand today would be more valuable than $10,000 to be received a year from today. In other words, if cash can be invested to earn 10% per year, the $10,000 on hand today will accumulate to $11,000 ($10,000 plus $1,000 earnings) by one year from today. The $10,000 on hand today can be referred to as the **present value** amount that is equivalent to $11,000 to be received a year from today.

Discounted Cash Flow Method. The **discounted cash flow method,** sometimes referred to as the **net present value method,** uses present value concepts to compute the present value of the cash flows expected from a proposal. To illustrate, if the rate of earnings is 12% and the cash to be received in one year is $1,000, the present value amount is $892.86 ($1,000 ÷ 1.12). If the cash is to be received one year later (two years in all), with the earnings compounded at the end of the first year, the present value amount would be $797.20 ($892.86 ÷ 1.12).

Instead of determining the present value of future cash flows by a series of divisions in the manner just illustrated, it is customary to find the present value of $1 from a table of present values and to multiply it by the amount of the future cash flow. Reference to the following partial table indicates that the present value of $1 to be received two years hence, with earnings at the rate of 12% a year, is .797. Multiplication of .797 by $1,000 yields $797, which is the same amount that was determined in the preceding paragraph by two successive divisions. The small difference is due to rounding the present value factors in the table to three decimal places.[1]

---

[1] More complete tables of both present values and future values are in Appendix B.

Year	6%	10%	12%	15%	20%
1	.943	.909	.893	.870	.833
2	.890	.826	.797	.756	.694
3	.840	.751	.712	.658	.579
4	.792	.683	.636	.572	.482
5	.747	.621	.567	.497	.402
6	.705	.564	.507	.432	.335
7	.665	.513	.452	.376	.279
8	.627	.467	.404	.327	.233
9	.592	.424	.361	.284	.194
10	.558	.386	.322	.247	.162

The particular rate of return selected in discounted cash flow analysis is affected by the nature of the business enterprise and its relative profitability, the purpose of the capital investment, the cost of securing funds for the investment, the minimum desired rate of return, and other related factors. If the present value of the net cash flow expected from a proposed investment, at the selected rate, equals or exceeds the amount of the investment, the proposal is desirable. For purposes of illustration, assume a proposal for the acquisition of $200,000 of equipment with an expected useful life of 5 years and a minimum desired rate of return of 10%. The anticipated net cash flow for each of the 5 years and the analysis of the proposal are as follows. The calculation shows that the proposal is expected to recover the investment and provide more than the minimum rate of return.

Year	Present Value of $1 at 10%	Net Cash Flow	Present Value of Net Cash Flow
1	.909	$ 70,000	$ 63,630
2	.826	60,000	49,560
3	.751	50,000	37,550
4	.683	40,000	27,320
5	.621	40,000	24,840
Total.....................		$260,000	$202,900
Amount to be invested			200,000
Excess of present value over amount to be invested			$ 2,900

When several alternative investment proposals of the same amount are being considered, the one with the largest excess of present value over the amount to be invested is the most desirable. If the alternative proposals involve different amounts of investment, it is useful to prepare a relative ranking of the proposals by using a **present value index**. The present value index for the previous illustration is computed by dividing the total present value of the net cash flow by the amount to be invested, as follows:

$$\text{Present Value Index} = \frac{\text{Total Present Value of Net Cash Flow}}{\text{Amount To Be Invested}}$$

$$\text{Present Value Index} = \frac{\$202,900}{\$200,000}$$

$$\text{Present Value Index} = 1.01$$

To illustrate the ranking of the proposals by use of the present value index, assume that the total present values of the net cash flow and the amounts to be invested for three alternative proposals are as follows:

	Proposal A	Proposal B	Proposal C
Total present value of net cash flow ...	$107,000	$86,400	$93,600
Amount to be invested	100,000	80,000	90,000
Excess of present value over amount to be invested	$ 7,000	$ 6,400	$ 3,600

The present value index for each proposal is as follows:

	Present Value Index
Proposal A......................	1.07 ($107,000 ÷ $100,000)
Proposal B......................	1.08 ($ 86,400 ÷ $ 80,000)
Proposal C......................	1.04 ($ 93,600 ÷ $ 90,000)

The present value indexes indicate that although Proposal A has the largest excess of present value over the amount to be invested, it is not as attractive as Proposal B in terms of the amount of present value per dollar invested. It should be noted, however, that Proposal B requires an investment of only $80,000, while Proposal A requires an investment of $100,000. The possible use of the $20,000 if B is selected should be considered before a final decision is made.

The primary advantage of the discounted cash flow method is that it gives consideration to the time value of money. A disadvantage of the method is that the computations are more complex than those for the methods that ignore present value. In addition, this method assumes that the cash received from the proposal during its useful life will be reinvested at the rate of return used to compute the present value of the proposal. Because of changing economic conditions, this assumption may not always be reasonable.

Discounted Internal Rate of Return Method. The discounted internal rate of return method, sometimes called the **internal rate of return** or **time-adjusted rate of return method,** uses present value concepts to compute the rate of return from the net cash flows expected from capital investment proposals. Thus, it is similar to the discounted cash flow method, in that it focuses on the present value of the net cash flows. However, the discounted internal rate of return method starts with the net cash flows and, in a sense, works backwards to determine the discounted rate of return expected from the proposal. The discounted cash flow method requires management to specify a minimum rate of return, which is then used to determine the excess (deficiency) of the present value of the net cash flow over the investment.

To illustrate the use of the discounted internal rate of return method, assume that management is evaluating a proposal to acquire equipment costing $33,530, which is expected to provide annual net cash flows of $10,000 per year for 5 years. If a rate of return of 12% is assumed, the present value of the net cash flows can be computed using the present value of $1 table on page 450, as follows:

Year	Present Value of $1 at 12%	Net Cash Flow	Present Value of Net Cash Flow
1	.893	$10,000	$ 8,930
2	.797	10,000	7,970
3	.712	10,000	7,120
4	.636	10,000	6,360
5	.567	10,000	5,670
Total		$50,000	$36,050

Since the present value of the net cash flow based on a 12% rate of return, $36,050, is greater than the $33,530 to be invested, 12% is obviously not the discounted internal rate of return. The following analysis indicates that 15% is the rate of return that equates the $33,530 cost of the investment with the present value of the net cash flows.

Year	Present Value of $1 at 15%	Net Cash Flow	Present Value of Net Cash Flow
1	.870	$10,000	$ 8,700
2	.756	10,000	7,560
3	.658	10,000	6,580
4	.572	10,000	5,720
5	.497	10,000	4,970
Total		$50,000	$33,530

In the illustration, the discounted internal rate of return was determined by trial and error. A rate of 12% was assumed before the discounted internal rate of return of 15% was identified. Such procedures are tedious and time consuming. When equal annual net cash flows are expected from a proposal, as in the illustration, the computations can be simplified by using a table of the present value of an annuity.[2]

---

[2]In the illustration, equal annual net cash flows are assumed, so that attention can be focused on the basic concepts. If the annual net cash flows are not equal, the procedures are more complex, but the basic concepts are not affected. In such cases, computers can be used to perform the computations.

A series of equal cash flows at fixed intervals is termed an **annuity.** The **present value of an annuity** is the sum of the present values of each cash flow. From another point of view, the present value of an annuity is the amount of cash that would be needed today to yield a series of equal cash flows at fixed intervals in the future. For example, reference to the following table of the present value of an annuity of $1 shows that the present value of cash flows at the end of each of five years, with a discounted internal rate of return of 15% per year, is 3.353. Multiplication of $10,000 by 3.353 yields the same amount ($33,530) that was determined in the preceding illustration by five successive multiplications.

Year	6%	10%	12%	15%	20%
1	.943	.909	.893	.870	.833
2	1.833	1.736	1.690	1.626	1.528
3	2.673	2.487	2.402	2.283	2.106
4	3.465	3.170	3.037	2.855	2.589
5	4.212	3.791	3.605	3.353	2.991
6	4.917	4.355	4.111	3.785	3.326
7	5.582	4.868	4.564	4.160	3.605
8	6.210	5.335	4.968	4.487	3.837
9	6.802	5.759	5.328	4.772	4.031
10	7.360	6.145	5.650	5.019	4.192

· · · · · · · · · ·
Present Value of an Annuity of $1 at Compound Interest

The procedures for using the present value of an annuity of $1 table to determine the discounted internal rate of return are as follows:

1. A present value factor for an annuity of $1 is determined by dividing the amount to be invested by the annual net cash flow, as expressed in the following formula:

$$\text{Present Value Factor for an Annuity of \$1} = \frac{\text{Amount To Be Invested}}{\text{Annual Net Cash Flow}}$$

2. The present value factor determined in (1) is located in the present value of an annuity of $1 table by first locating the number of years of expected useful life of the investment in the Year column and then proceeding horizontally across the table until the present value factor determined in (1) is found.
3. The discounted internal rate of return is then identified by the heading of the column in which the present value factor in (2) is located.

To illustrate the use of the present value of an annuity of $1 table, assume that management is considering a proposal to acquire equipment costing $97,360, which is expected to provide equal annual net cash flows of $20,000 for 7 years. The present value factor for an annuity of $1 is 4.868, computed as follows:

$$\text{Present Value Factor for an Annuity of \$1} = \frac{\text{Amount To Be Invested}}{\text{Annual Net Cash Flow}}$$

$$\text{Present Value Factor for an Annuity of \$1} = \frac{\$97,360}{\$20,000}$$

$$\text{Present Value Factor for an Annuity of \$1} = 4.868$$

For a period of 7 years, the following table for the present value of an annuity of $1 indicates that the factor 4.868 is associated with a percentage of 10%. Thus, 10% is the discounted internal rate of return for this proposal.

. . . .

Present Value of an Annuity of $1 at Compound Interest

Year	6%	10%	12%
1	.943	.909	.893
2	1.833	1.736	1.690
3	2.673	2.487	2.402
4	3.465	3.170	3.037
5	4.212	3.791	3.605
6	4.917	4.355	4.111
7	5.582	4.868	4.564
8	6.210	5.335	4.968
9	6.802	5.759	5.328
10	7.360	6.145	5.650

If the minimum acceptable rate of return for similar proposals is 10% or less, then the proposed equipment acquisition should be considered desirable. When several proposals are under consideration, management often ranks the proposals by their discounted internal rates of return, and the proposal with the highest rate is considered the most attractive.

The primary advantage of the discounted internal rate of return method is that the present values of the net cash flows over the entire useful life of the proposal are considered. An additional advantage of the method is that by determining a rate of return for each proposal, all proposals are automatically placed on a common basis for comparison, without the need to compute a present value index as was the case for the discounted cash flow method. The primary disadvantage of the discounted internal rate of return method is that the computations are somewhat more complex than for some of the other methods. In addition, like the discounted cash flow method, this method assumes that the cash received from a proposal during its useful life will be reinvested at the discounted internal rate of return. Because of changing economic conditions, this assumption may not always be reasonable.

The Discounted Internal Rate of Return Method — An Application Using the Microcomputer

The complexity of using the present value methods of evaluating capital investment proposals can be significantly reduced by using a microcomputer. The following computer pro- gram, which was written in the BASIC pro- gramming language, computes the discounted internal rate of return for an investment pro- posal with a series of equal net cash flows.

```
10   INPUT "periods";N: INPUT "investment";I: INPUT "annual net cash flow";C
20   INPUT "guess";G
30   X=(X+G)/100+1:S=I
40   FOR J=1 TO N:S=S+C/X^J:NEXT:X=(X-1)*100
50   IF ABS(Y-X)<=.001 THEN END
60   LPRINT X:Y=X:RESTORE:IF S>0 THEN 30
70   X=X-G:G=G/3:GOTO 30
```

To run this program, the user must have access to the BASIC programming system. The manual accompanying this system will describe the procedures for calling up the system and entering, saving, loading, and running a pro- gram. In using the above program, the program steps must be keyboarded exactly as shown. When the program is run, the user will be required to input (1) the number of periods for which the proposed capital investment will yield annual cash inflows, (2) the cost of the invest- ment expressed as a negative initial cash flow, (3) the annual net cash flows, and (4) an initial guess as to the approximate discounted internal rate of return. The initial guess does not neces- sarily have to be close to the true value, since the computer will estimate the true value regardless of the accuracy of the initial guess. The initial guess only adds efficiency to the estimation process. An example of the use of this com- puter program for the illustration presented on pages 453–454 is as follows:

```
periods? 7
investment? -97360
annual net cash flow? 20000
guess? 15
   15
   4.999995
   9.999991
   14.99999
   11.66666
   10.55554
   10.18517
   10.06172
   10.02057
   10.00685
   10.00227
   10.00456
   10.00303
```

The program will stop computing the esti- mated discounted internal rate of return when successive estimates are reasonably close to one another and additional precision is not war- ranted. In the above example, the approximate discounted internal rate of return is 10%. Note that the difference between the above estimate and the illustration in the text is due to rounding within the computer program.

Note: This program was written for the BASIC programming language using the IBM personal computer.

FACTORS THAT COMPLICATE CAPITAL INVESTMENT ANALYSIS

In the preceding paragraphs, the basic concepts for four widely used methods of evaluating capital investment proposals were discussed. In practice, additional factors may have an impact on a capital investment decision. Some of the most important of these factors, which are described in the following paragraphs, are the federal income tax, the unequal lives of alternate proposals, the leasing alternative, uncertainty, and changes in price levels.

Income Tax

In many cases, the impact of the federal income tax on capital investment decisions can be significant. One provision of the Internal Revenue Code (IRC) which should be considered in capital investment analysis is the allowable deduction for depreciation expense.

For determining **depreciation,** or the *cost recovery deduction,* which is the expensing of the cost of plant assets over their useful lives, the IRC specifies the use of the **Accelerated Cost Recovery System (ACRS). Modified ACRS (MACRS),** under the Tax Reform Act of 1986, provides for eight classes of useful lives for plant assets acquired after 1986. The two most common classes for assets other than real estate are the 5-year class and the 7-year class.[3] The 5-year class includes automobiles and light-duty trucks, and the 7-year class includes most machinery and equipment. Depreciation for these two classes approximates the use of the 200-percent declining-balance method.

The Internal Revenue Service has prescribed methods that result in annual percentages to be used in determining depreciation for each class. In using these rates, salvage value is ignored, and all plant assets are assumed to be placed in service in the middle of the year and taken out of service in the middle of the year. For the 5-year-class assets, for example, depreciation is spread over six years; for the 7-year-class assets, depreciation is spread over eight years, as shown in the following schedule of MACRS depreciation rates:

MACRS Depreciation Rate Schedule

Year	5-Year-Class Depreciation Rates	7-Year-Class Depreciation Rates
1	20.0%	14.3%
2	32.0	24.5
3	19.2	17.5
4	11.5	12.5
5	11.5	8.9
6	5.8	8.9
7		8.9
8		4.5
	100.0%	100.0%

MACRS simplifies depreciation accounting by eliminating the need to estimate useful life and salvage value and to decide on a depreciation method.

---

[3]Real estate is classified into 27½-year classes and 31½-year classes and is depreciated by the straight-line method.

Although a short-run tax saving can usually be realized by using the regular MACRS cost recovery allowance, a taxpayer may elect to use a straight-line deduction based on the property classes prescribed under MACRS. The accelerated write-off of depreciable assets provided by MACRS does not, however, effect a long-run net saving in income tax. The tax reduction of the early years of use is offset by higher taxes as the annual cost recovery allowance diminishes.

To illustrate the potential impact of MACRS depreciation on capital investment decisions, assume that Sierra Company is using the discounted cash flow method in evaluating a proposal.[4] The cost of the investment acquired in year 1 is $300,000, with an expected useful life of 5 years, no residual value, and a minimum desired rate of return of 12%. If Sierra Company elects the straight-line method of depreciation, the IRC requires one half of a full year's depreciation to be taken in the first year and one half of a full year's depreciation to be taken in the sixth year. Thus, Sierra Company would deduct the following depreciation amounts during the 5-year life of the asset:

	Depreciation Expense
First year........................	$30,000 [($300,000 ÷ 5) × 1/2]
Second year	$60,000 ($300,000 ÷ 5)
Third year.......................	$60,000 ($300,000 ÷ 5)
Fourth year......................	$60,000 ($300,000 ÷ 5)
Fifth year........................	$60,000 ($300,000 ÷ 5)
Sixth year	$30,000 [($300,000 ÷ 5) × 1/2]

During the six years in which depreciation expense is deducted, the investment is expected to yield annual operating income, before depreciation and income taxes, of $120,000, $100,000, $90,000, $70,000, $60,000, and $30,000, respectively. To simplify the illustration, all revenues and operating expenses except depreciation represent current period cash flows. If the income tax rate is 34%, the annual net aftertax cash flows from acquisition of the asset are as follows:

	Year					
	1	*2*	*3*	*4*	*5*	*6*
Net cash flow before income taxes	$120,000	$100,000	$90,000	$70,000	$60,000	$30,000
Income tax expense*..................	30,600	13,600	10,200	3,400	0	0
Net cash flow	$ 89,400	$ 86,400	$79,800	$66,600	$60,000	$30,000
*Income tax expense:						
Operating income before depreciation and income taxes..................	$120,000	$100,000	$90,000	$70,000	$60,000	$30,000
Depreciation expense	30,000	60,000	60,000	60,000	60,000	30,000
Income before income taxes	$ 90,000	$ 40,000	$30,000	$10,000	0	0
Income tax rate	34%	34%	34%	34%	0	0
Income tax expense	$ 30,600	$ 13,600	$10,200	$ 3,400	0	0

[4]The same general impact of depreciation on capital investment decisions would occur, regardless of which of the four capital investment evaluation methods was used. To simplify the discussion in this chapter, only the discounted cash flow method is illustrated.

Based on the preceding data and using the discounted cash flow method, a $2,899 deficiency of the present value over the amount to be invested is computed as follows:

Year	Present Value of 1 at 12%	Net Cash Flow	Present Value of Net Cash Flow
1	.893	$ 89,400	$ 79,834
2	.797	86,400	68,861
3	.712	79,800	56,818
4	.636	66,600	42,358
5	.567	60,000	34,020
6	.507	30,000	15,210
Total..........................		$412,200	$297,101
Amount to be invested......................................			300,000
Deficiency of present value over amount to be invested			$ 2,899

Because the discounted cash flow method indicates that there is a deficiency of the present value over the amount to be invested, the decision would be to reject the proposal. However, if the accelerated depreciation provided by the IRC is used, the present value of the acquisition changes significantly and might lead to a different decision. To illustrate, assume that Sierra Company is permitted to deduct depreciation over a 5-year period, beginning with the year the asset is acquired. Using the MACRS percentages shown on page 456, the depreciation for Sierra Company will be as follows:

	Depreciation Expense
First year	$60,000 ($300,000 × 20.0%)
Second year......................	$96,000 ($300,000 × 32.0%)
Third year........................	$57,600 ($300,000 × 19.2%)
Fourth year.......................	$34,500 ($300,000 × 11.5%)
Fifth year	$34,500 ($300,000 × 11.5%)
Sixth year........................	$17,400 ($300,000 × 5.8%)

The annual aftertax net cash flows from the acquisition of the plant asset, including the effect of MACRS depreciation, are as follows:

	Year					
	1	2	3	4	5	6
Net cash flow before income taxes	$120,000	$100,000	$90,000	$70,000	$60,000	$30,000
Income tax expense*...................	20,400	1,360	11,016	12,070	8,670	4,284
Net cash flow	$ 99,600	$ 98,640	$78,984	$57,930	$51,330	$25,716
*Income tax expense:						
Operating income before depreciation and income taxes.................	$120,000	$100,000	$90,000	$70,000	$60,000	$30,000
Depreciation expense	60,000	96,000	57,600	34,500	34,500	17,400
Income before income taxes	$ 60,000	$ 4,000	$32,400	$35,500	$25,500	$12,600
Income tax rate......................	34%	34%	34%	34%	34%	34%
Income tax expense	$ 20,400	$ 1,360	$11,016	$12,070	$ 8,670	$ 4,284

Based on the preceding data and using the discounted cash flow method, a $2,781 excess of the present value over the amount to be invested is computed as follows:

Year	Present Value of 1 at 12%	Net Cash Flow	Present Value of Net Cash Flow
1	.893	$ 99,600	$ 88,943
2	.797	98,640	78,616
3	.712	78,984	56,237
4	.636	57,930	36,843
5	.567	51,330	29,104
6	.507	25,716	13,038
Total		$412,200	$302,781
Amount to be invested			300,000
Excess of present value over amount to be invested................			$ 2,781

The specific dollar effects of tax considerations on the evaluation of capital investment proposals will depend on the deductions and credits allowed by the Internal Revenue Code at the time the capital investment decision is to be made. In this illustration, the discounted cash flow analysis indicates an excess of the present value over the amount to be invested, and the decision would be to invest in the asset.

Unequal Proposal Lives

In the preceding sections, the discussion of the methods of analyzing capital investment proposals was based on the assumption that alternate proposals had the same useful lives. In practice, however, alternate proposals may have unequal lives. In such cases, the proposals must be made comparable. One widely used method is to adjust the lives of projects with the longest lives to a time period that is equal to the life of the project with the shortest life. In this manner, the useful lives of all proposals are made equal. To illustrate, assume that the discounted cash flow method is being used to compare the following two proposals, each of which has an initial investment of $100,000:

	Net Cash Flows	
Year	Proposal X	Proposal Y
1	$30,000	$30,000
2	30,000	30,000
3	25,000	30,000
4	20,000	30,000
5	15,000	30,000
6	15,000	—
7	10,000	—
8	10,000	—

If the desired rate of return is 10%, the proposals have an excess of present value over the amount to be invested, as follows:

Proposal X

Year	Present Value of 1 at 10%	Net Cash Flow	Present Value of Net Cash Flow
1	.909	$ 30,000	$ 27,270
2	.826	30,000	24,780
3	.751	25,000	18,775
4	.683	20,000	13,660
5	.621	15,000	9,315
6	.564	15,000	8,460
7	.513	10,000	5,130
8	.467	10,000	4,670
Total		$155,000	$112,060

Amount to be invested 100,000

Excess of present value over amount to be invested . . . . . $ 12,060

Proposal Y

Year	Present Value of 1 at 10%	Net Cash Flow	Present Value of Net Cash Flow
1	.909	$ 30,000	$ 27,270
2	.826	30,000	24,780
3	.751	30,000	22,530
4	.683	30,000	20,490
5	.621	30,000	18,630
Total		$150,000	$113,700

Amount to be invested 100,000

Excess of present value over amount to be invested . . . . . $ 13,700

The two proposals cannot be compared by focusing on the amount of the excess of the present value over the amount to be invested, because Proposal Y has a life of 5 years while Proposal X has a life of 8 years. Proposal X can be adjusted to a 5-year life by assuming that it is to be terminated at the end of 5 years and the asset sold. This assumption requires that the residual value be estimated at the end of 5 years and that this value be considered a cash flow at that date. Both proposals will then cover 5 years, and the results of the discounted cash flow analysis can be used to compare the relative attractiveness of the two proposals. For example, assume that Proposal X has an estimated residual value at the end of year 5 of $40,000. For Proposal X, the excess of the present value over the amount to be invested is $18,640 for a 5-year life, as follows:

Proposal X

Year	Present Value of 1 at 10%	Net Cash Flow	Present Value of Net Cash Flow
1	.909	$ 30,000	$ 27,270
2	.826	30,000	24,780
3	.751	25,000	18,775
4	.683	20,000	13,660
5	.621	15,000	9,315
5 (Residual value)	.621	40,000	24,840
Total		$160,000	$118,640

Amount to be invested 100,000

Excess of present value over amount to be invested..... $ 18,640

Since the present value over the amount to be invested for Proposal X exceeds that for Proposal Y by $4,940 ($18,640 − $13,700), Proposal X may be viewed as the more attractive of the two proposals.

Lease Versus Capital Investment

Leasing of plant assets has become common in many industries in recent years. Leasing allows an enterprise to acquire the use of plant assets without the necessity of using large amounts of cash to purchase them. In addition, if management believes that a plant asset has a high degree of risk of becoming obsolete before the end of its useful life, then leasing rather than purchasing the asset may be more attractive. By leasing the asset, management reduces the risk of suffering a loss due to obsolescence. Finally, the Internal Revenue Code provisions which allow the lessor (the owner of the asset) to pass tax deductions on to the lessee (the party leasing the asset) have increased the popularity of leasing in recent years. For example, a company that leases for its use a $200,000 plant asset with a life of 8 years for $50,000 per year is permitted to deduct the annual lease payments of $50,000.

In many cases, before a final decision is made, management should consider the possibility of leasing assets instead of purchasing them. Ordinarily, leasing assets is more costly than purchasing because the lessor must include in the rental price not only the costs associated with owning the assets but also a profit. Nevertheless, using the methods of evaluating capital investment proposals, management should consider whether or not the profitability and cash flows from the lease alternative with its risks compares favorably to the profitability and cash flows from the purchase alternative with its risks.

Uncertainty

All capital investment analyses rely on factors that are uncertain; that is, the accuracy of the estimates involved, including estimates of expected revenues, expenses, and cash flows, are uncertain. Although the estimates are subject to varying degrees of risk or uncertainty, the long-term nature of capital investments suggests that many of the estimates are likely to involve considerable uncertainty. Errors in one or more of the estimates could lead to unwise decisions.

Because of the importance of capital investment decisions, management should be aware of the potential impact of uncertainty on their decisions. Some techniques that can be used to assist management in evaluating the effects of uncertainties on capital investment proposals are presented in Chapter 14.

Changes in Price Levels

The past three decades, which have been characterized by increasing price levels, are described as periods of **inflation.** In recent years, the rates of inflation have fluctuated widely, making the estimation of future revenues, expenses, and cash flows more difficult. Therefore, management should consider the expected future price levels and their likely effect on the estimates used in capital investment analyses. Fluctuations in the price levels assumed could significantly affect the analyses.

CAPITAL RATIONING

Capital rationing refers to the process by which management allocates available investment funds among competing capital investment proposals. Generally, management will use various combinations of the evaluation methods described in this chapter in developing an effective approach to capital rationing.

In capital rationing, an initial screening of alternative proposals is usually performed by establishing minimum standards for the cash payback and the average rate of return methods. The proposals that survive this initial screening are subjected to the more rigorous discounted cash flow and discounted internal rate of return methods of analysis. The proposals that survive this final screening are evaluated in terms of nonfinancial factors, such as employee morale. For example, the acquisition of new, more efficient equipment which eliminates several jobs could lower employee morale to a level that could decrease overall plant productivity.

The final step in the capital rationing process is a ranking of the proposals and a comparison of proposals with the funds available to determine which proposals will be funded. The unfunded proposals are reconsidered if funds subsequently become available. The flowchart on page 463 portrays the capital rationing decision process.

CAPITAL EXPENDITURES BUDGET

Once capital investment expenditures for a period have been approved, a **capital expenditures budget** should be prepared and procedures should be

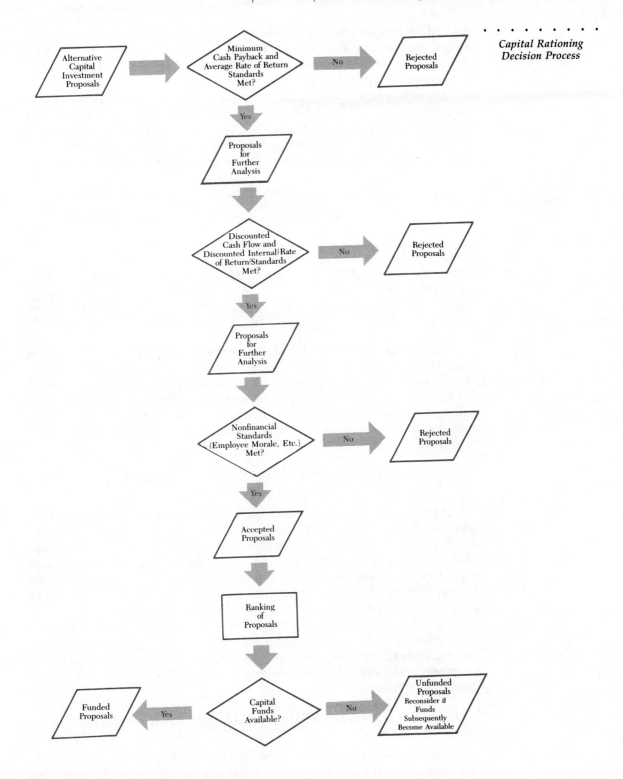

Capital Rationing
Decision Process

established for controlling the expenditures. After the assets are placed in service, the actual results of operations should be compared to the initial projected results to determine whether the capital expenditures are meeting management's expectations.

The capital expenditures budget facilitates the planning of operations and the financing of capital expenditures. A capital expenditures budget, which is integrated with the master budget as discussed in Chapter 8, summarizes acquisition decisions for a period typically ranging from one to five years. The following capital expenditures budget was prepared for Sealy Company:

Capital Expenditures Budget

Sealy Company
Capital Expenditures Budget
For Five Years Ending December 31, 1992

Item	1988	1989	1990	1991	1992
Machinery—Department A...	$240,000	—	—	$168,000	$216,000
Machinery—Department B...	108,000	$156,000	$336,000	120,000	—
Delivery equipment..........	—	54,000	—	—	36,000
Total....................	$348,000	$210,000	$336,000	$288,000	$252,000

The capital expenditures budget does not authorize the acquisition of plant assets. Rather, it serves as a planning device to determine the effects of the capital expenditures on operations after management has evaluated the alternative proposals, using the methods described in this chapter. Final authority for capital expenditures must come from the proper level of management. In some corporations, large capital expenditures must be approved by the board of directors.

CONTROL OF CAPITAL EXPENDITURES

Once the capital expenditures have been approved, control must be established over the costs of acquiring the assets, including the costs of installation and testing before the assets are placed in service. Throughout this period of acquiring the assets and readying them for use, actual costs should be compared to planned (budgeted) costs. Timely reports should be prepared, so that management can take corrective actions as quickly as possible and thereby minimize cost overruns and operating delays.

After the assets have been placed in service, attention should be focused on comparisons of actual operating expenses with budgeted operating expenses. Such comparisons provide opportunities for management to follow up on successful expenditures or to terminate or otherwise attempt to salvage failing expenditures.

USE OF COMPUTERS IN CAPITAL INVESTMENT ANALYSIS

Some of the computations for the capital investment evaluation methods discussed in this chapter can become rather complex. By use of the computer, the calculations can be performed easily and quickly. The most important use of the computer, however, is in developing various models which indicate the effect of changes in key factors on the results of capital investment proposals. For example, the effect of various potential changes in future price levels on a proposal could be simulated and the results presented to management for its use in decision making.

Chapter Review

KEY POINTS

1. Nature of Capital Investment Analysis.

The process by which management plans, evaluates, and controls investments involving property, plant, and equipment is called capital investment analysis. A capital investment program should include a plan for encouraging employees at all levels of an enterprise to submit proposals for capital investments. All reasonable proposals should be given serious consideration, and the effects of the economic implications expected from these proposals should be identified.

2. Methods of Evaluating Capital Investment Proposals.

The methods of evaluating capital investment proposals can be grouped into two general categories: (1) methods that ignore present value and (2) present value methods. The methods that ignore present value include (1) the average rate of return method and (2) the cash payback method. Methods that use present values in evaluating capital investment proposals are (1) the discounted cash flow method and (2) the discounted internal rate of return method.

The expected average rate of return is a measure of the expected profitability of an investment in plant assets. When several alternative capital investment proposals are being considered, the proposals can be ranked by their average rates of return. The higher the average rate of return, the more desirable the proposal. The primary advantage of the average rate of return method is its simplicity, and its primary disadvantage is its lack of consideration of expected cash flows from a proposal and the timing of those cash flows.

The cash payback method measures the cash payback period, which is the expected period of time that will pass between the date of a capital investment and the complete recovery in cash (or equivalent) of the amount invested. The cash payback method is especially useful to managers whose primary concern is liquidity. The primary disadvantage of the cash payback method is its failure to take into consideration the expected profitability of a proposal. Another disadvantage of the cash payback method is that the cash flows occurring after the payback period are ignored.

The discounted cash flow method uses present value concepts to compute the present value of the cash flows expected from a proposal. When several alternative investment proposals of the same amount are being considered, the one with the largest excess of present value over the amount to be invested is the most desirable. If the alternative proposals involve different amounts of investment, it is useful to prepare a ranking of the proposals by using a present value index. The primary advantage of the discounted cash flow method is that it gives consideration to the time value of money. A disadvantage of the method is that the computations are more complex than those for the methods that ignore present value. In addition, it assumes that the cash received from the proposal during its useful life will be reinvested at the rate of return used to compute the present value of the proposal.

The discounted internal rate of return method uses present value concepts to compute the rate of return from the net cash flows expected from capital investment proposals. When several proposals are under consideration, management often ranks proposals by their discounted internal rates of return, and the proposal with the highest rate is considered the most attractive. The primary advantage of the discounted internal rate of return method is that the present values of the net cash flows over the entire useful life of the proposal are considered. The primary disadvantage of the discounted internal rate of return method is that the computations are somewhat more complex than for some of the other methods. In addition, like the discounted cash flow method, this method assumes that the cash received from a proposal during its useful life will be reinvested at the discounted internal rate of return.

3. Factors that Complicate Capital Investment Analysis.

Factors that may complicate capital investment analysis include the impact of the federal income tax, unequal lives of alternative proposals, the leasing alternative, uncertainty, and changes in price levels.

4. Capital Rationing.

Capital rationing refers to the process by which management allocates available investment funds among competing capital investment proposals. In capital rationing, an initial screening of alternative proposals is usually performed by establishing minimum standards for the cash payback and the average rate of return methods. The final step in the capital rationing process is a ranking of the proposals and a comparison of proposals with the funds available to determine which proposals will be funded.

5. Capital Expenditures Budget.

Once capital investment expenditures for a period have been approved, a capital expenditures budget should be prepared and procedures should be established for controlling the expenditures.

6. Control of Capital Expenditures.

Throughout the period of acquiring plant assets and readying them for use, actual costs should be compared to planned costs, and timely reports should be prepared, so that management can minimize cost overruns and operating delays.

7. Use of Computers in Capital Investment Analysis.
Some of the computations for the capital investment evaluation methods can become complex. By the use of the computer, the calculations can be performed easily and quickly. In addition, the computer can be used in developing various models which indicate the effect of changes in key factors on the results of capital investment proposals.

KEY TERMS

capital investment analysis 445
average rate of return 446
cash payback period 448
present value 449
discounted cash flow method 449
present value index 450
discounted internal rate of
   return method 451

annuity 453
present value of an annuity 453
Modified Accelerated Cost Recovery
   System (MACRS) 456
inflation 462
capital rationing 462
capital expenditures budget 462

SELF-EXAMINATION QUESTIONS

(Answers at End of Chapter)

1. Methods of evaluating capital investment proposals that ignore present value include:
   A. average rate of return   C. both A and B
   B. cash payback   D. neither A nor B

2. Management is considering a $100,000 investment in a project with a 5-year life and no residual value. If the total income from the project is expected to be $60,000 and recognition is given to the effect of straight-line depreciation on the investment, the average rate of return is:
   A. 12%   C. 60%
   B. 24%   D. none of the above

3. As used in the analysis of proposed capital investments, the expected period of time that will elapse between the date of a capital investment and the complete recovery of the amount of cash invested is called:
   A. the average rate of return period C. the discounted cash flow period
   B. the cash payback period   D. none of the above

4. Which method of analyzing capital investment proposals determines the total present value of the cash flows expected from the investment and compares this value with the amount to be invested?
   A. Average rate of return
   B. Cash payback
   C. Discounted cash flow
   D. Discounted internal rate of return

5. The process by which management allocates available investment funds among competing capital investment proposals is referred to as:
   A. capital rationing
   B. capital expenditure budgeting
   C. leasing
   D. none of the above

ILLUSTRATIVE PROBLEM

The capital investment committee of Bormann Company is currently considering two projects. The estimated operating income and net cash flows expected from each project are as follows:

	Project A		Project B	
Year	Operating Income	Net Cash Flow	Operating Income	Net Cash Flow
1	$ 9,000	$19,000	$ 5,000	$15,000
2	7,000	17,000	6,000	16,000
3	6,000	16,000	8,000	18,000
4	5,000	15,000	7,000	17,000
5	3,000	13,000	4,000	14,000
	$30,000	$80,000	$30,000	$80,000

Each project requires an investment of $50,000. Straight-line depreciation will be used, and no residual value is expected. The committee has selected a rate of 15% for purposes of the discounted cash flow analysis.

Instructions:

1. Compute the following:
   a. The average rate of return for each project, giving effect to depreciation on the investment.
   b. The excess or deficiency of present value over the amount to be invested, as determined by the discounted cash flow method for each project. Use the present value of $1 table appearing in this chapter.
2. Prepare a brief report for the capital investment committee, advising it on the relative merits of the two projects.

SOLUTION

(1) (a) Average annual rate of return for both projects:

$$\frac{\$30,000 \div 5}{(\$50,000 + \$0) \div 2} = 24\%$$

(b) Discounted cash flow analysis:

Year	Present Value of 1 at 15%	Net Cash Flow Project A	Net Cash Flow Project B	Present Value of Net Cash Flow Project A	Present Value of Net Cash Flow Project B
1	.870	$19,000	$15,000	$16,530	$13,050
2	.756	17,000	16,000	12,852	12,096
3	.658	16,000	18,000	10,528	11,844
4	.572	15,000	17,000	8,580	9,724
5	.497	13,000	14,000	6,461	6,958
Total		$80,000	$80,000	$54,951	$53,672
Amount to be invested..................				50,000	50,000
Excess of present value over amount to be invested				$ 4,951	$ 3,672

(2) (a) Both projects offer the same average annual rate of return.
    (b) Although both projects exceed the selected rate established for dis-counted cash flows, Project A offers a larger excess of present value over the amount to be invested. Thus, if only one of the two projects can be accepted, Project A would be the more attractive.

Discussion Questions

13–1. Which two methods of capital investment analysis ignore present value?

13–2. Which two methods of capital investment analysis can be described as present value methods?

13–3. What is the "time value of money" concept?

13–4. (a) How is the average rate of return computed for capital investment analysis, assuming that consideration is given to the effect of straight-line depreciation on the amount of the investment? (b) If the amount of an 8-year investment is $100,000, the straight-line method of depreciation is used, there is no residual value, and the total income expected from the investment is $140,000, what is the average rate of return?

13–5. What are the principal objections to the use of the average rate of return method in evaluating capital investment proposals?

13–6. (a) As used in analyses of proposed capital investments, what is the cash payback period? (b) Discuss the principal limitations of the cash payback method for evaluating capital investment proposals.

13–7. What is the present value of $6,720 to be received one year from today, assuming an earnings rate of 12%?

13–8. Which method of evaluating capital investment proposals reduces their expected future net cash flows to present values and compares the total present values to the amount of the investment?

13–9. A discounted cash flow analysis used to evaluate a proposed equipment acquisition indicated an $18,000 excess of present value over the amount to be invested. What is the meaning of the $18,000 as it relates to the desirability of the proposal?

13–10. How is the present value index for a proposal determined?

13–11. What are the major disadvantages of the use of the discounted cash flow method of analyzing capital investment proposals?

13–12. What is an annuity?

13–13. What are the major disadvantages of the use of the discounted internal rate of return method of analyzing capital investment proposals?

13–14. What provision of the Internal Revenue Code is especially important for consideration in analyzing capital investment proposals?

13–15. What method can be used to place two capital investment proposals with unequal useful lives on a comparable basis?

13–16. What are the major advantages of leasing a plant asset rather than purchasing it?

13–17. What is capital rationing?

13–18. Which budget summarizes the acquisition decisions for a period?

13–19. Real World Focus. Boston Metal Products, a small manufacturer in Medford, Mass., was considering the purchase of a robot. The company controller was asked to calculate whether the $200,000 investment made financial sense. Using traditional accounting techniques, the controller concluded that the investment did not meet the financial criteria that had been established. However, the company went ahead and made the investment. What qualitative techniques could Boston Metal Products have used to justify the capital investment in a robot?

Exercises

13–20. **Average rate of return.** The following data are accumulated by Frantz Company in evaluating two competing capital investment proposals:

	Proposal E	Proposal F
Amount of investment.....................	$450,000	$180,000
Useful life	6 years	8 years
Estimated residual value	-0-	-0-
Estimated total income....................	$243,000	$108,000

Determine the expected average rate of return for each proposal, giving effect to straight-line depreciation on each investment.

13–21.   Cash payback period. Burke Company is evaluating two capital investment proposals, each requiring an investment of $150,000 and each with an 8-year life and expected total net cash flows of $240,000. Proposal 1 is expected to provide equal annual net cash flows of $30,000, and Proposal 2 is expected to have the following unequal annual net cash flows:

Year 1...............	$60,000
Year 2...............	50,000
Year 3...............	40,000
Year 4...............	20,000
Year 5...............	20,000
Year 6...............	20,000
Year 7...............	20,000
Year 8...............	10,000

Determine the cash payback period for both proposals.

13–22.   Discounted cash flow method. The following data are accumulated by Auerbach Company in evaluating the purchase of $120,000 of equipment having a 4-year useful life:

	Net Income	Net Cash Flow
Year 1	$25,000	$55,000
Year 2..................	10,000	40,000
Year 3..................	6,000	36,000
Year 4..................	4,000	34,000

(a) Assuming that the desired rate of return is 12%, determine the excess (deficiency) of present value over the amount to be invested for the proposal. Use the table of the present value of $1 appearing in this chapter. (b) Would management be likely to look with favor on the proposal? Explain.

13–23.   Present value index. Grayson Company has computed the excess of present value over the amount to be invested for capital expenditure proposals P and Q, using the discounted cash flow method. Relevant data related to the computation are as follows:

	Proposal P	Proposal Q
Total present value of net cash flow....................	$318,000	$441,000
Amount to be invested	300,000	420,000
Excess of present value over amount to be invested.....	$ 18,000	$ 21,000

Determine the present value index for each proposal.

13–24. Average rate of return, cash payback period, discounted cash flow method. Linston Company is considering the acquisition of machinery at a cost of $400,000. The machinery has an estimated life of 5 years and no residual value. It is expected to provide yearly income of $40,000 and yearly net cash flows of $120,000. The company's minimum desired rate of return for discounted cash flow analysis is 10%. Compute the following:

(a) The average rate of return, giving effect to straight-line depreciation on the investment.
(b) The cash payback period.
(c) The excess (deficiency) of present value over the amount to be invested, as determined by the discounted cash flow method. Use the table of the present value of $1 appearing in this chapter.

13–25. Discounted internal rate of return method. The discounted internal rate of return method is used by Ramsey Company in analyzing a capital expenditure proposal that involves an investment of $342,600 and annual net cash flows of $120,000 for each of the 4 years of useful life. (a) Determine a "present value factor for an annuity of $1" which can be used in determining the discounted internal rate of return. (b) Using the factor determined in (a) and the present value of an annuity of $1 table appearing in this chapter, determine the discounted internal rate of return for the proposal.

13–26. Discounted cash flow method and discounted internal rate of return method. Emerson Inc. is evaluating a proposed expenditure of $121,480 on a 4-year project whose estimated net cash flows are $40,000 for each of the four years.
   (a) Compute the excess (deficiency) of present value over the amount to be invested, using the discounted cash flow method and an assumed rate of return of 15%. (b) Based on the analysis prepared in (a), is the rate of return (1) more than 15%, (2) 15%, or (3) less than 15%? Explain. (c) Determine the discounted internal rate of return by computing a "present value factor for an annuity of $1" and using the table of the present value of an annuity of $1 presented in the text.

Problems
·

13–27. Average rate of return method, discounted cash flow method, and analysis. The capital investments budget committee is considering two projects. The estimated operating income and net cash flows from each project are as follows:

	Project G		Project H	
Year	Operating Income	Net Cash Flow	Operating Income	Net Cash Flow
1	$15,000	$ 39,000	$ 7,000	$ 31,000
2	10,000	34,000	9,000	33,000
3	8,000	32,000	10,000	34,000
4	6,000	30,000	10,000	34,000
5	6,000	30,000	9,000	33,000
Total	$45,000	$165,000	$45,000	$165,000

Each project requires an investment of $120,000. Straight-line depreciation will be used, and no residual value is expected. The committee has selected a rate of 10% for purposes of the discounted cash flow analysis.

Instructions:

(1) Compute the following:
  (a) The average rate of return for each project, giving effect to depreciation on the investment.
  (b) The excess (deficiency) of present value over the amount to be invested, as determined by the discounted cash flow method for each project. Use the present value of $1 table appearing in this chapter.
(2) Prepare a brief report for the capital investment committee, advising it on the relative merits of the two projects.

13–28.   Cash payback period, discounted cash flow method, and analysis.
Enders Company is considering two projects. The estimated net cash flows from each project are as follows:

Year	Project L	Project M
1	$ 50,000	$200,000
2	250,000	100,000
3	100,000	100,000
4	50,000	80,000
5	50,000	20,000
Total	$500,000	$500,000

Each project requires an investment of $300,000, with no residual value expected. A rate of 20% has been selected for the discounted cash flow analysis.

Instructions:

(1) Compute the following for each project:
  (a) Cash payback period.
  (b) The excess (deficiency) of present value over the amount to be invested, as determined by the discounted cash flow method. Use the present value of $1 table appearing in this chapter.
(2) Prepare a brief report advising management on the relative merits of each of the two projects.

13–29.   Discounted cash flow method, present value index, and analysis.
Farmer Company wishes to evaluate three capital investment proposals by using the discounted cash flow method. Relevant data related to the proposals are summarized as follows:

	Proposal A	Proposal B	Proposal C
Amount to be invested........	$100,000	$100,000	$150,000
Annual net cash flows:			
Year 1....................	60,000	45,000	75,000
Year 2....................	45,000	40,000	70,000
Year 3..................	30,000	30,000	60,000

Instructions:

(1) Assuming that the desired rate of return is 15%, prepare a discounted cash flow analysis for each proposal. Use the present value of $1 table appearing in this chapter.

(2) Determine a present value index for each proposal.

(3) Which proposal offers the largest amount of present value per dollar of investment? Explain.

13–30. Discounted cash flow method, discounted internal rate of return method, and analysis. Management is considering two capital investment proposals. The estimated net cash flows from each proposal are as follows:

Year	Proposal A	Proposal B
1	$50,000	$160,000
2	50,000	160,000
3	50,000	160,000
4	50,000	160,000

Proposal A requires an investment of $129,450, while Proposal B requires an investment of $456,800. No residual value is expected from either proposal.

Instructions:

(1) Compute the following for each proposal:
   (a) The excess (deficiency) of present value over the amount to be invested, as determined by the discounted cash flow method. Use a rate of 12% and the present value of $1 table appearing in this chapter.
   (b) A present value index.

(2) Determine the discounted internal rate of return for each proposal by (a) computing a "present value factor for an annuity of $1" and (b) using the present value of an annuity of $1 table appearing in this chapter.

(3) What advantage does the discounted internal rate of return method have over the discounted cash flow method in comparing proposals?

13–31. Effect of income tax on capital investment decision. Using the discounted cash flow method, the accountant for Collins Company prepared the following analysis of a project expected to be undertaken during Year 1:

Year	Present Value of 1 at 12%	Net Cash Flow	Present Value of Net Cash Flow
1	.893	$152,000	$135,736
2	.797	136,000	108,392
3	.712	136,000	96,832
4	.636	112,000	71,232
5	.567	100,000	56,700
6	.507	50,000	25,350
Total		$686,000	$494,242

Amount to be invested	500,000
Deficiency of present value over amount to be invested	$ 5,758

A review of the analysis and related items disclosed the following:
(a) The straight-line method was used for computing depreciation, with one half of a year's depreciation taken in the first year and the sixth year.
(b) Operating income (and net cash flow) before depreciation and taxes is expected to be $220,000, $160,000, $160,000, $120,000, $100,000, and $50,000 for the first through sixth years, respectively.
(c) The income tax rate is 40%.

Instructions:

(1) Assuming the use of the straight-line depreciation method with a 5-year life and no residual value, compute the following:
(a) Amount of depreciation expense for each of the six years covered by the project.
(b) Income tax expense for each of the six years covered by the project.
(c) Net cash flow for each of the six years covered by the project. (Note: The net cash flows calculated should agree with those included in the analysis presented in the first paragraph of this problem.)
(2) Compute the following:
(a) Depreciation expense for each of the six years covered by the project, assuming that the 5-year-class MACRS depreciation rates appearing in this chapter are used.
(b) Income tax expense for each of the six years, based on the use of MACRS depreciation.
(c) Net cash flow for each of the six years covered by the project, based on the income tax expense computed in (b).
(d) The excess (deficiency) of present value over the amount to be invested, based on the net cash flows determined in (c) and as determined by the discounted cash flow method. Use the present value of 1 table appearing in this chapter and round computations to the nearest dollar.
(3) Should the project be accepted? Explain.

13–32.   Evaluation of alternative capital investment decisions. The investment committee of Beaver Company is evaluating two projects. The projects have different useful lives, but each requires an investment of $160,000. The estimated net cash flows from each project are as follows:

	Net Cash Flows	
Year	Project A	Project B
1	$45,000	$60,000
2	45,000	60,000
3	45,000	60,000
4	45,000	60,000
5	45,000	
6	45,000	

The committee has selected a rate of 15% for purposes of discounted cash flow analysis. It also estimates that the residual value at the end of each project's useful life is $0, but at the end of the fourth year, Project A's residual value would be $90,000.

Instructions:

(1) For each project, compute the excess (deficiency) of present value over the amount to be invested, as determined by the discounted cash flow method. Use the present value of 1 table appearing in this chapter. (Ignore the unequal lives of the projects.)

(2) For each project, compute the excess (deficiency) of present value over the amount to be invested, as determined by the discounted cash flow method, assuming that Project A is adjusted to a four-year life for purposes of analysis. Use the present value of 1 table appearing in this chapter.

(3) In reporting to the investment committee, what advice would you give on the relative merits of the two projects?

ALTERNATE PROBLEMS

13–27A.   Average rate of return method, discounted cash flow method, and analysis.   The capital investments budget committee is considering two projects. The estimated operating income and net cash flows from each project are shown as follows:

| | Project J | | Project K | |
Year	Operating Income	Net Cash Flow	Operating Income	Net Cash Flow
1	$ 25,000	$ 75,000	$ 40,000	$ 90,000
2	25,000	75,000	30,000	80,000
3	25,000	75,000	20,000	70,000
4	15,000	65,000	6,000	56,000
5	10,000	60,000	4,000	54,000
Total	$100,000	$350,000	$100,000	$350,000

Each project requires an investment of $250,000. Straight-line depreciation will be used, and no residual value is expected. The committee has selected a rate of 12% for purposes of the discounted cash flow analysis.

Instructions:

(1) Compute the following:
   (a) The average rate of return for each project, giving effect to depreciation on the investment.
   (b) The excess (deficiency) of present value over the amount to be invested, as determined by the discounted cash flow method for each project. Use the present value of $1 table appearing in this chapter.
(2) Prepare a brief report for the capital investment committee, advising it on the relative merits of the two projects.

13–28A.   Cash payback period, discounted cash flow method, and analysis. Cuthbert Company is considering two projects. The estimated net cash flows from each project are as follows:

Year	Project D	Project E
1	$200,000	$ 50,000
2	200,000	150,000
3	100,000	300,000
4	100,000	100,000
5	100,000	100,000
Total	$700,000	$700,000

Each project requires an investment of $500,000, with no residual value expected. A rate of 12% has been selected for the discounted cash flow analysis.

Instructions:

(1) Compute the following for each project:
  (a) Cash payback period.
  (b) The excess (deficiency) of present value over the amount to be invested, as determined by the discounted cash flow method. Use the present value of 1 table appearing in this chapter.

(2) Prepare a brief report advising management on the relative merits of each of the two projects.

13–29A. Discounted cash flow method, present value index, and analysis. J. Wilson Company wishes to evaluate three capital investment projects by using the discounted cash flow method. Relevant data related to the projects are summarized as follows:

	Project P	Project Q	Project R
Amount to be invested........	$480,000	$240,000	$240,000
Annual net cash flows:			
Year 1....................	300,000	180,000	60,000
Year 2....................	240,000	120,000	120,000
Year 3....................	180,000	60,000	180,000

Instructions:

(1) Assuming that the desired rate of return is 20%, prepare a discounted cash flow analysis for each project. Use the present value of $1 table appearing in this chapter.

(2) Determine a present value index for each project.

(3) Which project offers the largest amount of present value per dollar of investment? Explain.

13–30A. Discounted cash flow method, discounted internal rate of return method, and analysis.   Management is considering two capital investment projects. The estimated net cash flows from each project are as follows:

Year	Project S	Project T
1	$120,000	$30,000
2	120,000	30,000
3	120,000	30,000
4	120,000	30,000

Project S requires an investment of $364,440, while Project T requires an investment of $85,650. No residual value is expected from either project.

Instructions:

(1) Compute the following for each project:
  (a) The excess (deficiency) of present value over the amount to be invested, as determined by the discounted cash flow method. Use a rate of 10% and the present value of $1 table appearing in this chapter.
  (b) A present value index.

(2) Determine the discounted internal rate of return for each project by (a) computing a "present value factor for an annuity of $1" and (b) using the present value of an annuity of $1 table appearing in this chapter.

(3) What advantage does the discounted internal rate of return method have over the discounted cash flow method in comparing projects?

Mini-Case 13

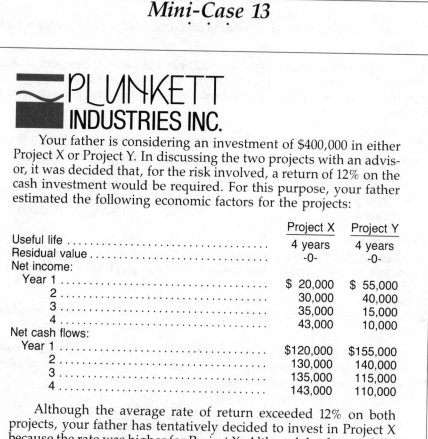

PLUNKETT INDUSTRIES INC.

Your father is considering an investment of $400,000 in either Project X or Project Y. In discussing the two projects with an advisor, it was decided that, for the risk involved, a return of 12% on the cash investment would be required. For this purpose, your father estimated the following economic factors for the projects:

	Project X	Project Y
Useful life	4 years	4 years
Residual value	-0-	-0-
Net income:		
Year 1	$ 20,000	$ 55,000
2	30,000	40,000
3	35,000	15,000
4	43,000	10,000
Net cash flows:		
Year 1	$120,000	$155,000
2	130,000	140,000
3	135,000	115,000
4	143,000	110,000

Although the average rate of return exceeded 12% on both projects, your father has tentatively decided to invest in Project X because the rate was higher for Project X. Although he doesn't fully understand the importance of cash flow, he has heard others talk about its importance in evaluating investments. In this respect, he noted that the total net cash flow from Project X is $528,000, which exceeds that from Project Y by $8,000.

Instructions:

(1) Determine the average rate of return for both projects.

(2) How would you explain the importance of net cash flows in the analysis of investment projects? Include a specific example to demonstrate the importance of net cash flows and their timing to these two projects.

Answers to Self-Examination Questions

· · ·

1. **C** Methods of evaluating capital investment proposals that ignore the time value of money are categorized as methods that ignore present value. This category includes the average rate of return method (answer A) and the cash payback method (answer B).

2. **B** The average rate of return is 24% (answer B), determined by dividing the expected average annual earnings by the average investment, as indicated below:

$$\frac{\$60,000 \div 5}{(\$100,000 + \$0) \div 2} = 24\%$$

3. **B** Of the three methods of analyzing proposals for capital investments, the cash payback method (answer B) refers to the expected period of time required to recover the amount of cash to be invested. The average rate of return method (answer A) is a measure of the anticipated profitability of a proposal. The discounted cash flow method (answer C) reduces the expected future net cash flows originating from a proposal to their present values.

4. **C** The discounted cash flow method (answer C) uses the concept of present value to determine the total present value of the cash flows expected from a proposal and compares this value with the amount to be invested. The average rate of return method (answer A) and the cash payback method (answer B) ignore present value. The discounted internal rate of return method (answer D) uses the present value concept to determine the discounted internal rate of return expected from the proposal.

5. **A** Capital rationing (answer A) is the process by which management allocates available investment funds among competing capital investment proposals. Capital expenditure budgeting (answer B) is the process of summarizing the decisions that have been made for the acquisition of plant assets and preparing a capital expenditures budget to reflect these decisions. Leasing (answer C) is an alternative that management should consider before making a final decision on the acquisition of assets.

Chapter Fourteen

CHAPTER OBJECTIVES

•

Describe and illustrate the use of the economic order quantity
for inventory control.

•

Describe and illustrate the use of the inventory order point and
safety stock for inventory control.

•

Describe and illustrate the use of linear programming for inventory control.

•

Describe the use of the expected value concept for
decision making under uncertainty.

•

Illustrate the use of payoff tables and decision trees in applying the
concept of expected value in managerial decision making.

•

Describe the value of information concept and illustrate its use in
managerial decision making.

•

Describe and illustrate the use of expected value concepts
in variance analysis.

•

Describe and illustrate the use of the maximin and maximax concepts in
managerial decision making under uncertainty.

•

Quantitative Techniques for Controlling Inventory and Making Decisions Under Uncertainty

Previous chapters have discussed many ways in which accounting data can be used by management in planning and controlling business operations, including such analyses as cost-volume-profit analysis, differential analysis, and capital investment analysis. These analyses can be performed using rather simple mathematical relationships, since they usually involve a limited number of objectives and variables. This chapter focuses on the use of quantitative techniques that rely on more sophisticated mathematical relationships and statistical methods. Such techniques enable management to consider a larger number of objectives and variables in planning and controlling operations.

The discussions and illustrations in this chapter relate to the use of quantitative techniques in controlling inventory and making decisions under uncertainty. These techniques often lead to a clarification of management decision alternatives and their expected effects on the business enterprise. For example, the most economical plan for purchasing materials for a single plant may be easily determined, based on the lowest overall cost per unit of materials. However, the most economical plan for purchasing materials for several plants may not be as easily determined, because transportation costs to the various plant locations may be different, and the amount of purchases from any one supplier may be limited. In this latter case, a quantitative technique known as linear programming may be useful in determining the most economical plan for purchasing materials.

The primary disadvantages of quantitative techniques are their complexity and their reliance on mathematical relationships and statistical methods which may be understood by only the most highly trained experts. When computers are used, however, it is less important to understand these complexities, so that quantitative techniques can be used by all levels of management.

Decision Support Systems for Managerial Use

A decision support system [DSS] is a computerized aid to ease or enhance the decision-making process. It is geared toward facilitating unstructured or semi-structured decisions. . . .

Unstructured decision situations are those that contain many unknowns, in the areas of both decision criteria and the variables upon which the decisions are based. For example, if we are dealing with a problem in which the interest rates and the unemployment rate a year from today will have some effect, but we are unsure of the exact relationship between those factors and the outcome, we are in an unstructured decision situation. We don't know what the interest rates or unemployment rate will be one year hence, nor do we know the exact relationship between those factors and our outcome.

Semistructured decision situations occur when either the decision criteria or the decision variables are unknown, but not both. For example, in a semistructured decision situation we know how to quantify the relationship between interest rates, the unemployment rate, and our outcome, but we don't know what the rates will be.

Decision support systems also may be employed to make structured decisions when the number of vari-ables is so great it becomes too difficult to organize and execute calculations manually. For example, if [a business enterprise is negotiating a mortgage to finance the acquisition of a plant asset and] different banks are offering different [mortgage] packages with different [interest] rates [and different loan provisions, such as compensating balance requirements, working capital requirements, payment options, and initiation fees,] we would have an ideal application for a decision support system. The [enterprise] would have to define the necessary criteria (for example, maximum [quarterly] payments. . .) and supply the variables offered by each of the banks.

. . . This is a fully structured decision as both the decision criteria and the decision variables are known. The automation of the tedious calculation process and the ability to change the decision criteria or decision variables quickly qualify it as a decision support system.

A DSS does not replace the decision maker by making the actual decision. As the name suggests, the DSS serves to support the decision-making process.

Source: Susan Davis-Stemp, Joshua E. Minkin, John Thomopoulos, Morris W. Stemp, and Robert Howell, *Decision Support Systems* (Montvale, New Jersey: National Association of Accountants, 1986).

INVENTORY CONTROL

For a business enterprise that needs large quantities of inventory to meet sales orders or production requirements, inventory is one of its most important assets. The lack of sufficient inventory can result in lost sales, idle production facilities, production bottlenecks, and additional purchasing costs due to placing special orders or rush orders. On the other hand, excess inventory can result in large storage costs and large spoilage losses, which reduce the profitability of the enterprise. Thus, it is important for a business enterprise to know the ideal quantity to be purchased in a single order and the minimum and maximum quantities to be on hand at any time. Such factors as economies of large-scale buying, storage costs, work interruption due to shortages, and seasonal and cyclical changes in production schedules need to be considered. Three quantitative techniques that are especially useful in inventory control are (1) the economic order quantity formula, (2) the inventory order point formula, and (3) linear programming.[1]

Economic Order Quantity
*   *   *

The optimum quantity of inventory to be ordered at one time is termed the **economic order quantity (EOQ).** Important factors to be considered in determining the optimum quantity are the costs involved in processing an order for the materials and the costs involved in storing the materials.

The annual cost of processing orders for a specified material (cost of placing orders, verifying invoices, processing payments, etc.) increases as the number of orders placed increases. On the other hand, the annual cost of storing the materials (taxes, insurance, occupancy of storage space, etc.) decreases as the number of orders placed increases. The economic order quantity is therefore that quantity that will minimize the combined annual costs of ordering and storing materials.

The combined annual cost incurred in ordering and storing materials can be computed under various assumptions as to the number of orders to be placed during a year. To illustrate, assume the following data for an inventoriable material which is used at the same rate during the year:

Units required during the year..........	1,200
Ordering cost, per order placed	$10.00
Annual storage cost, per unit..........	.60

If a single order were placed for the entire year's needs, the cost of ordering the 1,200 units would be $10. The average number of units held in inventory during the year would therefore be 600 (1,200 units ÷ 2) and would result in an annual storage cost of $360 (600 units × $.60). The combined order and storage costs for placing only one order during the year would thus be $370 ($10 + $360). If, instead of a single order, two orders were placed during the year, the order cost would be $20 (2 × $10), 600 units would need to be purchased on each order, the average inventory would be 300 units, and the annual storage cost would be $180 (300 units × $.60). Accordingly, the combined order and storage costs for placing two orders during the year would be $200 ($20 + $180). Successive computations will disclose the EOQ when the combined cost reaches its lowest point and starts upward. The following table shows an optimum of 200 units of materials per order, with 6 orders per year, at a combined cost of $120:

---

[1]The development and use of "just-in-time" inventory control procedures are discussed in Chapter 18, "Trends in Managerial Accounting."

Number of Orders	Number of Units per Order	Average Units in Inventory	Order and Storage Costs		
			Order Cost	Storage Cost	Combined Cost
1	1,200	600	$10	$360	$370
2	600	300	20	180	200
3	400	200	30	120	150
4	300	150	40	90	130
5	240	120	50	72	122
6	200	100	60	60	120
7	171	86	70	52	122

The economic order quantity may also be determined by a formula based on differential calculus. The formula and its application to the illustration is as follows:

$$EOQ = \sqrt{\frac{2 \times \text{Annual Units Required} \times \text{Cost per Order Placed}}{\text{Annual Storage Cost per Unit}}}$$

$$EOQ = \sqrt{\frac{2 \times 1,200 \times \$10}{\$.60}}$$

$$EOQ = \sqrt{40,000}$$

$$EOQ = 200 \text{ units}$$

Inventory Order Point

The **inventory order point,** usually expressed in units, is the level to which inventory is allowed to fall before an order for additional inventory is placed. The inventory order point depends on the (1) daily usage of inventory that is expected to be consumed in production or sold, (2) number of production days that it takes to receive an order for inventory, termed the **lead time,** and (3) **safety stock,** which is the amount of inventory that is available for use when unforeseen circumstances arise, such as delays in receiving ordered inventory as a result of a national truckers' strike. Once the order point is reached, the most economical quantity should be ordered.

The inventory order point is computed by using the following formula:

Inventory Order Point = (Daily Usage × Days of Lead Time) + Safety Stock

To illustrate, assume that Beacon Company, a printing company, estimates daily usage of 3,000 pounds of paper and a lead time of 30 days to receive an order of paper. Beacon Company desires a safety stock of 10,000 pounds. The inventory order point for the paper is 100,000 pounds, computed as follows:

Inventory Order Point = (Daily Usage × Lead Time) + Safety Stock
Inventory Order Point = (3,000 lbs. × 30 days) + 10,000 lbs.
Inventory Order Point = 90,000 lbs. + 10,000 lbs.
Inventory Order Point = 100,000 lbs.

In this illustration, a safety stock of 10,000 pounds of paper was assumed. This level of safety stock should be established by management after considering many factors, such as the uncertainty in the estimates of daily inventory usage and lead time. If management were 100% certain that estimates of the daily usage and lead time were correct, no safety stock would be required. As the uncertainty in these estimates increases, the amount of safety stock normally increases. In addition, the level of safety stock carried by an enterprise will also depend on the costs of carrying inventory and the costs of being out of inventory when materials are needed for production or sales. If the costs of carrying inventory are low and the costs of being out of inventory are high, then relatively large amounts of safety stock would normally be carried by a business enterprise.

Inventory Cardiogram

Henry C. Ekstein, the former chief financial officer of Remington Aluminum, developed an inventory cardiogram for use in controlling inventory. The cardiogram is a graph of inventory levels over time, which portrays the normal inventory usage cycle for a company. For example, the cardiogram indicates when and how many times inventory was overstocked and back ordered, the inventory reorder point, and the safety stock levels. In the following cardiogram,

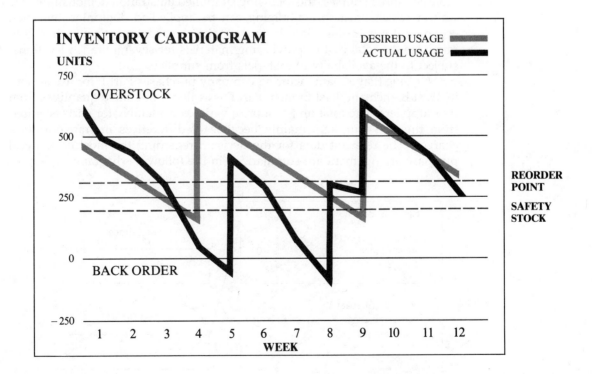

both desired and actual inventory usage are plotted. The reorder point is 275 units, the safety stock is 225 units, and the inventory was back ordered twice during the 12-week period. The economic order quantity is 400 units, indicated by the length of the vertical lines. The vertical lines also indicate the receipt of additional inventory.

Ekstein believes that the cardiogram is most effective in managing a limited number of inventory items that were previously uncontrolled. "Once you show someone the inventory cardiogram, " Ekstein claims, "all of a sudden it makes sense to them—how inventories behave, what the problem is, how many times it occurred over the past year, and what to do about it."

Source: Paul Susca, "Checking the Vital Signs," *CFO* (February, 1986), p. 13.

Quantitative techniques using statistics and probability theory may be useful to managers in establishing order point and safety stock levels. Such techniques are described in advanced texts.

Linear Programming for Inventory Control

Linear programming is a quantitative method that can provide data for solving a variety of business problems in which management's objective is to minimize costs or maximize profits, subject to several limiting factors. Although a thorough discussion of linear programming is appropriate for more advanced courses, the following simplified illustration demonstrates the way in which linear programming can be applied to determine the most economical purchasing plan. In this situation, management's objective is to minimize the total cost of purchasing materials for several branch locations, subject to the availability of materials from suppliers.

Assume that a manufacturing company purchases Part P for use at both its West Branch and East Branch. Part P is available in limited quantities from two suppliers. The total unit cost price varies considerably for parts acquired from the two suppliers mainly because of differences in transportation charges. The relevant data for the decision regarding the most economical purchase arrangement are summarized in the following diagram:

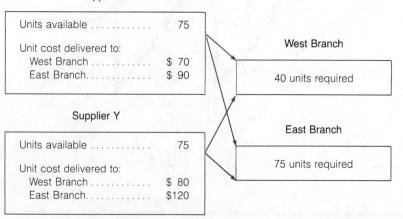

Supplier X

Units available	75
Unit cost delivered to:	
West Branch	$ 70
East Branch	$ 90

West Branch — 40 units required

Supplier Y

Units available	75
Unit cost delivered to:	
West Branch	$ 80
East Branch	$120

East Branch — 75 units required

It might appear that the most economical course of action would be to purchase (1) the 40 units required by West Branch from Supplier X at $70 a unit, (2) 35 units for East Branch from Supplier X at $90 a unit, and (3) the remaining 40 units required by East Branch from Supplier Y at $120 a unit. If this course of action were followed, the total cost of the parts needed by the two branches would amount to $10,750, as indicated by the following computation:

	Cost of Purchases		
	By West Branch	By East Branch	Total
From Supplier X:			
40 units at $70............	$2,800		$ 2,800
35 units at $90		$3,150	3,150
From Supplier Y:			
40 units at $120		4,800	4,800
Total......................	$2,800	$7,950	$10,750

Although many different purchasing programs are possible, the most economical course of action would be to purchase (1) the 75 units required by East Branch from Supplier X at $90 a unit and (2) the 40 units required by West Branch from Supplier Y at $80 a unit. If this plan were used, no units would be purchased at the lowest available unit cost, and the total cost of the parts would be $9,950, calculated as follows:

	Cost of Purchases		
	By West Branch	By East Branch	Total
From Supplier X:			
75 units at $90		$6,750	$6,750
From Supplier Y:			
40 units at $80	$3,200		3,200
Total......................	$3,200	$6,750	$9,950

Linear programming can be applied to this situation by using either a graphic approach or a mathematical equation approach. This latter approach, called the **simplex method,** uses algebraic equations and is often used more practically with a computer. Because of its complexity and because it is normally covered in advanced managerial accounting texts, the simplex method is not described in this chapter.

To illustrate the graphic approach to linear programming, the preceding facts for the purchase of Part P from Supplier X and Supplier Y by the West Branch and the East Branch will be used. The first step in solving this problem is to place all of the possible purchasing alternatives on a graph. Since the amount purchased from Supplier X will determine the amount purchased from Supplier Y, and vice versa, only a graph showing all possible purchase plans for Supplier X (or Supplier Y) is necessary. The following graph for Supplier X is based on the foregoing data.

· · · · · · · · · · ·

*Linear Programming
Graph—Units
Purchased From
Supplier X*

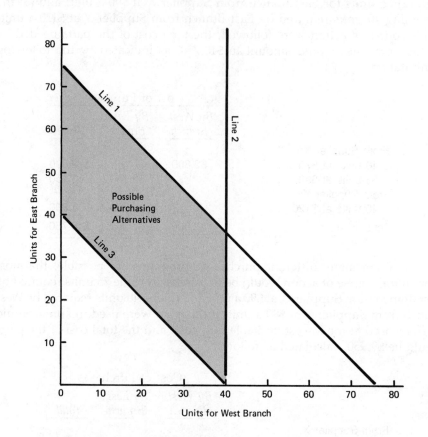

Line 1: Maximum number of units that can be purchased from Supplier X.

Line 2: Maximum number of units that will be purchased by West Branch.

Line 3: Minimum number of units that must be purchased from Supplier X.

The linear programming graph is constructed in the following manner:

1. Units for the West Branch are plotted on the horizontal axis, and units for the East Branch are plotted on the vertical axis.
2. A point representing the maximum number of units that could be purchased from Supplier X by the West Branch (75 units) is located on the horizontal axis. A point representing the maximum number of units that could be purchased from Supplier X by the East Branch (75 units) is located on the vertical axis.
3. A diagonal line (labeled Line 1) is drawn connecting the points representing the 75 units on the vertical axis with 75 units on the horizontal axis. This line represents the constraint on the maximum number

of units (75) that can be purchased from Supplier X by either branch or both branches.

4. The constraint on the number of units that the West Branch would purchase from Supplier X (40) is indicated by a line (labeled Line 2) which is drawn vertically upward from the point of 40 units on the horizontal axis to intersect Line 1.

5. A line (labeled Line 3) is drawn connecting 40 units on the vertical axis with 40 units on the horizontal axis. This line represents the constraint on minimum purchases from Supplier X (115 units required by the branches less 75 units available from each supplier).

6. The area bounded by the vertical axis and Lines 1, 2, and 3 is shaded. This area represents the set of all possible alternatives for purchases from Supplier X.

To illustrate the interpretation of a linear programming graph, assume that the West Branch purchased no units from Supplier X. The East Branch could then purchase between 40 and 75 units from Supplier X. This purchase alternative is indicated on the following graph between points A and B on the vertical axis. On the other hand, if the West Branch purchased 20 units from Supplier X, the East Branch could purchase between 20 and 55 units from Supplier X. This alternative is indicated on the following graph by the colored dotted line connecting points E and F.

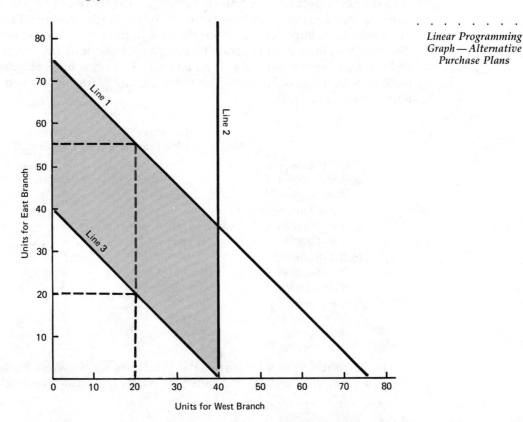

Linear Programming Graph—Alternative Purchase Plans

Although any point in the shaded area of the graph is a possible purchasing plan, managers are interested in selecting the most economical plan. According to the mathematical properties of linear programming, an economical purchase plan is located at one of the four points representing the corners of the shaded area of the graph. These corners are labeled A through D on the graph.

Each of the four corners represents the following purchases from Supplier X by the West Branch and the East Branch:

	Purchases by West Branch	Purchases by East Branch
Corner A:		
From Supplier X	0 units	40 units
Corner B:		
From Supplier X	0	75
Corner C:		
From Supplier X	40	0
Corner D:		
From Supplier X	40	35

Since the amount purchased from Supplier X affects the amount purchased from Supplier Y, the four corners identified above can be rewritten in terms of four separate purchase plans. In other words, if only 40 units are purchased from Supplier X and are shipped to the East Branch (Corner A), then the West Branch must obtain its purchases of 40 units from Supplier Y, and the East Branch must obtain an additional 35 units from Supplier Y to fulfill its total needs of 75 units. The four purchase plans represented by the four corners are as follows:

	Purchases by West Branch	Purchases by East Branch
Plan 1 (Corner A):		
From Supplier X	0 units	40 units
From Supplier Y	40	35
Plan 2 (Corner B):		
From Supplier X	0	75
From Supplier Y	40	0
Plan 3 (Corner C):		
From Supplier X	40	0
From Supplier Y	0	75
Plan 4 (Corner D):		
From Supplier X	40	35
From Supplier Y	0	40

By computing the total cost of the purchases for the West Branch and the East Branch for each of the purchase plans, the most economical purchase plan can be determined. As described earlier on page 487 and as shown in the following computation, Plan 2 is the most economical of the four purchase plans.

| | Cost of Purchases | | |
	By West Branch	By East Branch	Total
Plan 1:			
From Supplier X:			
40 units at $90.........		$3,600	$ 3,600
From Supplier Y:			
40 units at $80........	$3,200		3,200
35 units at $120........		4,200	4,200
Total...................	$3,200	$7,800	$11,000
Plan 2:			
From Supplier X:			
75 units at $90.........		$6,750	$ 6,750
From Supplier Y:			
40 units at $80.........	$3,200		3,200
Total..................	$3,200	$6,750	$ 9,950
Plan 3:			
From Supplier X:			
40 units at $70.........	$2,800		$ 2,800
From Supplier Y:			
75 units at $120........		$9,000	9,000
Total..................	$2,800	$9,000	$11,800
Plan 4:			
From Supplier X:			
40 units at $70.........	$2,800		$ 2,800
35 units at $90.........		$3,150	3,150
From Supplier Y:			
40 units at $120........		4,800	4,800
Total..................	$2,800	$7,950	$10,750

The preceding illustration of the graphic approach to linear programming required the construction of a graph and the consideration of four alternative purchase plans. Although an economical purchasing plan decision could have been determined by trial and error, such an approach can be time-consuming and costly. The trial and error approach could potentially require consideration of a much larger number of possible purchase plans before the most economical plan is found.

DECISION MAKING UNDER UNCERTAINTY

Quantitative techniques are especially useful to management in making decisions under uncertainty, which is characteristic of the environment in which managers must make decisions. The managerial accountant can aid management in making decisions under uncertainty by providing data useful in assessing the chances that future events will occur and the impact of those events. One technique useful for this purpose is the expected value concept. Two alternative concepts that managers may also find useful in special situations are the maximin and maximax concepts. These three concepts are discussed and illustrated in the remainder of this chapter.

MANAGERIAL USE OF THE EXPECTED VALUE CONCEPT

The concept of **expected value** involves identifying the possible outcomes from a decision and estimating the likelihood that each outcome will occur. By using the expected value concept, managers can better evaluate the uncertainty of the occurrence of predicted outcomes from decisions.

The likelihood that an outcome will occur from a decision is usually expressed in terms of a probability or chance of occurrence. For example, the probability or chance that, on the flip of a coin, a head will appear is .50 or 50%. Likewise, the probability or chance that the introduction of a new product will be successful might be expressed as .60 or 60%.

The expected value of a decision is the sum of the values that result when the dollar value of each outcome is multiplied by the probability or chance of its occurrence. Thus, expected value can be thought of as an average value. That is, each possible outcome is weighted by its chance of occurrence to obtain an average expected outcome. For example, assume that you are playing a game in which a coin is flipped. If a head appears, you win $10,000; if a tail appears, you lose $6,000. The expected value of this game is $2,000, computed as follows:

$$\text{Expected Value} = .50(\$10,000) + .50(-\$6,000)$$
$$\text{Expected Value} = \$5,000 - \$3,000$$
$$\text{Expected Value} = \$2,000$$

If you played the preceding game a large number of times, 50% of the time you would win $10,000, 50% of the time you would lose $6,000, and on the average you would win $2,000 per game. For example, if you played the game twice and won once and lost once, you would have won $10,000 and lost $6,000. Hence, you would have net winnings of $4,000 ($10,000 − $6,000). Since you played the game twice, your average winnings would be

$2,000 per game ($4,000 ÷ 2). Consequently, the expected value of playing the game is $2,000.

To illustrate the expected value concept within a managerial context, assume that the management of Faxon Company is faced with deciding on a location for a new hotel. The search for the best site has been narrowed to two choices within a large metropolitan area. One site is in the center of the city. The accessibility to the city's business and entertainment district makes this site attractive for conventions. The other location is twenty miles from the center of the city at the intersection of two interstate highways. The site is attractive because of its proximity to the city's international airport. After the hotel is constructed, the management of Faxon Company plans to operate the hotel for one year and then sell the hotel for a profit. Over the past five years, Faxon has successfully constructed and sold four hotels in this fashion.

The estimated profit or loss at each site depends on whether the occupancy rate the first year is high or low. Based on marketing studies, the following profit and loss data have been estimated:

City Site	Profit or Loss	Chance of Occurrence
High occupancy	$1,500,000	70%
Low occupancy	(500,000)	30

Interstate site	Profit or Loss	Chance of Occurrence
High occupancy	$1,000,000	60%
Low occupancy	100,000	40

The expected value of each site is computed by weighting each outcome by its chance of occurrence, as follows:

City Site

Expected value = .7($1,500,000) + .3(−$500,000)
Expected value = $1,050,000 − $150,000
Expected value = $900,000

Interstate Site

Expected value = .6($1,000,000) + .4($100,000)
Expected value = $600,000 + $40,000
Expected value = $640,000

Based on the expected values, the city site is more attractive than the interstate site because the city site has a higher expected value. Thus, on the average, the city site is expected to yield a higher profit than the interstate site.

The expected values for the city site and the interstate site of $900,000 and $640,000, respectively, will not actually occur. These values are weighted averages of the estimated profit or loss for each site. For the city site, the estimated outcome will be either a profit of $1,500,000 or a loss of $500,000. Likewise, for the interstate site, the estimated outcome will be either a profit of $1,000,000 or a profit of $100,000.

In the face of uncertainty, expected value is one of the most important pieces of information available to the manager for making a decision. Because expected value is an average concept, however, the range of possible outcomes (the variability of the outcomes) may also be valuable information for management's assessment of the uncertainty surrounding a decision. Although the city site in the preceding illustration has a higher expected value than the interstate site, the city site also has a wider range of possible outcomes (a profit of $1,500,000 or a loss of $500,000) than does the interstate site (a profit of $1,000,000 or $100,000). Consequently, the management of Faxon Company might select the interstate site in order to minimize the variability of the possible outcomes from the site decision. As with many other decisions, management must exercise judgment after weighing all available data and analyses.

The use of the expected value concept by management can be facilitated through the use of payoff tables and decision trees. In addition, the expected value concept may be used by managers in assessing the value of collecting additional information before a decision is made. The remainder of this section describes and illustrates the use of payoff tables and decision trees and discusses the value of obtaining additional information.

Payoff Tables

A **payoff table** presents a summary of the possible outcomes of one or more decisions. A payoff table is especially useful in managerial decision making when a wide variety of possible outcomes exists. One such situation might involve a decision facing a store manager who must decide on the amount of merchandise to purchase for various levels of possible consumer demand. To illustrate, assume that the new manager of Grocery Wholesalers Inc. must decide how many pounds of a perishable product to purchase on Monday for sale during the week. The product is purchased in 100-pound units, and by the end of the week, any unsold product is spoiled and lost. In the past, the former manager had noted that the maximum weekly sales had been 900 pounds. Therefore, to be assured that all demand could be met, 1,000 pounds were purchased.

The variable cost of the product is $1.50 per pound, and the selling price is $1.80 per pound. Thus, for each pound sold, Grocery Wholesalers Inc. earns a contribution margin of $.30 ($1.80 selling price − $1.50 variable cost per pound) to cover fixed costs and earn a profit. For each pound unsold at the end of the week, the $1.50 variable cost per pound is lost.

Based on sales records, it was determined that sales during the past ten weeks were as follows:

Number of Weeks	Actual Demand (Sales)
2	700 lbs.
5	800
3	900

The new manager must determine whether to purchase 700, 800, or 900 pounds. If the past ten weeks of sales data are used as an indication of future customer demand, the new manager should not purchase 1,000 pounds, since the recent sales data indicate that the maximum demand (sales) has not exceeded 900 pounds.

The outcomes (payoffs) in terms of contribution margin for each of the possible purchase amounts and possible levels of customer demand are summarized in the following payoff table:

Possible Demand	Contribution Margin of Purchases		
	700 lbs.	800 lbs.	900 lbs.
700 lbs.	$210	$ 60	$ (90)
800	210	240	90
900	210	240	270

Payoff Table of Possible Outcomes

The entries in the payoff table indicate that if 700 pounds are demanded and 700 pounds are purchased, for example, then 700 pounds will be sold and a total contribution margin of $210 (700 lbs. × $.30 per lb.) will result. If 700 pounds are demanded and 800 pounds are purchased, then 700 pounds will be sold and 100 pounds will spoil. In this case, the 700 pounds sold will generate a contribution margin of $210 (700 lbs. × $.30 per lb.), the 100 pounds that spoil will generate a loss of $150 (100 lbs. × $1.50 per lb.), and the net contribution margin will be $60 ($210 − $150). If 700 pounds are demanded and 900 pounds are purchased, then 700 pounds will be sold and 200 pounds will spoil. In this case, the 700 pounds sold will generate a contribution margin of $210 (700 lbs. × $.30 per lb.), the 200 pounds that spoil will generate a loss of $300 (200 lbs. × $1.50 per lb.), and the net contribution margin will be a loss of $90 ($210 − $300). If 800 pounds are demanded and 700 pounds are purchased, then 700 pounds will be sold and a total contribution margin of $210 (700 lbs. × $.30 per lb.) will result. The remaining entries in the payoff table are determined in a similar manner.

Based on the past ten weeks of sales data, the chances that the various levels of customer demand will occur can be estimated as follows:

Possible Demand	Number of Weeks	Chance of Occurrence
700 lbs.	2	20% (2/10)
800	5	50% (5/10)
900	3	30% (3/10)
	10	

A payoff table of expected values can now be constructed. Each entry in the payoff table of possible outcomes is multiplied by its chance of occurrence, as indicated above, to determine its expected value. The resulting amounts are entered in the following payoff table:

Possible Demand	Expected Value of Contribution Margin of Purchases		
	700 lbs.	800 lbs.	900 lbs.
700 lbs.	$ 42	$ 12	$ (18)
800	105	120	45
900	63	72	81
Totals	$210	$204	$ 108

The expected value of the outcome that 700 pounds are demanded and 700 pounds are purchased is computed by multiplying the contribution margin of $210 by the 20% chance that 700 pounds will be demanded. The resulting expected value is $42 ($210 × 20%). Likewise, the expected value of the outcome that 700 pounds are demanded and 800 pounds are purchased is computed by multiplying the contribution margin of $60 by the 20% chance that 700 pounds will be demanded. The resulting expected value is $12 ($60 × 20%). The expected value of the outcome that 700 pounds are demanded and 900 pounds are purchased is a loss of $18 (−$90 × 20%). Similarly, the expected value of the outcome that 800 pounds are demanded and 700 pounds are purchased is computed by multiplying the contribution margin of $210 by the 50% chance that 800 pounds will be demanded. The resulting expected value is $105 ($210 × 50%). The remaining entries in the payoff table are determined in a similar manner.

The total expected value of each possible purchase is determined by summing the individual expected values at each level of possible demand. In the above table, this total expected value is represented by the totals of each column. For example, the total expected value of a purchase of 700 pounds is equal to the sum of expected values of a purchase of 700 pounds and possible demand of 700 pounds ($42), a purchase of 700 pounds and possible demand of 800 pounds ($105), and a purchase of 700 pounds and possible demand of 900 pounds ($63). The resulting total expected value of purchasing 700 pounds is $210 (the total of the first column). Likewise, the total expected value of a purchase of 800 pounds is $204, and the total expected value of purchasing 900 pounds is $108.

Based solely on the above payoff table of expected values, the new manager should select that purchase with the highest total expected value. Thus, the best purchase decision, on the average, will be the purchase of 700 pounds, since its expected value of $210 is higher than any other purchase alternative. Even though this decision will result in lost sales in some weeks, on the average it will result in the largest possible profits.

Decision Trees

. . .

Decision trees are graphical representations of decisions, possible outcomes, and chances that outcomes will occur. Decision trees are especially useful to managers who are choosing among alternatives when possible outcomes are dependent on several decisions. For example, if management decides to produce a new product, it must consider whether to offer the product in all consumer markets or only in specific markets, whether to offer special introductory rebates, whether to offer special warranties, and whether and how much to advertise. In this case, the expected profit from producing the new product depends on many decisions, each of which has an effect on the profitability of the new product.

To illustrate the use of decision trees, assume that Lampe Company is considering disposing of unimproved land. If the unimproved land is to be sold as is, its sales price would be $80,000. If the land is improved, however, there is a 40% chance that it can be rezoned for commercial development and sold for $120,000 more than the cost incurred in making improvements. There is a 60% chance that the improved land would be rezoned for residential use, in which case the land could be sold to a real estate developer for $70,000 more than the cost of improvements.

The decision tree for the preceding example can be diagrammed as follows:

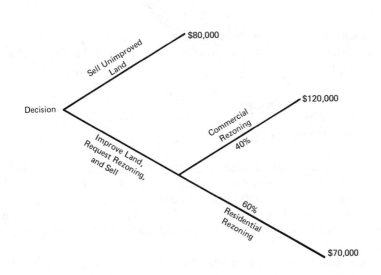

Decision Tree—Profit From Sale of Unimproved or Improved Land

The expected values can be computed directly from the decision tree by tracing back through each branch of the decision tree and multiplying each of the possible outcomes by the chance of its occurrence. For example, the expected value of the land being rezoned for commercial use and sold for $120,000 is $48,000 ($120,000 × .4). The expected value of the residential rezoning is computed in a similar manner and is $42,000 ($70,000 × .6). Since there is no uncertainty concerning the selling of the unimproved land for

$80,000, the expected value of selling the unimproved land is $80,000. These expected values are summarized in the following decision tree:

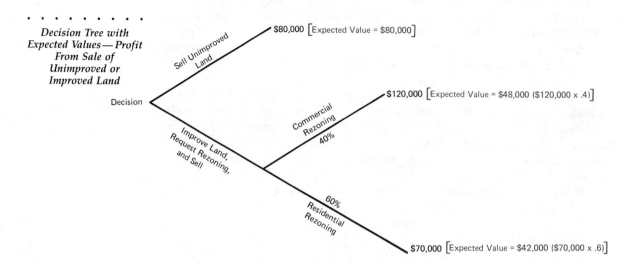

. . . .
Decision Tree with Expected Values — Profit From Sale of Unimproved or Improved Land

The total expected value of improving the land is equal to the sum of the expected values of the possible outcomes from the land improvement, or $90,000, computed as follows:

Commercial rezoning............................	$48,000
Residential rezoning.............................	42,000
Total expected value of improving the land	$90,000

The preceding analysis indicates that the land should be improved and sold, since the expected value of this course of action, $90,000, is higher than the expected value of selling the unimproved land, $80,000. Thus, on the average, a profit of $90,000 is expected from improving the land, with the worst possibility being a profit of $70,000 and the best possibility being a profit of $120,000.

Decision trees can be constructed to incorporate a large number of possible courses of action. The preceding illustration was intentionally brief in order to highlight the basic use of decision trees in aiding management's decision making under uncertainty.

Value of Information

In decision making, managers rarely have easy access to all the information they desire. In such cases, management must consider the information available and the value and the cost of seeking additional information relevant to the decision. If the expected value of acquiring additional information exceeds its expected cost, then the additional information should be acquired.

To illustrate, assume that an investment in Proposal A is expected to have a 60% chance of earning net income of $10,000 and a 40% chance of suffering a net loss of $5,000. This situation is diagrammed in the following decision tree:

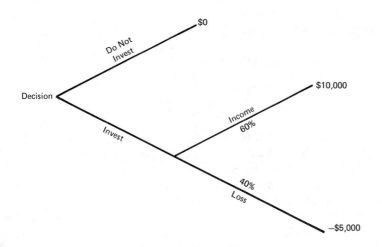

The expected value of investing in Proposal A is equal to the sum of the expected values of the possible outcomes, or $4,000, computed as follows:

Expected value of Proposal A = ($10,000 × .6) + (−$5,000 × .4)
Expected value of Proposal A = $6,000 − $2,000
Expected value of Proposal A = $4,000

Since the expected value of Proposal A is positive, the manager would normally invest in the proposal, even though there is a 40% chance of a loss of $5,000. Assume, however, that the manager could acquire additional information that would indicate with certainty whether Proposal A would earn the $10,000 income or suffer the loss of $5,000. How much would the manager be willing to pay for this additional (perfect) information?

The maximum amount (cost) that would be paid to obtain perfect information concerning a decision is termed the **value of perfect information**. It is the difference between (1) the expected value of a decision based on the perfect information and (2) the expected value of a decision based on existing information. To illustrate, the maximum amount that would be paid to obtain perfect information concerning Proposal A is determined by first computing the expected value of the proposal as if it is known beforehand whether the proposal would be successful or not. If the manager knows that the proposal will be successful, then a decision to invest would be made and income of $10,000 would be earned. If the manager knows that the proposal will be unsuccessful, then a decision not to invest would be made and no income or loss would result. For Proposal A, 60% of the time the perfect information will indicate that the proposal would be successful and therefore income of $10,000 would be earned. Also, 40% of the time the information will indicate that the proposal would be unsuccessful and therefore management would not invest. The expected value of perfect information is equal to the sum of the expected values of the possible outcomes, or $6,000, computed as follows:

Expected value of Proposal A,
  based on perfect information = ($10,000 × .6) + ($0 × .4)
Expected value of Proposal A,
  based on perfect information = $6,000

The value of perfect information concerning Proposal A is then determined by subtracting $4,000, the expected value of Proposal A, based on existing information, from the $6,000 computed above. Thus, as shown in the following computation, the manager would be willing to pay $2,000 to obtain perfect information concerning Proposal A.

Expected value of Proposal A, based on perfect information $6,000
Less expected value of Proposal A, based on existing information .   4,000
Value of perfect information concerning Proposal A $2,000

VARIANCE ANALYSIS USING EXPECTED VALUE

When variances from standard costs occur, management must decide whether to investigate the causes and attempt corrective actions. To assist management in making this decision, the managerial accountant can use the expected value concept to focus on the expected costs relevant to the decision.

In prior illustrations, the use of the expected value concept focused on choosing among alternatives, so that the alternative with the highest expected value in terms of profit was chosen. Since management's primary focus in variance analysis is to minimize costs, however, the decision whether to investigate a variance is one of choosing that alternative with the lowest expected cost. In other words, in deciding whether to investigate a variance, management should compare the expected costs if an investigation is made with the expected costs if no investigation is made. It will then choose the alternative (investigate or not investigate) that provides the lowest expected costs.

To illustrate, assume that an unfavorable direct materials quantity variance of $1,000 has been reported for July and is expected to continue for one month if not corrected. Past experience indicates that 60% of the time the variance is caused by poor quality materials and can be eliminated (is controllable) by switching suppliers. On the other hand, 40% of the time the variance is caused by machine wear and tear and cannot be eliminated (is uncontrollable) without a major overhaul of the machinery. Due to sales commitments, production cannot be delayed for a machinery overhaul until the end of August, when regular maintenance is scheduled.

If the variance is not investigated, it will continue for August and the expected cost is the amount of the variance, $1,000. If the variance is investigated, using personnel who are available to conduct the investigation at no additional cost, the investigation may indicate that the variance is caused by poor quality materials and therefore is controllable. Management will then change suppliers and there will be no variance in August. If the investigation indicates that the variance is caused by machine wear and tear (and therefore is uncontrollable), the variance will continue for August at a cost of $1,000. However, the variance will be caused by machine wear and tear only 40% of the time, and thus the expected cost is $400 ($1,000 × 40%). These possible outcomes are diagrammed in the following decision tree:

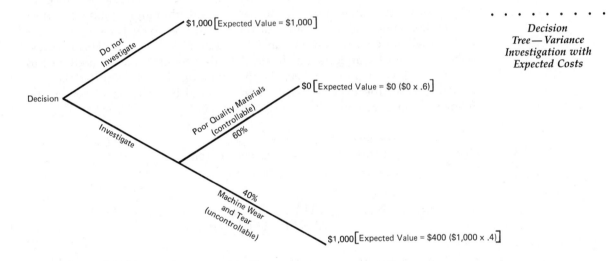

Decision Tree — Variance Investigation with Expected Costs

The total expected cost if the variance is investigated is the sum of the expected costs of the two possible outcomes, as shown in the following computation:

Expected cost if variance is caused by poor quality materials (controllable)... $ 0
Plus expected cost if variance is caused by machine wear
and tear (uncontrollable) 400
Total expected cost if variance is investigated $400

As indicated previously, management should select the alternative with the lowest expected cost. Since the total expected cost if the variance is investigated ($400) is less than the expected cost if no investigation is undertaken ($1,000), management should investigate the variance.

In this illustration, the cost of conducting the investigation was assumed to be zero. In practice, however, the cost may not be zero, and the important question therefore becomes: how much should management be willing to spend to investigate the variance? The answer for the direct materials variance illustration is $600, which is the difference between the total expected costs if (1) no investigation is undertaken and (2) an investigation is undertaken, as shown in the following computation:

Expected cost—no investigation.	$1,000
Less expected cost—investigation	400
Value of conducting an investigation	$ 600

In the above illustration, $600 is the maximum amount that management would spend to conduct an investigation of the direct materials variance. In other words, the value of conducting an investigation and obtaining perfect information concerning the cause of the variance is $600. Thus, if it is estimated that the cost to conduct an investigation would be $700, no investigation should be undertaken. If, on the other hand, the estimated cost to conduct an investigation is $500, the investigation should be undertaken. In the latter case, the expected cost savings would be $100, as shown in the following computation:

Value of conducting an investigation	$600
Less cost of conducting the investigation	500
Expected cost savings from investigation	$100

MAXIMIN AND MAXIMAX CONCEPTS OF DECISION MAKING UNDER UNCERTAINTY

Alternative concepts to expected value are useful to management when it is extremely difficult to estimate the chances of occurrence of the various outcomes or when the potential loss or gain for a proposal is so great that management would ignore the expected value in making the decision. For example, management might be considering the possibility of introducing a revolutionary new product, which has a chance of earning extraordinarily large profits but which requires a total commitment of company resources. If the product is successful, the company will earn record profits; but if the product fails, the company may go bankrupt. In such a situation, the expected value concept may not be useful because management may not be willing to risk bankruptcy. The remainder of this chapter describes and illustrates two alternative concepts to expected value: (1) the maximin concept and (2) the maximax concept. These concepts depend on different philosophies of risk and thus lead to different decisions.

Maximin Concept

The use of the **maximin concept** leads management to decide in favor of the alternative with the maximum (largest) minimum profit. The maximin concept is applied as follows:

1. The minimum (smallest) profit for each decision alternative is listed.
2. The decision alternative with the maximum (largest) profit from the list in (1) is chosen.

To illustrate, assume that the management of Hayes Company is considering building a condominium development in one of three locations. Because of limited funds, only one of the locations can be selected. The success of each location depends on demand. The estimated profit and loss from two levels of demand (low and high) for the condominium units for each location are as follows:

	Low Demand	High Demand
Location 1	$(500,000)	$4,000,000
Location 2	100,000	1,200,000
Location 3	150,000	800,000

In applying the maximin concept, the maximum minimum profit (or loss) from each alternative is selected. In this illustration, the minimum profit (loss) for each location appears in the low demand column. For Hayes Company, the maximin concept indicates that Location 3 should be chosen, since under conditions of low demand, Location 3 will earn more than either Locations 1 or 2. In this way, management is assured that in the worst possible case (that of low demand), a maximum profit of $150,000 will be earned. By using the maximin concept, management has avoided the possibility of losing $500,000 from the selection of Location 1 and earning only $100,000 profit from the selection of Location 2. At the same time, however, management has also forgone the possibility of earning a maximum profit of $4,000,000 from the selection of Location 1 under the most favorable (high demand) condition.

The maximin concept is used by managers when the primary concern is minimizing the risk of any loss. In such situations, managers are said to be risk averse.

Maximax Concept

The use of the **maximax concept** leads management to decide in favor of the alternative with the maximum (largest) profit. The maximax concept is applied as follows:

1. The maximum (largest) profit for each decision alternative is listed.
2. The decision alternative with the maximum (largest) profit from the list in (1) is chosen.

To illustrate, assume the same facts as in the preceding illustration for Hayes Company. In applying the maximax concept, only the maximum (largest) profit for each location is considered. In this illustration, the maximum profit for each location appears in the high demand column of the table on page 503. For Hayes Company, the maximax concept indicates that Location 1 should be selected, since under conditions of high demand, Location 1 will earn more than either Locations 2 or 3. In this way, management is assured that in the best possible case (that of high demand), the maximum profit of $4,000,000 will be earned. At the same time, however, management has also taken the risk of losing $500,000 from the selection of Location 1 under the worst (low demand) condition.

The maximax concept is used by managers when the primary concern is earning the largest possible profit, regardless of the risks. In such situations, managers are said to be risk takers.

Chapter Review

KEY POINTS

1. Inventory Control.

For a business enterprise that needs large quantities of inventory, one of the most important assets is inventory. The lack of sufficient inventory can result in lost sales, idle production facilities, production bottlenecks, and additional purchasing costs due to placing special orders or rush orders. On the other hand, excess inventory can result in large storage costs and large spoilage losses, which reduce the profitability of the enterprise.

The optimum quantity of inventory to be ordered at one time is the economic order quantity (EOQ). Important factors to be considered in determining the EOQ are the costs involved in processing an order for materials and the costs involved in storing materials. The EOQ can be determined in either tabular form or through the following formula:

$$EOQ = \sqrt{\frac{2 \times \text{Annual Units Required} \times \text{Cost per Order Placed}}{\text{Storage Cost per Unit}}}$$

The inventory order point is the level to which inventory is allowed to fall before an order for additional inventory is placed. The inventory order point depends on the (1) daily usage of inventory that is expected to be consumed in production or sold, (2) number of production days (lead time) that it takes to receive an order for inventory, and (3) the amount of inventory (safety stock) that is available for use when unforeseen circumstances arise. The inventory order point is computed using the following formula:

Inventory Order Point = (Daily Usage × Days of Lead Time) + Safety Stock

Linear programming is a quantitative method that can provide data for solving a variety of problems in which management's objective is to minimize costs or maximize profits, subject to several limiting factors. Linear programming can be used to determine the most economical merchandise purchasing plan.

2. Decision Making Under Uncertainty.
Quantitative techniques are especially useful to management in making decisions under uncertainty. The managerial accountant can aid management in making such decisions by providing data useful in assessing the chances that future events will occur and the impact of those events.

3. Managerial Use of the Expected Value Concept.
The concept of expected value involves identifying the possible outcomes from a decision and estimating the likelihood that each outcome will occur. The likelihood that an outcome will occur is usually expressed in terms of a probability or chance of occurrence. The expected value of the decision is the sum of the values that result when the dollar value of each outcome is multiplied by the probability of its occurrence. That is, each possible outcome is weighted by its chance of occurrence to obtain an average expected outcome.

The use of the expected value concept by management may be facilitated through the use of payoff tables and decision trees. A payoff table presents a summary of possible outcomes of one or more decisions. A payoff table is especially useful when a wide variety of possible outcomes exist. Decision trees are graphical representations of decisions, possible outcomes, and chances that outcomes will occur. Decision trees are especially useful when possible outcomes are dependent on several decisions.

In decision making, managers must consider the information available and the value and the cost of seeking additional information relevant to the decision. If the expected value of acquiring additional information exceeds its expected cost, then the additional information should be acquired. The maximum amount that would be paid to obtain perfect information concerning a decision is termed the value of perfect information. It is the difference between (1) the expected value of a decision based on perfect information and (2) the expected value of a decision based on existing information.

The expected value concept may be useful to managers in deciding whether to investigate the causes of variances from standard costs and to attempt corrective actions. Management should compare the expected cost if an investigation is made with the expected cost if no investigation is made, and then choose the alternative that provides the lowest expected cost.

4. Maximin and Maximax Concepts of Decision Making Under Uncertainty. Alternative concepts to expected value are useful when it is extremely difficult to estimate the chances of occurrence of the various outcomes or when the potential loss or gain for a proposal is so great that management would ignore the expected value in making the decision.

The maximin concept leads management to decide in favor of the alternative with the maximum (largest) minimum profit. The maximin concept is used when the primary concern is minimizing the risk of any loss. In such situations, managers are risk averse.

The use of the maximax concept leads management to decide in favor of the alternative with the maximum (largest) profit. The maximax concept is used when the primary concern is earning the largest possible profit, regardless of the risks. In such situations, managers are risk takers.

KEY TERMS
·

economic order quantity
  (EOQ) 483
inventory order point 484
lead time 484
safety stock 484
linear programming 486
simplex method 487

expected value 492
payoff table 494
decision trees 496
value of perfect information 499
maximin concept 503
maximax concept 503

SELF-EXAMINATION QUESTIONS
·
(Answers at End of Chapter)

1. In determing the economic order quantity, which, if any, of the following factors are important to consider?
   A. Storage cost per unit
   B. Annual units required
   C. Cost per order placed
   D. All of the above

2. Proposal R has a 60% chance of earning a profit of $80,000 and a 40% chance of incurring a loss of $60,000. What is the expected value of Proposal R?
   A. $24,000
   B. $48,000
   C. $72,000
   D. None of the above

3. Management's use of expected value can be facilitated through the use of payoff tables and:
   - A. the maximax concept
   - B. decision trees
   - C. the maximin concept
   - D. none of the above

4. The expected value of Proposal A, based on existing information, is $5,000, and the expected value of Proposal A, based on perfect information, is $8,000. What is the value of the perfect information concerning Proposal A?
   - A. $3,000
   - B. $5,000
   - C. $8,000
   - D. None of the above

5. The management of Freeman Co. is considering an investment in one of four real estate projects. The success of each project depends on whether demand is high or low. Based on the following data, which project would management select, using the maximin concept?

	Low Demand	High Demand
Project W.........................	$120,000	$600,000
Project X	(40,000)	800,000
Project Y	110,000	500,000
Project Z	(60,000)	900,000

   - A. Project W
   - B. Project X
   - C. Project Y
   - D. Project Z

ILLUSTRATIVE PROBLEM

Shiver News Distributors recently purchased a newsstand on the corner of 5th Avenue South and 2nd Street in downtown Clinton. The new manager of the newsstand must decide how many copies of the local newspaper to stock on a daily basis. The former manager had noted that the maximum daily sales, in the past, had been 175 papers, and to be assured that all demand could be met, 200 papers were purchased daily. The cost of the newspaper is $.20 per paper, and the paper is sold for $.30. Any papers remaining at the end of the day are worthless and are thrown away. The paper is published five days a week.

The records for the past month indicate the following sales:

Number of Days	Actual Demand (Sales)
2	100 papers
8	125
6	150
4	175

Instructions:

1. Prepare a payoff table of possible outcomes in terms of contribution margin, using the format shown in this chapter.

2. Based on the sales data for the past 20 days, estimate the chances of each level of possible demand for the newspaper.
3. Prepare a payoff table of expected values of possible outcomes in terms of contribution margin, using the format shown in this chapter.
4. Based on (3), how many newspapers should be purchased? Explain.

SOLUTION

(1)

Possible Demand	Contribution Margin of Purchases			
	100 papers	125 papers	150 papers	175 papers
100 papers	$10.00	$ 5.00	$ 0.00	$(5.00)
125	10.00	12.50	7.50	2.50
150	10.00	12.50	15.00	10.00
175	10.00	12.50	15.00	17.50

(2)

Possible Demand	Number of Days	Chance of Occurrence
100 papers	2	10% (2/20)
125	8	40% (8/20)
150	6	30% (6/20)
175	4	20% (4/20)

(3)

Possible Demand	Expected Value of Contribution Margin of Purchases			
	100 papers	125 papers	150 papers	175 papers
100 papers	$ 1.00	$ .50	$ 0.00	$(.50)
125	4.00	5.00	3.00	1.00
150	3.00	3.75	4.50	3.00
175	2.00	2.50	3.00	3.50
Totals	$10.00	$11.75	$10.50	$7.00

(4) 125 newspapers should be purchased, because the daily total expected value of this purchase is the highest. On the average, 125 papers is the best purchase.

Discussion Questions

14–1. What is the primary advantage of quantitative techniques?

14–2. What are the primary disadvantages of quantitative techniques?

14–3. For a business enterprise that needs large quantities of inventories to meet sales orders or production requirements, what can result from insufficient inventory?

14–4. What term is used to describe the optimum quantity of inventory to be ordered at one time?

14–5. Assuming that Product S is used at the same rate throughout the year, 10,000 units are required during the year, the cost per order placed is $5, and the storage cost per unit is $2.50, what is the economic order quantity for Product S?

14–6. The inventory order point depends on what factors?

14–7. Assuming that Parish Co. estimates daily usage of 1,200 pounds of Material X, the lead time to receive an order of Material X is 10 days. and a safety stock of 3,600 pounds is desired, what is the inventory order point?

14–8. If everything else remains the same, as the cost of carrying inventory decreases, would the level of safety stock normally carried by a company increase or decrease?

14–9. What quantitative technique is often useful in determining the most economical plan for purchasing materials for several locations?

14–10. How can the managerial accountant aid management in making decisions under uncertainty?

14–11. What concept involves identifying possible outcomes from a decision and estimating the likelihood that each outcome will occur?

14–12. How is the expected value of a decision calculated?

14–13. Assume that you are playing a game in which a coin is flipped. If a head appears, you win $1,000, and if a tail appears, you lose $700. What is the expected value of playing this game?

14–14. Rawlings Co. is considering an investment in a real estate project with the following outcomes and chances of occurrence. What is the expected value of the project?

Profit	Chance of Occurrence
$2,000,000	40%
1,000,000	60%

14–15. What term is used to describe a table frequently used by managers to summarize the possible outcomes of one or more decisions?

14–16. The following data have been taken from the sales records of Sims Co.:

Number of Weeks	Actual Demand (Sales)
5	5,000 units
2	8,000
6	7,000
4	4,000
3	6,000

Estimate the chance that each sales level will reoccur.

14–17. Based on the following payoff table of expected values, what should be the amount of monthly purchases?

Possible Demand	Expected Value of Contribution Margin of Purchases	
	20,000 units	30,000 units
20,000 units.........	$ 40,000	$ 30,000
30,000 units.........	60,000	90,000
Totals	$100,000	$120,000

14–18. What term is used to describe graphical representations of decisions, possible outcomes, and chances that outcomes will occur?

14–19. When are decision trees especially useful to managers in choosing among alternatives?

14–20. When should management acquire additional information before making a decision?

14–21. What term is used to describe the maximum amount that would be paid to obtain perfect information?

14–22. How is the value of perfect information computed?

14–23. Wolfe Co. is evaluating Proposal B as an investment. The expected value of Proposal B based on existing information is $30,000, and the expected value of Proposal B based on perfect information is $42,000. Wolfe Co. can obtain perfect information concerning Proposal B at a cost of $10,000. Should Wolfe Co. pay the $10,000 for the perfect information? Explain.

14–24. Using the expected value concept, how should management decide when to incur the costs necessary to investigate a variance?

14–25. What two alternative concepts to expected value can be used by management in making decisions under uncertainty?

14–26. When might the alternative concepts of maximax and maximin be more useful to management in decision making than the concept of expected value?

14–27. The president of Lundy Co. recently made the following statement concerning a proposed investment: "I don't care if the expected value is $3,000,000. I am not going to take the risk of losing $2,000,000 on Proposal X. I'm selecting Proposal W, with its expected value of $1,200,000, because its maximum possible loss is estimated to be $100,000." What decision-making concept was the president of Lundy Co. using?

14–28. Describe how the maximax concept of decision making is applied.

14–29. Would the use of the maximin and maximax concepts normally lead management to make the same decisions? Explain.

14–30. Real World Focus. On August 1, 1986, Grandview Resources Inc. reported in a news release the planned opening of a gold mine east of Stockton, California. The company expected to produce 60,000 to 80,000 ounces of gold annually from this mine. The chance of producing 60,000 ounces is equally as likely as producing 80,000 ounces annually. (a) What is the expected annual production of gold from the mine? (b) Assuming that gold will average $350 per ounce, what is the expected annual revenue from the gold mine?

Exercises

14–31. **Economic order quantity and inventory order point.** Jewell Company estimates that 4,080 units of Material W will be required during the coming year. The materials will be used at the rate of 15 units per day throughout the 272-day period of budgeted production for the year. Past experience indicates that the annual storage cost is $.15 per unit, the cost to place an order is $34, the lead time to receive an order is 30 days, and the desired amount of safety stock is 225 units. Determine (a) the economic order quantity, (b) the inventory order point, and (c) the number of units to be purchased when the inventory order point is reached.

14–32. **Linear programming graph.** Ralls Company purchases Part F for use at both its Austell and Tucker branches. Part F is available in limited quantities from two suppliers. The relevant data for determining an economical purchase plan are as follows:

Units required:	
Austell Branch..	50 units
Tucker Branch..	100 units
Supplier G:	
Total units available	100 units
Unit cost delivered to:	
Austell Branch...	$80 per unit
Tucker Branch...	$120 per unit
Supplier H:	
Total units available	100 units
Unit cost delivered to:	
Austell branch...	$90 per unit
Tucker Branch...	$150 per unit

The following linear programming graph for units purchased from Supplier G has been constructed, based on the above data:

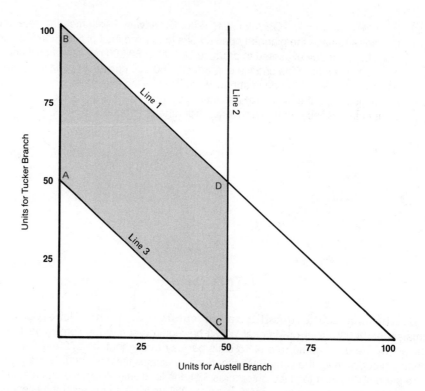

(a) For each of the four corners identified on the above graph by letters A through D, determine the purchases from Supplier G for the Austell and Tucker Branches. Use the same format as shown in this chapter.

(b) For each of the four corners in (a), indicate the units purchased from both Suppliers G and H for the Austell and Tucker Branches. Use the same format as shown in this chapter and identify Plan 1 with Corner A, Plan 2 with Corner B, Plan 3 with Corner C, and Plan 4 with Corner D.

(c) Determine the most economical purchase plan by computing the total cost of each purchase plan determined in (b).

14–33. Expected value of playing game. While on vacation in Atlantic City, you are offered the opportunity to play one game of chance in which a die is thrown. The die is numbered one through six, and each number has an equal chance of appearing on any throw of the die. The winnings and losses established for each number on a throw of the die are as follows:

Number	Winnings (Losses)
1	$1,500
2	900
3	600
4	450
5	(300)
6	(3,000)

(a) Determine the expected value of playing the game. (b) If the cost of playing the game is $20, would you play? Explain.

14–34. Expected value of exercising option to purchase land. Based on a rumor that a new shopping mall will locate near its office complex, Ritter Company is considering exercising an option to purchase thirty acres of land surrounding its offices. If the shopping mall is constructed, the land should increase substantially in value and be sold for a profit. The chance that the shopping mall will be built near the Ritter Company office complex and the potential profits that could result are as follows:

Outcome	Chance of Occurrence	Profit
Shopping mall locates near office complex	70%	$600,000
Shopping mall locates elsewhere	30%	20,000

(a) Determine the expected value of exercising the option and purchasing the land. (b) Assuming that exercising the option is one of several investments being considered, briefly discuss how the expected values computed in (a) might be compared with the alternatives.

14–35. Chances of occurrence and payoff table. The new manager of Gatlin Grocery must decide how many pounds of a perishable product to purchase on Monday for sale during the week. The outcomes for each of the possible purchases and the possible levels of customer demand are summarized in the following payoff table of possible outcomes:

Possible Demand	Contribution Margin of Purchases		
	500 lbs.	1,000 lbs.	1,500 lbs.
500 lbs.	$1,000	$ 250	$ (500)
1,000	1,000	2,000	1,250
1,500	1,000	2,000	3,000

The sales records for the past twenty weeks indicate the following levels of sales:

Number of Weeks	Actual Demand (Sales)
10	500 lbs.
6	1,000
4	1,500

(a) Based on the sales data for the past twenty weeks, determine the chances that the various levels of customer demand (500 lbs., 1,000 lbs., 1,500 lbs.) will occur. (b) Construct a payoff table of expected values of possible outcomes, using the format shown in this chapter. (c) What amount should Gatlin Grocery purchase?

14–36. Decision tree and analysis. Chapman Company is considering whether to offer a new product for sale in the Midwest or in the Northeast. Because of the uncertainty associated with introducing a new product, the decision will be made on the basis of expected annual income. The possible outcomes and chances of occurrence are summarized as follows:

Customer Demand	Midwestern Region		Northeastern Region	
	Annual Income	Chance of Occurrence	Annual Income	Chance of Occurrence
High	$20,000,000	40%	$35,000,000	35%
Moderate	10,000,000	35	15,000,000	20
Low...........	4,000,000	25	2,000,000	45

(a) To aid management in deciding in which region to offer the new product, prepare a decision tree with expected values. (b) Which region should be selected for the introduction of the new product, based on the expected value concept?

14–37. Value of perfect information. The management of Ramsay Company has the opportunity to invest in Proposal A, which is expected to have a 60% chance of earning income of $100,000 and a 40% chance of suffering a loss of $140,000. (a) What is the expected value of Proposal A, based on existing information? (b) What is the expected value of Proposal A, based on perfect information? (c) What is the value of perfect information concerning Proposal A? (d) If the management of Ramsay Company could purchase perfect information concerning Proposal A for $40,000, should the perfect information be purchased?

14–38. Expected cost of investigating a variance; analysis. The controller of Lien Company must decide whether to investigate an unfavorable direct labor quantity variance of $5,000 for July. The variance is expected to continue for August if no investigation is undertaken. Based on past experience, there is a 75% chance that the variance is controllable and can be eliminated for August if an investigation is conducted. There is a 25% chance that the variance is uncontrollable and cannot be eliminated for August. (a) Determine the expected cost if the variance is investigated, assuming that no additional cost will be incurred in conducting the investigation. (b) How much should management be willing to spend to investigate the variance?

14–39. Decision trees. Prepare a decision tree of expected values (costs) for (a) Exercise 14–37 and (b) Exercise 14–38.

14–40. Maximin and maximax concepts analysis. Siefer Company is considering an investment in one of three projects. The success of each project depends on whether customer demand is low or high. The possible profit or loss for each project is summarized as follows:

	Low Demand	High Demand
Project X.....................................	$300,000	$500,000
Project Y.....................................	(100,000)	400,000
Project Z.....................................	(200,000)	750,000

(a) Using the maximin concept, which project should management choose? (b) Using the maximax concept, which project should management choose? (c) Explain why the answers to (a) and (b) are not the same.

Problems

14–41. Economic order quantity and inventory order point. McCay Company has recently decided to implement a policy designed to control inventory better.

Based on past experience, the following data have been gathered for materials, which are used at a uniform rate throughout the year:

Units required during the year	2,760
Units of safety stock..	180
Days of scheduled production	230
Days of lead time to receive an order	25
Ordering cost, per order placed...................................	$34.50
Annual storage cost, per unit.....................................	$ .40

Instructions:

(1) Complete the following table for "number of orders" of 1 through 6.

Number of Orders	Number of Units per Order	Average Units in Inventory	Order and Storage Costs		
			Order Cost	Storage Cost	Combined Cost
1	2,760	1,380	$34.50	$552.00	$586.50

(2) Determine the economic order quantity, based on the table completed in (1).
(3) Determine the economic order quantity, using the economic order quantity formula.
(4) Determine the inventory order point.

14–42. Economic order quantity under present and proposed conditions. Based on the data presented in Problem 14–41, assume that McCay Company is considering the purchase of new automated storage equipment to facilitate access to materials and to increase storage capacity. In addition, the manager of the purchasing department has requested authorization to purchase five microcomputers to expedite the processing of purchase orders.

Instructions:

(1) Assuming that the new storage equipment will increase the storage cost from $.40 to $1.60 per unit, determine the economic order quantity for McCay Company, using the economic order quantity formula.
(2) Assuming that the new storage equipment is not purchased and the acquisition of the microcomputer equipment will decrease the cost per order placed fron $34.50 to $5.52, determine the economic order quantity, using the economic order quantity formula.
(3) Assuming that both the new storage equipment and the microcomputer equipment are purchased, determine the economic order quantity, using the economic order quantity formula. As indicated in (1) and (2), the purchase of the storage equipment is expected to increase the storage cost per unit from $.40 to $1.60, and the microcomputer equipment is expected to decrease the cost per order placed from $34.50 to $5.52.
(4) Based on the answers to Problem 14–41 and (1), (2), and (3) above, what generalizations can be made concerning how changes in the cost per order placed and the storage cost per unit affect the economic order quantity?

14–43. The most economical purchasing plan, using linear programming graph. Collins Company purchases Part Q for use at both its Comer and Lilburn branches. Part Q is available in limited quantities from two suppliers. The relevant data are as follows:

Units required:
  Comer Branch.. 100
  Lilburn Branch...................................... 150

Supplier E:
  Units available..................................... 150
  Unit cost delivered to:
    Comer Branch.................................... $40
    Lilburn Branch.................................. $70

Supplier F:
  Units available..................................... 150
  Unit cost delivered to:
    Comer Branch.................................... $50
    Lilburn Branch.................................. $90

The manager of the purchasing department has prepared the following purchase plan for the Comer and Lilburn branches:
  (1) Purchase all units for Comer Branch from Supplier E.
  (2) Purchase remaining available units of Supplier E for the Lilburn Branch.
  (3) Purchase any additional units required by the Lilburn Branch from Supplier F.

Instructions:

(1) Construct a linear programming graph for units to be purchased from Supplier E. Plot the units for the Comer Branch along the horizontal axis.

(2) Identify the four corners at which an economical purchase plan might be identified on the linear programming graph. Label the corners A through D, as shown in the illustration in this chapter.

(3) For each corner in (2), indicate purchases from Suppliers E and F for the Comer and Lilburn branches. Identify Plan 1 with Corner A, Plan 2 with Corner B, Plan 3 with Corner C, and Plan 4 with Corner D.

(4) Determine the most economical purchase plan by computing the total cost of purchases for each plan identified in (3).

(5) Was the purchasing department manager's plan the most economical? Explain.

14–44. Expected value and analysis. Interamerica Films Inc. is considering purchasing the rights to one of two autobiographies for the purposes of producing and marketing a motion picture. Each autobiography has the potential for development and sale as one of the following: (1) a cable TV movie, (2) a network (noncable) TV movie, (3) a weekly TV series, or (4) a commercial theater movie. The estimated profit for development and sale of each autobiography and the estimated chances of occurrence are as follows:

Autobiography S

	Estimated Profit	Chance of Occurrence
Cable TV movie	$15,000,000	25%
Network TV movie	8,000,000	15
Weekly TV series	20,000,000	30
Theater movie	10,000,000	30

Autobiography T

	Estimated Profit	Chance of Occurrence
Cable TV movie	$16,000,000	30%
Network TV movie	18,000,000	35
Weekly TV series	5,000,000	25
Theater movie	40,000,000	10

Instructions:

(1) Determine the expected value of each autobiography.
(2) Based on the results of (1), which autobiography rights should be purchased?

14–45. Payoff table, chances of occurrence, and analysis. Shugart News Distributors recently purchased a newsstand on the corner of Chase Street and Prince Avenue in downtown Hampton. The new manager of the newsstand must decide how many copies of a magazine to stock on a weekly basis. The magazine is published locally and features local civic and social events and has a large classified advertising section. The former manager had noted that the maximum weekly sales, in the past, had been 400 magazines, and to be assured that all demand could be met, 450 magazines were purchased. The cost of the magazine is $60 for quantities of 50 ($1.20 per magazine), and the magazine is sold for $2. Any magazines remaining at the end of the week are worthless and are thrown away.

The records for the past ten weeks indicate the following sales:

Number of Weeks	Actual Demand (Sales)
3	200
2	250
4	300
1	400

Instructions:

(1) Prepare a payoff table of possible outcomes in terms of contribution margin, using the format shown in this chapter.
(2) Based on the sales data for the past ten weeks, estimate the chances of each level of possible demand for the magazine.
(3) Prepare a payoff table of expected values of possible outcomes in terms of contribution margin, using the format shown in this chapter.
(4) Based on (3), how many magazines should be purchased? Explain.

14–46. Decision tree and analysis. Gem Mines Inc. is preparing to bid on the purchase of mining rights to one of two plats of federally owned land: Plat #600 and Plat #900. Both plats of land are known to contain deposits of coal; however, the quality of deposits will not be known until actual mining begins.

Preliminary estimates indicate that, for Plat #600, there is a 45% chance that the deposit is of high quality and will yield total profits of $20,000,000. There is a 30% chance that the deposit is of moderate quality and will yield total profits of $10,000,000. Finally, there is a 25% chance that the deposit is of low quality and will yield total profits of $2,000,000.

Preliminary estimates indicate that, for Plat #900, there is a 25% chance that the deposit is of high quality and will yield total profits of $40,000,000. There is a 20% chance that the deposit is of moderate quality and will yield total profits of $15,000,000. Finally, there is a 55% chance that the deposit is of low quality and will yield total profits of $1,000,000.

Instructions:

(1) Prepare a decision tree with expected values to aid management in deciding on which plat rights to bid.
(2) On which plat rights should the management of Gem Mines Inc. bid?

14–47.   Expected cost of conducting an investigation of a variance and analysis.   The controller of Crowley Company must decide whether to investigate an unfavorable direct labor rate variance of $8,000 reported for May. The variance is expected to continue for June if not corrected. Past experience indicates that 75% of the time the variance is caused by use of more experienced, higher paid employees in jobs budgeted for less experienced, lower paid employees. In this case, the variance can be eliminated by the rescheduling of job assignments. On the other hand, 25% of the time the variance is caused by overtime created by production commitments in excess of normal operations. If production demands continue, additional employees will be hired. However, because of training commitments, any new employees would not be available for assignment to normal operations until the end of June.

Instructions:

(1) Assuming that no additional costs would be incurred in conducting an investigation, what is the expected cost of investigation of the direct labor rate variance?
(2) What is the value of conducting an investigation of the direct labor rate variance?
(3) If the estimated cost to investigate the variance is $5,000, should the controller authorize an investigation? Explain.
(4) If the estimated cost to investigate the variance is $7,000, should the controller authorize an investigation? Explain.

14–48.   Maximin and maximax concepts and analysis.   The management of Dawson Realty Corporation is considering an investment in one of three real estate projects. The first project involves the construction of a medical office complex which will be sold to a group of practicing physicians.

The second project involves the construction of a professional office building in which space will be sold to nonmedical professional businesses, such as law firms and insurance agencies. The third project is the construction of a small shopping mall in which space will be sold to small businesses. The success of each project depends on whether demand for the constructed space is high, moderate, or low. The estimated profit or loss for each project is as follows:

Project	Demand for Space		
	High	Moderate	Low
Medical office complex	$2,000,000	$1,500,000	$1,200,000
Professional office complex ...	3,300,000	2,500,000	1,100,000
Shopping mall..............	4,000,000	2,000,000	(400,000)

Instructions:

(1) If the management of Dawson Realty Corporation uses the maximin concept, which of the three projects would be chosen?

(2) If the management of Dawson Realty Corporation uses the maximax concept, which of the three projects would be chosen?

(3) Assuming that the Moderate column is the most likely estimate of profit for each of the projects, what alternative decision concept can be used by Dawson Realty Corporation?

14–49. Expected value; maximin concept; maximax concept; and analysis. Kincaid Company is considering building a condominium development in one of three locations: a city location, a country club location, and a lakefront location. The success of each location depends on buyer demand. Based on marketing studies, the following profits and losses have been estimated for each location, along with the chances of occurrence:

	High Buyer Demand		Low Buyer Demand	
	Profit (Loss)	Chance of Occurrence	Profit (Loss)	Chance of Occurrence
City	$30,000,000	60%	$(12,000,000)	40%
Country club . .	60,000,000	70	(40,000,000)	30
Lakefront	50,000,000	75	(20,000,000)	25

Instructions:

(1) Determine the expected value of each location.

(2) Which location should be chosen, using the expected value concept?

(3) Which location should be chosen, using the maximin concept?

(4) Which location should be chosen, using the maximax concept?

(5) Which location should be chosen if management's primary objective is to choose that location with the smallest range of possible outcomes?

(6) Which location would be chosen if management uses the concept of selecting that location with the highest chance of profit?

ALTERNATE PROBLEMS

14–41A. Economic order quantity and inventory order point. Colson Company has recently decided to implement a policy designed to control inventory better. Based on past experience, the following data have been gathered for materials, which are used at a uniform rate throughout the year:

Units required during the year	3,960
Units of safety stock.	270
Days of scheduled production	220
Days of lead time to receive an order	20
Ordering cost, per order placed.	$33.00
Annual storage cost, per unit	$ .15

ADSHEET
BLEM

Instructions:

(1) Complete the following table for "number of orders" of 1 through 6.

Number of Orders	Number of Units per Order	Average Units in Inventory	Order and Storage Costs		
			Order Cost	Storage Cost	Combined Cost
1	3,960	1,980	$33.00	$297.00	$330.00

(2) Determine the economic order quantity, based on the table completed in (1).
(3) Determine the economic order quantity, using the economic order quantity formula.
(4) Determine the inventory order point.

14–43A. The most economical purchasing plan, using linear programming graph. Parks Company purchases Part R for use at both its Clinton and Moline branches. Part R is available in limited quantities from two suppliers. The relevant data are as follows:

Units required:	
Clinton Branch..	120
Moline Branch...	200
Supplier J:	
Units available.......................................	200
Unit cost delivered to:	
Clinton Branch......................................	$ 50
Moline Branch......................................	$100
Supplier K:	
Units available.......................................	200
Unit cost delivered to:	
Clinton Branch......................................	$ 60
Moline Branch......................................	$140

The new manager of the purchasing department of Parks Company has prepared the following purchase plan for the Clinton and Moline Branches:

	Purchases by Clinton Branch	Purchases by Moline Branch
From Supplier J	120 units	80 units
From Supplier K	0	120

Instructions:

(1) Construct a linear programming graph for units to be purchased from Supplier J. Plot the units for the Clinton Branch along the horizontal axis.
(2) Identify the four corners at which an economical purchase plan might be identified on the linear programming graph. Label the corners A through D, as shown in the illustration in this chapter.
(3) For each corner in (2), indicate purchases from Suppliers J and K for the Clinton and Moline branches. Identify Plan 1 with Corner A, Plan 2 with Corner B, Plan 3 with Corner C, and Plan 4 with Corner D.

(4) Determine the most economical purchase plan by computing the total cost of purchases for each plan identified in (3).

(5) Was the purchasing department manager's plan the most economical? Explain.

14–44A. Expected value and analysis. Fielder Science Corporation is considering purchasing the rights to one of two laser patents for purposes of research and development. Patent 1002 has potential developmental applications in the areas of medicine, computer science, pharmacology, and military weaponry. Patent 1010 has potential developmental applications in the areas of mining, automobile manufacturing, telecommunications, and energy. Whichever patent rights are purchased, it is likely that only one of the potential applications will yield research and development results promising enough to market commercially. The estimated profit for each patent application and the estimated chances of occurrence are as follows:

Patent 1002

Application	Estimated Profit	Chance of Occurrence
Medicine..................................	$15,000,000	20%
Computer science.........................	4,000,000	30
Pharmacology	6,000,000	35
Military weaponry	12,000,000	15

Patent 1010

Application	Estimated Profit	Chance of Occurrence
Mining....................................	$2,000,000	10%
Automobile manufacturing..................	8,000,000	30
Telecommunications.......................	10,000,000	40
Energy...................................	30,000,000	20

Instructions:

(1) Determine the expected value of each patent.

(2) Based on the results of (1), which patent rights should be purchased?

14–45A. Payoff table, chances of occurrence, and analysis. Martel News Distributors recently purchased a newsstand on the corner of 2nd Avenue South and 5th Avenue in downtown Morrison. The new manager of the newsstand must decide how many copies of the local newspaper to stock on a daily basis. The former manager had noted that the maximum daily sales, in the past, had been 200 papers, and to be assured that all demand could be met, 220 papers were purchased daily. The cost of the newspaper is $.20 per paper, and the paper is sold for $.40. Any papers remaining at the end of the day are worthless and are thrown away. The paper is published five days a week.

The records for the past month indicate the following sales:

Number of Days	Actual Demand (Sales)
2	100
4	150
8	175
6	200

Instructions:

(1) Prepare a payoff table of possible outcomes in terms of contribution margin, using the format shown in this chapter.
(2) Based on the sales data for the past 20 days, estimate the chances of each level of possible demand for the newspaper.
(3) Prepare a payoff table of expected values of possible outcomes in terms of contribution margin, using the format shown in this chapter.
(4) Based on (3), how many newspapers should be purchased? Explain.

14–46A. Decision tree and analysis. Jewel Mines Inc. is preparing to bid on the purchase of mining rights to one of two plats of federally owned land: Plat #100 and Plat #300. Both plats of land are known to contain deposits of uranium; however, the quality of the deposits will not be known until actual mining begins.

Preliminary estimates indicate that, for Plat #100, there is a 60% chance that the deposit is of high quality and will yield total profits of $50,000,000. There is a 25% chance that the deposit is of moderate quality and will yield total profits of $20,000,000. Finally, there is a 15% chance that the deposit is of low quality and will yield total profits of $5,000,000.

Preliminary estimates indicate that, for Plat #300, there is a 30% chance that the deposit is of high quality and will yield total profits of $80,000,000. There is a 30% chance that the deposit is of moderate quality and will yield total profits of $40,000,000. Finally, there is a 40% chance that the deposit is of low quality and will yield total profits of $1,000,000.

Instructions:

(1) Prepare a decision tree with expected values to aid management in deciding on which plat rights to bid.
(2) On which plat rights should the management of Jewel Mines Inc. bid?

14–47A. Expected cost of conducting an investigation of a variance and analysis. The controller of Hodges Company must decide whether to investigate an unfavorable direct labor time variance of $4,000 reported for August. The variance is expected to continue for September if not corrected. Past experience indicates that 80% of the time the variance is caused by lack of proper supervision and can be eliminated by reminding the supervisors of their responsibilities. On the other hand, 20% of the time the variance is caused by inexperienced personnel who lack proper training. Due to sales and production commitments, the appropriate training cannot be scheduled until the end of September.

Instructions:

(1) Assuming that no additional costs would be incurred in conducting an investigation, what is the expected cost of investigating the direct labor time variance?
(2) What is the value of conducting an investigation of the direct labor time variance?
(3) If the estimated cost to investigate the variance is $5,000, should the controller authorize an investigation? Explain.
(4) If the estimated cost to investigate the variance is $2,500, should the controller authorize an investigation? Explain.

14–48A. Maximin and maximax concepts and analysis. The management of Investors Systems Inc. is considering a speculative investment in one of three oil and gas ventures. The success or failure of each venture depends on the quantity of oil and gas discovered. The estimated profit or loss for each venture is as follows:

	Amount of Oil and Gas Discovered		
	Small Quantities	Moderate Quantities	Large Quantities
Venture X...............	$(100,000)	$8,000,000	$20,000,000
Venture Y...............	400,000	7,500,000	15,000,000
Venture Z...............	300,000	10,000,000	18,500,000

Instructions:

(1) If the management of Investors Systems Inc. uses the maximin concept, which of the three ventures would be chosen?
(2) If the management of Investors Systems Inc. uses the maximax concept, which of the three ventures would be chosen?
(3) Assuming that the Moderate Quantities column is the most likely estimate of profit from the oil and gas that will be discovered, what alternative decision concept can be used by Investors Systems Inc.?

Mini-Case 14

International Oil Inc.

International Oil Inc. must decide between two sites at which to drill for oil. At a desert site, there is a 70% chance that oil will be discovered, resulting in an estimated profit of $30,000,000. There is a 30% chance that no oil will be discovered at the desert site, resulting in an estimated loss of $5,000,000. At a mountain site, there is a 65% chance that oil will be discovered, resulting in an estimated profit of $40,000,000. There is a 35% chance that no oil will be discovered at the mountain site, resulting in an estimated loss of $20,000,000.

As a special assistant to the president, Susan Satterfield, you have been asked to analyze which site should be selected for drilling. In the past, Satterfield has selected that site with the largest possible profit.

Instructions:

(1) What decision concept has Satterfield used in the past?
(2) Using the concept identified in (1), which site should be selected?
(3) Prepare a decision tree with expected values to aid in the site selection decision. *(continued)*

(4) Based on the expected value concept, which site should be selected?

(5) Assuming that a new technology, using infrared photographs from satellites, can provide perfect information concerning the location of oil deposits, how much should International Oil Inc. be willing to pay for perfect information concerning (a) the desert site and (b) the mountain site?

(6) Assuming that the perfect information described in (5) costs $3,000,000 per site, should each site be analyzed at a cost of $3,000,000 per analysis to obtain perfect information?

(7) Assuming that Satterfield agrees to use the expected value concept in the selection of a drilling site, prepare a final recommendation using the results of (3) through (6).

Answers to Self-Examination Questions

· · ·

1. D Storage cost per unit (answer A), annual units required (answer B), and cost per order (answer C) are all important in the determination of economic order quantity.

2. A The expected value of Proposal R is $24,000 (answer A), computed as follows:

$$\text{Expected Value} = .60(\$80,000) + .40(-\$60,000)$$
$$\text{Expected Value} = \$48,000 - \$24,000$$
$$\text{Expected Value} = \$24,000$$

3. B Management's use of expected value can be facilitated through the use of payoff tables and decision trees (answer B). The maximax concept (answer A) and the maximin concept (answer C) do not use expected values.

4. A The value of perfect information concerning Proposal A is $3,000 (answer A), which is the difference between (1) the expected value of Proposal A based on perfect information, $8,000 (answer C), and (2) the expected value of a decision based on existing information, $5,000 (answer B).

5. A The maximin concept leads management to decide in favor of that alternative with the maximum minimum profit. For Freeman Co., the minimum profit (loss) for each alternative appears in the low demand column. This column indicates that Project W (answer A) has the highest minimum profit ($120,000) of the four alternatives.

*Part
Six*

*Financial
Analysis for
Management
Use*

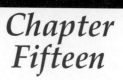

Chapter Fifteen

•

Describe the usefulness of financial statement analysis to management.

•

Describe the types of financial statement analysis.

•

Describe basic financial statement analytical procedures.

•

Illustrate the application of financial statement analysis in assessing solvency and profitability.

•

Identify and illustrate the content of corporate annual reports.

•

Describe the content of interim financial reports.

•

Financial Statement Analysis and Annual Reports

One of the primary objectives of accounting is to provide useful data to management for directing operations. In providing data to assist management, the accountant relies on a variety of concepts and techniques. Many of these concepts and techniques, such as budgeting, standard costs, differential analysis, break-even analysis, and variable costing, were discussed in preceding chapters. In this chapter, management's use of analyses of the data reported in the basic financial statements will be presented. In addition, the annual reports and the interim reports that are issued by corporations are discussed. These reports often contain some financial analyses as well as much of the basic information used by outsiders in evaluating management's performance.

USEFULNESS OF FINANCIAL STATEMENT ANALYSIS

The financial condition and the results of operations, as reported in the basic financial statements, are of interest to many groups external to the reporting enterprise. Since the basic statements will be evaluated by outsiders, such as creditors and owners, management is concerned with the basic financial statements and how they are viewed by these external parties. Management is also interested in the basic financial statements for other reasons. For example, the basic financial statements are used to assess the effectiveness of management in planning and controlling operations. In addition, management recognizes that the evaluation of past operations, as revealed by the analysis of the basic statements, represents a good starting point in planning future operations. Management uses financial statement analysis, therefore, as an important means of assessing past performance and in forecasting and planning future performance.

TYPES OF FINANCIAL STATEMENT ANALYSIS

Most of the items in the basic statements are of limited significance when considered individually. Their usefulness can be enhanced through studying relationships and comparisons of items (1) within a single year's financial statements, (2) in a succession of financial statements, and (3) with other enterprises. The selection and the preparation of analytical aids are a part of the work of the accountant.

Certain aspects of financial condition or of operations are of greater importance to management than are other aspects. However, management is especially interested in the ability of a business to pay its debts as they come due and to earn a reasonable amount of income. These two aspects of the status of an enterprise are called factors of **solvency** and **profitability**. An enterprise that cannot meet its obligations to creditors on a timely basis is likely to experience difficulty in obtaining credit, and this may lead to a decline in profitability. Similarly, an enterprise whose earnings are less than those of its competitors is likely to be at a disadvantage in obtaining credit or new capital from stockholders. In addition to this interrelationship between solvency and profitability, it is important to recognize that analysis of historical data is useful in assessing the past performance of an enterprise and in forecasting its future performance.

The basic analytical procedures and the various types of financial analysis useful in evaluating the solvency and profitability of an enterprise are discussed in the following paragraphs.

BASIC ANALYTICAL PROCEDURES

The analytical measures obtained from financial statements are usually expressed as ratios or percentages. For example, the relationship of $150,000 to $100,000 ($150,000/$100,000 or $150,000:$100,000) may be expressed as 1.5, 1.5:1, or 150%. This ease of computation and simplicity of form for expressing financial relationships are major reasons for the widespread use of ratios and percentages in financial analysis.

Analytical procedures may be used to compare the amount of specific items on a current statement with the corresponding amounts on earlier statements. For example, in comparing cash of $150,000 on the current balance sheet with cash of $100,000 on the balance sheet of a year earlier, the current amount may be expressed as 1.5 or 150% of the earlier amount. The relationship may also be expressed in terms of change, that is, the increase of $50,000 may be stated as a 50% increase.

Analytical procedures are also widely used to show the relationships of individual items to each other and of individual items to totals on a single statement. To illustrate, assume that included in the total of $1,000,000 of assets on a balance sheet are cash of $50,000 and inventories of $250,000. In relative terms, the cash balance is 5% of total assets and the inventories represent 25% of total assets. Individual items in the current asset group could also be related to total current assets. Assuming that the total of current assets in the example is $500,000, cash represents 10% of the total and inventories represent 50% of the total.

Increases or decreases in items may be expressed in percentage terms only when the base figure is positive. If the base figure is zero or a negative value, the amount of change cannot be expressed as a percentage. For example, if comparative balance sheets indicate no liability for notes payable on the first, or base, date and a liability of $10,000 on the later date, the increase of $10,000 cannot be stated as a percent of zero. Similarly, if a net loss of $10,000 in a particular year is followed by a net income of $5,000 in the next year, the increase of $15,000 cannot be stated as a percent of the loss of the base year.

In the following discussion and illustrations of analytical procedures, the basic significance of the various measures will be emphasized. The measures developed are not ends in themselves; they are only guides to the evaluation of financial and operating data. Many other factors, such as trends in the industry, changes in price levels, and general economic conditions and prospects, may also need consideration in order to arrive at sound conclusions.

Horizontal Analysis

The percentage analysis of increases and decreases in corresponding items in comparative financial statements is called **horizontal analysis**. The amount of each item on the most recent statement is compared with the corresponding item on one or more earlier statements. The increase or decrease in the amount of the item is then listed, together with the percent of increase or decrease. When the comparison is made between two statements, the earlier statement is used as the base. If the analysis includes three or more statements, there are two alternatives in the selection of the base: the earliest date or period may be used as the basis for comparing all later dates or periods, or each statement may be compared with the immediately preceding statement. The two alternatives are illustrated as follows:

BASE: EARLIEST YEAR

				Increase (Decrease*)			
				1989–90		*1989–91*	
Item	*1989*	*1990*	*1991*	*Amount*	*Percent*	*Amount*	*Percent*
A	$100,000	$150,000	$200,000	$ 50,000	50%	$100,000	100%
B	100,000	200,000	150,000	100,000	100%	50,000	50%

BASE: PRECEDING YEAR

				Increase (Decrease*)			
				1989–90		*1990–91*	
Item	*1989*	*1990*	*1991*	*Amount*	*Percent*	*Amount*	*Percent*
A	$100,000	$150,000	$200,000	$ 50,000	50%	$ 50,000	33%
B	100,000	200,000	150,000	100,000	100%	50,000*	25%*

Comparison of the amounts in the last two columns of the first analysis with the amounts in the corresponding columns of the second analysis reveals the effect of the base year on the direction of change and the amount and percent of change.

A condensed comparative balance sheet for two years, with horizontal analysis, is illustrated as follows:

Comparative Balance Sheet—Horizontal Analysis

	Chung Company Comparative Balance Sheet December 31, 1990 and 1989		Increase (Decrease*)	
	1990	1989	Amount	Percent
Assets				
Current assets..............	$ 550,000	$ 533,000	$ 17,000	3.2%
Long-term investments	95,000	177,500	82,500*	46.5%*
Plant assets (net)	444,500	470,000	25,500*	5.4%*
Intangible assets...........	50,000	50,000	—	
Total assets	$1,139,500	$1,230,500	$ 91,000*	7.4%*
Liabilities				
Current liabilities...........	$ 210,000	$ 243,000	$ 33,000*	13.6%*
Long-term liabilities	100,000	200,000	100,000*	50.0%*
Total liabilities	$ 310,000	$ 443,000	$133,000*	30.0%*
Stockholders' Equity				
Preferred 6% stock,				
$100 par.................	$ 150,000	$ 150,000	—	—
Common stock, $10 par	500,000	500,000	—	—
Retained earnings	179,500	137,500	$ 42,000	30.5%
Total stockholders' equity	$ 829,500	$ 787,500	$ 42,000	5.3%
Total liabilities and stockholders' equity	$1,139,500	$1,230,500	$ 91,000*	7.4%*

The significance of the various increases and decreases in the items shown cannot be fully determined without additional information. Although total assets at the end of 1990 were $91,000 (7.4%) less than at the beginning of the year, liabilities were reduced by $133,000 (30%) and stockholders' equity increased $42,000 (5.3%). It would appear that the reduction of $100,000 in long-term liabilities was accomplished, for the most part, through the sale of long-term investments.

The foregoing balance sheet may be expanded to include the details of the various categories of assets and liabilities, or the details may be presented in separate schedules. Opinions differ as to which method presents the clearer picture. A supporting schedule with horizontal analysis is illustrated by the following comparative schedule of current assets:

	1990	1989	Increase (Decrease*)	
			Amount	Percent
Cash	$ 90,500	$ 64,700	$25,800	39.9%
Marketable securities	75,000	60,000	15,000	25.0%
Accounts receivable (net)	115,000	120,000	5,000*	4.2%*
Inventories	264,000	283,000	19,000*	6.7%*
Prepaid expenses	5,500	5,300	200	3.8%
Total current assets	$550,000	$533,000	$17,000	3.2%

Chung Company
Comparative Schedule of Current Assets
December 31, 1990 and 1989

Comparative Schedule of Current Assets — Horizontal Analysis

The reduction in accounts receivable may have come about through changes in credit terms or improved collection policies. Similarly, a reduction in inventories during a period of increased sales probably indicates an improvement in the management of inventories.

The changes in the current assets would appear to be favorable, particularly in view of the 24.8% increase in net sales, shown in the following comparative income statement with horizontal analysis:

Chung Company
Comparative Income Statement
For Years Ended December 31, 1990 and 1989

Comparative Income Statement — Horizontal Analysis

	1990	1989	Increase (Decrease*)	
			Amount	Percent
Sales	$1,530,500	$1,234,000	$296,500	24.0%
Sales returns and allowances	32,500	34,000	1,500*	4.4%*
Net sales	$1,498,000	$1,200,000	$298,000	24.8%
Cost of goods sold	1,043,000	820,000	223,000	27.2%
Gross profit	$ 455,000	$ 380,000	$ 75,000	19.7%
Selling expenses	$ 191,000	$ 147,000	$ 44,000	29.9%
General expenses	104,000	97,400	6,600	6.8%
Total operating expenses	$ 295,000	$ 244,400	$ 50,600	20.7%
Operating income	$ 160,000	$ 135,600	$ 24,400	18.0%
Other income	8,600	11,000	2,400*	21.8%*
	$ 168,600	$ 146,600	$ 22,000	15.0%
Other expense	13,100	18,000	4,900*	27.2%*
Income before income tax	$ 155,500	$ 128,600	$ 26,900	20.9%
Income tax	64,500	52,100	12,400	23.8%
Net income	$ 91,000	$ 76,500	$ 14,500	19.0%

An increase in net sales, considered alone, is not necessarily favorable. The increase in Chung Company's net sales was accompanied by a somewhat greater percentage increase in the cost of goods (merchandise) sold, which indicates a narrowing of the gross profit margin. Selling expenses increased markedly and general expenses increased slightly, making an overall increase in operating expenses of 20.7%, as contrasted with a 19.7% increase in gross profit.

Although the increase in operating income and in the final net income figure is favorable, it would be incorrect for management to conclude that its operations were at maximum efficiency. A study of the expenses and additional analysis and comparisons of individual expense accounts should be made.

The income statement illustrated is in condensed form. Such a condensed statement usually provides enough information for all interested groups except management. If desired, the statement may be expanded or supplemental schedules may be prepared to present details of the cost of goods sold, selling expenses, general expenses, other income, and other expense.

A comparative retained earnings statement with horizontal analysis is illustrated as follows:

Comparative Retained Earnings Statement — Horizontal Analysis

			Increase (Decrease*)	
Chung Company Comparative Retained Earnings Statement For Years Ended December 31, 1990 and 1989				
	1990	1989	Amount	Percent
Retained earnings, January 1	$137,500	$100,000	$37,500	37.5%
Net income for year	91,000	76,500	14,500	19.0%
Total	$228,500	$176,500	$52,000	29.5%
Dividends: On preferred stock	$ 9,000	$ 9,000	—	—
On common stock	40,000	30,000	$10,000	33.3%
Total	$ 49,000	$ 39,000	$10,000	25.6%
Retained earnings, December 31	$179,500	$137,500	$42,000	30.5%

Examination of the statement reveals an increase of 30.5% in retained earnings for the year. The increase was attributable to the retention of $42,000 of the net income for the year ($91,000 net income − $49,000 dividends paid).

Vertical Analysis

• • •

Percentage analysis may also be used to show the relationship of the component parts to the total in a single statement. This type of analysis is called **vertical analysis.** As in horizontal analysis, the statements may be prepared in either detailed or condensed form. In the latter case, additional details of the changes in the various categories may be presented in supporting schedules. If such schedules are prepared, the percentage analysis may be based on either the total of the schedule or the balance sheet total. Although vertical analysis is confined within each individual statement, the significance of both the amounts and the percentages is increased by preparing comparative statements.

In vertical analysis of the balance sheet, each asset item is stated as a percent of total assets, and each liability and stockholders' equity item is stated as a percent of total liabilities and stockholders' equity. A condensed comparative balance sheet with vertical analysis is illustrated as follows:

• • • • • • • • •
*Comparative Balance
Sheet — Vertical
Analysis*

	1990		1989	
Chung Company Comparative Balance Sheet December 31, 1990 and 1989	Amount	Percent	Amount	Percent
Assets				
Current assets..............	$ 550,000	48.3%	$ 533,000	43.3%
Long-term investments	95,000	8.3	177,500	14.4
Plant assets (net)	444,500	39.0	470,000	38.2
Intangible assets...........	50,000	4.4	50,000	4.1
Total assets	$1,139,500	100.0%	$1,230,500	100.0%
Liabilities				
Current liabilities...........	$ 210,000	18.4%	$ 243,000	19.7%
Long-term liabilities	100,000	8.8	200,000	16.3
Total liabilities	$ 310,000	27.2%	$ 443,000	36.0%
Stockholders' Equity Preferred 6% stock, $100 par..................	$ 150,000	13.2%	$ 150,000	12.2%
Common stock, $10 par	500,000	43.9	500,000	40.6
Retained earnings	179,500	15.7	137,500	11.2
Total stockholders' equity	$ 829,500	72.8%	$ 787,500	64.0%
Total liabilities and stockholders' equity.......	$1,139,500	100.0%	$1,230,500	100.0%

The major relative changes in Chung Company's assets were in the current asset and long-term investment groups. In the lower half of the balance sheet, the greatest relative change was in long-term liabilities and retained earnings. Stockholders' equity increased from 64% of total liabilities and stockholders' equity at the end of 1989 to 72.8% at the end of 1990, with a corresponding decrease in the claims of creditors.

In vertical analysis of the income statement, each item is stated as a percent of net sales. A condensed comparative income statement with vertical analysis is illustrated as follows:

Comparative Income Statement — Vertical Analysis

	1990		1989	
	Amount	Percent	Amount	Percent
Sales	$1,530,500	102.2%	$1,234,000	102.8%
Sales returns and allowances	32,500	2.2	34,000	2.8
Net sales	$1,498,000	100.0%	$1,200,000	100.0%
Cost of goods sold..........	1,043,000	69.6	820,000	68.3
Gross profit	$ 455,000	30.4%	$ 380,000	31.7%
Selling expenses...........	$ 191,000	12.8%	$ 147,000	12.3%
General expenses	104,000	6.9	97,400	8.1
Total operating expenses	$ 295,000	19.7%	$ 244,400	20.4%
Operating income...........	$ 160,000	10.7%	$ 135,600	11.3%
Other income..............	8,600	.6	11,000	.9
	$ 168,600	11.3%	$ 146,600	12.2%
Other expense.............	13,100	.9	18,000	1.5
Income before income tax ...	$ 155,500	10.4%	$ 128,600	10.7%
Income tax................	64,500	4.3	52,100	4.3
Net income................	$ 91,000	6.1%	$ 76,500	6.4%

Chung Company
Comparative Income Statement
For Years Ended December 31, 1990 and 1989

Care must be used in judging the significance of differences between percentages for the two years. For example, the decline of the gross profit rate from 31.7% in 1989 to 30.4% in 1990 is only 1.3 percentage points. In terms of dollars of potential gross profit, however, it represents a decline of approximately $19,500 (1.3% × $1,498,000).

Common-Size Statements

Horizontal and vertical analyses with both dollar and percentage figures are helpful in disclosing relationships and trends in financial condition and operations of individual enterprises. Vertical analysis with both dollar and percentage figures is also useful in comparing one company with another or with industry averages. Such comparisons may be made easier by the use of **common-size statements,** in which all items are expressed only in relative terms.

Common-size statements may be prepared in order to compare percentages of a current period with past periods, to compare individual businesses, or to compare one business with industry percentages published by trade associations and financial information services. A comparative common-size income statement for two enterprises is illustrated as follows:

Common-Size Income Statement

Chung Company and Ross Corporation Condensed Common-Size Income Statement For Year Ended December 31, 1990	Chung Company	Ross Corporation
Sales	102.2%	102.3%
Sales returns and allowances	2.2	2.3
Net sales	100.0%	100.0%
Cost of goods sold	69.6	70.0
Gross profit	30.4%	30.0%
Selling expenses	12.8%	11.5%
General expenses	6.9	4.1
Total operating expenses	19.7%	15.6%
Operating income	10.7%	14.4%
Other income	.6	.6
	11.3%	15.0%
Other expense	.9	.5
Income before income tax	10.4%	14.5%
Income tax	4.3	5.5
Net income	6.1%	9.0%

Examination of the statement reveals that although Chung Company has a slightly higher rate of gross profit than Ross Corporation, the advantage is more than offset by its higher percentage of both selling and general expenses. As a consequence, the operating income of Chung Company is 10.7% of net sales as compared with 14.4% for Ross Corporation, an unfavorable difference of 3.7 percentage points.

Other Analytical Measures

In addition to the percentage analyses previously discussed, there are a number of other relationships that may be expressed in ratios and percentages. The items used in the measures are taken from the financial statements of the current period and hence are a further development of vertical analysis. Comparison of the items with corresponding measures of earlier periods is an extension of horizontal analysis.

Some of the more important ratios useful in the evaluation of solvency and profitability are discussed in the sections that follow. The examples are based on the illustrative statements presented earlier. In a few instances, data from a company's statements of the preceding year and from other sources are also used.

SOLVENCY ANALYSIS

Solvency is the ability of a business to meet its financial obligations as they come due. Solvency analysis, therefore, focuses mainly on balance sheet relationships that indicate the ability to liquidate current and noncurrent liabilities. Major analyses used in assessing solvency include (1) current position analysis, (2) accounts receivable analysis, (3) inventory analysis, (4) the ratio of plant assets to long-term liabilities, (5) the ratio of stockholders' equity to liabilities, and (6) the number of times interest charges are earned.

Current Position Analysis

To be useful, ratios relating to a firm's solvency must show the firm's ability to liquidate its liabilities. The use of ratios showing the ability to liquidate current liabilities is called **current position analysis** and is of particular interest to short-term creditors.

Working Capital. The excess of the current assets of an enterprise over its current liabilities at a certain moment of time is called **working capital.** The absolute amount of working capital and the flow of working capital during a period of time may be used in evaluating a company's ability to meet currently maturing obligations. Although useful for making intraperiod comparisons for a company, these absolute amounts are difficult to use in comparing companies of different sizes or in comparing such amounts with industry figures. For example, working capital of $250,000 may be very adequate for a small building contractor specializing in residential construction, but it may be completely inadequate for a large building contractor specializing in industrial and commerical construction.

Current Ratio. Another means of expressing the relationship between current assets and current liabilities is through the **current ratio,** sometimes referred to as the **working capital ratio** or **bankers' ratio.** The ratio is computed by dividing the total of current assets by the total of current liabilities.

The determination of working capital and the current ratio for Chung Company is illustrated as follows:

	1990	1989
Current assets	$550,000	$533,000
Current liabilities	210,000	243,000
Working capital	$340,000	$290,000
Current ratio	2.6:1	2.2:1

The current ratio is a more dependable indication of solvency than is working capital. To illustrate, assume that as of December 31, 1990, the working capital of a competing corporation is much greater than $340,000, but its current ratio is only 1.3:1. Considering these factors alone, Chung Company, with its current ratio of 2.6:1, is in a more favorable position to obtain short-term credit than the corporation with the greater amount of working capital.

Acid-Test Ratio. The amount of working capital and the current ratio are two solvency measures that indicate a company's ability to meet currently maturing obligations. However, these two measures do not take into account the composition of the current assets. To illustrate the significance of this additional factor, the following current position data for Chung Company and Randall Corporation as of December 31, 1990, are as follows:

	Chung Company	Randall Corporation
Current assets:		
Cash	$ 90,500	$ 45,500
Marketable securities	75,000	25,000
Accounts receivable (net)	115,000	90,000
Inventories	264,000	380,000
Prepaid expenses	5,500	9,500
Total current assets	$550,000	$550,000
Current liabilities	210,000	210,000
Working capital	$340,000	$340,000
Current ratio	2.6:1	2.6:1

Both companies have working capital of $340,000 and a current ratio of 2.6:1. But the ability of each company to meet its currently maturing debts is vastly different. Randall Corporation has more of its current assets in inventories, which must be sold and the receivables collected before the current liabilities can be paid in full. A considerable amount of time may be required to convert these inventories into cash. Declines in market prices and a reduction in demand could also impair the ability to pay current liabilities. Conversely, Chung Company has enough cash and current assets (marketable securities and accounts receivable) which can generally be converted to cash rather quickly to meet its current liabilities.

A ratio that measures the "instant" debt-paying ability of a company is called the **acid-test ratio** or **quick ratio.** It is the ratio of the total **quick assets,** which are the cash, the marketable securities, and the receivables, to the total current liabilities. The acid-test ratio data for Chung Company are as follows:

	1990	1989
Quick assets:		
Cash....................................	$ 90,500	$ 64,700
Marketable securities	75,000	60,000
Accounts receivable (net)	115,000	120,000
Total................................	$280,500	$244,700
Current liabilities	$210,000	$243,000
Acid-test ratio..............................	1.3:1	1.0:1

A thorough analysis of a firm's current position would include the determination of the amount of working capital, the current ratio, and the acid-test ratio. The current and acid-test ratios are most useful when viewed together and when compared with similar ratios for previous periods and with those of other firms in the industry.

Accounts Receivable Analysis

The size and composition of accounts receivable change continually during business operations. The amount is increased by sales on account and reduced by collections. Firms that grant long credit terms tend to have relatively greater amounts tied up in accounts receivable than those granting short credit terms. Increases or decreases in the volume of sales also affect the amount of outstanding accounts receivable.

Accounts receivable yield no revenue, hence it is desirable to keep the amount invested in them at a minimum. The cash made available by prompt collection of receivables improves solvency and may be used for purchases of merchandise in larger quantities at a lower price, for payment of dividends to stockholders, or for other purposes. Prompt collection also lessens the risk of loss from uncollectible accounts.

Accounts Receivable Turnover. The relationship between credit sales and accounts receivable may be stated as the **accounts receivable turnover.** It is computed by dividing net sales on account by the average net accounts receivable. It is preferable to base the average on monthly balances, which gives effect to seasonal changes. When such data are not available, it is necessary to use the average of the balances at the beginning and the end of the year. If there are trade notes receivable as well as accounts, the two should be combined. The accounts receivable turnover data for Chung Company are as follows. All sales were made on account.

	1990	1989
Net sales on account	$1,498,000	$1,200,000
Accounts receivable (net):		
Beginning of year	$ 120,000	$ 140,000
End of year...........................	115,000	120,000
Total.................................	$ 235,000	$ 260,000
Average..............................	$ 117,500	$ 130,000
Accounts receivable turnover	12.7	9.2

The increase in the accounts receivable turnover for 1990 indicates that there has been an acceleration in the collection of receivables, due perhaps to improvement in either the granting of credit or the collection practices used, or both.

Number of Days' Sales in Receivables. Another means of expressing the relationship between credit sales and accounts receivable is the **number of days' sales in receivables.** This measure is determined by dividing the net accounts receivable at the end of the year by the average daily sales on account (net sales on account divided by 365), illustrated as follows for Chung Company:

	1990	1989
Accounts receivable (net), end of year	$ 115,000	$ 120,000
Net sales on account	$1,498,000	$1,200,000
Average daily sales on account	$ 4,104	$ 3,288
Number of days' sales in receivables	28.0	36.5

The number of days' sales in receivables gives a rough measure of the length of time the accounts receivable have been outstanding. A comparison of this measure with the credit terms, with figures for comparable firms in the same industry, and with figures of Chung Company for prior years will help reveal the efficiency in collecting receivables and the trends in the management of credit.

Inventory Analysis

Although an enterprise must maintain sufficient inventory quantities to meet the demands of its operations, it is desirable to keep the amount invested in inventory to a minimum. Inventories in excess of the needs of business reduce solvency by tying up funds. Excess inventories may also cause increases in the amount of insurance, property taxes, storage, and other related expenses, further reducing funds that could be used to better advantage.

There is also added risk of loss through price declines and deterioration or obsolescence of the inventory.

Inventory Turnover. The relationship between the volume of goods (merchandise) sold and inventory may be stated as the **inventory turnover**. It is computed by dividing the cost of goods sold by the average inventory. If monthly data are not available, it is necessary to use the average of the inventories at the beginning and the end of the year. The inventory turnover data for Chung Company are as follows:

	1990	1989
Cost of goods sold	$1,043,000	$820,000
Inventories:		
Beginning of year	$ 283,000	$311,000
End of year.............................	264,000	283,000
Total.....................................	$ 547,000	$594,000
Average...................................	$ 273,500	$297,000
Inventory turnover........................	3.8	2.8

The improvement in the turnover resulted from an increase in the cost of goods sold, combined with a decrease in average inventory. The variation in types of inventories is too great to permit any broad generalizations as to what is a satisfactory turnover. For example, a firm selling food should have a much higher turnover than one selling furniture or jewelry, and the perishable foods department of a supermarket should have a higher turnover than the soaps and cleansers department. However, for each business or each department within a business, there is a reasonable turnover rate. A turnover below this rate means that the company or the department is incurring extra expenses such as those for administration and storage, is increasing its risk of loss because of obsolescence and adverse price changes, is incurring interest charges in excess of those considered necessary, and is failing to free funds for other uses.

Number of Days' Sales in Inventory. Another means of expressing the relationship between the cost of goods sold and inventory is the **number of days' sales in inventory**. This measure is determined by dividing the inventories at the end of the year by the average daily cost of goods sold (cost of goods sold divided by 365), illustrated as follows for Chung Company:

	1990	1989
Inventories, end of year.....................	$ 264,000	$283,000
Cost of goods sold	$1,043,000	$820,000
Average daily cost of goods sold.............	$ 2,858	$ 2,247
Number of days' sales in inventory	92.4	125.9

The number of days' sales in inventory gives a rough measure of the length of time it takes to acquire, sell, and then replace the average inventory. Although there was a substantial improvement in the second year, comparison of the measure with those of earlier years and of comparable firms is an essential element in judging the effectiveness of Chung Company's inventory control.

As with many attempts to analyze financial data, it is possible to determine more than one measure to express the relationship between the cost of goods sold and inventory. Both the inventory turnover and number of days' sales in inventory are useful for evaluating the efficiency in the management of inventory. Whether both measures are used or whether one measure is preferred over the other is a matter for the individual analyst to decide.

Ratio of Plant Assets to Long-Term Liabilities

Long-term notes and bonds are often secured by mortgages on plant assets. *The* **ratio of total plant assets to long-term liabilities** *provides a solvency measure that shows the margin of safety of the noteholders or bondholders. It also gives an indication of the potential ability of the enterprise to borrow additional funds on a long-term basis.* The ratio of plant assets to long-term liabilities of Chung Company is as follows:

	1990	1989
Plant assets (net)	$444,500	$470,000
Long-term liabilities.........................	$100,000	$200,000
Ratio of plant assets to long-term liabilities	4.4:1	2.4:1

The marked increase in the ratio at the end of 1990 was mainly due to the liquidation of one half of Chung Company's long-term liabilities. If the company should need to borrow additional funds on a long-term basis, it is in a stronger position to do so.

Ratio of Stockholders' Equity to Liabilities

Claims against the total assets of an enterprise are divided into two basic groups, those of the creditors and those of the owners. *The relationship between the total claims of the creditors and owners provides a solvency measure that indicates the margin of safety for the creditors and the ability of the enterprise to withstand adverse business conditions.* If the claims of the creditors are large in proportion to the equity of the stockholders, there are likely to be substantial charges for interest payments. If earnings decline to the point where the company is unable to meet its interest payments, control of the business may pass to the creditors.

The relationship between stockholder and creditor equity is shown in the vertical analysis of the balance sheet. For example, the balance sheet of Chung Company presented on page 533 indicates that on December 31, 1990, stockholders' equity represented 72.8% and liabilities represented 27.2% of the sum of the liabilities and stockholders' equity (100.0%). Instead of expressing each item as a percent of the total, the relationship may be expressed as a ratio of one to the other, as follows:

	1990	1989
Total stockholders' equity....................	$829,500	$787,500
Total liabilities...............................	$310,000	$443,000
Ratio of stockholders' equity to liabilities	2.7:1	1.8:1

The balance sheet of Chung Company shows that the major factor affecting the change in the ratio was the $100,000 reduction in long-term liabilities during 1990. The ratio at both dates shows a large margin of safety for the creditors.

Number of Times Interest Charges Earned

Some corporations, such as railroads and public utilities, have a high ratio of debt to stockholders' equity. In analyzing such corporations, it is customary to express *the solvency measure that shows the relative risk of the debtholders in terms of the* **number of times the interest charges are earned** during the year. The higher the ratio, the greater the assurance of continued interest payments in case of decreased earnings. *The measure also provides an indication of general financial strength,* which is of concern to stockholders and employees, as well as to creditors.

In the following data, the amount available to meet interest charges is not affected by taxes on income because interest is deductible in determining taxable income.

	1990	1989
Income before income tax.................	$ 900,000	$ 800,000
Add interest charges.....................	300,000	250,000
Amount available to meet interest charges .	$1,200,000	$1,050,000
Number of times interest charges earned	4	4.2

Analyses like the above can be applied to dividends on preferred stock. In such cases, net income would be divided by the amount of preferred dividends to yield the number of times preferred dividends were earned. This measure gives an indication of the relative assurance of continued dividend payments to preferred stockholders.

PROFITABILITY ANALYSIS

Profitability is the ability of an entity to earn income. It can be assessed by computing various relevant measures, including (1) the ratio of net sales to assets, (2) the rate earned on total assets, (3) the rate earned on stockholders' equity, (4) the rate earned on common stockholders' equity, (5) earnings per share on common stock, (6) the price-earnings ratio, and (7) dividend yield.

Ratio of Net Sales to Assets

The **ratio of net sales to assets** *is a profitability measure that shows how effectively a firm utilizes its assets.* Assume that two competing enterprises have equal amounts of assets, but the amount of the sales of one is double the amount of the sales of the other. Obviously, the former is making better use of its assets. In computing the ratio, any long-term investments should be excluded from total assets because they are wholly unrelated to sales of goods or services. Assets used in determining the ratio may be the total at the end of the year, the average of the beginning and end of the year totals, or the average of the monthly totals. The basic data and the ratio of net sales to assets for Chung Company are as follows:

	1990	1989
Net sales.....................................	$1,498,000	$1,200,000
Total assets (excluding long-term investments):		
Beginning of year	$1,053,000	$1,010,000
End of year..............................	1,044,500	1,053,000
Total......................................	$2,097,500	$2,063,000
Average...................................	$1,048,750	$1,031,500
Ratio of net sales to assets................	1.4:1	1.2:1

The ratio improved to a minor degree in 1990, largely due to the increased sales volume. A comparison of the ratio with those of other enterprises in the same industry would be helpful in assessing Chung Company's effectiveness in the utilization of assets.

Rate Earned on Total Assets

The **rate earned on total assets** *is a measure of the profitability of the assets, without regard to the equity of creditors and stockholders in the assets.* The rate is therefore not affected by differences in methods of financing an enterprise.

The rate earned on total assets is derived by adding interest expense to net income and dividing this sum by the average total assets held throughout the year. By adding interest expense to net income, the profitability of the assets is determined without considering the means of financing the acquisition of the assets. The rate earned by Chung Company on total assets is determined as follows:

	1990	1989
Net income	$ 91,000	$ 76,500
Plus interest expense	13,100	18,000
Total	$ 104,100	$ 94,500
Total assets:		
Beginning of year	$1,230,500	$1,187,500
End of year	1,139,500	1,230,500
Total	$2,370,000	$2,418,000
Average	$1,185,000	$1,209,000
Rate earned on total assets	8.8%	7.8%

The rate earned on total assets of Chung Company for 1990 indicates an improvement over that for 1989. A comparison with other companies and with industry averages would also be useful in evaluating the effectiveness of management performance.

It is sometimes preferable to determine the rate of operating income (income before nonoperating income, nonoperating expense, extraordinary items, and income tax) to total assets. If nonoperating income is not considered, the investments yielding such income should be excluded from the assets. The use of income before income tax eliminates the effect of changes in the tax structure on the rate of earnings. When considering published data on rates earned on assets, the reader should note the exact nature of the measure.

Rate Earned on Stockholders' Equity

Another relative measure of profitability is obtained by dividing net income by the total stockholders' equity. In contrast to the rate earned on total assets, **the rate earned on stockholders' equity** *emphasizes the income yield in relationship to the amount invested by the stockholders.*

The amount of the total stockholders' equity throughout the year varies for several reasons — the issuance of additional stock, the retirement of a class of stock, the payment of dividends, and the gradual accrual of net income. If monthly figures are not available, the average of the stockholders' equity at the beginning and the end of the year is used, as in the following illustration:

	1990	1989
Net income	$ 91,000	$ 76,500
Stockholders' equity:		
Beginning of year	$ 787,500	$ 750,000
End of year	829,500	787,500
Total	$1,617,000	$1,537,500
Average	$ 808,500	$ 768,750
Rate earned on stockholders' equity	11.3%	10.0%

The rate earned by a thriving enterprise on the equity of its stockholders is usually higher than the rate earned on total assets. The reason for the difference is that the amount earned on assets acquired through the use of funds provided by creditors is more than the interest charges paid to creditors. This tendency of the rate on stockholders' equity to vary disproportionately from the rate on total assets is sometimes called **leverage**. The Chung Company rate on stockholders' equity for 1990, 11.3%, compares favorably with the rate of 8.8% earned on total assets, as reported on the preceding page. The leverage factor of 2.5% (11.3% − 8.8%) for 1990 also compares favorably with the 2.2% (10.0% − 7.8%) differential for the preceding year. These leverage factors for Chung Company are illustrated graphically in the following charts:

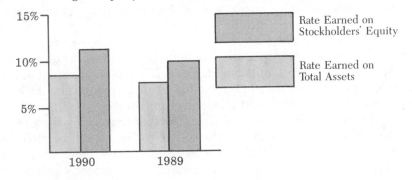

Chart of Rate Earned on Stockholders' Equity and Total Assets

Rate Earned on Common Stockholders' Equity

When a corporation has both preferred and common stock outstanding, the holders of the common stock have the residual claim on earnings. The **rate earned on common stockholders' equity** is the net income less preferred dividend requirements for the period, stated as a percent of the average equity of the common stockholders.

Chung Company has $150,000 of 6% nonparticipating preferred stock outstanding at both balance sheet dates, hence annual preferred dividends amount to $9,000. The common stockholders' equity is the total stockholders' equity, including retained earnings, reduced by the par of the preferred stock ($150,000). The basic data and the rate earned on common stockholders' equity are as follows:

	1990	1989
Net income.........................	$ 91,000	$ 76,500
Preferred dividends......................	9,000	9,000
Remainder—identified with common stock...	$ 82,000	$ 67,500
Common stockholders' equity:		
Beginning of year	$ 637,500	$ 600,000
End of year...........................	679,500	637,500
Total................................	$1,317,000	$1,237,500
Average..............................	$ 658,500	$ 618,750
Rate earned on common stockholders' equity .	12.5%	10.9%

The rate earned on common stockholders' equity differs from the rates earned by Chung Company on total assets and total stockholders' equity. This situation will occur if there are borrowed funds and also preferred stock outstanding, which rank ahead of the common shares in their claim on earnings. Thus the concept of leverage, as discussed in the preceding section, can be applied to the use of funds from the sale of preferred stock as well as from borrowing. Funds from both sources can be used in an attempt to increase the return on common stockholders' equity.

Earnings per Share on Common Stock

One of the profitability measures most commonly quoted by the financial press and included in the income statement in corporate annual reports is **earnings per share on common stock.** If a company has issued only one class of stock, the earnings per share are determined by dividing net income by the number of shares of stock outstanding. If there are both preferred and common stock outstanding, the net income must first be reduced by the amount necessary to meet the preferred dividend requirements.

Any changes in the number of shares outstanding during the year, such as would result from stock dividends or stock splits, should be disclosed in quoting earnings per share on common stock. Also if there are any non-recurring (extraordinary, etc.) items in the income statement, the income per share before such items should be reported along with net income per share. In addition, if there are convertible bonds or convertible preferred stock outstanding, the amount reported as net income per share should be stated without considering the conversion privilege, followed by net income per share assuming conversion had occurred.

The data on the earnings per share of common stock for Chung Company are as follows:

	1990	1989
Net income......................................	$91,000	$76,500
Preferred dividends.............................	9,000	9,000
Remainder — identified with common stock........	$82,000	$67,500
Shares of common stock outstanding.............	50,000	50,000
Earnings per share on common stock	$1.64	$1.35

Since earnings form the primary basis for dividends, earnings per share and dividends per share on common stock are commonly used by investors in weighing the merits of alternative investment opportunities. Earnings per share data can be presented in conjunction with dividends per share data to indicate the relationship between earnings and dividends and the extent to which the corporation is retaining its earnings for use in the business. The following chart shows this relationship for Chung Company:

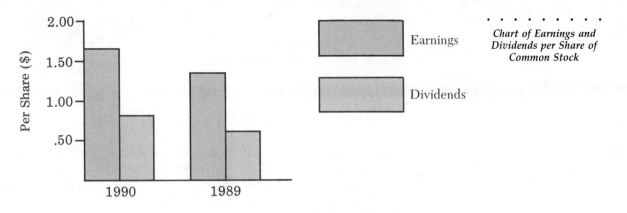

*Chart of Earnings and
Dividends per Share of
Common Stock*

Price-Earnings Ratio

A profitability measure commonly quoted by the financial press is the **price-earnings (P/E) ratio** on common stock. *The price-earnings ratio is used as an indicator of a firm's future earnings prospects.* It is computed by dividing the market price per share of common stock at a specific date by the annual earnings per share. Assuming market prices per common share of 20 1/2 at the end of 1990 and 13 1/2 at the end of 1989, the price-earnings ratio on common stock of Chung Company is as follows:

	1990	1989
Market price per share of common stock............	$20.50	$13.50
Earnings per share on common stock..............	$ 1.64	$ 1.35
Price-earnings ratio on common stock	12.5	10.0

The price-earnings ratio indicates that a share of common stock of Chung Company was selling for 12.5 and 10 times the amount of earnings per share at the end of 1990 and 1989 respectively.

Dividend Yield

The **dividend yield** on common stock is a profitability measure that shows the rate of return to common stockholders in terms of cash dividend distributions. It is of special interest to investors whose main investment objective is to receive a current return on the investment rather than an increase in the market price of the investment. The dividend yield is computed by dividing the annual dividends paid per share of common stock by the market price per share at a specific date. Assuming dividends of $.80 and $.60 per common share and market prices per common share of 20 1/2 and 13 1/2 at the end of 1990 and 1989 respectively, the dividend yield on common stock of Chung Company is as follows:

	1990	1989
Dividends per share on common stock..............	$ .80	$ .60
Market price per share of common stock............	$20.50	$13.50
Dividend yield on common stock..................	3.9%	4.4%

SUMMARY OF ANALYTICAL MEASURES

The following presentation is a summary of the method of computation and use of the analytical measures discussed in this chapter:

	Method of Computation	*Use*
Solvency measures		
Working capital	Current assets − current liabilities	To indicate the ability to meet currently maturing obligations
Current ratio	$\dfrac{\text{Current assets}}{\text{Current liabilities}}$	
Acid-test ratio	$\dfrac{\text{Quick assets}}{\text{Current liabilities}}$	To indicate instant debt-paying ability
Accounts receivable turnover	$\dfrac{\text{Net sales on account}}{\text{Average accounts receivable}}$	To assess the efficiency in collecting receivables and in the management of credit
Number of days' sales in receivables	$\dfrac{\text{Accounts receivable, end of year}}{\text{Average daily sales on account}}$	
Inventory turnover	$\dfrac{\text{Cost of goods sold}}{\text{Average inventory}}$	To assess the efficiency in the management of inventory
Number of days' sales in inventory	$\dfrac{\text{Inventory, end of year}}{\text{Average daily cost of goods sold}}$	
Ratio of plant assets to long-term liabilities	$\dfrac{\text{Plant assets (net)}}{\text{Long-term liabilities}}$	To indicate the margin of safety to long-term creditors
Ratio of stockholders' equity to liabilities	$\dfrac{\text{Total stockholders' equity}}{\text{Total liabilities}}$	To indicate the margin of safety to creditors
Number of times interest charges earned	$\dfrac{\text{Income before income tax + interest expense}}{\text{Interest expense}}$	To assess the risk to debt-holders in terms of number of times interest charges were earned
Profitability measures		
Ratio of net sales to assets	$\dfrac{\text{Net sales}}{\text{Average total assets (excluding long-term investments)}}$	To assess the effectiveness in the use of assets

	Method of Computation	*Use*
Rate earned on total assets	$\dfrac{\text{Net income} + \text{interest expense}}{\text{Average total assets}}$	To assess the profitability of the assets
Rate earned on stockholders' equity	$\dfrac{\text{Net income}}{\text{Average stockholders' equity}}$	To assess the profitability of the investment by stockholders
Rate earned on common stockholders' equity	$\dfrac{\text{Net income} - \text{preferred dividends}}{\text{Average common stockholders' equity}}$	To assess the profitability of the investment by common stockholders
Earnings per share on common stock	$\dfrac{\text{Net income} - \text{preferred dividends}}{\text{Shares of common stock outstanding}}$	
Dividends per share of common stock	$\dfrac{\text{Dividends}}{\text{Shares of common stock outstanding}}$	To indicate the extent to which earnings are being distributed to common stockholders
Price-earnings ratio	$\dfrac{\text{Market price per share of common stock}}{\text{Earnings per share on common stock}}$	To indicate future earnings prospects, based on the relationship between market value of common stock and earnings
Dividend yield	$\dfrac{\text{Dividends per common share}}{\text{Market price per common share}}$	To indicate the rate of return to common stockholders in terms of dividends

The analytical measures that have been discussed and illustrated are representative of many that can be developed for a medium-size merchandising enterprise. Some of them might well be omitted in analyzing a specific firm, or additional measures could be developed. The type of business activity, the capital structure, and the size of the enterprise usually affect the measures used.

Percentage analyses, ratios, turnovers, and other measures of financial position and operating results are useful analytical devices. They are helpful in appraising the present performance of an enterprise and in forecasting its future. They are not, however, a substitute for sound judgment, nor do they provide definitive guides to action. In selecting and interpreting analytical indexes, proper consideration should be given to any conditions peculiar to the enterprise or to the industry of which the enterprise is a part. The possible influence of the general economic and business environment should also be weighed.

To determine trends, the interrelationship of the measures used in appraising a certain enterprise should be carefully studied, as should comparable indexes of earlier fiscal periods. Data from competing enterprises may also be compared in order to determine the relative efficiency of the firm being analyzed. In making such comparisons, however, it is essential to consider the potential effects of any significant differences in the accounting methods used by the enterprises.

Perceptions of Financial Ratios

A survey of the views of financial executives on important issues relating to financial ratios indicated that financial ratios are an important tool in analyzing the financial results of a company and in managing a company. In addition, 93 of the 100 respondents to the survey indicated that their firms use financial ratios as part of their corporate objectives. The ratios most significant to the respondents are those that measure the ability of the firm to earn a profit.

Source: Charles H. Gibson, "How Industry Perceives Financial Ratios," *Management Accounting* (April, 1982), pp. 13–19.

Financial ratios are often more useful when they are compared with similar ratios of other companies or groups of companies. For this purpose, average ratios for many industries are compiled by various financial services and trade associations. In this process, however, it should be remembered that averages are just that— averages—and care should be taken in their use. The danger in interpreting averages was graphically illustrated by Eldon Grimm, a Wall Street analyst who said: "A statistician is an individual who has his head in the refrigerator, his feet in the oven and on the average feels comfortable."

Source: "Twenty-Five Years Ago in *Forbes*," *Forbes* (August 16, 1982), p. 107.

CORPORATE ANNUAL REPORTS

Corporations ordinarily issue to their stockholders and other interested parties annual reports summarizing activities of the past year and any significant plans for the future. Although there are many differences in the form and sequence of the major sections of annual reports, one section is always devoted to the financial statements, including the accompanying notes. In addition, annual reports usually include (a) selected data referred to as financial highlights, (b) a letter from the president of the corporation, which is sometimes also signed by the chairperson of the board of directors, (c) the independent auditors' report, (d) the management report, and (e) a five- or ten-year historical summary of financial data. A description of financial reporting for segments of a business and supplemental data on the effects of price-level changes may also be included, either separately or as footnotes to the financial statements. As a way to strengthen the relationship with stockholders, many corporations also include pictures of their products and officers or other materials. The following subsections describe the portions of annual reports commonly related to financial matters, with the exception of the principal financial statements, examples of which appear in Appendix F.

Financial Highlights

This section, sometimes called *Results in Brief*, typically summarizes the major financial results for the last year or two. It is usually presented on the first one or two pages of the annual report. Although there are many variations in format and content of this section, such items as sales, income before income taxes, net income, net income per common share, cash dividends, cash dividends per common share, and the amount of capital expenditures are typically presented. In addition to the selected income statement data, information about the financial position at year end, such as the amount of working capital, total assets, long-term debt, and stockholders' equity, is often provided. Other year-end data often reported are the number of common and preferred shares outstanding, number of common and preferred stockholders, and number of employees. An example of a financial highlights section from a corporation's annual report is as follows:

<table>
<tr><td colspan="3">FINANCIAL HIGHLIGHTS</td></tr>
<tr><td colspan="3">(Dollars in thousands except per share amounts)</td></tr>
<tr><td>For the Year</td><td>Current
Year</td><td>Preceding
Year</td></tr>
<tr><td>Sales.....................................</td><td>$1,336,750</td><td>$ 876,400</td></tr>
<tr><td>Income before income tax ....</td><td>149,550</td><td>90,770</td></tr>
<tr><td>Net income................................</td><td>105,120</td><td>66,190</td></tr>
<tr><td>   Per common share........................</td><td>4.03</td><td>2.62</td></tr>
<tr><td>Dividends declared on common stock ....</td><td>34,990</td><td>33,150</td></tr>
<tr><td>   Per common share........................</td><td>1.48</td><td>1.40</td></tr>
<tr><td>Capital expenditures and investments..........</td><td>265,120</td><td>157,050</td></tr>
<tr><td>At Year-End</td><td></td><td></td></tr>
<tr><td>Working capital.............................</td><td>$ 415,410</td><td>$ 423,780</td></tr>
<tr><td>Total assets ....</td><td>1,712,170</td><td>1,457,240</td></tr>
<tr><td>Long-term debt............................</td><td>440,680</td><td>457,350</td></tr>
<tr><td>Stockholders' equity.......................</td><td>840,350</td><td>692,950</td></tr>
</table>

*Financial Highlights
Section*

President's Letter

A letter by the president to the stockholders, discussing such items as reasons for an increase or decrease in net income, changes in existing plant or purchase or construction of new plants, significant new financing commitments, attention given to social responsibility issues, and future prospects, is also found in most annual reports. A condensed version of a president's letter adapted from a corporation's annual report is as follows:

To the Stockholders:

FISCAL YEAR REVIEWED

The record net income in this fiscal year resulted from very strong product demand experienced for about two thirds of the fiscal year, more complete utilization of plants, and a continued improvement in sales mix. Income was strong both domestically and internationally during this period.

PLANT EXPANSION CONTINUES

Capital expenditures during the year were $14.5 million. Expansions were in progress or completed at all locations. Portions of the Company's major new expansion at one of its West Coast plants came on stream in March of this year and will provide much needed capacity in existing and new product areas. Capital expenditures will be somewhat less during next year.

ENVIRONMENTAL CONCERN

The Company recognizes its responsibility to provide a safe and healthy environment at each of its plants. The Company expects to spend approximately $1 million in the forthcoming year to help continue its position as a constructive corporate citizen.

OUTLOOK

During the past 10 years the Company's net income and sales have more than tripled. Net income increased from $3.1 million to $10.7 million, and sales from $45 million to $181 million.

The Company's employees are proud of this record and are determined to carry the momentum into the future. The current economic slowdown makes results for the new fiscal year difficult to predict. However, we are confident and enthusiastic about the Company's prospects for continued growth over the longer term.

Respectfully submitted,

Frances B. Davis

Frances B. Davis
President

March 24, 1990

During recent years, corporate enterprises have become increasingly active in accepting environmental and other social responsibilities. In addition to the brief discussion that may be contained in the president's letter, a more detailed analysis of the company's social concerns may be included elsewhere in the annual report. Knowledgeable investors recognize that the failure of a business enterprise to meet acceptable social norms can have long-run unfavorable implications. In the near future, an important function of accounting may be to assist management in developing a statement covering the social responsibilities of corporate enterprises and what management is doing about them.

Independent Auditors' Report

Before issuing annual statements, all publicly held corporations, as well as many other corporations, engage independent public accountants, usually CPAs, to conduct an *examination* of the financial statements. Such an examination is for the purpose of adding credibility to the statements that have been prepared by management. Upon completion of the examination, which for large corporations may engage many accountants for several weeks or longer, an **independent auditors' report** is prepared. This report accompanies the financial statements. A typical report briefly describes, in two paragraphs, (1) the scope of the auditors' examination and (2) their opinion as to the fairness of the statements. The wording used in the following report for Walgreen Co. conforms with general usage.[1]

Independent Auditors' Report Section

To the Board of Directors and Shareholders of Walgreen Co.:
We have examined the consolidated balance sheet of Walgreen Co. (an Illinois corporation) and Subsidiaries as of August 31, 1986, and 1985, and the related consolidated statements of earnings and retained earnings and changes in financial position for each of the three years in the period ended August 31, 1986. Our examinations were made in accordance with generally accepted auditing standards and, accordingly, included such tests of the accounting records and such other auditing procedures as we considered necessary in the circumstances.

In our opinion, the financial statements referred to above present fairly the financial position of Walgreen Co. and Subsidiaries as of August 31, 1986, and 1985, and the results of their operations and the changes in their financial position for each of the three years in the period ended August 31, 1986, in conformity with generally accepted accounting principles applied on a consistent basis.

Arthur Andersen & Co.

Chicago, Illinois
October 7, 1986

---

[1]*Codification of Statements on Auditing Standards* (New York: American Institute of Certified Public Accountants, 1987), par. 509.07.

In most instances, the auditors can render a report such as the one illustrated, which may be said to be "unqualified." However, it is possible that accounting methods used by a client do not conform with generally accepted accounting principles or that a client has not been consistent in the application of principles. In such cases, a "qualified" opinion must be rendered and the exception briefly described. If the effect of the departure from accepted principles is sufficiently material, an "adverse" or negative opinion must be issued and the exception described. In rare circumstances, the auditors may be unable to perform sufficient auditing procedures to enable them to reach a conclusion as to the fairness of the financial statements. In such circumstances, the auditors must issue a "disclaimer" and briefly describe the reasons for their failure to be able to reach a decision as to the fairness of the statements.

Professional accountants cannot disregard their responsibility in attesting to the fairness of financial statements without seriously jeopardizing their reputations. This responsibility is described as follows:

> *The report shall either contain an expression of opinion regarding the financial statements, taken as a whole, or an assertion to the effect that an opinion cannot be expressed. When an overall opinion cannot be expressed, the reasons therefor should be stated. In all cases where an auditor's name is associated with financial statements, the report should contain a clear-cut indication of the character of the auditor's examination, if any, and the degree of responsibility he is taking.* [2]

Management Report

Responsibility for the accounting system and the resultant financial statements rests mainly with the principal officers of a corporation. In the **management report,** the chief financial officer or other representative of management (1) states that the financial statements are management's responsibility and that they have been prepared according to generally accepted accounting principles, (2) presents management's assessment of the company's internal accounting control system, and (3) comments on any other pertinent matters related to the accounting system, the financial statements, and the examination by the independent auditor.

Although the concept of a management report is relatively new, an increasing number of corporations are including such a report in the annual report. An example of such a report for Alcoa is as follows:

---

[2]*Ibid.,* par. 509.04.

Management's Report to Alcoa Shareholders

The accompanying financial statements of Alcoa and consolidated subsidiaries were prepared by management, which is responsible for their integrity and objectivity. The statements were prepared in accordance with generally accepted accounting principles and include amounts that are based on management's best judgments and estimates. The other financial information included in this annual report is consistent with that in the financial statements.

The company maintains a system of internal controls, including accounting controls, and a strong program of internal auditing. The system of controls provides for appropriate division of responsibility and the application of policies and procedures that are consistent with high standards of accounting and administration. The company believes that its system of internal controls provides reasonable assurance that assets are safeguarded against losses from unauthorized use or disposition and that financial records are reliable for use in preparing financial statements.

The Audit Committee of the Board of Directors, composed solely of directors who are not officers or employees, meets regularly with management, with the company's internal auditors, and with its independent certified public accountants, to discuss their evaluation of internal accounting controls and the quality of financial reporting. The independent auditors and the internal auditors have free access to the Audit Committee, without management's presence.

Management also recognizes its responsibility for conducting the company's affairs according to the highest standards of personal and corporate conduct. This responsibility is characterized and reflected in key policy statements issued from time to time regarding, among other things, conduct of its business activities within the laws of the host countries in which the company operates and potentially conflicting outside business interests of its employees. The company maintains a systematic program to assess compliance with these policies.

Charles W. Parry
Chairman of the Board
and Chief Executive Officer

James W. Wirth
Senior Vice President--Finance

Historical Summary

This section, for which there are many variations in title, reports selected financial and operating data of past periods, usually for five or ten years. It is usually presented in close proximity to the financial statements for the current year, and the types of data reported are varied. An example of a portion of such a report is as follows:

For the Year	1990	1989	1986
Five-Year Consolidated Financial and Statistical Summary for Years Ended December 31 (Dollar amounts in millions except for per share data)			
Net sales	$1,759.7	$1,550.1	$ 997.4
Gross profit	453.5	402.8	270.8
Percent to net sales	25.8%	26.0%	27.2%
Interest expense	33.9	21.3	15.0
Income before income tax	172.7	163.4	87.5
Income tax	62.8	57.8	30.2
Net income	109.9	105.6	57.3
Percent to net sales	6.2%	6.8%	5.7%
Per common share:			
Net income	5.19	4.84	2.54
Dividends	1.80	1.65	1.40
Return on stockholders' equity	19.4%	20.2%	13.6%
Common share market price:			
High	31	41 ½	40 ⅝
Low	18	22 ⅜	22 ¼
Depreciation and amortization	43.3	41.0	23.6
Capital expenditures	98.5	72.1	55.5
At Year End			
Working capital	$ 443.9	$ 434.8	$ 254.6
Plant assets—gross	704.7	620.3	453.7
Plant assets—net	420.0	362.7	263.4
Stockholders' equity	594.3	536.9	447.6
Stockholders' equity per common share	33.07	29.69	23.02
Number of holders of common shares	39,503	39,275	43,852
Number of employees	50,225	50,134	42,826

Segment of a Business

Many companies diversify their operations; that is, they are involved in more than one type of business activity. These companies may also operate in foreign markets. The individual segments of such diversified companies ordinarily experience differing rates of profitability, degrees of risk, and opportunities for growth. To help financial statement users in assessing past performance and future potential of diversified companies, financial statements should disclose such information as the enterprise's operations in different industries, its foreign markets, and its major customers. The required information for each significant reporting segment includes the following: revenue, income from operations, and identifiable assets associated with the segment.[3] An example of financial reporting for segments of a business is illustrated by the following note adapted from the 1987 financial statements of The Procter & Gamble Company:

| Millions of Dollars | Segments | | | | | |
	Laundry and Cleaning	Personal Care	Food and Beverage	Other	Corporate	Total
Net Sales						
1985	$4,884	$5,107	$2,815	$1,237	$(491)	$13,552
1986	5,348	6,451	2,923	1,161	(444)	15,439
1987	5,748	7,512	2,976	1,186	(458)	17,000
Earnings Before Income Taxes						
1985	691	332	(110)	104	(13)	1,004
1986	667	625	(64)	74	(127)	1,175
1987	510	498	(282)	148	(257)	617
Assets						
1985	2,038	3,776	1,717	1,244	908	9,683
1986	2,369	6,446	1,761	1,279	1,200	13,055
1987	2,690	6,679	1,690	1,273	1,383	13,715

Supplemental Data on the Effects of Price-Level Changes

Financial statements are expressed in terms of money. Because money changes in value as prices change, changing price levels will affect financial reporting. The means of disclosing the effects of these changing prices on financial reporting have been the subject of much experimentation by the accounting profession. Currently there are two widely discussed possibilities for supplementing conventional statements and thus resolving financial reporting problems created by changing price levels: (1) supplemental financial data based on current costs, and (2) supplemental financial data based on constant dollars. The discussion in the following sections is confined to the basic concepts and problems of these recommendations.

Current Cost Data. **Current cost** is the amount of cash that would have to be paid currently to acquire assets of the same age and in the same condition

---

[3]*Statement of Financial Accounting Standards, No. 14,* "Financial Reporting for Segments of a Business Enterprise" (Stamford: Financial Accounting Standards Board, 1976). Nonpublic corporations are exempted from this requirement by *Statement of Financial Accounting Standards, No. 21,* "Suspension of the Reporting of Earnings per Share and Segment Information by Nonpublic Enterprises" (Stamford: Financial Accounting Standards Board, 1978).

as existing assets. When current costs are used as the basis for financial reporting, assets, liabilities, and owner's equity are stated at current values, and expenses are stated at the current cost of doing business. The use of current costs permits the identification of gains and losses that result from holding assets during periods of changes in price levels. To illustrate, assume that a firm acquired land at the beginning of the fiscal year for $50,000 and that at the end of the year its current cost (value) is $60,000. The land could be reported at its current cost of $60,000, and the $10,000 increase in value could be reported as an unrealized gain from holding the land.

The major disadvantage in the use of current costs is the absence of established standards and procedures for determining such costs. However, many accountants believe that adequate standards and procedures will evolve through experimentation with actual applications.

Constant Dollar Data. **Constant dollar** data, also known as general price-level data, are historical costs that have been converted to constant dollars through the use of a price-level index. In this manner, financial statement elements are reported in dollars, each of which has the same (that is, constant) general purchasing power.

A **price-level index** is the ratio of the total cost of a group of commodities prevailing at a particular time to the total cost of the same group of commodities at an earlier base time. The total cost of the commodities at the base time is assigned a value of 100 and the price-level indexes for all later times are expressed as a ratio to 100. For example, assume that the cost of a selected group of commodities amounted to $12,000 at a particular time and $13,200 today. The price index for the earlier, or base, time becomes 100 and the current price index is 110 [(13,200 ÷ 12,000) × 100].

A general price-level index may be used to determine the effect of changes in price levels on certain financial statement items. To illustrate, assume a price index of 120 at the time of purchase of a plot of land for $10,000 and a current price index of 150. The **constant dollar equivalent** of the original cost of $10,000 may be computed as follows:

$$\frac{\text{Current Price Index}}{\text{Price Index at Date of Purchase}} \times \text{Original Cost} = \text{Constant Dollar Equivalent}$$

$$\frac{150}{120} \times \$10,000 = \$12,500$$

Current Annual Reporting Requirements for Price-Level Changes. In 1979, the Financial Accounting Standards Board undertook an experimental program for reporting the effects of changing prices by requiring approximately 1,300 large, publicly held enterprises to disclose certain current cost information and constant dollar information annually as supplemental data. In 1984, after reviewing the experiences with these 1979 disclosure requirements, the FASB concluded that current cost information was more useful than constant dollar information as a supplement to the basic financial statements. In addition, the FASB concluded that requiring two different methods of reporting the effects of changing prices may detract from the usefulness of the information. As a result, the requirement to report constant dollar information was dropped for those companies that report current cost information. Finally, in 1986, the FASB concluded that the supplemental data had been used very little and therefore made the supplemental disclosure of current cost/constant dollar information voluntary.[4] However, the FASB continues to encourage companies to experiment with different methods of providing the information.

The following footnote from the 1986 annual report of The Pillsbury Company illustrates the reporting of the effects of changing prices:

Information on effects of changing prices and inflation

Financial statements, prepared using historical costs as required by generally accepted accounting principles, may not reflect the full impact of current costs and general inflation.

The following supplementary disclosures attempt to remeasure certain historical financial information to recognize the effects of changes in current costs using specific price indices. The current cost information is then expressed in average Fiscal 1986 dollars to reflect the effects of general inflation based on the U.S. Consumer Price Index. . . .

Other Information

The preceding paragraphs described the most commonly presented sections of annual reports related to financial matters. Some annual reports may include other financial information, such as forecasts which indicate financial plans and expectations for the year ahead.

INTERIM FINANCIAL REPORTS

Corporate enterprises customarily issue interim financial reports to their stockholders. Corporations that are listed on a stock exchange or file reports with the Securities and Exchange Commission or other regulatory agencies are required to submit interim reports, usually on a quarterly basis. Such reports often have a significant influence on the valuation of a corporation's equity securities on stock exchanges.

Interim reports of an enterprise should disclose such information as gross revenue, costs and expenses, provision for income taxes, extraordinary or infrequently occurring items, net income, earnings per share, contingent

---

[4]*Statement of Financial Accounting Standards, No. 89,* "Financial Reporting and Changing Prices" (Stamford: Financial Accounting Standards Board, 1986).

items, and cash flows.[5] The particular accounting principles used on an annual basis, such as depreciation methods and inventory cost flow assumptions, are usually followed in preparing interim statements. However, if changes in accounting principles occur before the end of a fiscal year, there are detailed guidelines for their disclosure.[6]

Much of the value of interim financial reports to the investing public is based on their timeliness. Lengthy delays between the end of a quarter and the issuance of reports would usually greatly reduce their value. This is one of the reasons that interim reports are usually not audited by independent CPAs. In some cases, the interim reports are subjected to a "limited review" by the CPA and a report on this limited review is issued.

Chapter Review

KEY POINTS

1. Usefulness of Financial Statement Analysis.
The financial condition and the results of operations, as reported in the basic financial statements, are of interest to many groups external to the reporting enterprise. Because the basic financial statements are used to assess the effectiveness of management in planning and controlling operations and because financial statements can be used to plan future operations, financial statement analysis is also important to management.

2. Types of Financial Statement Analysis.
Users of financial statements often gain a clearer picture of the economic condition of an entity by studying relationships and comparisons of items (1) within a single year's statements, (2) in a succession of statements, (3) with other enterprises, and (4) with industry averages. Users are especially interested in solvency and profitability. Analysis of historical data in financial statements is useful in assessing the past performance of an enterprise and in forecasting its future performance.

3. Basic Analytical Procedures.
The analytical measures obtained from financial statements are usually expressed as ratios or percentages. The basic measures developed through the use of analytical procedures are not ends in themselves. They are only guides to the evaluation of financial and operating data. Many other factors,

---

[5]*Opinions of the Accounting Principles Board*, No. 28, "Interim Financial Reporting" (New York: American Institute of Certified Public Accountants, 1973).

[6]*Statement of Financial Accounting Standards*, No. 3, "Reporting Accounting Changes in Interim Financial Statements" (Stamford: Financial Accounting Standards Board, 1974).

such as trends in the industry, changes in price levels, and general economic conditions and prospects, may also need consideration in order to arrive at sound conclusions.

The percentage analysis of increases and decreases in corresponding items in comparative financial statements is called horizontal analysis. Percentage analysis may also be used to show the relationship of the component parts to the total in a single statement. This type of analysis is called vertical analysis. Although vertical analysis is confined within each individual statement, the significance of both the amounts and the percentages is increased by preparing comparative statements. Vertical analysis with both dollar and percentage figures is also useful in comparing one company with another or with industry averages. Such comparisons may be made easier by the use of common-size statements, in which all items are expressed only in relative terms.

4. Solvency Analysis.
Solvency is the ability of a business to meet its financial obligations as they come due. Solvency analysis, therefore, focuses mainly on balance sheet relationships that indicate the ability to liquidate liabilities. Major analyses used in assessing solvency include (1) current position analysis, (2) accounts receivable analysis, (3) inventory analysis, (4) the ratio of plant assets to long-term liabilities, (5) the ratio of stockholders' equity to liabilities, and (6) the number of times interest charges are earned.

Current position analysis includes the assessment of working capital, the current ratio, and the acid-test ratio. Accounts receivable analysis includes the assessment of accounts receivable turnover and number of days' sales in receivables. Inventory analysis includes the assessment of inventory turnover and number of days' sales in inventory. The ratio of plant assets to long-term liabilities shows the margin of safety for the creditors. The ratio of stockholders' equity to liabilities indicates the margin of safety for the creditors and the ability of the enterprise to withstand adverse business conditions. The number of times interest charges are earned indicates the relative risk of the debtholders' continuing to receive interest payments.

5. Profitability Analysis.
Profitability is the ability of an entity to earn income. It can be assessed by computing various relevant measures, including (1) the ratio of net sales to assets, (2) the rate earned on total assets, (3) the rate earned on stockholders' equity, (4) the rate earned on common stockholders' equity, (5) the earnings per share on common stock, (6) the price-earnings ratio, and (7) the dividend yield.

6. Summary of Analytical Measures.
The type of business activity, the capital structure, and the size of the enterprise usually affect the measures used in financial statement analysis. These analytical measures, however, are not a substitute for sound judgment, nor do they provide definitive guides to action. In selecting and interpreting analytical indexes, proper consideration should be given to any conditions peculiar to the enterprise or to the industry of which the enterprise is a part.

7. Corporate Annual Reports.

Corporations ordinarily issue to their stockholders and other interested parties annual reports summarizing activities of the past year and any significant plans for the future. These reports normally include the financial highlights section, the president's letter, the independent auditors' report, the management report, and a historical summary of operations. Reporting of segments and supplementary data on the effects of price-level changes may also be included.

8. Interim Financial Reports.

Corporations customarily issue interim financial reports to their stockholders. Interim reports disclose such information as gross revenue, expenses, net income, and cash flows, following the accounting principles that are used on an annual basis.

KEY TERMS

solvency 528
profitability 528
horizontal analysis 529
vertical analysis 533
common-size statements 535
working capital 536
current ratio 536
acid-test ratio 538
quick assets 538
accounts receivable turnover 538
number of days' sales in
   receivables 539
inventory turnover 540
number of days' sales in
   inventory 540

rate earned on total assets 543
rate earned on stockholders'
   equity 544
leverage 545
rate earned on common
   stockholders' equity 545
earnings per share on common
   stock 546
price-earnings (P/E) ratio 547
current cost 557
constant dollar 558
price-level index 558

SELF-EXAMINATION QUESTIONS

(Answers at End of Chapter)

1. What type of analysis is indicated by the following?

	Amount	Percent
Current assets	$100,000	20%
Plant assets.....................	400,000	80
Total assets.....................	$500,000	100%

A. Vertical analysis
B. Horizontal analysis
C. Current position analysis
D. None of the above

2. Which of the following measures is useful as an indication of the ability of a firm to liquidate current liabilities?
   A. Working capital
   B. Current ratio
   C. Acid-test ratio
   D. All of the above

3. The ratio determined by dividing total current assets by total current liabilities is:
   A. current ratio
   B. working capital ratio
   C. bankers' ratio
   D. all of the above

4. The ratio of the quick assets to current liabilities, which indicates the "instant" debt-paying ability of a firm, is:
   A. current ratio
   B. working capital ratio
   C. acid-test ratio
   D. none of the above

5. A measure useful in evaluating the efficiency in the management of inventories is:
   A. inventory turnover
   B. number of days' sales in inventory
   C. both A and B
   D. none of the above

ILLUSTRATIVE PROBLEM

Fleming Inc.'s comparative financial statements for the years ended December 31, 1990 and 1989, are as follows. The market price of Fleming Inc.'s common stock was $30 on December 31, 1989, and $25 on December 31, 1990.

Fleming Inc.
Comparative Income Statement
For Years Ended December 31, 1990 and 1989

	1990	1989
Sales (all on account)	$5,125,000	$3,257,600
Sales returns and allowances	125,000	57,600
Net sales	$5,000,000	$3,200,000
Cost of goods sold	3,400,000	2,080,000
Gross profit	$1,600,000	$1,120,000
Selling expenses	$ 785,000	$ 499,000
General expenses	325,000	224,000
Total operating expenses	$1,110,000	$ 723,000
Operating income	$ 490,000	$ 397,000
Other income	25,000	19,200
	$ 515,000	$ 416,200
Other expense (interest)	105,000	64,000
Income before income tax	$ 410,000	$ 352,200
Income tax	165,000	141,000
Net income	$ 245,000	$ 211,200

Fleming Inc.
Comparative Retained Earnings Statement
For Years Ended December 31, 1990 and 1989

	1990	1989
Retained earnings, January 1	$ 723,000	$ 581,800
Add net income for year	245,000	211,200
Total..	$ 968,000	$ 793,000
Deduct dividends:		
On preferred stock	$ 40,000	$ 40,000
On common stock...........................	45,000	30,000
Total.....................................	$ 85,000	$ 70,000
Retained earnings, December 31	$ 883,000	$ 723,000

Fleming Inc.
Comparative Balance Sheet
December 31, 1990 and 1989

Assets	1990	1989
Current assets:		
Cash	$ 175,000	$ 125,000
Marketable securities........................	150,000	50,000
Accounts receivable (net)	425,000	325,000
Inventories	720,000	480,000
Prepaid expenses...........................	30,000	20,000
Total current assets	$1,500,000	$1,000,000
Long-term investments	250,000	225,000
Plant assets (net)	2,093,000	1,948,000
Total assets	$3,843,000	$3,173,000

Liabilities	1990	1989
Current liabilities..............................	$ 750,000	$ 650,000
Long-term liabilities:		
Mortgage note payable, 10%, due 1995	$ 410,000	—
Bonds payable, 8%, due 1997................	800,000	$ 800,000
Total long-term liabilities	$1,210,000	$ 800,000
Total liabilities	$1,960,000	$1,450,000

Stockholders' Equity	1990	1989
Preferred 8% stock, $100 par	$ 500,000	$ 500,000
Common stock, $10 par	500,000	500,000
Retained earnings............................	883,000	723,000
Total stockholders' equity	$1,883,000	$1,723,000
Total liabilities and stockholders' equity	$3,843,000	$3,173,000

Instructions:

Determine the following measures for 1990:
    (1) Working capital.
    (2) Current ratio.
    (3) Acid-test ratio.

(4) Accounts receivable turnover.
(5) Number of days' sales in receivables.
(6) Inventory turnover.
(7) Number of days' sales in inventory.
(8) Ratio of plant assets to long-term liabilities.
(9) Ratio of stockholders' equity to liabilities.
(10) Number of times interest charges earned.
(11) Number of times preferred dividends earned.
(12) Ratio of net sales to assets.
(13) Rate earned on total assets.
(14) Rate earned on stockholders' equity.
(15) Rate earned on common stockholders' equity.
(16) Earnings per share on common stock.
(17) Price-earnings ratio.
(18) Dividend yield.

SOLUTION

(1) Working capital: $750,000
$1,500,000 − $750,000

(2) Current ratio: 2.0:1
$1,500,000 ÷ $750,000

(3) Acid-test ratio: 1.0:1
$750,000 ÷ $750,000

(4) Accounts receivable turnover: 13.3

$$\$5,000,000 \div \frac{\$425,000 + \$325,000}{2}$$

(5) Number of days' sales in receivables: 31 days
$5,000,000 ÷ 365 = $13,699
$ 425,000 ÷ $13,699

(6) Inventory turnover: 5.7

$$\$3,400,000 \div \frac{\$720,000 + \$480,000}{2}$$

(7) Number of days' sales in inventory: 77.3 days
$3,400,000 ÷ 365 = $9,315
$ 720,000 ÷ $9,315

(8) Ratio of plant assets to long-term liabilities: 1.7:1
$2,093,000 ÷ $1,210,000

(9) Ratio of stockholders' equity to liabilities: 1.0:1
$1,883,000 ÷ $1,960,000

(10) Number of times interest charges earned: 4.9
($410,000 + $105,000) ÷ $105,000

(11) Number of times preferred dividends earned: 6.1
$245,000 ÷ $40,000

(12) Ratio of net sales to assets: 1.5:1

$$\$5,000,000 \div \frac{\$3,593,000 + \$2,948,000}{2}$$

(13) Rate earned on total assets: 10.0%

$$(\$245,000 + \$105,000) \div \frac{\$3,843,000 + \$3,173,000}{2}$$

(14) Rate earned on stockholders' equity: 13.6%

$$\$245,000 \div \frac{\$1,883,000 + \$1,723,000}{2}$$

(15) Rate earned on common stockholders' equity: 15.7%

$$(\$245,000 - \$40,000) \div \frac{\$1,383,000 + \$1,223,000}{2}$$

(16) Earnings per share on common stock: $4.10
($245,000 − $40,000) ÷ 50,000

(17) Price-earnings ratio: 6.1
$25 ÷ $4.10

(18) Dividend yield: 3.6%

$$\frac{(\$45,000 \div 50,000 \text{ shares})}{\$25}$$

Discussion Questions

15–1. In the analysis of the financial status of an enterprise, what is meant by *solvency* and *profitability*?

15–2. Using the following data taken from a comparative balance sheet, illustrate (a) horizontal analysis and (b) vertical analysis.

	Current Year	Preceding Year
Accounts payable..........................	$ 600,000	$ 400,000
Total current liabilities	1,250,000	1,000,000

15–3. What is the advantage of using comparative statements for financial analysis rather than statements for a single date or period?

15–4. The current year's amount of net income (after income tax) is 20% larger than that of the preceding year. Does this indicate an improved operating performance? Discuss.

15–5. What are common-size financial statements?

15–6. (a) Name the major ratios useful in assessing solvency and profitability.
(b) Why is it important not to rely on only one ratio or measure in assessing the solvency or profitability of an enterprise?

15–7. Identify the measure of current position analysis described by each of the following: (a) the excess of current assets over current liabilities, (b) the ratio of current assets to current liabilities, (c) the ratio of quick assets to current liabilities.

15–8. Selected condensed data taken from the balance sheet of Young Corporation at June 30, the end of the current fiscal year, are as follows:

Cash, marketable securities, and receivables	$300,000
Other current assets	450,000
Total current assets.....................................	$750,000
Current liabilities.......................................	$250,000

At June 30, what are (a) the working capital, (b) the current ratio, and (c) the acid-test ratio?

15–9. For Stapp Company, the working capital at the end of the current year is $75,000 greater than the working capital at the end of the preceding year, reported as follows. Does this mean that the current position has improved? Explain.

	Current Year	Preceding Year
Current assets:		
Cash, marketable securities, and receivables .	$360,000	$300,000
Inventories	540,000	325,000
Total current assets......................	$900,000	$625,000
Current liabilities	450,000	250,000
Working capital.............................	$450,000	$375,000

15–10. A company that grants terms of n/30 on all sales has an accounts receivable turnover for the year, based on monthly averages, of 6. Is this a satisfactory turnover? Discuss.

15–11. What does an increase in the number of days' sales in receivables ordinarily indicate about the credit and collection policy of the firm?

15–12. (a) Why is it advantageous to have a high inventory turnover? (b) Is it possible for the inventory turnover to be too high? Discuss. (c) Is it possible to have a high inventory turnover and a high number of days' sales in inventory? Discuss.

15–13. What does the following data taken from a comparative balance sheet indicate about the company's current ability to borrow additional funds on a long-term basis as compared to the preceding year?

	Current Year	Preceding Year
Plant assets (net).........................	$1,800,000	$1,700,000
Long-term liabilities	600,000	850,000

15–14. What does an increase in the ratio of stockholders' equity to liabilities indicate about the margin of safety for the firm's creditors and the ability of the firm to withstand adverse business conditions?

15–15. In determining the number of times interest charges are earned, why are interest charges added to income before income tax?

15–16. In computing the ratio of net sales to assets, why are long-term investments excluded in determining the amount of the total assets?

15–17. In determining the rate earned on total assets, why is interest expense added to net income before dividing by total assets?

15–18. (a) Why is the rate earned on stockholders' equity by a thriving enterprise ordinarily higher than the rate earned on total assets?
(b) Should the rate earned on common stockholders' equity normally be higher or lower than the rate earned on total stockholders' equity? Explain.

15–19. The net income (after income tax) of Olson Company was $20 per common share in the latest year and $30 per common share for the preceding year. At the beginning of the latest year, the number of shares outstanding was doubled by a stock split. There were no other changes in the amount of stock outstanding. What were the earnings per share in the preceding year, adjusted to place them on a comparable basis with the latest year?

15–20. The price-earnings ratio for the common stock of Daytona Company was 12 at December 31, the end of the current fiscal year. What does the ratio indicate about the selling price of the common stock in relation to current earnings?

15–21. Why would the dividend yield differ significantly from the rate earned on common stockholders' equity?

15–22. Favorable business conditions may bring about certain seemingly unfavorable ratios, and unfavorable business operations may result in apparently favorable ratios. For example, Almond Company increased its sales and net income substantially for the current year, yet the current ratio at the end of the year is lower than at the beginning of the year. Discuss some possible causes of the apparent weakening of the current position while sales and net income have increased substantially.

15–23. (a) What are the major components of an annual report? (b) Indicate the purpose of the financial highlights section and the president's letter.

15–24. (a) The typical independent auditors' report expressing an unqualified opinion consists of two paragraphs. What is reported in each paragraph? (b) Under what conditions does an auditor give a qualified opinion?

15–25. Conventional financial statements do not give recognition to the instability of the purchasing power of the dollar. How can the effect of the fluctuating dollar on business operations be presented to the users of the financial statements?

15–26. What is the current cost of an asset?

15–27. If land was purchased for $80,000 when the general price-level index was 220, and the general price-level index has risen to 242, what is the constant dollar equivalent of the original cost of the land?

15–28. Real World Focus. Tandy Corporation's 1987 annual report indicates that the rate earned on total assets was 13.2% for the year ended June 30, 1987. For the same period, the rate earned on stockholders' equity was 18%. What is the explanation for the difference in the two rates?

Exercises

·

15–29. **Vertical analysis of income statement.** Revenue and expense data for P. A. Good Company are as follows:

	1990	1989
Sales	$900,000	$800,000
Cost of goods sold	531,000	464,000
Selling expenses	135,000	144,000
General expenses	63,000	64,000
Income tax	63,000	48,000

(a) Prepare an income statement in comparative form, stating each item for both 1990 and 1989 as a percent of sales.
(b) Comment on the significant changes disclosed by the comparative income statement.

READSHEET
PROBLEM

15–30. **Horizontal analysis of balance sheet.** Balance sheet data for Dennis Company on December 31, the end of the fiscal year, are as follows:

	1990	1989
Current assets	$451,000	$410,000
Plant assets	449,000	413,800
Intangible assets	50,000	56,200
Current liabilities	100,000	90,000
Long-term liabilities	250,000	275,000
Common stock	400,000	350,000
Retained earnings	200,000	165,000

Prepare a comparative balance sheet with horizontal analysis, indicating the increase (decrease) for 1990 when compared with 1989.

15–31. Current position analysis. The following data were abstracted from the balance sheet of Concepcion Company:

	Current Year	Preceding Year
Cash....................................	$ 95,500	$112,500
Marketable securities	45,000	50,000
Accounts and notes receivable (net).........	189,500	187,500
Inventories	279,500	189,000
Prepaid expenses	20,500	11,000
Accounts and notes payable (short-term)......	275,000	222,500
Accrued liabilities.........................	25,000	27,500

(a) Determine for each year (1) the working capital, (2) the current ratio, and (3) the acid-test ratio. (Present figures used in your computations.)

(b) What conclusions can be drawn from these data as to the company's ability to meet its currently maturing debts?

15–32. Accounts receivable analysis. The following data are taken from the financial statements for Shula Company:

	Current Year	Preceding Year
Accounts receivable, end of year............	$ 662,100	$ 601,350
Monthly average accounts receivable (net) ...	627,000	550,100
Net sales on account	5,016,000	3,850,700

Terms of all sales are 1/10, n/60.

(a) Determine for each year (1) the accounts receivable turnover and (2) the number of days' sales in receivables.

(b) What conclusions can be drawn from these data concerning the composition of the accounts receivable?

15–33. Inventory analysis. The following data were abstracted from the income statement of McHale Corporation:

	Current Year	Preceding Year
Sales	$4,275,500	$4,160,000
Beginning inventories.....................	648,000	558,000
Purchases................................	2,664,000	2,790,000
Ending inventories........................	672,000	648,000

(a) Determine for each year (1) the inventory turnover and (2) the number of days' sales in inventory.

(b) What conclusions can be drawn from these data concerning the composition of the inventories?

15–34. Six measures of solvency or profitability. The following data were taken from the financial statements of John Britz and Co. for the current fiscal year:

Plant assets (net)...	$1,250,000

Liabilities:	
Current liabilities..	$ 400,000
Mortgage note payable, 10%, issued 1982, due 1992	500,000
Total liabilities	$ 900,000

Stockholders' equity:

Preferred 8% stock, $100 par, cumulative, nonparticipating (no change during year).......................................			$ 200,000
Common stock, $10 par (no change during year)...................			1,000,000
Retained earnings:			
Balance, beginning of year...............	$687,500		
Net income	193,500	$881,000	
Preferred dividends	$ 16,000		
Common dividends	65,000	81,000	
Balance, end of year......................................			800,000
Total stockholders' equity......................................			$2,000,000

Net sales	$3,975,000
Interest expense..	50,000

Assuming that long-term investments totaled $150,000 throughout the year and that total assets were $2,700,000 at the beginning of the year, determine the following, presenting figures used in your computations: (a) ratio of plant assets to long-term liabilities, (b) ratio of stockholders' equity to liabilities, (c) ratio of net sales to assets, (d) rate earned on total assets, (e) rate earned on stockholders' equity, (f) rate earned on common stockholders' equity.

15–35. Five measures of solvency or profitability. The balance sheet for Culp Corporation at the end of the current fiscal year indicated the following:

Bonds payable, 12% (issued in 1975, due in 1995)	$2,000,000
Preferred 8% stock, $100 par...........................	1,000,000
Common stock, $50 par................................	2,500,000

Income before income tax was $720,000, and income taxes were $320,000 for the current year. Cash dividends paid on common stock during the current year totaled $300,000. The common stock was selling for $64 per share at the end of the year. Determine each of the following: (a) number of times bond interest charges were earned, (b) number of times preferred dividends were earned, (c) earnings per share on common stock, (d) price-earnings ratio, and (e) dividend yield.

15–36. Earnings per share. The net income reported on the income statement of Burger and Co. was $2,900,000. There were 500,000 shares of $10 par common stock and 100,000 shares of $8 preferred stock outstanding throughout the current year. The income statement included two extraordinary items: a $900,000 gain from condemnation of land and a $300,000 loss arising from flood damage, both after applicable income tax. Determine the per share figures for common stock for (a) income before extraordinary items and (b) net income.

15–37. Effect of price-level change on investment in land. Several years ago, Manley Company purchased land as a future building site for $60,000. The price-level index at that time was 120. On October 11 of the current year, when the price-level index was 132, the land was sold for $71,500.

    (a) Determine the amount of the gain that would be realized according to conventional accounting.

    (b) Indicate the amount of the gain that may be (1) attributed to the change in purchasing power and (2) considered a true gain in terms of current dollars.

15–38. Real World Focus. The following comparative income statement (in thousands of dollars) for the years ending December 31, 1986 and 1985, was adapted from the 1986 annual report of William Wrigley Jr. Company:

	1986	1985
Revenues:		
Net sales..................................	$698,982	$620,267
Investment income	6,980	6,787
Total revenues	$705,962	$627,054
Cost and expenses:		
Cost of sales	$318,280	$295,430
Selling, distribution, and general		
administrative...........................	283,480	250,375
Interest...................................	544	788
Total costs and expenses	$602,304	$546,593
Earnings before income taxes	$103,658	$ 80,461
Income taxes	49,840	36,963
Net earnings................................	$ 53,818	$ 43,498

    (a) Prepare a comparative income statement for 1986 and 1985 in vertical form, stating each item as a percent of revenues. (b) Based upon (a), which 1986 income statement item(s) might warrant additional investigation?

Problems

·

15–39. Horizontal analysis for income statement. For 1990, Talman Company reported its most significant increase in net income in years. At the end of the year, Ann Talman, the president, is presented with the following condensed comparative income statement:

Talman Company
Comparative Income Statement
For Years Ended December 31, 1990 and 1989

	1990	1989
Sales	$909,000	$804,500
Sales returns and allowances.	9,000	4,500
Net sales.	$900,000	$800,000
Cost of goods sold	548,000	480,000
Gross profit.	$352,000	$320,000
Selling expenses . :	$117,000	$144,000
General expenses.	81,000	65,000
Total operating expenses.	$198,000	$209,000
Operating income	$154,000	$111,000
Other income	2,000	1,000
Income before income tax.	$156,000	$112,000
Income tax	58,000	42,000
Net income.	$ 98,000	$ 70,000

Instructions:

(1) Prepare a comparative income statement with horizontal analysis for the two-year period, using 1989 as the base year.
(2) To the extent the data permit, comment on the significant relationships revealed by the horizontal analysis prepared in (1).

READSHEET
ROBLEM

15–40. Vertical analysis for income statement. For 1990, Knight Company initiated an extensive sales promotion campaign that included the expenditure of an additional $75,000 for advertising. At the end of the year, John Knight, the president, is presented with the following condensed comparative income statement:

Knight Company
Comparative Income Statement
For Years Ended December 31, 1990 and 1989

	1990	1989
Sales	$841,500	$687,480
Sales returns and allowances.	16,500	7,480
Net sales.	$825,000	$680,000
Cost of goods sold	519,750	435,200
Gross profit.	$305,250	$244,800
Selling expenses	$198,000	$102,000
General expenses.	36,300	40,800
Total operating expenses.	$234,300	$142,800
Operating income	$ 70,950	$102,000
Other expense.	2,475	2,720
Income before income tax.	$ 68,475	$ 99,280
Income tax	14,850	24,480
Net income.	$ 53,625	$ 74,800

Instructions:

(1) Prepare a comparative income statement for the two-year period, presenting an analysis of each item in relationship to net sales for each of the years.
(2) To the extent the data permit, comment on the significant relationships revealed by the vertical analysis prepared in (1).

15–41. Common-size income statement. Revenue and expense data for the current calendar year for Regal Publishing Company and for the publishing industry are as follows. The Regal Publishing Company data are expressed in dollars; the publishing industry averages are expressed in percentages.

	Regal Publishing Company	Publishing Industry Average
Sales	$8,080,000	100.6%
Sales returns and allowances...............	80,000	.6
Cost of goods sold	5,760,000	69.0
Selling expenses..........................	656,000	9.0
General expenses.........................	496,000	8.2
Other income	40,000	.6
Other expense...........................	96,000	1.4
Income tax	384,000	5.0

Instructions:

(1) Prepare a common-size income statement comparing the results of operations for Regal Publishing Company with the industry average.
(2) As far as the data permit, comment on significant relationships revealed by the comparisons.

15–42. Effect of transactions on current position analysis. Data pertaining to the current position of Mullins Company are as follows:

Cash.....................................	$ 90,000
Marketable securities......................	40,000
Accounts and notes receivable (net)	120,000
Inventories...............................	225,000
Prepaid expenses	25,000
Accounts payable.........................	140,000
Notes payable (short-term).................	75,000
Accrued liabilities	35,000

Instructions:

(1) Compute (a) the working capital, (b) the current ratio, and (c) the acid-test ratio.
(2) List the following captions on a sheet of paper:

Transaction	Working Capital	Current Ratio	Acid-Test Ratio

Compute the working capital, the current ratio, and the acid-test ratio after each of the following transactions, and record the results in the appropriate columns. Consider each transaction separately and assume that only that transaction affects the data given above.

(a) Declared a cash dividend, $50,000.
(b) Issued additional shares of stock for cash, $100,000.
(c) Purchased goods on account, $50,000.
(d) Paid accounts payable, $60,000.
(e) Borrowed cash from bank on a long-term note, $50,000.
(f) Paid cash for office supplies, $20,000.
(g) Received cash on account, $75,000.
(h) Paid notes payable, $75,000.
(i) Declared a common stock dividend on common stock, $100,000.
(j) Sold marketable securities, $40,000.

15–43. Effect of errors on current position analysis. Prior to approving an application for a short-term loan, Tolono National Bank required that Morgan Company provide evidence of working capital of at least $300,000, a current ratio of at least 1.5:1, and an acid-test ratio of at least 1.0:1. The chief accountant of Morgan Company compiled the following data pertaining to the current position:

Morgan Company
Schedule of Current Assets and Current Liabilities
December 31, 1989

Current assets:	
Cash...	$ 54,750
Marketable securities	72,500
Accounts receivable	341,500
Notes receivable	125,000
Interest receivable..........................	6,250
Inventories	188,250
Supplies....................................	11,750
Total current assets.....................	$800,000
Current liabilities:	
Accounts payable	$300,000
Notes payable	100,000
Total current liabilities.................	$400,000

Instructions:

(1) Compute (a) the working capital, (b) the current ratio, and (c) the acid-test ratio.
(2) At the request of the bank, a firm of independent auditors was retained to examine data submitted with the loan application. This examination disclosed several errors. Prepare correcting entries for each of the following errors:

(a) A canceled check indicates that a bill for $28,750 for repairs on factory equipment had not been recorded in the accounts.
(b) Accounts receivable of $41,500 are uncollectible and should be immediately written off. In addition, it was estimated that of the remaining receivables, 5% would eventually become uncollectible. An allowance should be made for these future uncollectible accounts.
(c) Six months' interest had been accrued on the $125,000, 10%, six-month note receivable dated October 1, 1989.

(continued)

(d) Supplies on hand at December 31, 1989, total $4,750.

(e) The marketable securities portfolio includes $50,000 of Dixon Company stock that is held as a long-term investment.

(f) The notes payable account consists of a 12%, 90-day note dated November 1, 1989. No interest had been accrued on the note.

(g) Accrued wages as of December 31, 1989, totaled $30,000.

(h) Rental Income had been credited upon receipt of $72,000, which was the full amount of a year's rent for warehouse space leased to C. A. Cox Inc., effective July 1, 1989.

(3) Giving effect to each of the preceding errors separately and assuming that only that error affects the current position of Morgan Company, compute (a) the working capital, (b) the current ratio, and (c) the acid-test ratio. Use the following column headings for recording your answers:

Error	Working Capital	Current Ratio	Acid-Test Ratio

(4) Prepare a revised schedule of working capital as of December 31, 1989, and recompute the current ratio and the acid-test ratio, giving effect to the corrections of all of the preceding errors.

(5) Discuss the action you would recommend that the bank take regarding the pending loan application.

<table>
<tr><td>SPREADSHEET
PROBLEM</td></tr>
</table>

15–44. Eighteen measures of solvency and profitability. The comparative financial statements of C. L. Ames Inc. are as follows. The market price of C. L. Ames Inc.'s common stock was $60.50 on December 31, 1989, and $51 on December 31, 1990.

C. L. Ames Inc.
Comparative Income Statement
For Years Ended December 31, 1990 and 1989

	1990	1989
Sales (all on account).....................	$9,396,750	$8,024,000
Sales returns and allowances..............	46,750	24,000
Net sales................................	$9,350,000	$8,000,000
Cost of goods sold	5,984,000	4,800,000
Gross profit.............................	$3,366,000	$3,200,000
Selling expenses........................	$1,496,000	$1,232,000
General expenses........................	673,200	658,000
Total operating expenses..................	$2,169,200	$1,890,000
Operating income	$1,196,800	$1,310,000
Other income	149,600	136,000
	$1,346,400	$1,446,000
Other expense (interest)	240,000	210,000
Income before income tax.................	$1,106,400	$1,236,000
Income tax	506,400	596,000
Net income..............................	$ 600,000	$ 640,000

C. L. Ames Inc.
Comparative Retained Earnings Statement
For Years Ended December 31, 1990 and 1989

	1990	1989
Retained earnings, January 1...............	$2,770,000	$2,420,000
Add net income for year....................	600,000	640,000
Total.....................................	$3,370,000	$3,060,000
Deduct dividends:		
On preferred stock	$ 90,000	$ 90,000
On common stock.......................	210,000	200,000
Total.................................	$ 300,000	$ 290,000
Retained earnings, December 31............	$3,070,000	$2,770,000

C. L. Ames Inc.
Comparative Balance Sheet
December 31, 1990 and 1989

Assets	1990	1989
Current assets:		
Cash.....................................	$ 412,500	$ 363,000
Marketable securities	137,500	132,000
Accounts receivable (net)	550,000	495,000
Inventories	792,000	726,000
Prepaid expenses	88,000	44,000
Total current assets....................	$1,980,000	$1,760,000
Long-term investments.....................	275,000	220,000
Plant assets (net)	5,665,000	5,280,000
Total assets	$7,920,000	$7,260,000

Liabilities		
Current liabilities	$1,100,000	$ 990,000
Long-term liabilities:		
Mortgage note payable, 12%, due 1997....	$ 250,000	—
Bonds payable, 14%, due 2007	1,500,000	$1,500,000
Total long-term liabilities...............	$1,750,000	$1,500,000
Total liabilities...........................	$2,850,000	$2,490,000

Stockholders' Equity		
Preferred 9% stock, $100 par..............	$1,000,000	$1,000,000
Common stock, $10 par...................	1,000,000	1,000,000
Retained earnings........................	3,070,000	2,770,000
Total stockholders' equity	$5,070,000	$4,770,000
Total liabilities and stockholders' equity	$7,920,000	$7,260,000

Instructions:

Determine the following measures for 1990, presenting the figures used in your computations:

(1) Working capital.

(2) Current ratio.

(3) Acid-test ratio.

(4) Accounts receivable turnover.

(5) Number of days' sales in receivables.

(6) Inventory turnover.

(7) Number of days' sales in inventory.

(8) Ratio of plant assets to long-term liabilities.

(9) Ratio of stockholders' equity to liabilities.

(10) Number of times interest charges earned.

(11) Number of times preferred dividends earned.

(12) Ratio of net sales to assets.

(13) Rate earned on total assets.

(14) Rate earned on stockholders' equity.

(15) Rate earned on common stockholders' equity.

(16) Earnings per share on common stock.

(17) Price-earnings ratio.

(18) Dividend yield.

15–45. Report on detailed financial analysis. Ralph Lamor is considering making a substantial investment in C. L. Ames Inc. The company's comparative financial statements for 1990 and 1989 are given in Problem 15–44. To assist in the evaluation of the company, Lamor secured the following additional data taken from the balance sheet at December 31, 1988:

Accounts receivable (net)	$ 440,000
Inventories	674,000
Long-term investments...............................	100,000
Total assets	6,700,000
Total stockholders' equity (preferred and common stock outstanding same as in 1989)......................	4,200,000

Instructions:

Prepare a report for Lamor, based on an analysis of the financial data presented. In preparing your report, include all ratios and other data that will be useful in arriving at a decision regarding the investment.

ALTERNATE PROBLEMS

15–40A. Vertical analysis for income statement. For 1990, Paret Company initiated an extensive sales promotion campaign that included the expenditure of an additional $50,000 for advertising. At the end of the year, Ray Paret, the president, is presented with the following condensed comparative income statement:

Paret Company
Comparative Income Statement
For Years Ended December 31, 1990 and 1989

	1990	1989
Sales	$609,000	$361,800
Sales returns and allowances.	9,000	1,800
Net sales.	$600,000	$360,000
Cost of goods sold	372,000	216,000
Gross profit.	$228,000	$144,000
Selling expenses	$108,000	$ 57,600
General expenses	24,000	16,200
Total operating expenses.	$132,000	$ 73,800
Operating income	$ 96,000	$ 70,200
Other income	1,800	1,440
Income before income tax	$ 97,800	$ 71,640
Income tax	24,000	18,000
Net income	$ 73,800	$ 53,640

Instructions:

(1) Prepare a comparative income statement for the two-year period, presenting an analysis of each item in relationship to net sales for each of the years.
(2) To the extent the data permit, comment on the significant relationships revealed by the vertical analysis prepared in (1).

15–42A. Effect of transactions on current position analysis. Data pertaining to the current position of D. Ellis Inc. are as follows:

Cash.	$132,500
Marketable securities.	50,000
Accounts and notes receivable (net)	297,500
Inventories.	482,500
Prepaid expenses	37,500
Accounts payable.	302,500
Notes payable (short-term).	75,000
Accrued liabilities	22,500

Instructions:

(1) Compute (a) the working capital, (b) the current ratio, and (c) the acid-test ratio.
(2) List the following captions on a sheet of paper:

Transaction	Working Capital	Current Ratio	Acid-Test Ratio

Compute the working capital, the current ratio, and the acid-test ratio after each of the following transactions, and record the results in the appropriate columns. Consider each transaction separately and assume that only that transaction affects the data given above.
(a) Paid accounts payable, $100,000.

(b) Sold marketable securities, $50,000.
(c) Purchased goods on account, $80,000.
(d) Paid notes payable, $75,000.
(e) Declared a cash dividend, $50,000.
(f) Declared a common stock dividend on common stock, $72,500.
(g) Borrowed cash from bank on a long-term note, $200,000.
(h) Received cash on account, $150,000.
(i) Issued additional shares of stock for cash, $150,000.
(j) Paid cash for office supplies, $30,000.

15–44A. Eighteen measures of solvency and profitability. The comparative financial statements of A. B. Peters Company are as follows. The market price of A. B. Peters Company's common stock was $64 on December 31, 1989, and $82 on December 31, 1990.

A. B. Peters Company
Comparative Income Statement
For Years Ended December 31, 1990 and 1989

	1990	1989
Sales (all on account).....................	$6,860,000	$4,880,000
Sales returns and allowances...............	110,000	80,000
Net sales.................................	$6,750,000	$4,800,000
Cost of goods sold	4,590,000	3,120,000
Gross profit..............................	$2,160,000	$1,680,000
Selling expenses	$ 877,500	$ 741,000
General expenses.........................	438,750	336,000
Total operating expenses..................	$1,316,250	$1,077,000
Operating income	$ 843,750	$ 603,000
Other income	33,750	30,000
	$ 877,500	$ 633,000
Other expense (interest)	193,800	120,000
Income before income tax..................	$ 683,700	$ 513,000
Income tax	316,200	226,500
Net income	$ 367,500	$ 286,500

A. B. Peters Company
Comparative Retained Earnings Statement
For Years Ended December 31, 1990 and 1989

	1990	1989
Retained earnings, January 1...............	$1,084,500	$ 903,000
Add net income for year...................	367,500	286,500
Total.....................................	$1,452,000	$1,189,500
Deduct dividends:		
On preferred stock	$ 60,000	$ 60,000
On common stock........................	67,500	45,000
Total.....................................	$ 127,500	$ 105,000
Retained earnings, December 31............	$1,324,500	$1,084,500

A. B. Peters Company
Comparative Balance Sheet
December 31, 1990 and 1989

Assets	1990	1989
Current assets:		
Cash....................................	$ 337,500	$ 262,500
Marketable securities	150,000	—
Accounts receivable (net)	637,500	487,500
Inventories	1,080,000	720,000
Prepaid expenses	45,000	30,000
Total current assets...................	$2,250,000	$1,500,000
Long-term investments...................	375,000	337,500
Plant assets (net)	3,139,500	2,922,000
Total assets	$5,764,500	$4,759,500

Liabilities		
Current liabilities	$1,125,000	$ 975,000
Long-term liabilities:		
Mortgage note payable, 12%, due 1999....	$ 615,000	—
Bonds payable, 10%, due 1997	1,200,000	$1,200,000
Total long-term liabilities...............	$1,815,000	$1,200,000
Total liabilities...........................	$2,940,000	$2,175,000

Stockholders' Equity		
Preferred $8 stock, $100 par...............	$ 750,000	$ 750,000
Common stock, $25 par...................	750,000	750,000
Retained earnings.......................	1,324,500	1,084,500
Total stockholders' equity	$2,824,500	$2,584,500
Total liabilities and stockholders' equity	$5,764,500	$4,759,500

Instructions:

Determine the following measures for 1990, presenting the figures used in your computations:

(1) Working capital.
(2) Current ratio.
(3) Acid-test ratio.
(4) Accounts receivable turnover.
(5) Number of days' sales in receivables.
(6) Inventory turnover.
(7) Number of days' sales in inventory.
(8) Ratio of plant assets to long-term liabilities.
(9) Ratio of stockholders' equity to liabilities.
(10) Number of times interest charges earned.
(11) Number of times preferred dividends earned.
(12) Ratio of net sales to assets.
(13) Rate earned on total assets.
(14) Rate earned on stockholders' equity.

(continued)

(15) Rate earned on common stockholders' equity.
(16) Earnings per share on common stock.
(17) Price-earnings ratio.
(18) Dividend yield.

Mini-Case 15

You and your sister are both presidents of companies in the same industry, CDP Inc. and RST Inc., respectively. Both companies were originally operated as a single-family business; but, shortly after your father's death in 1975, the business was divided into two companies. Your sister took over CDP Inc., located in Indianapolis, while you took over RST Inc., located in Cincinnati.

During a recent family reunion, your sister referred to the much larger rate of return to her stockholders than was the case in your company and suggested that you consider rearranging the method of financing your corporation. The difference is highlighted by the following chart, which compares the rates earned on the stockholders' equity and the assets of the two companies:

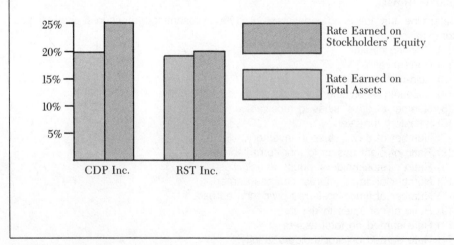

Since 1975, the growth in your sister's company has been financed largely through borrowing and yours largely through the issuance of additional common stock. Both companies have about the same volume of sales, gross profit, operating income, and total assets.

The income statements for the year ended December 31, 1990, and the balance sheets at December 31, 1990, for both companies are as follows:

Income Statements

	CDP Inc.	RST Inc.
Sales	$2,029,500	$1,952,500
Sales returns and allowances	29,500	22,500
Net sales	$2,000,000	$1,930,000
Cost of goods sold	1,225,000	1,179,000
Gross profit	$ 775,000	$ 751,000
Selling expenses	$ 335,000	$ 305,750
General expenses	195,000	175,250
Total operating expenses	$ 530,000	$ 481,000
Operating income	$ 245,000	$ 270,000
Interest expense	31,000	10,500
Income before income tax	$ 214,000	$ 259,500
Income tax	86,000	103,500
Net income	$ 128,000	$ 156,000

Balance Sheets

Assets	CDP Inc.	RST Inc.
Current assets	$ 62,500	$ 65,000
Plant assets (net)	775,000	810,000
Intangible assets	12,500	25,000
Total assets	$ 850,000	$ 900,000
Liabilities		
Current liabilities	$ 25,000	$ 40,000
Long-term liabilities	310,000	100,000
Total liabilities	$ 335,000	$ 140,000
Stockholders' Equity		
Common stock ($10 par)	$ 100,000	$ 400,000
Retained earnings	415,000	360,000
Total stockholders' equity	$ 515,000	$ 760,000
Total liabilities and stockholders' equity	$ 850,000	$ 900,000

In addition to the 1990 financial statements, the following data were taken from the balance sheet at December 31, 1989:

	CDP Inc.	RST Inc.
Total assets	$ 800,000	$ 860,000
Total stockholders' equity..................	495,000	740,000

Instructions:

(1) Determine for 1990 the following ratios and other measures for both companies.
   (a) Ratio of plant assets to long-term liabilities.
   (b) Ratio of stockholders' equity to liabilities.
   (c) Ratio of net sales to assets.
   (d) Rate earned on total assets.
   (e) Rate earned on stockholders' equity.
(2) For both CDP Inc. and RST Inc., the rate earned on stockholders' equity is greater than the rate earned on total assets. Explain.
(3) Why is the rate of return on stockholders' equity for CDP Inc. approximately 20% greater than for RST Inc.?
(4) Comment on your sister's suggestion for rearranging the financing of RST Inc.

Answers to Self-Examination Questions
· · ·

1. **A** Percentage analysis indicating the relationship of the component parts to the total in a financial statement, such as the relationship of current assets to total assets (20% to 100%) in the question, is called vertical analysis (answer A). Percentage analysis of increases and decreases in corresponding items in comparative financial statements is called horizontal analysis (answer B). An example of horizontal analysis would be the presentation of the amount of current assets in the preceding balance sheet along with the amount of current assets at the end of the current year, with the increase or decrease in current assets between the periods expressed as a percentage. Current position analysis (answer C), relates to analysis of various current asset and current liability items.

2. D Various solvency measures, categorized as current position analysis, indicate a firm's ability to meet currently maturing obligations. Each measure contributes in the analysis of a firm's current position and is most useful when viewed with other measures and when compared with similar measures for other periods and for other firms. Working capital (answer A) is the excess of current assets over current liabilities; the current ratio (answer B) is the ratio of current assets to current liabilities; and the acid-test ratio (answer C) is the ratio of the sum of cash, receivables, and marketable securities to current liabilities.

3. D The ratio of current assets to current liabilities is usually referred to as the current ratio (answer A) and is sometimes referred to as the working capital ratio (answer B) or bankers' ratio (answer C).

4. C The ratio of the sum of cash, receivables, and marketable securities (sometimes called quick assets) to current liabilities is called the acid-test ratio (answer C) or quick ratio. The current ratio (answer A) and working capital ratio (answer B) are two terms that describe the ratio of current assets to current liabilities.

5. C As with many attempts at analyzing financial data, it is possible to determine more than one measure that is useful for evaluating the efficiency in the management of inventories. Both the inventory turnover (answer A), which is determined by dividing the cost of goods sold by the average inventory, and the number of days' sales in inventory (answer B), which is determined by dividing the inventories at the end of the year by the average daily cost of goods sold, express the relationship between the cost of goods sold and inventory.

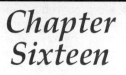

Chapter
Sixteen

CHAPTER
OBJECTIVES

•

Describe the nature and purpose of the statement of cash flows.

•

Describe and illustrate the following types of cash flow activities:
Cash flows from operating activities
Cash flows from financing activities
Cash flows from investing activities

•

Describe and illustrate the preparation of the statement of cash flows.

•

Statement of Cash Flows

The preparation of various accounting reports for management's use has been described in preceding chapters. This chapter is devoted to an in-depth discussion of the nature and purpose of the statement of cash flows. Such a statement is useful to managers in evaluating past and planning future financing and investing activities. It is also useful to creditors and investors in their analysis of a firm's financial condition and profitability.

NATURE OF THE STATEMENT OF CASH FLOWS

In 1987, the Financial Accounting Standards Board (FASB) issued Statement of Financial Accounting Standards No. 95, which requires the inclusion of a statement of cash flows as part of the basic set of financial statements. The statement of cash flows replaces the statement of changes in financial position (frequently called the funds statement).

The statement of changes in financial position reported a firm's significant financing and investing activities for a period. These activities were generally described in terms of the inflow and outflow of "funds," with funds defined either as "cash" or "working capital" (current assets − current liabilities). After considerable research and experimentation, the FASB decided that a statement of cash flows would better meet the objectives of financial reporting, expressed as follows:

Financial reporting should provide information to help present and potential investors and creditors and other users in assessing the amounts, timing, and uncertainty of prospective cash receipts from dividends or interest and the proceeds from the sale, redemption, or maturity of securities or loans. The prospects for those cash receipts are affected by an enterprise's ability to generate enough cash to meet its obligations when due and its other cash operating needs, to reinvest in operations, and to pay cash dividends....[1]

---

[1]*Statement of Financial Accounting Concepts, No. 1,* "Objectives of Financial Reporting by Business Enterprises" (Stamford: Financial Accounting Standards Board, 1978), par. 37.

The **statement of cash flows** reports a firm's major sources of cash receipts and major uses of cash payments for a period.[2] Such a statement provides useful information about a firm's activities in generating cash from operations, meeting its financial obligations, paying dividends, and maintaining and expanding operating capacity. Such information, when used in conjunction with the other financial statements, assists investors, creditors, and others in assessing the entity's profitability and solvency (the ability to meet currently maturing debt). For example, the receipt of cash from issuing bonds indicates that the firm is not only committed to the payment of periodic interest expense (which affects profitability and solvency), but also to the redemption of the bonds at maturity (which affects solvency). Thus, the statement of cash flows is useful in analyzing both past and future profitability and solvency of the firm.

Focus on Cash Flow

In the past, investors have relied almost exclusively on a company's earnings information in judging the company's performance. But this information may be misleading. Therefore, as described in the following excerpt from an article in *The Wall Street Journal,* more and more investors are focusing on cash flows.

Follow the money.

That's a guiding principle for the increasing number of stock analysts and investors who study corporate cash flows. While none of them advocates using cash-flow analysis by itself, they say it can be an important tool in piercing the camouflage that sometimes makes reported earnings misleading.

As the term suggests, cash flow is basically a measure of the money flowing into—or out of—a business. If large companies were run, like lemonade stands, on a cash basis, earnings and cash flow would be identical.

Every major corporation, however, keeps its books on an accrual basis. When it builds a new plant or receives a large multiyear contract, it generally staggers the expense or income over a period of years.

That can give a truer picture of corporate profitability, but sometimes it obscures important developments.

Take a company that spent $140 million on new machinery last year. If it depreciates the equipment over a seven-year period, it will be subtracting $20 million from reported profits each year.

But if the machines will stay up-to-date and useful for 25 years, the company's reported earnings may understate its true strength....

...Sometimes the reverse is true. If a company has been neglecting capital spending, its earnings may look good. But on a cash-flow basis, it will look no better, and perhaps worse, than its competitors.

Thus, focusing on cash flow makes the investor confront an important question: whether...assets being depreciated really do wear out as rapidly as they are being depreciated....

...Joseph Battipaglia, an analyst with Gruntal & Co. in New York, says that cash-flow trends gave alert investors an early warning of the auto industry's problems in the 1970's. By the end of the decade, he notes, poor earnings made those problems apparent to everyone. But by then, he says, "everyone was going through the same door at the same time."

Source: John R. Dorfman, "Stock Analysts Increase Focus on Cash Flow," *The Wall Street Journal* (February 17, 1987), Section 2, page 1.

---

[2]Cash is the most useful concept for the statement of cash flows. However, cash in excess of immediate needs may be invested in income-producing, short-term, highly liquid investments, called cash equivalents, such as Treasury bills and money market funds. In such cases, the statement of cash flows may report changes during the period in cash and cash equivalents.

FORM OF THE STATEMENT OF CASH FLOWS

The statement of cash flows classifies cash receipts and cash payments by three types of activities:

1. **Cash flows from operating activities,** which include cash transactions that enter into the determination of net income.
2. **Cash flows from financing activities,** which include receipts from the issuance of equity and debt securities; and payments for dividends, re-purchase of equity securities, and redemption of debt securities.
3. **Cash flows from investing activities,** which include receipts from the sale of investments and plant assets and other noncurrent assets; and payments for the acquisition of investments and plant assets and other noncurrent assets.

By grouping cash flows by operating, financing, and investing activities, significant relationships within and among the activities can be evaluated. For example, cash receipts from borrowings can easily be related to repayments of borrowings when both are reported as financing activities. Also, the impact of each of the three activities (operating, financing, and investing) on cash flows can be evaluated. Such relationships assist investors and creditors in evaluating the effects of cash flows on profitability and solvency.

The common transactions giving rise to cash flows that would be reported in one of the three sections of the statement of cash flows are presented in the diagram below and are discussed in the following paragraphs. The focus in this chapter is on presenting the basic concept of cash flows and on providing an understanding of the preparation, interpretation, and use of the statement of cash flows.

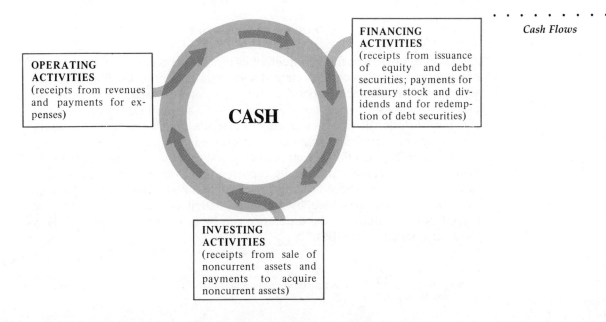

Cash Flows

Operating Activities

The most frequent and often the most important cash flows relate to operating activities entered into for the purpose of earning net income. There are two alternatives to reporting cash flows from such operating activities in the statement of cash flows: (1) the direct method and (2) the indirect method. The **direct method** reports the major classes of operating cash receipts (cash collected from customers and cash received from interest and dividends, for example) and of operating cash payments (cash paid to suppliers for merchandise and services, to employees for wages, and to creditors for interest, for example). The difference between these operating cash receipts and cash payments would be reported as the net cash flow from operating activities. The principal advantage of the direct method is that it presents the major categories of cash receipts and cash payments. Its principal disadvantage is that the necessary data are often costly to accumulate.

When the **indirect method** is used, the effects of all deferrals of past cash receipts and payments and all accruals of expected future cash receipts and payments are removed from the net income reported on the income statement. This removal is accomplished by adjusting the amount reported as net income upward or downward to determine the net amount of cash flows from operating activities. One of the major advantages of the indirect method is that it focuses on the differences between net income and cash flows from operating activities. In addition, the data needed for the indirect method are generally more readily available and less costly to obtain than the data needed for the direct method.

Because of its more frequent usage, the indirect method will be used in this chapter.[3] Regardless of which method is used, the same amount of net cash flow from operating activities will be reported in the statement of cash flows.

Financing Activities

Cash inflows from financing activities include proceeds from the issuance of equity securities, such as preferred and common stocks. Cash inflows also arise from the issuance of bonds, mortgage notes payable, and notes and other long-term and short-term borrowings. Cash outflows from financing activities include the payment of cash dividends, the acquisition of treasury stock, and the repayment of amounts borrowed.

In reporting cash flows from financing activities on the statement of cash flows, the cash inflows are usually reported first, followed by the cash outflows. If the inflows exceed the outflows, the net cash flow can be described as "Net cash flow provided by financing activities." If the cash outflows exceed the cash inflows, the difference can be described as "Net cash flow used for financing activities."

---

[3]A brief discussion of the direct method of reporting cash flows from operating activities is presented in Appendix C.

Investing Activities
. . .

Cash inflows from investing activities generally arise from the sale of investments, plant assets, and intangible assets. Cash outflows generally include payments to acquire investments, plant assets, and intangible assets.

In reporting cash flows from investing activities on the statement of cash flows, the cash inflows are usually reported first, followed by the cash outflows. If the inflows exceed the outflows, the net cash flow can be described as "Net cash flow provided by investing activities." If the cash outflows exceed the cash inflows, the difference can be described as "Net cash flow used for investing activities."

Noncash Financing and Investing Activities
. . .

In addition to the financing and investing activities described in the preceding sections, financing and investing may be affected by transactions that do not involve cash. If such transactions have occurred during the period, their effect, if significant, should be reported in a separate schedule to accompany the statement of cash flows. This broadened concept recognizes that some financing and investing transactions do not involve cash receipts and payments but have a significant effect on future cash flows. For example, the issuance of common stock in liquidation of long-term debt has no effect on cash. However, the transaction will eliminate the future cash payments to retire the bonds and future cash payments for interest. Therefore, it should be reported.

A complete discussion of the kinds of noncash transactions that usually have a significant effect on financing and investing activities is beyond the scope of discussion here. The following transactions are illustrative of the many possibilities: issuance of bonds or capital stock in exchange for plant assets, issuance of common stock in exchange for convertible preferred stock, and issuance of long-term investments in exchange for machinery and equipment.

ASSEMBLING DATA FOR THE STATEMENT OF CASH FLOWS
.

To collect the data for the statement of cash flows, all the cash receipts and disbursements for a period could be analyzed and then reported by activity (operating, financing, or investing) on the statement. However, this direct method of analyzing and reporting cash flows is expensive and time consuming. An indirect method is the more efficient procedure of examining the noncash balance sheet accounts and determining the type of cash flow activity that leads to changes in these accounts during the period. In performing this analysis, supplementary explanatory data can be obtained from the income statement and other records as needed. Such a procedure is not only efficient but also logical, because all transactions eventually affect balance sheet accounts. For example, although revenues and expenses are not shown directly on the balance sheet, the retained earnings account on the balance sheet is affected as revenues and expenses are closed at the end of a period.

Although there is no order in which the noncash balance sheet accounts must be analyzed, time can be saved and greater accuracy can be achieved by selecting the accounts in the reverse order in which they appear on the balance sheet. Therefore, the retained earnings account provides the starting point for determining the cash flows from operating activities that normally appear first on the statement of cash flows.

To illustrate this approach to assembling the data for the statement of cash flows, the following comparative balance sheet for T. R. Morgan Corporation for the year ended December 31, 1990, will be used. Selected ledger

Comparative Balance Sheet

T. R. Morgan Corporation
Comparative Balance Sheet
December 31, 1990 and 1989

	1990	1989	Increase Decrease*
Assets			
Cash	$ 49,000	$ 26,000	$ 23,000
Trade receivables (net)	74,000	65,000	9,000
Inventories	172,000	180,000	8,000*
Prepaid expenses	4,000	3,000	1,000
Investments (long-term)	—	45,000	45,000*
Land	90,000	40,000	50,000
Building	200,000	200,000	—
Accumulated depreciation — building	(36,000)	(30,000)	(6,000)
Equipment	290,000	142,000	148,000
Accumulated depreciation — equipment	(43,000)	(40,000)	(3,000)
Total assets	$800,000	$631,000	$169,000
Liabilities			
Accounts payable (merchandise creditors)	$ 50,000	$ 32,000	$ 18,000
Income tax payable	2,500	4,000	1,500*
Dividends payable	15,000	8,000	7,000
Bonds payable	120,000	245,000	125,000*
Total liabilities	$187,500	$289,000	$101,500*
Stockholders' Equity			
Preferred stock	$150,000	—	$150,000
Premium on preferred stock	10,000	—	10,000
Common stock	280,000	$230,000	50,000
Retained earnings	172,500	112,000	60,500
Total stockholders' equity	$612,500	$342,000	$270,500
Total liabilities and stockholders' equity	$800,000	$631,000	$169,000

accounts will be presented as needed, along with supplementary data taken from the income statement.[4]

Retained Earnings

According to the comparative balance sheet for T. R. Morgan Corporation, there was an increase of $60,500 in retained earnings during the year. The retained earnings account, as shown below, indicates the nature of the entries made during the year that resulted in this increase.

ACCOUNT RETAINED EARNINGS   ACCOUNT NO.

Date		Item	Debit	Credit	Balance Debit	Balance Credit
1990						
Jan.	1	Balance				112,000
Dec.	31	Net income		90,500		
	31	Cash dividends	30,000			172,500

The retained earnings account indicates net income of $90,500 and cash dividends declared of $30,000. The determination of the amount of cash flows from operating activities and the cash flows for the payment of dividends is discussed in the following paragraphs. It should be noted that there may be entries in the retained earnings account that do not affect cash, such as a transfer of retained earnings to paid-in capital accounts in the issuance of a stock dividend. Similarly, transfers between the retained earnings account and appropriations accounts have no effect on cash. Such transactions would not be reported on the statement of cash flows.

Cash Flows from Operating Activities. The amount of net income, $90,500, which is reported on the income statement, was determined by the accrual method of accounting. It is therefore necessary to recognize the relationship of the accrual method to the movement of cash. Usually, a part of some of the costs and expenses reported on the income statement, as well as a part of the revenue earned, is not accompanied by cash outflow or inflow.

There is often a period of time between the accrual of a revenue and the receipt of the related cash. Perhaps the most common example is the sale of merchandise or a service on account, for which payment is received at a later point in time. Hence, the amount reported on the income statement as revenue from sales is not likely to correspond with the amount of the related cash inflow for the same period.

[4]When the volume of data is substantial, experienced accountants may first assemble all relevant facts in working papers designed for the purpose. Specialized working papers are not essential, however. Because of their complexity, they tend to obscure the basic concepts of cash flow analysis for anyone who is not already familiar with the subject. For this reason, special working papers will not be used in the following discussion. Instead, the emphasis will be on the basic analyses. The use of a work sheet as an aid in assembling data for the statement of cash flows is presented in Appendix D.

Timing differences between the incurrence of an expense and the related cash outflow must also be considered in determining the amount of cash flows from operating activities. For example, the amount reported on the income statement as insurance expense is the amount of insurance premiums expired rather than the amount of premiums paid during the period. Similarly, supplies paid for in one year may be used and thus converted to an expense in a later year. Conversely, a portion of some of the expenses incurred near the end of one period, such as wages and taxes, may not require a cash outlay until the following period.

Some revenues and expenses related to noncurrent accounts do not provide or use cash. For example, depreciation expense is a proper expense for the purpose of determining net income, but it does not require an outlay of cash.

To determine the amount of cash flows from operating activities, the accrual basis net income, as reported on the income statement, must be converted to the cash basis. For purposes of illustration, the types of accounts that must be analyzed to convert net income from the accrual basis to the cash basis can be placed in two categories, described as follows:

1. Expenses affecting noncurrent accounts but not cash. For example, depreciation of plant assets and amortization of intangible assets are deducted from revenue but have no effect on cash. Similarly, the amortization of premium on bonds payable, which decreases interest expense and therefore increases operating income, does not affect cash.
2. Revenues and expenses affecting current asset and current liability accounts in amounts that differ from cash flows. For example, a sale of $10,000 on account, on which $8,000 has subsequently been collected, increases revenue by $10,000 but increases cash by only $8,000. In this case, to convert the revenue reported on the income statement ($10,000) to the cash basis, the increase in accounts receivable of $2,000 ($10,000 sale less $8,000 collection) can be deducted from the $10,000 of revenue to yield a cash flow of $8,000.

Generally accepted accounting principles require that cash flows be classified according to the nature of the underlying transaction.[5] This requirement means that cash flows from operating activities should not include transactions which are financing activities or investing activities. For example, the gain or loss from the sale of noncurrent assets would be reported as part of the total cash flows from investing activities arising from the sale of noncurrent assets. To illustrate, assume that land costing $50,000 was sold for $90,000 (a gain of $40,000). The sale should be reported in the investing activities section as "Cash receipts from the sale of land, $90,000." Since the $40,000 gain on the sale of the land is reported in the income statement, the $40,000 must be deducted from net income in converting the reported net income to cash flows

[5]*Statement of Financial Accounting Standards*, No. 95, "Statement of Cash Flows" (Stamford: Financial Accounting Standards Board, 1987).

from operations. Otherwise, the $40,000 gain would be reported twice on the statement of cash flows. Similarly, losses resulting from such transactions would be added to net income in determining the net cash flow from operating activities. Also, gains or losses arising from the retirement of debt would need to be deducted from or added to net income as reported on the income statement to determine the net cash flow from operating activities.

The conversion of the net income reported on the income statement to cash flows from operating activities can be summarized as follows:

Net income, per income statement			$XX
Add:	Depreciation of plant assets	$XX	
	Amortization of bond discount and intangible assets	XX	
	Decreases in current assets (receivables, inventories, prepaid expenses)	XX	
	Increases in current liabilities (accounts and notes payable, accrued liabilities)	XX	
	Losses on disposal of assets and retirement of debt	XX	XX
Deduct:	Amortization of bond premium	$XX	
	Increases in current assets (receivables, inventories, prepaid expenses)	XX	
	Decreases in current liabilities (accounts and notes payable, accrued liabilities)	XX	
	Gains on disposal of assets and retirement of debt	XX	XX
Net cash flow from operating activities			$XX

Note that two current accounts—cash and dividends payable—are not included in this conversion schedule. Cash is omitted because it is the focus of the analysis. Dividends payable is omitted because dividends are a distribution of earnings and do not affect net income. The treatment of dividends as they affect the statement of cash flows will be discussed later in the chapter. In the following paragraphs, the manner in which the net income reported by T. R. Morgan Corporation is converted to "Cash flows from operating activities" is discussed.

Depreciation. The comparative balance sheet for T. R. Morgan Corporation indicates that Accumulated Depreciation—Equipment increased by $3,000, and Accumulated Depreciation—Building increased by $6,000. Reference to these two accounts, shown as follows, indicates that depreciation for the year was $12,000 for the equipment and $6,000 for the building, or a total of $18,000.

ACCOUNT ACCUMULATED DEPRECIATION—EQUIPMENT   ACCOUNT NO.

Date		Item	Debit	Credit	Balance Debit	Balance Credit
1990						
Jan.	1	Balance				40,000
May	9	Discarded, no salvage	9,000			
Dec.	31	Depreciation for year		12,000		43,000

ACCOUNT ACCUMULATED DEPRECIATION — BUILDING   ACCOUNT NO.

Date		Item	Debit	Credit	Balance Debit	Balance Credit
1990						
Jan.	1	Balance				30,000
Dec.	31	Depreciation for year		6,000		36,000

Since the $18,000 of depreciation expense reduces net income but did not require an outlay of cash, $18,000 is added to net income in the process of determining the cash flows from operating activities, as follows:

Cash flows from operating activities:

Net income	$90,500	
Add: Depreciation	18,000	$108,500

Current assets and current liabilities. In the process of determining cash flows from operating activities, decreases in the noncash current assets and increases in the current liabilities must be added to the amount reported as net income. Conversely, increases in the noncash current assets and decreases in the current liabilities must be deducted from the amount reported as net income. The relevant current asset and current liability accounts of T. R. Morgan Corporation are as follows:

Accounts	December 31 1990	December 31 1989	Increase Decrease*
Trade receivables (net).....................	$ 74,000	$ 65,000	$ 9,000
Inventories................................	172,000	180,000	8,000*
Prepaid expenses	4,000	3,000	1,000
Accounts payable (merchandise creditors).....	50,000	32,000	18,000
Income tax payable........................	2,500	4,000	1,500*

The additions to **trade receivables** for sales on account during the year were $9,000 more than the deductions for amounts collected from customers on account. The amount reported on the income statement as sales therefore included $9,000 that did not yield cash inflow during the year. Accordingly, $9,000 must be deducted from net income.

The $8,000 decrease in **inventories** indicates that the merchandise sold exceeded the cost of the merchandise purchased by $8,000. The amount reported on the income statement as a deduction from the revenue therefore included $8,000 that did not require cash outflow during the year. Accordingly, $8,000 must be added to net income.

The outlay of cash for **prepaid expenses** exceeded by $1,000 the amount deducted as an expense during the year. Hence, $1,000 must be deducted from net income.

The effect of the increase in **accounts payable**, which is the amount owed creditors for goods and services, was to include in expired costs and expenses the sum of $18,000 for which there had been no cash outlay during the year. Income was thereby reduced by $18,000, though there was no cash outlay. Hence, $18,000 must be added to net income.

The outlay of cash for **income taxes** exceeded by $1,500 the amount of income tax deducted as an expense during the period. Accordingly, $1,500 must be deducted from net income.

The foregoing adjustments to income, including the adjustment for depreciation, may be summarized as follows:

Cash flows from operating activities:			
Net income			$ 90,500
Add: Depreciation	$18,000		
Decrease in inventories	8,000		
Increase in accounts payable	18,000	44,000	
		$134,500	
Deduct: Increase in trade receivables..........	$ 9,000		
Increase in prepaid expenses	1,000		
Decrease in income tax payable.......	1,500	11,500	$123,000

Gain on sale of investments. Reference to the ledger or income statement would indicate that the sale of investments resulted in a gain of $30,000. As discussed in preceding paragraphs, to avoid the double reporting of this $30,000 in the statement of cash flows, it must be deducted from the net income reported on the income statement as follows:[6]

Cash flows from operating activities:		
Net income	$90,500	
Deduct: Gain on sale of investments.....................	30,000	$60,500

Reporting cash flows from operating activities. All the adjustments that are necessary to convert the net income to cash flows from operating activities for T. R. Morgan Corporation are presented in a format suitable for the statement of cash flows, as follows:

Cash flows from operating activities:			
Net income, per income statement..............			$ 90,500
Add: Depreciation	$18,000		
Decrease in inventories	8,000		
Increase in accounts payable	18,000	44,000	
		$134,500	
Deduct: Increase in trade receivables..........	$ 9,000		
Increase in prepaid expenses	1,000		
Decrease in income tax payable.......	1,500		
Gain on sale of investments..........	30,000	41,500	
Net cash flow from operating activities			$93,000

---

[6]The reporting of the cash flows from the sale of investments, which is an investing activity, is discussed in a later paragraph.

Cash Flows for Payment of Dividends. According to the retained earnings account of T. R. Morgan Corporation (page 593), cash dividends of $30,000 were declared during the year. However, according to the dividends payable account, shown as follows, dividend payments during the year totaled $23,000, revealing a timing difference between the declaration and the payment.

ACCOUNT DIVIDENDS PAYABLE   ACCOUNT NO.

Date		Item	Debit	Credit	Balance Debit	Balance Credit
1990						
Jan.	1	Balance				8,000
	10	Cash paid	8,000		—	—
June	20	Dividend declared		15,000		15,000
July	10	Cash paid	15,000		—	—
Dec.	20	Dividend declared		15,000		15,000

The $23,000 of cash dividend payments would be reported in the financing activities section and may be noted on the statement of cash flows as follows:

Cash flows from financing activities:
Cash paid for dividends $23,000

Common Stock
· · ·

The increase of $50,000 in the common stock account, shown as follows, is the result of stock being issued in exchange for land valued at $50,000.

ACCOUNT COMMON STOCK   ACCOUNT NO.

Date		Item	Debit	Credit	Balance Debit	Balance Credit
1990						
Jan.	1	Balance				230,000
Dec.	28	Issued at par in exchange for land		50,000		280,000

Although cash was not involved, the transaction represents a significant financing and investing transaction that should be reported in a separate schedule to the statement of cash flows, as discussed previously. In this schedule, the transaction may be noted as follows:

Noncash financing and investing activities:
Issuance of common stock at par for land $50,000

Preferred Stock

The increase of $150,000 in the preferred stock account and the increase of $10,000 in the premium on preferred stock account, shown as follows, is the result of an issuance of preferred stock for $160,000.

ACCOUNT PREFERRED STOCK, $50 PAR   ACCOUNT NO.

Date		Item	Debit	Credit	Balance Debit	Balance Credit
1990 Nov.	1	3,000 shares issued for cash		150,000		150,000

ACCOUNT PREMIUM ON PREFERRED STOCK   ACCOUNT NO.

Date		Item	Debit	Credit	Balance Debit	Balance Credit
1990 Nov.	1	3,000 shares issued for cash		10,000		10,000

This cash flow would be reported in the financing activities section and may be noted on the statement of cash flows as follows:

Cash flows from financing activities:
Cash received from sale of preferred stock $160,000

Bonds Payable

The next item listed on the balance sheet, bonds payable, decreased $125,000 during the year. Examination of the bonds payable account, which appears as follows, indicates that $125,000 of the bonds payable were retired by payment of the face amount.

ACCOUNT BONDS PAYABLE   ACCOUNT NO.

Date		Item	Debit	Credit	Balance Debit	Balance Credit
1990 Jan.	1	Balance				245,000
June	30	Retired by payment of cash at face amount	125,000			120,000

This cash flow would be reported in the financing activities section and may be noted as follows:

Cash flows from financing activities:
Cash paid to retire bonds payable $125,000

Equipment
· · ·

The comparative balance sheet indicates that the cost of equipment increased $148,000. The following equipment account and the accumulated depreciation account reveal that the net change of $148,000 was the result of two separate transactions—the discarding of equipment that had cost $9,000 and the purchase of equipment for $157,000. The equipment discarded had been fully depreciated, as indicated by the debit of $9,000 in the accumulated depreciation account, and no salvage was realized from its disposal. Hence, the transaction had no effect on cash and is not reported on the statement of cash flows.

ACCOUNT EQUIPMENT   ACCOUNT NO.

Date		Item	Debit	Credit	Balance Debit	Balance Credit
1990						
Jan.	1	Balance			142,000	
May	9	Discarded, no salvage		9,000		
Dec.	7	Purchased for cash	157,000		290,000	

ACCOUNT ACCUMULATED DEPRECIATION—EQUIPMENT   ACCOUNT NO.

Date		Item	Debit	Credit	Balance Debit	Balance Credit
1990						
Jan.	1	Balance				40,000
May	9	Discarded, no salvage	9,000			
Dec.	31	Depreciation for year		12,000		43,000

The effect on cash flows from the purchase of equipment for $157,000 would be reported in the investing activities section and may be noted as follows:

Cash flows from investing activities:
Cash paid for purchase of equipment **$157,000**

The credit in the accumulated depreciation account had the effect of reducing the book value of equipment by $12,000 but caused no change in cash. The depreciation was treated previously as an addition to net income in determining cash flows from operating activities.

Building
· · ·

According to the comparative balance sheet, there was no change in the $200,000 balance in the building account between the beginning and end of the year. Reference to the ledger confirms the absence of entries in the building account during the year, and hence the account is not shown here. The credit in the related accumulated depreciation account reduced the book value of the building, but, as indicated previously, cash was not affected. The depreciation was treated previously as an addition to net income in determining cash flows from operating activities.

Land
· · ·

The comparative balance sheet indicates that land increased by $50,000. The notation in the land account, which follows, indicates that the land was acquired by issuance of common stock at par.

ACCOUNT LAND   ACCOUNT NO.

Date		Item	Debit	Credit	Balance Debit	Balance Credit
1990						
Jan.	1	Balance			40,000	
Dec.	28	Acquired by issuance of common stock at par	50,000		90,000	

Although cash was not involved in this transaction, as indicated previously, the acquisition represents a significant financing and investing activity. Therefore, the transaction would be reported in a separate schedule as follows:

Noncash financing and investing activities:
Issuance of common stock at par for land $50,000

Investments
· · ·

The comparative balance sheet indicates that investments decreased by $45,000. The notation in the following investments account indicates that the investments were sold for $75,000 in cash.

ACCOUNT INVESTMENTS   ACCOUNT NO.

Date		Item	Debit	Credit	Balance Debit	Balance Credit
1990						
Jan.	1	Balance			45,000	
June	8	Sold for $75,000 cash		45,000	—	—

The $75,000 received from the sale of the investments must be reported as a cash flow from investing activities. Accordingly, the notation in the statement of cash flows is as follows:

Cash flows from investing activities:
Cash received from sale of investments (includes $30,000 gain reported
 in net income). $75,000

Note that the $30,000 gain on the sale is included in the net income reported on the income statement. As indicated previously, this gain was deducted from the net income in determining the cash flows from operating activities.

ILLUSTRATION OF THE STATEMENT OF CASH FLOWS

As mentioned previously, the statement of cash flows is divided into three sections—cash flows from operating activities, cash flows from financing activities, and cash flows from investing activities. Although different formats are possible, the cash flows from operating activities section is generally presented first, followed by the sections for cash flows from financing activities and investing activities. The total of the net cash flows from the three sections is the increase or decrease in cash for the period. If there were noncash financing and investing activities during the period, a separate schedule reporting such transactions would accompany the statement of cash flows.

An analysis of the statement of cash flows for T. R. Morgan Corporation, presented on page 603, indicates that the cash position increased by $23,000 during the year. The most significant increase in net cash flows was from operating activities ($93,000). The investing activities used $82,000 of cash flows during the year.

CASH FLOW PER SHARE

The term "cash flow per share" is sometimes encountered in the financial press. In many cases, the reference is to cash flows from operations per share. Such reporting of cash flow per share might mislead readers into thinking that cash flow is equivalent to or perhaps superior to earnings per share in appraising the relative success of operations. For example, users might interpret the cash flow from operations per share as being the amount available for dividends, when most of the cash generated by operations may be required for repaying loans or for reinvesting in the business. The financial statements, including the statement of cash flows, should therefore not report a cash flow per share amount.

T. R. Morgan Corporation
Statement of Cash Flows
For Year Ended December 31, 1990

Cash flows from operating activities:			
Net income, per income statement......		$ 90,500	
Add: Depreciation..................	$ 18,000		
Decrease in inventories	8,000		
Increase in accounts payable....	18,000	44,000	
		$134,500	
Deduct: Increase in trade receivables..	$ 9,000		
Increase in prepaid expenses.	1,000		
Decrease in income tax			
payable..................	1,500		
Gain on sale of investments...	30,000	41,500	
Net cash flow from operating activities ..			$93,000
Cash flows from financing activities:			
Cash received from sale of preferred			
stock............................		$160,000	
Less: Cash paid for dividends.........	$ 23,000		
Cash paid to retire bonds			
payable	125,000	148,000	
Net cash flow provided by financing			
activities			12,000
Cash flows from investing activities:			
Cash received from sale of investments .		$ 75,000	
Less: Cash paid for purchase of			
equipment		157,000	
Net cash flow used for investing			
activities			(82,000)
Increase in cash........................			$23,000
Cash at the beginning of the year........			26,000
Cash at the end of the year			$49,000

Schedule of Noncash Financing and Investing Activities	
Issuance of common stock at par for land	$50,000

Chapter Review

KEY POINTS

1. Nature of the Statement of Cash Flows.

The statement of cash flows reports a firm's major sources of cash receipts and major uses of cash payments for a period. The statement of cash flows provides useful information about a firm's activities in generating cash from operations, meeting its financial obligations, paying dividends, and maintaining and expanding operating capacity. When used in conjunction with the other financial statements, the statement of cash flows is useful in analyzing both past and future profitability and solvency of a firm.

2. Form of the Statement of Cash Flows.

The statement of cash flows reports cash receipts and cash payments by three types of activities: (1) operating activities, (2) financing activities, and (3) investing activities. Operating activities include cash transactions that enter into the determination of net income. Financing activities include receipts from the issuance of equity and debt securities and payments for dividends, repurchase of equity securities, and redemption of debt securities. Investing activities include receipts from the sale of noncurrent assets, such as investments and plant assets, and payments for the acquisition of noncurrent assets. If financing and investing transactions that do not involve cash have occurred during the period, their effect should be reported in a separate schedule to the statement of cash flows.

3. Assembling Data for the Statement of Cash Flows.

The common and most efficient procedure for determining the data for the statement of cash flows is to examine the noncash balance sheet accounts and determine the type of cash flow activity related to changes in these accounts.

4. Illustration of the Statement of Cash Flows.

The statement of cash flows is divided into three sections, with the cash flows from operating activities generally placed first, followed by the cash flows from financing activities and the cash flows from investing activities. A separate schedule is used to report noncash financing and investing activities.

5. Cash Flow per Share.

Sometimes the financial press refers to cash flows from operations per share. Such reporting of cash flow per share data might mislead readers into thinking that cash flow is equivalent to or perhaps superior to earnings per share in appraising the relative success of operations. The financial statements, including the statement of cash flows, should therefore not report a cash flow per share amount.

KEY TERMS
·

statement of cash flows 588
cash flows from operating
  activities 589

cash flows from financing
  activities 589

cash flows from investing
activities 589

direct method 590
indirect method 590

SELF-EXAMINATION QUESTIONS

(Answers at End of Chapter)

1. A full set of financial statements for a corporation would include:
   A. a balance sheet
   B. an income statement
   C. a statement of cash flows
   D. all of the above

2. An example of a cash flow from an operating activity is:
   A. receipt of cash from the sale of capital stock
   B. receipt of cash from the sale of bonds
   C. payment of cash for dividends
   D. none of the above

3. An example of a cash flow from a financing activity is:
   A. receipt of cash from the sale of capital stock
   B. receipt of cash from the sale of bonds
   C. payment of cash for dividends
   D. all of the above

4. An example of a cash flow from an investing activity is:
   A. receipt of cash from the sale of equipment
   B. receipt of cash from the sale of capital stock
   C. payment of cash for dividends
   D. payment of cash to repurchase equity securities

5. The net income reported on the income statement for the year was $55,000 and depreciation on plant assets for the year was $22,000. The balances of the current asset and current liability accounts at the beginning and end of the year are as follows:

	End	Beginning
Cash	$ 65,000	$ 70,000
Trade receivables	100,000	90,000
Inventories	145,000	150,000
Prepaid expenses.	7,500	8,000
Accounts payable (merchandise creditors)	51,000	58,000

The total amount reported for cash flows from operating activities in the statement of cash flows would be:

A. $33,000   C. $77,000
B. $55,000   D. none of the above

ILLUSTRATIVE PROBLEM

.

The comparative balance sheet of Jones Inc. for December 31, 1990 and 1989, is as follows:

Assets	1990	1989
Cash	$ 65,100	$ 42,500
Trade receivables (net)	91,350	61,150
Inventories	104,500	109,500
Prepaid expenses.............................	3,600	2,700
Land	30,000	50,000
Buildings....................................	345,000	245,000
Accumulated depreciation — buildings	(120,600)	(110,400)
Machinery and equipment......................	255,000	255,000
Accumulated depreciation — machinery and equipment.	(92,000)	(65,000)
Patents	35,000	40,000
	$716,950	$630,450

Liabilities and Stockholders' Equity	1990	1989
Accounts payable (merchandise creditors)	$ 61,150	$ 75,000
Dividends payable	15,000	10,000
Salaries payable	6,650	7,550
Mortgage note payable, due 1995.................	60,000	—
Bonds payable	—	75,000
Common stock, $20 par	300,000	250,000
Premium on common stock	100,000	75,000
Retained earnings..............................	174,150	137,900
	$716,950	$630,450

An examination of the income statement and the accounting records revealed the following additional information applicable to 1990:

(a) Net income, $96,250.
(b) Depreciation expense reported on the income statement: buildings, $10,200; machinery and equipment, $27,000.
(c) Land costing $20,000 was sold for $20,000.
(d) Patent amortization reported on the income statement, $5,000
(e) A mortgage note was issued for $60,000.
(f) A building costing $100,000 was constructed.
(g) 2,500 shares of common stock were issued at 30 in exchange for the bonds payable.
(h) Cash dividends declared, $60,000.

Instructions:
Prepare a statement of cash flows.

SOLUTION

Jones Inc.
Statement of Cash Flows
For Year Ended December 31, 1990

Cash flows from operating activities:		
Net income, per income statement......		$ 96,250
Add: Depreciation	$ 37,200	
Amortization of patents	5,000	
Decrease in inventories..........	5,000	47,200
		$143,450
Deduct: Increase in trade receivables (net)	$ 30,200	
Increase in prepaid expenses ..	900	
Decrease in accounts payable..	13,850	
Decrease in salaries payable...	900	45,850
Net cash flow from operating activities ..		$97,600
Cash flows from financing activities:		
Cash received from issuance of mortgage note payable.......................	$ 60,000	
Less: Cash paid for dividends.........	55,000	
Net cash flow provided by financing activities............................		5,000
Cash flows from investing activities:		
Cash received from sale of land.........	$ 20,000	
Less: Cash paid for construction of building	100,000	
Net cash flow used for investing activities...........................		(80,000)
Increase in cash........................		$22,600
Cash at the beginning of the year.........		42,500
Cash at the end of the year		$65,100

Schedule of Noncash Financing and Investing Activities	
Issuance of common stock to retire bonds payable............	$75,000

Discussion Questions

16–1. Which financial statement is most useful in evaluating past and planning future financing and investing activities?

16–2. What financial statement was replaced by the statement of cash flows?

16–3. For the statement of changes in financial position, the working capital basis was often employed. What is working capital?

16–4. What are the three types of activities reported on the statement of cash flows?

16–5. State the effect of each of the following transactions, considered individually, on cash flows (cash receipt or payment, and amount):
(a) Sold a new issue of $100,000 of bonds at 102.
(b) Sold equipment with a book value of $37,500 for $40,000.
(c) Sold 5,000 shares of $50 par common stock at $45 per share.
(d) Retired $500,000 of bonds on which there was $2,500 of unamortized bond discount for $501,000.

16–6. Identify each of the following as to type of cash flow activity (operating, financing, or investing):
(a) sale of investments
(b) issuance of common stock
(c) purchase of buildings
(d) net income
(e) issuance of bonds
(f) payment of cash dividends
(g) purchase of treasury stock
(h) redemption of bonds
(i) sale of equipment
(j) issuance of preferred stock
(k) purchase of patents

16–7. Name the two alternatives to reporting cash flows from operating activities in the statement of cash flows.

16–8. What is the principal disadvantage of the direct method of reporting cash flows from operating activities?

16–9. What are the major advantages of the indirect method of reporting cash flows from operating activities?

16–10. On the statement of cash flows, if the cash inflows from financing activities exceed the cash outflows, how is the difference described?

16–11. On the statement of cash flows, if the cash outflows from financing activities exceed the cash inflows, how is the difference described?

16–12. On the statement of cash flows, if the cash inflows from investing activities exceed the cash outflows, how is the difference described?

16–13. On the statement of cash flows, if the cash outflows from investing activities exceed the cash inflows, how is the difference described?

16–14. A corporation issued $250,000 of common stock in exchange for $250,000 of plant assets. Where would this transaction be reported on the statement of cash flows?

16–15. A corporation acquired as a long-term investment all of the capital stock of AJC Co., valued at $5,000,000, by issuance of $5,000,000 of its own common stock. Where should the transaction be reported on the statement of cash flows?

16–16. (a) What is the effect on cash flows of the declaration and issuance of a stock dividend?
(b) Is the stock dividend reported on the statement of cash flows?

16–17. On its income statement for the current year, a company reported a net loss of $50,000 from operations. On its statement of cash flows, it reported $25,000 of cash flows from operating activities. Explain the seeming contradiction between the loss and the cash flows.

16–18. What is the effect on cash flows of an appropriation of retained earnings for bonded indebtedness?

16–19. A retail enterprise, employing the accrual method of accounting, owed merchandise creditors (accounts payable) $295,000 at the beginning of the year and $320,000 at the end of the year. What adjustment for the $25,000 increase must be made to net income in determining the amount of cash flows from operating activities? Explain.

16–20. If revenue from sales amounted to $940,000 for the year and trade receivables totaled $120,000 and $135,000 at the beginning and end of the year respectively, what was the amount of cash received from customers during the year?

16–21. If salaries payable was $95,000 and $85,000 at the beginning and end of the year respectively, should $10,000 be added to or deducted from income to determine the amount of cash flows from operating activities? Explain.

16–22. The board of directors declared cash dividends totaling $120,000 during the current year. The comparative balance sheet indicates dividends payable of $25,000 at the beginning of the year and $30,000 at the end of the year. What was the amount of cash payments to stockholders during the year?

16–23. A long-term investment in bonds with a cost of $70,000 was sold for $75,000 cash. (a) What was the gain or loss on the sale? (b) What was the effect of the transaction on cash flows? (c) How should the transaction be reported in the statement of cash flows?

16–24. A corporation issued $5,000,000 of 20-year bonds for cash at 105. How would the transaction be reported on the statement of cash flows?

16–25. Fully depreciated equipment costing $75,000 was discarded. What was the effect of the transaction on cash flows if (a) $5,000 cash is received, (b) there is no salvage value?

16–26. Real World Focus.   Tandy Corporation converted approximately $100 million of 6½% debenture bonds into shares of common stock. How would this transaction be reported on the statement of cash flows?

Exercises

16–27.   **Cash flows from operating activities section.**   The net income reported on the income statement for the current year was $87,100. Depreciation recorded on equipment and a building amounted to $32,250 for the year. Balances of the current asset and current liability accounts at the beginning and end of the year are as follows:

SPREADSHEET PROBLEM

	End of Year	Beginning of Year
Cash.	$ 61,125	$58,725
Trade receivables (net).	87,500	80,000
Inventories	110,000	95,000
Prepaid expenses	6,900	7,650
Accounts payable		
(merchandise creditors)	77,200	72,700
Salaries payable	3,750	6,250

Prepare the cash flows from operating activities section of the statement of cash flows.

16–28. Cash flows from operating activities section. The net income reported on an income statement for the current year was $92,125. Depreciation recorded on store equipment for the year amounted to $43,500. Balances of the current asset and current liability accounts at the beginning and end of the year are as follows:

	End of Year	Beginning of Year
Cash.	$ 69,750	$61,250
Trade receivables (net).	80,500	85,000
Merchandise inventory	110,000	97,000
Prepaid expenses	7,900	7,400
Accounts payable		
(merchandise creditors)	69,700	72,700
Wages payable	7,500	6,250

Prepare the cash flows from operating activities section of a statement of cash flows.

16–29. Reporting changes in equipment on statement of cash flows. An analysis of the general ledger accounts indicated that office equipment, which had cost $60,000 and on which accumulated depreciation totaled $52,500 on the date of sale, was sold for $7,000 during the year. Using this information, indicate the items to be reported on the statement of cash flows.

16–30. Reporting changes in equipment on statement of cash flows. An analysis of the general ledger accounts indicated that delivery equipment, which had cost $35,000 and on which accumulated depreciation totaled $29,750 on the date of sale, was sold for $7,000 during the year. Using this information, indicate the items to be reported on the statement of cash flows.

16–31. Reporting land transactions on statement of cash flows. On the basis of the details of the following plant asset account, indicate the items to be reported on the statement of cash flows.

ACCOUNT LAND

ACCOUNT NO.

Date		Item	Debit	Credit	Balance Debit	Balance Credit
19--						
Jan.	1	Balance			650,000	
Aug.	29	Purchased for cash	200,000			
Nov.	20	Sold for $75,000		40,000	810,000	

16–32. Reporting stockholders' equity items on statement of cash flows. On the basis of the following stockholders' equity accounts, indicate the items, exclusive of net income, to be reported on the statement of cash flows. There were no unpaid dividends at either the beginning or end of the year.

ACCOUNT COMMON STOCK, $10 PAR   ACCOUNT NO.

Date		Item	Debit	Credit	Balance Debit	Balance Credit
19--						
Jan.	1	Balance, 50,000 shares				500,000
	20	5,000 shares issued for cash		50,000		
June	25	2,750-share stock dividend		27,500		577,500

ACCOUNT PREMIUM ON COMMON STOCK   ACCOUNT NO.

Date		Item	Debit	Credit	Balance Debit	Balance Credit
19--						
Jan.	1	Balance				50,000
	20	5,000 shares issued for cash		10,000		
June	25	Stock dividend		5,000		65,000

ACCOUNT RETAINED EARNINGS   ACCOUNT NO.

Date		Item	Debit	Credit	Balance Debit	Balance Credit
19--						
Jan.	1	Balance				225,000
June	25	Stock dividend	32,500			
Dec.	15	Cash dividend	55,000			
	31	Net income		97,500		235,000

16–33. Reporting land acquisition for cash and mortgage note on statement of cash flows. On the basis of the details of the following plant asset account, indicate the items to be reported on the statement of cash flows.

ACCOUNT LAND   ACCOUNT NO.

Date		Item	Debit	Credit	Balance Debit	Balance Credit
19--						
Jan.	1	Balance			750,000	
Mar.	2	Purchased for cash	100,000			
Oct.	29	Purchased with long-term				
		mortgage note	300,000		1,150,000	

Problems

16–34. Statement of cash flows. The comparative balance sheet of R. N. Corley Inc. for December 31 of the current year and the preceding year is as follows:

	December 31	
	Current Year	Preceding Year
Cash.	$ 72,000	$ 50,500
Trade receivables (net).	88,000	80,000
Inventories	105,900	91,400
Investments	—	50,000
Land.	50,000	—
Equipment.	375,000	275,000
Accumulated depreciation	(149,000)	(114,000)
	$541,900	$432,900
Accounts payable (merchandise creditors).	$ 57,000	$ 55,000
Dividends payable.	15,000	10,000
Common stock, $40 par.	320,000	250,000
Premium on common stock.	17,000	12,000
Retained earnings.	132,900	105,900
	$541,900	$432,900

The following additional information was taken from Corley's records:

(a) The investments were sold for $60,000 cash.
(b) Equipment and land were acquired for cash.
(c) There were no disposals of equipment during the year.
(d) The common stock was issued for cash.
(e) There was a $64,500 credit to Retained Earnings for net income.
(f) There was a $37,500 debit to Retained Earnings for cash dividends declared.

Instructions:

Prepare a statement of cash flows.

16–35. Statement of cash flows. The comparative balance sheet of AZCO Company at June 30 of the current year and the preceding year is as follows:

Assets	Current Year	Preceding Year
Cash.	$ 40,750	$ 55,250
Trade receivables (net).	85,400	95,000
Merchandise inventory	255,300	249,200
Prepaid expenses	3,825	2,700
Plant assets	321,500	289,500
Accumulated depreciation—plant assets.	(172,100)	(197,500)
	$534,675	$494,150
Liabilities and Stockholders' Equity		
Accounts payable (merchandise creditors).	$ 53,525	$ 49,150
Mortgage note payable	—	75,000
Common stock, $20 par.	250,000	200,000
Premium on common stock.	40,000	25,000
Retained earnings.	191,150	145,000
	$534,675	$494,150

Additional data obtained from the income statement and from an examination of the accounts in the ledger are as follows:

(a) Net income, $91,150.
(b) Depreciation reported on the income statement, $28,600.
(c) An addition to the building was constructed at a cost of $86,000, and fully depreciated equipment costing $54,000 was discarded, with no salvage realized.
(d) The mortgage note payable was not due until 1992, but the terms permitted earlier payment without penalty.
(e) 2,500 shares of common stock were issued at 26 for cash.
(f) Cash dividends declared and paid, $45,000.

Instructions:

Prepare a statement of cash flows.

16–36. **Statement of cash flows.** The comparative balance sheet of A. R. Katz Corporation at December 31 of the current year and the preceding year is as follows:

Assets	Current Year	Preceding Year
Cash	$ 89,900	$ 82,400
Trade receivables (net)	117,200	132,700
Inventories	260,070	238,070
Prepaid expenses............................	4,500	3,900
Land	100,000	100,000
Buildings....................................	622,500	422,500
Accumulated depreciation—buildings	(210,000)	(192,000)
Machinery and equipment.....................	275,000	275,000
Accumulated depreciation—machinery and equipment..................................	(130,600)	(108,400)
Patents	40,500	50,000
	$1,169,070	$1,004,170

Liabilities and Stockholders' Equity		
Accounts payable (merchandise creditors)	$ 36,280	$ 51,780
Dividends payable	25,000	20,000
Salaries payable.............................	10,550	19,400
Mortgage note payable, due 1995..............	150,000	—
Bonds payable...............................	—	100,000
Common stock, $15 par	550,000	475,000
Premium on common stock	75,000	50,000
Retained earnings............................	322,240	287,990
	$1,169,070	$1,004,170

An examination of the income statement and the accounting records revealed the following additional information applicable to the current year:

(a) Net income, $84,250.
(b) Depreciation expense reported on the income statement: buildings, $18,000; machinery and equipment, $22,200.

(c) Patent amortization reported on the income statement, $9,500.
(d) A building was constructed for $200,000 cash.
(e) A mortgage note for $150,000 was issued for cash.
(f) 5,000 shares of common stock were issued at 20 in exchange for the bonds payable.
(g) Cash dividends declared, $50,000.

Instructions:

Prepare a statement of cash flows.

16–37.   Statement of cash flows.   The comparative balance sheet of C. R. Lucas Inc. at December 31 of the current year and the preceding year is as follows:

Assets	Current Year	Preceding Year
Cash	$ 97,600	$ 84,500
Trade receivables (net)	140,500	125,250
Income tax refund receivable..................	7,500	—
Inventories	214,150	225,650
Prepaid expenses...........................	8,100	9,250
Investments................................	70,000	200,000
Land	110,000	150,000
Buildings..................................	650,000	375,000
Accumulated depreciation—buildings	(173,100)	(161,500)
Equipment	507,000	392,000
Accumulated depreciation—equipment.........	(181,620)	(171,420)
	$1,450,130	$1,228,730

Liabilities and Stockholders' Equity		
Accounts payable (merchandise creditors)	$ 71,400	$ 90,600
Income tax payable	—	9,000
Bonds payable..............................	300,000	—
Discount on bonds payable	(24,375)	—
Common stock, $5 par	525,000	500,000
Premium on common stock	70,000	60,000
Appropriation for plant expansion	200,000	175,000
Retained earnings...........................	308,105	394,130
	$1,450,130	$1,228,730

The noncurrent asset, the noncurrent liability, and the stockholders' equity accounts for the current year are as follows:

ACCOUNT INVESTMENTS   ACCOUNT NO.

Date		Item	Debit	Credit	Balance Debit	Balance Credit
19--						
Jan.	1	Balance			200,000	
May	5	Realized $155,000 cash from sale		130,000	70,000	

ACCOUNT LAND   ACCOUNT NO.

Date		Item	Debit	Credit	Balance Debit	Balance Credit
19--						
Jan.	1	Balance			150,000	
Aug.	15	Realized $50,000 from sale		40,000	110,000	

ACCOUNT BUILDINGS   ACCOUNT NO.

Date		Item	Debit	Credit	Balance Debit	Balance Credit
19--						
Jan.	1	Balance			375,000	
June	30	Acquired for cash	275,000		650,000	

ACCOUNT ACCUMULATED DEPRECIATION — BUILDINGS   ACCOUNT NO.

Date		Item	Debit	Credit	Balance Debit	Balance Credit
19--						
Jan.	1	Balance				161,500
Dec.	31	Depreciation for year		11,600		173,100

ACCOUNT EQUIPMENT   ACCOUNT NO.

Date		Item	Debit	Credit	Balance Debit	Balance Credit
19--						
Jan.	1	Balance			392,000	
Apr.	4	Discarded, no salvage		40,000		
July	11	Purchased for cash	80,000			
Oct.	10	Purchased for cash	75,000		507,000	

ACCOUNT ACCUMULATED DEPRECIATION — EQUIPMENT   ACCOUNT NO.

Date		Item	Debit	Credit	Balance Debit	Balance Credit
19--						
Jan.	1	Balance				171,420
Apr.	4	Equipment discarded	40,000			
Dec.	31	Depreciation for year		50,200		181,620

ACCOUNT BONDS PAYABLE   ACCOUNT NO.

Date		Item	Debit	Credit	Balance Debit	Balance Credit
19--						
June	30	Issued 20-year bonds		300,000		300,000

ACCOUNT DISCOUNT ON BONDS PAYABLE   ACCOUNT NO.

Date		Item	Debit	Credit	Balance Debit	Balance Credit
19--						
June	30	Bonds issued	25,000		25,000	
Dec.	31	Amortization		625	24,375	

ACCOUNT COMMON STOCK, $5 PAR   ACCOUNT NO.

Date		Item	Debit	Credit	Balance Debit	Balance Credit
19--						
Jan.	1	Balance				500,000
July	1	Stock dividend		25,000		525,000

ACCOUNT PREMIUM ON COMMON STOCK   ACCOUNT NO.

Date		Item	Debit	Credit	Balance Debit	Balance Credit
19--						
Jan.	1	Balance				60,000
July	1	Stock dividend		10,000		70,000

ACCOUNT APPROPRIATION FOR PLANT EXPANSION   ACCOUNT NO.

Date		Item	Debit	Credit	Balance Debit	Balance Credit
19--						
Jan.	1	Balance				175,000
Dec.	31	Appropriation		25,000		200,000

ACCOUNT RETAINED EARNINGS   ACCOUNT NO.

Date		Item	Debit	Credit	Balance Debit	Balance Credit
19--						
Jan.	1	Balance				394,130
July	1	Stock dividend	35,000			
Dec.	31	Net loss	1,025			
	31	Cash dividends	25,000			
	31	Appropriated	25,000			308,105

Instructions:

Prepare a statement of cash flows.

16–38. Statement of cash flows. An income statement and a comparative balance sheet for Lee Company are as follows:

Lee Company
Income Statement
For Current Year Ended December 31

Sales		$962,500
Cost of merchandise sold		617,500
Gross profit		$345,000
Operating expenses (including depreciation of $32,200)		220,600
Income from operations		$124,400
Other income:		
Gain on sale of land	$15,000	
Gain on sale of investments	7,500	
Interest income	1,600	24,100
		$148,500
Interest expense		24,000
Income before income tax		$124,500
Income tax		43,000
Net income		$ 81,500

Lee Company
Comparative Balance Sheet
December 31, Current and Preceding Year

Assets	Current Year	Preceding Year
Cash	$ 39,900	$ 46,600
Trade receivables (net)	109,750	94,250
Inventories	169,200	152,100
Prepaid expenses	4,150	4,900
Investments	27,600	75,000
Land	70,000	60,000
Buildings	330,000	180,000
Accumulated depreciation—buildings	(73,000)	(65,000)
Equipment	395,000	350,000
Accumulated depreciation—equipment	(143,800)	(119,600)
Total assets	$928,800	$778,250
Liabilities and Stockholders' Equity		
Accounts payable (merchandise creditors)	$ 64,750	$ 50,400
Income tax payable	5,000	7,800
Dividends payable	12,500	10,000
Mortgage note payable	150,000	—
Bonds payable	100,000	200,000
Common stock, $25 par	350,000	300,000
Premium on common stock	38,000	33,000
Retained earnings	208,550	177,050
Total liabilities and stockholders' equity	$928,800	$778,250

618 · Part 6 · Financial Analysis for Management Use

The following additional information on funds flow during the year was obtained from an examination of the ledger:

(a) Investments (long-term) were purchased for $27,600.
(b) Investments (long-term) were sold for $82,500.
(c) Equipment was purchased for $45,000. There were no disposals.
(d) A building valued at $150,000 and land valued at $50,000 were acquired by a cash payment of $200,000.
(e) Land which cost $40,000 was sold for $55,000 cash.
(f) A mortgage note payable for $150,000 was issued for cash.
(g) Bonds payable of $100,000 were retired by the payment of their face amount.
(h) 2,000 shares of common stock were issued for cash at 27 1/2.
(i) Cash dividends of $50,000 were declared.

Instructions:

Prepare a statement of cash flows.

16–39. Real World Focus. The current asset and current liability sections of the May 31, 1987 and 1986 balance sheets of The Pillsbury Company are as follows (dollars in millions):

	1987	1986
Current assets:		
Cash and equivalents........................	$ 80.7	$ 96.5
Receivables	522.7	492.7
Inventories	572.2	490.2
Prepaid and other assets....................	98.0	79.7
Total current assets........................	$1,273.6	$1,159.1
Current liabilities:		
Notes payable	$ 51.9	$ 22.1
Current portion of long-term debt.............	44.9	52.1
Accounts and drafts payable.................	620.7	513.6
Advances on sales	113.7	91.4
Employee compensation payable............	121.7	118.6
Income taxes payable......................	—	49.8
Other liabilities	289.7	287.9
Total current liabilities.....................	$1,242.6	$1,135.5

Selected data from Pillsbury Company's 1987 income statement (dollars in millions) were as follows:

Net income	$181.9
Depreciation	197.6
Amortization	23.9
Deferred income taxes (expense)	54.0

Instructions:

Prepare the cash flows from operating activities section of the statement of cash flows for The Pillsbury Company.

ALTERNATE PROBLEMS

16–34A. Statement of cash flows. The comparative balance sheet of C.D. Collins Co. for June 30 of the current year and the preceding year is as follows:

	June 30	
	Current Year	Preceding Year
Cash...................................	$ 64,200	$ 49,900
Trade receivables (net)......................	91,500	80,000
Inventories	105,900	90,500
Investments	—	75,000
Land.....................................	85,000	—
Equipment................................	355,000	275,000
Accumulated depreciation	(149,000)	(119,000)
	$552,600	$451,400
Accounts payable (merchandise creditors)......	$ 62,450	$ 55,000
Dividends payable..........................	12,000	10,000
Common stock, $20 par......................	300,000	250,000
Premium on common stock..................	22,000	12,000
Retained earnings..........................	156,150	124,400
	$552,600	$451,400

The following additional information was taken from the records of Collins:

(a) Equipment and land were acquired for cash.
(b) There were no disposals of equipment during the year.
(c) The investments were sold for $80,000 cash.
(d) The common stock was issued for cash.
(e) There was a $76,750 credit to Retained Earnings for net income.
(f) There was a $45,000 debit to Retained Earnings for cash dividends declared.

Instructions:
Prepare a statement of cash flows.

16–35A. Statement of cash flows. The comparative balance sheet of AIA Corporation at December 31 of the current year and the preceding year is as follows:

Assets	Current Year	Preceding Year
Cash	$ 62,600	$ 51,250
Trade receivables (net)	55,800	58,500
Merchandise inventory......................	97,500	77,300
Prepaid expenses...........................	5,300	4,650
Plant assets.................................	375,000	337,500
Accumulated depreciation—plant assets	(110,000)	(125,000)
	$486,200	$404,200

Liabilities and Stockholders' Equity	Current Year	Preceding Year
Accounts payable (merchandise creditors)	$ 55,600	$ 40,100
Mortgage note payable	—	50,000
Common stock, $25 par	250,000	200,000
Premium on common stock	55,000	25,000
Retained earnings...............................	125,600	89,100
	$486,200	$404,200

Additional data obtained from the income statement and from an examination of the accounts in the ledger are as follows:

(a) Net income, $72,500.
(b) Depreciation reported on the income statement, $27,500.
(c) An addition to the building was constructed at a cost of $80,000, and fully depreciated equipment costing $42,500 was discarded, with no salvage realized.
(d) The mortgage note payable was not due until 1993, but the terms permitted earlier payment without penalty.
(e) 2,000 shares of common stock were issued at 40 for cash.
(f) Cash dividends declared and paid, $36,000.

Instructions:

Prepare a statement of cash flows.

SPREADSHEET PROBLEM

16–36A. **Statement of cash flows.** The comparative balance sheet of Dina Corporation at December 31 of the current year and the preceding year is as follows:

Assets	Current Year	Preceding Year
Cash	$ 53,400	$ 46,200
Trade receivables (net)	82,100	67,450
Inventories	110,500	119,750
Prepaid expenses..............................	4,000	2,900
Land	60,000	60,000
Buildings.....................................	345,000	265,000
Accumulated depreciation — buildings	(140,600)	(130,400)
Machinery and equipment.......................	275,000	275,000
Accumulated depreciation — machinery and equipment...................................	(92,000)	(65,000)
Patents	30,000	35,000
	$727,400	$675,900

Liabilities and Stockholders' Equity		
Accounts payable (merchandise creditors)	$ 52,750	$ 80,000
Dividends payable	10,000	7,500
Salaries payable...............................	4,500	4,950
Mortgage note payable, due 1992.................	50,000	—
Bonds payable	—	100,000
Common stock, $20 par	380,000	300,000
Premium on common stock	80,000	60,000
Retained earnings..............................	150,150	123,450
	$727,400	$675,900

An examination of the income statement and the accounting records revealed the following additional information applicable to the current year:

(a) Net income, $66,700.

(b) Depreciation expense reported on the income statement: buildings, $10,200; machinery and equipment, $27,000.

(c) A building was constructed for $80,000 cash.

(d) Patent amortization reported on the income statement, $5,000.

(e) A mortgage note for $50,000 was issued for cash.

(f) 4,000 shares of common stock were issued at 25 in exchange for the bonds payable.

(g) Cash dividends declared, $40,000.

Instructions:

Prepare a statement of cash flows.

16–37A. Statement of cash flows. The comparative balance sheet of ACF Inc. at December 31 of the current year and the preceding year is as follows:

Assets	Current Year	Preceding Year
Cash	$ 56,125	$ 60,525
Trade receivables (net)	110,500	99,400
Inventories	218,750	192,700
Prepaid expenses...............................	6,400	6,750
Investments	—	75,000
Land	47,500	47,500
Buildings.......................................	305,000	210,000
Accumulated depreciation — buildings	(76,400)	(69,000)
Equipment	470,500	395,500
Accumulated depreciation — equipment.............	(143,500)	(129,000)
	$994,875	$889,375

Liabilities and Stockholders' Equity		
Accounts payable (merchandise creditors)	$ 64,500	$ 80,500
Income tax payable	5,900	4,800
Bonds payable	100,000	—
Discount on bonds payable	(4,875)	—
Common stock, $20 par	550,000	500,000
Premium on common stock	67,000	55,000
Appropriation for plant expansion	75,000	50,000
Retained earnings................................	137,350	199,075
	$994,875	$889,375

The noncurrent asset, the noncurrent liability, and the stockholders' equity accounts for the current year are as follows:

ACCOUNT INVESTMENTS   ACCOUNT NO.

Date		Item	Debit	Credit	Balance Debit	Balance Credit
19--						
Jan.	1	Balance			75,000	
Aug.	3	Realized $67,500 cash from				
·		sale		75,000	—	—

ACCOUNT LAND   ACCOUNT NO.

Date		Item	Debit	Credit	Balance Debit	Balance Credit
19-- Jan.	1	Balance			47,500	

ACCOUNT BUILDINGS   ACCOUNT NO.

Date		Item	Debit	Credit	Balance Debit	Balance Credit
19-- Jan.	1	Balance			210,000	
July	1	Acquired for cash	95,000		305,000	

ACCOUNT ACCUMULATED DEPRECIATION — BUILDINGS   ACCOUNT NO.

Date		Item	Debit	Credit	Balance Debit	Balance Credit
19-- Jan.	1	Balance				69,000
Dec.	31	Depreciation for year		7,400		76,400

ACCOUNT EQUIPMENT   ACCOUNT NO.

Date		Item	Debit	Credit	Balance Debit	Balance Credit
19-- Jan.	1	Balance			395,500	
Mar.	28	Discarded, no salvage		35,000		
Sept.	12	Purchased for cash	65,000			
Nov.	21	Purchased for cash	45,000		470,500	

ACCOUNT ACCUMULATED DEPRECIATION — EQUIPMENT   ACCOUNT NO.

Date		Item	Debit	Credit	Balance Debit	Balance Credit
19-- Jan.	1	Balance				129,000
Mar.	28	Equipment discarded	35,000			
Dec.	31	Depreciation for year		49,500		143,500

ACCOUNT BONDS PAYABLE   ACCOUNT NO.

Date		Item	Debit	Credit	Balance Debit	Balance Credit
19-- July	1	Issued 20-year bonds		100,000		100,000

ACCOUNT DISCOUNT ON BONDS PAYABLE   ACCOUNT NO.

Date		Item	Debit	Credit	Balance Debit	Balance Credit
19--						
July	1	Bonds issued	5,000		5,000	
Dec.	31	Amortization		125	4,875	

ACCOUNT COMMON STOCK, $20 PAR   ACCOUNT NO.

Date		Item	Debit	Credit	Balance Debit	Balance Credit
19--						
Jan.	1	Balance				500,000
July	22	Stock dividend		50,000		550,000

ACCOUNT PREMIUM ON COMMON STOCK   ACCOUNT NO.

Date		Item	Debit	Credit	Balance Debit	Balance Credit
19--						
Jan.	1	Balance				55,000
July	22	Stock dividend		12,000		67,000

ACCOUNT APPROPRIATION FOR PLANT EXPANSION   ACCOUNT NO.

Date		Item	Debit	Credit	Balance Debit	Balance Credit
19--						
Jan.	1	Balance				50,000
Dec.	31	Appropriation		25,000		75,000

ACCOUNT RETAINED EARNINGS   ACCOUNT NO.

Date		Item	Debit	Credit	Balance Debit	Balance Credit
19--						
Jan.	1	Balance				199,075
July	22	Stock dividend	62,000			
Dec.	31	Net income		100,275		
	31	Cash dividends	75,000			
	31	Appropriated	25,000			137,350

Instructions:

Prepare a statement of cash flows.

Mini-Case 16

a.j.jenkins inc.

Ann Jenkins is the president and majority shareholder of A. J. Jenkins Inc., a small retail store chain. Recently, Jenkins submitted a loan application for A. J. Jenkins Inc. to Paxton State Bank. It called for a $150,000, 13%, 10-year loan to help finance the construction of a building and the purchase of store equipment costing a total of $200,000 to enable A. J. Jenkins Inc. to open another store in Paxton. Land for this purpose was acquired last year. The bank's loan officer requested a statement of cash flows in addition to the most recent income statement, balance sheet, and retained earnings statement that Jenkins had submitted with the loan application.

As a close family friend, Jenkins asked you to prepare a statement of cash flows. From the records provided, you prepared the following statement:

A. J. Jenkins Inc.
Statement of Cash Flows
For Year Ended December 31, 19--

Cash flows from operating activities:			
Net income, per income statement		$ 82,500	
Add: Depreciation.........................	$25,500		
Decrease in trade receivables	9,000	34,500	
		$117,000	
Deduct: Increase in inventory................	$ 7,500		
Increase in prepaid expenses........	500		
Decrease in accounts payable	2,000		
Gain on sale of investments	5,000	15,000	
Net cash flow from operating activities			$102,000
Cash flows from financing activities:			
Cash paid for dividends		$ 50,000	
Net cash flow used for financing activities			(50,000)
Cash flows from investing activities:			
Cash received from investments sold		$ 35,000	
Less: Cash paid for purchase of store			
equipment.........................		30,000	
Net cash flow from investing activities			5,000
Increase in cash			$ 57,000
Cash at the beginning of the year			30,000
Cash at the end of the year			$ 87,000

Schedule of Noncash Financing and Investing Activities

Issuance of common stock at par for land...........................	$40,000

After reviewing the statement, Jenkins telephoned you and commented, "Are you sure this statement is right?" Jenkins then raised the following questions:

(a) "How can depreciation be a cash flow?"

(b) "The issuance of common stock for the land is listed in a separate schedule. This transaction has nothing to do with cash! Shouldn't this transaction be eliminated from the statement?"

(c) "How can the gain on sale of investments be a deduction from net income in determining the cash flow from operating activities?"

(d) "Why does the bank need this statement anyway? They can compute the increase in cash from the balance sheets for the last two years."

After jotting down Jenkins' questions, you assured her that this statement was "right". However, to alleviate Jenkins' concern, you arranged a meeting for the following day.

Instructions:

(1) How would you respond to each of Jenkins' questions?

(2) Do you think that the statement of cash flows enhances the chances of A. J. Jenkins Inc. receiving the loan? Discuss.

Answers to Self-Examination Questions

· · ·

1. **D** A full set of financial statements for a corporation includes a balance sheet (answer A), an income statement (answer B), a statement of cash flows (answer C), and a statement of retained earnings.

2. **D** Cash flows from operating activities relate to transactions that enter into the determination of net income (answer D). Receipts of cash from the sale of capital stock (answer A) and the sale of bonds (answer B) and payments of cash for dividends (answer C) are cash flows from financing activities.

3. **D** Cash flows from financing activities include receipts from the issuance of equity (answer A) and debt (answer B) securities and payments for dividends (answer C), repurchase of equity securities, and redemption of debt securities.

4. **A** Cash flows from investing activities include receipts from the sale of noncurrent assets, such as equipment (answer A), and payments for the acquisition of noncurrent assets. Receipts of cash from the sale of capital stock (answer B) and payments of cash for dividends (answer C) and for the repurchase of equity securities (answer D) are cash flows from financing activities.

5. **D** The cash flows from operating activities section of the statement of cash flows would report net cash flow from operating activities of $65,500, determined as follows:

Net income		$55,000
Add:		
Depreciation	$22,000	
Decrease in inventories	5,000	
Decrease in prepaid expenses	500	27,500
		$82,500
Deduct:		
Increase in trade receivables	$10,000	
Decrease in accounts payable	7,000	17,000
Net cash flow from operating activities		$65,500

Part
Seven

Modern Uses of Managerial Accounting

Chapter
Seventeen

CHAPTER
OBJECTIVES

Describe the characteristics of nonprofit organizations.

Describe and illustrate the concepts and principles of fund accounting for nonprofit organizations.

Describe and illustrate budgeting concepts useful to management in planning and controlling operations of nonprofit organizations.

Describe and illustrate the flow of data through an accounting system for a nonprofit organization.

Describe and illustrate the preparation and use of the principal financial statements for a nonprofit organization.

Nonprofit Organizations

Entities engaged in business transactions may be classified as profit making or nonprofit. Profit-making organizations respond to a demand for a product or a service, with the objective of earning net income. The accounting concepts and their use by the management of such organizations were discussed in preceding chapters.

Nonprofit organizations provide goods or services that fulfill a social need, often for those who do not have the purchasing power to acquire these goods or services for themselves. These organizations are usually operated as informal associations or as corporations in accordance with the applicable laws and regulations. Nonprofit organizations may be classified as either (1) governmental units or (2) charitable, religious, or philanthropic units (hereafter referred to simply as "charitable"). Governmental organizations include the United States, states, cities, and counties. The second category includes churches, hospitals, private schools and universities, medical research facilities, and many other types of organizations that are financed wholly or in part by donations.

As the sense of social responsibility to society has increased in recent years, there has been a corresponding increase in the number of nonprofit organizations and in the volume of their activities. Approximately one third of the volume of business in the United States is conducted by approximately 750,000 governmental units and charitable organizations with annual spending of approximately one trillion dollars ($1,000,000,000,000).

As nonprofit organizations play an increasingly significant role, managers of such organizations have as much need for accounting information to assist them in planning and controlling operations and in decision making as do managers of profit-making organizations. This chapter is devoted to the accounting concepts applicable to nonprofit organizations and their use by management.

CHARACTERISTICS OF NONPROFIT ORGANIZATIONS

Profit-making organizations are characterized by (1) the private ownership of the organization's assets and (2) the objective of earning net income for the private ownership interests, whether these interests are represented by sole proprietors, partners, or stockholders. The distinguishing characteristics of nonprofit organizations are: (1) no individuals own any equity shares or interests; (2) there is neither a conscious profit motive nor an expectation of earning net income; (3) no part of any excess of revenues over expenditures is distributed to those who contributed support through taxes or voluntary donations; and (4) any excess of revenues over expenditures that results from operations in the short run is ordinarily used in later years to further the purposes of the organization.

Some nonprofit organizations, such as a governmental-owned electric utility or a public transportation company, are created to provide services to the citizens of the area for a fee that is close to the cost of providing the service. After the initial investment, they tend to be self-sustaining; that is, the revenues earned support their operations. Because the activities of such organizations are financed mainly by charges to the customers using the services, the accounting concepts used are those appropriate to a commercial enterprise. Most nonprofit organizations, however, are established to provide a service to society without levying against the user a direct charge equal to the full cost of the service.

On Governmental Accounting

"I think it an object of great importance... to simplify our system of finance, and to bring it within the comprehension of every member of Congress... the whole system [has been] involved in impenetrable fog. [T]here is a point... on which I should wish to keep my eye... a simplication of the form of accounts... so as to bring everything to a single center[;] we might hope to see the finances of the Union as clear and intelligible as a merchant's books, so that every member of Congress, and every man of any mind in the Union, should be able to comprehend them to investigate abuses, and consequently to control them."

Thomas Jefferson
April 1802

Source: *Sound Financial Reporting in the U. S. Government* (Chicago: Arthur Andersen & Co, 1986).

FUND ACCOUNTING

The accounting systems for all nonprofit organizations must provide financial data to management for use in planning and controlling operations as well as for reporting to external parties, such as taxpayers and donors, for their use in determining the effectiveness of operations. Therefore, most of the basics of accounting for profit-making enterprises are essential for nonprofit organizations. In addition, accounting systems for nonprofit organizations should include mechanisms (1) to ensure that management observes the restrictions imposed upon it by law, charter, by laws, etc., and (2) to provide for reports to taxpayers and donors that such restrictions have been respected. For these reasons, a nonprofit organization often applies the concept of "fund accounting" in conjunction with a budget and appropriations technique to account for the assets received by the organization and to ensure that expenditures are made only for authorized purposes.

The term "fund" was used in the preceding chapter in the context of the funds statement, where funds can be interpreted to mean "cash" or more broadly to mean "working capital." The term **fund,** as used in accounting for nonprofit organizations, is defined as an accounting entity with accounts maintained for recording assets, liabilities, **fund equity** (the excess of assets over liabilities), revenues, and expenditures for a particular purpose according to specified restrictions or limitations. The following description of fund accounting appeared in an annual report for the District of Columbia:

> *The accounts of the District are organized in funds and account groups, each of which is considered a separate accounting entity. The accompanying financial statements include all funds and account groups of the District.*

> *The operations of each fund are accounted for with a separate set of self-balancing accounts that comprise its assets, liabilities, fund equity, revenues, and expenditures or expenses, as appropriate. Government resources are allocated to and accounted for in individual funds based upon the purposes for which they are to be spent.*

Funds may be established by law, provisions of a charter, administrative action, or by a special contribution to a charitable organization. Most nonprofit organizations maintain a General Fund in which to record transactions related to day-to-day operations. For example, cities usually maintain a "General Fund" for recording transactions related to many community services, such as fire and police protection, street lighting and repairs, and maintenance of water and sewer mains. Cities may maintain additional funds for special tax assessments, bond redemption, and for other specified purposes. It is possible to have transactions between funds, as when one fund borrows money from another fund, in which case the transaction is recorded in the accounts of both funds.

Both public and private universities usually maintain a number of separate funds in addition to a General Fund. For example, there may be a number of scholarship funds, named for alumni or other donors, with many restrictions concerning the recipients, such as high scholastic attainment, residence in a specified area, and enrollment in a particular course of study. Charitable organizations also often have a number of funds, sometimes called "endowment funds," from which only the income may be spent. The amounts contributed to such funds are often invested in various income-yielding bonds and stocks.

Budgeting

The essentials of budgeting are the same for both profit and nonprofit organizations. In both cases, the budget is prepared by management and subsequently reviewed, revised, and approved by the appropriate body. For the nonprofit organization, the budget is approved by the governing body (council, directors, or trustees) of the organization. The concept of zero-base budgeting can also be applied in developing the budget estimates for both types of organizations. (The **zero-base budgeting** concept requires all levels of management to start from zero and estimate revenues and expenditures as if there had been no previous activities in their unit.)

The budgeting process in profit-oriented organizations generally starts with the preparation of the sales or revenue budget. In nonprofit organizations, however, the budgeting process often begins with the estimation of the expenditures for the various programs provided by the organization. The organization then seeks means of financing these programs or, if adequate financing cannot be provided, the expenditures are reduced to levels that can be financed from expected revenues. For example, a hospital, a church, or a governmental organization proposes specific programs and activities and the related expenditures for the coming year. Then the organization seeks financing from such sources as donations or taxes. For the final budget, the proposed expenditures should not exceed the estimated revenues. In many cases, this restriction requires a downward revision of the original estimates for expenditures.

Since the main function of most nonprofit organizations is to provide nonrevenue-producing goods or services, the most critical element in the budgetary control process is the control of expenditures. Therefore, in an attempt to make the budgetary process more useful in controlling expenditures and operations, budget performance reporting has received increased attention in recent years by nonprofit organizations. The manner of identifying expenditures has become the focus of the budget format, which may follow one of three basic types: (1) line budget, (2) program budget, and (3) combined line-program budget.

Line Budgets. The **line** or functional **budget** is very popular because its format closely parallels that of the profit-making organization. In the line budget, items of expenditure are presented by the "object" of the expenditure, that is, by the "reason" for the expenditure. Objects of expenditures for a nonprofit organization would include salaries, supplies, and travel, just as wages, power and light, and maintenance would be identified for the factory overhead cost budget for a profit-making organization. A budget in the line format, severely condensed to focus on the basic concept of the format, is illustrated as follows:

Line Budget

Gates Community College Budget of Expenditures For Year Ending June 30,19--	
Faculty salaries	$ 6,270,000
Administrative salaries	1,862,000
Maintenance salaries	990,000
Supplies	695,000
Utilities	655,000
Miscellaneous	553,000
Total expenditures	$11,025,000

Program Budgets. The **program budget** focuses on the services or programs provided by the nonprofit organization. For example, the budget of expenditures for a small community college may focus on such programs as basic education, adult education, athletic programs, and community service programs, as illustrated in the following budget:

Program Budget

Gates Community College
Budget of Expenditures
For Year Ending June 30, 19--

	Basic Education	Adult Education	Athletic Programs	Community Service Programs
Faculty salaries.........	$5,200,000	$ 850,000	$120,000	$100,000
Administrative salaries...	1,750,000	85,000	15,000	12,000
Maintenance salaries....	900,000	65,000	15,000	10,000
Supplies..............	640,000	37,000	10,000	8,000
Utilities..............	600,000	35,000	10,000	10,000
Miscellaneous..........	510,000	28,000	5,000	10,000
Total expenditures.......	$9,600,000	$1,100,000	$175,000	$150,000

Since the program budget requires management to identify the programs to be provided and their related costs, the principal advantage of the program budget is that the effectiveness of the program can be easily evaluated in terms of the benefits provided and the expenditures made on each program.

Combined Line-Program Budgets. The advantages of both the line and program budget can be achieved by adding a total column to the program budget. In effect, this **combined line-program budget** adds the features of the line budget to the program budget, as shown in the following illustration:

Combined Line-Program Budget

Gates Community College
Budget of Expenditures
For Year Ending June 30, 19--

	Basic Education	Adult Education	Athletic Programs	Community Service Programs	Total
Faculty salaries	$5,200,000	$ 850,000	$120,000	$100,000	$ 6,270,000
Administrative salaries.....	1,750,000	85,000	15,000	12,000	1,862,000
Maintenance salaries.....	900,000	65,000	15,000	10,000	990,000
Supplies......	640,000	37,000	10,000	8,000	695,000
Utilities........	600,000	35,000	10,000	10,000	655,000
Miscellaneous.	510,000	28,000	5,000	10,000	553,000
Total expenditures	$9,600,000	$1,100,000	$175,000	$150,000	$11,025,000

Management Reports and Special Analysis

Some of the reports and special analyses discussed in preceding chapters relate specifically to the profit motive and thus, in general, are not applicable to nonprofit organizations. Such analyses would include gross profit analysis and differential analysis for evaluating a proposal to discontinue an unprofitable segment. Many of the profit-making concepts, however, are applicable to the nonprofit organization. As mentioned previously, for example, budget performance reports that compare actual results with budgeted figures can be helpful in controlling the costs and operations of a nonprofit organization. A nonprofit organization may use the differential analysis concepts described in preceding chapters in evaluating a proposal either to lease equipment or to purchase it. Likewise, a proposal to replace old equipment with new and more efficient equipment could be evaluated in terms of the differential costs associated with both the old and new equipment. Similarly, the basic concept of economic order quantities would be equally applicable to nonprofit and profit-making organizations.

BASIC FUND ACCOUNTING SYSTEM

The basic double-entry system, the determination of financial position, and the reporting of financial position and results of operations are essential for the planning and controlling of the activities of nonprofit organizations. In addition, the integration of budgetary data into the system and the extensive use of other control techniques, such as subsidiary ledgers, increase the effectiveness of the accounting system in aiding management's control of expenditures and operations. The fundamentals of the basic fund accounting system and its use in providing data for management are discussed in the remainder of the chapter.

Estimated Revenues and Appropriations

The official budget for a nonprofit organization sets the specific goals for the fiscal period. Through **appropriations** (authorization to spend the budgeted expenditures), the budget designates the manner in which the revenues of each fund are to be used to accomplish the organization's goals. The estimated revenues may be viewed as potential assets and the appropriations as potential liabilities.

Budgeting is an important part of an accounting system for nonprofit organizations. By integrating the budget amounts into the accounting system, the comparison of these budgeted amounts with actual amounts assists management in controlling operations. Therefore, after the budget for the General Fund has been approved by the governing body, the estimated revenues and appropriations are recorded in controlling accounts. Any difference between the estimated revenues and appropriations is recorded in the fund equity account, Fund Balance. The amount in the fund balance account represents unrestricted, spendable resources of the General Fund. An example of such an entry is as follows:

Estimated Revenues	1,900,000	
Appropriations		1,850,000
Fund Balance		50,000

The effect of the recording of the budgeted amounts in the General Fund accounts is presented in the following diagram:

GENERAL FUND ACCOUNTS

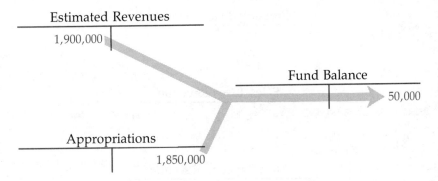

When the budget shows an excess of estimated revenues over appropriations, as in the preceding illustration, Fund Balance is credited. If the budget had shown an excess of appropriations over estimated revenues, the excess would be debited to Fund Balance. The subsidiary ledgers for Estimated Revenues and Appropriations contain accounts for the various sources of expected revenue (property taxes, sales taxes, etc.) and the various purposes of appropriations (general government, streets and roads, libraries, etc.). By recording this budgetary information in the accounts, periodic reports comparing actual amounts with budgeted amounts can be prepared readily.

Revenues
· · ·

The realization of revenues requires an entry debiting accounts for the assets acquired and crediting the revenues account. For example, a portion of the estimated revenues from property taxes, sales taxes, etc., may be realized in the form of cash during the first month of the fiscal year. To summarize these receipts, an entry would be made as follows:

Cash	152,500	
Revenues		152,500

Revenues is a controlling account. In practice, it is customary to use a single subsidiary ledger, called the **revenue ledger,** for both Estimated Revenues and Revenues. Each subsidiary account is used for recording the estimated revenues and the actual revenues. The relationship between the general ledger accounts and the subsidiary revenue ledger is illustrated in the following diagram:

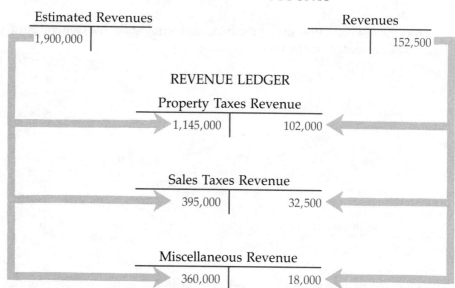

GENERAL LEDGER ACCOUNTS

Estimated Revenues	Revenues
1,900,000	152,500

REVENUE LEDGER

Property Taxes Revenue

1,145,000	102,000

Sales Taxes Revenue

395,000	32,500

Miscellaneous Revenue

360,000	18,000

At any point in time, the difference between the two general ledger controlling accounts, Estimated Revenues and Revenues, would be equal to the sum of the balances of the accounts in the subsidiary revenue ledger. A debit balance in a subsidiary ledger account indicates the amount of the excess of estimated revenues over actual revenues. If actual revenues exceed the amount estimated, the account balance would be a credit.

Expenditures

As regularly recurring expenditures, such as payrolls, are incurred, the account Expenditures is debited and the appropriate liability accounts or cash are credited. For example, the entry for the biweekly payroll would be as follows:

Expenditures	31,200	
Wages Payable		31,200

Encumbrances

There is usually a lapse of time between the placing of an order and delivery of the goods or services ordered. When contracts such as those for road or building construction are executed, the time lag may extend over relatively long periods. All legally binding commitments to pay money eventually become expenditures. These commitments, called **encumbrances**, should be recorded in the accounts when a contract is entered into in order to ensure that expenditures do not exceed amounts appropriated. The means of preventing overexpenditures is illustrated by the following entry:

Encumbrances..	10,000	
Fund Balance Reserved for Encumbrances		10,000

When orders are filled or contracts completed for amounts encumbered, the entry that recorded the encumbrance is reversed and the expenditure is recorded, as illustrated by the following entries:

Fund Balance Reserved for Encumbrances	10,000	
Encumbrances.......................................		10,000
Expenditures	10,000	
Accounts Payable....................................		10,000

The effect of these two entries is to (1) cancel the original entry in which the encumbrance was recorded and (2) record the expenditure and the related liability.

When encumbrances are recorded, the sum of the balances of the accounts Encumbrances and Expenditures can be viewed as offsets to the account Appropriations. The difference obtained by subtracting the balances of Encumbrances and Expenditures from the amount of Appropriations is the amount of commitments that can still be made. For example, if appropriations of $1,850,000 were approved when the budget was adopted and $1,500,000 and $240,000 have been recorded in Expenditures and Encumbrances, respectively, only $110,000 is available for commitment during the remainder of the fiscal year.

Expenditure Ledger

Appropriations, Encumbrances, and Expenditures are controlling accounts. In practice, it is customary to use a single subsidiary ledger, called the **expenditure ledger,** in which each account indicates appropriations, encumbrances, and expenditures.

When a budget is approved, appropriations are recorded in the proper accounts in the expenditure ledger to indicate the unencumbered or uncommitted balance. As order commitments are made, the amounts of the encumbrances are recorded in the proper expenditure ledger account (by a debit) and the unencumbered balance is adjusted accordingly. When orders are filled, the expenditure and the credit to encumbrances are recorded in the proper columns. At any point in time, the accounts in the expenditure ledger indicate the balance of the encumbrances outstanding and the unencumbered balance.

In the following illustration of an account in the expenditure ledger, the budget appropriation for police department supplies is $250,000 as of July 1. On July 5, a purchase order that encumbered $10,000 was recorded and the encumbrances balance of $10,000 and the unencumbered balance of $240,000 were recorded. When the invoice of $10,000 was received on July 17, the encumbrances balance was reduced to zero and the $10,000 expenditure was recorded.

ACCOUNT POLICE DEPARTMENT—SUPPLIES   ACCOUNT NO. 200-21

Date		Item	Encumbrances			Expenditures		Unencumbered Balance
			Debit	Credit	Balance	Item	Total	
July	1	Budget appropriation						250,000
	5	Purchase order	10,000		10,000			240,000
	17	Invoice		10,000	—	10,000	10,000	240,000
	30	Purchase order	7,500		7,500			232,500

Long-Lived Assets

When long-lived assets are purchased, they are usually recorded as debits to the account Expenditures in the same manner as supplies and other ordinary expenses. A separate record, called the General Fixed Assets Account Group, can be maintained for the purpose of assigning responsibility for the custody and use of the individual assets.

The practice of recording the purchase of long-lived assets as an expenditure and the related failure to record depreciation expense has been debated for many years. Most governmental units do not differentiate between long-lived assets and ordinary recurring expenses. This practice is supported by the fact that the acquisition of plant assets is often authorized by a special appropriation, perhaps financed by a bond issue for a local government unit.[1]

PERIODIC REPORTING

A nonprofit organization should prepare interim statements comparing actual revenues and expenditures with the related budgeted amounts. Variations between the two should be investigated immediately to determine their cause and to consider possible corrective actions.

---

[1]Most charitable organizations are required to recognize depreciation for general-purpose external financial statements (*Statement of Financial Accounting Standards, No. 93*). In such cases, the recording and reporting of depreciation follows the concepts for profit-making enterprises.

At the end of the fiscal year, closing entries are recorded and the operating data are summarized and reported. The entry to close the revenues and estimated revenues accounts is illustrated as follows:

Revenues..	1,920,000	
Estimated Revenues		1,900,000
Fund Balance		20,000

In the illustration, actual revenues exceeded the amount estimated. If the actual revenues had been less than the amount estimated, the fund equity account, Fund Balance, would have been decreased by a debit. The effect of this entry is to adjust Fund Balance to indicate the actual amount of the revenues for the period.

The entry to close the appropriations and expenditures accounts is illustrated as follows:

Appropriations...................................	1,850,000	
Expenditures		1,825,000
Fund Balance		25,000

In the illustration, appropriations exceeded the actual expenditures. If the appropriations had been less than the actual expenditures, Fund Balance would have been decreased by a debit. The effect of this entry is to adjust Fund Balance to indicate the actual amount of the expenditures for the period.

The entry to close the encumbrances account, which represents the commitments outstanding at the end of the year, is illustrated as follows:

Fund Balance	20,000	
Encumbrances.....................................		20,000

Inevitably, some orders placed during the year will remain unfilled at the end of the year. To indicate the commitment to pay for these orders, Fund Balance Reserved for Encumbrances is not closed and is included in the fund equity section of the year-end balance sheet. When the orders are filled in the next year, Fund Balance Reserved for Encumbrances will be debited and Accounts Payable credited.

FINANCIAL STATEMENTS

Financial statements for each fund and combined financial statements for all funds should be prepared periodically. The principal financial statements prepared at the end of each fiscal year are: (1) a balance sheet, which is similar to a commercial enterprise balance sheet, and (2) a statement of revenues, expenditures, and changes in fund balance. The objective of the **statement of revenues, expenditures, and changes in fund balance** is to provide users with information on a nonprofit entity's operating performance for a period. The nature of this statement emphasizes the absence of the profit motive and the importance of controlling expenditures within the revenue limits imposed by law or the dictate of donors. The first part of the statement presents a comparison of the budgeted and actual revenues and expenditures, but not a net income amount. The second part, which is similar to the retained earnings statement for a commercial enterprise, presents the effects of operations and encumbrances on the unreserved fund balance. Both the balance sheet and the statement of revenues, expenditures, and changes in fund balance are illustrated in the following section.

The financial statements for the funds should also be accompanied by adequate disclosures, including a summary of significant accounting policies. Two excerpts from the summary of significant accounting policies section of the District of Columbia's annual report are as follows:

Encumbrances

Encumbrances are commitments to acquire goods and services. The recording of purchase orders and contracts in order to reserve that portion of the applicable appropriation is employed as an extension of allocation in the General Fund.

Fixed Assets

Costs to acquire fixed assets used in governmental funds are charged as current expenditures in the General Fund.

ILLUSTRATION OF NONPROFIT ACCOUNTING

To illustrate further the concepts and procedures that have been described, assume that the trial balance of the General Fund of the City of Lewiston, as of July 1, 1989, the beginning of the fiscal year, is as follows:

City of Lewiston — General Fund
Trial Balance
July 1, 1989

Cash	242,500	
Savings Accounts	250,000	
Property Taxes Receivable	185,000	
Investment in U.S. Treasury Notes	350,000	
Accounts Payable		162,600
Wages Payable		30,000
Fund Balance		834,900
	1,027,500	1,027,500

The transactions completed during the year for the General Fund are summarized and recorded as follows:

(a) Estimated revenues and appropriations.

Entry: Estimated Revenues................. 9,100,000
      Appropriations   9,070,000
      Fund Balance....................   30,000

(b) Revenues from property tax levy.

Entry: Property Taxes Receivable........... 6,500,000
      Revenues   6,500,000

(c) Collection of property taxes and other taxes on a cash basis, such as sales taxes, motor vehicle license fees, municipal court fines, etc.

Entry: Cash............................ 9,105,000
      Property Taxes Receivable.........   6,470,000
      Revenues   2,635,000

(d) Expenditures for payrolls.

Entry: Expenditures...................... 3,280,000
      Wages Payable   3,280,000

(e) Expenditures encumbered.

Entry: Encumbrances..................... 5,800,000
      Fund Balance Reserved for
        Encumbrances.................   5,800,000

(f) Liquidation of encumbrances and receipt of invoices.

Entry: Fund Balance Reserved for
      Encumbrances..................... 5,785,000
        Encumbrances...................   5,785,000

      Expenditures...................... 5,785,000
        Accounts Payable   5,785,000

(g) Cash disbursed.

Entry: Accounts Payable 5,800,000
      Wages Payable 3,270,000
        Cash..........................   9,070,000

(h) Revenues and estimated revenues accounts closed.

Entry: Revenues 9,135,000
      Estimated Revenues..............   9,100,000
      Fund Balance...................   35,000

(i) Appropriations and expenditures accounts closed.

Entry:	Appropriations	9,070,000	
	Expenditures.		9,065,000
	Fund Balance.		5,000

(j) Encumbrances account closed.

Entry:	Fund Balance.	15,000	
	Encumbrances		15,000

After the foregoing entries have been posted, the general ledger accounts and the trial balance for the General Fund appear as follows. Entries in the accounts are identified by letters to facilitate comparison with the summary journal entries.

Cash

Balance	242,500	(g)	9,070,000	
(c)	9,105,000	Balance	277,500	
	9,347,500		9,347,500	
Balance	277,500			

Savings Accounts

Balance	250,000	

Property Taxes Receivable

Balance	185,000	(c)	6,470,000	
(b)	6,500,000	Balance	215,000	
	6,685,000		6,685,000	
Balance	215,000			

Investment in U.S. Treasury Notes

Balance	350,000	

Accounts Payable

(g)	5,800,000	Balance	162,600	
Balance	147,600	(f)	5,785,000	
	5,947,600		5,947,600	
		Balance	147,600	

Wages Payable

(g)	3,270,000	Balance	30,000	
Balance	40,000	(d)	3,280,000	
	3,310,000		3,310,000	
		Balance	40,000	

Fund Balance Reserved for Encumbrances

(f)	5,785,000	(e)	5,800,000	
Balance	15,000			
	5,800,000		5,800,000	
		Balance	15,000	

Fund Balance

(j)	15,000	Balance	834,900	
Balance	889,900	(a)	30,000	
		(h)	35,000	
		(i)	5,000	
	904,900		904,900	
		Balance	889,900	

Estimated Revenues

(a)	9,100,000	(h)	9,100,000	

	Revenues				Expenditures		
(h)	9,135,000	(b)	6,500,000	(d)	3,280,000	(i)	9,065,000
		(c)	2,635,000	(f)	5,785,000		
	9,135,000		9,135,000		9,065,000		9,065,000

	Appropriations				Encumbrances		
(i)	9,070,000	(a)	9,070,000	(e)	5,800,000	(f)	5,785,000
						(j)	15,000
					5,800,000		5,800,000

City of Lewiston — General Fund
Trial Balance
June 30, 1990

Cash	277,500	
Savings Accounts	250,000	
Property Taxes Receivable	215,000	
Investment in U.S. Treasury Notes	350,000	
Accounts Payable		147,600
Wages Payable		40,000
Fund Balance Reserved for Encumbrances		15,000
Fund Balance		889,900
	1,092,500	1,092,500

The balance sheet for the City of Lewiston General Fund, as of June 30, 1990, is as follows. On the balance sheet, the fund balance reserved for encumbrances is reported as a separate item in the fund equity section. The balance of the account Fund Balance, $889,900, is described as "Unreserved fund balance." As mentioned previously, this amount represents the unrestricted, spendable resources of the General Fund.

City of Lewiston — General Fund
Balance Sheet
June 30, 1990

Assets		
Cash		$ 277,500
Savings accounts[2]		250,000
Property taxes receivable		215,000
Investment in U.S. Treasury notes		350,000
Total assets		$1,092,500
Liabilities		
Accounts payable	$147,600	
Wages payable	40,000	
Total liabilities		$ 187,600
Fund Equity		
Fund balance reserved for encumbrances	$ 15,000	
Unreserved fund balance	889,900	
Total fund equity		904,900
Total liabilities and fund equity		$1,092,500

Although there are many variations in form, the statement of revenues, expenditures, and changes in fund balance reports the following:

1. Differences (in terms of over or under budget) between budgeted revenues and actual revenues.
2. Differences (in terms of over or under budget) between budgeted expenditures and actual expenditures.
3. The excess or deficiency of revenues (both actual and budgeted) over expenditures.
4. The fund balance at the beginning of the year and the amount of the encumbrances closed to fund balance at the end of the year.
5. The fund balance at the end of the year.

The statement of revenues, expenditures, and changes in fund balance for the City of Lewiston General Fund is as follows:

---

[2]*Statement No. 3,* "Deposits with Financial Institutions, Investments (including Repurchase Agreements), and Reverse Repurchase Agreements" (Stamford: Governmental Accounting Standards Board, 1986), requires specific disclosures about deposits with financial institutions. A discussion of these disclosures is beyond the scope of this chapter.

City of Lewiston—General Fund
Statement of Revenues, Expenditures, and Changes in Fund Balance
For Year Ended June 30, 1990

	Budget	Actual	Over	Under
Revenues:				
General property taxes	$6,480,000	$6,500,000	$20,000	
Sales taxes......................	1,835,500	1,850,500	15,000	
Motor vehicle licenses...........	312,250	310,250		$ 2,000
Municipal court fines	257,000	255,750		1,250
Interest	35,000	35,000		
Building permits	27,100	27,500	400	
Miscellaneous	153,150	156,000	2,850	
Total revenues..................	$9,100,000	$9,135,000	$38,250	$ 3,250
Expenditures:				
General government.............	$2,450,000	$2,465,250	$15,250	
Police department—				
personnel services	1,250,000	1,256,000	6,000	
Police department—supplies	299,000	290,500		$ 8,500
Police department—equipment ...	190,000	182,750		7,250
Police department—				
other charges	30,000	27,500		2,500
Fire department—				
personnel services	1,035,000	1,039,000	4,000	
Fire department—supplies	320,600	315,600		5,000
Fire department—equipment	200,500	197,750		2,750
Fire department—				
other charges	16,400	18,200	1,800	
Streets and roads...............	1,530,000	1,521,850		8,150
Sanitation	741,000	739,500		1,500
Public welfare	630,000	632,600	2,600	
Libraries	377,500	378,500	1,000	
Total expenditures	$9,070,000	$9,065,000	$30,650	$35,650
Excess of revenues over				
expenditures	$ 30,000	$ 70,000		
Fund balance, July 1, 1989		834,900		
		$ 904,900		
Less encumbrances..............		15,000		
Fund balance, June 30, 1990.......		$ 889,900		

The data for the preparation of the preceding statement would be provided by the various subsidiary ledgers for the City of Lewston General Fund. These ledgers were not presented in order to simplify the illustration.

Chapter Review

KEY POINTS

1. Characteristics of Nonprofit Organizations.

The distinguishing characteristics of nonprofit organizations are: (1) no individuals own any equity shares or interests; (2) there is neither a conscious profit motive nor an expectation of earning net income; (3) no part of any excess of revenues over expenditures is distributed to those who contributed support through taxes or voluntary donations; and (4) any excess of revenues over expenditures that results from operations in the short run is ordinarily used in later years to further the purposes of the organization.

2. Fund Accounting.

Accounting systems for nonprofit organizations include procedures to ensure that the management of the organization observes restrictions imposed upon it by law, charter, bylaws, etc., and to provide for reports to taxpayers and donors that such restrictions have been respected. Fund is defined as an accounting entity with accounts maintained for recording assets, liabilities, fund equity, revenues, and expenditures for a particular purpose according to specified restrictions or limitations.

The essentials of budgeting are the same for both profit and nonprofit organizations. In nonprofit organizations, the budgeting process often begins with the estimation of the expenditures for the organization's programs. Thus, the focus of the budget format is the manner of identifying expenditures. A line budget presents items of expenditure by the "object" of the expenditure, that is, by the reason for the expenditure. A program budget focuses on the services or programs provided by the organization. The advantages of both the line and program budget can be achieved by adding a total column to the program budget. This budget format is called a combined line-program budget.

3. Basic Fund Accounting System.

In a basic double-entry fund accounting system, estimated revenues, viewed as potential assets, and appropriations, viewed as potential liabilities, are recorded directly in the accounts. Any excess or deficiency of estimated revenues over appropriations is recorded in the fund balance account. The receipt of revenues is recorded by debiting an asset account and crediting the revenues controlling account. Recurring expenditures are recorded by debiting the expenditures controlling account and crediting an asset or liability account. When there is a lapse of time between the placing of an order and the delivery of the goods or services ordered, expenditures are recorded by use of encumbrances and fund balance reserved for encumbrances accounts. When encumbrances are recorded, the sum of the balances of the accounts Encumbrances and Expenditures can be viewed as offsets to the account

Appropriations. The difference is the amount of commitments that can still be made. Appropriations, Expenditures, and Encumbrances are controlling accounts.

When long-lived assets are purchased, they are usually recorded as debits to the account Expenditures. A separate record is maintained for the purpose of assigning responsibility for the custody and use of these assets.

4. Periodic Reporting.

At the end of a reporting period, actual revenues and expenditures should be compared with the related budgeted amounts. The revenues, estimated revenues, appropriations, expenditures, and encumbrances accounts are closed to the fund balance account. The fund balance reserved for encumbrances account is not closed and appears in the year-end balance sheet.

5. Financial Statements.

The principal financial statements for a nonprofit organization are: (1) a balance sheet and (2) a statement of revenues, expenditures, and changes in fund balance.

KEY TERMS

fund 631
fund equity 631
zero-base budgeting 631
line budget 632
program budget 632
combined line-program
 budget 633

appropriations 634
encumbrances 637
statement of revenues,
 expenditures, and changes
 in fund balance 640

SELF-EXAMINATION QUESTIONS

(Answers at End of Chapter)

1. In accounting for nonprofit organizations, the term employed to represent an accounting entity with accounts for assets, liabilities, fund equity, revenues, and expenditures for a particular purpose is:
   A. fund
   B. appropriation
   C. encumbrance
   D. none of the above

2. In accounting for nonprofit organizations, the account that represents the fund equity of an accounting entity is:
   A. Retained Earnings
   B. Accumulated Earnings
   C. Fund Balance
   D. none of the above

3. The budgeting concept that requires all levels of management to start from zero and estimate revenues and appropriations as if there had been no previous activities in their unit is:
   A. fund budgeting
   B. encumbrance budgeting
   C. zero-base budgeting
   D. estimation budgeting

4. Legally binding commitments by a nonprofit organization to pay money are referred to as:
   A. encumbrances
   B. appropriations
   C. fund equity
   D. none of the above

5. The principal financial statements for a nonprofit organization are a balance sheet and a (an):
   A. statement of revenues, expenditures, and changes in fund balance
   B. trial balance
   C. income statement
   D. none of the above

ILLUSTRATIVE PROBLEM

The City of Yatesville's fiscal period ends June 30. The trial balance of the General Fund as of July 1, 1989, was as follows:

City of Yatesville — General Fund
Trial Balance
July 1, 1989

Cash.	12,600	
Savings Accounts	66,800	
Property Taxes Receivable	480,600	
Accounts Payable		7,300
Wages Payable		4,450
Fund Balance		548,250
	560,000	560,000

The operations for the year ended June 30, 1990, are summarized as follows:

(a) Estimated revenues, $2,400,000; appropriations, $2,350,000.
(b) Revenues from property tax levy, $1,925,500.
(c) Cash received from property taxes, $2,005,600, and other revenues, $485,700.
(d) Expenditures encumbered and evidenced by purchase orders, $1,760,000.
(e) Liquidation of encumbrances and vouchers prepared for purchase order billings, $1,755,000.
(f) Expenditures for payrolls, $602,000.
(g) Cash disbursed for vouchers, $1,740,000; for payment of wages, $598,000; for savings accounts, $150,000.

Instructions:

1. Open T accounts for the accounts appearing in the trial balance and enter the balances as of July 1, 1989, identifying them as "Bal."
2. Open T accounts for Fund Balance Reserved for Encumbrances, Estimated Revenues, Revenues, Appropriations, Expenditures, and Encumbrances.
3. Prepare the entries to record the foregoing summarized operations.
4. Post the entries recorded in 3 to the accounts, using the identifying letters in place of dates.
5. Prepare the appropriate entries to close the accounts as of June 30, 1990, and post to the accounts using the letter "C" to identify the postings.
6. Prepare a balance sheet as of June 30, 1990.

SOLUTION

(1), (2), (4), and (5)

Cash			
Bal.	12,600	(g)	2,488,000
(c)	2,491,300		

Fund Balance			
C	7,000	Bal.	548,250
C	5,000	(a)	50,000
		C	11,200

Savings Accounts		
Bal.	66,800	
(g)	150,000	

Estimated Revenues			
(a)	2,400,000	C	2,400,000

Property Taxes Receivable			
Bal.	480,600	(c)	2,005,600
(b)	1,925,500		

Revenues			
C	2,411,200	(b)	1,925,500
		(c)	485,700

Accounts Payable			
(g)	1,740,000	Bal.	7,300
		(e)	1,755,000

Appropriations			
C	2,350,000	(a)	2,350,000

Wages Payable			
(g)	598,000	Bal.	4,450
		(f)	602,000

Expenditures			
(e)	1,755,000	C	2,357,000
(f)	602,000		

Fund Balance Reserved for Encumbrances			
(e)	1,755,000	(d)	1,760,000

Encumbrances			
(d)	1,760,000	(e)	1,755,000
		C	5,000

(3)

(a)	Estimated Revenues	2,400,000	
	Appropriations		2,350,000
	Fund Balance		50,000
(b)	Property Taxes Receivable	1,925,500	
	Revenues		1,925,500
(c)	Cash	2,491,300	
	Property Taxes Receivable		2,005,600
	Revenues		485,700
(d)	Encumbrances	1,760,000	
	Fund Balance Reserved for Encumbrances		1,760,000
(e)	Fund Balance Reserved for Encumbrances	1,755,000	
	Encumbrances		1,755,000
	Expenditures	1,755,000	
	Accounts Payable		1,755,000
(f)	Expenditures	602,000	
	Wages Payable		602,000
(g)	Accounts Payable	1,740,000	
	Wages Payable	598,000	
	Savings Accounts	150,000	
	Cash		2,488,000

(5)

Revenues	2,411,200	
Estimated Revenues		2,400,000
Fund Balance		11,200
Appropriations	2,350,000	
Fund Balance	7,000	
Expenditures		2,357,000
Fund Balance	5,000	
Encumbrances		5,000

(6)

City of Yatesville—General Fund
Balance Sheet
June 30, 1990

Assets

Cash	$ 15,900
Savings accounts	216,800
Property taxes receivable	400,500
Total assets	$633,200

Liabilities

Accounts payable	$ 22,300	
Wages payable.	8,450	
Total liabilities		$ 30,750

Fund Equity

Fund balance reserved for encumbrances.	$ 5,000	
Unreserved fund balance	597,450	
Total fund equity		602,450
Total liabilities and fund equity.		$633,200

Discussion Questions

17–1. (a) What types of organizations are classified as nonprofit? (b) Give three examples of nonprofit organizations.

17–2. Approximately how much of the volume of business in the United States is conducted by governmental units and charitable organizations?

17–3. What characteristics distinguish commercial enterprises from nonprofit organizations?

17–4. As the term is used in reference to accounting for nonprofit organizations, what is meant by "fund"?

17–5. As used in accounting for nonprofit organizations, what is meant by "fund equity"?

17–6. What concept requires all levels of management of a governmental unit to start from zero and estimate revenues and appropriations as if there had been no previous activities in their unit?

17–7. How are expenditures presented in a line budget?

17–8. What is the principal advantage of the program budget format?

17–9. In the budget for nonprofit organizations, what items are viewed as (a) potential assets, (b) potential liabilities?

17–10. In recording estimated revenues and appropriations as expressed in the budget, would Fund Balance be debited or credited if appropriations exceed estimated revenues?

17–11. If an account in the revenue ledger indicated that estimated revenues exceeded revenues, will the account have a debit balance or a credit balance?

17–12. What is the name given to binding commitments to pay money?

17–13. What is the purpose of recording encumbrances in the accounts?

17–14. If the appropriations, expenditures, and encumbrances accounts have balances of $950,000, $750,000 and $125,000 respectively, what amount is available for commitments during the remainder of the fiscal year?

17–15. What is the name of the subsidiary ledger that is controlled by the appropriations, encumbrances, and expenditures accounts?

17–16. In the subsidiary expenditure ledger, the libraries account shows an unencumbered balance. Does this balance indicate that appropriations for the year exceed the sum of encumbrances outstanding and expenditures incurred to date?

17–17. What account in the general ledger of a nonprofit organization is debited for purchases of long-lived assets?

17–18. When the closing entry for the revenues and estimated revenues accounts is prepared, what is the name of the account in which the difference between the balances in the two accounts is recorded?

17–19. If, in the closing process, the estimated revenues are $3,500,000 and the revenues are $3,625,000, will the fund balance account be debited or credited?

17–20. When the closing entry for the appropriations and expenditures accounts is prepared, in what account is the difference between the balances in the two accounts recorded?

17–21. If, in the closing process, the appropriations are $2,800,000 and the expenditures are $2,760,000, will the fund balance account be debited or credited?

17–22. At the end of the fiscal year, to what account is the balance in Encumbrances closed?

17–23. In which financial statements will the year-end balance of the following accounts appear: (a) Expenditures and (b) Fund Balance Reserved for Encumbrances?

17–24. What are the two principal financial statements for nonprofit organizations?

17–25. Describe the two parts of the statement of revenues, expenditures, and changes in fund balance.

17–26. Real World Focus. The following General Fund items are included in the annual report for the City of Athens, Georgia, for the year ended June 30, 1986:

Total assets...............	$2,475,535
Liabilities	152,050
Encumbrances	99,695

What is the unreserved fund balance as of June 30,1986?

Exercises

17–27. **Combined line-program budget.** The estimates of the expenditures of the Parks and Recreation Department of the City of Woodstock, as submitted by the departmental supervisors for the fiscal year ending June 30, 1990, are as follows:

Parks:

Supervisory salaries...............................	$240,000
Maintenance salaries.............................	210,000
Clerical salaries...................................	180,000
Utilities	177,000
Payroll taxes	57,000
Maintenance	48,000
Equipment purchases	40,000
Miscellaneous	30,000

Recreation:

Supervisory salaries...............................	$186,000
Utilities	150,000
Lifeguard salaries.................................	108,000
Instructors' salaries...............................	100,000
Clerical salaries...................................	70,000
Maintenance	63,000
Payroll taxes	40,000
Equipment purchases	36,000
Miscellaneous	25,000

Prepare a combined line-program budget.

17–28. Entries from budget for nonprofit enterprise. The budget approved for the fiscal year by the city council of Marble Hill for the General Fund indicated appropriations of $1,850,000 and estimated revenues of $1,910,000. Present the entry to record the financial data indicated by the budget.

17–29. Entries from budget and for revenues and expenditures. Present entries to record the following selected data related to the General Fund of Villa Grove:
(a) The budget indicated appropriations of $3,350,000 and estimated revenues of $3,400,000.
(b) Cash received from revenues, $490,000.
(c) Cash paid for regularly recurring expenditures, $275,000.

17–30. Entries for placement of orders and their receipt for nonprofit enterprise. An order was placed by a nonprofit organization for $8,560 of supplies. Subsequently, $7,110 of the supplies were received and $1,450 were back ordered. Present entries to record (a) the placement of the order and (b) the receipt of the supplies and the invoice of $7,110, terms n/eom.

17–31. Closing entries for nonprofit enterprise. Selected account balances from the General Fund ledger of McNair Park District at the end of the current fiscal year are as follows:

Appropriations.............................	$580,000
Encumbrances	35,000
Estimated Revenues.......................	600,000
Expenditures..............................	542,000
Fund Balance	71,300
Fund Balance Reserved for Encumbrances...	35,000
Revenues.................................	605,500

Prepare the appropriate closing entries.

17–32. Balance sheet for General Fund of nonprofit enterprise. Selected account balances from the ledger of the Paxton Forest Preserve District—General Fund are as follows:

Accounts Payable	$ 12,700
Cash in Bank	15,600
Fund Balance	198,550
Marketable Securities	180,000
Petty Cash	650
Fund Balance Reserved for Encumbrances	10,000
Savings Accounts	25,000

Prepare a balance sheet as of July 31.

17–33. Statement of revenues, expenditures, and changes in fund balance. Data from two subsidiary ledgers of Village of Savoy—General Fund, at August 31, 1990, are as follows:

Revenue Ledger

	Debits	Credits
Property taxes	100,000	102,100
Sales taxes	350,000	334,800
Other	10,000	12,200

Expenditure Ledger

	Expenditures	Budget Appropriations
Administration	38,750	40,000
Fire	75,300	75,000
Library	15,800	13,200
Police	235,900	240,000
Streets and roads	55,600	50,000
Other	27,400	30,000

The beginning balance of the fund balance account as of September 1, 1989, was $187,500. Assuming that the encumbrances account has a balance of $5,000 on August 31, 1990, prepare a statement of revenues, expenditures, and changes in fund balance for the year ended August 31, 1990.

17–34. Computation of unreserved fund balance. Selected account balances before closing on June 30, the end of the current fiscal year for Rankin—General Fund, are as follows. The fund balance account had a balance of $396,400 on July 1, 1989, the beginning of the current fiscal year.

Appropriations	$2,080,000
Encumbrances	10,000
Estimated Revenues	2,120,000
Expenditures	2,008,000
Revenues	2,060,000

Compute the balance of the fund balance account as of June 30, 1990, the end of the current fiscal year.

Problems

·

17–35. Combined line-program budget. The Oyster Bay Police Department prepared the following line budget for the current fiscal year:

Oyster Bay Police Department
Budget of Expenditures
For Year Ending June 30, 1990

Salaries...	$ 800,000
Patrol cars	320,000
Utilities	120,000
Building maintenance...............................	80,000
Supplies	40,000
Miscellaneous	10,000
Total expenditures	$1,370,000

Estimates of the percent of each line item for each of the three principal programs of the police department are as follows:

	Percent of Cost by Program		
	Crime Prevention	Criminal Investigation	Community Education
Salaries.........................	30%	60%	10%
Patrol cars	50	30	20
Utilities	80	15	5
Building maintenance..............	25	55	20
Supplies	70	10	20
Miscellaneous	40	35	25

Instructions:

Prepare a combined line-program budget for the current year.

17–36. Statements for nonprofit enterprise. After the closing entries were posted, selected accounts in the ledger of the General Fund for Woodbury on June 30, the end of the current year, are as follows:

Accounts Payable..	$ 52,500
Cash in Bank...	18,400
Cash on Hand..	5,600
Investments in Marketable Securities...........................	150,000
Property Taxes Receivable....................................	72,650
Savings Accounts...	50,000
Wages Payable...	32,400

Data from the revenue ledger are as follows:

	Estimated Revenues	Revenues
General property taxes	$4,140,000	$4,165,200
Sales taxes	1,332,000	1,324,000
Motor vehicle taxes	228,000	229,600
Municipal court fines	119,400	125,200
Interest on investments................	31,800	27,000
Miscellaneous	88,800	85,200

Data from the expenditures ledger are as follows:

	Appropriations	Expenditures
General government	$1,740,000	$1,729,000
Police department—personnel services	978,000	984,000
Police department—equipment and supplies..	242,000	248,400
Police department—other charges..........	34,000	29,200
Fire department—personnel services	636,000	652,000
Fire department—equipment and supplies....	294,000	297,600
Fire department—other charges............	18,000	22,200
Streets and roads........................	1,050,000	1,060,000
Public welfare	624,000	621,600
Libraries	264,000	267,600

There were no encumbrances at the beginning or end of the year. The fund balance account had a balance of $167,150 on July 1, the beginning of the current year.

Instructions:

(1) Prepare the statement of revenues, expenditures, and changes in fund balance for the year ended June 30.

(2) Prepare a balance sheet as of June 30.

If the working papers correlating with the textbook are not used, omit Problem 17–37.

SPREADSHEET
PROBLEM

17-37. Statements for nonprofit enterprise. After the closing entries were posted, the accounts in the ledger of the General Fund for Santa Rosa on July 31, 1990, the end of the current fiscal year, are as follows:

Accounts Payable	$ 63,000
Cash in Bank	22,000
Cash on Hand	6,750
Fund Balance...	204,100
Fund Balance Reserved for Encumbrances..................	50,000
Investments in Marketable Securities	180,000
Property Taxes Receivable	87,150
Savings Accounts	60,000
Wages Payable	38,800

Estimated revenues, revenues, appropriations, and expenditures from the respective subsidiary ledgers have been entered in the working papers in the statement of revenues, expenditures, and changes in fund balance. The fund balance account had a balance of $243,500 on August 1, 1989, the beginning of the current fiscal year. The amount of encumbrances closed to fund balance at July 31, 1990, was $50,000.

Instructions:

(1) Complete the statement of revenues, expenditures, and changes in fund balance for the year ended July 31, 1990.
(2) Prepare a balance sheet.

17–38. Entries for summarized operations and closing for nonprofit enterprise; accounts; trial balance. The trial balance for the City of San Angelo— General Fund at the beginning of the current fiscal year is as follows:

City of San Angelo—General Fund
Trial Balance
July 1, 19--

Cash	110,000	
Savings Accounts	300,000	
Property Taxes Receivable	250,000	
Investment in U.S. Treasury Notes	120,000	
Accounts Payable		105,800
Wages Payable		42,100
Fund Balance		632,100
	780,000	780,000

The following data summarize the operations for the current year:

(a) Estimated revenues, $7,000,000; appropriations, $6,850,000.
(b) Revenues from property tax levy, $5,000,000.
(c) Cash received from property taxes, $4,910,000, and other revenues, $2,150,000.
(d) Expenditures encumbered and evidenced by purchase orders, $4,000,000.
(e) Expenditures for payrolls, $2,775,000.
(f) Liquidation of encumbrances and vouchers prepared for purchase order billings, $3,900,000.
(g) Cash disbursed for vouchers, $3,800,000; for payment of wages, $2,760,000; for savings accounts, $475,000.

Instructions:

(1) Open T accounts for the accounts appearing in the trial balance and enter the balances as of July 1, identifying them as "Bal."
(2) Open T accounts for Fund Balance Reserved for Encumbrances, Estimated Revenues, Revenues, Appropriations, Expenditures, and Encumbrances.
(3) Prepare entries to record the foregoing summarized operations.
(4) Post the entries recorded in (3) to the accounts, using the identifying letters in place of dates.
(5) Prepare the appropriate entries to close the accounts as of June 30 and post to the accounts, using the letter "C" to identify the postings.
(6) Prepare a trial balance as of June 30.

17–39. Statements for nonprofit enterprise. The account balances in the General Fund ledger of the City of Irving on June 30, 1990, the end of the current fiscal year, are as follows:

Cash on Hand..	$ 3,600
Cash in Bank	245,000
Savings Accounts......................................	300,000
Property Taxes Receivable	120,000
Accounts Payable	48,200
Wages Payable..	30,900
Fund Balance Reserved for Encumbrances...................	13,500
Estimated Revenues	4,045,400
Revenues..	4,068,000
Appropriations..	4,020,700
Expenditures...	4,023,800
Encumbrances	13,500

The total of the debits and credits in the revenue ledger are as follows:

	Debits	Credits
General property taxes......................	$3,090,000	$3,120,000
Sales taxes................................	735,000	721,200
Motor vehicle licenses	140,000	141,600
Interest on savings accounts.................	30,000	31,800
Miscellaneous..............................	50,400	53,400

Data from the expenditure ledger are as follows:

	Expenditures	Budget Appropriations
General government..................	$1,348,200	$1,332,000
Police department....................	792,000	800,000
Fire department......................	617,500	633,500
Streets and roads	597,600	578,400
Sanitation	423,700	424,800
Public welfare.......................	244,800	252,000

The encumbrances balances in the expenditure ledger are as follows:

General government.......................................	$5,200
Fire department..	3,000
Sanitation	5,300

Instructions:

(1) Prepare a statement of revenues, expenditures, and changes in fund balance for the year ended June 30, 1990. The fund balance account had a balance of $545,300 on July 1, 1989, the beginning of the current fiscal year.

(2) Prepare a balance sheet as of June 30, 1990.

ALTERNATE PROBLEMS

17–35A. Combined line-program budget. The Austell Police Department prepared the following line budget for the current fiscal year:

Austell Police Department
Budget of Expenditures
For Year Ending June 30, 1990

Salaries...	$400,000
Patrol cars	120,000
Utilities	60,000
Building maintenance.................................	30,000
Supplies	25,000
Miscellaneous	5,000
Total expenditures	$640,000

Estimates of the percent of each line item for each of the three principal programs of the police department are as follows:

	Percent of Cost by Program		
	Crime Prevention	Criminal Investigation	Community Education
Salaries..........................	80%	15%	5%
Patrol cars	75	10	15
Utilities	60	30	10
Building maintenance..............	30	50	20
Supplies	50	35	15
Miscellaneous	40	40	20

Instructions:

Prepare a combined line-program budget for the current year.

17–36A. Statements for nonprofit enterprise. After the closing entries were posted, selected balances in the ledger of the General Fund for Woodbury on June 30, the end of the current year, are as follows:

Accounts Payable..	$114,300
Cash in Bank..	162,900
Cash on Hand...	23,500
Investments in Marketable Securities.........................	240,000
Property Taxes Receivable..................................	213,000
Savings Accounts..	180,000
Wages Payable...	29,100

Data from the revenue ledger are as follows:

	Estimated Revenues	Revenues
General property taxes	$4,140,000	$4,165,200
Sales taxes	1,332,000	1,324,000
Motor vehicle taxes	228,000	229,600
Municipal court fines	119,400	125,200
Interest on investments................	31,800	27,000
Miscellaneous	88,800	85,200

Data from the expenditure ledger are as follows:

	Appropriations	Expenditures
General government	$1,740,000	$1,729,000
Police department—personnel services	978,000	984,000
Police department—equipment and supplies..	242,000	248,400
Police department—other charges..........	34,000	29,200
Fire department—personnel services	636,000	652,000
Fire department—equipment and supplies....	294,000	297,600
Fire department—other charges............	18,000	22,200
Streets and roads........................	1,050,000	1,060,000
Public welfare	624,000	621,600
Libraries	264,000	267,600

There were no encumbrances at the beginning or end of the year. The fund balance account had a balance of $631,400 on July 1, the beginning of the current year.

Instructions:

(1) Prepare the statement of revenues, expenditures, and changes in fund balance for the year ended June 30.

(2) Prepare a balance sheet as of June 30.

If the working papers correlating with the textbook are not used, omit Problem 17–37A.

17–37A. Statements for nonprofit enterprise. After the closing entries were posted, the account balances in the ledger of the General Fund for Santa Rosa on July 31, 1990, the end of the current fiscal year, are as follows:

Accounts Payable	$ 57,500
Cash in Bank	28,700
Cash on Hand	8,400
Fund Balance..	205,300
Fund Balance Reserved for Encumbrances................	40,000
Investments in Marketable Securities	150,000
Property Taxes Receivable	92,000
Savings Accounts	45,800
Wages Payable	22,100

Estimated revenues, revenues, appropriations, and expenditures from the respective subsidiary ledgers have been entered in the working papers in the statement of revenues, expenditures, and changes in fund balance. The fund balance account had a balance of $234,700 on August 1, 1989, the beginning of the current fiscal year. The amount of encumbrances closed to fund balance at July 31, 1990, was $40,000.

Instructions:

(1) Complete the statement of revenues, expenditures, and changes in fund balance for the year ended July 31, 1990.
(2) Prepare a balance sheet.

17–38A. Entries for summarized operations and closing for nonprofit enterprise; accounts; trial balance. The trial balance for the City of Maple Heights—General Fund at the beginning of the current fiscal year is as follows:

Maple Heights—General Fund
Trial Balance
July 1, 19--

Cash..	225,000	
Savings Accounts	80,000	
Property Taxes Receivable	122,500	
Investment in U.S. Treasury Notes	100,000	
Accounts Payable		52,700
Wages Payable		19,200
Fund Balance...............................		455,600
	527,500	527,500

The following data summarize the operations for the current year:

(a) Estimated revenues, $2,180,000; appropriations, $2,150,000.
(b) Revenues from property tax levy, $1,450,000.
(c) Cash received from property taxes, $1,460,000, and other revenues, $760,000.
(d) Expenditures for payrolls, $1,150,000.
(e) Expenditures encumbered and evidenced by purchase orders, $1,210,000.
(f) Liquidation of encumbrances and vouchers prepared for purchase order billings, $1,050,000.
(g) Cash disbursed for vouchers, $1,065,000; for payment of wages, $1,155,800; for savings accounts, $40,000.

Instructions:

(1) Open T accounts for the accounts appearing in the trial balance and enter the balances as of July 1, identifying them as "Bal."
(2) Open T accounts for Fund Balance Reserved for Encumbrances, Estimated Revenues, Revenues, Appropriations, Expenditures, and Encumbrances.
(3) Prepare entries to record the foregoing summarized operations.
(4) Post the entries recorded in (3) to the accounts, using the identifying letters in place of dates.
(5) Prepare the appropriate entries to close the accounts as of June 30 and post to the accounts, using the letter "C" to identify the postings.
(6) Prepare a trial balance as of June 30.

Mini-Case 17

UNIT 🏫 SCHOOL DISTRICT

During a recent visit with your parents over Thanksgiving vacation, your mother was discussing her recent election to the Unit 4 School Board. At the first board meeting, she was presented with the following operating statement for the recently completed fiscal year:

Unit 4 School District
Operating Statement
For Year Ended August 31, 19--

Revenues		$9,050,000
Expenditures:		
Teachers' salaries	$4,250,000	
Administrative salaries	1,150,000	
Transportation	1,000,000	
Utilities	900,000	
Maintenance	850,000	
Equipment purchases	750,000	
Supplies	200,000	
Miscellaneous	400,000	9,500,000
Operating deficit		$ 450,000

The school district has limited resources available to conduct its programs. These resources are generally from taxes, and knowing that the likelihood of tax increases is almost nil in the near future, your mother is especially interested in studying the allocation of these scarce resources. She is also concerned with the operating deficit. Your mother has asked you how the operating statement can be used to assist her in evaluating past operations and in planning for future operations.

Instructions:

Briefly discuss the usefulness of the operating statement for your mother's purposes. Include any suggestions for modified or additional statements that your mother might request from the school district's accountant.

Answers to Self-Examination Questions

$\cdot$ $\cdot$ $\cdot$

1. **A** In accounting for nonprofit organizations, the term used to represent an accounting entity with appropriate accounts for a particular purpose is "fund" (answer A). Potential liabilities of a fund are referred to as appropriations (answer B), and a fund's binding commitments to pay money eventually are referred to as encumbrances (answer C).

2. **C** The account that represents the equity for a nonprofit organization is termed Fund Balance (answer C). For a commercial enterprise, the equity resulting from earnings retained in the enterprise is referred to by various terms, including Retained Earnings (answer A) and Accumulated Earnings (answer B).

3. **C** Zero-base budgeting (answer C), which requires management to start from zero and estimate revenues and appropriations as if there had been no previous activities in a unit, is useful in budgeting for both commercial and nonprofit organizations.

4. **A** In accounting for nonprofit organizations, the commitments to pay money eventually are termed encumbrances (answer A). Potential liabilities are referred to as appropriations (answer B), and the term used to represent the equity for a nonprofit organization is fund equity (answer C).

5. **A** One of the two principal financial statements for a nonprofit organization is the statement of revenues, expenditures, and changes in fund balance (answer A). The trial balance (answer B) is not a financial statement. Because of the lack of a profit motive or the expectation of earning net income, an income statement (answer C) is normally not prepared for a nonprofit organization.

Chapter
Eighteen

Trends in Managerial Accounting

The preceding chapters of this text have described and illustrated traditional managerial accounting techniques useful to managers for planning and controlling operations. For example, Chapters 3 and 4 described and illustrated job order and process cost accounting systems, Chapter 5 described cost behavior and cost estimation, and Chapters 6 and 7 described cost-volume-profit analysis and profit reporting.

This chapter describes trends in the development and use of managerial accounting concepts. These trends reflect responses to a rapidly changing business environment.

CHANGES IN THE UNITED STATES ECONOMY

The stimulus for many of the trends in managerial accounting is changes in the economy of the United States. During the 1970s and throughout the 1980s, the competitive advantage in the manufacture and production of goods shifted from the United States to foreign producers. In 1970, the United States exported $42.5 billion of merchandise and imported $39.9 billion, for a net surplus of exports over imports of $2.6 billion. In 1985, the United States exported $214.4 billion of merchandise and imported $338.9 billion, for a net trade deficit (i.e., imports exceeded exports) of $124.5 billion.[1] This shift in exports and imports has been blamed on such factors as the high cost of American labor, trade barriers to foreign markets, unfavorable exchange rates, and the poor quality of American goods.

In response to competitive world markets, the U.S. economy has become more service oriented. In addition, many manufacturers have been forced to adopt new manufacturing techniques and processes. In turn, the managerial accounting methods which provide the basic information that management uses in planning and controlling operations have changed. Many of these changes are described in the remainder of this chapter.

---

[1]Council of Economic Advisers, *Economic Report of the President* (United States Printing Office: Washington, D.C., 1987), p. 358.

MANAGERIAL ACCOUNTING FOR SERVICE ENTERPRISES

Accounting for the rendering of services is less complex than accounting for the production of products from raw materials. Specifically, for planning and controlling the operations of a service enterprise, management does not need detailed product cost information on a timely basis. Although most of the managerial concepts and techniques described and illustrated for manufacturing enterprises are also relevant for service enterprises, some techniques are less relevant. For example, although capital investment analysis may be used by service enterprises, by their very nature service enterprises are not capital intensive. Therefore, fewer capital investment decisions are made, and those that are made tend to have less of an impact on profitability and solvency than do the capital investment decisions of a manufacturing enterprise. Likewise, inventory analysis is generally not as important for service enterprises, since the only inventory for a service enterprise is usually supplies. Finally, since fixed costs are normally a small portion of the total costs, cost-volume-profit analysis and the computation of the break-even point is not as relevant for a service enterprise.

The managerial accounting concepts and procedures that are especially relevant for service enterprises include job order cost accounting systems, budgeting, responsibility accounting, standard costs, and pricing (setting professional fees). These concepts are described in the following paragraphs.[2]

Job Order Cost Accounting

A cost accounting system is useful to management for planning and controlling the operations of a service enterprise. Since services are usually tailored to a particular client, a job order cost accounting system rather than a process cost system is generally appropriate for a service enterprise. The procedures described and illustrated in Chapter 3 are applicable to service enterprises. The major difference in a job order costing system for a service enterprise is that the planning and control of costs focus on direct labor and overhead. The cost of any materials or supplies used in rendering services for a client is usually small in amount and is normally included as part of the overhead.

The direct labor and overhead costs of rendering services to clients are accumulated in a work in process account, which is supported by a cost ledger. A job cost sheet is used to accumulate the costs for each client's job. When a job is completed and the client is billed, the costs are transferred to a cost of services account. This account is similar to the cost of merchandise sold account for a merchandising enterprise or the cost of goods sold account for a manufacturing enterprise. A finished goods account is not necessary, since the revenues associated with the services are recorded after the services

---

[2]The application of these concepts and procedures to service enterprises is described and illustrated in more detail in Appendix E.

have been rendered. The flow of costs through a service enterprise using a job order cost accounting system is illustrated as follows:

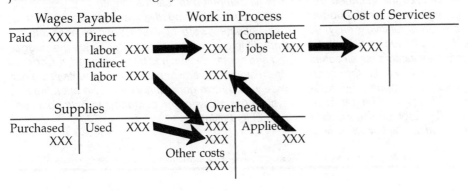

Flow of Costs Through a Service Enterprise

In practice, additional accounting considerations unique to service enterprises may need to be considered. For example, a service enterprise may bill clients on a weekly or monthly basis rather than waiting until a job is completed. In these situations, a portion of the costs related to each billing should be transferred from the work in process account to the cost of services account. This treatment is similar to the percentage-of-completion method used by construction contractors. A service enterprise may also have advance billings which would be accounted for as deferred revenue until the services have been completed.

Job Order Cost Accounting for an Advertising Agency

An article in the December, 1983 issue of *Management Accounting* discussed the importance of good financial planning and control for a service enterprise. The article described how an advertising agency, which develops advertising campaigns for clients, implemented a job order cost accounting system for planning and controlling its operations. Excerpts from the article follow:

... Formed in 1970 by the merging of two smaller agencies, the [New York-based advertising agency] grew [by the late 1970s] from $6 million in billings [revenues] ... to $80 million in billings a year. ... [Business expanded] so rapidly that management had its hands full just taking care of day-to-day business. This left little time to develop a formal accounting system. ... The firm knew its total expenses (by adding employee salaries and overhead) and its total revenues, but had no idea which individual accounts [clients] were mak-

ing or losing money. ... Despite this lack of planning and control, [the company] remained profitable. ... Then ... the company suffered a major loss and senior management attempted to discover why the loss had occurred.

... [A] major reason for the loss was deemed to be the company's inadequate cost control system. Some accounts were highly profitable and others extremely unprofitable, but top management had no idea which were which. ...

... [The company] developed a [two-part] program [to address its problems]. First ... a budgeting/cost control system designed to forecast revenue and expenses at least three to six months into the future by individual account [was established]. This system assured management that, well in advance of a given period, it would have a good idea of revenue and expenses, which would enable it to plan accordingly. ...

The second part of the program was to develop a control system which would monitor the actual amount of revenue or expense derived from each account on a monthly basis, and then analyze the variance between the actual amount and the original budget. Determining the actual revenue is relatively easy.... [Actual] direct costs are derived through a time sheet system which was developed to encompass all actual work performed by every employee in the company.... [The direct labor cost is computed by multiplying] the total number of hours worked by each employee on the account... [by] each person's cost to the agency [hourly wage rate].... Overhead is then calculated on a [direct labor cost] basis and a profit or loss [is computed for each account].

...Since devising the...system [the company] has become aware of which specific accounts are unprofitable and the reasons why. Since the budgeting and control system has been instituted, the agency has resigned several unprofitable accounts that otherwise would have gone unnoticed.... In brief, the new system has allowed [the company] to better plan and control its business.

Source: William B. Mills, "Drawing Up a Budgeting System for an Ad Agency," *Management Accounting* (December, 1983), pp. 46–51, 59.

Budgeting

The planning and control of service enterprises may be facilitated through management's use of budgeting. The budgeting process for a service enterprise is similar to that for a manufacturing enterprise, except that less emphasis is placed on materials budgets and more emphasis is placed on direct labor and overhead budgets.

A revenue (professional fees) budget is the first budget normally prepared by a service enterprise. An estimate of the billable hours serves as a foundation upon which the other budgets are based. The direct labor cost budget is based upon the revenue budget and indicates the number of professional staff hours required to meet the revenue projections. The overhead cost budget is based primarily on the projected number of professional staff hours and indicates the amount of overhead costs for the number of clients that will be served during the period. The operating expenses budget indicates amounts for administrative expenses and for marketing efforts. The revenue, direct labor, overhead, and operating expense budgets are supporting budgets for the development of the budgeted income statement.

The capital expenditures budget and the cash budget for a service enterprise do not differ significantly from those of a manufacturing enterprise. The budgeted balance sheet presents the estimated details of the enterprise's financial condition, assuming that all budgeted operating and financial plans are fulfilled. A budgeted balance sheet for a service enterprise would not differ from that for a manufacturing enterprise, except that no raw materials or finished goods inventories would be reported. A work in process account might be listed for those jobs for which services are partially completed at the end of the period.

Responsibility Accounting

The concept of responsibility accounting would be applied to a service enterprise in a manner similar to that for a manufacturing enterprise. Most service enterprises are organized as profit centers, with each different service offered established as a separate profit center. In these profit centers, the departmental manager has control over costs and revenues. Other departments within a service organization, such as a typing and reproduction department or a computer processing department, could be organized as cost centers. The departmental manager in such a cost center would be responsible for costs incurred in the department. Normally, service enterprises are not organized as investment centers, since service enterprises are not capital intensive. However, a branch office of a service enterprise might be organized as an investment center, in which case the branch manager would have responsibility for costs, revenues, and investment in the center.

The responsibility accounting reports for a service enterprise would be similar to those for a manufacturing enterprise. Cost center reports normally take the form of budget performance reports that compare budgeted costs with actual costs. Profit center reports emphasize profit measures, such as gross profit, departmental margin, or operating income. Budgeted profit measures could be compared with actual profit, using analyses such as gross profit analysis. Investment center performance reports emphasize the rate of return on investment or residual income as performance measures.

Standard Costs

A full standard cost system associated with manufacturing enterprises would normally not be used by a service enterprise because it emphasizes standard costs for materials, direct labor, and factory overhead. Of these costs, a service enterprise would generally use only standard costs for direct labor to assist in planning and controlling operations. When direct labor standards are developed, variances may be computed for direct labor cost. These variances would normally include the direct labor time variance and the direct labor rate variance.

Although overhead costs may be significant for a service enterprise, these costs are normally controlled through the use of budget performance reports, as illustrated in Chapter 8. Because service enterprises are not capital intensive, overhead volume variances are not applicable. Therefore, the only overhead variance generally analyzed for a service enterprise is the controllable (spending) variance, which is reported in a budget performance report.

Pricing

The pricing concepts for determining product prices, described and illustrated in Chapter 12, are also relevant for setting professional fees for service enterprises. The product cost approach is generally not appropriate, since a product is not being manufactured. However, the total cost and variable cost approaches may be applicable for a service enterprise. Because of the difficulties mentioned in Chapter 12, the economic approach to setting professional fees is rarely used by service enterprises.

MAJOR TRENDS IN MANUFACTURING

The major trends in manufacturing in the United States in recent years can be grouped into five general categories: (1) just-in-time manufacturing systems, (2) automation, (3) product quality, (4) inventory control, and (5) information technology. In the following paragraphs, each of these trends is briefly described, and its implications for managerial accounting are discussed.[3]

Just-In-Time Manufacturing Systems

Recently, manufacturers have begun to reorganize the traditional production line to achieve greater efficiency and to improve product quality. One such system that has received much attention by industry is the **just-in-time manufacturing system**, sometimes referred to as the **flexible flow manufacturing system.**

In a traditional production process, a product moves through the process according to functional flows along a continuous production line. That is, the product moves from process to process as each function or step is completed. Each worker is assigned a specific job, which is performed repeatedly as unfinished products are received from the preceding department. In such a process, a product is often said to be "pushed through" production, since each manufacturing department "pushes" the unfinished product to the next stage (department) of manufacturing. For example, a furniture manufacturer might use seven production departments to perform the operating functions necessary to manufacture furniture, as shown in the diagram on page 671.

For the furniture maker in the illustration, manufacturing would begin in the Cutting Department, where the wood would be cut to design specifications. Next, the Drilling Department would perform the drilling function, after which the Sanding Department would sand the wood, the Staining Department would stain the furniture, and the Varnishing Department would apply varnish and other protective coatings. Then, the Upholstery Department would add fabric and other materials. Finally, the Assembly Department would assemble the furniture to complete the manufacturing process.

In the traditional production process, production supervisors attempt to enter enough materials into the manufacturing process to keep all the manufacturing departments operating. Some departments, however, may process materials more rapidly than others. In addition, if one department stops production because of machine breakdowns, for example, the preceding

---

[3]These manufacturing trends and the implications for managerial accounting are described and illustrated in more detail in the articles, books, and monographs listed in the Selected Bibliography on pages 686–688.

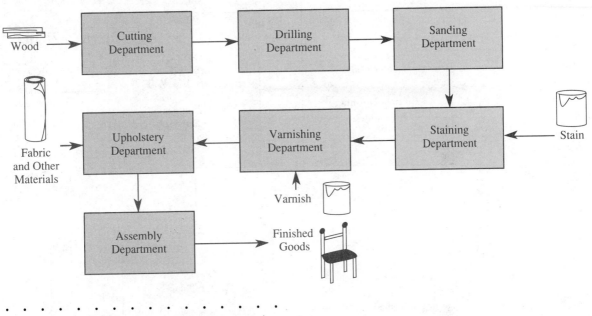

Wood

Fabric and Other Materials

Stain

Varnish

Finished Goods

Traditional Production Line—Furniture Manufacturer

departments usually continue production in order to avoid idle time. This unevenness may result in a build-up of work in process between departments. Furthermore, if bottlenecks occur, the entire production line stops because the unfinished product is not passed on to the successive departments.

In a just-in-time manufacturing system, a primary emphasis is on the reduction of work in process inventories. Large amounts of work in process represent a large dollar investment in inventory that is not earning a return to the enterprise. Ideally, no work in process would exist among departments, but each department's processing finishes "just in time" for the next department's processing to begin. In a just-in-time system, the product is often said to be "pulled through" production, since a department finishing its processing "pulls" (demands) more materials from the preceding department.

One way in which just-in-time manufacturing systems attempt to reduce work in process is by combining processing functions into **work centers.** The seven departments illustrated above for the furniture manufacturer might be reorganized into three work centers, for example. As shown in the following diagram, Work Center One would perform the cutting, drilling, and sanding functions; Work Center Two would perform the staining and varnishing functions; and Work Center Three would perform the upholstery and assembly functions.

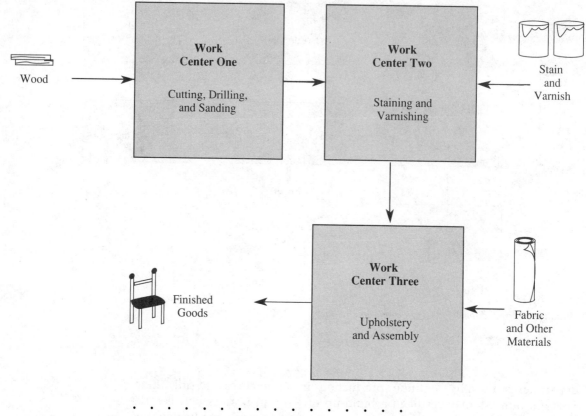

Just-In-Time Production Line—Furniture Manufacturer

In the traditional production line, as described previously, a worker typically performs only one function on a continous basis. However, in a work center in which several manufacturing functions take place, the workers are often cross-trained to perform more than one function. Research has indicated that workers who perform several manufacturing functions identify better with the end product. This identification creates pride in the products and improves quality and productivity.

The just-in-time reorganization of the manufacturing departments may also result in a reorganization of activities involving services to these departments. Specifically, the service activities may be assigned to individual work centers, rather than to the traditional centralized service departments. For example, each work center may be assigned the responsibility for the repair and maintenance of its machinery and equipment. The acceptance of this responsibility creates an environment in which workers gain a better understanding of the production process and machinery limitations. In turn, workers tend to take better care of the machinery, which decreases repairs and maintenance costs, reduces machine downtime, and improves product quality.

Another trend in just-in-time manufacturing systems is the splitting or "decoupling" of the traditional production process into one or more mini-production lines. For example, the mini-production lines of General Motors were described in Chapter 4 on page 98. Each mini-production line operates as if it were independent of the other production lines. Thus, the continuous nature of the traditional production line is eliminated, and there is less emphasis on pushing materials into production to keep all departments operating. Examples of a traditional production line and a decoupled, just-in-time manufacturing system are shown below and at the top of page 674.

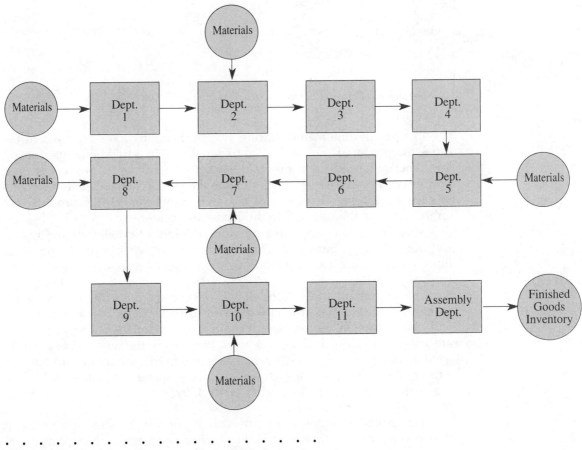

Traditional Production System—Continuous Production Line

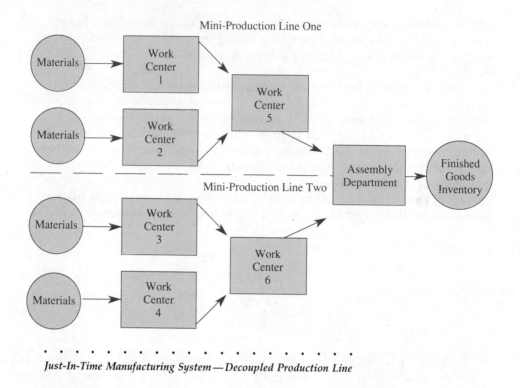

Just-In-Time Manufacturing System—Decoupled Production Line

In a just-in-time manufacturing system, handling costs are reduced because the product is not moved as frequently as in a traditional production line. The mini-production line is often set up so that the product is on a movable carrier that is centrally located in the work center. When the workers in each work center have completed their activities with the product, the entire carrier is then moved to the next work center.

Mini-production lines also provide additional flexibility in the manufacturing process. Since each line is viewed as separate from the other lines, a line having a slow period might contract for special jobs outside the company.

The important implications of just-in-time manufacturing systems for managerial accountants are in the areas of cost allocation, cost accumulation, and cost control. When service functions, such as repairs and maintenance, are assigned to individual work centers, the costs of the services are accumulated in each work center, rather than allocated from a service department. As a result, the direct costs for each work center are determined more easily and are more accurate. In turn, cost control by work center and by mini-production line are facilitated.

The reduction of the amount of work in process inventory may make it unnecessary to account for work in process as a separate inventory item. Costs are accumulated in each work center as they enter the manufacturing process, and at the end of the period, these costs are transferred directly to finished goods inventory and to cost of goods sold, without flowing through the work in process account. Any work in process at the end of the period could be reported with the materials as "Materials and In Process Inventory."

Automation

One of the more visible trends in manufacturing is the increased use of automated machinery to perform routine, repetitive tasks with minimum human involvement in the manufacturing process. Automated machinery can take many forms, including computer-aided machinery and robots.

The use of automated machinery in the manufacturing process is often justified on the basis of labor and material savings. Other factors, however, such as improved quality control and reduced product development time, are often benefits of the use of automated machinery. For example, with the use of robotics, changes in products can be easily introduced into the manufacturing process by reprogramming robots. This ability to add or modify products quickly allows a company to react to changing market preferences and conditions.

The use of automated machinery increases overhead costs through increases in depreciation, maintenance, repairs, property taxes, and insurance. Automation also reduces the amount of direct labor required in the manufacturing process. Twenty-five years ago, for example, direct labor costs frequently accounted for 40% of production costs. With the use of automated machinery, direct labor costs may now represent no more than 5% of production costs. In such an environment, direct labor costs may be charged to overhead rather than accounted for as a separate product cost.[4] As a result, overhead as a percentage of product costs increases.

When a manufacturing process is automated, there is likely to be a greater emphasis on the control of overhead costs through analysis of cost trends. Activity measures may be developed to aid managers in determining the nature of overhead costs for control and allocation purposes. These activity measures, known as **cost drivers**, may include the number of orders received and processed for Receiving Department costs; the number of pounds, gallons, or liters shipped for Shipping Department costs; the number of repairs for Maintenance Department costs; and the number of engineering orders completed for Engineering Department costs. These cost drivers rather than traditional allocation bases, such as direct labor hours, direct labor costs, or units produced, would be used for allocating overhead costs to products.

An example of the results of a cost analysis brought about by automation was a company that found that 23% of its products accounted for 85% of its total sales and all of its profits. The remaining 77% of its products lost money. The cost analysis revealed that the direct-labor-based overhead allocation system was shifting costs from low-volume, special-order products to more

---

[4]Ford S. Worthy, "Accounting Bores You? Wake Up," *Fortune* (October 12, 1987), p. 44.

profitable high-volume products. The allocation system was thereby disguising the true profitability of the products. The company immediately analyzed its product line and discontinued those products that were losing money.[5]

The increasing automation of manufacturing processes has also changed the way that managerial accountants use the traditional methods of capital investment analysis. In many situations, using the traditional quantitative methods, such as the average rate of return, discounted cash flow, and discounted internal rate of return methods, the purchase of automated equipment would not be recommended. However, companies often find that qualitative considerations achieved through automation, such as improved product quality and reliability, reduced development time for introducing new products, and manufacturing flexibility, often outweigh the quantitative considerations. To illustrate, Boston Metal Products purchased a robot, even though traditional capital investment analysis techniques did not justify the investment. The investment paid off quickly, and the robot improved the speed and the quality of welding. As a result, the company was able to speed up deliveries and to grow fourfold in three years with a higher quality product.[6]

Product Quality

During the 1950s and 1960s, price was a primary vehicle for competition among manufacturers. During that period, for example, Japanese products were primarily known for their low prices. During the last decade, however, foreign competitors, such as Japan, have implemented new manufacturing techniques and stringent quality control standards and have supplied world markets with higher quality products at lower prices than those of U.S. manufacturers. As a result, many U.S. manufacturers have been forced to move toward superior product quality as a major manufacturing goal in order to compete effectively.

To improve product quality, U.S. manufacturers have begun to use a Japanese method of organizing workers into **quality circles,** sometimes referred to as **quality control teams.** A quality circle is a group of employees who meet periodically to identify and discuss problems and, when appropriate, to implement solutions to those problems. The use of such quality circles generates greater worker interest and commitment to the manufacturing process and to product quality. The team concept also generates a greater number of suggestions for improving manufacturing processes and cutting costs.

Quality control may be enhanced through the automation of manufacturing processes that allow robots or computer-controlled machinery to monitor the manufacturing process directly. When a weakness or defect in the

---

[5]H. Thomas Johnson and Robert S. Kaplan, *Relevance Lost,* Harvard Business School Press (Boston: 1987).
[6]John Holusha, "Cost Accounting's Blind Spot," *The New York Times* (October 14, 1986).

manufactured product is detected, production is stopped and corrective action is taken.

Managerial accountants aid managers in their efforts to control product quality by analyzing defects and defective rates and by providing timely information on customer complaints, service calls, and warranty expenses. The monitoring of scrap provides managers with information on the quality of materials received from suppliers. In a quality control environment, less emphasis is placed on the price of materials and price variances, and more emphasis is placed on how the quality of the materials affects the final product.

The managerial accountant also aids managers in the control of the quality of production by preparing and interpreting quality control charts. **Quality control charts,** which may be developed by using statistical methods, show desired operating conditions and limits within which production may vary. Production observations outside these limits require investigation and possible corrective action.

In the following example of a quality control chart, the rate of defective units is represented by the vertical axis. The horizontal axis represents samples (1–14) taken from the production process over a period of time. The upper limit for the rate of defective units is 4%. The actual rates of defective units are plotted on the chart, based on the sample observations. For example, observation 3 indicates a rate of defective units of 2%.

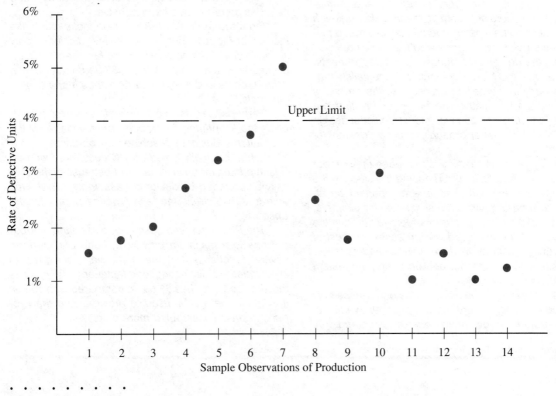

Quality Control Chart

Quality control charts aid managers in determining trends in the rate of defective units and whether the manufacturing process is in control or out of control. For example, in the preceding quality control chart, observations 1–6 indicate increasing rates of defective units, ending with observation 7. At this point, management took corrective action to bring the rate of defective units back into an acceptable range, as indicated by observations 8–14.

Designing Products for Assembly—How To Improve Quality

Increasing concern over product quality has resulted in greater emphasis on product design to meet consumer needs better. Associated with this responsiveness is an emphasis on reducing the number of parts required to manufacture a product. Generally, as described in the following excerpt from an article in *The New York Times*, reducing the number of parts required for a product reduces the difficulty of monitoring quality control and increases product quality.

Until recently, industrial designers and manufacturing engineers did not have much to do with each other.... But some major corporations have found that substantial gains await those who tear down the wall between the design and manufacturing departments.

The idea is to have manufacturing specialists participate early in the design process, so the problems of putting parts together on an assembly line are given equal consideration with more traditional design concerns. The new approach is called "design for assembly."

One goal of the strategy is to reduce the number of parts in a product, in turn reducing the steps in the assembly process. Why should a component be attached to a casing with several screws, for example, when it could be snapped into a molded fitting in the base piece? The improved design saves the cost of the screws, the labor to drive them in and costs involved in ordering, storing, and delivering the fasteners to the line....

As an example of what a design-for-assembly approach can do, [a Ford Motor Company executive] demonstrated an overhead-console clock-and-light

unit from the 1984 Ford Escort. Seen from the back, the unit consists of 22 components connected by wires and held together by different sizes of fasteners driven in at different angles. It could be assembled only by hand, and it took 12 people to meet production targets.

On the 1987 model, the console clock was redesigned according to principles...[that] emphasize minimizing the number of parts and assign numerical values to different methods of putting things together. That enables an engineer to measure how efficient a design is from an assembly standpoint.

Ford used a computerized system... to evaluate its redesign of the overhead console.

From the front, the 1987 version looks much like the earlier models. But the back view discloses only six parts in all, with no wires and no fasteners. Assembly has been automated, with an 83 percent reduction in labor costs and a 39 percent savings in the cost of materials....

Perhaps the classic example of design for assembly is the Proprinter, a computer printer made by the International Business Machines Corporation.

I.B.M. originally provided PC customers with an Epson printer, made in Japan. But because of the cost savings provided by design for assembly, I.B.M. was able to substitute its made-in-America printer for the Epson.

The Proprinter was designed to keep the number of parts to a minimum by having each part perform several functions. And the parts were designed to snap together, eliminating long fasteners. The result is that the Proprinter has 61 parts, compared with 152 on the Epson that I.B.M. used to provide. And the Proprinter can be assembled more quickly....

Source: John Holusha, "Designing for Assembly Lines," *The New York Times* (August 12, 1987).

Inventory Control

· · ·

Inventory control has been a major concern for managers for many years. The use of the economic order quantity, order point, and linear programming techniques for inventory control were described and illustrated in Chapter 14. Two additional techniques of inventory control—materials requirements planning and just-in-time inventory systems—are briefly described in the following paragraphs.

Materials Requirements Planning. **Materials requirements planning (MRP),** also known as **materials resource planning,** is a system developed in the 1970s. An MRP system uses computers to project materials requirements by developing purchasing schedules and manufacturing schedules based on projected demand. Included in the materials projections are allowances for such factors as machine breakdowns, which cause shortages or delays in receiving or processing materials. An MRP system is also reviewed and updated for such factors as changes in the product and in customer demand for the product.

The major disadvantages of MRP are that the models used to project materials requirements are often complex, require lengthy periods to develop, and must be used with computers. Therefore, an MRP system is costly. Although these disadvantages are significant, it has been estimated that between 2,000 and 5,000 companies in the United States are using an MRP system.[7] Most of these companies have annual sales exceeding \$20 million. Black & Decker, for example, with sales of over \$1 billion and nearly 20,000 products, has had remarkable success in using MRP.[8]

In the development of materials requirements planning systems, managerial accountants provide the product cost information necessary for the development of the computer models that are used to minimize materials and inventory costs. For example, the purchase cost of each item of material going into the final product must be estimated, along with handling and storage costs. Managerial accountants must also notify managers of any significant changes in costs, so that the system can be updated.[9]

Just-In-Time Inventory Systems. **Just-in-time inventory systems** were initially developed by the Japanese, who refer to such systems as **Kanban systems.** The goal of just-in-time inventory systems is to reduce inventories to the lowest possible point. The optimum of just-in-time systems would be to acquire just enough inventory to keep the production line moving on a continuous basis. No excess inventory would ever exist, and no interruptions

---

[7]Sumer C. Aggarwal, "MRP, JIT, OPT, FMS?" *Harvard Business Review* (September-October 1985), p. 8.

[8]*Ibid.*, p. 9.

[9]Billy B. Bowers, "Product Costing in the MRP Environment," *Management Accounting* (December, 1982), pp. 24–27.

in the production process would occur because of inventory shortages. The impact of a just-in-time inventory system on the profitability of an enterprise can be significant. For example, General Motors has used a just-in-time inventory approach since 1980 and has reduced its annual inventory-related costs from $8 billion to $2 billion.[10]

The implementation of a just-in-time inventory system usually requires major changes in an enterprise's purchasing system. These changes generally involve agreements with suppliers that will assure the receipt of high quality materials and a timely (just-in-time) delivery of the materials. Manufacturers may require suppliers to locate warehouses near production facilities in order to expedite delivery of materials. In some cases, a manufacturer's computer system is connected directly to a supplier's system, so that purchases may be made electronically when production reaches predetermined levels.

Just-in-time inventory systems are normally implemented with just-in-time manufacturing systems. In these cases, the managerial accountant provides input into the selection of suppliers and the design of innovative purchasing systems. Since materials may be shipped directly from suppliers to mini-production lines, where they will immediately enter production, methods are needed to assure the enterprise that proper quantities of materials have been received. Rather than delaying production by counting materials at the point of receipt, emphasis is likely to be placed on an analysis of the output of the manufacturing process and a reconciliation of the output quantities with the invoices received from the suppliers.

With just-in-time inventory and manufacturing systems, less emphasis is placed on traditional variance analysis, such as the computation of materials price variances, and more emphasis is placed on the timely delivery of materials. Long-term supplier-manufacturer relationships are negotiated with an emphasis on the quality of materials rather than the lowest possible price. As inventories are reduced, relevant product costs become more significant for managerial decision making in such areas as product pricing, cost control, and discontinuance of unprofitable products. The emphasis also changes in performance evaluations, where more nonfinancial measures are used, such as the time to produce a product from start to finish, or **throughput time,** the quantity of scrap generated, and numbers of service calls.

Information Technology
• • •

The use of advanced computer information technology in the manufacturing process allows managers to maintain real-time contact with the manufacturing process. With this information, managers can monitor and control operations on a minute-by-minute basis. This continuous monitoring of inputs and outputs of the manufacturing process increases production efficiency and product quality. For example, production supervisors can moni-

---

[10]David Whiteside and Jules Arbose, "Unsnarling Industrial Production: Why Top Management Is Starting to Care?" *International Management* (March, 1984), p. 20.

tor the amount of scrap that is being generated at each stage of production and can take any corrective action that might be necessary on a timely basis. In contrast, in a traditional manufacturing system, managers often receive weekly or monthly scrap reports.

A primary concern of managerial accountants is providing managers with accurate and timely information on which to base decisions. Managerial accountants may need to become directly involved in the development and implementation of the advanced computer systems that are integrated with the manufacturing process. The challenge to managerial accountants is to develop innovative methods for providing information, so that managers are not overwhelmed by the amount of data, but are able to identify the essential information for decision-making purposes.

Designing the Factory Floor

Computer simulations can be used to design manufacturing operations to maximize efficiency and productivity. The following excerpts were taken from an article in *Business Week* that described how these simulations are used.

You pass by the factory manager's office, and what do you see? He and his top engineers are huddled around a computer screen where cute little symbols are threading their way through mazes. Are these well-paid professionals playing video games on company time?

Look again: The screen display is a recreation of the factory floor, replete with machine tools, robots, flexible manufacturing cells, and materials-handling vehicles. The goal of this game is to exploit those resources in the most efficient way and turn out the highest-quality, lowest-cost product. Welcome to the era of manufacturing simulation.

While the exercise may have make-believe overtones, the payoff can be real. That's what the engineers at Northern Research & Engineering Corp., a consulting subsidiary of Ingersoll-Rand Co., learned when they designed a complicated line for making ball bearings. They figured they would need 77 machine tools performing 16 different processes. But when they fed the information into a computer and simulated the line in operation, they quickly realized the plan could be improved. They were able to [save] $750,000 for their client, Torrington Co. With computer simulation, says Northern Research senior engineer James M. Hanson, savings of several million dollars are "not unusual...."

Source: William G. Wild Jr. and Otis Port, "This Video 'Game' Is Saving Manufacturers Millions," *Business Week* (August 17, 1987), pp. 82 and 84.

Chapter Review

KEY POINTS

1. Changes in the United States Economy.
In response to competitive world markets, the U.S. economy has become more service oriented. In addition, many manufacturers have been forced to

adopt new manufacturing techniques and processes. These changes have led to changes in the managerial accounting methods which provide the basic information that management uses in planning and controlling operations.

2. Managerial Accounting for Service Enterprises.

A cost accounting system is useful to management in planning and controlling the operations of a service enterprise. Since services are usually tailored to a particular client, a job order cost accounting system is generally appropriate for a service enterprise. The cost of any materials or supplies used in rendering services for a client is usually small in amount and is normally included as part of the overhead. The direct labor and overhead costs of rendering services are accumulated in a work in process account. When a job is completed and the client is billed, the costs are transferred to a cost of services account.

The planning and control of service enterprises may be facilitated through management's use of budgeting. A revenue (professional fees) budget is the first budget normally prepared by a service enterprise. The revenue, direct labor, overhead, and operating expense budgets are supporting budgets for the budgeted income statement. The budgeted balance sheet presents the estimated financial condition, assuming that all budgeted operating and financial plans are fulfilled.

Most service enterprises are organized as profit centers, with each different service offered established as a separate profit center. Other departments within a service organization, such as a typing and reproduction department, could be organized as cost centers. Profit center reports emphasize profit measures, such as gross profit, departmental margin, or operating income. Cost center reports normally take the form of budget performance reports that compare budgeted costs with actual costs.

When standard costs are used for a service enterprise, they normally include only standards for direct labor. When direct labor standards are developed, variances would normally include the direct labor time variance and the direct labor rate variance.

The pricing concepts for determining product prices, as described for manufacturing enterprises, are also relevant for setting professional fees for a service enterprise. Service enterprises normally use the total cost and variable cost concepts of pricing.

3. Major Trends in Manufacturing.

In a just-in-time manufacturing system, processing functions are combined into work centers. In this way, manufacturing departments are consolidated and work in process inventories are reduced. Within each work center, employees are often cross-trained to perform a variety of functions. In addition, centralized service department functions may be reassigned to individual work centers. The traditional production process may be "decoupled" into mini-production lines. The use of mini-production lines reduces handling costs and adds flexibility to the manufacturing process. When service functions are assigned to individual work centers, the costs are accumulated in each work center. In addition, accounting for work in process as a separate inventory item may no longer be necessary.

The use of automated machinery in the manufacturing process may be justified on the basis of labor and materials savings, improved quality control, flexibility, and reduced product development time. As automation increases, direct labor cost may be included as part of the factory overhead costs. As a result, factory overhead costs are a larger percentage of total product costs. Activity measures known as cost drivers may be developed to aid managers in controlling and allocating overhead costs. In addition, qualitative factors should be considered in analyzing capital investments involving the use of automated equipment.

Superior product quality is a major goal of manufacturers who compete in world markets. To improve product quality, manufacturers have organized workers into quality circles, implemented the use of automated equipment, placed greater emphasis on the quality of materials, and prepared quality control charts.

Inventory control is a major concern of managers. Materials requirements planning systems use sophisticated models for minimizing materials and handling costs. A disadvantage of these systems is their cost.

The goal of just-in-time inventory systems is the reduction of inventory to a minimal level. Just-in-time inventory systems are normally implemented with just-in-time manufacturing systems. These systems generally require major changes in an enterprise's purchasing system. These changes generally involve agreements with suppliers that will assure the receipt of high quality materials on a timely basis. Less emphasis is placed on traditional materials price variances and inventory valuation for financial statement purposes. Instead, increased emphasis is placed on product costs and performance evaluations.

The use of advanced computer information technology in the manufacturing process allows managers to maintain real-time contact with the manufacturing process. Managerial accountants may need to become directly involved in the development and implementation of these systems in order to assure that managers receive timely and useful information for decision-making purposes.

KEY TERMS

just-in-time manufacturing
  system 670
cost drivers 675
quality circle 676

quality control chart 677
materials requirements
  planning (MRP) 679
just-in-time inventory system 679

SELF-EXAMINATION QUESTIONS

(Answers at End of Chapter)

1. Which of the following managerial accounting techniques is most applicable to service enterprises?
   A. Break-even analysis
   B. Inventory analysis
   C. Job order cost accounting
   D. Capital investment analysis

2. Most processing functions are often combined in a just-in-time manufacturing system into:
   A. work centers
   B. departments
   C. divisions
   D. none of the above

3. The use of automated machinery in the manufacturing process often:
   A. decreases labor costs
   B. increases overhead costs
   C. improves product quality
   D. all of the above

4. Just-in-time inventory systems:
   A. have the goal of reducing inventory to the lowest possible level
   B. aim to have just enough inventory to keep the production line moving on a continuous basis
   C. if operating optimally would have no excess inventory and no work interruptions due to inventory shortages
   D. all of the above

5. Which of the following activity measures would be the best cost driver for Receiving Department costs?
   A. Number of orders shipped
   B. Direct labor costs
   C. Units produced
   D. Pounds of materials received

Discussion Questions

18–1. How has the United States economy responded in recent years to competitive pressures from world-wide producers of goods?

18–2. Which managerial accounting concepts and procedures are especially relevant for service enterprises?

18–3. Why are capital investment analysis and inventory analysis generally not as important for service enterprises as for manufacturing enterprises?

18–4. Which type of cost accounting system, a job order cost system or a process cost system, is most appropriate for a service enterprise?

18–5. For a service enterprise using a job order cost accounting system, the direct labor and overhead costs of rendering services to clients are accumulated in a work in process account. What separate ledger supports the work in process account?

18–6. When a job is completed for a service enterprise using a job order cost accounting system, to what account are the costs transferred?

18–7. In comparison to a manufacturing enterprise, a service enterprise places less emphasis on what type of budget (materials, labor, overhead)?

18–8. For a service enterprise, which budget is normally prepared first?

18–9. What are three profit measures emphasized in responsibility accounting for a profit center?

18–10. For a service enterprise using responsibility accounting, would a reproduction department normally be treated as a profit center, a cost center, or an investment center?

18–11. For a service enterprise using a standard cost system for direct labor, which two variances would normally be computed?

18–12. Which of the following price concepts would normally not be appropriate for a service enterprise: product cost concept, total cost concept, or variable cost concept?

18–13. What term is sometimes used to refer to just-in-time manufacturing systems?

18–14. Describe the differences in worker assignments for a traditional production line and a just-in-time manufacturing system.

18–15. What term is used to describe the combined processing functions in a just-in-time manufacturing system?

18–16. In a just-in-time manufacturing system, what is the primary advantage of assigning repair and maintenance responsibilities directly to individual work centers?

18–17. For managerial accountants, what are two implications of just-in-time manufacturing systems?

18–18. What is a primary characteristic of automated machinery?

18–19. What term is used to refer to an activity measure used to allocate overhead costs for cost control and allocation purposes?

18–20. In allocating overhead costs for an engineering department to individual production departments, what would be a good cost driver?

18–21. Give an example of a qualitative factor which should be considered in a capital investment analysis involving automated equipment.

18–22. During the 1950s and 1960s, what was the primary vehicle for competition among manufacturers?

18–23. What are some of the benefits of using quality circles to improve product quality?

18–24. The managerial accountant can aid managers in controlling the quality of production through the preparation and interpretation of what type of chart?

18–25. What term is given to inventory systems that use computers to project materials requirements and then develop purchase schedules and manufacturing schedules?

18–26. What is the ultimate goal of just-in-time inventory systems?

18–27. Why does the implementation of a just-in-time inventory system usually require major changes in an enterprise's purchasing system?

18–28. How can a managerial accountant aid in the implementation of a just-in-time inventory system?

18–29. What are some nonfinancial indicators of product quality?

18–30. What is a primary managerial accounting concern with respect to advanced computer information technology?

18–31. Real World Focus. The bar codes designed to speed groceries through checkout lanes are now being applied to manufacturing assembly lines. For example, North American automobile makers now require the use of bar codes by virtually all their suppliers. Why would manufacturers insist on the use of bar codes by their suppliers?

Selected Bibliography

Aggarwal, Sumer C. *"MRP, JIT, OPT, FMS?"* Harvard Business Review (September–October, 1985), pp. 8–10, 12, 16.

Bennett, Robert E., James A. Hendricks, David E. Keys, and Edward J. Rudnicki. *Cost Accounting for Factory Automation.* Montvale, N.J.: National Association of Accountants, 1987.

Bennett, Robert E., and James A. Hendricks. "Justifying the Acquisition of Automated Equipment." *Management Accounting* (July, 1987), pp. 39–46.

Bowers, Billy. "Product Costing in the MRP Environment." *Management Accounting* (December, 1982), pp. 24–27.

Cook, James. "Kanban, American-Style." *Forbes* (October 8, 1984), pp. 66, 70.

Foster, George, and Charles T. Horngren. "JIT: Cost Accounting and Cost Management Issues." *Management Accounting* (June, 1987), pp. 19–25.

Holusha, John. "Cost Accounting's Blind Spot." *The New York Times*, October 14, 1986.

Holusha, John. "Designing for Assembly Lines." *The New York Times*, August 12, 1987.

Howell, Robert A., and Stephen R. Soucy. "Capital Investment in the New Manufacturing Environment." *Management Accounting* (November, 1987), pp. 26–32.

Howell, Robert A., and Stephen R. Soucy. "Cost Accounting in the New Manufacturing Environment." *Management Accounting* (August, 1987), pp. 42–48.

Howell, Robert A., James D. Brown, Stephen R. Soucy, and Allen H. Seed, III. *Management Accounting in the New Manufacturing Environment.* Montvale, N.J.: National Association of Accountants, 1987.

Howell, Robert A., and Stephen R. Soucy. "Operating Controls in the New Manufacturing Environment." *Management Accounting* (October, 1987), pp. 23–31.

Howell, Robert A., and Stephen R. Soucy. The New Manufacturing Environment: Major Trends for Management Accounting." *Management Accounting* (July, 1987), pp. 21–27.

Jayson, Susan. "Cost Accounting for the 90s." *Management Accounting* (July, 1986), pp. 58–59.

Johnson, H. Thomas, and Robert S. Kaplan. "The Rise and Fall of Management Accounting." *Management Accounting* (January, 1987), pp. 22–30.

Johnson, H. Thomas, and Robert S. Kaplan. *Relevance Lost: The Rise and Fall of Management Accounting.* Boston: Harvard Business School Press, 1987.

Kaplan, Robert S. "Must CIM Be Justified by Faith Alone?" *Harvard Business Review* (March–April, 1986), pp. 87–95.

Lammert, Thomas B., and Robert Ehrsam. "The Human Element: The Real Challange in Modernizing Cost Systems." *Management Accounting* (July, 1987), pp. 32–37.

Mackey, James T. "11 Key Issues in Manufacturing Accounting." *Management Accounting* (January, 1987), pp. 32–37.

Marcom, John Jr. "Slimming Down: IBM Is Automating, Simplifying Products to Beat Asian Rivals." *The Wall Street Journal,* April 14, 1986, pp. 1, 10.

McIlhattan, Robert D. "How Cost Management Systems Can Support The JIT Philosophy." *Management Accounting* (September, 1987), pp. 20–26.

McNair, C.J., and William Mosconi. "Measuring Performance in an Advanced Manufacturing Environment." *Management Accounting* (July, 1987), pp. 28–31.

Neumann, Bruce R., and Pauline R. Jaouen. "Kanban, Zips and Cost Accounting: A Case Study." *Journal of Accountancy* (August, 1986), pp. 132–141.

Sadhwani, A.T., and M.H. Sarhan. "The Impact of Just-In-Time Inventory Systems on Small Businesses." *Journal of Accountancy* (January, 1987), pp. 118–130.

Sadhwani, Arjan T., M.H. Sarhan, and Dayal Kiringoda. "Just-In-Time: An Inventory System Whose Time Has Come." *Journal of Accountancy* (December, 1985), pp. 36–44.

Sauers, Dale G. "Analyzing Inventory Systems." *Management Accounting* (May, 1986), pp. 30–36.

Seglund, Ragnor, and Santiago Ibarreche. "Just-In-Time: The Accounting Implications." *Management Accounting* (August, 1984), pp. 43–45.

Whiteside, David, and Jules Arbose. "Unsnarling Industrial Production: Why Top Management Is Starting to Care?" *International Management* (March, 1984).

Wild, William G., Jr., and Otis Port. "This 'Video Game' is Saving Manufacturers Millions." *Business Week* (August 17, 1987), pp. 82, 84.

Worthy, Ford S. "Accounting Bores You? Wake Up." *Fortune* (October 12, 1987), pp. 43, 44, 48–50.

Answers to Self-Examination Questions

· · ·

1. **C** A job order cost accounting system (answer C) is most applicable to an enterprise that renders services to individual clients. Break-even analysis (answer A) is generally not applicable, since fixed costs are normally a small portion of the total costs of a service enterprise. Inventory analysis (answer B) is generally not applicable, since service enterprises do not carry much inventory. Capital investment analysis (answer D) is generally not applicable, since service enterprises are generally not capital intensive.

2. **A** In a just-in-time manufacturing system, several manufacturing and service functions may be combined into work centers (answer A), in which workers perform a variety of tasks. The traditional production line is organized according to departments (answer B) or divisions (answer C).

3. **D** Automation in the manufacturing process decreases labor costs (answer A) because fewer people are needed to perform routine tasks. It increases overhead costs (answer B) because costs associated with machinery, such as depreciation and maintenance, increase. It improves product quality (answer C) because machines tend to perform more consistently in the manufacturing process.

4. **D** The goal of just-in-time inventory systems is to reduce inventory to the lowest possible level (answer A). When such systems operate optimally, just enough inventory is acquired to keep the production line moving on a continuous basis (answer B), and no excess inventory exists and no work interruptions due to inventory shortages occur (answer C).

5. **D** The best cost driver for Receiving Department costs is the pounds of materials received (answer D). This activity measure is more closely associated with the Receiving Department costs than is the number of orders shipped (answer A), direct labor costs (answer B), or units produced (answer C).

Appendixes

Appendix A
Glossary
• • •

A

Absorption costing. The concept that considers the cost of manufactured products to be composed of direct materials, direct labor, and factory overhead.

Accounting. An information system that communicates economic information for use by various groups and individuals in making informed judgments and decisions.

Accounts receivable turnover. The relationship between credit sales and accounts receivable, computed by dividing net sales on account by the average net accounts receivable.

Acid-test ratio. The ratio of the sum of cash, receivables, and marketable securities to current liabilities.

Annuity. A series of equal cash flows at fixed intervals.

Appropriation. A designated use of revenues for which a potential liability is recognized by nonprofit organizations.

Average cost method. A method of determining product costs in which all costs incurred in manufacturing the goods completed during a period are averaged, and this average is used in determining the unit product cost of the goods completed during the period and the work in process at the end of the period.

Average rate of return. A method of evaluating capital investment proposals that focuses on the expected profitability of the investment.

B

Break-even point. The point in the operations of an enterprise at which revenues and expired costs are equal.

Budget. A formal written statement of management's plans for the future, expressed in financial terms.

Budget performance report. A report comparing actual results with budget figures.

By-product. A product resulting from a manufacturing process and having little value in relation to the principal product or joint products.

C

Capital expenditures budget. The budget summarizing future plans for acquisition of plant facilities and equipment.

Capital investment analysis. The process by which management plans, evaluates, and controls long-term capital investments involving property, plant, and equipment.

Capital rationing. The process by which management allocates available investment funds among competing capital investment proposals.

Cash flows from financing activities. The section of the statement of cash flows in which is reported the transactions involving cash receipts from the issuance of equity and debt securities; and cash payments for dividends, repurchase of equity securities, and redemption of debt securities.

Cash flows from investing activities. The section of the statement of cash flows in which is reported the activities involving cash receipts from the sale of investments, plant assets, and other noncurrent assets; and cash payments for the acquisition of investments, plant assets, and other noncurrent assets.

Cash flows from operating activities. The section of the statement of cash flows in which is reported the cash transactions that entered into the determination of net income.

Cash payback period. The expected period of time that will elapse between the date of a capital investment and the complete recovery in cash (or equivalent) of the amount invested.

Combined line-program budget. A budget in which the items of expenditure are presented by the object of the expenditure and the program associated with the expenditure.

Common-size statement. A financial statement in which all items are expressed only in relative terms.

Constant dollar. Historical costs that have been converted into dollars of constant value through the use of a price-level index.

Continuous budgeting. A method of budgeting that provides for maintenance of a twelve-month projection into the future.

Contribution margin. Sales less variable cost of goods sold and variable selling and general expenses.

Contribution margin ratio. The percentage of each sales dollar that is available to cover the fixed expenses and provide an operating income. Sometimes called the profit-volume ratio.

Controllable cost. For a specific level of management, a cost that can be directly controlled.

Controller. The chief managerial accountant of an organization.

Controlling. The process by which managers attempt to achieve the goals identified in an enterprise's strategic and operational plans.

Conversion costs. The combination of direct labor and factory overhead costs.

Cost accounting system. An accounting system which uses the perpetual system of inventory accounting for the three manufacturing inventories: direct materials, work in process, and finished goods.

Cost behavior. The manner in which a cost changes in relation to its activity base.

Cost center. A decentralized unit in which the responsibility for control of costs incurred and the authority to make decisions that affect these costs is the responsibility of the unit's manager.

Cost driver. An activity measure used to allocate overhead cost.

Cost estimation. The method or methods used to estimate costs for use in managerial decision making.

Cost ledger. A subsidiary ledger employed in a job order cost system and which contains an account for each job order.

Cost of goods sold. The cost of a product (direct materials, direct labor, and factory overhead costs) that has been sold during a period by a manufacturing enterprise.

Cost of merchandise sold. The cost of merchandise that has been sold during a period by a merchandising enterprise.

Cost of production report. A report prepared periodically by a processing department, summarizing (1) the units for which the department is accountable and the disposition of these units and (2) the costs charged to the department and the allocation of these costs.

Cost price approach. An approach to transfer pricing that uses cost as the basis for setting the transfer price.

Costs. The disbursement of cash (or the commitment to pay cash in the future) for the purpose of generating revenues.

Cost-volume-profit analysis. The systematic examination of the interrelationships between selling prices, volume of sales and production, costs, expenses, and profits.

Cost-volume-profit chart. A chart used to assist management in understanding the relationships between costs, expenses, sales, and operating profit or loss. Sometimes referred to as a break-even chart.

Current cost. The amount of cash that would have to be paid currently to acquire assets of the same age and in the same condition as existing assets.

Currently attainable standards. Standards which represent levels of operation that can be attained with reasonable effort.

Current ratio. The ratio of current assets to current liabilities.

D

Decentralization. The separation of a business into more manageable units.

Decision making. The process by which managers determine to follow one course of action as opposed to an alternative.

Decision tree. A graphical representation of decisions, possible outcomes, and chances that outcomes will occur.

Departmental margin. Departmental gross profit less direct departmental expenses.

Differential analysis. The area of accounting concerned with the effect of alternative courses of action on revenues and costs.

Differential cost. The amount of increase or decrease in cost that is expected from a particular course of action as compared with an alternative. Sometimes referred to as incremental cost.

Differential revenue. The amount of increase or decrease in revenue expected from a particular course of action as compared with an alternative.

Direct cost. A cost that can be traced directly to a unit within an enterprise or organization.

Direct expense. An expense directly traceable to or incurred for the sole benefit of a specific department and ordinarily subject to the control of the department manager.

Directing. The process by which managers, given their assigned level of responsibilities, run day-to-day operations.

Direct labor cost. The cost of wages paid to employees directly involved in changing direct materials into finished products.

Direct labor rate variance. The cost associated with the difference between the actual rate paid for direct labor used in producing a commodity and the standard rate for the commodity.

Direct labor time variance. The cost associated with the difference between the actual direct labor hours spent producing a commodity and the standard hours for the commodity.

Direct materials cost. The cost of materials entering directly into the manufactured product. Sometimes referred to as raw materials costs.

Direct materials inventory. The cost of direct materials which have not yet entered into the manufacturing process.

Direct materials price variance. The cost associated with the difference between the actual price of direct materials used in producing a commodity and the standard price for the commodity.

Direct materials quantity variance. The cost associated with the difference between the actual quantity of direct materials used in producing a commodity and the standard quantity for the commodity.

Direct method. A method of reporting the cash flows from operating activities as the difference between the operating cash receipts and the operating cash payments.

Discounted cash flow method. A method of analysis of proposed capital investments that focuses on the present value of the cash flows expected from the investment.

Discounted internal rate of return method. A method of analysis of proposed capital investments that focuses on using present value concepts to compute the rate of return from the net cash flows expected from the investment.

Discretionary cost. A cost that is not essential to short-term operations.

E

Earnings per share (EPS) on common stock. The profitability ratio of net income available to common shareholders to the number of common shares outstanding.

Economic order quantity (EOQ). The optimum quantity of specified inventoriable materials to be ordered at one time.

Economies of scale. An economic concept that recognizes that over a wide range of production, costs vary in differing proportions to changes in an activity base. When production facilities are limited, costs tend to increase but at a decreasing rate as production increases from a relatively low level.

Elastic demand. An economic concept in which a price increase or decrease for a product will have a significant effect on the number of units of the product sold.

Elasticity of demand. The degree to which the number of units sold changes because of a change in product price.

Encumbrance. A commitment by a nonprofit organization to incur expenditures in the future.

Engineering method. A cost estimation method in which engineers estimate total cost, as well as variable and fixed components, based on studies of such factors as production methods, materials and labor requirements, equipment needs, and utility demands.

Equivalent units of production. The number of units that could have been manufactured from start to finish during a period.

Expected value. A concept useful for managers in decision making which involves identifying the possible outcomes from a decision and estimating the likelihood that each outcome will occur.

Expenses. The cost of assets used up in the generation of revenues.

F

Factory overhead controllable variance. The difference between the actual amount of factory overhead cost incurred and the amount of factory overhead budgeted for the level of operations achieved.

Factory overhead cost. Costs other than direct materials cost and direct labor cost incurred in the manufacturing process. Sometimes referred to as manufacturing overhead or factory burden.

Factory overhead volume variance. The cost or benefit associated with operating at a level above or below 100% of productive capacity.

Financial accounting. The area of accounting that is concerned with the recording of transactions using generally accepted accounting principles (GAAP) for a business enterprise or other economic unit and with a periodic preparation of various statements from such records.

Finished goods inventory. The cost of finished products on hand that have not been sold.

Finished goods ledger. The subsidiary ledger that contains the individual accounts for each kind of commodity produced.

First-in, first-out method. A method of determining product costs in which the beginning work in process inventory costs are kept separate from the costs incurred during the period, and the beginning work in process is assumed to be completed first.

Fixed cost. A cost that remains constant in total dollar amount as the level of activity changes.

Flexible budgets. A series of budgets for varying rates of activity.

Fund. In accounting for nonprofit organizations, an accounting entity with accounts maintained for recording assets, liabilities, fund equity, revenues, and expenditures for a particular purpose.

Fund equity. The excess of assets over liabilities in a nonprofit organization.

G

General accounting system. An accounting system which extends the periodic system of inventory accounting used by merchandising enterprises to the three manufacturing inventories: direct materials, work in process, and finished goods.

Generally accepted accounting principles. Generally accepted guidelines for the preparation of financial statements.

Gross profit analysis. The procedure used to develop information concerning the effect of changes in quantities and unit prices on sales and cost of goods sold.

H

High-low method. A method used to estimate total cost, as well as variable and fixed components, by using the highest and lowest total costs revealed by past cost patterns.

Horizontal analysis. The percentage analysis of increases and decreases in corresponding items in comparative financial statements.

I

Indirect cost. A cost that for a specific unit within an enterprise or organization cannot be traced directly to that unit.

Indirect expense. An expense that is incurred for an entire business enterprise as a unit and that is not subject to the control of individual department managers.

Indirect method. A method of reporting the cash flows from operating activities as the net income from operations adjusted for all deferrals of past cash receipts and payments and all accruals of expected future cash receipts and payments.

Inelastic demand. An economic concept in which a price increase or decrease for a product will have little or no effect on the number of units of the product sold.

Inflation. A period when prices in general are rising and the purchasing power of money is declining.

Inventory order point. The level to which inventory is allowed to fall before an order for additional inventory is placed.

Inventory turnover. The relationship between the volume of goods sold and inventory, computed by dividing the cost of goods sold by the average inventory.

Investment center. A decentralized unit in which the manager has the responsibility and authority to make decisions that affect not only cost and revenues, but also the plant assets available to the center.

Investment turnover. A component of the rate of return on investment, computed as the ratio of sales to invested assets.

J

Job cost sheet. An account in the cost ledger in which the costs charged to a particular job order are recorded.

Job order cost system. A type of cost accounting system that provides for a separate record of the cost of each particular quantity of product that passes through the factory.

Joint costs. The costs common to the manufacture of two or more products (joint products).

Joint products. Two or more commodities of significant value produced from a single principal direct material.

Judgmental method. A cost estimation method in which managers estimate total cost, as well as variable and fixed components, using experience and past observations of cost-volume-relationships.

Just-in-time inventory system. A system whose goal is to reduce inventories to the lowest possible point. Sometimes referred to as a kanban system.

Just-in-time manufacturing system. A system of manufacturing in which a primary emphasis is on the reduction of work in process inventories by combining processing functions and organizing mini-production lines.

L

Lead time. The time, usually expressed in days, that it takes to receive an order for inventory.

Learning effect (learning curve). The effect on costs determined by how rapidly new employees learn their jobs or by how rapidly experienced employees learn new job assignments.

Least squares method. A cost estimation method that uses statistics to estimate total cost and the fixed and variable cost components.

Leverage. The tendency of the rate earned on stockholders' equity to vary from the rate earned on total assets because the amount earned on assets acquired through the use of funds provided by creditors varies from the interest paid to these creditors.

Linear programming. A quantitative method that can be used in providing data for solving a variety of business problems in which management's objective is to minimize cost or maximize profits, subject to several limiting factors.

Line budget. A budget in which the items of expenditure are presented by the object of the expenditure. Sometimes referred to as a functional budget.

M

Management. Individuals who are charged with the responsibility of directing the operations of enterprises.

Management by exception. The philosophy of managing which involves monitoring the operating results of implemented plans and comparing the expected results with the actual results. This feedback allows management to isolate significant variations for further investigation and possible remedial action.

Management process. The four basic functions of (1) planning, (2) organizing and directing, (3) controlling, and (4) decision making used in managing an organization.

Managerial accounting. The area of accounting that provides relevant information to management for use in planning, organizing and directing, controlling, and decision making.

Manufacturing margin. Sales less variable cost of goods sold.

Marginal cost. The increase in total cost of producing and selling an additional unit of product.

Marginal revenue. The increase in total revenue realized from the sale of an additional unit of product.

Margin of safety. The difference between current sales revenue and the sales at the break-even point.

Market price approach. An approach to transfer pricing that uses the price at which the product or service transferred could be sold to outside buyers as the transfer price.

Markup. An amount which is added to a "cost" amount to determine product price.

Market (sales) value method. A method of allocating joint costs among products according to their relative sales values.

Master budget. The comprehensive budget plan encompassing all the individual budgets related to sales, cost of goods sold, operating expenses, capital expenditures, and cash.

Materials ledger. The subsidiary ledger containing the individual accounts for each type of material.

Materials requirements planning (MRP). A system which uses computers to project materials requirements by developing purchasing schedules and manufacturing schedules based on projected demand. Sometimes termed materials resource planning.

Materials requisition. The form used by the appropriate manufacturing department to authorize the issuance of materials from the storeroom.

Maximax concept. A concept useful for managerial decision making, which leads management to decide in favor of that alternative with the maximum (largest) profit.

Maximin concept. A concept useful for managerial decision making, which leads management to decide in favor of that alternative with the maximum (largest) minimum profit.

Mixed cost. A cost with both variable and fixed characteristics, sometimes referred to as semivariable or semifixed cost.

Modified Accelerated Cost Recovery System (MACRS). The system described in the Internal Revenue Code for determining depreciation (cost recovery) of plant asset acquisitions.

Monopolistic competitive market. A market in which there exists many sellers of similar products with no one seller having a large enough share of the market to influence the total sales of the other products.

Monopoly market. A market in which no directly competing products exist.

N

Negotiated price approach. An approach to transfer pricing that allows the managers of decentralized units to agree (negotiate) among themselves as to the proper transfer price.

Noncontrollable cost. For a specific level of management, a cost that cannot be directly controlled.

Number of days' sales in inventory. The relationship between the volume of goods sold and inventory, computed by dividing the inventory at the end of the year by the average daily cost of goods sold.

Number of days' sales in receivables. The relationship between credit sales and accounts receivable, computed by dividing the net accounts receivable at the end of the year by the average daily sales on account.

O

Oligopoly market. A market in which there exists a few large sellers competing against each other with similar products, and the amount sold by each seller has a direct effect on the sales of the other companies.

Operational planning. The development of short-term plans to achieve goals identified in an enterprise's strategic plan. Sometimes referred to as tactical planning.

Opportunity cost. The amount of income that is foregone by selecting one alternative over another.

Organizing. The process by which management assigns responsibility to individuals for achieving enterprise goals.

Overapplied overhead. The amount of overhead applied in excess of the actual overhead costs incurred for production during a period.

P

Payoff table. A table that summarizes the possible outcomes of one or more decisions for management's use in decision making.

Period costs. Those costs that are used up in generating revenue during the current period and that are not involved in the manufacturing process. These costs are recognized as expenses on the current period's income statement.

Planning. The process by which management develops a course of action to attain enterprise goals.

Predetermined factory overhead rate. The rate used to apply factory overhead costs to the goods manufactured.

Present value. The estimated present worth of an amount of cash to be received (or paid) in the future.

Present value index. An index computed by dividing the total present value of the net cash flow to be received from a proposed capital investment by the amount to be invested.

Present value of an annuity. The sum of the present values of a series of equal cash flows to be received at fixed intervals.

Price-earnings (P/E) ratio. The ratio of the market price per share of common stock, at a specific date, to the annual earnings per share.

Price graph. A graph used to determine the price-cost combination that maximizes the total profit of an enterprise by plotting the marginal revenues and marginal costs.

Price-level index. The ratio of the total cost of a group of commodities prevailing at a particular time to the total cost of the same group of commodities at an earlier base time.

Price theory. A separate discipline in the area of micro-economics which studies the setting of product prices.

Prime costs. The combination of direct materials and direct labor costs.

Process cost system. A type of cost accounting system that accumulates costs for each of the various departments or processes within a factory.

Product cost concept. A concept used in applying the cost-plus approach to product pricing in which only the costs of manufacturing the product, termed the product cost, are included in the cost amount to which the markup is added.

Product costs. The three components of manufacturing cost: direct materials, direct labor, and factory overhead costs.

Product life cycle. A concept that assumes that a product passes through various stages from the time that it is introduced until the time that it disappears from the market.

Program budget. A budget in which the items of expenditure are presented by the program associated with the expenditure.

Profitability. The ability of a firm to earn income.

Profit center. A decentralized unit in which the manager has the responsibility and the authority to make decisions that affect both cost and revenues (and thus profits).

Profit margin. A component of the rate of return on investment, computed as the ratio of operating income to sales.

Profit-volume chart. A chart used to assist management in understanding the relationship between profit and volume.

Purchase orders. The form issued by the purchasing department to suppliers, requesting the delivery of materials.

Purchase requisitions. The form used to inform the purchasing department that materials are needed by an enterprise.

Purely competitive market. A market in which the price for a product is established solely by the market conditions, and the quantity that a firm sells has no impact on the total market for the product. Thus, a firm can sell all it produces at the market price.

Q

Quality circle. A group of employees who meet periodically to identify and discuss problems and, when appropriate, to implement solutions to those problems.

Quality control chart. A chart, often developed using statistical methods, which shows desired operating conditions and limits within which production may vary.

Quick assets. The sum of cash, receivables and marketable securities.

R

Rate earned on common stockholders' equity. A measure of profitability computed by dividing net income, reduced by preferred dividend requirements, by common stockholders' equity.

Rate earned on stockholders' equity. A measure of profitability computed by dividing net income by total stockholders' equity.

Rate earned on total assets. A measure of the profitability of assets, without regard to the equity of creditors and stockholders in the assets.

Rate of return on investment (ROI). A measure of managerial efficiency in the use of investments in assets, computed by dividing operating income by invested assets.

Receiving report. The form used by the receiving department to indicate that materials have been received and inspected.

Relevant range. The range of activity within which the enterprise is planning to operate.

Residual income. The excess of divisional operating income over a "minimum" amount of desired operating income.

Responsibility accounting. The process of measuring and reporting operating data by areas of responsibility.

S

Safety stock. The amount of inventory that serves as a reserve for unforeseen circumstances, and therefore is not normally used in regular operations.

Sales mix. The relative distribution of sales among the various products available for sale.

Scattergraph method. A cost estimation method that uses a graph to estimate total cost and the fixed and variable cost components.

Semivariable cost. A cost with both variable and fixed characteristics, sometimes referred to as a mixed or semifixed cost.

Service departments. Factory departments that do not process materials directly, but render services for the benefit of production departments.

Simplex method. A mathematical equation approach to linear programming, which is often used more practically with a computer.

Solvency. The ability of a firm to pay its debts as they come due.

Standard costs. Detailed estimates of what a product should cost.

Standard cost system. An accounting system that uses standards for each element of manufacturing costs entering into the finished product.

Statement of cash flows. A summary of the major cash receipts and cash payments for a period.

Statement of cost of goods manufactured. A separate statement for a manufacturer that reports the cost of goods manufactured during a period.

Statement of revenues, expenditures, and changes in fund balance. The statement for a nonprofit enterprise that provides a comparison of budgeted and actual revenues and expenditures along with the effect of operations on the unreserved fund balance.

Step-wise fixed cost. A cost which varies in a step-wise fashion with changes in an activity base. Because of the long width of the range of production (steps) over which the total cost changes, the cost is classified as a fixed cost for managerial decision making.

Step-wise variable cost. A cost which varies in a step-wise fashion with changes in an activity base. Because of the short width of the range of production (steps) over which the total cost changes, the cost is classified as a variable cost for managerial decision making.

Strategic planning. The development of a long-range course of action to achieve enterprise goals.

Sunk cost. Costs which have been incurred and cannot be reversed by subsequent decisions.

T

Theoretical standards. Standards that represent levels of performance that can be achieved only under perfect operating conditions, such as no idle time, no machine breakdowns, and no materials spoilage.

Time tickets. The form on which the amount of time spent by each employee and the labor cost incurred for each individual job, or for factory overhead, are recorded.

Total cost concept. A concept used in applying the cost-plus approach to product pricing in which all costs of manufacturing a product plus the selling and general expenses are included in the cost amount to which the markup is added.

Transfer price. The price charged one decentralized unit by another for the goods or services provided.

U

Underapplied overhead. The amount of actual overhead in excess of the overhead applied to production during a period.

V

Value of perfect information. The maximum amount (cost) that will be paid to obtain perfect information concerning a decision.

Variable cost. A cost that varies in total dollar amount as the level of activity changes.

Variable cost concept. A concept used in applying the cost-plus approach to product pricing in which only variable costs and expenses are included in the cost amount to which the markup is added.

Variable costing. The concept that considers the cost of products manufactured to be composed only of those manufacturing costs that increase or decrease as the volume of production rises or falls (direct materials, direct labor, and variable factory overhead).

Variance. The difference between what a product should cost (standard) and how much it does cost (actual).

Vertical analysis. The percentage analysis of component parts in relation to the total of the parts in a single financial statement.

W

Working capital. The excess of total current assets over total current liabilities at some point in time.

Work in process inventory. The direct materials costs, the direct labor costs, and the factory overhead costs which have entered into the manufacturing process, but are associated with products that have not been finished.

Z

Zero-base budgeting. A concept of budgeting that requires all levels of management to start from zero and estimate budget data as if there had been no previous activities in their unit.

Appendix B
Interest Tables
· • ·

The following present value and future value tables contain factors carried to six decimal places for interest rates of 1% to 15% for 50 periods.

Future Amount of 1 at Compound Interest Due in n Periods: $a = (1 + i)^n$

Table 1

n	1%	2%	3%	4%	5%	6%	7%	8%	9%	10%	12%	15%
1	1.010000	1.020000	1.030000	1.040000	1.050000	1.060000	1.070000	1.080000	1.090000	1.100000	1.120000	1.150000
2	1.020100	1.040400	1.060900	1.081600	1.102500	1.123600	1.144900	1.166400	1.188100	1.210000	1.254400	1.322500
3	1.030301	1.061208	1.092727	1.124864	1.157625	1.191016	1.225043	1.259712	1.295029	1.331000	1.404928	1.520875
4	1.040604	1.082432	1.125509	1.169859	1.215506	1.262477	1.310796	1.360489	1.411582	1.464100	1.573519	1.749006
5	1.051010	1.104081	1.159274	1.216653	1.276282	1.338226	1.402552	1.469328	1.538624	1.610510	1.762342	2.011357
6	1.061520	1.126162	1.194052	1.265319	1.340096	1.418519	1.500730	1.586874	1.677100	1.771561	1.973823	2.313061
7	1.072135	1.148686	1.229874	1.315932	1.407100	1.503630	1.605781	1.713824	1.828039	1.948717	2.210681	2.660020
8	1.082857	1.171659	1.266770	1.368569	1.477455	1.593848	1.718186	1.850930	1.992563	2.143589	2.475963	3.059023
9	1.093685	1.195093	1.304773	1.423312	1.551328	1.689479	1.838459	1.999005	2.171893	2.357948	2.773079	3.517876
10	1.104622	1.218994	1.343916	1.480244	1.628895	1.790848	1.967151	2.158925	2.367364	2.593742	3.105848	4.045558
11	1.115668	1.243374	1.384234	1.539454	1.710339	1.898299	2.104852	2.331639	2.580426	2.853117	3.478550	4.652391
12	1.126825	1.268242	1.425761	1.601032	1.795856	2.012196	2.252192	2.518170	2.812665	3.138428	3.895976	5.350250
13	1.138093	1.293607	1.468534	1.665074	1.885649	2.132928	2.409845	2.719624	3.065805	3.452271	4.363493	6.152788
14	1.149474	1.319479	1.512590	1.731676	1.979932	2.260904	2.578534	2.937194	3.341727	3.797498	4.887112	7.075706
15	1.160969	1.345868	1.557967	1.800944	2.078928	2.396558	2.759032	3.172169	3.642482	4.177248	5.473566	8.137062
16	1.172579	1.372786	1.604706	1.872981	2.182875	2.540352	2.952164	3.425943	3.970306	4.594973	6.130394	9.357621
17	1.184304	1.400241	1.652848	1.947901	2.292018	2.692773	3.158815	3.700018	4.327633	5.054470	6.866041	10.761264
18	1.196147	1.428246	1.702433	2.025817	2.406619	2.854339	3.379932	3.996019	4.717120	5.559917	7.689966	12.375454
19	1.208109	1.456811	1.753506	2.106849	2.526950	3.025600	3.616528	4.315701	5.141661	6.115909	8.612762	14.231772
20	1.220190	1.485947	1.806111	2.191123	2.653298	3.207135	3.869684	4.660957	5.604411	6.727500	9.646293	16.366537
21	1.232392	1.515666	1.860295	2.278768	2.785963	3.399564	4.140562	5.033834	6.108808	7.400250	10.803848	18.821518
22	1.244716	1.545980	1.916103	2.369919	2.925261	3.603537	4.430402	5.436540	6.658600	8.140275	12.100310	21.644746
23	1.257163	1.576899	1.973587	2.464716	3.071524	3.819750	4.740530	5.871464	7.257874	8.954302	13.552347	24.891458
24	1.269735	1.608437	2.032794	2.563304	3.225100	4.048935	5.072367	6.341181	7.911083	9.849733	15.178629	28.625176
25	1.282432	1.640606	2.093778	2.665836	3.386355	4.291871	5.427433	6.848475	8.623081	10.834706	17.000064	32.918953
26	1.295256	1.673418	2.156591	2.772470	3.555673	4.549383	5.807353	7.396353	9.399158	11.918177	19.040072	37.856796
27	1.308209	1.706886	2.221289	2.883369	3.733456	4.822346	6.213868	7.988061	10.245082	13.109994	21.324881	43.535315
28	1.321291	1.741024	2.287928	2.998703	3.920129	5.111687	6.648838	8.627140	11.167140	14.420994	23.883866	50.065612
29	1.334504	1.775845	2.356566	3.118651	4.116136	5.418388	7.114257	9.317275	12.172182	15.863093	26.749930	57.575454
30	1.347849	1.811362	2.427262	3.243398	4.321942	5.743491	7.612255	10.062657	13.267678	17.449402	29.959922	66.211772
31	1.361327	1.847589	2.500080	3.373133	4.538039	6.088101	8.145113	10.867669	14.461770	19.194342	33.555113	76.143538
32	1.374941	1.884541	2.575083	3.508059	4.764941	6.453387	8.715271	11.737083	15.763329	21.113777	37.581726	87.565068
33	1.388690	1.922231	2.652335	3.648381	5.003189	6.840590	9.325340	12.676050	17.182028	23.225154	42.091533	100.699829
34	1.402577	1.960676	2.731905	3.794316	5.253348	7.251025	9.978114	13.690134	18.728411	25.547670	47.142517	115.804803
35	1.416603	1.999890	2.813862	3.946089	5.516015	7.686087	10.676581	14.785344	20.413968	28.102437	52.799620	133.175523
40	1.488864	2.208040	3.262038	4.801021	7.039989	10.285718	14.974458	21.724521	31.409420	45.259256	93.050970	267.863546
45	1.564811	2.437854	3.781596	5.841176	8.985008	13.764611	21.002452	31.920449	48.327286	72.890484	163.987604	538.769269
50	1.644632	2.691588	4.383906	7.106683	11.467400	18.420154	29.457025	46.901613	74.357520	117.390853	289.002190	1083.657442

Table 2

Future Amount of Ordinary Annuity of 1 per Period: $A_{\overline{n}|i} = \dfrac{(1+i)^n - 1}{i}$

n	1%	2%	3%	4%	5%	6%	7%	8%	9%	10%	12%	15%
1	1.000000	1.000000	1.000000	1.000000	1.000000	1.000000	1.000000	1.000000	1.000000	1.000000	1.000000	1.000000
2	2.010000	2.020000	2.030000	2.040000	2.050000	2.060000	2.070000	2.080000	2.090000	2.100000	2.120000	2.150000
3	3.030100	3.060400	3.090900	3.121600	3.152500	3.183600	3.214900	3.246400	3.278100	3.310000	3.374400	3.472500
4	4.060401	4.121608	4.183627	4.246464	4.310125	4.374616	4.439943	4.506112	4.573129	4.641000	4.779328	4.993375
5	5.101005	5.204040	5.309136	5.416323	5.525631	5.637093	5.750740	5.866601	5.984711	6.105100	6.352847	6.742381
6	6.152015	6.308121	6.468410	6.632975	6.801913	6.975319	7.153291	7.335929	7.523335	7.715610	8.115189	8.753738
7	7.213535	7.434283	7.662462	7.898294	8.142008	8.393838	8.654021	8.922803	9.200435	9.487171	10.089012	11.066799
8	8.285671	8.582969	8.892336	9.214226	9.549109	9.897468	10.259803	10.636628	11.028474	11.435888	12.299693	13.726819
9	9.368527	9.754628	10.159106	10.582795	11.026564	11.491316	11.977989	12.487558	13.021036	13.579477	14.775656	16.785842
10	10.462213	10.949721	11.463879	12.006107	12.577893	13.180795	13.816448	14.486562	15.192930	15.937425	17.548735	20.303718
11	11.566835	12.168715	12.807796	13.486351	14.206787	14.971643	15.783599	16.645487	17.560293	18.531167	20.654583	24.349276
12	12.682503	13.412090	14.192030	15.025805	15.917127	16.869941	17.888451	18.977126	20.140720	21.384284	24.133133	29.001667
13	13.809328	14.680332	15.617790	16.626838	17.712983	18.882138	20.140643	21.495297	22.953385	24.522712	28.029109	34.351917
14	14.947421	15.973938	17.086324	18.291911	19.598632	21.015066	22.550488	24.214920	26.019189	27.974983	32.392602	40.504705
15	16.096896	17.293417	18.598914	20.023588	21.578564	23.275970	25.129022	27.152114	29.360916	31.772482	37.279715	47.580411
16	17.257864	18.639285	20.156881	21.824531	23.657492	25.672528	27.888054	30.324283	33.003399	35.949730	42.753280	55.717472
17	18.430443	20.012071	21.761588	23.697512	25.840366	28.212880	30.840217	33.750226	36.973705	40.544703	48.883674	65.075093
18	19.614748	21.412312	23.414435	25.645413	28.132385	30.905653	33.999033	37.450244	41.301338	45.599173	55.749715	75.836357
19	20.810895	22.840559	25.116868	27.671229	30.539004	33.759992	37.378965	41.446263	46.018458	51.159090	63.439681	88.211811
20	22.019004	24.297370	26.870374	29.778079	33.065954	36.785591	40.995492	45.761964	51.160120	57.274999	72.052442	102.443583
21	23.239194	25.783317	28.676486	31.969202	35.719252	39.992727	44.865177	50.422921	56.764530	64.002499	81.698736	118.810120
22	24.471586	27.298984	30.536780	34.247970	38.505214	43.392290	49.005739	55.456755	62.873338	71.402749	92.502584	137.631638
23	25.716302	28.844963	32.452884	36.617889	41.430475	46.995828	53.436141	60.893296	69.531939	79.543024	104.602894	159.276384
24	26.973465	30.421862	34.426470	39.082604	44.501999	50.815577	58.176671	66.764759	76.789813	88.497327	118.155241	184.167841
25	28.243200	32.030300	36.459264	41.645908	47.727099	54.864512	63.249038	73.105940	84.700896	98.347059	133.333870	212.793017
26	29.525632	33.670906	38.553042	44.311745	51.113454	59.156383	68.676470	79.954415	93.323977	109.181765	150.333934	245.711970
27	30.820888	35.344324	40.709634	47.084214	54.669126	63.705766	74.483823	87.350768	102.723135	121.099942	169.374007	283.568766
28	32.129097	37.051210	42.930923	49.967583	58.402583	68.528112	80.697691	95.338830	112.968217	134.209936	190.698887	327.104080
29	33.450388	38.792235	45.218850	52.966286	62.322712	73.639798	87.346529	103.965936	124.135356	148.630930	214.582754	377.169693
30	34.784892	40.568079	47.575416	56.084938	66.438848	79.058186	94.460786	113.283211	136.307539	164.494023	241.332684	434.745146
31	36.132740	42.379441	50.002678	59.328335	70.760790	84.801677	102.073041	123.345868	149.575217	181.943425	271.292606	500.956918
32	37.494068	44.227030	52.502759	62.701469	75.298829	90.889778	110.218154	134.213537	164.036987	201.137767	304.847719	577.100456
33	38.869009	46.111570	55.077841	66.209527	80.063771	97.343165	118.933425	145.950620	179.800315	222.251544	342.429446	644.665525
34	40.257699	48.033802	57.730177	69.857909	85.066959	104.183755	128.258765	158.626670	196.982344	245.476699	384.520979	765.365353
35	41.660276	49.994478	60.462082	73.652225	90.320307	111.434780	138.236878	172.316804	215.710755	271.024368	431.663496	881.170156
40	48.886373	60.401983	75.401260	95.025516	120.799774	154.761966	199.635112	259.056519	337.882445	442.592556	767.091420	1779.090308
45	56.481075	71.892710	92.719861	121.029392	159.700156	212.743514	285.749311	386.505617	525.858734	718.904837	1358.230032	3585.128460
50	64.463182	84.579401	112.796867	152.667084	209.347996	290.335905	406.528929	573.770156	815.083556	1163.908529	2400.018249	7217.716277

Table 3

Present Value of 1 at Compound Interest Due in n Periods: $P_{\overline{n}|i} = \dfrac{1}{(1+i)^n}$

n	1%	2%	3%	4%	5%	6%	7%	8%	9%	10%	12%	15%
1	0.990099	0.980392	0.970874	0.961538	0.952381	0.943396	0.934580	0.925926	0.917431	0.909091	0.892857	0.869565
2	0.980296	0.961169	0.942596	0.924556	0.907029	0.889996	0.873439	0.857339	0.841680	0.826446	0.797194	0.756144
3	0.970590	0.942322	0.915142	0.888996	0.863838	0.839619	0.816298	0.793832	0.772183	0.751315	0.711780	0.657516
4	0.960980	0.923845	0.888487	0.854804	0.822702	0.792094	0.762895	0.735030	0.708425	0.683013	0.635518	0.571753
5	0.951466	0.905731	0.862609	0.821927	0.783526	0.747258	0.712986	0.680583	0.649931	0.620921	0.567427	0.497177
6	0.942045	0.887971	0.837484	0.790315	0.746215	0.704961	0.666342	0.630170	0.596267	0.564474	0.506631	0.432328
7	0.932718	0.870560	0.813092	0.759918	0.710681	0.665057	0.622750	0.583490	0.547034	0.513158	0.452349	0.375937
8	0.923483	0.853490	0.789409	0.730690	0.676839	0.627412	0.582009	0.540269	0.501866	0.466507	0.403883	0.326902
9	0.914340	0.836755	0.766417	0.702587	0.644609	0.591898	0.543934	0.500249	0.460428	0.424098	0.360610	0.284262
10	0.905287	0.820348	0.744094	0.675564	0.613913	0.558395	0.508349	0.463193	0.422411	0.385543	0.321973	0.247185
11	0.896324	0.804263	0.722421	0.649581	0.584679	0.526788	0.475093	0.428883	0.387533	0.350494	0.287476	0.214943
12	0.887449	0.788493	0.701380	0.624597	0.556837	0.496969	0.444012	0.397114	0.355535	0.318631	0.256675	0.186907
13	0.878663	0.773033	0.680951	0.600574	0.530321	0.468839	0.414964	0.367698	0.326179	0.289664	0.229174	0.162528
14	0.869963	0.757875	0.661118	0.577475	0.505068	0.442301	0.387817	0.340461	0.299246	0.263331	0.204620	0.141329
15	0.861349	0.743015	0.641862	0.555265	0.481017	0.417265	0.362446	0.315242	0.274538	0.239392	0.182696	0.122894
16	0.852821	0.728446	0.623167	0.533908	0.458112	0.393646	0.338735	0.291890	0.251870	0.217629	0.163122	0.106865
17	0.844377	0.714163	0.605016	0.513373	0.436297	0.371364	0.316574	0.270269	0.231073	0.197845	0.145644	0.092926
18	0.836017	0.700159	0.587395	0.493628	0.415521	0.350344	0.295864	0.250249	0.211994	0.179859	0.130040	0.080805
19	0.827740	0.686431	0.570286	0.474642	0.395734	0.330513	0.276508	0.231712	0.194490	0.163508	0.116107	0.070265
20	0.819544	0.672971	0.553676	0.456387	0.376889	0.311805	0.258419	0.214548	0.178431	0.148644	0.103667	0.061100
21	0.811430	0.659776	0.537549	0.438834	0.358942	0.294155	0.241513	0.198656	0.163698	0.135131	0.092560	0.053131
22	0.803396	0.646839	0.521893	0.421955	0.341850	0.277505	0.225713	0.183941	0.150182	0.122846	0.082643	0.046201
23	0.795442	0.634156	0.506692	0.405726	0.325571	0.261797	0.210947	0.170315	0.137781	0.111678	0.073788	0.040174
24	0.787566	0.621721	0.491934	0.390121	0.310068	0.246979	0.197147	0.157699	0.126405	0.101526	0.065882	0.034934
25	0.779768	0.609531	0.477606	0.375117	0.295303	0.232999	0.184249	0.146018	0.115968	0.092296	0.058823	0.030378
26	0.772048	0.597579	0.463695	0.360689	0.281241	0.219810	0.172195	0.135202	0.106393	0.083905	0.052521	0.026415
27	0.764404	0.585862	0.450189	0.346817	0.267848	0.207368	0.160930	0.125187	0.097608	0.076278	0.046894	0.022970
28	0.756836	0.574375	0.437077	0.333477	0.255094	0.195630	0.150402	0.115914	0.089548	0.069343	0.041869	0.019974
29	0.749342	0.563112	0.424346	0.320651	0.242946	0.184557	0.140563	0.107328	0.082155	0.063039	0.037383	0.017369
30	0.741923	0.552071	0.411987	0.308319	0.231377	0.174110	0.131367	0.099377	0.075371	0.057309	0.033378	0.015103
31	0.734577	0.541246	0.399987	0.296460	0.220359	0.164255	0.122773	0.092016	0.069148	0.052099	0.029802	0.013133
32	0.727304	0.530633	0.388337	0.285058	0.209866	0.154957	0.114741	0.085200	0.063438	0.047362	0.026609	0.011420
33	0.720103	0.520229	0.377026	0.274094	0.199873	0.146186	0.107235	0.078889	0.058200	0.043057	0.023758	0.009931
34	0.712973	0.510028	0.366045	0.263552	0.190355	0.137912	0.100219	0.073045	0.053395	0.039143	0.021212	0.008635
35	0.705914	0.500028	0.355383	0.253415	0.181290	0.130105	0.093663	0.067635	0.048986	0.035584	0.018940	0.007509
40	0.671653	0.452890	0.306557	0.208289	0.142046	0.097222	0.066780	0.046031	0.031838	0.022095	0.010747	0.003733
45	0.639055	0.410197	0.264439	0.171198	0.111297	0.072650	0.047613	0.031328	0.020692	0.013719	0.006098	0.001856
50	0.608039	0.371528	0.228107	0.140713	0.087204	0.054288	0.033948	0.021321	0.013449	0.008519	0.003460	0.000923

Present Value of Ordinary Annuity of 1 per Period: $P_{\overline{n}|i} = \dfrac{1 - \dfrac{1}{(1+i)^n}}{i}$

Table 4

n	1%	2%	3%	4%	5%	6%	7%	8%	9%	10%	12%	15%
1	0.990099	0.980392	0.970874	0.961538	0.952381	0.943396	0.934579	0.925926	0.917431	0.909091	0.892857	0.869565
2	1.970395	1.941561	1.913470	1.886095	1.859410	1.833393	1.808018	1.783265	1.759111	1.735537	1.690051	1.625709
3	2.940985	2.883883	2.828611	2.775091	2.723248	2.673012	2.624316	2.577097	2.531295	2.486852	2.401831	2.283225
4	3.901966	3.807729	3.717098	3.629895	3.545951	3.465106	3.387211	3.312127	3.239720	3.169865	3.037349	2.854978
5	4.853431	4.713460	4.579707	4.451822	4.329477	4.212364	4.100197	3.992710	3.889651	3.790787	3.604776	3.352155
6	5.795476	5.601431	5.417191	5.242137	5.075692	4.917324	4.766540	4.622880	4.485919	4.355261	4.111407	3.784483
7	6.728195	6.471991	6.230283	6.002055	5.786373	5.582381	5.389289	5.206370	5.032953	4.868419	4.563757	4.160420
8	7.651678	7.325481	7.019692	6.732745	6.463213	6.209794	5.971299	5.746639	5.534819	5.334926	4.967640	4.487322
9	8.566018	8.162237	7.786109	7.435332	7.107822	6.801692	6.515232	6.246888	5.995247	5.759024	5.328250	4.771584
10	9.471305	8.982585	8.530203	8.110896	7.721735	7.360087	7.023582	6.710081	6.417658	6.144567	5.650223	5.018769
11	10.367628	9.786848	9.252624	8.760477	8.306414	7.886875	7.498674	7.138964	6.805191	6.495061	5.937699	5.233712
12	11.255077	10.575341	9.954004	9.385074	8.863252	8.383844	7.942686	7.536078	7.160725	6.813692	6.194374	5.420619
13	12.133740	11.348374	10.634955	9.985648	9.393573	8.852683	8.357651	7.903776	7.486904	7.103356	6.423548	5.583147
14	13.003703	12.106249	11.296073	10.563123	9.898641	9.294984	8.745468	8.244237	7.786150	7.366687	6.628168	5.724476
15	13.865053	12.849264	11.937935	11.118387	10.379658	9.712249	9.107914	8.559479	8.060688	7.606080	6.810864	5.847370
16	14.717874	13.577709	12.561102	11.652296	10.837770	10.105895	9.446649	8.851369	8.312558	7.823709	6.973986	5.954235
17	15.562251	14.291872	13.166118	12.165669	11.274066	10.477260	9.763223	9.121638	8.543631	8.021553	7.119630	6.047161
18	16.398269	14.992031	13.753513	12.659297	11.689587	10.827603	10.059087	9.371887	8.755625	8.201412	7.249670	6.127966
19	17.226009	15.678462	14.323799	13.133939	12.085321	11.158116	10.335595	9.603599	8.950115	8.364920	7.365777	6.198231
20	18.045553	16.351433	14.877475	13.590326	12.462210	11.469921	10.594014	9.818147	9.128546	8.513564	7.469444	6.259331
21	18.856983	17.011209	15.415024	14.029160	12.821153	11.764077	10.835527	10.016803	9.292244	8.648694	7.562003	6.312462
22	19.660379	17.658048	15.936917	14.451115	13.163003	12.041582	11.061241	10.200744	9.442425	8.771540	7.644646	6.358663
23	20.455821	18.292204	16.443608	14.856842	13.488574	12.303379	11.272187	10.371059	9.580207	8.883218	7.718434	6.398837
24	21.243387	18.913926	16.935542	15.246963	13.798642	12.550358	11.469334	10.528758	9.706612	8.984744	7.784316	6.433771
25	22.023156	19.523456	17.413148	15.622080	14.093945	12.783356	11.653583	10.674776	9.822580	9.077040	7.843139	6.464149
26	22.795204	20.121036	17.876842	15.982769	14.375185	13.003166	11.825779	10.809978	9.928972	9.160945	7.895660	6.490564
27	23.559608	20.706898	18.327031	16.329586	14.643034	13.210534	11.986709	10.935165	10.026580	9.237223	7.942554	6.513534
28	24.316443	21.281272	18.764108	16.663063	14.898127	13.406164	12.137111	11.051078	10.116128	9.306567	7.984423	6.533508
29	25.065785	21.844385	19.188455	16.983715	15.141074	13.590721	12.277674	11.158406	10.198283	9.369606	8.021806	6.550877
30	25.807708	22.396456	19.600441	17.292033	15.372451	13.764831	12.409041	11.257783	10.273654	9.426914	8.055184	6.565980
31	26.542285	22.937702	20.000428	17.588494	15.592811	13.929086	12.531814	11.349799	10.342802	9.479013	8.084986	6.579113
32	27.269589	23.468335	20.388766	17.873552	15.802677	14.084043	12.646555	11.434999	10.406240	9.526376	8.111594	6.590503
33	27.989693	23.988564	20.765792	18.147646	16.002549	14.230230	12.753790	11.513888	10.464441	9.569432	8.135352	6.600463
34	28.702666	24.498592	21.131837	18.411198	16.192904	14.368141	12.854009	11.586934	10.517835	9.608575	8.156564	6.609099
35	29.408580	24.998619	21.487220	18.664613	16.374194	14.498246	12.947672	11.654568	10.566821	9.644159	8.175504	6.616607
40	32.834686	27.355479	23.114772	19.792774	17.159086	15.046297	13.331709	11.924613	10.757360	9.779051	8.243777	6.641778
45	36.094508	29.490160	24.518713	20.720040	17.774070	15.455832	13.605522	12.108402	10.881197	9.862808	8.282516	6.654293
50	39.196118	31.423606	25.729764	21.482185	18.255925	15.761861	13.800746	12.233485	10.961683	9.914814	8.304498	6.660515

Appendix C
The Direct Method of Reporting Cash Flows From Operating Activities
· · ·

There are two alternative formats for reporting cash flows from operating activities on the statement of cash flows: (1) the indirect method and (2) the direct method. The amount reported as the net cash flow from operating activities will not be affected by the format used. The indirect method is more widely used in practice and was discussed and illustrated in Chapter 16. The basic concepts of reporting cash flows from operating activities by the direct method are briefly discussed in this appendix.

In reporting cash flows from operating activities by the direct method, the major classes of operating cash receipts (cash received from customers, for example) and operating cash payments (cash payments to suppliers for merchandise, for example) are presented on the statement of cash flows. The difference between the total cash receipts by major classes and the total cash payments by major classes is the net cash flow from operating activities.[1]

ASSEMBLING DATA FOR CASH FLOWS FROM OPERATING ACTIVITIES
·

To collect data for reporting cash flows from operating activities by the direct method, all of the operating cash receipts and operating cash payments for a period could be analyzed and classified for reporting on the statement of cash flows. However, this procedure would be expensive and time consuming. A more efficient procedure is to examine the revenues and expenses reported on the income statement and to determine the cash flows related to these revenues and expenses. In performing this analysis, supplementary data can be obtained from other records as needed. To illustrate this approach to assembling data for reporting cash flows from operating activities, the following income statement for Johnson Company for the year ended December 31, 1989, will be used:

---

[1]A reconciliation of net income and net cash flow from operating activities, as illustrated in the footnote on page C-5, should be included as a supplement to the cash flow statement when the direct method of reporting cash flows from operating activities is used.

```
                    Johnson Company
                    Income Statement
              For Year Ended December 31, 1989
```

Sales	$990,000
Cost of merchandise sold.	580,000
Gross profit	$410,000
Operating expenses:	
Depreciation expense . . . . $ 38,000	
Other operating expenses 256,500	
Total operating expenses	294,500
Income before income tax	$115,500
Income tax.	27,500
Net income.	$ 88,000

Additional data showing the change in relevant account balances from the beginning to the end of 1989 are as follows:

	December 31		Increase
Accounts	1989	1988	Decrease*
Trade receivables (net)	$ 72,500	$ 65,000	$ 7,500
Inventories	155,000	165,000	10,000*
Prepaid expenses.	6,500	5,000	1,500
Accounts payable (merchandise creditors)	60,000	46,000	14,000
Accrued operating expenses	13,000	8,500	4,500
Income tax payable	5,500	7,500	2,000*

The determination of the cash receipts and cash payments by major classes are discussed and illustrated in the following paragraphs.

Cash Received from Customers

The $990,000 of sales reported on the income statement for Johnson Company is determined by the accrual method. To determine the cash received from sales made to customers, the $990,000 must be converted to the cash basis. The procedure to convert the sales reported on the income statement to the cash received from customers can be summarized as follows:

	+ decrease in trade receivables	
Sales (reported on the income statement)	**or**	= Cash Received from Customers
	− increase in trade receivables	

For Johnson Company, the cash received from customers is $982,500, determined as follows:

Sales...	$990,000
Less increase in trade receivables	7,500
Cash received from customers	$982,500

The additions to **trade receivables** for sales on account during the year were $7,500 more than the deductions for amounts collected from customers on account. The amount reported on the income statement as sales therefore included $7,500 that did not yield cash inflow during the year. In other words, the increase in trade receivables of $7,500 during 1989 indicates that sales exceeded cash received from customers by $7,500. Accordingly, $7,500 must be deducted from sales to determine the cash received from customers.

The $982,500 of cash received from customers would be reported in the cash flows from operating activities section of the cash flow statement. For Johnson Company, this section is presented on page C-5.

Cash Payments for Merchandise

The $580,000 of cost of merchandise sold reported on the income statement for Johnson Company is determined by the accrual method. The conversion of the cost of merchandise sold to the cash payments made during 1989 for merchandise can be summarized as follows:

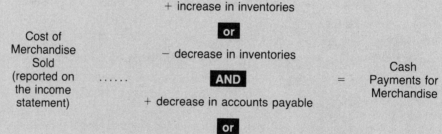

In the illustration for Johnson Company, the cash payments for merchandise is $556,000, determined as follows:

Cost of merchandise sold............................			$580,000
Deduct: Decrease in inventories.....................		$10,000	
Increase in accounts payable...............		14,000	24,000
Cash payments for merchandise......................			$556,000

The $10,000 decrease in **inventories** indicates that the merchandise sold exceeded the cost of the merchandise purchased by $10,000. The amount reported on the income statement as a deduction from sales revenue therefore included $10,000 that did not require cash outflow during the year. Accordingly, $10,000 must be deducted from cost of merchandise sold in determining the cash payments for merchandise.

The effect of the increase in **accounts payable,** which is the amount owed creditors for merchandise, was to include in merchandise purchases the sum of $14,000 for which there had been no cash outlay during the year. In other words, the increase in accounts payable indicates that cash payments for merchandise was $14,000 less than purchases made during 1989. Hence, $14,000 must be deducted from the cost of merchandise sold in determining the cash payments for merchandise.

Cash Payments for Operating Expenses

Since the $38,000 of depreciation expense reported on the income statement did not require an outlay of cash, it is not reported on the statement of cash flows. The conversion of the $256,500 reported for the other operating expenses to cash payments for operating expenses can be summarized as follows:

+ increase in prepaid expenses

or

Operating Expenses other than Depreciation (reported on the income statement) .... − decrease in prepaid expenses

AND

+ decrease in accrued expenses

or

− increase in accrued expenses

= Cash Payments for Operating Expenses

For Johnson Company, the cash payments for operating expenses is $253,500, determined as follows:

Operating expenses other than depreciation.	$256,500
Add increase in prepaid expenses	1,500
	$258,000
Deduct increase in accrued operating expenses	4,500
Cash payments for operating expenses.	$253,500

The outlay of cash for **prepaid expenses** exceeded by $1,500 the amount deducted as an expense during the year. Hence, $1,500 must be added to the amount of operating expenses (other than depreciation) reported on the income statement in determining the cash payments for operating expenses.

The increase in **accrued operating expenses** indicates that the amount reported as an expense during the year exceeded the cash payments by $4,500. Hence, $4,500 must be deducted from the amount of operating expenses on the income statement in determining the cash payments for operating expenses.

Cash Payments for Income Taxes

The procedure to convert the amount of income tax reported on the income statement to the cash basis can be summarized as follows:

Income Tax (reported on income statement)	....	+ decrease in income tax payable **or** − increase in income tax payable	=	Cash Payments for Income Tax

For Johnson Company, the cash payments for income tax is $29,500, determined as follows:

Income tax	$27,500
Add decrease in income tax payable	2,000
Cash payments for income tax	$29,500

The outlay of cash for **income taxes** exceeded by $2,000 the amount of income tax deducted as an expense during the period. Accordingly, $2,000 must be added to the amount of income tax reported on the income statement to determine the cash payments for income tax.

REPORTING CASH FLOWS FROM OPERATING ACTIVITIES

The main classes of operating cash receipts and operating cash payments for Johnson Company, as determined in the preceding paragraphs, may be reported in the statement of cash flows as follows:

Cash flows from operating activities:			
Cash received from customers		$982,500	
Deduct: Cash payments for merchandise..............	$556,000		
Cash payments for operating expenses	253,500		
Cash payments for income tax	29,500	839,000	
Net cash flow from operating activities..			$143,500[2]

---

[2]Regardless of whether the direct method or the indirect method is used, the same amount of net cash flow from operating activities will be reported in the cash flow statement. For example, as described and illustrated in Chapter 16, the indirect method would report net cash flow from operating activities of $143,500, which would be presented as follows:

Net income, per income statement.................		$88,000	
Add: Depreciation	$38,000		
Decrease in inventories	10,000		
Increase in accounts payable	14,000		
Increase in accrued operating expenses......	4,500	66,500	
		$154,500	
Deduct: Increase in trade receivables.............	$ 7,500		
Increase in prepaid expenses	1,500		
Decrease in income tax payable..........	2,000	11,000	
Net cash flow from operating activities		$143,500	

Exercises

C–1. Cash flows from operating activities section. The income statement of BCD Company for the current year ended June 30 is as follows:

Sales..		$735,000
Cost of merchandise sold......................		440,000
Gross profit		$295,000
Operating expenses:		
Depreciation expense	$ 22,500	
Other operating expenses...................	177,500	
Total operating expenses		200,000
Income before income tax......................		$ 95,000
Income tax....................................		20,000
Net income...................................		$ 75,000

Changes in the balance of selected accounts from the beginning to the end of the current year are as follows:

	Increase (Decrease)
Trade receivables (net)	$(15,000)
Inventories	8,000
Prepaid expenses....................................	(750)
Accounts payable (merchandise creditors)	(12,500)
Accrued operating expenses	5,000
Income tax payable	(1,500)

Prepare the cash flows from operating activities section of the statement of cash flows, using the direct method of presentation.

C–2. Cash flows from operating activities section. The income statement for AB&T Co. for the current year ended March 31 and the balances of selected accounts at the end and beginning of the year are as follows:

Sales..		$975,000
Cost of merchandise sold......................		610,000
Gross profit		$365,000
Operating expenses:		
Depreciation expense	$ 55,000	
Other operating expenses...................	210,000	
Total operating expenses		265,000
Income before income tax......................		$100,000
Income tax....................................		24,500
Net income...................................		$ 75,500

	End of Year	Beginning of Year
Trade receivables (net)	$ 98,000	$ 89,000
Inventories	110,000	115,000
Prepaid expenses.......................	4,500	3,000
Accounts payable (merchandise creditors) .	67,500	75,000
Accrued operating expenses	9,000	6,000
Income tax payable	3,000	2,000

Prepare the cash flows from operating activities section of the statement of cash flows, using the direct method of presentation.

C–3. Cash flows from operating activities section. The income statement for the current year and balances of selected accounts at the beginning and end of the current year are as follows:

Sales...		$870,000
Cost of merchandise sold.........................		510,000
Gross profit		$360,000
Operating expenses:		
Depreciation expense	$ 32,250	
Other operating expenses......................	213,750	
Total operating expenses		246,000
Income before income tax.........................		$114,000
Income tax......................................		26,900
Net income.....................................		$ 87,100

	End of Year	Beginning of Year
Trade receivables......................	$87,500	$ 80,000
Inventories	110,000	95,000
Prepaid expenses......................	6,900	7,650
Accounts payable (merchandise creditors) .	77,200	72,700
Accrued operating expenses	3,750	6,250
Income tax payable	1,100	1,100

Prepare the cash flows from operating activities section of the statement of cash flows, using the direct method of presentation.

C–4. Cash flows from operating activities section. The income statement for the current year and the balances of selected accounts at the beginning and end of the current year are as follows:

Sales...		$1,300,000
Cost of merchandise sold.........................		760,000
Gross profit		$ 540,000
Operating expenses:		
Depreciation expense	$ 43,500	
Other operating expenses......................	367,875	
Total operating expenses		411,375
Operating income...............................		$ 128,625
Other expense:		
Interest expense		9,000
Income before income tax........................		$ 119,625
Income tax.....................................		27,500
Net income.....................................		$ 92,125

	End of Year	Beginning of Year
Accounts receivable (trade)	$ 80,500	$ 85,000
Inventories	110,000	97,000
Prepaid expenses..........................	7,900	7,400
Accounts payable (merchandise creditors) .	69,700	72,700
Accrued operating expenses	7,500	6,250
Interest payable..........................	1,500	1,500
Income tax payable	2,500	4,000

Prepare the cash flows from operating activities section of a statement of cash flows, using the direct method of presentation.

Problems

C–5. Statement of cash flows.

The comparative balance sheet of R. N. Corley Inc. for December 31 of the current year and the preceding year and the income statement for the current year are as follows:

	December 31	
	Current Year	Preceding Year
Cash	$ 72,000	$ 50,500
Trade receivables (net)	88,000	80,000
Inventories	105,900	91,400
Investments	—	50,000
Land	50,000	—
Equipment	375,000	275,000
Accumulated depreciation..................	(149,000)	(114,000)
	$541,900	$432,900
Accounts payable (merchandise creditors)	$ 59,000	$ 57,000
Accrued operating expenses	5,000	7,000
Dividends payable	15,000	10,000
Common stock, $40 par	320,000	250,000
Premium on common stock	17,000	12,000
Retained earnings............................	125,900	96,900
	$541,900	$432,900
Sales......................................		$919,500
Cost of merchandise sold....................		550,000
Gross profit		$369,500
Operating expenses:		
Depreciation expense	$ 35,000	
Other operating expenses...................	260,000	
Total operating expenses		295,000
Operating income...........................		$ 74,500
Other income:		
Gain on sale of investments.................		10,000
Income before income tax....................		$ 84,500
Income tax		20,000
Net income................................		$ 64,500

The following additional information was taken from Corley's records:
  (a) The investments were sold for $60,000 cash at the beginning of the year.
  (b) Equipment and land were acquired for cash.
  (c) There were no disposals of equipment during the year.
  (d) The common stock was issued for cash.
  (e) There was a $35,500 debit to Retained Earnings for cash dividends declared.

Instructions:

Prepare a statement of cash flows, using the direct method of presenting cash flows from operating activities.

C–6. Statement of Cash Flows. The comparative balance sheet of C. D. Collins Co. for June 30 of the current year and the preceding year is as follows:

	June 30 Current Year	June 30 Preceding Year
Cash	$ 64,200	$ 49,900
Trade receivables (net)	91,500	80,000
Inventories	105,900	90,500
Investments	—	75,000
Land	85,000	—
Equipment	355,000	275,000
Accumulated depreciation........................	(149,000)	(119,000)
	$552,600	$451,400
Accounts payable (merchandise creditors)	$ 62,450	$ 55,000
Accrued operating expenses	6,000	4,000
Dividends payable	12,000	10,000
Common stock, $20 par	300,000	250,000
Premium on common stock	22,000	12,000
Retained earnings................................	150,150	120,400
	$552,600	$451,400

The income statement for the current year ended June 30 is as follows:

Sales...		$995,000
Cost of merchandise sold		590,750
Gross profit		$404,250
Operating expenses:		
Depreciation expense	$ 30,000	
Other operating expenses......................	280,000	
Total operating expense		310,000
Operating income.................................		$ 94,250
Other income:		
Interest income................................		5,000
Income before income tax..........................		$ 99,250
Income tax		22,500
Net income......................................		$ 76,750

The following additional information was taken from the records of Collins:
  (a) Equipment and land were acquired for cash.
  (b) There were no disposals of equipment during the year.
  (c) The investments were sold for $75,000 cash.
  (d) The common stock was issued for cash.
  (e) There was a $47,000 debit to Retained Earnings for cash dividends declared.

Instructions:

Prepare a statement of cash flows, using the direct method of presenting cash flows from operating activities.

Appendix D
Work Sheet for Statement of Cash Flows

· • ·

Some accountants prefer to use a work sheet to assist them in assembling data for the statement of cash flows. Although a work sheet is not essential, it is especially useful when a large number of transactions must be analyzed. Also, whether or not a work sheet is used, the concept of cash flows and the statement of cash flows are not affected.

The following sections describe and illustrate the use of the work sheet in preparing the statement of cash flows for T. R. Morgan Corporation, based on the data in Chapter 16.

WORK SHEET PROCEDURES FOR STATEMENT OF CASH FLOWS

The comparative balance sheet and additional data obtained from the accounts of T. R. Morgan Corporation are presented on page D-2. The work sheet prepared from these data is presented on page D-3. The procedures to prepare the work sheet for the statement of cash flows are outlined as follows:

1. List the title of each *noncash* account in the Description column. For each account, enter the debit or credit representing the change (increase or decrease) in the account balance for the year in the Change During Year column.
2. Add the debits and credits in the Change During Year column and determine the subtotals. Enter the change (increase or decrease) in cash during the year in the appropriate column to balance the totals of the debits and credits.
3. Provide space in the bottom portion of the work sheet for later use in identifying the various cash flows from (1) operating activities, (2) financing activities, and (3) investing activities.
4. Analyze the change during the year in each noncash account to determine the cash flows by type of activity related to the transactions recorded in each account. Record these activities in the bottom portion of the work sheet by means of entries in the Work Sheet Entries columns.
5. Complete the work sheet.

These procedures are explained in detail in the following paragraphs.

T. R. Morgan Corporation
Comparative Balance Sheet
December 31, 1990 and 1989

	1990	1989	Increase Decrease*
Assets			
Cash...........................	$ 49,000	$ 26,000	$ 23,000
Trade receivables (net)	74,000	65,000	9,000
Inventories	172,000	180,000	8,000*
Prepaid expenses......................	4,000	3,000	1,000
Investments (long-term).................	—	45,000	45,000*
Land...................................	90,000	40,000	50,000
Building	200,000	200,000	—
Accumulated depreciation — building.......	(36,000)	(30,000)	(6,000)
Equipment..............................	290,000	142,000	148,000
Accumulated depreciation — equipment	(43,000)	(40,000)	(3,000)
Total assets...........................	$800,000	$631,000	$169,000
Liabilities			
Accounts payable (merchandise creditors) ...	$ 50,000	$ 32,000	$ 18,000
Income tax payable	2,500	4,000	1,500*
Dividends payable	15,000	8,000	7,000
Bonds payable..........................	120,000	245,000	125,000*
Total liabilities........................	$187,500	$289,000	$101,500*
Stockholders' Equity			
Preferred stock	$150,000	—	$150,000
Premium on preferred stock	10,000	—	10,000
Common stock..........................	280,000	$230,000	50,000
Retained earnings.......................	172,500	112,000	60,500
Total stockholders' equity	$612,500	$342,000	$270,500
Total liabilities and stockholders' equity.....	$800,000	$631,000	$169,000

Additional data:

(1) Net income, $90,500.
(2) Cash dividends declared, $30,000.
(3) Common stock issued at par for land, $50,000.
(4) Preferred stock issued for cash, $160,000.
(5) Bonds payable retired for cash, $125,000.
(6) Depreciation for year: equipment, $12,000; building, $6,000.
(7) Fully depreciated equipment discarded, $9,000.
(8) Equipment purchased for cash, $157,000.
(9) Book value of investments sold for $75,000 cash, $45,000.

T. R. Morgan Corporation
Work Sheet for Statement of Cash Flows
For Year Ended December 31, 1989

Description	Change During Year Debit	Change During Year Credit	Work Sheet Entries Debit		Work Sheet Entries Credit	
Trade receivables	9,000				(q)	9,000
Inventories........................		8,000	(p)	8,000		
Prepaid expenses	1,000				(o)	1,000
Accounts payable		18,000	(n)	18,000		
Income tax payable................	1,500				(m)	1,500
Dividends payable.................		7,000	(l)	7,000		
Investments.......................		45,000	(k)	45,000		
Land..............................	50,000				(j)	50,000
Building	—	—				
Accumulated depreciation—building..		6,000	(i)	6,000		
Equipment.........................	148,000		(g)	9,000	(h)	157,000
Accumulated depreciation— equipment.......................		3,000	(f)	12,000	(g)	9,000
Bonds payable.....................	125,000				(e)	125,000
Preferred stock....................		150,000	(d)	150,000		
Premium on preferred stock		10,000	(d)	10,000		
Common stock.....................		50,000	(c)	50,000		
Retained earnings		60,500	(a)	90,500	(b)	30,000
	334,500	357,500				
Increase in cash...................	23,000					
Totals	357,500	357,500				

			Debit		Credit	
Operating activities:						
Net income					(a)	90,500
Depreciation of equipment...........................					(f)	12,000
Depreciation of building.............................					(i)	6,000
Gain on sale of investments			(k)	30,000		
Decrease in income tax payable			(m)	1,500		
Increase in accounts payable........................					(n)	18,000
Increase in prepaid expenses........................			(o)	1,000		
Decrease in inventories					(p)	8,000
Increase in trade receivables			(q)	9,000		
Financing activities:						
Declaration of cash dividends........................			(b)	30,000		
Increase in dividends payable					(l)	7,000
Issuance of common stock for land...................					(c)	50,000
Issuance of preferred stock..........................					(d)	160,000
Retirement of bonds payable			(e)	125,000		
Investing activities:						
Purchase of equipment..............................			(h)	157,000		
Acquisition of land by issuance of common stock......			(j)	50,000		
Sale of investments.................................					(k)	75,000
Totals				809,000		809,000

Noncash Accounts

Since the analysis of transactions recorded in the noncash accounts reveals the cash flows, the work sheet focuses on noncash accounts. For this purpose, the titles of the noncash accounts are entered in the Description column. To facilitate reference in the illustration, noncash current accounts are listed first, followed by the noncurrent accounts. The order of the listing is not important. Next, the debit or credit change for the year in each account balance is entered in the Change During Year column. For example, the beginning and ending balances of Trade Receivables were $65,000 and $74,000, respectively. Thus, the change for the year was an increase, or debit, of $9,000. The beginning and ending balances of Inventories were $180,000 and $172,000, respectively. Thus, the change for the year was a decrease, or credit, of $8,000. The changes in the other accounts are determined in a like manner.

Change in Cash

Since transactions that result in changes in cash also result in changes in the noncash accounts, the change in cash for the period will equal the change in the noncash accounts for the period. Thus, if a subtotal of the debits and credits for the noncash accounts (as indicated in the Change During Year column) is determined, the increase or decrease in cash for the period can be inserted in the appropriate column and the two columns will balance. In the illustration, the subtotal of the credit column ($357,500) exceeds the subtotal of the debit column ($334,500) by $23,000, which is identified as the increase in cash. By entering the $23,000 as a debit in the Change During Year column, the debit and credit columns are balanced. This $23,000 increase in cash will also be reported on the statement of cash flows.

If the subtotals in the Change During Year columns indicate that the debits exceed the credits, the balancing figure would be identified as a decrease in cash.

Cash Flow Activities

After the Change During Year columns are totaled and ruled, "Operating activities," "Financing activities," and "Investing activities" are written in the Description column. Several lines are skipped between each category, so that at a later time the various cash flows can be entered, by type of activity. When the work sheet is completed, this bottom portion will contain the data necessary to prepare the statement.

To determine the various cash flows by activity for the year, the changes in the noncash accounts are analyzed. As each account is analyzed, entries made in the work sheet relate specific types of cash flows to the noncash accounts. For purposes of discussion, the noncash accounts can be classified as (1) noncurrent accounts and (2) current accounts (except cash).

Analysis of Noncurrent Accounts
· · ·

As was discussed in Chapter 16, transactions that increase or decrease noncurrent accounts often result in cash flows. Therefore, the changes in the noncurrent accounts are analyzed to determine the various cash flows for the year. As each account is analyzed, entries that relate specific types of cash flow activity to the noncurrent account are made in the work sheet. It should be noted that the work sheet entries are not entered into the accounts. They are, as is the entire work sheet, strictly an aid in assembling the data for later use in preparing the statement.

The sequence in which the noncurrent accounts are analyzed is unimportant. However, because it is more convenient and efficient, and the chance for errors is reduced, the analysis illustrated will begin with the retained earnings account and proceed upward in the listing in sequential order.

Retained Earnings. The work sheet indicates that there was an increase of $60,500 in retained earnings for the year. The additional data, taken from an examination of the account, indicate that the increase was the result of two factors: (1) net income of $90,500 and (2) declaration of cash dividends of $30,000. To identify the cash flows by activity, two entries are made on the work sheet. These entries also serve to account for, or explain, the increase of $60,500.

Net income. In closing the accounts at the end of the year, the retained earnings account was credited for $90,500, representing the net income. The $90,500 is also reported on the statement of cash flows as "cash flows from operating activities." An entry on the work sheet to debit retained earnings and to credit "Operating activities — net income" accomplishes the following: (1) the credit portion of the closing entry (to retained earnings) is accounted for, or in effect canceled, and (2) the cash flow is identified in the bottom portion of the work sheet. The entry on the work sheet is as follows:

(a) Retained Earnings.................................... 90,500
    Operating Activities — Net Income   90,500

The cash flows from operating activities is affected by expenses that did not decrease cash. It is also affected by differences between the time an expense is incurred and the time cash flows out, and differences between the time a revenue is recognized and the time cash flows in to the business. In addition, gains and losses from investing and financing transactions affect the determination of cash flows from operating activities. These effects are discussed later in this appendix.

Dividends. In closing the accounts at the end of the year, the retained earnings account was debited for $30,000, representing the cash dividends declared. The $30,000 is also reported on the statement as a financing activity. An entry on the work sheet to debit "Financing Activities— declaration of cash dividends" and to credit retained earnings accomplishes the following: (1) the debit portion of the closing entry (to retained earnings) is accounted for, or in effect canceled, and (2) the cash flow is identified in the bottom portion of the work sheet. The entry on the work sheet is as follows:

(b) Financing Activities—Declaration		
of Cash Dividends	30,000	
Retained Earnings		30,000

The cash used for the payment of dividends is affected by a difference between the time a dividend is declared and the time it is paid. This effect is discussed later in this appendix.

Common Stock. The next noncurrent item on the work sheet, common stock, increased by $50,000 during the year. The additional data, taken from an examination of the account, indicate that the stock was exchanged for land. Although this is a noncash transaction, it should be reported in a separate schedule on the statement of cash flows. To account fully for the change of $50,000 in the common stock account and to provide the data for the separate schedule, the following entry is made on the work sheet:

(c) Common Stock	50,000	
Financing Activities—Issuance of Common Stock		
for Land		50,000

It should be noted that the effect of the exchange will also be analyzed when the land account is examined.

Preferred Stock. The work sheet indicates that the preferred stock account increased by $150,000 and the premium on preferred stock account increased by $10,000. The additional data indicate that these increases resulted from the sale of preferred stock for $160,000. The work sheet entry to account for these increases and to identify the cash flow is as follows:

(d) Preferred Stock	150,000	
Premium on Preferred Stock	10,000	
Financing Activities—Issuance of Preferred Stock		160,000

Bonds Payable. The decrease of $125,000 in the bonds payable account during the year resulted from the retirement of the bonds for cash. The work sheet entry to record the effect of this transaction on cash is as follows:

(e) Financing Activities—Retirement of Bonds Payable	125,000	
Bonds Payable		125,000

Accumulated Depreciation—Equipment. The work sheet indicates that the accumulated depreciation—equipment account increased by $3,000 during the year. The additional data indicate that the increase resulted from (1) depreciation expense of $12,000 (credit) for the year and (2) discarding $9,000 (debit) of fully depreciated equipment. Since depreciation expense does not affect cash but does decrease the amount of net income, it should be added to net income to determine the amount of cash flows from operating activities. This effect is indicated on the work sheet by the following entry:

(f) Accumulated Depreciation—Equipment.............	12,000	
Operating Activities—Net Income:		
Depreciation of Equipment........................		12,000

It should be noted that the notation in the Description column is placed so that the $12,000 can be added to "Operating activities—net income."

Since the discarding of the fully depreciated equipment did not affect cash, the following entry is made on the work sheet in order to fully account for the change of $3,000 in the accumulated depreciation—equipment account:

(g) Equipment..	9,000	
Accumulated Depreciation—Equipment...........		9,000

It should be noted that this entry, like the transaction that was recorded in the accounts, does not affect cash. It serves only to complete the accounting for all transactions that resulted in the change in the account during the year and thus helps assure that no transactions affecting cash are overlooked in the analysis.

Equipment. The work sheet indicates that the equipment account increased by $148,000 during the year. The additional data, determined from an examination of the ledger account, indicates that the increase resulted from (1) discarding $9,000 of fully depreciated equipment and (2) purchasing $157,000 of equipment. The discarding of the equipment was included in, or accounted for, in (g) and needs no additional attention. The use of cash to purchase equipment is recognized by the following entry on the work sheet:

(h) Investing Activities—Purchase of Equipment	157,000	
Equipment......................................		157,000

Accumulated Depreciation—Building. The $6,000 increase in the accumulated depreciation—building account during the year resulted from the entry to record depreciation expense. Since depreciation expense does not affect cash but does decrease the amount of net income, it should be added to net income to determine the amount of cash flows from operating activities. This effect is accomplished by the following entry on the work sheet:

(i) Accumulated Depreciation—Building	6,000	
Operating Activities—Net Income:		
Depreciation of Building		6,000

Building. There was no change in the balance of the building account during the year, and reference to the account confirms that no entries were made in it during the year. Hence, no entry is necessary on the work sheet.

Land. As indicated in the analysis of the common stock account, the $50,000 increase in land resulted from an acquisition by issuance of common stock. To account fully for the change of $50,000 in the land account and to provide the data for the separate schedule reporting this noncash transaction, the following entry is made on the work sheet:

(j) Investing Activities—Acquisition of Land by		
Issuance of Common Stock......................	50,000	
Land		50,000

Investments. The work sheet indicates that investments decreased by $45,000. The examination of the ledger account indicates that investments were sold for $75,000. As was explained on page 597, the $30,000 gain on the sale is included in net income and must be deducted from net income in the operating activities section. The $75,000 of cash flows from investments sold would be reported as an investing activity. To indicate this cash flow on the work sheet, the following entry is made:

(k) Operating Activities—Net Income:		
Gain on Sale of Investments......................	30,000	
Investments.....................................	45,000	
Investing Activities—Sale of Investments		75,000

Analysis of Current Accounts (Except Cash)

· · ·

The amount of cash used to pay dividends may differ from the amount of cash dividends declared. Timing differences between the incurrence of an expense and the related cash outflow and between the recognition of revenue and the receipt of cash must be considered in determining the amount of cash flows from operating activities. Therefore, the current accounts (other than cash) are analyzed to determine (1) cash flows for payment of dividends and (2) cash flows from operating activities.

Cash Flows for Payment of Dividends. The additional data indicate that $30,000 of dividends had been declared, which was identified as a financing activity in entry (b). The $7,000 credit in the Change During Year column of the work sheet for Dividends Payable reveals a timing difference between the declaration and the payment. In other words, the $7,000 increase in Dividends

Payable for the year indicates that dividends paid were $7,000 less than dividends declared. The work sheet entry to adjust the dividends declared of $30,000 to reflect the dividends paid of $23,000 is as follows:

(l) Dividends Payable..................................	7,000	
Financing Activities—Declaration of Cash		
Dividends: Increase in Dividends Payable		7,000

When the $7,000, which represents the increase in dividends payable, is deducted from the $30,000 of "financing activities—declaration of cash dividends," $23,000 is subsequently reported on the statement as a cash flow from financing activity.

Cash Flows From Operating Activities. The starting point in the analysis of the effect of operations on cash is net income for the period. The effect of this amount, $90,500, is indicated by entry (a). As indicated in the earlier analysis, depreciation expense of $18,000 must be added [(f) and (i)] to the $90,500 because depreciation expense did not decrease the amount of cash. Also as explained in entry (k), the gain on the sale of investments, $30,000, must be deducted. In addition, it is necessary to recognize the relationship of the accrual method of accounting to the movement of cash. Ordinarily, a portion of some of the other costs and expenses reported on the income statement, as well as a portion of the revenue earned, is not accompanied by cash outflow or inflow.

The effect of timing differences is indicated by the amount and the direction of change in the balances of the asset and liability accounts affected by operations. Decreases in such assets and increases in such liabilities during the period must be added to the amount reported as net income to determine the amount of cash flows from operating activities. Conversely, increases in such assets and decreases in such liabilities must be deducted from the amount reported as net income.

The noncash current accounts (except Dividends Payable) provide the following data that indicate the effect of timing differences on the amount of cash inflow and outflow from operating activities:

Accounts	Increase Decrease*
Trade receivables (net)	$ 9,000
Inventories	8,000*
Prepaid expenses..................................	1,000
Accounts payable (merchandise creditors)	18,000
Income tax payable	1,500*

The sequence in which the noncash current accounts are analyzed is unimportant. However, to continue the sequence used in analyzing preceding accounts, the analysis illustrated will begin with the income tax payable account and proceed upward in the listing in sequential order.

Income tax payable decrease. The outlay of cash for income taxes exceeded by $1,500 the amount of income tax deducted as an expense during the period. Accordingly, $1,500 must be deducted from income to determine the amount of cash flows from operating activities. This procedure is indicated on the work sheet by the following entry:

```
(m) Operating Activities — Net Income:
      Decrease in Income Tax Payable.................   1,500
        Income Tax Payable ...........................              1,500
```

Accounts payable increase. The effect of the increase in the amount owed creditors for goods and services was to include in expired costs and expenses the sum of $18,000. Income was thereby reduced by $18,000 for which there had been no cash outlay during the year. Hence, $18,000 must be added to income to determine the amount of cash flows from operating activities. The work sheet entry is as follows:

```
(n) Accounts Payable ...............................   18,000
      Operating Activities — Net Income:
        Increase in Accounts Payable...................              18,000
```

Prepaid expenses increase. The outlay of cash for prepaid expenses exceeded by $1,000 the amount deducted as an expense during the year. Hence $1,000 must be deducted from income to determine the amount of cash flows from operating activities. The work sheet entry is as follows:

```
(o) Operating Activities — Net Income:
      Increase in Prepaid Expenses....................   1,000
        Prepaid Expenses ..............................              1,000
```

Inventories decrease. The $8,000 decrease in inventories indicates that the merchandise sold exceeded the cost of the merchandise purchased by $8,000. The amount reported on the income statement as a deduction from the revenue therefore included $8,000 that did not require cash outflow during the year. Accordingly, $8,000 must be added to income to determine the amount of cash flows from operations. The work sheet entry is as follows:

```
(p) Inventories.....................................   8,000
      Operating Activities — Net Income:
        Decrease in Inventories ......................              8,000
```

Trade receivables (net) increase. The additions to trade receivables for sales on account during the year exceeded by $9,000 the deductions for amounts collected from customers on account. The amount reported on the income statement as sales therefore included $9,000 that did not yield cash inflow during the year. Accordingly, $9,000 must be deducted from income to determine the amount of cash flows from operating activities. The work sheet entry is as follows:

(q) Operating Activities—Net Income:
    Increase in Trade Receivables 9,000
        Trade Receivables................................... 9,000

Completing the Work Sheet

After all of the noncash accounts have been analyzed, all of the operating, financing, and investing activities are identified in the bottom portion of the work sheet. To assure the equality of the work sheet entries, the last step is to total the Work Sheet Entries columns.

Preparation of the Statement of Cash Flows

The data for the three sections of the statement of cash flows are obtained from the bottom portion of the work sheet. Some modifications are made to the work sheet data for presentation on the statement. For example, in presenting the cash flows from operating activities, the total depreciation expense ($18,000) is reported instead of the two separate amounts ($12,000 and $6,000). The cash paid for dividends is reported as $23,000 instead of the amount of dividends declared ($30,000), less the increase in dividends payable ($7,000). The issuance of the common stock for land ($50,000) is reported in a separate schedule. The increase (or decrease) in cash that is reported on the statement is also identified on the work sheet. The statement prepared from the work sheet is illustrated on page D-12.

T. R. Morgan Corporation
Statement of Cash Flows
For Year Ended December 31, 1990

Cash flows from operating activities:			
Net income, per income statement.......		$ 90,500	
Add: Depreciation	$ 18,000		
Decrease in inventories	8,000		
Increase in accounts payable.....	18,000	44,000	
		$134,500	
Deduct: Increase in trade receivables...	$ 9,000		
Increase in prepaid expenses..	1,000		
Decrease in income tax			
payable...................	1,500		
Gain on sale of investments....	30,000	41,500	
Net cash flow from operating activities ...			$ 93,000
Cash flows from financing activities:			
Cash received from sale of preferred			
stock		$160,000	
Less: Cash paid for dividends..........	$ 23,000		
Cash paid to retire bonds payable.	125,000	148,000	
Net cash flow provided by financing			
activities			12,000
Cash flows from investing activities:			
Cash received from sale of investments ..		$ 75,000	
Less: Cash paid for purchase of			
equipment		157,000	
Net cash flow used for investing activities .			(82,000)
Increase in cash........................			$ 23,000
Cash at the beginning of the year.........			26,000
Cash at the end of the year			$ 49,000

Schedule of Noncash Financing and Investing Activities

Issuance of common stock for land.........................	$50,000

Appendix E
Managerial Accounting for Service Enterprises and Activities

. . .

The primary emphasis of this text has been to describe and illustrate managerial accounting concepts and techniques for manufacturing enterprises. The accounting for such enterprises, which produce products from raw materials, is more complex than the accounting for the rendering of services. However, as described in Chapter 18, many of the managerial concepts and techniques described and illustrated for manufacturing enterprises are also relevant for service enterprises and activities. This appendix illustrates the application of job order cost accounting, budgeting, responsibility accounting, standard costs, and pricing for a service enterprise.

JOB ORDER COST ACCOUNTING

Since a service enterprise performs services for a particular client, the procedures described in Chapter 3 for a job order cost accounting system are appropriate. To illustrate, assume that Grant and Lewis, CPAs, have organized as a professional corporation (designated by the initials *P.C.*) to practice public accounting. Selected transactions for November, followed by the entries to record them, are presented below.

(a) Labor incurred as reported by time reports for November:

Direct labor:	
Smith Co. (Job 101)	$ 12,000
Abel Inc. (Job 102)	50,000
Lybrand Co. (Job 103)	35,000
Martin Inc. (Job 104)	60,000
Young Inc. (Job 105)	23,000
	$180,000
Indirect labor	8,000
Total	$188,000

Work in Process	180,000	
Overhead	8,000	
Wages Payable		188,000

(b) Other costs incurred:

Overhead	33,800	
Advertising Expense.	12,000	
Rent Expense	9,000	
Office Supplies Expense	4,000	
Accounts Payable.		56,100
Supplies		2,700

(c) Application of overhead costs to jobs (the predetermined rate is 20% of direct labor cost):

Work in Process	36,000	
Overhead		36,000

(d) Cases completed and billed to clients:

Client	Amount Billed	Cost
Smith Co. (Job 101).	$ 35,000	$ 14,400
Able Inc. (Job 102).	120,000	60,000
Lybrand Co. (Job 103).	90,000	42,000
Total billings.	$245,000	$116,400

Accounts Receivable	245,000	
Professional Fees.		245,000
Cost of Services	116,400	
Work in Process		116,400

Assuming that there was no work in process on November 1, 1989, the balance of the work in process account on November 30, $99,600, should agree with the subsidiary cost ledger, as shown below. Note that, for a service enterprise, any materials or supplies cost is included in overhead cost, and hence, no direct materials account is needed.

Client	Direct Labor Cost	Overhead Cost	Total Cost
Martin Inc. (Job 104)	$60,000	$12,000	$72,000
Young Inc. (Job 105)	23,000	4,600	27,600
Total.			$99,600

The financial statements of a service enterprise are similar to those for a merchandising and manufacturing enterprise and therefore are not illustrated. On the income statement, the balance of the cost of services account is deducted from the balance of the professional fees account to determine gross profit. Any underapplied or overapplied overhead cost is either transferred to the cost of services account or allocated between the cost of services account and the work in process account.

BUDGETING

For a service enterprise, a revenue (professional fees) budget is normally the first budget prepared. An estimate of the billable hours serves as the basis upon which the other budgets are prepared. To illustrate, the professional fees budget for Grant and Lewis, CPAs, is as follows:

Grant and Lewis, CPAs, P.C.
Professional Fees Budget
For the Year Ending December 31, 1989

	Billable Hours	Hourly Rate	Total Revenue
Audit Department:			
Staff	12,000	$30	$ 360,000
Supervisors	8,000	$40	320,000
Managers	6,000	$60	360,000
Partners	4,000	$80	320,000
Total	30,000		$1,360,000
Tax Department:			
Staff	22,000	$25	$ 550,000
Supervisors	15,000	$30	450,000
Managers	10,000	$50	500,000
Partners	8,000	$75	600,000
Total	55,000		$2,100,000
Consulting Group:			
Staff	4,000	$30	$ 120,000
Supervisors	3,000	$40	120,000
Managers	6,000	$60	360,000
Partners	2,000	$80	160,000
Total	15,000		$ 760,000
Total professional fees			$4,220,000

The direct labor cost budget is based upon the professional fees budget and indicates the number of professional staff hours required to meet the fee projections. To illustrate, the direct labor cost budget for Grant and Lewis, CPAs, is as follows:

Grant and Lewis, CPAs, P.C. Direct Labor Cost Budget For the Year Ending December 31, 1989				
	Billable Hours Required			
	Staff	Supervisors	Managers	Partners
Audit Department	12,000	8,000	6,000	4,000
Tax Department.	22,000	15,000	10,000	8,000
Consulting Group	4,000	3,000	6,000	2,000
Total.	38,000	26,000	22,000	14,000
Average compensation per hour	× $15	× $20	× $35	× $60
Total direct labor cost	$570,000	$520,000	$770,000	$840,000

The remaining budgets for a service enterprise are similar to those for a merchandising or manufacturing enterprise. These budgets include the overhead cost budget, the operating expenses budget, the cash budget, and the capital expenditures budget. In combination, these supporting budgets form the master budget and are the basis for the preparation of the budgeted income statement and the budgeted balance sheet.

RESPONSIBILITY ACCOUNTING

The responsibility accounting reports for the profit centers or the cost centers of service enterprises are similar to those for a merchandising or manufacturing enterprise. To illustrate, a profit center and a cost center responsibility report for Grant and Lewis, CPAs, P.C., are as follows:

Responsibility Report — Profit Center

Grant and Lewis, CPAs, P.C. Tax Department For Month Ended April 30, 1989		
Professional fees.		$500,000
Cost of services		420,000
Gross profit		$ 80,000
Operating expenses:		
Marketing expenses.	$20,000	
General expenses	18,000	
Total operating expenses		38,000
Income from operations		$ 42,000

Grant and Lewis, CPAs, P. C. Budget Performance Report — Typing and Reproduction Department For Month Ended April 30, 1989				
	Budget	Actual	Over	Under
Supervisory salaries...............	$ 45,000	$ 45,000		
Secretarial wages................	30,000	31,500	$1,500	
Depreciation on equipment	15,000	15,000		
Supplies	11,000	14,100	3,100	
Power and light.................	8,000	7,500		$500
Rent..........................	1,000	1,000		
	$110,000	$114,100	$4,600	$500

STANDARD COSTS

Standards may be developed for the direct labor costs of a service enterprise. When direct labor standards are developed, the total direct labor cost variance, the direct labor time variance, and the direct labor rate variance can be determined as follows:

Total Direct Labor Cost Variance

$$\text{Total Direct Labor Cost Variance} = \text{Actual Direct Labor Cost} - \text{Standard Direct Labor Cost}$$

Direct Labor Time Variance

$$\text{Direct Labor Time Variance} = \text{Actual Hours Worked} - \text{Standard Hours} \times \text{Standard Rate per Hour}$$

Direct Labor Rate Variance

$$\text{Direct Labor Rate Variance} = \text{Actual Rate per Hour} - \text{Standard Rate} \times \text{Actual Hours Worked}$$

To illustrate, assume that the following data were gathered for the direct labor costs used in completing the audit of a client of Grant and Lewis, CPAs:

Actual: 1,500 hours at $28.00	$42,000	
Standard: 1,400 hours at $28.50	39,900	
Total variance	$ 2,100	unfavorable

The total unfavorable direct labor cost variance of $2,100 is made up of an unfavorable time variance and a favorable rate variance. The direct labor time variance is $2,850 unfavorable, computed as follows:

$$\text{Direct Labor Time Variance} = \frac{\text{Actual Hours Worked} - \text{Standard Hours}}{} \times \frac{\text{Standard Rate per Hour}}{}$$

Time variance = (1,500 hours − 1,400 hours) × $28.50

Time variance = 100 hours × $28.50

Time variance = $2,850 unfavorable

The direct labor rate variance is $750 favorable, computed as follows:

$$\text{Direct Labor Rate Variance} = \frac{\text{Actual Rate per Hour} - \text{Standard Rate}}{} \times \frac{\text{Actual Hours Worked}}{}$$

Rate variance = ($28.50 per hour − $28.50 per hour) × 1,500 hours

Rate variance = −$.50 per hour × 1,500 hours

Rate variance = −$750 favorable

To assist service enterprise managers in controlling direct labor costs, reports analyzing the cause of the variances may be prepared. For example, the direct labor time variance could have been caused by the use of inexperienced staff or staff with inadequate training. The direct labor rate variance could have been generated through the use of lower-paid staff for duties normally performed by higher-paid staff. For example, a tax manager rather than a tax partner might have reviewed a tax return.

PRICING

·

The total cost and variable cost concepts for determining product prices, described and illustrated in Chapter 12, are also relevant for setting professional billing rates for service enterprises. As indicated in Chapter 18, the product cost concept is generally not appropriate for service enterprises.

To illustrate the total cost concept of setting professional fees, assume the following costs and expenses for the rendering of 100,000 billable hours by Grant and Lewis, CPAs.

Variable costs and expenses:
Direct labor... $27 per billable hour
Overhead... 4
Marketing and general............................. 4
Fixed costs and expenses:
Overhead... $140,000
Marketing and general............................. 360,000

Assume that Grant and Lewis, CPAs, desire a total income of $900,000 from the rendering of accounting services. The total cost for 100,000 billable hours during the year is $4,000,000 or $40 per billable hour, computed as follows:

Variable costs and expenses		
($35 × 100,000 hours)		$3,500,000
Fixed costs and expenses:		
Overhead	$140,000	
Marketing and general..........................	360,000	500,000
Total costs and expenses		$4,000,000

The markup percentage on each billable hour is 22.5%, computed as follows:

$$\text{Markup Percentage} = \frac{\text{Desired Income}}{\text{Total Costs and Expenses}}$$

$$\text{Markup Percentage} = \frac{\$900,000}{\$4,000,000}$$

$$\text{Markup Percentage} = 22.5\%$$

Based on the total cost per billable hour of $40 and the markup percentage of 22.5%, Grant and Lewis, CPAs, would charge an average billable rate per hour of $49, as shown in the following computation:

Total cost per billable hour	$40
Markup ($40 × 22.5%)	9
Rate per billable hour...	$49

The variable cost concept of product pricing could also have been used by Grant and Lewis, CPAs. The markup percentage using the variable cost concept is 40%, computed as follows:

$$\text{Markup Percentage} = \frac{\text{Desired Income} + \text{Total Fixed Costs and Expenses}}{\text{Total Variable Costs and Expenses}}$$

$$\text{Markup Percentage} = \frac{\$900,000 + \$500,000}{\$3,500,000}$$

$$\text{Markup Percentage} = \frac{\$1,400,000}{\$3,500,000}$$

$$\text{Markup Percentage} = 40\%$$

Based on the variable cost per billable hour of $35 and the markup percentage of 40%, Grant and Lewis, CPAs, would charge an average billable rate per hour of $49, as shown in the following computation:

Variable cost per billable hour	$35
Markup ($35 × 40%)..	14
Rate per billable hour...	$49

As indicated in Chapter 12, the total cost and variable cost concepts of pricing only provide a general guide to setting prices. Other factors, such as competitive market pressures and general economic conditions, must also be considered. For example, because of uncertain economic conditions, Grant and Lewis, CPAs, might decide to round the estimated billable rate of $49 upward to $50 per hour. In addition, the billable rate of $49 is an average rate, and Grant and Lewis might establish different rates for each level of employee within the firm. For example, the services of new staff would normally be billed at a lower rate than the services of managers or partners.

Exercises

·

E-1. Job order cost accounting entries. Selected transactions for September for Marlowe and Sparkman, CPAs, are as follows:
(a) Labor incurred as reported by time reports for September:

Direct labor:	
Abel Inc. (Job 1)	$ 4,000
Nobel Co. (Job 2)	2,800
Anderson Co. (Job 3)	3,500
Nash Inc. (Job 4)	12,250
Thomas Inc. (Job 5)	1,250
	$23,800
Indirect labor	6,200
Total	$30,000

(b) The following other costs were incurred on account: overhead cost, $15,000; advertising expense, $3,000; rent expense, $5,000; and office supplies expense, $1,800.
(c) Overhead is applied to individual jobs at a rate of 60% of direct labor cost.
(d) Jobs completed and billed to clients:

Client	Amount Billed
Abel Inc. (Job 1)	$ 7,000
Nobel Co. (Job 2)	5,500
Anderson Co. (Job 3)	6,000
Total billings	$18,500

Instructions:

(1) Prepare journal entries to record the preceding transactions.
(2) Prepare a summary of jobs in work in process as of September 30.

E-2. Professional fees budget. Mitchell and Momper, CPAs, offer three types of services to clients: auditing, tax, and computer installation. Based upon past experience and projected growth, the following billable hours have been estimated for the year ending December 31, 1989:

	Billable Hours
Audit Department:	
Staff	18,000
Partners	6,000
Tax Department:	
Staff	15,000
Partners	3,000
Computer Installation:	
Staff	12,000
Partners	2,000

The average billing rate for staff is $40 per hour, and the average billing rate for partners is $80 per hour.

Instructions:

Prepare a professional fees budget for Mitchell and Momper, CPAs, for the year ending December 31, 1989, showing the estimated professional fees by type of service rendered.

E-3. Direct labor cost budget. Based upon the data in Exercise E-2 and assuming that the average compensation per hour for staff and partners is $25 and $50 respectively, prepare a direct labor cost budget for Mitchell and Momper, CPAs, for the year ending December 31, 1989.

E-4. Budget performance report. The Typing and Reproduction Department budget for March for Simpson and Ingram, CPAs, is as follows:

Simpson and Ingram, CPAs
Typing and Reproduction Department Budget
For Month Ended March 31, 1989

Supervisory salaries	$24,500
Secretarial wages	8,600
Depreciation on equipment	2,500
Supplies	1,000
Power and light	850
Rent	650
Total	$38,100

Simpson and Ingram, CPAs, treats the Typing and Reproduction Department as a cost center. The actual costs of the Typing and Reproduction Department for March were as follows: supervisory salaries, $24,500; secretarial wages, $9,000; depreciation on equipment, $2,500; supplies, $930; power and light, $1,200; and rent, $650.

Instructions:

Prepare a budget performance report for the Typing and Reproduction Department for the month of March.

E-5. Direct labor cost variances. The following direct labor cost data for the Dysan Case have been gathered by Davis and Grainger, P.C., attorneys at law:

Actual: 2,200 hours at $19.50 .... $42,900
Standard: 2,000 hours at $20.00 40,000

Instructions:

(1) Determine the total direct labor cost variance, the direct labor time variance, and the direct labor rate variance. Indicate whether each variance is favorable or unfavorable.
(2) Briefly describe possible causes of the time and rate variances determined in (1).

E-6. Total cost and variable cost concepts of pricing. Borman and Beeman, P.C., attorneys at law, have gathered the following cost data for the purpose of setting a billing rate for the rendering of professional services:

Variable costs and expenses:
  Direct labor....................................... $20 per billable hour
  Overhead 3
  Marketing and general............................ 2
Fixed costs and expenses:
  Overhead $50,000
  Marketing and general............................ 10,000

Borman and Beeman desire a total income of $280,000, based upon the rendering of 20,000 hours of professional service.

Instructions:

(1) Using the total cost concept of pricing, determine the markup percentage and estimated billing rate per hour.
(2) Using the variable cost concept of pricing, determine the markup percentage and estimated billing rate per hour.

Appendix F
Specimen Financial Statements
· • ·

This appendix contains financial statements based on the actual statements of a small, privately held manufacturing company and selected statements and notes for other companies. Because privately held companies are not required to release their financial statements to the public, the Carter Manufacturing Company statements were modified to protect the confidentiality of the company. We are grateful for the assistance of the public accounting firm of Deloitte Haskins & Sells and Mr. Mark Young in developing these statements.

AUDITOR'S OPINION

Carter Manufacturing Company:

We have examined the balance sheets of Carter Manufacturing Company as of December 31, 1986 and 1985, and the related statements of income and retained earnings and of changes in financial position for the years then ended. Our examinations were made in accordance with generally accepted auditing standards and, accordingly, included such tests of the accounting records and such other auditing procedures as we considered necessary in the circumstances.

In our opinion, the accompanying financial statements present fairly the financial position of Carter Manufacturing Company as of December 31, 1986 and 1985, and the results of its operations and the changes in its financial position for the years then ended, in conformity with generally accepted accounting principles consistently applied.

February 22, 1987
Atlanta, Georgia

CARTER MANUFACTURING COMPANY

BALANCE SHEETS, DECEMBER 31, 1986 and 1985

ASSETS	NOTES	1986	1985
CURRENT ASSETS:			
Cash:			
Cash in bank.........................		$ 38,526	$ 88,443
Petty cash...........................		7,650	12,300
Savings certificates..................		375,000	235,344
Marketable securities.................	2, 5	332,238	361,842
Receivables:			
Customers—less allowance for doubtful accounts of $486,000 in 1986 and $45,000 in 1985	3	2,979,197	2,809,352
Interest.............................		16,680	6,288
Other		22,893	10,125
Inventories	4	5,927,631	6,033,126
Prepaid insurance.....................		38,604	45,234
Other prepayments....................		22,566	32,586
Total current assets		9,760,985	9,634,640
PLANT AND EQUIPMENT:			
Machinery and equipment..............		2,901,148	2,788,225
Delivery equipment....................		745,893	771,873
Furniture and fixtures..................		214,119	214,437
Leasehold improvements...............		97,758	94,011
Total................................		3,958,918	3,868,546
Less accumulated depreciation and amortization		2,172,171	2,085,417
Plant and equipment—net..............		1,786,747	1,783,129
TOTAL ASSETS......................		$11,547,732	$11,417,769

See notes to financial statements.

LIABILITIES AND SHAREHOLDERS' EQUITY

	NOTES	1986	1985
CURRENT LIABILITIES:			
Trade accounts payable..................		$ 1,804,807	$ 1,700,652
Due under line of credit..................	5	120,000	180,000
Current portion of long-term debt	6	266,676	236,709
Accrued salaries, wages and commissions .		369,009	194,910
Accrued and withheld payroll taxes........		69,267	144,111
Income taxes payable		48,081	37,287
Contributions to employee benefit plans ...	8	277,521	100,647
Accrued rent............................		67,500	270,000
Total current liabilities....................		3,022,861	2,864,316
LONG-TERM DEBT	6, 7, 9	1,028,682	1,295,358
DEFERRED INCOME TAXES		56,091	44,877
SHAREHOLDERS' EQUITY:			
Capital stock—authorized and outstanding, 172,000 shares of $3 par value..........................		516,000	516,000
Additional paid-in capital		36,927	36,927
Retained earnings.......................		6,887,171	6,660,291
Shareholders' equity.....................		7,440,098	7,213,218
TOTAL LIABILITIES AND SHAREHOLDERS' EQUITY		$11,547,732	$11,417,769

CARTER MANUFACTURING COMPANY

STATEMENTS OF INCOME AND RETAINED EARNINGS FOR THE YEARS ENDED DECEMBER 31, 1986 AND 1985

	NOTE	1986	1985
SALES (Less returns of $237,782 in 1986 and $345,762 in 1985)................		$23,555,271	$23,401,635
COST OF GOODS SOLD		17,130,648	17,767,857
GROSS PROFIT		6,424,623	5,633,778
SELLING AND GENERAL EXPENSES		6,136,161	5,406,762
INCOME FROM OPERATIONS........		288,462	227,016
OTHER INCOME (EXPENSES):			
Interest................................		167,978	84,732
Dividends		50,268	50,124
Sale of waste materials, etc.............		183,526	91,365
Gain from sale of property and equipment.		4,581	3,600
Unrealized loss on marketable securities ..	2	(28,824)	(80,388)
Interest expense		(233,385)	(112,641)
Cash discount lost		(63,924)	(108,987)
Total...................................		80,220	(72,195)
INCOME BEFORE INCOME TAXES...		368,682	154,821
INCOME TAX EXPENSE:			
Federal:			
Current...............................		112,336	31,410
Deferred		9,303	18,036
Total federal............................		121,639	49,446
State:			
Current...............................		18,252	11,955
Deferred		1,911	3,021
Total state..............................		20,163	14,976
Total...................................		141,802	64,422
NET INCOME		226,880	90,399
RETAINED EARNINGS, BEGINNING OF YEAR		6,660,291	6,569,892
RETAINED EARNINGS, END OF YEAR		$ 6,887,171	$ 6,660,291

See notes to financial statements.

CARTER MANUFACTURING COMPANY

STATEMENTS OF CHANGES IN FINANCIAL POSITION FOR THE YEARS ENDED DECEMBER 31, 1986 AND 1985

	1986	1985
SOURCES OF WORKING CAPITAL:		
Net income...	$ 226,880	$ 90,399
Add charges not requiring an outlay of working capital:		
Depreciation and amortization......................	173,145	181,638
Deferred income taxes.............................	11,214	21,057
Total from operations.................................	411,239	293,094
Proceeds from sale of plant and equipment—net of		
gains included in operations........................	11,019	1,800
Increase in long-term debt		1,295,358
Total...	422,258	1,590,252
USES OF WORKING CAPITAL:		
Purchase of plant and equipment.....................	187,782	1,322,398
Reduction of long-term debt.........................	266,676	
Total...	454,458	1,322,398
INCREASE (DECREASE) IN WORKING CAPITAL ..	$ (32,200)	$ 267,854
COMPONENTS OF CHANGE IN WORKING CAPITAL:		
Cash and savings certificates and account	$ 85,089	$ 325,572
Marketable securities	(29,604)	(80,388)
Receivables	193,005	290,889
Inventories	(105,495)	(3,918)
Prepaid expenses...................................	(16,650)	77,820
Trade accounts payable	(104,155)	(1,177)
Due under line of credit	60,000	(60,000)
Current portion of long-term debt	(29,967)	(236,709)
Accrued salaries, wages and commissions	(174,099)	(28,560)
Accrued and withheld payroll taxes	74,844	(102,966)
Income taxes payable—net..........................	(10,794)	(35,937)
Contributions to employee benefits plans	(176,874)	123,228
Accrued rent.......................................	202,500	
INCREASE (DECREASE) IN WORKING CAPITAL..	$ (32,200)	$ 267,854

See notes to financial statements.

CARTER MANUFACTURING COMPANY

NOTES TO FINANCIAL STATEMENTS FOR THE YEARS ENDED DECEMBER 31, 1986 AND 1985

1. SIGNIFICANT ACCOUNTING POLICIES

Nature of Business—The Company is principally engaged in the manufacture and sale of metal products.

Inventories

For the year ended December 31, 1984, the Company changed its method of accounting for inventories to a last-in, first-out (lifo) method. During a time of rapid price increases, the lifo method provides a better matching of revenue and expense than does the fifo method. The total effect of the change was included in the 1984 financial statements, and no restatement was made of amounts reported in prior years. The effect of this change was to reduce net income for 1984 by $298,944.

Plant and Equipment

Plant and equipment are stated at cost less accumulated depreciation and amortization. Depreciation on plant and equipment acquired after 1978 is computed using the straight-line method for financial reporting and accelerated methods for income tax purposes. Depreciation on previously acquired plant and equipment is computed using accelerated methods for financial reporting and income tax purposes, except that the straight-line method is used for tax purposes at such time as it results in a greater deduction than would result from continued use of an accelerated method. Rates are based upon the following estimated useful lives:

Classification	Useful Life
Machinery and equipment	7–10 Years
Delivery equipment	6–7 Years
Furniture and fixtures	8–10 Years
Leasehold improvements	5–6 Years

Revenue Recognition—Revenue from merchandise sales is recognized when the merchandise is shipped to the customer.

Deferred Income Taxes

Deferred income taxes are provided for timing differences between reported financial income before income taxes and taxable income. The timing differences arise from depreciation deductions for income tax purposes in excess of depreciation expense for financial reporting purposes.

2. MARKETABLE SECURITIES

The Company's marketable securities are stated at the lower of cost or market. At December 31, 1986 and 1985, the Company's investments had a cost of $582,876 and $583,656 respectively. To reduce the carrying amount of this investment to market, which was lower than cost at December 31, 1986 and 1985, valuation allowances of $250,638 and $221,814, respectively, were established. This resulted in a charge to earnings of $28,824 in 1986 and a charge to earnings of $80,388 in 1985.

3. RECEIVABLE DUE FROM A SINGLE CUSTOMER

At December 31, 1986, approximately $700,000 was due from a single distributor. Approximately $435,000 of the allowance for doubtful accounts at December 31, 1986, relates specifically to this receivable.

At December 31, 1985, approximately $350,000 was due from the distributor.

4. INVENTORIES

At December 31, 1986 and 1985, inventories (see Note 1) consisted of the following:

	1986	1985
Raw materials	$1,654,563	$1,491,876
Work in process	2,427,513	2,255,574
Finished goods	2,684,409	2,839,278
Total cost	6,766,485	6,586,728
Less lifo reserve	838,854	553,602
Total lifo	$5,927,631	$6,033,126

5. LINE OF CREDIT

The Company has an agreement with a bank for a line of credit, of which $180,000 was unused at December 31, 1986. Borrowings under the line are at an interest rate (12% at December 31, 1986) of 2% above the bank's prime lending rate. The Company's marketable securities are pledged as collateral for borrowing under the line.

6. LONG-TERM DEBT

At December 31, 1986 and 1985, the Company had three installment notes, payable to a bank as follows:

	1986	1985
Note dated February 2, 1986, due in $60,000 semi-annual installments, with interest payable monthly at 12.625%	$ 120,000	$ 240,000
Note dated March 2, 1985, due in $10,000 semiannual installments, with interest payable monthly at 14.125%	20,000	40,000
Note dated December 12, 1985, due in 120 monthly payments of increasing amounts with interest at 14.00%	1,155,358	1,252,067
Total	1,295,358	1,532,067
Less amount due within one year	266,676	236,709
Total	$1,028,682	$1,295,358

CARTER MANUFACTURING COMPANY

NOTES TO FINANCIAL STATEMENTS FOR
THE YEARS ENDED DECEMBER 31, 1986 AND 1985

7. LONG-TERM LIABILITIES

The long-term liabilities have the following aggregate minimum maturities during the next five years:

1987...................	$ 266,676
1988	131,122
1989	135,103
1990	140,503
1991	146,299
After 1991.............	475,655
Total.................	$1,295,358

8. EMPLOYEE BENEFIT PLANS

The Company has a profit-sharing plan for its salaried employees and a defined benefit retirement plan for its hourly paid employees. Both plans are noncontributory, are funded annually, and have been amended to comply with the Employee Retirement Income Security Act of 1974.

The contributions to the profit-sharing plan are made at the discretion of the Board of Directors and were $138,261 for 1986 and $57,750 for 1985.

Annual contributions to the retirement plan were $139,260 for 1986 and $42,897 for 1985. The plan is being funded based upon actuarial computations of costs which include consideration of normal cost, interest on the unfunded prior service cost, and amortization of the prior service cost over a forty-year period.

At January 1, 1986 and 1985, net assets available for retirement plan benefits were $824,214 and $622,518 respectively; the actuarial present values of vested plan benefits were $984,666 and $885,435, respectively; and nonvested accumulated plan benefits were $87,522 and $90,788, respectively. The assumed rate of return used in determining the actuarial present values of accumulated plan benefits was 5%.

9. OPERATING LEASE

The Company leases land and buildings under a 5-year noncancelable operating lease which expires on December 31, 1989. Future minimum lease payments are as follows:

1987...................	$300,000
1988...................	330,000
1989...................	360,000
Total..................	$990,000

Consolidated Statements of Earnings
Tonka Corporation and Subsidiaries

(In millions, except per share data)	Fiscal Year		
	1986	1985	1984
Net revenues	$ 293.4	$ 244.4	$ 139.0
Cost of goods sold	159.3	131.9	93.9
Gross profit	134.1	112.5	45.1
Advertising expense	45.7	40.2	13.8
Selling, general and administrative expenses	43.1	29.9	19.4
Other expense (income)	1.2	2.6	(1.9)
Interest expense — net	3.8	3.6	5.5
Earnings before income taxes	40.3	36.2	8.3
Income taxes	18.0	16.7	3.3
Net earnings	$ 22.3	$ 19.5	$ 5.0
Net earnings per share	$ 3.04	$ 2.99	$ .78
Average number of common shares	7.3	6.5	6.5

Consolidated Statements of Retained Earnings
Tonka Corporation and Subsidiaries

(In millions)	Fiscal Year		
	1986	1985	1984
Retained earnings at beginning of year	$ 46.4	$ 27.3	$ 22.7
Net earnings	22.3	19.5	5.0
Cash dividends	(.5)	(.4)	(.4)
Retained earnings at end of year	$ 68.2	$ 46.4	$ 27.3

Consolidated Balance Sheets
Tonka Corporation and Subsidiaries

(In millions)	January 3, 1987	December 28, 1985
Assets		
Current assets:		
Cash and short-term investments	$ 44.8	$ 22.9
Accounts receivable — net	58.4	44.1
Inventories	20.8	25.7
Prepaid expenses and other current assets	5.8	6.0
Deferred income taxes	4.8	4.5
Total current assets	134.6	103.2
Land, buildings and equipment:		
Land	2.0	2.0
Buildings	9.9	10.4
Equipment	44.6	40.6
Total land, buildings and equipment	56.5	53.0
Less accumulated depreciation	(34.1)	(33.1)
Net land, buildings and equipment	22.4	19.9
Other assets	1.6	.2
Total assets	$ 158.6	$ 123.3
Liabilities and Stockholders' Equity		
Current liabilities:		
Accounts payable	$ 17.6	$ 21.4
Accrued taxes	4.5	22.2
Accrued payroll	5.8	4.3
Accrued advertising	6.8	6.6
Accrued royalties	6.4	1.6
Current portion of long-term debt	7.9	.1
Other current liabilities	4.5	6.0
Total current liabilities	53.5	62.2
Long-term debt	8.2	8.1
Deferred income taxes and other	.6	1.7
Total liabilities	62.3	72.0
Stockholders' equity:		
Common stock, $.66 2/3 par, issued and outstanding 7.7 and 6.6 shares, respectively	5.1	4.3
Additional paid-in capital	25.3	3.0
Retained earnings	68.2	46.4
Cumulative translation adjustments	(2.3)	(2.4)
Total stockholders' equity	96.3	51.3
Total liabilities and stockholders' equity	$ 158.6	$ 123.3

Notes to Consolidated Financial Statements

Tonka Corporation and Subsidiaries
January 3, 1987, December 28, 1985 and December 29, 1984
(In millions, except share and per share data)

Note One — Summary of Significant Accounting Policies

Principles of Consolidation

The consolidated financial statements include the accounts of Tonka Corporation and subsidiaries (The "Company" or "Tonka"), all of which are wholly-owned. All material intercompany balances and transactions have been eliminated.

Short-term Investments

Short-term investments are carried at the lower of cost or market.

Land, Buildings, and Equipment

Land, buildings and equipment are stated on the basis of cost. Depreciation is computed by the straight-line method at rates expected to amortize the cost of buildings and equipment over their estimated useful lives.

Inventory Valuation

Inventories are valued at the lower of cost or market. Domestic inventories are valued using the last-in, first-out (LIFO) method, while other inventories are generally valued using the first-in, first-out (FIFO) method.

Research and Development

All expenditures for research and development are charged against operations in the year incurred. The charges for fiscal 1986, 1985 and 1984 were $8.3, $4.5 and $1.7, respectively.

Income Taxes

Deferred income taxes are provided for all significant timing differences between financial and taxable income. Investment tax credits are accounted for as a reduction of income tax expense in the year realized (flow-through method).

Reclassifications

The 1984 and 1985 financial statements have been reclassified to conform to 1986 presentations.

Earnings Per Share

Earnings per share are calculated based upon the weighted average number of shares outstanding during the year.

Note Two — Other Significant Transactions

In 1986, the Company decided to close out the GoBots product line. Proceeds from the GoBots inventory closeout were $7.9, which approximated the inventory value. All proceeds and inventory costs were included in cost of goods sold.

Consolidated Statements of Changes in Financial Position

Tandy Corporation and Subsidiaries

In thousands.

	Year Ended June 30,				
	1987	1986	1985	1984	1983
Cash provided by (used for) operations:					
Net income	$242,329	$197,659	$189,060	$281,871	$278,521
Charges (credits) to income not requiring (providing) cash:					
Depreciation and amortization	62,591	55,388	46,720	40,623	33,792
Equity in net (income) loss of companies spun off	2,837	2,919	(2,052)	(6,931)	(9,628)
Deferred income taxes and other items	13,497	32,653	(13,179)	5,435	3,340
Cash provided by (used for) current assets and liabilities:					
Receivables	(6,899)	(17,737)	11,411	(640)	(20,070)
Inventories	(145,554)	58,397	(236,547)	(69,616)	(161,127)
Other current assets	3,806	(7,850)	(4,710)	(3,308)	(8,760)
Accounts payable, accrued expenses and income taxes	51,204	(1,241)	3,334	(18,240)	23,792
Total cash provided by (used for) operations	223,811	320,188	(5,963)	229,194	139,860
Investment activities:					
Additions to property, plant and equipment, net of retirements	(93,136)	(55,029)	(70,677)	(50,825)	(58,445)
Net assets of companies acquired for cash	—	(13,155)	(15,770)	(93,065)	—
Investments in and advances to companies spun off	(32,482)	(20,122)	(25,881)	(5,214)	12,721
Investment in Tandy Credit Corporation	(38,051)	—	—	—	—
Other investment activities	(1,507)	(6,592)	(5,533)	(7,885)	(7,433)
Net investment activities	(165,176)	(94,898)	(117,861)	(156,989)	(53,157)
Financing activities:					
Purchases of treasury stock	(39,267)	(5)	(144,448)	(92,535)	—
Purchase and retirement of stock through tender offer	—	—	—	(355,000)	—
Sales of treasury stock to employee stock purchase program	43,312	37,753	37,889	38,863	33,654
Dividends declared	(33,693)	—	—	—	—
Changes in short-term borrowings—net	1,755	(70,867)	74,585	3,142	7,140
Additions to long-term borrowings	4,610	—	299,249	208,000	370
Redemption of subordinated debentures	(100,044)	—	—	—	—
Repayments of long-term borrowings	(150,520)	(1,687)	(207,022)	(3,762)	(8,535)
Net financing activities	(273,847)	(34,806)	60,253	(201,292)	32,629
Increase (decrease) in cash and short-term investments	(215,212)	190,484	(63,571)	(129,087)	119,332
Cash and short-term investments at the beginning of the year	273,634	83,150	146,721	275,808	156,476
Cash and short-term investments at the end of the year	$ 58,422	$273,634	$ 83,150	$146,721	$275,808

The Review of Operations and Financial Information, pages 12 to 38, is an integral part of these statements.

Consolidated Balance Sheets

General Mills, Inc. and Subsidiaries

ASSETS	Fiscal Year Ended	
	May 25, 1986	May 26, 1985
	(In Millions)	
CURRENT ASSETS:		
Cash	$ 56.4	$ 49.4
Short-term investments	133.9	17.4
Receivables, less allowance for doubtful accounts of $6.3 in 1986 and $4.0 in 1985	220.0	284.5
Inventories	350.9	377.7
Prepaid expenses	32.8	31.5
Net assets of discontinued operations and redeployments	10.4	517.5
TOTAL CURRENT ASSETS	804.4	1,278.0
LAND, BUILDINGS AND EQUIPMENT, AT COST:		
Land	100.9	93.3
Buildings	583.2	524.4
Equipment	894.7	788.1
Construction in progress	132.2	80.2
Total Land, Buildings and Equipment	1,711.0	1,486.0
Less accumulated depreciation	(626.1)	(530.0)
NET LAND, BUILDINGS AND EQUIPMENT	1,084.9	956.0
OTHER ASSETS:		
Net noncurrent assets of businesses to be spun off	—	206.5
Intangible assets, principally goodwill	53.4	50.8
Investments and miscellaneous assets	143.5	162.7
TOTAL OTHER ASSETS	196.9	420.0
TOTAL ASSETS	$2,086.2	$2,654.0

LIABILITIES AND STOCKHOLDERS' EQUITY		
CURRENT LIABILITIES:		
Accounts payable	$ 382.4	$ 352.2
Current portion of long-term debt	10.5	59.4
Notes payable	4.7	379.8
Accrued taxes	97.5	1.4
Accrued payroll	100.6	91.8
Other current liabilities	167.1	164.0
TOTAL CURRENT LIABILITIES	762.8	1,048.6
LONG-TERM DEBT	458.3	449.5
DEFERRED INCOME TAXES	49.7	29.8
DEFERRED INCOME TAXES—TAX LEASES	78.1	60.8
OTHER LIABILITIES AND DEFERRED CREDITS	54.8	42.0
TOTAL LIABILITIES	1,403.7	1,630.7
STOCKHOLDERS' EQUITY:		
Common stock	215.9	213.7
Retained earnings	812.9	1,201.7
Less common stock in treasury, at cost	(314.1)	(333.9)
Cumulative foreign currency adjustment	(32.2)	(58.2)
TOTAL STOCKHOLDERS' EQUITY	682.5	1,023.3
TOTAL LIABILITIES AND STOCKHOLDERS' EQUITY	$2,086.2	$2,654.0

See accompanying notes to consolidated financial statements.

Consolidated Statements of Earnings

General Mills, Inc. and Subsidiaries

	Fiscal Year Ended		
	May 25, 1986	May 26, 1985	May 27, 1984
	(Amounts in Millions, Except Per Share Data)		
CONTINUING OPERATIONS:			
SALES	$4,586.6	$4,285.2	$4,118.4
COSTS AND EXPENSES:			
Cost of sales, exclusive of items below	2,563.9	2,474.8	2,432.8
Selling, general and administrative expenses	1,545.7	1,381.7	1,263.9
Depreciation and amortization expenses	113.1	110.4	99.0
Interest expense, net	38.8	46.6	19.1
TOTAL COSTS AND EXPENSES	4,261.5	4,013.5	3,814.8
EARNINGS FROM CONTINUING OPERATIONS—PRETAX	325.1	271.7	303.6
GAIN (LOSS) FROM REDEPLOYMENTS	(1.5)	(75.8)	53.0
EARNINGS FROM CONTINUING OPERATIONS AFTER REDEPLOYMENTS—PRETAX	323.6	195.9	356.6
INCOME TAXES	140.1	80.5	153.9
EARNINGS FROM CONTINUING OPERATIONS AFTER REDEPLOYMENTS	183.5	115.4	202.7
EARNINGS PER SHARE—CONTINUING OPERATIONS AFTER REDEPLOYMENTS	$ 4.11	$ 2.58	$ 4.32
DISCONTINUED OPERATIONS AFTER TAX	—	(188.3)	30.7
NET EARNINGS (LOSS)	$ 183.5	$ (72.9)	$ 233.4
NET EARNINGS (LOSS) PER SHARE	$ 4.11	$ (1.63)	$ 4.98
AVERAGE NUMBER OF COMMON SHARES	44.6	44.7	46.9

Consolidated Statements of Retained Earnings

	Fiscal Year Ended		
	May 25, 1986	May 26, 1985	May 27, 1984
	(Amounts in Millions, Except Per Share Data)		
RETAINED EARNINGS AT BEGINNING OF YEAR	$1,201.7	$1,375.0	$1,237.6
Net earnings (loss)	183.5	(72.9)	233.4
Deduct dividends of $2.26 per share in 1986, $2.24 per share in 1985 and $2.04 per share in 1984	(100.9)	(100.4)	(96.0)
Distribution of equity to stockholders from spin-off of Toy and Fashion operations	(471.4)	—	—
RETAINED EARNINGS AT END OF YEAR	$ 812.9	$1,201.7	$1,375.0

See accompanying notes to consolidated financial statements.

KMART CORPORATION
CONSOLIDATED STATEMENTS OF INCOME

	Fiscal Year Ended		
(Millions, except per-share data)	January 28, 1987	January 29, 1986	January 30, 1985
Sales	$23,812	$22,035	$20,762
Licensee fees and rental income	234	223	206
Equity in income of affiliated retail companies	83	76	65
Interest income	23	23	39
	24,152	22,357	21,072
Cost of merchandise sold (including buying and occupancy costs)	17,258	15,987	15,095
Selling, general and administrative expenses	4,936	4,673	4,268
Advertising	581	554	543
Interest expense:			
Debt	171	205	147
Capital lease obligations	178	181	184
	23,124	21,600	20,237
Income from continuing retail operations before income taxes	1,028	757	835
Income taxes	458	285	332
Income from continuing retail operations	570	472	503
Discontinued operations (Note B)	28	(251)	(4)
Extraordinary item (Note I)	(16)	—	—
Net income for the year	$ 582	$ 221	$ 499
Earnings per common and common equivalent share:			
Continuing retail operations	$ 2.84	$ 2.42	$ 2.58
Discontinued operations	.14	(1.27)	(.02)
Extraordinary item	(.08)	—	—
Net income	$ 2.90	$ 1.15	$ 2.56
Weighted average shares outstanding	201.5	197.4	197.3

See accompanying Notes to Consolidated Financial Statements.

The consolidated statements of income for prior periods have been restated for discontinued operations.

Per share amounts and weighted average shares outstanding have been adjusted to reflect the three-for-two stock split declared March 24, 1987.

KMART CORPORATION
CONSOLIDATED BALANCE SHEETS

(Millions)	January 28, 1987	January 29, 1986
Assets		
Current Assets:		
Cash (includes temporary investments of $296 and $352, respectively)	$ 521	$ 627
Merchandise inventories	5,153	4,537
Accounts receivable and other current assets	390	363
Total current assets	6,064	5,527
Investments in Affiliated Retail Companies	317	293
Property and Equipment—net	3,594	3,644
Other Assets and Deferred Charges	603	527
	$10,578	$9,991
Liabilities and Shareholders' Equity		
Current Liabilities:		
Long-term debt due within one year	$ 4	$ 15
Notes payable	296	127
Accounts payable—trade	2,207	1,908
Accrued payrolls and other liabilities	639	624
Taxes other than income taxes	223	218
Income taxes	162	198
Total current liabilities	3,531	3,090
Capital Lease Obligations	1,600	1,713
Long-Term Debt	1,011	1,456
Other Long-Term Liabilities	315	345
Deferred Income Taxes	182	114
Shareholders' Equity	3,939	3,273
	$10,578	$9,991

See accompanying Notes to Consolidated Financial Statements.

KMART CORPORATION
CONSOLIDATED STATEMENTS OF SHAREHOLDERS' EQUITY

($ Millions)	Common Stock Shares	Amount	Capital in Excess of Par Value	Retained Earnings	Treasury Shares	Foreign Currency Translation Adjustment	Total Shareholders' Equity
Balance at January 25, 1984	**188,866,208**	**$126**	**$293**	**$2,569**	**$**	**$ (48)**	**$2,940**
Net income for the year				499			499
Cash dividends declared, $.84 per share				(155)			(155)
Common stock sold under stock option and employees' savings plans and conversion of debentures	1,178,232	1	20				21
Purchase of 2,517,750 treasury shares, at cost					(51)		(51)
Foreign currency translation adjustment						(20)	(20)
Balance at January 30, 1985	**190,044,440**	**127**	**313**	**2,913**	**(51)**	**(68)**	**3,234**
Net income for the year				221			221
Cash dividends declared, $.92 per share				(176)			(176)
Common stock sold under stock option and employees' savings plans and conversion of debentures	1,478,041	1	30				31
Foreign currency translation adjustment						(37)	(37)
Balance at January 29, 1986	**191,522,481**	**128**	**343**	**2,958**	**(51)**	**(105)**	**3,273**
Net income for the year				582			582
Cash dividends declared, $1.00 per share				(193)			(193)
Three-for-two stock split		67	(67)				—
Common stock sold under stock option and employees' savings plans	2,792,834	2	63				65
Common stock issued for conversion of debentures	7,867,995	5	181				186
Reissue of 666,328 treasury shares for employees' savings plan			8		14		22
Foreign currency translation adjustment						4	4
Balance at January 28, 1987	**202,183,310**	**$202**	**$528**	**$3,347**	**$(37)**	**$(101)**	**$3,939**

Common stock, authorized 250,000,000 shares, $1.00 par value.

Ten million shares of no par value preferred stock with voting and cumulative dividend rights are authorized but unissued. Currently there are no plans for its issuance.

See accompanying Notes to Consolidated Financial Statements.

Cash dividends declared and common stock shares have been adjusted to reflect the three-for-two stock split declared March 24, 1987 [Note C].

Kmart Corporation 1986 Annual Report

Consolidated Statement of Income

(in millions except per share amounts)
PepsiCo, Inc. and Subsidiaries
Fifty-two weeks ended December 27, 1986, December 28, 1985 and December 29, 1984

	1986	1985	1984
Net Sales	$9,290.8	$7,653.4	$7,107.6
Costs and Expenses			
Cost of sales	3,731.8	3,148.3	2,974.4
Marketing, administrative and other expenses	4,738.4	3,760.4	3,407.4
Refranchising (credit) charge	–	(25.9)	156.0
Interest expense	263.2	195.4	205.1
Interest income	(122.9)	(96.4)	(86.1)
	8,610.5	6,981.8	6,656.8
Income From Continuing Operations Before Income Taxes	680.3	671.6	450.8
Provision for Income Taxes	222.5	251.5	175.8
Income From Continuing Operations	457.8	420.1	275.0
Discontinued Operations			
Income (loss) from discontinued operations (net of income tax provision of $6.7 in 1985 and none in 1984)	–	9.6	(47.5)
Gain (loss) on disposals (net of income tax provision of $28.8 in 1985 and benefit of $1.0 in 1984)	–	114.0	(15.0)
	–	123.6	(62.5)
Net Income	$ 457.8	$ 543.7	$ 212.5
Income (Loss) Per Share			
Continuing operations	$1.75	$1.50	$ .97
Discontinued operations	–	.44	(.22)
Net Income Per Share	$1.75	$1.94	$ .75
Average shares outstanding used to calculate income per share	262.2	280.7	287.5

See accompanying Notes to Consolidated Financial Statements.

Allocation of 1986 Net Sales

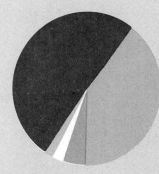

- Marketing, Administrative and Other Expenses 51.0%
- Cost of Sales 40.2%
- Net Interest Expense 1.5%
- Income Taxes 2.4%
- Net Income 4.9%

Consolidated Statement of Financial Condition

(in millions except per share amount)
PepsiCo, Inc. and Subsidiaries
December 27, 1986 and December 28, 1985

	1986	1985
Assets		
Current Assets		
Cash	$ 34.9	$ 26.0
Short-term investments	885.6	912.9
	920.5	938.9
Receivable from sale of North American Van Lines	–	375.5
Notes and accounts receivable, less allowance: 1986-$43.2, 1985-$30.4	820.2	653.3
Inventories	431.5	380.1
Prepaid expenses, taxes and other current assets	331.6	478.0
	2,503.8	2,825.8
Long-term Receivables, Investments and Other Assets	400.1	309.6
Property, Plant and Equipment	3,840.1	2,571.8
Goodwill	1,284.6	185.7
	$8,028.6	$5,892.9
Liabilities and Shareholders' Equity		
Current Liabilities		
Notes payable	$ 232.7	$ 344.1
Accounts payable	858.9	623.7
Income taxes payable	195.2	150.0
Other current liabilities	936.3	738.2
	2,223.1	1,856.0
Long-term Debt	2,492.9	1,035.6
Capital Lease Obligations	139.7	127.1
Other Liabilities and Deferred Credits	336.2	222.8
Deferred Income Taxes	777.6	813.7
Shareholders' Equity		
Capital stock, par value 1 2/3¢ per share: authorized 600.0 shares, issued 287.7 shares	4.8	4.8
Capital in excess of par value	287.0	282.5
Retained earnings	2,356.6	2,061.4
Cumulative translation adjustment	(40.0)	(40.9)
Cost of treasury stock: 1986-27.4 shares, 1985-24.6 shares	(549.3)	(470.1)
	2,059.1	1,837.7
	$8,028.6	$5,892.9

See accompanying Notes to Consolidated Financial Statements.

Consolidated Statement of Changes in Financial Condition

(in millions)
PepsiCo, Inc. and Subsidiaries
Fifty-two weeks ended December 27, 1986, December 28, 1985 and December 29, 1984

	1986	1985	1984
Cash was Generated by (Used for):			
Continuing operations:			
Income	$ 457.8	$ 420.1	$ 275.0
Depreciation and amortization	400.7	290.8	249.6
Deferred income taxes	54.0	81.1	121.3
Other noncash charges and credits, net	84.4	95.8	85.4
Refranchising (credit) charge	–	(14.9)	62.0
Changes in operating working capital accounts (see details below)	234.4	(53.0)	188.2
Cash generated by continuing operations	1,231.3	819.9	981.5
Cash generated by (used for) discontinued operations	–	1.4	(1.0)
Investment activities:			
Acquisitions	1,678.3	160.0	–
Purchases of property, plant and equipment	886.3	785.9	555.8
Receivable from sale of North American Van Lines	(375.7)	375.5	–
Proceeds from sale of North American Van Lines	–	(369.0)	–
Proceeds from sales of property, plant and equipment	(45.5)	(49.4)	(42.2)
Proceeds from sale of Wilson Sporting Goods	–	(134.1)	–
Other, net	.7	4.5	26.8
Cash used for investment activities	2,144.1	773.4	540.4
Financing activities*:			
Increase in long-term debt and capital lease obligations	1,371.1	689.9	41.4
Cash dividends declared	(162.6)	(161.2)	(156.2)
(Decrease) increase in notes payable	(159.9)	63.3	5.5
Purchase of treasury stock	(158.0)	(458.2)	–
Issuance of capital stock	83.2	51.5	11.3
Safe Harbor leases	(1.1)	114.0	115.6
Reduction in long-term debt and capital lease obligations	(78.3)	(220.5)	(197.9)
Cash generated by (used for) financing activities	894.4	78.8	(180.3)
Resulting in:			
(Decrease) increase in cash and short-term investments during the year	$ (18.4)	$ 126.7	$ 259.8
Details of Changes in Operating Working			
Capital Accounts Which Generated (Used) Cash*:			
Notes and accounts receivable	$ (48.7)	$ (65.9)	$ (45.0)
Inventories	24.2	(39.4)	(81.0)
Prepaid expenses, taxes and other current assets	27.7	(125.1)	17.8
Accounts payable	126.5	136.2	130.5
Income taxes payable	29.9	.5	58.9
Other current liabilities	74.8	40.7	107.0
	$ 234.4	$ (53.0)	$ 188.2

*Does not include amounts related to Acquisitions (at the dates of acquisition),
divestitures and discontinued operations.

See accompanying Notes to Consolidated Financial Statements.

Business Segments

Net Sales

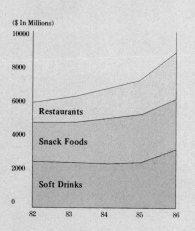

($ In Millions)

Restaurants

Snack Foods

Soft Drinks

Operating Profits

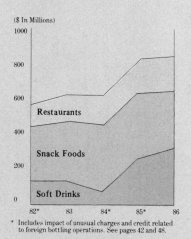

($ In Millions)

Restaurants

Snack Foods

Soft Drinks

* Includes impact of unusual charges and credit related
  to foreign bottling operations. See pages 42 and 48.

PepsiCo operates within three distinct business segments on a worldwide basis: soft drinks, snack foods and restaurants. Management's discussion and analysis of PepsiCo's business segments appears on pages 17, 23 and 30 under Management's Analysis.

The soft drinks segment primarily manufactures and markets Pepsi-Cola, Slice and their allied brands worldwide and Seven-Up internationally. For purposes of this Note, the operations of the soft drink concentrate manufacturing facility in Puerto Rico are allocated between domestic and foreign based upon the actual concentrate shipments to the respective markets. The snack foods segment primarily manufactures and markets salty snacks. The restaurants segment primarily includes the operations of Pizza Hut, Taco Bell and Kentucky Fried Chicken. The 1986 soft drinks and restaurants segment data included the results of the soft drink business of MEI Corporation, the international franchise soft drink business of The Seven-Up Company and Kentucky Fried Chicken operations from their respective dates of acquisition (see Note to the Consolidated Financial Statements on page 41).

In 1986 PepsiCo made three reclassifications to conform the reporting of segment net sales and operating profits to industry practices. Certain promotional discounts previously included in the soft drinks segment as marketing expense were reclassified as a reduction of net sales. State income taxes and net foreign currency translation gains previously included in the determination of segment operating profits were excluded and reclassified to "Provision for income taxes" and "Corporate expenses, net," respectively. The 1985 and 1984 amounts were reclassified on a comparable basis.

In December 1986 the Securities and Exchange Commission issued guidelines that clarified the reporting of certain unusual items. As a result, soft drinks segment operating profits were restated to include a $26 million credit recorded in 1985 and a $156 million charge recorded in 1984 related to the sale of several foreign company-owned bottling operations (see Note to the Consolidated Financial Statements on page 42).

Operating profits included research and development expenses of $82 million, $66 million and $49 million in 1986, 1985 and 1984, respectively.

Corporate expenses included unallocated corporate items, net interest expense and net foreign currency translation gains, which arose principally from the translation of foreign local currency borrowings. These foreign exchange translation gains were $33 million, $32 million and $53 million in 1986, 1985 and 1984, respectively.

Corporate identifiable assets principally consisted of short-term investments. Included in 1985 were the receivable from the sale of North American Van Lines and the investment in the Allegheny Pepsi-Cola Bottling Company, and in 1985 and 1984, the investment in Safe Harbor leases.

	1986	1985	1984
Net Sales:			
Soft drinks	$3,588.4	2,725.1	2,565.0
Snack foods	3,018.4	2,847.1	2,709.2
Restaurants	2,684.0	2,081.2	1,833.4
Total continuing operations	$9,290.8	7,653.4	7,107.6
Foreign portion	$1,225.8	951.9	963.9
Operating Profits:			
Soft drinks	$ 348.6	283.4	86.6
Snack foods	342.8	392.5	393.9
Restaurants	210.1	198.1	183.8
Corporate expenses, net	(221.2)	(202.4)	(213.5)
Income from continuing operations before income taxes	$ 680.3	671.6	450.8
Foreign portion	$ 64.7	70.0	(139.9)
Capital Spending:			
Soft drinks	$ 193.9	160.7	83.6
Snack foods	298.6	286.3	188.9
Restaurants	384.6	331.0	252.5
Corporate	9.2	7.9	30.8
Total continuing operations	$ 886.3	785.9	555.8
Foreign portion	$ 81.4	67.3	36.4
Identifiable Assets:			
Soft drinks	$2,617.7	1,318.6	1,038.9
Snack foods	1,603.8	1,487.1	1,254.5
Restaurants	2,659.5	1,326.7	1,020.7
Corporate	1,147.6	1,760.5	1,277.0
Total continuing operations	$8,028.6	5,892.9	4,591.1
Foreign portion	$2,275.0	1,054.3	687.5
Depreciation and Amortization Expense:			
Soft drinks	$ 104.3	69.2	71.1
Snack foods	135.3	107.7	93.6
Restaurants	156.4	109.2	75.7
Corporate	4.7	4.7	9.2
Total continuing operations	$ 400.7	290.8	249.6
Foreign portion	$ 36.3	25.3	36.8

This information constitutes a Note to the Consolidated
Financial Statements.

Capital Spending

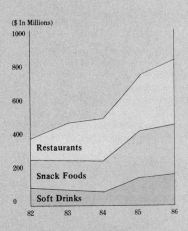

Identifiable Assets

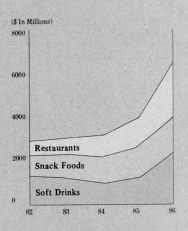

UNITED CABLE TELEVISION CORPORATION and Subsidiaries
CONSOLIDATED BALANCE SHEETS

(In Thousands) As of May 31,	1986	1985
Assets		
Cash and cash equivalents	$ 1,400	$ 11,845
Trade accounts receivable, less allowance for doubtful		
receivables of $402,000 in 1986 and $401,000 in 1985	3,758	3,369
Notes and other receivables	3,956	6,264
Prepaid expenses and other assets	8,739	6,405
Investments in and advances to managed limited		
partnerships (Note 3)	45,557	16,602
Investments in and advances to affiliated companies (Note 1)	982	989
Investment in cable television systems (Notes 1, 2, 3, 4 and 12)		
Property, plant and equipment, at cost	459,876	383,411
Less—accumulated depreciation	(164,927)	(132,205)
	294,949	251,206
Cost in excess of net tangible assets of subsidiaries at acquisition, net of accumulated amortization of $3,863,000 in 1986 and $1,635,000 in 1985	68,572	33,783
Deferred cable television permit costs, net of accumulated amortization of $1,585,000 in 1986 and $1,279,000 in 1985	7,013	9,390
Total investment in cable television systems	370,534	294,379
Investments in broadcast television entities (Note 13)	19,206	7,639
Net assets of discontinued segment at estimated net realizable value (Notes 1 and 13)	—	10,991
	$454,132	$358,483

The accompanying notes to consolidated financial statements are an integral part of these balance sheets.

UNITED CABLE TELEVISION CORPORATION and Subsidiaries
CONSOLIDATED BALANCE SHEETS

(In Thousands) As of May 31,	1986	1985
Liabilities and stockholders' investment		
Accounts payable and accrued liabilities	$ 31,140	$ 17,402
Subscriber prepayments and deposits	11,590	9,879
Debt (Note 4)	347,996	276,842
Total liabilities	390,726	304,123
Minority interests	462	450
Deferred income taxes (Note 6)	3,921	3,702
Commitments (Note 11)		
Preferred stock, Series A, $1 par value, 10¼% cumulative, 100,000 shares authorized and outstanding in 1986 and 150,000 shares authorized and outstanding in 1985, issued at $100 per share, convertible into common stock, mandatory redemption requirements (Note 5)	9,894	14,828
Stockholders' investment (Notes 1, 2, 7, 8 and 9)		
Preferred stock, $1 par value, authorized 900,000 shares, none issued	—	—
Convertible preferred stock, Series B, $1 par value, none authorized or issued in 1986, 4,000 shares authorized and 3,650 shares outstanding in 1985	—	14,600
Common stock, $.10 par value, 40,000,000 shares authorized and 24,383,306 issued in 1986 and 20,000,000 shares authorized and 15,135,914 issued in 1985	2,438	1,513
Additional paid-in capital	44,325	18,232
Retained earnings (Note 4)	2,459	1,256
Treasury stock	(93)	(221)
Total stockholders' investment	49,129	35,380
	$454,132	$358,483

The accompanying notes to consolidated financial statements are an integral part of these balance sheets.

UNITED CABLE TELEVISION CORPORATION and Subsidiaries

CONSOLIDATED STATEMENTS OF OPERATIONS

(In Thousands Except Per Share Data) For The Years Ended May 31,	1986	1985	1984
Revenues	**$195,766**	$168,996	$140,741
Operating expenses	**68,223**	61,339	53,463
General and administrative expenses	**45,604**	39,154	33,782
Depreciation and amortization	**39,172**	32,465	27,008
	152,999	132,958	114,253
Operating income after depreciation	**42,767**	36,038	26,488
Other income (expense)			
Interest expense	**(33,477)**	(19,770)	(18,374)
Interest capitalized during construction (Note 1)	**1,224**	554	1,337
Acquisition cost write-off	**—**	(1,937)	—
Other, net	**(694)**	(538)	(476)
Income from continuing operations before income taxes	**9,820**	14,347	8,975
Income tax provision (benefit) (Note 6)			
Current	**18**	(10)	7
Deferred	**901**	1,890	807
	919	1,880	814
Income from continuing operations	**8,901**	12,467	8,161
Loss on disposal of discontinued segment, net of applicable income tax benefits of $575,000 in 1986 and $350,000 in 1984 (Note 13)	**(4,857)**	—	(4,226)
Net earnings before extraordinary item	**4,044**	12,467	3,935
Extraordinary loss, net of applicable income tax benefit of $224,000 (Note 4)	**—**	(1,925)	—
Net earnings	**$ 4,044**	$ 10,542	$ 3,935
Earnings (loss) per common and common equivalent share (Note 1)			
Primary and fully diluted			
Continuing operations	**$ .32**	$ .40	$ .27
Discontinued operations	**(.20)**	—	(.17)
Extraordinary item	**—**	(.07)	—
Net earnings	**$ .12**	$ .33	$ .10
Average number of common and common equivalent shares (Note 1)			
Primary	**24,511**	27,059	24,898
Fully diluted	**24,554**	27,108	24,916
Dividends per common share	**$ .07**	$ .06	$ .06

The accompanying notes to consolidated financial statements are an integral part of these statements.

The Pillsbury Company and Subsidiaries
Consolidated Statement of Earnings

	Year ended May 31		
	1987	1986	1985
	(In millions except per share amounts)		
Net sales	$6,127.8	$5,847.9	$4,843.4
Costs and expenses:			
Cost of sales	4,292.2	4,102.6	3,465.5
Selling, general and administrative expenses	1,387.5	1,270.9	984.7
Interest expense, net	95.6	97.3	53.0
	5,775.3	5,470.8	4,503.2
Earnings before taxes on income	352.5	377.1	340.2
Taxes on income	170.6	169.0	148.4
Net earnings	$ 181.9	$ 208.1	$ 191.8
Average number of shares outstanding	86.7	87.3	86.8
Earnings per share	$ 2.10	$ 2.38	$ 2.21

Notes to Consolidated Financial Statements are an integral part of this statement.

General Motors Corporation

STATEMENT OF CONSOLIDATED INCOME

For the Years Ended December 31, 1986, 1985 and 1984 (Dollars in Millions Except Per Share Amounts)	1986	1985	1984
Net Sales and Revenues (Notes 1 and 2)			
Manufactured products	$101,506.9	$95,268.4	$83,699.7
Computer systems services	1,306.8	1,103.3	190.2
Total Net Sales and Revenues	102,813.7	96,371.7	83,889.9
Cost and Expenses			
Cost of sales and other operating charges, exclusive of items listed below	88,298.0	81,654.6	70,217.9
Selling, general and administrative expenses	5,203.5	4,294.2	4,003.0
Depreciation of real estate, plants and equipment	3,499.6	2,777.9	2,663.2
Amortization of special tools	2,596.1	3,083.3	2,236.7
Amortization of intangible assets (Note 1)	498.0	347.3	69.1
Special provision for scheduled plant closings and other restructurings (Note 6)	1,287.6	—	—
Total Costs and Expenses	101,382.8	92,157.3	79,189.9
Operating Income	1,430.9	4,214.4	4,700.0
Other income less income deductions—net (Note 7)	983.1	1,299.2	1,713.5
Interest expense (Note 1)	(953.7)	(892.3)	(909.2)
Income before Income Taxes	1,460.3	4,621.3	5,504.3
United States, foreign and other income taxes (credit) (Note 9)	(300.3)	1,630.3	1,805.1
Income after Income Taxes	1,760.6	2,991.0	3,699.2
Equity in earnings of nonconsolidated subsidiaries and associates (dividends received amounted to $1.7 in 1986, $100.5 in 1985 and $706.1 in 1984)	1,184.1	1,008.0	817.3
Net Income	2,944.7	3,999.0	4,516.5
Dividends on preferred stocks	10.8	11.6	12.5
Earnings on Common Stocks	$ 2,933.9	$ 3,987.4	$ 4,504.0
Earnings attributable to:			
$1-2/3 par value common stock	$ 2,607.7	$ 3,883.6	$ 4,498.3
Class E common stock (issued in 1984)	$ 136.2	$ 103.8	$ 5.7
Class H common stock (issued in December 1985)	$ 190.0	—	—
Average number of shares of common stocks outstanding (in millions):			
$1-2/3 par value common	317.6	316.3	315.3
Class E common (issued in 1984)	63.8	66.5	36.3*
Class H common (issued in December 1985)	63.9	—	—
Earnings Per Share Attributable to (Note 10):			
$1-2/3 par value common stock	$8.21	$12.28	$14.27
Class E common stock (issued in 1984)	$2.13	$1.57	$0.16*
Class H common stock (issued in December 1985)	$2.97	—	—

Reference should be made to notes on pages 30 through 41. Certain amounts for 1984 have been reclassified to conform with 1985 classifications.
Earnings and earnings per share attributable to common stocks in 1985 and 1984 have been restated to reflect the Class E common stock amendment approved by the stockholders in December 1985.

*Adjusted to reflect the two-for-one stock split in the form of a 100% stock dividend distributed on June 10, 1985.

CONSOLIDATED BALANCE SHEET

December 31, 1986 and 1985 (Dollars in Millions Except Per Share Amounts)

ASSETS	1986	1985
Current Assets		
Cash	$ 150.7	$ 179.1
United States Government and other marketable securities and time deposits—at cost, which approximates market of $3,881.0 and $4,933.1	3,868.1	4,935.3
Total cash and marketable securities	4,018.8	5,114.4
Accounts and notes receivable (Note 11):		
Nonconsolidated subsidiaries and associates (including GMAC and its subsidiaries—$1,387.1 and $4,038.7)	1,607.0	4,126.9
Other (less allowances)	9,697.3	3,155.1
Inventories (less allowances) (Note 1)	7,235.1	8,269.7
Contracts in process (less advances and progress payments of $2,345.7 and $2,525.3) (Note 1)	1,590.6	1,453.8
Prepaid expenses	2,619.6	2,136.1
Total Current Assets	26,768.4	24,256.0
Equity in Net Assets of Nonconsolidated Subsidiaries and Associates (principally GMAC and its subsidiaries—Note 11)	7,232.3	5,718.5
Other Investments and Miscellaneous Assets—at cost (less allowances)	2,308.4	3,069.8
Common Stocks Held for the GM Incentive Program (Note 3)	190.3	190.2
Property		
Real estate, plants and equipment—at cost (Note 12)	55,240.7	47,267.1
Less accumulated depreciation (Note 12)	27,658.0	24,325.0
Net real estate, plants and equipment	27,582.7	22,942.1
Special tools—at cost (less amortization)	2,793.7	1,710.9
Total Property	30,376.4	24,653.0
Intangible Assets—at cost (less amortization) (Note 1)	5,717.2	5,945.3
Total Assets	$72,593.0	$63,832.8

LIABILITIES AND STOCKHOLDERS' EQUITY	1986	1985
Current Liabilities		
Accounts payable (principally trade)	$ 6,368.0	$ 7,322.2
Loans payable (Note 14)	2,730.1	2,655.2
United States, foreign and other income taxes payable	333.1	243.1
Accrued liabilities and deferred income taxes (Note 13)	13,416.9	12,078.0
Total Current Liabilities	22,848.1	22,298.5
Long-Term Debt (Note 14)	4,007.3	2,500.2
Payable to GMAC (Note 11)	5,500.0	300.0
Capitalized Leases (including GMAC and its subsidiaries—$35.8 and $76.1)	318.0	367.0
Other Liabilities	6,991.7	6,879.8
Deferred Credits (including investment tax credits—$1,505.3 and $1,328.8)	2,249.9	1,962.6
Stockholders' Equity (Notes 3, 4, 5 and 15)		
Preferred stocks ($5.00 series, $153.0 and $169.3; $3.75 series, $81.4)	234.4	250.7
Common stocks:		
$1-2/3 par value common (issued, 319,383,830 and 318,853,315 shares)	532.3	531.4
Class E common (issued, 53,507,119 and 66,227,137 shares)	5.4	6.6
Class H common (issued, 66,585,332 and 65,495,316 shares)	6.6	6.6
Capital surplus (principally additional paid-in capital)	6,332.6	6,667.8
Net income retained for use in the business	23,888.7	22,606.6
Subtotal	31,000.0	30,069.7
Accumulated foreign currency translation and other adjustments (Note 1)	(322.0)	(545.0)
Total Stockholders' Equity	30,678.0	29,524.7
Total Liabilities and Stockholders' Equity	$72,593.0	$63,832.8

Reference should be made to notes on pages 30 through 41. Certain amounts for 1985 have been reclassified to conform with 1986 classifications.

American Greetings

CONSOLIDATED STATEMENTS OF INCOME

Years ended February 28, 1987, 1986 and 1985
Thousands of dollars except per share amounts

	1987	1986	1985
Net sales	$1,102,532	$1,012,451	$919,371
Other income	23,463	23,200	26,287
Total Revenue	1,125,995	1,035,651	945,658
Costs and expenses:			
Material, labor and other production costs	471,503	416,322	377,755
Selling, distribution and marketing	340,980	308,745	274,095
Administrative and general	145,012	131,928	123,750
Depreciation and amortization	29,059	23,471	18,799
Interest	24,875	19,125	15,556
Divestiture loss	12,371	—	—
	1,023,800	899,591	809,955
Income Before Income Taxes	102,195	136,060	135,703
Income taxes	38,834	61,635	61,338
Net Income	$ 63,361	$ 74,425	$ 74,365
Net Income Per Share	$1.97	$2.32	$2.35

See notes to consolidated financial statements

CONSOLIDATED STATEMENTS OF CHANGES IN FINANCIAL POSITION

Years ended February 28, 1987, 1986 and 1985
Thousands of dollars

	1987	1986	1985
Cash From Operations:			
Net income	$ 63,361	$ 74,425	$ 74,365
Items not requiring outlay of current funds:			
Depreciation and amortization	29,059	23,471	18,799
Deferred income taxes	13,321	16,634	18,517
Other	6,012	2,134	2,560
	111,753	116,664	114,241
Working Capital Changes:			
(Increase) in receivables	(32,479)	(66,834)	(26,741)
(Increase) in inventories	(14,133)	(36,584)	(34,430)
(Increase) decrease in other current assets	7,618	(5,086)	(7,107)
Increase (decrease) in current liabilities	(10,626)	16,870	17,366
	(49,620)	(91,634)	(50,912)
Cash From Operations After Changes in Working Capital	62,133	25,030	63,329
Cash From Long-Term Financing:			
Increases in long-term debt	116,325	81,997	3,517
Reduction of long-term debt	(48,774)	(54,593)	(5,318)
Sale of stock under option plans	8,322	7,557	7,531
	75,873	34,961	5,730
Cash Required For Long-Term Items:			
Property, plant and equipment:			
Additions	(68,740)	(61,799)	(43,575)
Disposals—net	3,995	1,133	1,947
Purchase of treasury shares	(14,113)	(1,743)	—
Acquisitions of businesses	(36,690)	—	—
Other—net	(10,798)	(17,182)	(6,505)
	(126,346)	(79,591)	(48,133)
Dividends to Shareholders	(21,288)	(19,910)	(17,114)
Increase (Decrease) in Cash and Equivalents	$ (9,628)	$(39,510)	$ 3,812

See notes to consolidated financial statements

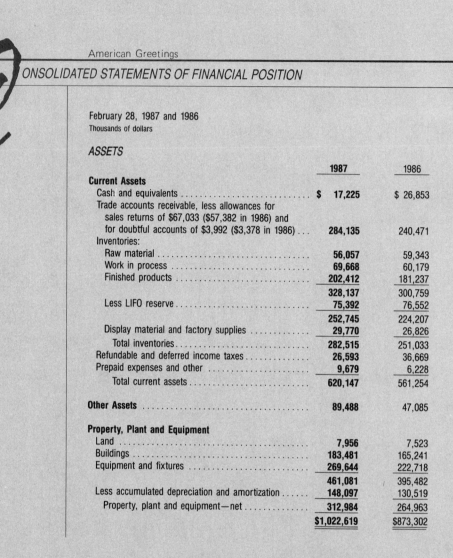

American Greetings

ONSOLIDATED STATEMENTS OF FINANCIAL POSITION

February 28, 1987 and 1986
Thousands of dollars

ASSETS

	1987	1986
Current Assets		
Cash and equivalents	$ 17,225	$ 26,853
Trade accounts receivable, less allowances for sales returns of $67,033 ($57,382 in 1986) and for doubtful accounts of $3,992 ($3,378 in 1986)	284,135	240,471
Inventories:		
Raw material	56,057	59,343
Work in process	69,668	60,179
Finished products	202,412	181,237
	328,137	300,759
Less LIFO reserve	75,392	76,552
	252,745	224,207
Display material and factory supplies	29,770	26,826
Total inventories	282,515	251,033
Refundable and deferred income taxes	26,593	36,669
Prepaid expenses and other	9,679	6,228
Total current assets	620,147	561,254
Other Assets	89,488	47,085
Property, Plant and Equipment		
Land	7,956	7,523
Buildings	183,481	165,241
Equipment and fixtures	269,644	222,718
	461,081	395,482
Less accumulated depreciation and amortization	148,097	130,519
Property, plant and equipment—net	312,984	264,963
	$1,022,619	$873,302

LIABILITIES AND SHAREHOLDERS' EQUITY

	1987	1986
Current Liabilities		
Notes payable	$ 25,092	$ 15,921
Accounts payable	69,175	66,685
Payrolls and payroll taxes	31,230	28,675
Retirement plans...................	10,966	11,697
State and local taxes	3,056	2,763
Dividends payable	5,343	5,317
Income taxes.....................	—	18,988
Sales returns.....................	29,964	23,889
Current maturities of long-term debt ...	10,894	4,786
Total current liabilities	185,720	178,721
Long-Term Debt	235,005	147,592
Deferred Income Taxes	77,451	64,025
Shareholders' Equity		
Common shares—par value $1:		
Class A.........................	29,552	29,203
Class B.........................	2,588	2,982
Capital in excess of par value	102,718	94,744
Treasury stock.....................	(15,409)	(1,689)
Cumulative translation adjustment	(11,604)	(16,801)
Retained earnings	416,598	374,525
Total shareholders' equity..........	524,443	482,964
	$1,022,619	$873,302

See notes to consolidated financial statements

American Greetings

MANAGEMENT ANALYSIS

Years ended February 28, 1987, 1986 and 1985

RESULTS OF OPERATIONS

Total revenue increased 8.7% in 1987 to $1.126 billion after increasing 9.5% in 1986. Although greeting card sales continued to increase, particularly everyday card sales, higher than expected returns of seasonal merchandise negatively affected net sales. Net greeting card dollar sales increased 7% in 1987 and 13% in 1986 while unit sales increased 2% in 1987 and 3% in 1986. Significant sales increases were also recorded by the Corporation's AmToy Division.

Sales by major product classification for the past three years, stated as a percent of net sales, were as follows:

	1987	1986	1985
Everyday greeting cards	38%	37%	37%
Holiday greeting cards	27	29	27
Gift wrapping and party goods	18	18	19
Consumer products (toys, candles and giftware)	8	7	8
Stationery and miscellaneous	9	9	9

Other income increased 1.1% in 1987, after being down 11.7% in 1986. Licensing income totaled $18.3 million in 1987, compared to $17.6 million in 1986 and $20.9 million in 1985. The decrease in 1986 was primarily due to the poor retail environment experienced by many of our licensees in that year.

Material, labor and other production costs were 41.9% of total revenue in 1987, up from 40.2% in 1986 after a slight increase from 39.9% in 1985. Higher costs associated with increased sales volume from non-greeting card subsidiaries and $7.5 million in unfavorable year end inventory adjustments were the significant factors responsible for the increased costs. Principally because of the inventory adjustments, material, labor and other production costs for the three months ended February 28, 1987 increased to 42.1% of total revenue from 36.3% in 1986.

Selling, distribution and marketing expenses were 30.3% of total revenue in 1987 as compared to 29.8% in 1986 and 29.0% in 1985. These increases are primarily the result of costs associated with competition for market share, revenues being less than original expectations, and in 1987, increased advertising costs.

As a percent of total revenue, administrative and general expenses did not change significantly from prior year levels, increasing slightly to 12.9% of revenue compared to 12.7% in 1986 and 13.1% in 1985.

Reflecting the Corporation's increased level of capital spending in recent years, depreciation expense increased $5.6 million in 1987 to 2.6% of total revenue (2.3% in 1986 and 2.0% in 1985).

Interest expense increased $5.8 million in 1987 and $3.6 million in 1986. Higher borrowing levels to fund capital expenditures, acquisitions, and (in 1987) treasury stock, along with increased inventory and accounts receivable levels, were the reasons for the increases.

During February, 1987 the assets and business of the Corporation's unprofitable German operations were sold. Although the pre-tax loss associated with the sale was $12.4 million, it was largely offset by income tax benefits of $11.9 million.

Because of the tax rate change resulting from the Tax Reform Act of 1986, the Corporation's investment in purchased tax benefits (made in 1983) was required under generally accepted accounting principles to be revalued and resulted in an unanticipated tax benefit of $8.2 million in 1987.

The tax benefits associated with the sale of the Corporation's German operations and the revaluation of the investments in tax benefits, both recorded in the fourth fiscal quarter of 1987, were the primary factors causing the effective tax rate to decrease to 38.0% in 1987, compared to 45.3% in 1986 and 45.2% in 1985.

During 1987, the Corporation adopted the installment sales method of tax accounting for certain domestic seasonal sales. Although this change had no impact on tax expense and reported earnings in 1987, it will have a significant overall favorable impact on cash flow in 1988.

ANAGEMENT ANALYSIS—CONTINUED

CHANGES IN FINANCIAL POSITION

Cash provided from operations totaled $111.8 million in 1987 as compared to $116.7 million in 1986 and $114.2 million in 1985. Net cash from long-term financing (long-term debt and sale of stock under option plans) increased to $75.9 million in 1987 from $35.0 million in 1986 and $5.7 million in 1985. These funds were used to finance the Corporation's working capital requirements and other investments.

Accounts receivable as a percent of prior twelve months' net sales increased to 25.8% at the end of 1987 compared to 23.8% in 1986 and 18.9% in 1985. The difficult retail environment continued to cause slower collections from our accounts. Inventories, measured on the same basis, increased

to 25.6% in 1987 from 24.8% in 1986 and 23.3% in 1985, principally due to higher inventories of non-greeting card products, display fixtures and factory supplies.

The Corporation invested $68.7 million in property, plant and equipment in 1987 ($61.8 million in 1986 and $43.6 million in 1985). To provide for future growth and productivity improvements, capital expenditures are expected to increase further in 1988. In addition, the Corporation acquired various businesses for $36.7 million as discussed in Note B to the Consolidated Financial Statements.

Dividend payments to shareholders increased to $21.3 million in 1987 from $19.9 million in 1986 and $17.1 million in 1985.

As a result of the Corporation's higher year-end 1987 borrowing levels, the ratio of total debt to total capitalization (equity plus short and long-term debt) increased to 34.1% from 25.8% in 1986 and 22.2% in 1985.

Shareholders' equity increased 8.6% to $524 million at February 28, 1987. Shareholders' equity per share was $16.32 at year-end 1987 ($15.01 in 1986 and $13.35 in 1985).

The Corporation finances its peak working capital requirements in the United States primarily through the issuance of commercial paper. Note C to the Consolidated Financial Statements more fully describes the Corporation's domestic and foreign credit facilities.

CASH FROM OPERATIONS
IN MILLIONS

$125

100

75

50

25

0

83 84 85 86 87

CAPITAL ADDITICNS
IN MILLIONS

$70

56

42

28

14

0

83 84 85 86 87

CAPITALIZATION
IN MILLIONS

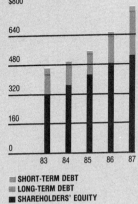

$800

640

480

320

160

0

83 84 85 86 87

 SHORT-TERM DEBT
LONG-TERM DEBT
SHAREHOLDERS' EQUITY

EFFECTS OF INFLATION

The effect of inflation on inventory is mitigated by the Corporation's use of the last-in, first-out method of inventory valuation for its principal domestic

inventories. In addition, the Corporation attempts to offset any increase in costs through productivity improvements. For these reasons, as well as

the moderate inflation rate experienced during fiscal year 1987, inflation had a negligible impact on the operating results of the Corporation.

AMERICAN GREETINGS

Index

Check Figures
for Selected Problems
• •

Agreement between the following "check" figures and those obtained in solving the problems is an indication that a significant portion of the solution is basically correct, aside from matters of form and procedure.

Problem 2–33   Cost of goods manufactured, $327,300

2–35   Net income, $74,000

2–33A   Cost of goods manufactured, $1,780,000

2–35A   Net income, $50,000

Problem 3–27   Finished goods, $22,825

3–29   Total assets, $509,986

3–30   Trial balance totals, $2,017,680

3–27A   Finished goods, $11,590

3–30A   Trial balance totals, $1,150,585

Problem 4–30   Work in process, June 30, Department 2, $74,760

4–31   Equivalent units of production, 11,670 units

4–32   Total assets, $1,454,620

4–33   Equivalent units of production, 24,000 units

4–35   Work in process, Aug. 31, $4,000

4–36   Equivalent units of production, 23,200 units

4–30A   Work in process, April 30, Department 2, $45,024

4–33A   Equivalent units of production, 34,500 units

4–35A   Work in process, July 31, $17,250

Problem 5–43   Variable cost per unit, $1.50

5–43A   Variable cost per unit, $2.85

Problem 6–29   Break-even point, (1), $1,000,000

6–30   Maximum operating profit: (2), $160,000; (4), $120,000

6–31   Maximum operating profit: (2), $75,000; (4) $62,500

6–32   Break-even point, $1,360,000

6–33   Break-even point, $900,000

6–34   Present break-even point, $2,000,000

6–29A   Break-even point, (1), $350,000

6–30A   Maximum operating profit: (2), $125,000; (4), $100,000

6–31A   Maximum operating profit: (2), $50,000: (4), $40,000

6–33A   Break-even point, $750,000

Problem 7–24   Decrease in gross profit, $4,900

7–25   Income from operations, (2), $180,000

7–26   Operating loss, $56,500

7–27   Contribution to company profit, Thom, $89,100

7–28   Total contribution margin, (1), $464,000; (3), $511,280

7–24A   Decrease in gross profit, $25,600

7–25A   Loss from operations, (2), $2,000

7–26A   Operating loss, $38,500

Problem 8–25   Total production, Product A, 73,000 units

8–26   Net income, $425,900

8–27   Deficiency, June, $18,200

8–28   Total revenue from sales, $1,840,230

8–30   Net income, $215,100; cash, $116,100

8–27A   Deficiency, November, $22,500

8–28A   Total revenue from sales, $5,524,200

Problem 9–25   Total factory overhead cost variance — unfavorable, $5,600

9–26   Total factory overhead cost variance — unfavorable, $5,725

9–27   Total factory overhead cost variance — unfavorable, $12,000

9–28   Work in process account balance (debit), $11,200

9–25A   Total factory overhead cost variance—unfavorable, $7,060

927A   Total factory overhead cost variance—favorable, $3,150

9–28A   Work in process account balance (debit), $10,140

Problem 10–24   Net income, $111,290

10–27   Total departmental margin, $138,670

10–24A   Net income, $37,050

Problem 11–32   ROI, Division C, 16.5%

11–33   ROI, Proposal 3, 18.1%

11–34   Division A is most profitable

11–35   ROI, Division F, 18%

11–38   Total company income would increase by $500,000

11–32A   ROI, Division Z, 24%

11–32A   Division O is most profitable

11–35A   ROI, Division Y, 24%

11–38A   Total company income would increase by $160,000

Problem 12–36   Gain from operating warehouse, $200,000

12–37   Net cost reduction, $330,000

12–38   Gain from promotion campaign, Product D, $95,000

12–39   Net advantage, $1,250

12–40   Net advantage, $4,300

12–41   Selling price, $21.60

12–36A   Gain from operating warehouse, $80,000

12–37A   Net cost reduction, $235,000

12–41A   Selling price, $19.20

Problem 13–27   Excess of present value over amount to be invested, Project H, $4,686

13–28   Excess of present value over amount to be invested, Project M, $40,500

13–29   Present value index, Proposal C, 1.05

13–30   Discounted internal rate of return, Proposal B, 15%

13–31   (2), Excess of present value over amount to be invested, $5,381

13–32   (2), Excess of present value over amount to be invested, Project A, $20,000

13–27A   Excess of present value over amount to be invested, Project K, $10,204

13–28A   Excess of present value over amount to be invested, Project D, $29,500

13–29A   Present value index, Project Q, 1.12

13–30A   Discounted internal rate of return, Project T, 15%

Problem 14–41   EOQ, 690 units

14–42   EOQ, (3), 138 units

14–43   Plan 2 is the most economical plan

14–44   Expected value, T, $16,350,000

14–45   250 magazines should be purchased

14–46   Expected value, Plat #900, $13,550,000

14–47   Value of conducting an investigation, $6,000

14–48   (1), medical office complex

14–49   (2), lakefront location

14–41A   EOQ, 1,320 units

14–43A   Plan 2 is the most economical plan

14–44A   Expected value, Patent #1010, $12,600,000

14–45A   175 newspapers should be purchased

14–46A   Expected value, Plat #100, $35,750,000

14–47A   Value of conducting an investigation, $3,200

14–48A   (2), Venture X

Problem 15–43   Working capital, Dec. 31, 1989, $186,625

Problem 16–34   Increase in cash, $21,500

16–35   Decrease in cash, $14,500

16–36   Net cash flow from operating activities, $102,500

16–37   Net cash flow from operating activities, $(11,900)

16–38   Net cash flows used for investing activities, $(135,100)

16–34A   Increase in cash, $14,300

16–35A   Increase in cash, $11,350

16–36A   Net cash flow from operating activities, $74,700

16–37A Net cash flow from operating
activities, $113,100

Problem 17–35 Total expenditures, Crime
Prevention, $548,000

17–36 Excess of revenues over
expenditures, $44,600

17–37 Fund balance, July 31, 1990,
$204,100

17–38 Trial balance totals, $1,370,000

17–39 Fund balance, June 30, 1990,
$576,000

17–35A Total expenditures, Crime
Prevention, $469,500

17–36A Excess of revenues over
expenditures, $44,600

17–37A Fund balance, July 31, 1990,
$205,300

17–38A Trial balance totals, $516,700